Soviet National Income, 1958-1964

Soviet National Income 1958-1964

National Accounts of the USSR in the Seven Year Plan Period

ABRAHAM S. BECKER

UNIVERSITY OF CALIFORNIA PRESS
BERKELEY & LOS ANGELES

1969

University of California Press
Berkeley and Los Angeles, California

University of California Press, Ltd.
London, England

Library of Congress Catalog Card Number: 70–77483

Preface

The publication of this book brings to a close an extended study of Soviet national income during the Seven Year Plan period. Early results of the research were reported in four RAND Memoranda: *Soviet National Income and Product in 1965: The Goals of the Seven Year Plan,* RM-3520-PR, March 1963; *Soviet Military Outlays Since 1955,* RM-3886-PR, July 1964; *Soviet National Income and Product, 1958–1962: Part I—National Income at Established Prices,* RM-4394-PR, June 1965; and *Part II—National Income at Factor Cost and Constant Prices,* RM-4881-PR, May 1966. Not all the themes explored in those four papers are taken up again in this book, but for that subset the present work supersedes its predecessors.

Completion of this study also represents the addition of a new link to the chain of RAND-sponsored studies of Soviet national income, a series which has been notably associated with Abram Bergson. It is he who stands first and foremost in the long list of my intellectual debts accumulated in the generation of the book. Abram Bergson first introduced me to the intricacies of the study of Soviet economic growth, and his pioneering work in this field provides the core of the theoretical and procedural framework for the present work. No reader of my book will fail to note the extent of my debt to him. In addition, I have greatly benefited from his comments and criticisms on the draft text of the book as well as on one of my earlier RAND papers.

The creation of this work in all its stages has been aided and abetted by a great many people. Raymond P. Powell and Norman M. Kaplan very generously provided searching critiques of the entire manuscript, text and appendixes. Norman Kaplan's physical presence at RAND Santa Monica in the fall of 1968 provided me with a windfall opportunity to discuss the issues with him at length. I am deeply grateful to them for their valuable aid.

The papers that served as steppingstones to the present work also benefited from the advice and criticisms of a number of people. These debts are acknowledged in full in the prefaces to the respective papers, but I should particularly like to repeat here my gratitude to Charles A. Cooper, Hans Heymann, Jr., Oleg Hoeffding, Richard H. Moorsteen, Raymond P. Powell, and T. Paul Schultz for their critiques of early drafts of the aforementioned RAND Memoranda and to Nancy Nimitz for her invaluable counsel on the knotty problems of agricultural income and organization. I am also grateful to Miss Nimitz for her kind permission to cite from several of her unpublished manuscripts.

Marvin H. Kosters, Douglas F. Loveday, Evsey D. Domar and Oleg Hoeffding also read and commented upon an early version of Chapters 1–3, and I acknowledge their contribution with thanks. The arduous labor of interpreting and transcribing my scrawled over drafts has been cheerfully borne largely by Jane Bickner, Marnie Pratt, and Bernadine Siuda; and for their patience and unflappability I express my appreciation. Thanks are also due and willingly rendered to Janina Bonczek, who assiduously and cheerfully checked the calculations and references of the sources to Tables 1–4; to Marjorie S. Behrens, who compiled the Bibliography; and to Evangeline O. Johnson for research assistance in connection with Chapter 11. Apart from the author only one other person can be said to have been associated with the manuscript from its early stages until its completion—RAND Economics Department editor, Helen B. Turin. Her contribution, alas, will not be entirely visible, but she has done her valiant best to defend the cause of clarity, simplicity, and felicity of expression. I absolve her of complicity in any and all sins that still remain in print.

This list of acknowledgments would be grievously incomplete without the expression of deepfelt appreciation to my wife and children. They bore the long travail with me and maintained a perfect faith, at which I could only marvel, that though it tarry the day of completion must yet come. Without that sustaining confidence, this book would not have seen the light of day.

This book was written under Project RAND, the continuing program of research conducted by The RAND Corporation for the U.S. Air Force. I wish to express to both of these organizations my appreciation for their support.

A NOTE ON TABLES, REFERENCES, AND RUBLE VALUES

Text tables are numbered consecutively. Appendix tables carry the letter designation of the appendix plus an arabic numeral—for example, K-1—and are located at the end of their respective appendixes. In all tables, the symbol "-" means zero or insignificant; the symbol ". ." means not available; the symbol "n.a." means not applicable. Differences between totals and sums of components are due to rounding unless otherwise indicated.

For brevity, references in text footnotes, table sources, and the appendixes supply only the author's last name and omit titles of articles: for example, Karcz, *American Economic Review,* June 1964. When reference is to an article other than in a journal, the author's name will be followed by the word "in" and the title of the work: for example, Karcz, in *New Directions in the Soviet Economy,* 1966. Complete references will be found in the bibliography under the author's name. Explanation of the abbreviations of references used in the footnotes, tables, and appendixes is provided in a list of short titles preceding the Bibliography.

Unless otherwise specified, all values in this book are expressed in "new" domestic rubles, in force from 1961. One "new" ruble equals ten (pre-1961) "old" rubles. The foreign trade ruble at which Soviet imports and exports are valued externally has no necessary relation to the domestic ruble. One "new" foreign trade ruble equals 4.4 (pre-1961) "old" foreign trade rubles.

Contents

APPENDIXES

TEXT TABLES

FIGURES

APPENDIX TABLES

1

Introduction

Purpose of the Study

The subject of this book is the pattern of change in Soviet national income and output during the years 1958–1964. The bulk of the book consists of a presentation and analysis of an independently constructed set of national accounts for each of the years in the period indicated. With minor modifications (set out in Chapter 2), the accounting structure and concepts of this study are those of the Soviet National Income and Product (hereafter, SNIP) system devised by Abram Bergson and utilized in calculations by Oleg Hoeffding, Abram Bergson, Hans Heymann, Jr., and Nancy Nimitz, covering the period 1928–1955.[1] Accounts for 1958 were previously compiled by Nimitz,[2] and the present estimates for that year rely in part on her work. Because of the appearance of substantial new data and for methodological consistency with my estimates for subsequent years, it appeared necessary to redo the accounts for 1958.

The period that is the focus of this study virtually coincides with that of the Seven Year Plan (hereafter SYP), scheduled to run from 1959 through 1965. A secondary focus of this book is therefore a set of national accounts for the plan year 1965, representing an attempt to translate the SYP's targets for 1965 into national income and product flows. The targets in question are those formulated in 1958–1959 when the general directives of the SYP, called the Control Figures, were developed. These goals are to be distinguished from those of the annual

---

[1] *SNIP 1928, SNIP 1937, SNIP 1940–1948, SNIP 1949–1955,* and *Real SNIP.*

[2] *SNIP 1956–1958.*

plan for 1965 formulated at the end of 1964.[8] To avoid confusion, the SYP terminal year is hereafter designated "1965S." The function of the *ex ante* accounts for 1965S is to provide an ordered view of economic policy as it was conceived at the beginning of the period. Comparison of the *ex ante* and the *ex post* data should illuminate the transformation of policy under the pressure of various forces.

The completion of these calculations extends the coverage of SNIP estimates to a significant transitional period in Soviet affairs. A half century after the October Revolution and on the 40th anniversary of what has been called the Second Bolshevik Revolution—the inauguration of full-speed industrialization in 1928–1929—the estimates to be presented extend SNIP coverage to a rather different era in Soviet economic history, one of retardation of growth under nonwar conditions. Even disregarding the catastrophes of war, Soviet growth has not been uniform, and slowdowns have been observed before, most notably in 1938–1940. But the SYP period is unique in the duration of the retardation. It is one, moreover, in which the concern over diminished growth prospects has very likely served as the "impelling force" (*puskovoi impuls*), to use A. M. Birman's phrase, for the first serious effort at major reform of the Soviet body economic. If the reform announced in the fall of 1965 still seems mild and hesitant at the moment, the potential effects of further steps along this path are powerful. The ultimate repercussions of the retardation could drastically alter the shape and functioning of Soviet economic institutions.

It is not just in the record of economic growth or the pattern of institutional change that we may observe the transition, but also in the character of the society's directing figures. The SYP period is, of course, the era of Khrushchev, the time of his triumph and of his downfall. No less Khrushchev's is the SYP itself, a personal identification symbolized by the departure from the orthodox time-span of five years. A capsule comparison of the man with his predecessor and inheritors points up his bifarious stance. The Stalinist economy was a growth machine, to use an oversimplified but still evocative image, propelled by the single-minded will of the man of steel. The present regime consists of pragmatic repairmen, aware that the old engine isn't what it used to be and concerned at how extensive an overhaul will be needed. Khrushchev

---

[8] To complicate matters still further, goals for 1965 were formulated at the end of 1963 as part of a two year plan for 1964 and 1965. However, no further reference to this plan appears in the book.

himself was a Janus-like figure, facing backward and forward in time. As the last of the leadership line who believed with perfect faith in the power of Bolshevik will, he was a throwback to the earlier era. His successors are unlikely to be accused as he was of "voluntarism" and "subjectivism." On the other hand, other aspects of Khrushchev's style of leadership—for example, his concern for communication between leaders and led, and for "goulash" communism—link him to the present directorship. In his time, after all, currents of thought were allowed to spring forth that are the source of the current reform and possibly of more radical change to follow. It is hoped that this study will contribute to our understanding of a remarkable era in Soviet history.

The *explanation* of Soviet growth is *not* the concern of this book. It makes no pretense at explaining the recent retardation in the rate of growth of national product, a task requiring a disaggregation by branch of origin, in addition to the estimates by final use attempted here. Discussion of the topic is not totally forsworn, but the essential aim is rather to broaden our perception of Soviet growth and structural change. It hardly seems necessary to argue that if growth is to be explained, a study of national income along the lines of this study is at least a useful point of departure.

Having sketched in the general framework of the book, I should now elaborate on the separate though related themes, national income 1958–1964 and national income in the SYP.

NATIONAL INCOME 1958–1964

In the past, independent calculation of Soviet national income by non-Soviet scholars was a natural response to the paucity and, as most observers agreed, unreliability of Soviet official data. For two decades, beginning in the mid-1930s, information on the structure of Soviet national income, whether by origin or disposition, was suppressed. Published Soviet figures relating to total output aroused doubt of their trustworthiness because of the obscurity of the calculations on which they were based.

It is generally recognized that the situation described applied to Soviet statistics in the Stalin era; that after his death the flow of information became faster, broader, and deeper. If we look at relevant changes with regard to national income alone, we find very significant innovations: the use of the long obsolete and statistically suspect 1926–1927 prices as index weights was abandoned even before Stalin's death; since 1958, valuation of output for intertemporal comparisons is at 1958 prices;[4] since 1959, the statistical handbooks have published percentage distributions of aggregate output at current prices by branch of origin, with the series now carried back as far as 1958; since 1960, absolute values have been published for total national income, its branch origin and its final use distribution, all in current prices.[5]

Why, then, should we continue to compile independent national income estimates? Unfortunately—in view of the immense labor such computations require, there is still reason to believe, in Bergson's phrase, "that the measurement of Russian national income is too important a task to leave to Russian statisticians." [6] This would be true if only because the theoretical foundation of national income accounting in the USSR is the Soviet version of Marxian economics. In consequence, the published Soviet national income data are of quite different scope from income estimates generated by noncommunist social accounting systems. Soviet statisticians have not yet published any reconciliations of the official Soviet data with noncommunist income concepts.[7]

Second, the methodology of the official calculations has never been set out in detail. The statistical yearbooks contain scattered notes on methods and procedures, and these are virtually the only official statements available. There are, of course, numerous Soviet works on the subject, some of which are written by authoritative figures in the statistical and planning apparatus, but it is often difficult to distinguish official practice from personal predilection in these writings.[8] Moreover, the Soviet literature focuses on normative issues, particularly with respect to valuation, and leaves large areas of current procedure obscure. To cite but one example, the treatment of the balance of payments in Soviet national accounts is, to my knowledge, nowhere discussed in sufficient

---

[4] Indexes for earlier years have not been recomputed with the new price weights. The old indexes—using 1926/1927 prices through 1950, 1951 prices for the period 1951–1955, and 1956 prices for 1956–1958—have been chain-linked to the new 1958 price indexes.

[5] The final use distributions have now been carried back as far as 1950, in *VS*, 1966, No. 4, p. 96.

[6] *Real SNIP*, p. 3.

[7] There have been a number of Soviet attempts to recompute national income of the United States or western European countries on a Marxist basis but none to recast Soviet national income.

[8] Riabushkin voiced a similar complaint with regard to the literature on the so-called "balance of the national economy." Riabushkin, in *Uchenye zapiski po statistike*, IV, 1959, p. 49.

detail to answer the most elementary questions concerning the scope of published data.[9]

Soviet national income statistics are on occasion still released in a manner to stir dormant suspicions. A case in point concerns the magnitude of the aggregate increase in 1964. On December 9, 1964, Premier Kosygin reported an anticipated increase of 5 percent. According to the plan fulfillment report, published in the central press of January 30, 1965, national income rose 7 percent in 1964. The annual *SSSR v tsifrakh v 1964 godu,* sent to the printers on April 3, 1965, gave the figure as "over" 7 percent. With the appearance of the yearbook, *Narodnoe khoziaistvo SSSR v 1964 godu,* sent to the printers on November 22, 1965, the increase mushroomed to 9.0 percent. Confusion also attaches to the 1965 figure and is related to the fuzzy distinction between income produced and income utilized.[10]

Third, although material is now being published that had not been seen in Soviet sources since the early 1930s, it is being released in aggregated form. Disposition of Soviet national income is shown in the yearbooks as a twofold breakdown into "consumption" and "accumulation and other expenditure"; only three subcategories appear under each of the major headings. The precise definition, scope, and content of the categories are uncertain.

Finally, the USSR has not yet published a complete, integrated set of accounts. Except for a skeletal structure of gross product—in terms of the shares of all material outlays, wages, and surplus product—in the single year 1959,[11] no official data have been released on the structure of incomes generated and received.

For the period since 1958 there exist two published sets of independent estimates of Soviet GNP compiled outside of the USSR, one by Stanley Cohn for the Joint Economic Committee of the U.S. Congress, and the other by Richard Moorsteen and Raymond Powell.[12] Both the Cohn and Moorsteen–Powell estimates represent aggregations of branch of origin indexes. As far as is known, the material to be presented makes up the only independent reconstruction of Soviet national accounts during the period indicated.

---

[9] See, for example, Nove, *Soviet Studies,* July 1966, pp. 83–84.

[10] For details see Nove, *Soviet Studies,* July 1965, pp. 99–101, and the same author's article cited in note 9 above.

[11] *NKh 1960,* p. 144.

[12] See Chapter 10 for a detailed comparison of the Cohn and Moorsteen–Powell results with those of the present study.

SYP AND SNIP

In developing estimates of Soviet national income *ex post* I tread a well-worn path, but *ex ante* income accounts are a novelty; I believe that the accounts for 1965S are the first calculations of planned flows in terms of a national income framework. As already indicated, their purpose is to provide a more ordered view of economic policy than can be obtained from mere inspection of the mixed bag of plan goals using a variety of units of measure. The comparison of plan and implementation is intended to highlight the alteration of policy as the period unfolded.

My accounts terminate with the year 1964; the SYP was scheduled to run through 1965. Does not the absence of *ex post* accounts for 1965 seriously impair the comparison of plan and fulfillment? Khrushchev was dismissed from office at the end of 1964, and I shall argue in the conclusion that the SYP and the economic policy of the period until his overthrow bear a common stamp of his mode of operation. But I also want to make clear that the comparison of plan and fulfillment in this study is not directed to the evaluation of the relative success or failure of the plan. Although this is a popular exercise, its rationale is frequently dubious. It is clear, of course, that important SYP goals, such as growth of national income and agricultural output, were not met. Few Soviet "perspective" plans (that is, a plan covering a period of more than a year or two) have ever achieved more than indifferent success. Indeed, before World War II, the gulf between the five year plan (hereafter, FYP) goal and fulfillment was so wide and the obsolescence of original targets so rapid that it seems fruitless to make the FYPs the criterion of periodization of Soviet economic history. This is a point on which Naum Jasny was insistent,[13] and with considerable justification. Nor were the postwar FYPs conspicuously more successful. The sixth and last, scheduled to run from 1956 through 1960, was abandoned after two years when it became apparent that its targets were hopelessly out of reach.

It is also clear that the planners themselves must expect actual results to differ substantially from the stated goals of a medium or long term plan. Soviet dogma asserts that perspective plans are the basis of all planning in the USSR, and it is frequently suggested that perspective plans are as operational as short range plans. On the other hand, Stalin called the First FYP "a first approximation" to be "improved and rendered more precise on the basis of local experience of the working of

---

[13] Jasny, *Soviet Industrialization 1928–1952,* 1961, Chapter 1; also his *Essays on the Soviet Economy,* 1962, Essay VI.

the Plan." Speaking of the Third FYP, Molotov declared that "planning does not consist in a piling-up of figures and tables irrespective of how the plan is progressing. . . . Corrections have to be introduced into the planned figures and time-limits to bring them into accord with the actual process of carrying out the plan." [14] Over a long period of time, even in a planned and regimented economy, events have a way of unpredictably unsettling the best laid plans. Logic and experience must have convinced Soviet planners and policy-makers of this, and the conviction is reflected in the fact that "the operational plan in the Soviet Union is not the long-term plan, but the short-term plan, the annual plan." [15] Only the short term plan in fact has a directive character, legally compelling enterprise behavior.

However seriously Soviet leaders may have taken the SYP's goals in 1958–1959, when they were framed, Soviet expectations with respect to 1965 must have quickly changed in important respects. Before the SYP period was half over, Soviet agriculture had performed poorly after the bumper harvest year of 1958, to the unconcealed disappointment of the government; changes had been made in investment allocations for particular branches and sectors of the economy; a projected military demobilization had been countermanded and the identified military budget in 1961 increased sharply in midyear, followed by a further increase in the following year; where the private sector was originally expected to contribute significantly to the fulfillment of the housing space target, the pace of growth declined after 1959, and a 1962 decree sharply curtailed further individual housing construction and ownership; [16] prices of meat and butter were raised in mid-1962, and the gradual abrogation of direct income taxes was halted in mid-course. By March 1963, the government had apparently seen enough and ordered work begun on a special two year plan covering 1964 and 1965. Soviet sources insisted that the 1964–1965 plan was an organic part of the SYP and would serve only to "concretize" the assignments for these two years set out in the SYP.[17] Outside the USSR, the March 1963 announcement was taken as effective notice of the demise of the SYP.

Nevertheless, it is a mistake to judge either the realism or success of a

[14] Cited in Dobb, *Soviet Economic Development Since 1917,* 1960, pp. 356–357.

[15] Levine, in *Comparisons of the United States and Soviet Economies,* 1959, p. 152.

[16] *Pravda,* August 7, 1962.

[17] "Novym khoziaistvennym planam . . . ," *PKh,* 1963, No. 5, p. 1.

Soviet perspective plan *just* by the gap between original goal and realization. A true measure of the degree of fulfillment would require that we know what the plan would have been had planners and policy-makers foreseen at least the exogenously determined changes in plan indicators. It follows that the essential criterion of plan realism is whether goals are consistent with the means available, as indicated by information existing at the time of plan formulation. By this standard, the SYP impressed unbiased observers at the time as a distinct change from the past.[18] The very fact that the Plan's *raison d'être* was a replacement for the abortive Sixth FYP suggested that realism and relevance were considerations of weight in formulating Plan objectives (with a conspicuous exception to be mentioned shortly). Indeed, rates of growth of key indicators in the SYP were all lower than those of the Sixth FYP, as shown in the following tabulation: [19]

	Average Annual Rates of Growth	
	Sixth FYP	*SYP*
National income	9.9	7.2–7.5
Gross industrial production	10.6	8.6
Gross grain harvest	11.0	2.2–3.6
Railroad freight transportation	7.3	4.9–5.3
Retail trade, state-cooperative sector	8.5	7.2

Additional interest is lent to the SYP particulars by the reforms in economic administration, revisions in the mechanism of central planning, and the changes in planning methods that took place in 1957–1959.[20] In 1957, most of the central industrial ministries were abolished and control was transferred to regional councils of national economy in the first instance. The State Planning Commission received many of the executive powers formerly vested in the central ministries.[21]

---

[18] See, for example, Hoeffding, *Foreign Affairs,* April 1959.

[19] Compound rates implied by percent increases between initial and terminal years given in *Pravda,* January 15, 1956 and January 28, 1959. No gross agricultural output target was given in the Sixth Plan directives; since the SYP gross agricultural output target was 7.7 percent per year, and in view of the Sixth Plan national income and industrial production targets, the difference compared with the Sixth Plan target probably would be small.

[20] For a survey, see Kaser, *Soviet Studies,* April 1959, pp. 321–338.

[21] On the 1957 industrial reorganization see Hoeffding, *American Economic Review, Papers and Proceedings,* May 1959, pp. 65–77; and Kaser, in Grossman, ed., *Value and Plan,* 1960, pp. 213–234.

In 1958 the MTS (machine-tractor stations) were abolished and their machinery sold to the collective farms. The system of multiple prices of agricultural products was abolished, thereby immensely simplifying the task of rational calculation.[22] Of particular interest here are the attempts to improve the methodology of planning: the adoption of an improved and elaborated set of national economic balances recommended by a conference of statisticians in 1957;[23] the proposal to institute annual directives within the overall guidelines of the SYP to insure continuity in planning, and the overhauling of the instructions on the formulation of annual plans;[24] the increased use of the "synthetic," nonmaterial balances for greater integration and consistency of parts of the plan.[25]

All this suggests that a particular effort may have been made to turn out a consistent and meaningful set of directives for the SYP period. This is not to say that realism is the hallmark of all parts of the plan. The agricultural targets were regarded in the West with considerable skepticism almost from the time of the publication of the draft in the fall of 1958, but they were viewed as more likely an indication of overoptimism than of arbitrariness.

Realism in a plan is a measure of the clarity of the planners' perception of the economic environment and of the policy-makers' restraint in keeping goals linked to objective possibilities. But neither of these is an absolute good. In Soviet-style planning, anchored on material balances, the marginal cost of reducing *small* anticipated imbalances may be high, and for perspective planning the incremental returns are probably too meager relative to the required effort. Because the future is essentially unpredictable, the system must be prepared to meet the unexpected, changing stance as required. It must strive, in Holland Hunter's phrase, for "an equilibrium of flexible consistency," a "stochastic equilibrium."[26] Within obvious limits, the Napoleonic device, *on s'engage et puis on*

---

[22] Nimitz, in *Comparison of the United States and Soviet Economies,* 1959, pp. 267–268; Volin, *Problems of Communism,* January–February 1959, pp. 35–43.

[23] *Vsesoiuznoe soveshchanie statistikov, 4–8 iunia 1957g.,* 1958, pp. 177–261.

[24] Kotov and Krylov, *PKh,* 1958, No. 9, pp. 11–24.

[25] V. Kats, *Promyshlenno-ekonomicheskaia gazeta,* August 3, 1958, p. 2.

[26] Hunter, *Economic Development and Cultural Change,* Part 1, July 1961, p. 570. (The second term is attributed by Hunter to Jack Faucett of CEIR.) Hunter is discussing current planning in this article. If the point is valid for the short run, it is true *a fortiori* of long-run planning with its greater unpredictability.

voit, makes considerable sense.[27] So long, too, as Soviet planning relies on buffer sectors and reserves to open bottlenecks in high priority sectors, such an attitude may produce more or less severe dislocations but is not *prima facie* evidence of lack of realism in plan construction. Nor must we forget, as Hunter and others have reminded us, the hortatory function of taut planning, mobilizing effort for maximum pressure against the frontiers of production possibilities. To this we might add informational and incentive functions—for example, directing attention to priority objectives and holding out hope for better living standards.

This line of reasoning cannot be pushed very far, clearly. An excess of flexibility must inevitably bring on not equilibrium but disruption and spinning of the wheels. Moreover, it is a far cry from this kind of descriptive analysis to an operational definition of realism. It must be hastily added that such a definition is outside the scope of this study. However, my point is that in the absence of indications of material failures of realism, we are justified in an interest in the plan as a reflection of contemporary policy, independent of the fate of particular targets. That is, to the degree that the plan faithfully reflects planners' and policy-makers' judgments of the time, it provides a guide to the paths in which they hope to lead the economy, knowing and expecting that there will be twists and turns along the way. These are the terms of reference for the analysis of the SYP in this book.

Still, time effects unforeseen changes in means and ends—if not in ultimate objectives, very likely in short or intermediate range goals. Eugène Zaleski views the transition from one long term plan to another not in terms of the decision of the central authority and the promulgation of a decree, but as the crossing of a threshold. That crossing is identified with the "moment where the tide of partial adjustments," in terms of both means and ends, and with respect to exogenous and endogenous change, "empties the original plan of content." [28] Was not the SYP emptied of content long before the actual end of the period it embraced? Is it permissible to attach the SYP label *ex post* to the entire seven year span?

---

[27] These limits are considerably short of the gulf between "engaging" and "seeing" which Alexander Erlich found so characteristic of both Leninist and Stalinist economic policy. See Erlich's article in Simmons, ed., *Continuity and Change in Russian and Soviet Thought*, 1955, p. 81.

[28] Zaleski, *Planification de la croissance et fluctuations économiques en U.R.S.S., I, 1918–1932*, 1962, p. xx (preface by André Piatier).

It is implicit in my remarks to this point that I approach the matter somewhat differently from Zaleski, at least with respect to the period of direct concern to me. I am less concerned with the applicability of particular targets at post-inception points in time than in the insights into aims and policies to be derived from analysis of the plan itself. That same concern motivates the comparisons of plan and fulfillment undertaken in this study.

At the beginning of this section, previewing a conclusion of Chapter 12, I contended that the *ex post* economic patterns of the years 1959–1964 are of the same mold from which the SYP was cast, despite the differences between plan and realization, set out at length in Chapter 9. That consistency, it seems to me, was broken with the fall from power of Khrushchev and his replacement by a new regime with a new set of objectives and instrumentalities. I do not pretend that the goals of the SYP remained or indeed ever were operational targets, only that there is a broad overarching unity in the period that entitles us to amalgamate plan and realization, deviant as the latter was from the former, in a single analytic time unit. The reader will be able to judge for himself whether the claim is justified.

Plan of the Work

The substance of the book is set out in Parts II and III, dealing with analysis of the national income data and some of the implications of this analysis. Part II has a core of three chapters dealing with financial flows, resource allocation, and growth in 1958–1964. Two additional chapters focus on military expenditures and investment. The analysis of the SYP accounts is the subject of Chapter 9. Part III draws a variety of comparisons. The findings of this study are compared with those of others for the same period in Chapter 10. Intertemporal comparisons in the interval 1950–1964 for both the USSR and leading noncommunist economies are attempted in Chapter 11. The final chapter summarizes the findings and presents some conclusions, particularly with respect to the SYP and economic policy in the period of the Plan.

Methodological problems are the subject of the two chapters of Part I. Chapter 2 summarizes the SNIP accounting system, presents the set of accounts compiled at prevailing prices of the given years, and attempts to weigh their reliability. The data at prevailing prices supply the raw material for the analysis (in Chapters 4 and 9) of financial flows—sources of incomes, patterns of outlays, the relation of the budget to national aggregates. Analysis of Soviet resource allocation, in the framework of the economist's concern with the ultimate categories of welfare and productive potential, must first grapple with the deficiencies of Soviet prices as measuring rods of either of the two categories. Therefore, Chapter 3 is largely devoted to a consideration of the adjustments in prevailing-price values required as a result of a critical analysis of the Soviet price system. The standard of judgment in this effort is a valuation standard developed by Abram Bergson. I am also concerned with growth and hence with the isolation of real changes from those reflecting only movements of the price level. A discussion of the criteria governing the deflation of current-price time series is included in Chapter 3; details of the deflation procedure are relegated to an Appendix.

The reader interested in getting directly at the results of the study will probably want to skim Part I, concentrate on the rest of the text, and avoid the Appendixes. However, should he desire to examine the artificer's toolbox and scrutinize his procedure the means will be at hand. In particular, the appendixes are intended to facilitate reproduction of every link in the estimating process. Anyone with a taste for exploring the thickets of Soviet statistics is warmly invited to make the armchair journey as far as his interest and patience will sustain him.

Part I

The SNIP Accounts and Their Methodology

2

National Income and Product at Established Prices

This chapter provides the data and the attendant methodological explanation of the established-price accounts for 1958–1964 and 1965S. It also attempts to appraise the reliability of the 1958–1964 established-price estimates and explores the meaning of the 1965S account entries.

The Accounting System

To avoid unnecessary repetition of Bergson's extensive treatment of these topics,[1] I try to limit the following discussion to the essential principles of the system and to areas of difference between Bergson's and my approaches.

SECTORING

For income and outlay accounting, the economy is divided into a household sector and the public sectors. The former includes households not only in their capacity as consumers, but as producers as well—notably, in connection with the small garden plots and livestock holdings owned by collective and state farmers, as well as by other rural elements of the population. Included in the public sectors are state, nonfarm cooperative, and collective farm enterprises and institutions, along with such social organizations as the Communist Party, trade unions, and voluntary societies, in their capacity as economic entities. These organizations make up the collective farm, state, and state-cooperative (in-

---

[1] See *SNIP 1937*, Chapter 2, and *Real SNIP*, Chapter 2.

cluding the social organizations) sectors, collectively termed the public sectors.[2]

PRODUCTION BOUNDARIES

The outstanding issue is the distinction between intermediate and final product and, in that connection, of the appropriate treatment of government activity. Bergson opted to follow Department of Commerce rather than Kuznets procedure and consider as final product all government outlays—social welfare (except transfer payments), administration, defense, internal security, and a variety of minor production expenditures financed through the government budget. This study, in turn, follows Bergson on this matter,[3] but some clarifying comments should be made:

(1) As the border between governmental and nongovernmental activities of the public sector, Bergson settled on the distinction between *khozraschet* and budget organizations. *Khozraschet* (usually and somewhat inadequately translated as "economic" or "business accounting") organizations are generally required to meet current outlays out of current revenues, hence relate to the budget primarily on a capital rather than current basis. Budget organizations, as the term suggests, have all their expenditures financed by the budget and transmit to it all their revenues. By this test administrative outlays of ministries were regarded as final product but those of subordinate organs intermediate between enterprises and ministries were not. As Bergson recognized, this criterion allowed room for unintended change in the volume of administrative activity included as final product through shifts in the Soviet administrative code. Fortunately, there was little change in this regard during the SYP period, but for longer intertemporal comparisons, it should be borne in mind that the SYP period is virtually coextensive with the era of *sovnarkhoz* ("councils of national economy") administration, as distinct from the ministerial form that both preceded and followed it. Most *sovnarkhozy,* it appears, were budget institutions, but some were not;[4] to what extent the elimination of most economic ministries in 1957 was compensated by the subsequent proliferation of state committees, also budget organizations, is not clear.

---

[2] Production divisions of the economy—industry, agriculture, transport and so forth—will be designated by the term "branch."

[3] In a sense my choice is easier than was his inasmuch as I opt for an exclusively production potential interpretation of the estimates. See the first section of Chapter 3.

[4] *Gosudarstvennyi biudzhet,* 1965, p. 186.

(2) From time to time Soviet administrative practice has seen fit to deny *khozraschet* status to what are in effect production organizations. The outstanding example is provided by the machine tractor stations (MTS) which, until their dissolution in 1958, serviced collective farms. Bergson wisely treated these as if they had been on *khozraschet*. Project design (*proektno-izyskatel'skie*) organizations were transferred in 1959 from budget to *khozraschet* status, and that part of their expenditures connected with specific investment projects is now financed from investment funds; the rest continue to be financed from operating grants by the budget. In the present accounts all outlays of these organizations appear as final product. Although it would perhaps be preferable to consider the outlays now financed from the budget as intermediate, both the absence of adequate data and the advantage of consistency with Bergson's treatment indicate acceptance of these and similar government-financed operational outlays as final product.[5]

(3) However, such liberalism does not extend to budget subsidies to *khozraschet* enterprises to cover ordinary operating losses. These "conventional subsidies," as they are designated in this study, and a number of other loss-compensating grants (subsidies to procurement organizations and accounting subsidies to foreign trade organizations) are transfers considered to reflect intermediate outlays.

(4) Although he accepted the Soviet distinction between "capital" and "current" repairs to plant and equipment, Bergson nevertheless was skeptical that the principle was being correctly observed in practice. The general assumption of this study is that all Soviet capital repairs outlays are appropriately considered final product.[6] However, I shall test the sensitivity of the results to this assumption by omitting half of capital repairs in a number of illustrative calculations in Chapters 5 and 6.

IMPUTATIONS

Production boundaries in national income calculations are extended by imputations. In this study imputations are made in four cases, three of which follow the usual SNIP practice. (1) A rental value is imputed to owner-occupied housing, calculated at the average rate paid in state housing. (2) Income of households from agriculture consumed or invested in kind is valued at average prices realized in sales by all sectors. (3) Military subsistence allowances are not only a component of public

---

[5] For examples see below, p. 395.

[6] For additional discussion of this point, see below, pp. 57, 104–105.

sector outlays on defense, as a partial measure of defense services, but are also entered in both income and outlay sides of the household sector account. The rate of imputation is, of course, given by state sector prices. (4) An imputation new to SNIP procedure is valuation of building services contributed by prospective owners in the construction of privately owned housing. Since the estimates of the value of these services derive from official data on the value of private housing construction, it seems likely that state wage rates serve as the basis for imputation, but this is by no means certain. The appropriateness of the first two imputation rates will be taken up in Chapter 3, in a discussion of the general valuation problem.

The treatment of collective farm incomes and outlays poses a special problem. Until well into the 1950s the calculation of costs was unknown in collective farm accounting, and it is only since 1963 that farms have begun to compute net income in a sense reasonably comparable to profits of state enterprises. Detailed information on investment in fixed capital and inventories was and remains scarce. The most readily available data were on money income and its disposition. Hence from *SNIP 1949–1955* on, retained collective farm income is considered to be money income allocated to investment and cultural funds; that volume of income is also entered as collective farm outlays in the accounts. This procedure has the obvious disadvantage of ignoring outlays financed from income in kind and increases of debt (bank loans and procurement advances).[7] On the other hand, investment estimated from data on changes in collective farm assets may be overstated because of purchases of livestock from households and other farms.[8] Frequently, the sources conjoin new livestock investment and acquisitions from other producers. The data on collective farm working capital are particularly deficient, and it is often difficult to distinguish real and financial assets. Pending further clarification of collective farm accounts, it appears necessary to restrict coverage in these accounts to farm money income and outlays.[9]

Income and Outlay Categories

The basic national income and product accounts for 1958–1964 and 1965S are set out in Tables 1–6. Tables 1–2 provide a sources and uses

---

[7] In a consolidated public sector account, intra-sector debt changes cancel out but this is not true of the increments in real assets they finance.

[8] But understated because of the netting out of retirements.

[9] This summary of the present state of collective farm accounting and statistics owes much to an unpublished paper by Sally Anderson.

TABLE 1

HOUSEHOLD INCOMES, 1958–1964, 1965S
(billion rubles)

	1958	1959	1960	1961	1962	1963	1964	1965S
1. Wages and salaries, farm and nonfarm								
A. Worker and employee wage and salary bill	52.19 [a]	54.89 [a]	59.62	65.91	70.65	74.14	79.21	80.0
B. Bonuses not included in wage and salary bill	.55	.67	.59	.74	.73	.62	.84	[b]
C. Wages in kind	.50	.55	.60	.65	.70	.75	.80	[b]
D. Total	53.24	56.11	60.81	67.30	72.08	75.51	80.85	
2. Net income of households from agriculture, excluding wages of state employed farm labor								
A. Money payments by collective farms	5.00	4.76	4.94	5.51	6.20	6.73	7.87	. .
B. Net income from sales of farm products	6.22	6.33	5.98	6.04	7.35	7.92	7.00	. .
C. Net farm income in kind	10.57	9.99	9.80	10.08	9.98	8.55	10.12	. .
D. Total	21.79	21.08	20.72	21.63	23.53	23.20	24.99	26.4
3. Income of armed forces								
A. Military pay	2.60	2.50	2.39	2.26	2.53	2.34	2.14	2.6
B. Military subsistence	1.51	1.45	1.38	1.31	1.47	1.36	1.24	1.5
C. Total	4.11	3.95	3.77	3.57	4.00	3.70	3.38	4.1
4. Other income currently earned; statistical discrepancy	7.71	9.82	10.87	6.02	7.05	9.08	9.08	11.0 [c]
5. Imputed net rent of owner-occupied dwellings	1.10	1.14	1.18	1.21	1.24	1.26	1.29	1.4
6. Imputed value of owner-supplied building services	1.18	1.36	1.22	1.05	.92	.80	.74	1.6
7. Total income currently earned	88.13	93.46	98.57	100.78	108.82	113.55	120.33	124.5
8. Transfer receipts								
A. Pensions and allowances	8.90	9.45	9.88	10.90	11.60	12.00	12.60	15.0
B. Stipends	.72	.76	.73	.75	.81	.84	.92	1.0
C. Interest receipts	.25	.28	.31	.33	.36	.34	.38	.5
D. Net new bank loans to households	.08	.14	.06	(−).02	(−).07	(−).14	(−).08	—
E. Total	9.95	10.63	10.98	11.96	12.70	13.04	13.82	16.5
9. Total income	99.08	104.09	109.55	112.74	121.52	126.59	134.15	141.0

Notes:

[a] Includes earnings of members of producer cooperatives absorbed into the state sector in 1960.

[b] Included with item 4.

[c] Includes items 1.B and 1.C; excludes statistical discrepancy, recorded on outlay side.

Sources:

Appendixes A and E.

TABLE 2

HOUSEHOLD OUTLAYS, 1958–1964, 1965S

(billion rubles)

	1958	1959	1960	1961	1962	1963	1964	1965S
1. Retail sales of goods for consumption								
A. State-cooperative trade	60.33	64.47	71.13	73.41	79.64	84.29	88.18	93.2
B. Extravillage farm markets	4.43	4.23	4.00	4.31	4.36	4.29	4.42	[a]
C. Total	64.76	68.70	75.13	77.72	84.00	88.58	92.60	
2. Consumer services								
A. Housing (including imputed rent)	1.71	1.80	1.89	1.97	2.06	2.14	2.22	2.4
B. Trade union and other dues	.91	.94	1.02	1.12	1.19	1.26	1.35	1.3
C. Other services	6.58	7.09	7.65	8.48	9.36	10.06	10.88	13.2
D. Total	9.20	9.83	10.56	11.57	12.61	13.46	14.45	16.9
3. Consumption of income in kind								
A. Farm income in kind	9.92	9.52	9.12	9.36	9.55	9.39	9.67	[a]
B. Nonfarm wages in kind	.50	.55	.60	.65	.70	.75	.80	.8
C. Military subsistence	1.51	1.45	1.38	1.31	1.47	1.36	1.24	1.5
D. Total	11.93	11.52	11.10	11.32	11.72	11.50	11.71	
4. Other outlays for consumption	3.00	3.19	2.66	2.21	3.34	3.81	4.00	19.1 [b]
5. Total outlays for consumption	88.89	93.24	99.45	102.82	111.67	117.35	122.76	131.5
6. Investment								
A. Private housing construction	2.65	3.05	2.74	2.37	2.07	1.79	1.66	3.5
B. Farm investment in kind	.65	.47	.68	.72	.43	−.84	.45	—
C. Total	3.30	3.52	3.42	3.09	2.50	.95	2.11	3.5
7. Total outlays for consumption and investment	92.19	96.76	102.87	105.91	114.17	118.30	124.87	135.0
8. Transfer outlays								
A. Net savings	1.11	1.41	.65	.57	.89	1.47	2.00	2.2
B. Direct taxes	5.19	5.52	5.60	5.83	6.00	6.31	6.75	3.0
C. Other payments to the state	.59	.40	.43	.43	.46	.51	.53	.8
D. Total	6.89	7.33	6.68	6.83	7.35	8.29	9.28	6.0
9. Total outlays	99.08	104.09	109.55	112.74	121.52	126.59	134.15	141.0

Notes:

[a] Included with item 4.

[b] Includes extravillage farm market sales, consumption of farm income in kind, and statistical discrepancy.

Sources:

Appendixes B and F.

TABLE 3

PUBLIC SECTOR INCOMES, 1958–1964, 1965S
(billion rubles)

	1958	1959	1960	1961	1962	1963	1964	1965S
1. Net income retained by economic organizations								
A. Retained income of collective farms	2.66	2.85	2.62	2.65	2.79	2.52	2.73	5.4
B. Retained profits of state enterprises	4.58	4.95	4.58	4.66	5.32	3.54	4.66	10.0
C. Retained profits of nonfarm cooperatives	.90	.92	.85	.36	.42	.52	.55	2.3 (C and D)
D. Retained profits of other organizations	.51	.51	.57	.21	.12	.18	.18	
E. Total	8.65	9.23	8.62	7.88	8.65	6.76	8.12	17.7
2. Charges to economic enterprises for special funds								
A. Social insurance budget	3.26	3.58	3.74	4.15	4.41	4.63	4.95	5.0
B. Training of workers; research	.52	.67	.73	.80	.95	1.00	1.00	.7
C. Total	3.78	4.25	4.47	4.95	5.36	5.63	5.95	5.7
3. Taxes and other payments out of income by economic organizations to budget								
A. Tax on income of collective farms	1.03	1.24	1.21	.93	1.01	1.04	.98	..
B. Tax on income of nonfarm cooperatives and other organizations	.63	.66	.63	.30	.31	.35	.37	..
C. Deductions from profits of state enterprises	13.57	15.88	18.65	20.70	23.74	25.55	28.55	..
D. Turnover tax	30.45	31.07	31.34	30.92	32.95	34.52	36.69	..
E. Miscellaneous charges	6.34	9.28	9.95	10.64	10.62	11.52	11.83	..
F. Total	52.02	58.13	61.78	63.49	68.63	72.98	78.42	95.0
4. Net accounting profits of foreign trade organizations	.12	−.02	.14	..	..	..	..	—
5. Allowance for subsidized losses, n.e.c.	−3.60	−3.30	−2.95	−2.15	−2.70	−2.35	−2.30	−1.0
6. Consolidated total charges against current product, net of depreciation	60.97	68.29	72.06	74.17	79.94	83.02	90.19	117.4
7. Depreciation	7.96	9.00	10.14	11.30	12.59	17.12	18.71	14.5
8. Consolidated total charges against current product	68.93	77.29	82.20	85.47	92.53	100.14	108.90	131.9
9. Transfer receipts								
A. Net savings of households	1.11	1.41	.65	.57	.89	1.47	2.00	2.2
B. Direct taxes	5.19	5.52	5.60	5.83	6.00	6.31	6.75	3.0
C. Other payments to the state	.59	.40	.43	.43	.46	.51	.53	.8
D. Total	6.89	7.33	6.68	6.83	7.35	8.29	9.28	6.0
10. Consolidated net income	75.82	84.62	88.88	92.30	99.88	108.43	118.18	137.9

Sources:
Appendixes C and G.

TABLE 4

PUBLIC SECTOR OUTLAYS, 1958–1964, 1965S
(billion rubles)

	1958	1959	1960	1961	1962	1963	1964	1965S
1. Communal services								
A. Education, excluding R&D	5.91	6.30	6.88	7.70	8.20	9.40	10.40	11.0
B. Health care and physical culture	4.41	4.85	5.13	5.30	5.40	5.70	6.20	7.0
C. Other	.21	.22	.23	.23	.23	.23	.23	.3
D. Total	10.53	11.37	12.24	13.23	13.83	15.33	16.83	18.3
2. Government administration	1.20	1.12	1.09	1.08	1.09	1.09	1.11	1.5
3. Gross investment								
A. Fixed capital	33.39	37.04	41.13	43.98	46.93	50.69	55.00	60.4
B. Inventories	7.90	9.41	4.80	6.06	5.74	7.97	11.63	7.3
C. Total	41.29	46.45	45.93	50.04	52.67	58.66	66.63	67.7
4. Research and development	2.06	2.31	2.52	2.90	3.30	3.80	4.20	33.9 (items 4–7)
5. Internal security	1.50	1.50	1.50	1.50	1.50	1.50	1.50	
6. Defense (budget) [a]	9.06	9.07	9.00	11.29	12.34	13.57	12.98	
7. Outlays n.e.c.; statistical discrepancy	.23	2.17	5.62	.30	2.45	1.44	1.11	
8. Consolidated total value of goods and services, exclusive of sales to households	65.87	73.99	77.90	80.34	87.18	95.39	104.36	121.4
9. Transfer outlays								
A. Pensions and allowances	8.90	9.45	9.88	10.90	11.60	12.00	12.60	15.0
B. Stipends	.72	.76	.73	.75	.81	.84	.92	1.0
C. Interest payments to households	.25	.28	.31	.33	.36	.34	.38	.5
D. Net new bank loans to households	.08	.14	.06	−.02	−.07	−.14	−.08	—
E. Total	9.95	10.63	10.98	11.96	12.70	13.04	13.82	16.5
10. Consolidated total outlays	75.82	84.62	88.88	92.30	99.88	108.43	118.18	137.9

Note:
[a] Net of pensions paid from defense funds.

Sources:
Appendixes D and H.

TABLE 5

Gross National Product Account, 1958–1964, 1965S
(billion rubles)

	1958	1959	1960	1961	1962	1963	1964	1965S
Incomes								
1. Total income of households currently earned	89.13	93.46	98.57	100.78	108.82	113.55	120.33	124.5
2. Consolidated charges of government, social, and economic organizations against current product net of depreciation	60.97	68.29	72.06	74.17	79.94	83.02	90.19	117.4
3. Net national product	150.10	161.75	170.63	174.95	188.76	196.57	210.52	241.9
4. Depreciation	7.96	9.00	10.14	11.30	12.59	17.12	18.71	14.5
5. Gross national product	158.06	170.75	180.77	186.25	201.35	213.69	229.23	256.4
Outlays								
6. Total outlays of households for consumption and investment	92.19	96.76	102.87	105.91	114.17	118.30	124.87	135.0
7. Consolidated total value of goods and services disposed of by government, social, and economic organizations	65.87	73.99	77.90	80.34	87.18	95.39	104.36	121.4
8. Gross national product	158.06	170.75	180.77	186.25	201.35	213.69	229.23	256.4

Sources:
Incomes from Tables 1 and 3, outlays from Tables 2 and 4.

TABLE 6

Gross National Product by Use, at Established Prices, 1958–1964, 1965S
(billion rubles)

	1958	1959	1960	1961	1962	1963	1964	1965S
1. Retail sales to households								
A. State-cooperative trade	60.33	64.47	71.13	73.41	79.64	84.29	88.18	93.2
B. Extravillage farm markets	4.43	4.23	4.00	4.31	4.36	4.29	4.42	[a]
C. Total	64.76	68.70	75.13	77.72	84.00	88.58	92.60	
2. Consumer services								
A. Housing (including imputed rent)	1.71	1.80	1.89	1.97	2.06	2.14	2.22	2.4
B. Dues	.91	.94	1.02	1.12	1.19	1.26	1.35	1.3
C. Other services	6.58	7.09	7.65	8.48	9.36	10.06	10.88	13.2
D. Total	9.20	9.83	10.56	11.57	12.61	13.46	14.45	16.9
3. Consumption of income in kind								
A. Farm income in kind	9.92	9.52	9.12	9.36	9.55	9.39	9.67	[a]
B. Nonfarm wages in kind	.50	.55	.60	.65	.70	.75	.80	.8
C. Military subsistence	1.51	1.45	1.38	1.31	1.47	1.36	1.24	1.5
D. Total	11.93	11.52	11.10	11.32	11.72	11.50	11.71	
4. Other outlays for consumption	3.00	3.19	2.66	2.21	3.34	3.81	4.00	19.1 [b]
5. Total outlays for consumption	88.89	93.24	99.45	102.82	111.67	117.35	127.76	131.5
6. Communal services								
A. Education, excluding science	5.91	6.30	6.88	7.70	8.20	9.40	10.40	11.0
B. Health care and physical culture	4.41	4.85	5.13	5.30	5.40	5.70	6.20	7.0
C. Other	.21	.22	.23	.23	.23	.23	.23	.3
D. Total	10.53	11.37	12.24	13.23	13.83	15.33	16.83	18.3
7. Government administration	1.20	1.12	1.09	1.08	1.09	1.09	1.11	1.5
8. Gross investment								
A. Fixed capital								
(1) Households	3.30	3.52	3.42	3.09	2.50	.95	2.11	3.5
(2) Public sector	33.39	37.04	41.13	43.98	46.93	50.69	55.00	60.4
(3) Total	36.69	40.56	44.55	47.07	49.43	51.64	57.11	63.9
B. Inventories	7.90	9.41	4.80	6.06	5.74	7.97	11.63	7.3
C. Total	44.59	49.97	49.35	53.13	55.17	59.61	68.74	71.2

TABLE 6 (continued)

	1958	1959	1960	1961	1962	1963	1964	1965S
9. Research and development	2.06	2.31	2.52	2.90	3.30	3.80	4.20	
10. Internal security	1.50	1.50	1.50	1.50	1.50	1.50	1.50	
11. Defense (budget)								
A. Pay and subsistence	4.11	3.95	3.77	3.57	4.00	3.70	3.38	33.9
B. Other	4.95	5.12	5.23	7.72	8.34	9.87	9.60	
C. Total	9.06	9.07	9.00	11.29	12.34	13.57	12.98	
12. Outlays n.e.c.; public sector statistical discrepancy	.23	2.17	5.62	.30	2.45	1.44	1.11	
13. Gross national product	158.06	170.75	180.77	186.25	201.35	213.69	229.23	256.4

Notes.

[a] Included with item 4.

[b] Includes extravillage farm market sales, consumption of farm income in kind, and statistical discrepancy for household sector.

Sources:
Tables 2 and 4.

statement for households; Tables 3–4 are the corresponding accounts of the public sector. Current income and outlay aggregates are combined in a gross national product account in Table 5. Finally, Table 6 shows the disposition of GNP by final use category. The derivation of the estimates is explained in detail in Appendixes A through H.

Income of households in money and in kind is shown in Table 1 as the sum of wages and salaries of workers and employees,[10] net income from agriculture excluding wages and salaries,[11] military pay and subsistence, other current income, imputed income associated with private housing construction and occupation, and transfer receipts from the public sector. For years other than 1965S, "other income currently earned" is the balancing item of the household sector account and as such includes changes in cash balances (for which no estimates are attempted). With respect to 1958–1964, "other income currently earned" is computed as the difference between the sum of household income explicitly accounted for and total household outlays, and carries the supplementary designation "statistical discrepancy." Household outlays, which include savings, are shown distributed in Table 2 between outlays for consumption (purchases in retail markets, outlays on consumer services and consumption in kind), and outlays for investment, along with transfer payments to the public sector.[12] Because of relatively more severe data gaps on the outlay side, the household sector balance for 1965S is obtained with an expenditure category (farm income in kind, market sales, and other outlays for consumption), rather than "other current income," as the residual.

Under retail sales are included purchases in state and cooperative outlets and in the extravillage markets; the latter consist of the collective

---

[10] The term "workers and employees" is used throughout this report as the equivalent of the Russian *rabochie i sluzhashchie* and embraces the entire civilian labor force except for collective farmers, members of other cooperatives, and individual peasants and artisans. In 1960 the producer cooperatives were absorbed by state industry. My estimates of wages and salaries for 1958–1960 include an allowance for earnings by members of the cooperatives.

[11] Because of the form in which wage and salary data appear, it has been more convenient not to attempt separate estimation of the wages and salaries of state-employed farm labor.

[12] To label personal savings as a transfer payment may appear strange. In Bergson's view this called attention to the parallelism between incomes for which no goods or services are provided and uses of income for which goods and services are not received. *SNIP 1937*, pp. 17, 19.

farm markets proper and sales by consumer cooperatives at market prices. Intravillage market sales are omitted from retail sales. In principle, the method of calculation of farm consumption in kind indicates inclusion there of the intravillage market sales. However, the data suggest that these sales are in fact to be found in the residual category, "other outlays for consumption," of which they are the major component. This residual category is new to SNIP accounts, having been made possible by recent detailed Soviet breakdowns of consumption outlays. Farm investment in kind is limited to investment in livestock; private sector investment in other fixed capital as well as in inventories are omitted for want of data.

Income of the public sectors is shown in Table 3 as the sum of income retained (by state enterprises, collective farms, cooperatives, and other organizations), payments from income to the budget or to special funds, depreciation charges, and transfer receipts from households, less allowances for subsidized losses not elsewhere counted. That is, while retained incomes are reckoned net of what I call "conventional subsidies," they are believed to exclude certain classes of revenue and to include certain types of budget subsidy. The revenues excluded are those of the MTS (and their successors the RTS—repair tractor stations—until their complete dissolution in 1960) and of the project-design organizations (all income before 1959 and part thereafter). Budget subsidies believed included are grants in connection with the wage reform of the 1950s and 1960s as well as those to cover the gap between prices paid by agricultural procurement organizations to farms and households on one hand, and the prices received by these organizations from industry and trade on the other. Specific account is taken of the operating deficit of the MTS-RTS and of the indicated non-"conventional" budget subsidies; the income of project design organizations is presumed encompassed by the "miscellaneous charges" item of organization payments to the budget. Bookkeeping profits and losses of foreign trade organizations, which arise from the difference between internal prices and those of the world market, are viewed apart from ordinary profits. I do not distinguish between customs duties and foreign trade accounting profits, although as acknowledged in Appendix C there is some question whether this is correct.[13]

Table 4 embodies the most significant departures from previous SNIP practice. Customarily, total outlays were shown as the sum of expendi-

---

[13] See below, pp. 369–370.

tures on communal services (health care, education, and other), government administration, internal security, defense (the explicit budget allocation), gross investment, and transfer payments to households. Gross investment was computed as a residual, the difference between all other public sector outlays explicitly identified and total public sector income. In this study, I separate out research and development (R&D) outlays from expenditures on education and compute gross investment independently as the sum of investment in fixed capital[14] and in inventories. The residual row 7 in Table 4 is now conceptually a vastly smaller aggregate. Owing again to lack of information, the residual for 1965S includes defense, internal security, and R&D.

Perhaps I should make explicit that my approach to balancing the separate household and public sector income-outlay accounts is pragmatic. There is no principle of national income accounting that dictates a particular choice. In my household accounts the availability of data is decisive: expenditures determine total incomes in 1958–1964 because of the existence of relatively detailed information on household consumption, contrasted with the vagueness of our information on miscellaneous household incomes and Soviet secrecy on currency in circulation. For the public sectors in 1958–1964 expenditures might just as well have been treated as determining incomes instead of the reverse; the uncertainties with respect to miscellaneous public sector incomes, which would be the balancing item in such a case, are about as severe as those relating to miscellaneous public sector outlays. An alternative procedure would be to omit outlays n.e.c. altogether, allowing the sum of all other expenditures to determine the total. It seems to me that this is the least desirable solution, for it makes it easy to ignore the significant problems of concealed military outlays and of investment expenditures not covered by item 3 of Table 4. The volatility of outlays n.e.c. does pose a problem, and I shall attempt to deal with it at several points in the study.

Since R&D expenditures have not previously been separated out in SNIP accounts, it may be useful to append a comment on the scope of the category. The figures shown are reported outlays on "science," financed from both government budget and other sources. There is no

---

[14] Including some livestock (see Chapter 8). Fixed investment also includes warehouse stocks of equipment requiring installation. It seems to me that these differ in no substantive way from warehouse stocks of equipment not requiring installation. The latter are included in reported new fixed investment; the former are not, but I choose to classify them with fixed rather than inventory investment.

comparable entry in the Department of Commerce's national accounts but the Soviet data seem to be both more and less inclusive than figures on U.S. R&D expenditures estimated by the National Science Foundation.[15] The Soviet data are more inclusive in terms of coverage of fields of research and type of R&D expenditure. "Science," in Soviet parlance, embraces all aspects of learning, and much, if not all, of Soviet research in social sciences and humanities is included in outlays on "science." Investment in R&D facilities may also be included,[16] in contrast to the American data. On the other hand, the scope of development activities is probably understated in the reported Soviet outlays, by virtue of the omission of certain enterprise expenditures. The most important of these are charged to the production cost category "expenditures of future periods" and are recovered in the form of higher product prices.[17] Whether, on balance, reported total USSR outlays are under or overstated compared to the coverage of reported U.S. R&D expenditures is not clear. The magnitude of Soviet research outlays in the fields of humanities and social sciences is probably not very sizable, but it is difficult to appraise the relative significance of R&D investment versus omitted development expenditures.

For present purposes, of course, a more pertinent issue is the comparative scope of R&D expenditures in the U.S. national accounts relative to those for the USSR presented here. Since outlays on social science and humanities research as well as investment in R&D facilities are entered under various headings in the U.S. national product accounts, the only remaining issue is of the possible understatement of develop-

---

[15] The following is drawn largely from Nimitz, *An Addendum to Soviet Expenditures on Scientific Research* (forthcoming) Section II, to which the reader is referred for details.

[16] There is also evidence to the contrary, *ibid.* The issue is discussed in the sources to Table D-2, below.

[17] Davies, Barker, and Fakiolas (in Freeman and Young, *The Research and Development Effort in Western Europe, North America and the Soviet Union,* 1965, p. 119) believe that expenditures by "project and design" (*proektnye i konstruktorskie*) organizations are not included in budget outlays on science. At least since January 1, 1962 and for work of "theoretical or general state significance," this is not the case: Bashin, *Planirovanie nauchno-issledovatel'skikh i opytno-konstruktorskikh rabot,* 1966, p. 7; Rogovtsev, *Planirovanie i finansirovanie novoi tekhniki na predpriiatii,* 1965, p. 51. The latter source suggests that the project-design organizations were all financed by the budget prior to 1962.

For additional discussion of financing arrangements in Soviet R&D, see *The Soviet Financial System,* 1968, Chapter III.

ment expenditures. On the other hand, total Soviet outlays on science may include R&D financed from the budget appropriation to "defense." If this is so, the SNIP "defense" component would be double counted.

A possibility of double counting also exists in the SNIP accounts with respect to investment and the public sector outlay categories of administration, internal security, and defense. This is because the state-cooperative investment entries in my accounts are supplied largely by official investment statistics, whereas the entries for administration, defense, and internal security are taken from budget data or represent rule-of-thumb estimates. The most significant investment component is presumably that of military outlays; Soviet sources are laconic in their discussion of this sensitive subject (see Chapter 7).[18]

Reliability of the 1958–1964 Estimates

This section attempts to appraise the accuracy[19] of major income and outlay aggregates for 1958–1964 shown in Tables 1–6. Evaluation of the estimates at constant prices will be found in Chapters 6 and 10, but the reliability of the current factor cost values cannot be judged in the same manner because of the absence of comparable Soviet or non-Soviet series. As for the 1965S accounts, the issue there is one of internal consistency rather than reliability as commonly understood, and that problem is treated separately at the end of this chapter.

The evidence assembled or summarized below is bulky and the discussion lengthy. Nevertheless, the ultimate conclusion must be equivocal. I believe the estimates for 1958–1964 warrant some confidence in their reliability. On the other hand, there are divergences of the estimates from the few exogenous standards cited below. The more substantial discrepancies may have plausible explanations other than error in the estimates, but the confidence that can be placed in such reconciliations must be left to the reader's judgment.

---

[18] For further clarification of the scope of SNIP income and outlay categories, see *Real SNIP,* Chapter 2, and Appendixes A-H of the present study.

[19] It may be appropriate here to note that in Tables 1–6 values for SNIP 1958–1964 are shown to the nearest ten, and those for SNIP 1965S, to the nearest hundred million rubles. This is not to be considered a claim for accuracy of measurement at the indicated levels but merely a procedural convenience.

In general, values for the predominant share of incomes and outlays have been obtained from official Soviet sources, directly or at only slight remove. On the other hand, despite the relative abundance of official statistics in recent years, some important gaps in information still remain, and it is not yet possible to short-circuit that painstaking search for minutiae so familiar to students of Soviet affairs. A prime example is the estimation of farm personal incomes, which has required extensive manipulation of a mass of isolated bits of information on production, prices, inputs, and the like. For some items even a fine grain sifting of the literature produces little yield. There are no explicit entries in the accounts for changes in household cash balances because of a complete lack of information. The estimates of military incomes and of internal security outlays rest on educated guesses. Among public sector incomes, the determination of miscellaneous payments to the state budget, item 3.E of Table 3, is arbitrary because of the absence of information on minor categories of budget revenues. There are similar and not unrelated difficulties with unspecified public sector outlays, part of item 7 of Table 4. The interested reader is urged to make a careful inspection of the appendixes, without which a complete picture of the reliability of the estimates cannot be obtained.

The discussion of the 1958–1964 estimates considers, in turn, income and outlays of households, then of the public sector, and concludes with a reconciliation of SNIP net national product with official Soviet data on "national income."

HOUSEHOLD INCOME AND OUTLAYS

A number of statements may be found in the Soviet literature, directly or indirectly derived from official sources, on the magnitude of changes in aggregate household money income. Since my estimates are independently built up from individual components, the statements referred to may serve as yardsticks of the reliability of my estimated totals. The statements are cited and discussed in Appendix N. Regrettably, they are ambiguous, susceptible to contradictory interpretation, and do not extend beyond 1962. As tests of the accuracy of the SNIP estimates, they leave much to be desired, but at a minimum my estimates of aggregate household money income (and, hence, of money outlays) in 1958–1962 are not necessarily inconsistent with the independent yardsticks. Allowance for changes in cash hoards held by households may be the key to resolving the small inconsistencies noted, and I shall return to this question in Chapter 4.

THE PUBLIC SECTORS

I know of no exogenous, independent yardsticks by which to measure the reliability of my estimates of public sector incomes and outlays. The chief components derive generally from official or other reliable sources. The weak links in the chain of estimates consist of two residuals: item 3.E of Table 3, "miscellaneous charges," and item 7 of Table 4, "outlays n.e.c.; statistical discrepancy." "Miscellaneous charges" are a portion of unidentified state budget revenues from the public sectors. SNIP studies have always used a rule of thumb assigning half of the total of these miscellaneous revenues as charges against current product and considering the other half as items on capital account. In this study, for reasons explained in Appendix C, three-quarters of the miscellaneous revenues are viewed as current charges. Since the miscellaneous revenues have aggregated about 10 billion rubles on the average in this period (Table C-1), the difference between half and three-quarters of the total is not negligible. Moreover, the choice affects the outlay side of the public sector accounts as well and impacts most heavily on the Table 4 residual, item 7. Testing the sensitivity of the public sector estimates to the choice of the fraction of residual budget revenues considered a charge on current account is obviously a matter of first importance. The calculations are set forth in Appendix M and the conclusions are introduced at appropriate points in the discussion of Part II. Here it should be said that alternative assumptions on the current account share of miscellaneous revenues result in increments or decrements of values that are *multiples* of the existing entries for outlays n.e.c. in Table 4; with respect to item 3.E of Table 3, the difference is far smaller and on GNP the effect is negligible.

That the figures on outlays n.e.c. of the public sector are to be handled with great care seems self-evident. But there are real expenditures reflected there—operating and investment expenditures not elsewhere accounted for. What little information can be mustered in Appendix D suggests that the entries in 1959 and 1962–1964 may be of the right order of magnitude. On the other hand, those of 1958 and 1961 seem too low and that of 1960 too high as estimates of these omitted expenditures. The relatively low value of item 7 in 1958 may reflect an overstatement of state-cooperative inventory investment in that year, which was estimated differently from counterparts for the remaining years in the series.

Another striking feature of Table 4 is the sharp decline in inventory investment in 1960 followed by partial recovery in 1961. These changes are opposite in direction to those exhibited by item 7. Possibly, significant changes in the rate of additions to the so-called "state reserves" were also taking place in these years—sharp decline in 1959 and sharper increase in 1960 (Table 25). Conceivably, these phenomena are related, to be at least partially explained by bookkeeping transfers of stocks.

The uncertainties that I have been discussing arise because of the absence of detail in the available distributions of state budget expenditures (Table 24). Budget outlays on social-cultural measures are wholly represented in the SNIP accounts,[20] as are the appropriations to defense and administration and that part of loan service expenditures flowing to households. The SNIP estimate of internal security outlays would be found in the miscellaneous category of Table 24, item 6. However, my investment estimates are not derived from budget data and the distribution of budget outlays on the "national economy" by type and function is not known.[21]

Finally, mention must be made of the role of the budget surplus. It is possible, as is sometimes alleged, that all or part of the reported surplus in a given year is not a true excess of revenues over expenditures but a disguised expenditure. Soviet discussions stress the credit-expansion function of budget surpluses, and some Western scholars have accepted the contention that the surpluses are in fact net additions to budget bank balances.[22] As such, they would represent not a new expenditure but the counterpart of various investment outlays already entered under item 3 of Table 4. However, some unpublished estimates by Raymond Powell relating to the early and middle 1950s cast considerable doubt on the validity of the accepted interpretation.[23]

---

[20] Current outlays net of transfer payments are entered as communal services and research and development. Stipends, pensions, and allowances are the major elements of state sector transfer payments. Investment in social-cultural facilities forms part of the official data entered in item 3.A of Table 4.

[21] Relatively more information is available for planned than for realized magnitudes. See for example, CIA, *The 1960 Soviet Budget,* November 1960; *The Soviet Budget for 1961,* June 1961; *The Soviet Budget for 1962,* November 1962.

[22] See *SNIP 1940–1948,* pp. 213–215; and Holzman, *Soviet Taxation,* 1955, Chapter 2, esp. pp. 23–25.

[23] Private communication to the author. Powell concludes: "On balance, I regard the budget surplus as one of the least understood mysteries of Soviet financial accounting."

TABLE 7

RECONCILIATION OF NET NATIONAL PRODUCT AND NET MATERIAL PRODUCT, 1958–1964

(billion rubles)

	1958	1959	1960	1961	1962	1963	1964
1. Net national product	150.10	161.75	170.63	174.95	188.76	196.57	210.52
2. Less: nonmaterial services							
A. Housing	1.78	1.88	1.98	2.07	2.16	2.25	2.35
B. Trade union and other dues	.91	.94	1.02	1.12	1.19	1.26	1.35
C. Household outlays on other services	3.96	4.22	4.50	4.92	5.38	5.72	6.16
D. Communal services, R&D, administration and internal security	11.22	11.95	12.70	13.68	14.41	15.85	17.25
E. Military pay and subsistence	4.11	3.95	3.77	3.57	4.00	3.70	3.38
F. Total	21.98	22.94	23.97	25.36	27.14	28.78	30.49
3. Add: Farm income in kind valuation adjustment	.40	.40	.50	.51	.53	.46	.63
4. Add: Depreciation on nonproductive capital	4.40	4.92	5.50	6.08	6.76	7.55	8.35
5. Less: Omitted capital consumption allowances	4.6	5.8	5.5	6.1	7.1	7.0	7.4
6. Equals: Computed net material product	128.3	138.3	147.2	150.1	161.8	168.8	181.6
7. Reported net material product	127.7	136.2	145.0	152.9	164.6	168.8	181.3
8. Deviation of computed from reported net material product							
A. Billion rubles	+ .6	+2.1	+2.2	−2.8	−2.8	0	+ .3
B. Percent	+0.5	+1.5	+1.5	−1.8	−1.7	0	+0.2

Sources:

1. *Net national product.* Table 5.
2. *Nonmaterial services.*

A. *Housing.* Entries represent the sum of imputed rent (p. 335) plus nonmaterial outlays on maintenance of state housing (maintenance of private housing is ignored as negligible). The calculation is as follows:

	1958	*1959*	*1960*	*1961*	*1962*	*1963*	*1964*
Imputed rent on private housing	1.10	1.14	1.18	1.21	1.24	1.26	1.29
Nonmaterial outlays on maintenance of state housing	.68	.74	.80	.86	.92	.99	1.06
Total	1.78	1.88	1.98	2.07	2.16	2.25	2.35

TABLE 7 (continued)

For estimates of nonmaterial outlays on maintenance see the sources to Table 25, item 1.B(2).

B. *Trade union and other dues.* Table 2.

C. *Household outlays on other services.* Total outlays less utilities (considered a "productive" service) and the material component of (1) education, health care and physical culture; (2) entertainment and culture; (3) transportation and communication; (4) other public sector services for consumption. Table J-2 and p. 486.

D. *Communal services, R&D,* administration and internal security. Table J-2.

E. *Military pay and subsistence.* Table 1. In SNIP accounts, military subsistence appears twice, once as a household outlay in kind and once as a part of the public sector's outlay on "defense." In Soviet national accounting, military subsistence is included in household consumption, but as a measure of the services of the armed forces, subsistence along with pay are excluded from public sector outlays.

3. *Farm income in kind valuation adjustment.* Table 25, item 1.A(7).

4. *Depreciation on nonproductive capital.* Soviet national accounting treats depreciation on nonproductive capital as an element of consumption. The figures are taken from Table 25, items 1.A(8) and 1.B(3).

5. *Omitted capital consumption allowances.* This is the sum of (a) the residual book value of capital retirements and (b) the difference between depreciation in the net material product account, by my estimate, and the SNIP depreciation entries, as follows (billion rubles):

	1958	*1959*	*1960*	*1961*	*1962*	*1963*	*1964*
Book value of capital retirements	1.1	1.7	1.1	1.2	1.8	1.2	1.2
NMP depreciation	11.5	13.1	14.5	16.2	17.9	22.9	24.9
Less: SNIP depreciation	8.0	9.0	10.1	11.3	12.6	17.1	18.9
	4.6	5.8	5.5	6.1	7.1	7.0	7.2

The SNIP figures are from Table 5, the others from Table 26 (items 6.D and 8). The difference between NMP and SNIP depreciation represents allowances imputed by the Central Statistical Administration for entities that do not ordinarily compute amortization allowances.

7. *Reported net material product. NKh 1965,* p. 589.

SNIP AND OFFICIAL SOVIET INCOME ESTIMATES

Table 7 attempts a reconciliation of net national product (NNP) as estimated in this study with official Soviet values of "national income" (*natsional'nyi dokhod*), often referred to in the West as "net material product" (NMP). The concept of NMP shown in Table 7 is NMP produced, which exceeds NMP utilized by the foreign trade balance and accidental loss of or damage to fixed and working capital charged to national income rather than cost of production.[24] The essential difference between NNP and NMP is the latter's exclusion of most services, or at least the wage component of these services. More precisely, NMP may be derived from NNP by the addition of an adjustment for differences between SNIP and NMP methods of valuing farm income in kind and the subtraction of (1) the nonmaterial component of services and (2) the difference between (a) capital consumption allowances deducted by Soviet statisticians to obtain NMP and not so deducted from GNP to obtain NNP and (b) depreciation on nonproductive capital, considered an element of consumption in the NMP accounts.

Item 8 of Table 7 indicates actual or virtual identity of the theoretical (item 6) and reported (item 7) NMP magnitudes in 1958, and 1963–1964; the divergence is two billion rubles and about 1½ percent in 1959–1960; theoretical values understate reported values by about 3 billion rubles or 2 percent in 1961–1962. An alternative method of appraisal is to compare year-to-year differences in the two series:

Annual Increases in Computed and Reported NMP

	Billion Rubles		*Percent*	
	Reported	*Computed*	*Reported*	*Computed*
1959	8.5	10.0	6.7	7.8
1960	8.8	8.9	6.5	6.4
1961	7.9	2.9	5.4	2.0
1962	11.7	11.7	7.7	7.8
1963	4.2	7.0	2.6	4.3
1964	12.5	12.8	7.4	7.6
1959–1964 average	8.9	8.9	6.1	6.0

Except for 1961, the annual increases in theoretical NMP differ from those of reported NMP by at most 2.8 billion rubles or 1.7 percentage points. In 1961 the computed series understates the year's increase shown in the reported series by 5 billion rubles or 3.4 percentage points. Over the period as a whole, the average difference is insignificant.

---

[24] See Chapter 7, note 41.

Thus, by the test of reconciliation with reported NMP, (1) absolute values of SNIP estimates seem very close to the mark in three of the seven years and off by 2–3 billion rubles in 1959–1962, (2) annual increments in the SNIP estimates are of the appropriate size for the period as a whole and in all years except 1961 (underestimate, 5 billion rubles) and 1963 (overestimate, 3 billions). The 1961 shortfall may be reflected in the sharp drop of residual public sector outlays (Tables 4 and 6), from 5.91 billion rubles in 1960 to .43 billions in 1961. If the 1961 and 1962 deviations of computed from reported NMP are not the consequence of error either in reported NMP or in the estimate of NNP, they must be traced to overestimation of the net deduction from NNP. The latter is entirely conceivable but cannot be independently demonstrated.

It is tempting to conclude that the test of reconciliation with official Soviet aggregates should add to our confidence in the overall estimates at established prices compiled in this study, with the qualifications already noted. After all, the Central Statistical Administration does have access to relatively complete information on the Soviet economy. But as I have already indicated, there are still on occasion grounds to suspect the official reports of political motivation. The Soviet NMP data will not command full confidence until the sources and methods of estimation are made public to a far greater degree than has yet been done.

The Meaning of SNIP 1965S

I said earlier that the SNIP 1965S estimates are intended as translations into GNP terms of the original goals embodied in the SYP. The implications of this statement are explored below.

SCOPE OF THE "SEVEN YEAR PLAN"

As a public document, the SYP is available only in the form of the so-called Control Figures, proposed by Khrushchev in a speech to the 21st Party Congress on January 27, 1959 [25] and adopted by the Congress on February 5, 1959.[26] Theoretically the set of control figures represents only a stage in the development of a Soviet plan, which is followed by the elaboration and articulation of the control figures into a

---

[25] *Pravda* and *Izvestiia,* January 28, 1959. Khrushchev's report presented a revised version of the theses adopted by the November 1958 Plenum of the Party Central Committee and published in the central press on November 14, 1958.

[26] *Pravda* and *Izvestiia,* February 8, 1959.

final plan.[27] A final SYP document was never published and Soviet sources make clear that the process of plan formulation in fact terminated at or near the control figure stage.[28]

I am not now concerned with the quality of the SYP as plan, with its realism and relevance, only with the degree to which SNIP 1965S faithfully reflects the Plan, however immature the latter's form. From this point of view, the truncation of the plan formulation process in mid-course does not necessarily constitute a serious limitation for me. A considerable amount of supporting data was necessary to the formulation of even the major goals appearing in the Control Figures and such information was submitted by lower order enterprises and organizations to the planners.[29] The construction of a value-unit, "synthetic" balance of the economy was apparently an important part of the preparation of the SYP,[30] a process which by its nature is calculated to provide the integration of plan targets set out in control figures. In summary, the nonavailability of a detailed final plan has complicated the process of estimating 1965S magnitudes and added to the bulk of this study's appendixes, but it is not necessarily an insuperable obstacle to the pursuit of my objective.

For the purposes of this study, the SYP is considered to encompass not only the Control Figures but also the supplementary detail that underlies them. Therefore, the first criterion of acceptability of any figure as an entry in the SNIP accounts is that the particular datum represent an element of the complete SYP, as defined. Although the criterion seems clear in principle, its application encounters a major difficulty in the frequent absence of explicit Soviet source indications of the required numbers. The estimates of SNIP 1965S depend to a considerable extent on roundabout estimation, projections of past trends, or even educated guesses, rather than on data specifically and positively identified in Soviet sources as components of the SYP. As in all independent reconstructions of Soviet national income, including the *ex post*

---

[27] For a description of the process see Kerblay, *Cahiers du Monde Russe et Soviétique,* May 1959, p. 175.

[28] See Chapter 12, note 7.

[29] An impression of the kind of detail accumulated in the preliminary stages of plan formulation may be derived from the scope and categories of the SYP data forms that appear in French translation in *Le Plan Septennal Soviétique,* November 1960.

[30] Bor and Notkin, *VE,* 1961, No. 5, p. 39. See, however, Chapter 12 for summary evaluations of these efforts.

estimates of this book, there is no sharp line of demarcation nor any clear order of acceptability of these estimating procedures. Soviet sources are frequently deficient in explanation of the quantitative information they provide. The confidence that can be placed in roundabout estimates depends on the confidence to be attached to the links in the chain of reasoning. Whether projections or educated guesses may be used depends on the nature and importance of the particular block in the overall structure. Nevertheless, we have far less direct information from Soviet sources on 1965S than on realized 1958–1964 magnitudes, and it is necessary to appraise the results of the 1965S estimates from this point of view.

Only a few income and outlay components could be directly estimated from reliable, authoritative Soviet sources. Fortunately, however, the relative weight of these estimates in the balance is great. The values of the worker and employee wage bill, of retail trade turnover, and of total state budget incomes were published in Soviet sources. The announced cumulated seven year investment targets together with published 1958 investment data required "only" the assumption of a constant annual rate of growth to be translated into 1965S goals. The estimates of public sector expenditures on health care and education (excluding outlays on "science") are examples of categories where in the absence of direct information on 1965S planned values, other SYP targets, such as school enrollment or hospital beds, served as multipliers to lead from 1958 to 1965S estimates. This method also characterizes the estimates of, for example, pensions and allowances paid households, housing rent (including imputed rent), outlays on building materials and building services. The use of related SYP targets along with other information in a roundabout process of estimation of 1965S income and product flows is most laboriously illustrated in the calculation of net income of households from agriculture, which takes up 11 pages in Appendix E. Similar examples of estimates delicately suspended on particular SYP pegs are household net savings and outlays on other services, private housing construction (Appendix F), and retained income of collective farms (Appendix G). On the other hand, the estimates of military manpower (which underlie estimates of income of the armed forces), nonfarm wages in kind, and budget subsidies cannot be characterized as other than educated guesses.

I make reference above to the use of an assumption of constant annual rates of growth in order to derive 1965S figures for investment. The same assumption is used at a number of other points in the estimates—with respect to retained income of collective farms and of other public sector organizations, depreciation in the state-cooperative sector, and outlays on health care. In most cases the estimates thereby derived can be supported by other procedures, but the figures for state-cooperative depreciation and public sector gross investment depend completely on the validity of that assumption. I know of no evidence to dispute its acceptability but the assumption is a critical one, particularly in connection with the problems of the credibility of the estimated public sector residual for 1965S, which is discussed at length in Chapter 9.

In short, I am painfully aware of the number of places in which the estimates of particular components depend heavily on projections, heroic assumptions, and the liberal use of unvarnished intuition. Where such recourse was required, it is made explicit in Appendixes E through H, and the interested reader is urged to explore them. It is to be hoped, nevertheless, that the reader brought to this point will not be discouraged: the interest of his study resides not in the values of military pay and subsistence or of "other income currently earned," but in the overall values and in the use made of them. In the sense discussed, there is a firmer basis for confidence in the reliability of the overall results.

ORIGINAL VERSUS REVISED GOALS

The 1965S accounts are supposed to reflect the original goals of the SYP. In all cases of conflicting data the criterion of choice has been selection of the alternative most likely to represent an original rather than a revised target. Minor examples of the kind of problem involved here are the estimates of the number of cooperative artisans and of the volume of income taxes to be paid by households in 1965S. It has been assumed here that the absorption of the cooperative artisans into the state labor force which took place in 1960 was not part of the SYP, but the amounts involved are so small that even if the assumption is wrong the effect on household incomes is negligible. The intention to dispense with direct income taxes on the population was announced in Khrushchev's SYP report to the 21st Congress, but he indicated then that the details had not yet been worked out. My estimate of proceeds in 1965S is based on the detailed timetable announced early in 1960. It is not likely that the estimate is substantially different from the one that was current in the Central Statistical Administration only a year earlier.

There are, however, two elements of public sector incomes where an error in distinction between original and revised targets may have considerable impact. These elements are the total size of the state budget and the volume of state and cooperative sector profits in 1965S. More particularly, the issue is the derivation of four 1965S entries in Table 3—items 1.B, 1.C, and 1.D, state-cooperative sector retained profits, and item 3.F, total organization payments to the budget. These items account for 9 and 69 percent, respectively, of the consolidated net income of the public sector. Since public sector outlays are defined equal to public sector incomes, substantial errors in the items indicated have a sizable effect not only on Table 3 itself but also on Table 4 and, consequently, on an important part of the gross national product account.

In the process of estimating retained profits of the state-cooperative sector, total profits of the sector in 1965S are estimated very roughly in Appendix G as in the range 44–63 billion rubles. The Soviet Minister of Finance, V. Garbuzov, declared in 1962 that total profits in 1965 would "exceed" 50 billion rubles.[31] The date of Garbuzov's statement suggests the likelihood that he was referring to a revised 1965 target. Unfortunately, neither the size nor the direction of the difference between the original and revised goals is apparent. The calculation of total profits in Appendix G is rough, and the possibility of substantial error can certainly not be discounted. However, total profits do not enter directly into the 1965S accounts at any point. Retained profits are specified in Table 3, but profits taxes are subsumed within the lumped sum of all current enterprise contributions to the state budget. The estimate of retained profits seems conservative: growth between 1958 and 1965S of the major element, retained profits of state enterprises, is estimated as 100 percent, or slightly less than the margin of increase of noncentralized investment outlays, which bear a close relation to retained profits.

As for organization contributions to the state budget, these depend in turn on estimates of total budget revenues and the share of household payments. The latter estimate is too small for any likely margin of error to affect the outcome sizably. This is not true of the value of the total state budget. In an article published in the spring of 1960 Garbuzov wrote: "The volume of the state budget already now is 773 billion [old] rubles and at the end of the SYP is to be 1.2 trillion [old] rubles."[32] Garbuzov was apparently referring to revenues, since his base of comparison, 77.3 billion rubles, was the planned 1960 volume of budget revenues.[33] A year after the appearance of this statement, in the fall of

---

[31] *Ekon.gazeta,* April 23, 1962.
[32] Garbuzov, *FinSSSR,* 1960, No. 5, p. 9.
[33] *Izvestiia,* October 31, 1959.

1961, he declared that "according to preliminary calculations the state budget of the USSR will reach 110 billion [new] rubles in 1965." [34]

It is not clear whether Garbuzov was referring in the latter statement to revenues or expenditures, for in a previous paragraph he discussed both total expenditures and the structure of revenues. If he had expenditures in mind, the two statements could be consistent, since Soviet budgets traditionally allow for a revenue surplus. On the alternative assumption, the question is whether the second reference is to a revised 1965S goal. There is obviously considerable room for rounding error in comparing the two citations: "1.2 trillion" [old] rubles is compatible with a value in the range 115–124 billion, while Garbuzov's second 1965S figure could perhaps be stretched to 112 billions.

The consequence of choice among these figures is not negligible, as already stated. The absolute change in every entry in the accounts where change would be necessary would be the same, but the relative impact is heaviest on the sum of items 4–7 in Table 4. The figure used in this study is 115 billion rubles, more consistent with the earlier Garbuzov statement but at the lower end of the indicated range. At the appropriate points in the discussion to follow, the reader will be reminded of the consequences of alternative choices.

PRICES

SNIP 1965S estimates are valued at established prices, prices planned for 1965S or constant prices of 1958. No attempt has been made to estimate income and product in adjusted factor costs because of complete absence of information on the incidence of subsidies and turnover taxes in 1965S. With the exception of prices in retail trade, it is assumed in these accounts that the SYP provided for no change in the level and structure of prices. A price decrease on the order of 5 percent was announced as planned for retail trade by 1965S. The Control Figures also hinted at possible cuts in procurement prices for some farm products.[35] However, not until the July 1960 Plenum of the Party's Central Committee was a review of wholesale prices of producers' goods actually ordered. This review was to have taken place in 1961–1962, but was subsequently postponed several times and not actually implemented until 1967. Thus, there would appear to be justification for assuming constancy of the general price level in the SYP, with the minor exception noted above.

---

[34] *Pravda*, September 30, 1961, p. 3.

[35] See Appendix E, pp. 425–426.

3

The Problem of Valuation

As indicated previously, this study's approach to Soviet national income valuation in essentials follows that of Abram Bergson. The literature on this subject is extensive and there is no need to resurvey the territory so well explored by Bergson, his critics, and his defenders. Discussion of the general theory is restricted here to a brief summary of the problem and Bergson's approach to its solution. The chief task of this chapter is to determine the nature of the adjustments to Soviet values that appear to be called for by the Bergsonian approach. The first section summarizes the theory of measurement of production potential in a Soviet type of economy and within a given unit of time. In the second and longest section, the adequacy of Soviet prices as measures of scarcity is appraised in the light of the theory presented. Intertemporal growth of potential and its measurement is treated briefly in the third section.

Production Potential at a Point in Time and the AFCS

Chapter 2 is concerned with national income accounts at prices prevailing in the separate years of the period. For certain purposes—for example, the study of financial flows—such data are appropriate and of considerable interest. No problems of the meaning of existing prices are posed because the goal of the inquiry is limited to the measurement and analysis of flows at exactly these prices. National income data are also used to measure resource allocation and economic growth, and on this more abstract plane of analysis the meaning of prevailing relative prices must be scrutinized closely. Confronted by the necessity to define such terms as "growth," the economist has distinguished two ultimate categories or standards of income measurement: economic welfare, relating to the utility of goods and services viewed through the prism of a collection of preference functions; and efficiency, or the capacity of the community to produce varying quantities of goods and services with given technology and resource endowment. Each of these standards of national income measurement implies particular valuation rules, and it is by these rules that the appropriateness of existing relative prices is judged.

The theory of national income measurement was developed in relation to a market economy. Even on this model, the theory provides an imperfect fit. What is its relevance to a society with centralized control of resource allocation, making limited use of a price system that, in any case, has obvious elements of arbitrariness? To this problem Bergson has responded with a modification of the usual efficiency standard, the adjusted factor cost standard (hereafter, AFCS). If the efficiency standard presupposes that the community is operating on its production possibilities schedule, showing the maximum quantities of goods and services in various combinations capable of being produced in a given period of time, the AFCS is applicable to an economy whose inefficiencies prevent it from reaching such a production frontier. Bergson pictures the economy as operating instead on its "feasibility locus," short of the frontier.

From this modification of the efficiency standard, Bergson deduces a modified set of pricing rules. The AFCS calls for an average cost valuation. Commodity prices, uniform within a market, represent average costs of primary factors: wage differences reflect average differences in productivity and disutility; a charge for capital consists of depreciation and interest, the latter being levied at a uniform rate derived from the average productivity of capital in the economy as a whole; rent is also charged and corresponds on the average to the differential return to superior land or natural resource deposits. To the extent that valuation under these rules results in relative prices that approximate the rates of substitution of decisionmakers in the system, Bergson notes, the production potential standard may also serve as one of welfare, but in terms of decisionmakers' rather than consumers' preferences.[1]

It seems difficult to believe, even for sectoral or branch aggregates, that the relative prices implied by the valuation adjustments undertaken in this study are proportional to Soviet decisionmakers' rates of substitution. To assume so would be to assert either that (1) decisionmakers themselves make such adjustments in established prices, which then

---

[1] In *Real SNIP* (p. 39 and Chapter 10) Bergson also considers a variant of a consumer welfare standard but in relation to consumption only.

serve as the basis for choice; or (2) a coincidental confluence of prevailing prices, AFC, and decisionmakers' rates of substitution is self-perpetuating. The first is clearly untenable, the second not demonstrable. This study's preference, therefore, is to have the calculations gauged by a production potential standard only.

There remains the question of whether faulty prices can be adjusted to an acceptable degree of approximation to the theoretical criteria. The reader can make his own judgment on this after reading the next section of this chapter. But it is necessary to emphasize the inevitability of imprecision. As Bergson concluded: [2] "In sum, theory provides the basis not for the precise measurement of abstract ultimates but for the organization of broadly meaningful statistical inquiries. If the moral holds generally, it certainly applies also to the USSR. If we are to proceed, it must be on this basis." [3]

---

[2] *Ibid.*, p. 41.

[3] In *Real SNIP*, Bergson considers at length what controversy has arisen over his calculations. It may be worthwhile to append a note on the argument of one of his sharpest critics, Peter Wiles, because (1) the latter implicitly continued the debate in a later book (Wiles, *The Political Economy of Communism*, 1962); (2) this later work crystallizes the difference between him and Bergson; and (3) on the fundamental point at issue between them hinges the validity of a modified factor cost standard such as is used in this study.

Wiles' original argument (*Soviet Studies*, October 1955, pp. 143–160, and *Soviet Studies*, October 1956, pp. 134–143) appeared to bear on the application of the AFCS to Soviet prices; in fact, it represented a challenge to the validity of the AFCS itself. If actual relative prices depart from true measures of relative scarcity, he argued, adjustments for the observed divergences do not yield a set of weights appropriate to the aggregation of actual outputs. The adjusted prices are correct weights only "for the relative outputs that *would have been* established in a free economy employing the current supply of land, labor, and capital to its best advantage" (Wiles, *Soviet Studies*, October 1955, p. 145; emphasis in original). "Irrational" relative prices engender "irrational" relative outputs. Indeed, he insisted that the former, paradoxically, are the appropriate weights for the latter.

The first volley in the counterattack mounted against Wiles, by Hodgman, Granick, Montias, and Holzman (*Soviet Studies*, July 1956, April 1957, and July 1957), was directed to a major premise of his argument—that rationality was to be defined solely in terms of consumer satisfaction, if not necessarily consumer sovereignty—and to his claim that Soviet retail prices were a theoretically acceptable set of weights to measure Soviet output. However, it remained for Bergson to deal with the heart of the matter. Wiles had argued that failure of Soviet interindustry wage differentials to corre-

The AFCS and Soviet Prices

I turn now to a critique of the Soviet price system during the period under review, guided by the principles of the AFCS. In its essentials the

---

spond to relative values of marginal product precluded a meaningful measure of Soviet national income in terms of factor costs. To this Bergson replied (*Real SNIP*, p. 116) that

> a factor cost valuation ordinarily is used where the concern is primarily to measure production potential . . . For purposes of the efficiency standard valuation, the prices finally used to value different commodities must measure marginal rates of transformation. This is fully achieved if prices correspond to marginal costs. *There is no further requirement that the prices that correspond to marginal costs also correspond to marginal utilities or planners' preferences.* (Emphasis supplied.)

In other words, Wiles' concern is with the rationality of output prices, in the sense of correspondence to marginal utilities; Bergson's rebuttal is that a production potential standard utilizes factor costs, bypassing the problem.

That this is not a satisfactory response from Wiles' point of view is shown in his later study, especially in the following passage (*The Political Economy of Communism*, 1962, p. 230):

> *Factor costs* on the other hand represent merely the marginal transformation ratios between *products* (not, to repeat, factors) for enterprises. It is difficult to see why they should be of any special interest to the statistical theorist, since the entrepreneur's or manager's valuations of his products have far less status in welfare economics than the consumer's valuation of them; the consumer, not the entrepreneur represents "social benefit." (Emphasis in original.)

If Wiles acknowledges the usefulness of factor costs it is only as a *pis aller:* empirically, when data are scarce; theoretically, for the determination of the relation between aggregate consumption and investment. Even here, however, "on a free market this ratio might just as well be expressed in output prices (consumption forgone) as in input prices (factors released)."

Thus, Wiles opts generally for a welfare standard of national income measurement and tends to slight the distinction between welfare and production potential standards. This study follows Bergson in believing that production potential is a valid independent standard and that the required measuring rod is only the terms on which alternatives are offered, to use Lange's phrase. It is agreed that the relative desirability of outputs engendered or accompanied by faulty pricing is pertinent in a welfare measure. The bill of goods produced in a Soviet type of economy, valued at adjusted factor costs, will probably diverge from the optimum, in the sense of failing to maximize an objective function. But such a finding would not invalidate the AFCS; it would only highlight the pair of distinctions Bergson uses—between location on the production possibilities schedule and location on the feasibility locus, and between production potential and welfare.

Soviet price system during the period of the SYP[4] differed little from that described in *Real SNIP*. Those aspects of Soviet prices on which prior SNIP discussion focused are by and large still the relevant problems in our period and no significantly new problems were added. The discussion below will successively treat the turnover tax, interest and profits, budget subsidies, depreciation, farm prices and incomes, and wages.

TURNOVER TAXES; NONAGRICULTURAL RENT

Proceeds from the turnover tax, although considerably shrunken in relative importance since the middle 1950s, still accounted for more than 30 percent of all public sector income in 1964, almost 40 percent of budget revenue alone.[5] Here, as in previous SNIP studies, the tax is regarded as inconsistent with the AFCS, for the following reasons: [6]

(1) Though it is levied on some producer goods—oil, gas, and electric power, predominantly—it is primarily a tax on consumer goods. Roughly three-fifths of all tax proceeds are derived from levies on alcoholic beverages, tobacco, cosmetics, food products, cloth, knitwear, clothing, and footwear.[7]

(2) Manipulation of rates appears to have much more to do with the tax's function as an instrument of fiscal balance than with considerations of resource allocation or proper cost accounting.

(3) The rate system is extraordinarily complex, with great variation in the method of computing the tax, a multiplicity of rates in the same industry, and partial or complete exemptions for certain categories of sales (depending on, among other things, the producer, consumer, or intended use of the product).

The question is frequently raised whether the turnover tax, even if not generally intended as a factor charge, can be viewed as a surrogate for charges absent from Soviet pricing but required by the AFCS—for example, interest or differential rent. To a large extent, a negative reply is implicit in the previous characterization of the tax system: the network of tax rates must bear little resemblance to a conceivable structure of interest or rent charges. Apart from the question of the relation of the

---

[4] Here and elsewhere in this study reference is to the system in force before the 1965 reforms.

[5] Table 3 and Table C-1.

[6] The following discussion relies in part on *The Soviet Financial System*, 1968, Chapter VI, Part A.

[7] Smirnov, *Ekonomicheskoe soderzhanie naloga s oborota*, 1963, p. 260.

tax on food to agricultural rent, an issue discussed later in this chapter,[8] the only interesting possibility of a contrary conclusion is with respect to rent and the tax on gas and petroleum products, the sole extractive industry products taxed at the time. However, the basic tax on petroleum is levied as a flat charge per ton, reported in 1962 to be 40 percent of the industry wholesale price charged by sales offices, and hence, presumably, a whopping two-thirds of the wholesale price excluding tax. Prices at retail contain an additional tax.[9]

The role of rent in Soviet pricing of extractive industry output and the implications for the AFCS are considerably more complex than is implied by the above comments on petroleum taxes. Briefly, a few of the relevant considerations are as follows:

(1) Suppose prices paid mining enterprises are based on average costs of a heterogeneous group of producers, plus a profit margin calculated as percent of costs, with high-cost producers compensated by subsidy. Average cost pricing, whether industry-wide or regionally, is the rule in a number of mining activities—coal and nonferrous ores, for example. Adjustment of established price values would require assignment of the subsidies to the values of product on which they are incident. Whether rent is then considered to be included in prices to users depends on whether costs and profits are viewed as meeting other theoretical requirements—for example, adequacy of depreciation charges, equivalence of profits to an appropriate interest charge.

(2) Pricing of oil and gas is far more differentiated. Prices *received by crude oil producers* are differentiated according to more or less individual field cost with a ratio of low to high of 1:25. Prices *paid by refineries* are uniform for the particular refinery or group of refineries and reflect average costs of production and transportation for the particular locality. The range of these prices is on the order of 1:13. Prices *charged by refineries* to sales organizations (f.o.b. point of origin) are based on individual cost. Finally, *industry wholesale prices on refinery output* (f.o.b. destination) are differentiated by zone, within which prices are uniform for a given quality, regardless of point of origin and production costs therein. Turnover tax is levied at this final stage.[10]

---

[8] Below, pp. 61–63.

[9] Anchishkin, *Nalog s oborota—Konkretnaia forma pribavochnogo produkta sotsialisticheskogo proizvodstva,* 1962, p. 22, cited in *The Soviet Financial System,* 1968, p. 93, note 29.

[10] Iakovets, *Metodologiia tsenoobrazovaniia v gornodobyvaiushchei promyshlennosti,* 1964, pp. 180–184. Oil and gas prices exclude prospecting costs (p. 64).

Thus, prices paid by refineries for crude oil and by sales organizations for refined output appear to include a measure of differential rent. That measure would also be reflected in prices paid by final users, net of the turnover tax. How much of the tax could be then equated to the uncharged rent would depend on the actual numbers—costs, prices, and quantities relative to the various production and consumption localities on one hand, and the tax proceeds on the other. Given the size of the tax it seems likely that total proceeds are a multiple of the uncharged rent.[11]

(3) This discussion itself oversimplifies the issues in that it fails to distinguish between rent and depletion charges, the latter representing compensation for the consumption of an asset with limited life. There does not appear to be any allowance for depletion in Soviet accounting.

(4) Finally, it should be noted that Soviet loggers pay a rentlike charge to the budget in the form of stumpage fees. An American student of the Soviet timber industry found that the structure of Soviet stumpage fees did tend to encourage economy of operation, but the general level was too low for efficient practice.[12]

In sum, and again apart from the issue of agricultural rent in food taxes, it seems appropriate to deduct all turnover taxes from final output values. Net of tax, the latter undoubtedly fail to reflect a substantial share of nonagricultural differential rent. In view of the complexity of the issue, it does not seem advisable to attempt imputation.

INTEREST AND PROFITS

No substantive changes took place during the period under review with respect to the role of profits and interest in the Soviet price system. In terms of its explicit functions, profit was as far removed from a factor charge as before.[13] Interest was still charged only on bank loans, in which the share of short term credit for working capital was overwhelming.[14] Fixed capital investment was financed predominantly outside the

---

[11] Revenue from the tax on petroleum exceeded 2 billion rubles by 1959 (Broide, *Finansirovanie neftianoi i gazovoi promyshlennosti,* 1960, pp. 100–101, cited in *The Soviet Financial System,* 1968, p. 90, note 14). It appears that the 1967 price reform was expected to produce around 1 billion rubles of rent. See *Ekon.gazeta,* No. 25, June 1967, pp. 10–11; Sitarian and Afremov, *FinSSSR,* 1967, No. 4, p. 10.

[12] Bowles, *Soviet Studies,* July 1961, pp. 28–31.

[13] Bergson notes a possible exception, unplanned profits due to superior management (*Real SNIP,* p. 109). To determine the share of unplanned profits that is in fact due to managerial skill rather than to behavioral characteristics of the system would be a difficult assignment.

[14] The ratio of the volume of short term loans outstanding to that of long

banking system. Interest rates were low—for example, 2 percent on long term investment loans to state enterprises and even lower on the same loans to collective farms.[15] Interest was intended as a stimulus to prudent use of loan funds but also as the means by which banks maintained themselves as *khozraschet* institutions.[16] On the assumption that interest paid on credit was a charge for intermediate services,[17] and in view of the insignificant role of interest in investment, a divergence from the AFCS may be perceived in the absence of an explicit net charge for capital.

However, can profits be viewed as a surrogate? It is clear from the Soviet literature on pricing and profits that profit rates were not set in any conscious relation to the volume of capital employed. Indeed, the suggestion that this is an appropriate criterion for price setting is one of the novel features of the Soviet price discussions in the last decade. It was not until 1967 that the criterion was slated to be implemented in actual price revisions. Some provisional conclusions may be drawn by treating the question statistically, examining the actual relations between profits and capital.

Table 8 compares net profits earned in the various branches of the economy in the split year 1959–1960 with the sum of fixed capital and inventories held on January 1, 1960. The fixed capital stock values shown are net of reported wear and tear (presumably the charge called for by the AFCS is on depreciated values of capital), include livestock and housing, but exclude capital in social-cultural services (health, education, science, and so on.) [18]

---

term loans arose from 8.3:1 in 1958 to 10.5:1 in 1964. Loans to collective farms dominate the long term balance (almost three-quarters in 1964). *NKh 1964*, p. 774.

[15] *Finansovo-kreditnyi slovar'*, I, 1961, p. 398; II, 1964, p. 252.

[16] *Ibid.*, II, p. 252.

[17] *Real SNIP*, p. 109, note 7.

[18] Possibly excluded as well is capital in administration, internal security, and the military establishment, although no specific guidance is provided in the Soviet sources.

Unfortunately, the three sets of data as provided in official sources differ considerably in scope and classification. Therefore, it has been necessary to undertake some adjustment of the original data:

(1) The profits data relate to "balance [sheet] profits," (see Appendix I) hence, profits and losses of housing and communal service establishments operated by, for example, an industrial or transport enterprise are incorporated in the net profits of industry and transportation shown in Table 8. The

classification underlying the inventory data is probably roughly similar. On the other hand, the official capital stock data separate out nonproductive from productive assets, with the category of housing including all housing, whether operated by an industrial enterprise or by the local Soviets. Thus, it is necessary to separate out housing operated by branches of the economy other than the communal economy and to add the relevant values to the particular branch's capital stock. The basis for the adjustment is explained in the sources to Table 8.

(2) Profits of consumer cooperatives have been added to those of state trade organizations. Trade inventories include the inventories of cooperatives.

(3) The gross values of collective farm and private sector capital (for which no profits are reported in the official data) have been inferred by Kaplan (see sources to Table 8) as, respectively, over 21.3 and 51–55 billion rubles. The estimate for the private sector breaks down to 47–49 billions of housing and 4–6 billions of livestock and other items (Kaplan, in Bergson and Kuznets, *Economic Trends in the Soviet Union,* 1963, pp. 111–112). Collective farm capital is assumed here to have been 22.5 billion rubles, private housing 48 billions, and private agricultural capital 5 billions. These amounts are subtracted from reported gross capital values for agriculture and housing in compiling the data for Table 8.

In two other instances, adjustments are called for but not made:

(1) The capital stock category "trade and catering" presumably includes the capital of foreign trade organizations; the trade category in the official profits data most likely excludes foreign trade (*SNIP 1956–1958,* pp. 76–77). The latter is probably a component of the residual category of the profits distribution, "other branches." It also seems likely that inventories held by foreign trade organizations are not entered under "trade" but under "other branches." Lack of information precludes adjustment of the capital entry for trade, but the resulting distortion is not likely to be serious; the profit rate in trade is slightly understated, the rate for the residual category slightly overstated.

(2) Whereas the profits series for construction refers to contract construction alone, the capital stock classification subsumes all construction. (Kaplan, in Bergson and Kuznets, *Economic Trends in the Soviet Union,* 1963, p. 103. It is not clear whether construction capital in intercollective farm organizations is included, but the amount is insignificant for present purposes. See *NKh 1961,* p. 421.) Because force account construction is undertaken in a number of branches of the economy, it is impossible to adjust for the indicated differences in coverage. However, the consequent distortion is not as serious as appears at first glance, inasmuch as contract construction accounts for 85 percent of all construction-installation in the state-cooperative sector. It seems doubtful that the construction profits figure is understated by very much more than 10–15 percent and the calculated profit rate by much more than 1–2 percentage points.

TABLE 8

PROFITS AND CAPITAL BY BRANCH OF THE PUBLIC SECTOR, 1959–1960

	Billion Rubles				Profit Rates, Column (1) Divided by Column (4) (percent)
	Net Profits,[a] Average 1959–1960	Capital on January 1, 1960			
		Net Fixed[b]	Inventories	Total	
	(1)	(2)	(3)	(4)	(5)
1. Industry	13.27	74.23	30.57	104.80	13
2. Construction	.98	6.34	2.63	8.97	11
3. Transportation-communication	4.17	32.24	1.07	33.31	13
4. Collective farms	3.96[c]	15.98	7.78	23.76	17
5. State agriculture		13.04	4.28	17.32	
	.35				2
6. Procurement		1.55	4.30	5.85	
7. Trade	2.18	3.08	20.06	23.14	9
8. Supply-sales organizations	1.09	.86	7.46	8.32	13
9. Other branches of material production; municipal economy and services	2.04	16.68	3.00	19.68	10
Total	28.04	164.00	81.15	245.15	11

Notes:

[a] Before deductions from profits.

[b] Net of wear and tear; including livestock.

[c] Retained money income net of depreciation, before income taxes.

Sources:

Net profits. Retained income of collective farms: pp. 362 and 383. All other entries: *NKh 1962*, p. 627. Profits of consumer cooperatives are included here with those of trade.

Net fixed capital. Except for collective farms, the estimates are obtained in three steps:

1. Values of gross capital by branch (except in agriculture) are taken from *NKh 1959*, p. 67.

2. Gross values of housing and their distribution by branch are obtained as follows:

(a) The total gross value of housing capital given in *NKh 1959*, 94.15 billion rubles, consists of 48.00 billion rubles of private housing (Norman M. Kaplan, in Bergson and Kuznets, *Economic Trends in the Soviet Union*, 1963, p. 133) and 46.15 billions of publicly owned housing, of which that operated by local Soviets is estimated as one-third and "enterprise" housing (i.e., operated by enterprises, *sovnarkhozy*, or ministries) as two-thirds (V. Maslakov *et al.*, *Finansy zhilishchnogo i kommunal'nogo khoziaistva*, 1960, p. 9).

(b) Enterprise housing, 30.78 rubles, is assigned 60 percent to industry, 10 percent each to construction and agriculture, and 20 percent to transportation-communication. The allocation takes into account the structure of employment in these branches in 1959 (*NKh 1962*, p. 453) but allows for private rural housing belonging to employees of the public sector and the predominance of industry and transportation in enterprise housing.

3. The value of capital held by state agriculture is obtained by subtracting collective farm (22.5 billion rubles) and private agricultural capital, 5.0 billions (Kaplan, in Bergson and Kuznets, pp. 111–112; but see also note 18 of this chapter) from reported total capital in agriculture of 41.92 billions and adding 3.08 billions for housing operated by state agriculture.

4. Gross capital values except those of collective farms are reduced by wear-and-tear percentages cited in *NKh 1959*, p. 75; for collective farms I use the percentage for agricultural artels as of 1 January 1962, given in *NKh 1961*, p. 425.

Inventories. Collective farms: *SNIP 1958–1962, Part II*, 1966, p. 190. All other entries: Table L-1.

The profit rates shown in Column 5 of Table 8 may be surprising. In view of the known principles of Soviet price formation, according to which profit rates are set in relation to average branch prime costs, it was hardly to be expected that the computed profit rates in all branches except agriculture[19] and procurement should display so little variation from the sectoral average, a respectable 11 percent of all fixed capital and inventories.[20] If the calculation used gross rather than net profits—that is, with conventional subsidies added back[21]—the economy-wide average profit ratio would be raised to 14 percent, the industrial average to 17 percent, and the average for nonindustrial branches other than agriculture and procurement to 12 percent. State agriculture and procurement appear to be exceptions, but if we should add both conventional subsidies to agriculture and subsidies received by procurement organizations[22] to the entry in Table 8, their joint profit rate would rise to 14 percent. True, the procurement subsidies are the consequence less of transactions with state farms than with collective farms and households, but our concern is the incidence on final use, and from this point of view we need not be troubled by the distinction.[23]

Even with allowance for the deficiencies of the profits and capital data, these findings suggest that an attempt to excise profits and substitute an imputed interest charge would hardly be worth the effort. However, there are several important qualifications to be made.

(1) The 13 percent profit rate computed for industry in Table 8 is an average of widely disparate component rates. The dispersion may be

---

[19] The collective farm profit rate is somewhat misleading as it conceals undervaluation of farm labor. See below, pp. 63 ff.

[20] The 1967 price reform, according to indications furnished by Sitnin (*Kommunist,* No. 14, 1966, pp. 38, 41) intended a rate of profit in relation to productive fixed and working capital of 8–15 percent in most industrial branches; the industrial average was to be 15 percent.

[21] By "conventional subsidies" I mean grants to *khozraschet* enterprises operating at a loss. Subsidies are discussed in the section immediately following. For the branch origin of conventional subsidies see p. 478.

[22] See p. 373.

[23] Alternatively, consider collective farms, state agriculture, and procurement as a group and add all subsidies to net profits. Then the group profit rate is 15 percent.

Since the profits of state agriculture as well as the retained income of collective farms include differential rent, the indicated profit rates are overstated. An offsetting consideration with respect to collective farms is the omission of agricultural profits in kind.

illustrated with official data for 1964, showing profit rates by branch of industry, but unfortunately based only on gross fixed capital at original cost: [24]

All industry	14.0
Electric power	4.6
Petroleum extraction and refining	9.5
Coal	−15.9
Ferrous metals	8.7
Chemicals	17.9
Machine building and metal working	16.5
Timber, wood, and paper	8.3
Construction materials	4.7
Light	32.1
Food	30.8

If we consider the light and food branches consumer goods industry and everything else producer goods, equality of profit rates in the two subaggregates would require the deduction of some 5 billion rubles of consumer goods profits in 1964 and their reallocation to producer goods. The listed branches of industry are in fact far from homogeneous with respect to output classification, but it seems clear that to retain profits as a surrogate for interest means to overvalue consumer goods relative to producer goods and consumption relative to other final uses. I shall attempt to gauge the significance of this error in the discussion of the adjusted values presented in Chapter 5.

(2) Table 8 omits the private sector, for the obvious reason that no profits are ascribed to it in Soviet accounting. Assuming, say, a 10 percent rate of return and the negligibility of inventories, capital values and imputed interest for the sector are as follows (billion rubles): [25]

	Net Fixed Capital on January 1, 1960	*Imputed Interest*
Private agricultural sector	3.75	.38
Private housing	36.00	3.60
Total	39.75	3.98

[24] *NKh 1965*, p. 760. The numerator of the profit rates represents balance profits (see note 18 above); the denominator embraces all capital (average annual stock) recorded on the balance sheets of enterprises classified in industry. Fixed capital is valued at original cost gross of depreciation. *Ibid.*, p. 847.

[25] Sources are those described in Table 8. I gladly refrain from speculating on the rate of return appropriate to government service capital.

Thus, even if we accept reported profits as a suitable proxy for the required interest return in those branches of the economy where profits are recorded, established price values omit a sizable volume of interest, estimated at 4 billion rubles in 1959–1960, the imputed return to private sector capital. My accounts provide for an imputed rent on private housing, but the rate is that on state housing and the aggregate amount, 1.16 billion rubles in 1959–1960, is obviously inadequate in the light of the calculation above. Indeed, it would appear sensible to impute an interest return to state housing as well. Because of the form in which the profits data appear, it was necessary in Table 8 to lump state housing with other capital in the major branches. This procedure screens the undervaluation of Soviet housing returns resulting from the state subsidized rentals. Hence, the imputed interest on all housing (with a depreciated capital value of 72 billion rubles) should be on the order of 7 billions and the total gross imputed interest in excess of profits recorded in Soviet accounts about 7½ billion rubles in 1959–1960.[26] Again, this difficulty will be handled separately in Chapter 5.

SUBSIDIES

Subsidies on current accounts are, of course, also a departure from factor cost pricing. Five kinds of subsidies are considered in this study: conventional subsidies; budget financing of the operating deficit of the MTS and RTS (applicable only to 1958 and 1959); budget grants to enterprises to raise wages in connection with the wage reform of the late 1950s and early 1960s; budget subsidies to agricultural procurement organizations whose sale prices lagged behind their rapidly increasing purchase prices; and financing of losses sustained in socialized housing in consequence of the low rentals charged.

The last four types of subsidies are discussed and the relevant values are estimated in Appendixes C and J. The special problem of conventional subsidies is dealt with in Appendix I. For the purposes of factor cost adjustment, it is necessary to know the value of all losses incurred by unprofitable enterprises and organizations—that is, not only those covered by budget subsidies, but also those financed by redistributions of profits below the level of the state budget.[27] Each of these categories of

---

[26] However, see the discussion in Chapter 5 on the relative merits of a 5 or 10 percent rate of imputation.

[27] Strictly, this assumes that gross profits is the best approximation to imputed interest required by the AFCS. See above, p. 53. Hereafter, the term "conventional subsidies" will denote all grants to cover ordinary operat-

operating losses turns out to be difficult to measure reliably. If the estimates and interpretations made in Appendix I are correct, and considerable reservations are expressed there on this score, total conventional subsidies grew from 4.1 billion rubles in 1958 to 7.6–7.7 billions in 1963–1964.

In view of the general assumption heretofore accepted by writers on Soviet economic affairs, that conventional subsidies dwindled in importance during the 1950s, the indicated estimates may seem unacceptably large. They may indeed be inexact, as Appendix I makes clear, but there are two aspects of Soviet price policy that should not be lost sight of. First, although Soviet sources emphasize the importance of the 1949 price reform (which sharply increased prices) in "liquidating" subsidies to industry,

> in practice what was liquidated were basically subsidies to *branches* of industry and not to separate enterprises. . . . Chief administrations (*glavki*) having unprofitable enterprises covered their losses from the profits of profit-making enterprises. Accounts with the budget were placed on a net basis (*sal'dirovalis'*), showing in the final reckoning a normal financial condition for an industrial branch as a whole.[28]

After the industrial reorganization of 1957, the method of subsidizing losses remained substantially unchanged, except that profit redistribution now took place within the regional *sovnarkhoz*, uniting profitable and unprofitable enterprises of different branches of industry.

Second, wide disparities between the costs of different enterprises in the same branch of industry or *sovnarkhoz* along with average cost pricing guarantee that some enterprises will incur substantial losses.[29] Since general price changes are infrequent in the Soviet Union, one might imagine that the level of such planned losses should decline after a general price reform, as productivity rises and if there were no wage inflation. However, just as an average profit rate for a branch of industry conceals great variations in the relations between cost and price of sub-branches, so do increases in average productivity and declines in average cost for major branches of industry reveal little about move-

---

ing losses. Grants from the budget will be called "conventional budget subsidies" and those from *sovnarkhozy* or ministries, "conventional agency subsidies."

[28] Pervushin, *Problema differentsiatsii proizvoditel'nosti obshchestvennogo truda*, 1963, p. 193 (emphasis in the original).

[29] Bornstein, *American Economic Review*, March 1962, pp. 74–77.

ments at the tails of the distribution.[30] The fact is that four or five years after the major price reform of 1955, 21.5 percent of all industrial enterprises under the jurisdiction of *sovnarkhozy* were expected to incur losses.[31]

In the light of these two considerations, total operating losses on the order of 4–8 billion rubles may not seem so unlikely.

DEPRECIATION

Depreciation is an explicit cost charged by *khozraschet* enterprises. To postpone for the moment the question of collective farm costs, the issue is whether depreciation charges are high enough. By my estimate, depreciation—of which about half represents allowances for capital repairs—averaged 5.7 percent of GNP in 1958–1962.[32] In the United States, where major repairs are far more frequently charged off to current cost, capital consumption allowances made up about 8.5 percent of GNP in the same period.[33] Thus, the pure replacement depreciation ratio was perhaps 2 or 2½ times higher in the United States than in the Soviet Union.

Such a statistical comparison, however, is of limited significance. The U.S. ratio is affected by institutional idiosyncrasies—government-encouraged depletion allowances and accelerated depreciation, tax incentives to charge capital expenses off to current cost, and exclusion of depreciation on government capital. Moreover, there is no *a priori* reason why the relation of net to gross product should be identical in the two countries. One would, in fact, expect the contrary, that in a rapidly growing economy with a high rate of investment, depreciation would absorb a smaller share of total resources than it would in an economy of less rapid growth and a tendency to marked underutilization of capacity.[34] In the past, depreciation has taken both larger and smaller shares

---

[30] It must also be noted that available data on productivity changes in industry or its components concern value of gross output per worker and employee, while information on costs is restricted to changes in outlays per ruble of marketed output.

[31] Kondrashev, *DiK,* 1962, No. 6, p. 29. Although this article appeared in 1962, the context suggests reference to 1959 or 1960.

[32] Tables 3 and 5.

[33] U.S. Bureau of the Census, *Statistical Abstract of the United States: 1964,* p. 322.

[34] See Domar, *Essays in the Theory of Economic Growth,* 1957, Chapter VII.

of U.S. GNP than indicated above—larger during most of the depression years, smaller during the boom years of World War II.[35]

This is not to deny that Soviet depreciation practice has been deficient. It is clear that Soviet planners were also dissatisfied on this score,[36] for higher depreciation rates were introduced in 1963. The new rates raised the annual total of depreciation charges in the state-cooperative sector by about 3 billion rubles, or roughly one-quarter,[37] and the ratio of depreciation charges to GNP to 8.1 percent in 1963–1964.

However, with qualifications to be noted, it seems doubtful that revaluation of the 1958–1962 SNIP estimates using the revised depreciation rates would significantly affect either the level or broad structure of output at factor cost. The aggregate increase in amortization allowances in 1963 amounts to less than 2 percent of 1962 GNP (at factor cost), while the impact seems to have been distributed among consumer and producer goods industries.[38]

---

[35] U.S. Department of Commerce, *U.S. Income and Output,* 1958, pp. 138–139.

[36] The literature on this subject is considerable. A good summary of Soviet views is provided in Filippov, *Novye normy amortizatsii,* 1963, Chapters III–V. The standard work in English is Campbell, *Accounting in Soviet Planning and Management,* 1963, Chapters 3 and 4.

[37] *NKh 1963,* pp. 637, note, and 653.

[38] Especially large increases in rates were reported for the coal, timber, construction materials, light, food, and salt industries and for river transportation. Filippov, *Novye normy amortizatsii,* 1963, p. 97.

Additional evidence is provided by a crude comparison of branch changes in the flow of amortization deductions between 1962 and 1963 and the corresponding changes in average annual capital stock values: (1) The increase in depreciation rates is likely to have been smallest in trade and distribution. Increases in allowances were 24 percent in trade, 25 percent in procurement, and 27 percent in supply and sales. Growth of capital in this part of the economy was around 15 percent. (2) The gross capital stock in industry, agriculture, construction, and transportation-communication in each case increased by 10 percent or less. The growth of amortization was 38, 55, 28, and 32 percent, respectively. Most likely the relative change in depreciation rates was about the same in the first three branches, with the growth in state agriculture considerably higher. (3) It may be concluded that the new depreciation rates tended to raise the value of agricultural output relative to that of other sectors. If consumer goods and producer goods industries were equally affected by the other changes, the net effect of the revised depreciation rates would be to raise the value of consumption slightly relative to that of investment. However, the impact is undoubtedly too small to trouble about.

Sources of the data used in this comparison are as follows: Amortization

The implicit assumption in this discussion is that the 1963 depreciation rates fulfill the requirements of AFCS pricing. Without attempting a detailed analysis of the new rate structure, it may be sufficient to indicate that the combination of the rate revision and the previously enacted capital revaluation (as of January 1, 1960) should have tackled the most serious deficiencies in Soviet depreciation accounting—the large gap between book and replacement value of assets, faulty estimation of asset service lives, inadequate differentiation of rates, neglect of obsolescence, and jumbling of capital repair and depreciation.[39] The corollary of this argument is that the inadequacy of Soviet depreciation charges should have been greater in 1958 and 1959 than in subsequent years, because the revaluation of fixed capital at the beginning of 1960 raised capital values to which unchanged depreciation rates were presumably applied and raised them unevenly between branches of the economy.[40] Unfortunately, the actual depreciation series shows no substantial change that would reflect the introduction of higher capital asset values in the depreciation formula denominator; it does reflect the sharply increased depreciation norms in 1963.[41] Why this is so remains unexplained, but I do not propose to impute additional depreciation allowances for the reasons advanced earlier.

The foregoing has related to the state-cooperative sector. Collective

---

allowances are from *NKh 1963*, p. 653. Average annual capital stock values are computed as follows: (1) The capital stock at the end of 1963 is given directly, and that for the end of 1962 may be computed indirectly from indexes in *NKh 1963*, pp. 55–56. (2) To compute the stocks at the end of 1961, index numbers for that year in *NKh 1961*, p. 68 are adjusted, divided by the corresponding index numbers for end-1963 (*NKh 1963*), and the results applied to the end-1963 values. (3) The adjustments to the index numbers are required for construction, housing, all nonproductive capital, and total capital, because of minor revisions evidently incorporated in these series in later yearbooks. The adjustments as well as the magnitudes are determined by comparing index numbers for 1960 as given in *NKh 1961* and *NKh 1963*. (4) Stocks at the end of 1961 and 1962 and those at the end of 1962 and 1963 are averaged to obtain average annual values.

Comparability of the capital values and amortization deductions suffers from the same general discrepancies in coverage and classification as does that of the capital values and profits in Table 8. Because of the qualifications discussed in connection with Table 8, the comparison of changes in capital stocks with increases in amortization allowances is necessarily tentative in tone.

[39] See sources indicated in note 36 above.

[40] *NKh 1959*, p. 73.

[41] See Chapter 8, note 11.

farm accounting has only partly incorporated depreciation practices of other public sector enterprises: amortization allowances are not counted a production expense and are not isolated in a separate bank account as is the rule with state enterprises. However, depreciation is computed and in a bookkeeping sense taken out of additions to "indivisible funds." The rates used are those of state farm accounting. Since prices on collective farm output cover depreciation via additions to indivisible funds, leaving a volume of retained income, which in relation to the capital stock is more than equal to the average "profit" rate of the public sector as a whole (Table 8), the question here too is whether the depreciation rates are high enough. The remarks in the previous paragraphs apply here as well.

Not all state-cooperative capital is depreciated, or depreciated to the same extent. Enterprise housing accounting computes amortization only for capital repair, not for full replacement. Until 1963 housing operated by local Soviets was generally not depreciated, and capital repairs were financed from the government budget.[42] Budget organization capital is not depreciated at all. The magnitude of the consequent understatement of depreciation may be estimated as about 1.8 billion rubles in 1959–1960[43] or almost one-fifth of the sum of charges recorded in Table 3. Imputation of depreciation on this category of capital will be attempted in Chapter 5.

FARM PRICES

Two questions are at issue here, the multiplicity of prices for farm output and the inclusion of a charge for differential agricultural rent in farm prices. In 1958, the complex system of agricultural procurement was radically revised: the MTS were abolished along with payments in kind to them by collective farms; at the same time, single state procurement prices were fixed for collective farms and households, in place of the dual or triple price system previously in force.

---

[42] Filippov, *Novye normy amortizatsii,* 1963, p. 127.

[43] The calculation uses estimates of service lives of structures compiled by Moorsteen and Powell, *The Soviet Capital Stock 1928–1962,* 1966, p. 63: Municipal economy and services, 50 years; private housing, 60 years; state housing, 90 years; social-cultural services, 80 years. To allow for the shorter life of equipment the indicated service lives are here reduced to 35 years for municipal economy capital and 70 years for social-cultural service capital. Straight line depreciation is assumed. For gross capital stock values, see the sources to Table 8 above.

Nevertheless, multiplicity of prices continued to characterize Soviet agriculture even after 1958. The prices at which state farms delivered their production to the state were different from purchase prices paid collective farms and households. Purchase and state farm delivery prices were substantially below collective farm market prices. Minor variations were introduced by consumer cooperatives selling surpluses from both collective farms and households on commission or at some form of market prices.[44]

For agricultural raw materials, the system poses no challenge to the AFCS. Although they bought at varying price levels from farms and farmers, procurement organizations sold to processing organizations at a single price. Subsidies and turnover taxes regulated the margins between the different price levels.[45] However, any divergence between the price levels of state retail sales and of the extravillage farm market does violate the single-price criterion of the AFCS. A calculation explained in Appendix J suggests that market prices were roughly 5 percent higher than state retail prices in 1958–1960. The gap increased to 15–20 percent in 1961–1963 and 25 percent in 1964.[46]

As for agricultural rent, there was still no explicit charge for the use of land. The issue is the extent to which rent is (1) retained by producers, hence constitutes an implicit charge in prices paid by users, or (2) absorbed by the turnover tax, hence absent from prices net of the tax. Those who would argue that the turnover tax is an implicit charge for differential rent, that little or no rent is retained on the farm, imply that farm prices covered the costs of only the lowest-cost producers. In the state sector, although subsidies were prevalent, a number of farms earned a profit, and adjustment of prevailing prices for these subsidies renders the statement entirely inapplicable to state farms. Regarding collective farms and considering all channels of marketing, the statement was unlikely to have been completely true before 1958 and was certainly not thereafter. For example, the margin over average cost in the country as a whole provided by 1958 procurement prices ranged from 19 to 363 percent for mutton, potatoes, tobacco, wool, vegetables, grain, sugar beets, cotton, flax, and sunflower; although production of beef, pork, poultry, milk, and eggs was unprofitable, on the average the margin of

---

[44] On the size of the differences between purchase, state farm delivery, and collective farm market prices, see Table A-2 and sources thereto. The system of consumer cooperative sales is explained below, pp. 315–316.

[45] See below, pp. 373–379.

[46] See pp. 489–491.

loss did not exceed 41 percent of cost.[47] Collective farm market prices were considerably higher, of course.[48]

It might be argued that the costs in these comparisons are themselves deficient. However, since the cost data are based on state farm wage norms rather than actual collective farm distributions, the deficiencies relate to such matters as interest and rent;[49] the first is treated separately elsewhere, the second brings us back to the point at hand.

When agricultural output was procured by the state in large part at near-confiscatory prices and sold to the consumer at a huge markup absorbed by the turnover tax, the state's differential pricing could be viewed as, among other things, a redistribution of differential rent. After the price and institutional reforms of 1954–1958, such a view is questionable. Under the 1958 procurement price system producers were enabled to keep a greater proportion than before of differential rent. The new regional price and delivery structure tended to penalize less productive regions and to accentuate the inequality of farm incomes.[50] True,

---

[47] Zverev, *Natsional'nyi dokhod i finansy SSSR*, 1961, p. 306.

[48] Despite losses sustained on livestock production, collective farms are said to have earned .81 billion rubles of "profits" on all sales to the state in 1960, with a "profit" margin of 8.4 percent over costs. If sales on the collective farm market are taken into account, the "profit" rate is raised to 18.6 percent. (Koroviakovskii, *Sovershenstvovanie sistemy gosudarstvennykh zagotovok sel'skokhoziaistvennykh produktov v SSSR*, 1963, p. 122.) The meaning of these rates is obviously sensitive to judgment on the appropriateness of collective farmer earnings levels.

This rebuttal ignores the redistributive role of agricultural income taxation but the effect seems slight: (1) The magnitudes involved are not appreciable. After the 1953 reform, which effectively cut the tax in half, the agricultural tax on private plots brought in less than half a billion rubles annually. Proceeds from the income tax on collective farms were 1.03 billion rubles in 1958, rose to 1.24 billions in 1959 and then remained below that level in 1960–1964. In the 1960s income from livestock production was largely exempted from taxation. (2) For both taxes the rates were fixed rather than progressive. (3) Agricultural tax rates were regionally differentiated, those of the collective farm income tax considerably less so. (On the actual tax revenues, see *Gosbiudzhet I* and *II*, pp. 8–9 and 11, respectively. The nature of the collective farm income tax is outlined in *Vedomosti Verkhovnogo soveta*, January 1, 1959, pp. 5–6. On the agricultural tax, see Garbuzov, *FinSSSR*, 1953, No. 9, pp. 9–15.)

[49] That is, assuming correspondence of the state farm wage system to the requirements of the AFCS. More on this shortly.

[50] Nimitz, *Problems of Communism*, May–June 1965, p. 15.

higher prices were paid in poorer than in richer regions but the disparities in costs were far greater than the price premia. The price differential between extreme RSFSR zones was but 30 percent for grain, 58 percent for sunflower, 48 percent for sugar beets, 29 percent for large cattle, 50 percent for hogs, and 19 percent for poultry. Cost disparities ranged from 2:1 for livestock to 5:1 for grain.[51] In consequence, sharp regional differences in unit farm income are noted. Among *raiony* (that is, large regions) of the RSFSR the spread between highest and lowest levels of net income of collective farms per ruble of production outlays was 2.7:1 in 1959–1961.[52] Net income of farms per able-bodied collective farmer was 6.9 times as high in the Altai krai in 1958–1959 as in Gorkii oblast; the level in the Turkmen SSSR was 3.3 times as high as in Lithuania.[53] The "immiseration" of the poor farms to the benefit of the rich farms tended to perpetuate itself, short of state intervention. The data show a strong direct relation between the level of pay per man day and the share of gross income (after production outlays) devoted to investment.[54]

At the same time, the abolition of payments in kind to MTS eliminated a major channel of absorption of rent, turnover taxes on food products were diminishing, and substantial subsidies to procurement organizations were required to support a high and rising level of prices paid to farms and farmers. Thus, more and more rent tended to be retained by producers rather than extracted by the state, and the implicit charge may be largely reflected in farm incomes and in the structure of final use.

AGRICULTURAL–NONAGRICULTURAL INCOME DIFFERENTIALS

The main issue here is whether the peculiarities of the collective farm institution create a gap in earnings between collective farmers and workers of comparable skill in the state labor force, a gap that might constitute a deviation from AFCS pricing. I estimate that the average hourly earnings of collective farmers came to 63 percent of those of industrial wage earners in 1958. Collective farmer earnings were probably slightly less than average wages and salaries in the food industry but

---

[51] Emel'ianov, *Ekonomicheskie nauki,* 1965, No. 1, p. 5.

[52] An SSSR, *Material'noe stimulirovanie razvitiia kolkhoznogo proizvodstva,* 1963, p. 12.

[53] Sidirova, *VE,* 1961, No. 10, p. 94.

[54] Venzher, in Venzher *et al., Proizvodstvo, nakoplenie, protreblenie,* 1965, p. 291.

fell farther short of the average wage and salary earned in light industry.[55]

Comparison with earnings on state farms is more difficult because of uncertainty on the distribution of private sector sales and incomes in kind between state farm employees and other noncollective farmers, as well as the absence of information on actual hours worked. The reported average monthly wage and salary of state farm personnel in 1958, 53.1 rubles,[56] was 62 percent as high as the industrial average wage. That is, state farm average wages and salaries alone approximately equaled collective farmer unit earnings. Addition of income from the private plot to the reported figure would raise earnings per man on state farms considerably above those on collective farms. Whether the two sets of data are entirely comparable is not clear.[57]

In any case, Soviet writers have been unanimous in proclaiming collective farmer earnings below those of state farmers. For example, a 1963 source declares: "In recent years, average income of collective farmers (from the collective farm and the private plot) per man day worked came to about three-quarters of the earnings of a state farm worker and ⅔ of the earnings of a worker in local industry." [58] A 1966 source similarly places the ratio of average collective farm family member income "in recent years" as 75–83 percent of the income of state farm workers, including in both cases income from the plot.[59]

To a smaller extent on state farms and to a more considerable extent on collective farms, household incomes include differential rent and a return on privately owned capital. Since the AFCS requires a correspondence of farm labor incomes (that is, net of returns to land or capital), to wages elsewhere of comparable labor, the real difference between incomes of collective farmers and average wages in industry is greater than apparent.

The gap may be the larger for the additional reason that the compari-

---

[55] For details of the calculation see Appendix O.

[56] *NKh 1964*, p. 555.

[57] Additional complications enter in considering the diverse prices at which state and collective farms sell farm products to households. For example, state farm workers purchase food at cost (*VS*, 1965, No. 1, p. 75, note); collective farms sell to farmers at a mixture of costs and procurement, market, and retail prices.

[58] Alekseeva and Voronin, *Nakoplenie i razvitie kolkhoznoi sobstvennosti*, 1963, p. 29.

[59] Palladina and Grebennikova, *VE*, 1966, No. 11, p. 27.

son has been drawn in terms of real earnings. Hence, we must take account of urban-rural differentials in state-cooperative retail trade prices. During the 1950s higher prices were charged in rural areas for goods accounting for about 40 percent of retail trade turnover. The differential, which amounted to about 7 percent, was reduced in stages: partial reductions were decreed on January 1, 1960 (whose value to the rural population was said to be 76 million rubles a year), January 1, 1961 (annual value, 160 million rubles), and April 25, 1965 (annual value, 67.5 million rubles). The differentials were to be abolished after January 1, 1966 (annual saving, 400 million rubles).[60] Allegedly the differential was required originally to cover higher trading costs in rural localities.[61] To the extent that was the case, the differential is, of course, legitimate for the purpose of my comparison. In principle, I should also take account of the relative availability of goods and of other services, among them housing. One would guess that the advantage is to the side of the urban nonagricultural population.[62]

An appraisal of the relation between collective farmers' and industrial earnings after 1958 is hampered by absence of data on the structure of private sector output and marketings. From the fragmentary information available I estimate the development of collective farmer earnings per man hour in relation to those of industrial wage earners as follows (indexes, 1958 = 100; income in current prices): [63]

	1958	*1959*	*1960*	*1961*	*1962*	*1963*	*1964*
Collective farmer income	100	95	88	90	97	96	104
Collective farmer man hours	100	98	93	92	90	87	87
Income per collective farmer man hour	100	97	95	98	108	110	120
Industrial wage bill	100	106	120	130	137	144	152
Industrial man hours	100	101	102	107	110	113	118
Industrial wage per man hour	100	105	117	122	125	127	129
Gap, collective farmer income/industrial wage	100	92	81	80	86	87	93

[60] Vorkunov, *ESKh,* 1966, No. 5, p. 99; Sarkisian, *VE,* 1966, No. 6, p. 81.
[61] Bauman and Tolkushkin, *VS,* 1965, No. 4, p. 33.
[62] For scattered evidence on this question, see below, pp. 335–339, 351–352.
[63] The sources are provided in Appendix O.

The tabulation indicates that the income differential widened sharply in favor of industrial wages in 1959–1960. Thereafter, as incomes of collective farmers increased while their labor inputs continued to decease, the differential began to narrow. Nevertheless, the 1958 relation between the two was not yet restored by 1964. A contrary trend is visible in comparing just wages and salaries of state agricultural workers with earnings in industry. At least this is so after 1960, when the wage reform reached state agriculture. By 1963 average earnings in the latter branch were 26 percent greater than in 1958 and an additional 5 percent increase occurred in 1964. During the same period average earnings in industry rose 15 percent.[64]

To what extent do the earnings differentials revealed above exceed differences in productivity and disutility, hence contradict the requirements of AFCS pricing? In part the gaps disclosed may be explained by the operation of the same factors—higher productivity in industry, lower levels of skill in agriculture—that make urban-rural income differentials virtually universal in the development process. Thus, the age-sex-education structure of the two work forces in the Soviet Union differed substantially in the late 1950s. According to the 1959 census, the proportion of the rural population with better than a primary education was only half as large as that of the urban population. Per 1000 employees there were three times as many specialists employed in industry as in agriculture; the ratio for specialists with higher education was almost 8:1.[65]

To repeat, such differences, although not necessarily of the same magnitude, are characteristic of many other economies, including that of the United States. As I have noted, there was in 1958 a small gap between earnings on the collective farms and those in light and food industry, where the labor force is composed predominantly of unskilled women. Differences in the qualitative structure of the industrial and collective farm work forces probably were magnified in subsequent years. A significant rural emigration took place in the SYP period, and male youths tended to form a disportionately large share of the emigrants.[66] Between 1957 and 1963, there was no change in the number of specialists per able-bodied collective farmer, but the number of in-

[64] *NKh 1964,* p. 555.
[65] Lagutin and Lemeshev, *ESKh,* 1962, No. 5, pp. 35–36.
[66] Markov, *PKh,* 1965, No. 10, p. 5.

dustrial specialists per unit of employment jumped more than 50 percent by 1964.[67]

On the other hand, the income disparities also reflect the intended and unintended consequences of Khrushchev's economic policy—the nature of the 1958 farm price system, the burden of MTS machinery payments, increases in prices for new machinery and parts, and the vagaries of his crop policy.[68] After his departure, it was possible to declare that

> the average skill level of agricultural personnel, the complexity and intensity of their labor, is lower than in industry. But the social-economic conditions of agricultural labor lower its attractiveness. Thus, the socially necessary level of labor payment in agriculture hardly needs to be lower than that in other branches of material production.[69]

Evidently, the new leadership shared this sentiment and very substantial wage-price measures were taken after Khrushchev's removal to raise agricultural incomes.[70]

I conclude that agricultural output is probably undervalued at existing prices, net of turnover taxes. The undervaluation is greatest in the early 1960s and less consequential at both the beginning and end of the SYP period.

WAGES

There is little that needs to be said about the correspondence of wage differentials with productivity and disutility in this period. The restrictive labor controls introduced on the eve of World War II were no longer in force, and an open labor market was the rule. Similarly, rationing had been abolished in 1947 and an open consumers' goods market re-established. Neither the structure of Soviet wage differentials nor their

---

[67] On the number of specialists see *NKh 1964*, pp. 421 and 562. Industrial employment is taken from *NKh 1959*, p. 138 and *NKh 1964*, p. 135; agricultural employment from Nimitz, *Farm Employment in the Soviet Union 1928–1963*, November 1965, p. 112. The absolute number of specialists on collective farms rose by about 9 percent in 1964; employment at collective farms probably declined.

[68] On agricultural policy, see Nimitz, *Problems of Communism*, May–June 1965, and her *Farm Employment in the Soviet Union 1928–1963*, November 1965, pp. 90–108; also Karcz, in *New Directions in the Soviet Economy*, 1966, pp. 383–450.

[69] Marinko and Sabadakha, *Ekonomicheskie nauki*, 1966, No. 5, p. 64.

[70] See Bush, in *New Directions in the Soviet Economy*, 1966, pp. 451–472; Karcz, *Soviet Studies*, October 1965, pp. 129–161.

correspondence with labor market conditions in the present period is precisely known, but a recent study of industrial wage differentials concludes that "earnings differentials among the branches of industry in the Soviet socialized and centrally managed economy resemble fairly closely the differentials that result from the operation of free market economies." [71] Since the essential principles and institutions of Soviet labor policy have not changed, Bergson's position with respect to prewar wages would seem valid for the SYP period as well.[72] No substantive conflict with the AFCS is seen in the Soviet wage structure.

SUMMARY

Turnover taxes, subsidies, and the divergence between collective farm market and retail prices are viewed as in clear conflict with valuation under the AFCS. No such conflict is seen with respect to differentials in wages and salaries. Collective farm labor incomes per unit of input fall far short of industrial earnings, especially in the early 1960s. It seems likely that agricultural output is undervalued on this account. There are no explicit levies for either interest (as a net charge for capital) or rent, but profits may be a rough approximation to interest, except that separate imputation seems necessary for private sector capital. An increasing share of differential rent in agriculture is believed to have been retained by producers during the SYP period, hence reflected in the factor cost valuation of income and output. Soviet depreciation practice clearly left something to be desired before the revision of rates in 1963, but a revaluation of output on this score alone does not appear worth the effort. Partial or complete imputation of depreciation would be necessary for housing and social-cultural capital.

The operational implications of this critique of the Soviet price system are developed in Chapters 5 and 6, where values at established prices are recast in closer conformity to the AFCS. The recasting is performed in two steps. A basic set of AFC values is developed first, incorporating adjustments for the major divergences from AFCS valuation revealed earlier—turnover taxes, subsidies, and multiple prices on the retail market. For varying years within the period under review, the

[71] Schroeder, *Soviet Studies*, January 1966, p. 312. The relatively depressed levels of earnings in the service branches are to be explained presumably by the low valuation attached to these occupations in the planners' preferences.

[72] *Real SNIP*, pp. 113–117; *SNIP 1937*, pp. 63–68.

sensitivity of the basic series to various alterations will be tested: (1) imputation of interest to private sector capital, (2) imputation of depreciation to private sector and government service capital, and (3) adjustment for undervaluation of agricultural output. The effect of the latter adjustment should also suggest the impact of imputing agricultural rent, although the imputation is not undertaken explicitly.

Growth of Production Potential

So far the discussion has concerned productive potential in a single unit of time and, correspondingly, prices as reflections of transformation rates during that time unit. I turn now to the problem of measuring growth of potential, to be expressed in indexes relating values of final product of different years. Again we note the importance of correspondence between relative prices and underlying transformation rates; only if we can assume some "reasonable" correspondence are we entitled to use price-weighted aggregates of quantities as measures of growth of potential, understood in the usual sense as an outward extension of the production possibilities frontier, or, in the special case of the AFCS, of the feasibility locus.

Moorsteen and Bergson have elaborated the theoretical criteria relevant to choice of appropriate indexes.[73] I think it worth summarizing the theory in more than the barest outline because my calculations will be forced to depart from the ideal, and the reader will have to gauge the extent of the distortions thereby incurred.

Consider first a comparison of two periods. As measures of change in aggregate output, we have a choice between the Laspeyres quantity index

$$\frac{\sum P_o Q_i}{\sum P_o Q_o} \tag{1}$$

and the Paasche index

$$\frac{\sum P_i Q_i}{\sum P_i Q_o} \tag{2}$$

Where *P* and *Q* refer to prices and quantities in the base (*o*) or given year (*i*).

[73] Moorsteen, *Quarterly Journal of Economics,* August 1961, pp. 451–459; *Real SNIP,* pp. 26–34.

Depending on assumptions with regard to the curvature of the underlying production possibility schedules (p.p.s.), one or the other index may be a better approximation of the "true" change in capacity to produce a particular mix.[74] Specifically, if we may assume the p.p.s. nonlinear and concave to the origin (that is, characterized by diminishing marginal rates of transformation) with price lines tangent to the p.p.s. at observed outputs, the Laspeyres quantity index generally provides a better approximation of the actual change in capacity to produce the mix of the given year; the reverse is true with respect to the capacity to produce the base year mix. The conclusions hold even if the schedules are convex to the origin, provided they exhibit only moderate curvature.

As stated, the findings assume a comparison where a large increase in the capacity to produce a particular commodity (or class of commodities) is associated with a large decline in its relative real resource cost. This is the postulated reality behind the Gerschenkron hypothesis that in the initial stages of industrialization an early-year weighted quantity index shows much larger growth than an index with price weights drawn from a relatively late industrialization year. Should the p.p.s. change in the opposite way—if a commodity becomes more expensive in real terms to produce as a large change in capacity to produce it takes place—the indicated matching of Laspeyres and Paasche quantity indexes with given and base year indexes holds where the schedules are convex, or concave with moderate curvature.

Corresponding to the choice of the quantity indexes is an appropriate price deflator. If we opt for the Laspeyres quantity index, the appropriate price deflator is

$$\frac{\sum P_i Q_i}{\sum \frac{P_o}{P_i} P_i Q_i} \tag{3}$$

that is, a given-year (variable-weight), value-weighted price index—in effect, a Paasche price index. Conversely, choice of formula (2) requires a base-year (fixed weight), value-weighted price index—a Laspeyres price index,

$$\frac{\sum \frac{P_i}{P_o} P_o Q_o}{\sum P_o Q_o} \tag{4}$$

[74] The theory expressed in terms of p.p.s. should presumably be equally applicable in terms of a feasibility locus.

Consider now three or more periods of time, say years, and let the objective be to obtain a series of indexes enabling comparisons between any pair of years in the series. If such comparisons require that the individual indexes refer to the same output mix, and on the assumption of concave p.p.s. and price lines tangent to them at observed output, the result will be obtained only with the use of variable price weights of the given year—that is, with Paasche quantity indexes (2). The appropriate deflator of a current-price series is then, as indicated, formula (4), the Laspeyres price index. Use of formula (3) would result in a series where the binary comparisons on the base year referred in each case to a different mix. Such would also be the result of chained indexes.

Assurance of an index series referring to a particular and constant output mix conveys no information on the margin of error with respect to the correspondence of the computed indexes to the true relation between p.p.s. It is possible that in such a series the computed index bias would be greater than in a conventional series weighted by base year prices, whose binary comparisons refer, as we have seen, to constantly changing output mixes. The answer would depend on the length of the period, the shapes of the schedules, and the degree to which observed relative prices approximated p.p.s. transformation rates.[75] It is likely that the choice would be between measurements with a constant output mix (where in any binary comparison conceivably neither year's actual output would reflect the mix in question) or measurements intended to minimize the degree of index number bias.

Unhappily, the uncertainties besetting the theory of production indexes must be compounded by the defects of the empirical tools at our disposal. Because of insufficient information on price level changes and the heterogeneity of the few price indexes or constant-price series available, it appears impossible in this study to apply a consistent deflation procedure. To redress the balance slightly, it should be noted in fairness that the calculations cover a relatively short period of time during which there were no general revisions in the wholesale or retail structure of nonagricultural prices. Possibly the relatively limited scope of structural change during the SYP period may partly counterweigh any distortions resulting from inadequate information. The reader will have to judge for himself how much confidence can be placed in the results in the light of these theoretical and practical considerations.

---

[75] Bergson, pointing out these empirical uncertainties, suggests that the likelihood rests with concave curves and decreasing relative cost of the rapidly increasing product.

Nevertheless, some guidelines must be set. How shall this be done? To begin with, use of 1958 prices seems an obvious choice, for comparison with official Soviet data on net material product, valued at 1958 prices (since 1959). It would also seem useful to make alternative calculations using the prices of a later year. Although no general wholesale or retail price revisions took place during the SYP period, agricultural procurement prices were substantially increased in 1962 and to a lesser extent in 1963. To provide a test of the sensitivity of the indexes to a change in weight year, perhaps an appropriate alternative would be prices of 1964. Price-level change was minimal during that year, whereas in the following year the new regime instituted a significant reform in agricultural prices and delivery regulations. Thus, the revaluation will aim at obtaining fixed-weight quantity indexes, using two alternative weight years, 1958 and 1964. How close I come to that goal is appraised in Chapter 6 and can be independently judged by turning to Appendix K, which explains the deflation procedure in detail.

Part II

Analysis of Findings

4

Incomes and Outlays at Current Prevailing Prices

Analysis of the findings of this study begins with a consideration of the first-stage results of the *ex post* national accounts, values at current prevailing or established prices. Succeeding chapters will take up the results of calculations yielding *ex post* values at current factor cost and constant prices, the latter at both prevailing prices and factor cost. This chapter is largely concerned with the structure of incomes and outlays of households and the public sectors. It concludes with a brief discussion of changes in the relation between the state budget and GNP.

Sectoral Incomes and Outlays

INCOMES OF HOUSEHOLDS

Changes in the originating structure of household income are shown in Table 9. The period began with wages and salaries, farm and nonfarm, as the dominant elements in household incomes and that dominance was magnified in the succeeding years. By 1964 six of every ten rubles of household income, actual and imputed, were earned as wages and salaries, compared with somewhat more than five in 1958.

To some extent, this growth in employment and aggregate earnings reflects mere bookkeeping changes: a large number of collective farms were transformed into state farms, and overnight collective farmers were transformed into workers and employees. Conversion of collective to state farms has been taking place irregularly since the middle 1950s. The process was particularly intensive in 1957, 1960, and 1961, in which

TABLE 9

Structure of Household Income, 1958–1964
(percent)

	1958	1959	1960	1961	1962	1963	1964
1. Wages and salaries, farm and nonfarm	53.7	53.9	55.5	59.7	59.3	59.6	60.3
2. Net income of households from agriculture (excluding wages and salaries of state employed farm labor)	22.0	20.6	18.9	19.2	19.4	18.3	18.6
3. Military pay and subsistence	4.1	3.8	3.4	3.2	3.3	2.9	2.5
4. Other income currently earned, statistical discrepancy	7.8	9.4	9.9	5.3	5.8	7.2	6.8
5. Imputed rent and imputed value of owner-supplied building services	2.3	2.4	2.2	2.0	1.8	1.6	1.5
6. Transfer receipts	10.0	10.2	10.0	10.6	10.5	10.3	10.3
7. Total income	100.0	100.0	100.0	100.0	100.0	100.0	100.0

Source:

Table 1.

years more than 3 million households were converted.[1] Also in 1960 producer cooperatives were absorbed by state industry and the 1.3 million artisans thereby became workers and employees. The downward pull on average wages exerted by these status transformations was counterweighted by the effects of a wage reform.[2] Under the wage reform carried out between 1956 and 1965 minimum wage rates were raised twice, and adjustments were made in the general wage and salary system which also raised average earnings.[3] These developments help explain the relatively sharp upswing in the wage and salary group's share between 1959 and 1961.

The share of income from agriculture (excluding wages and salaries) declined over this period. The small increase in the weight of agricultural income in 1961 and 1962 was due to a 27 percent increase in cash payments to member households by collective farms in these two years.[4] A 22 percent growth of income from sales in 1962 was the consequence of a sharp increase in state purchase prices for livestock products decreed in the middle of that year. Although income from sales rose again in 1963, by about .6 billion rubles, income in kind dropped by more than twice that amount. The pattern was reversed in 1964.

As indicated, the cited estimates of agricultural incomes exclude wages and salaries paid to state-employed labor; the latter incomes are counted as part of the wage and salary bill. However, allowance for changes in agricultural wages and salaries would not alter the general finding, that between 1958 and 1964 the share of income derived from agricultural employment declined and the share of nonagricultural wages and salaries increased markedly.[5]

---

[1] Based on unpublished research by N. Nimitz.

[2] Average earnings of collective farmers and cooperative artisans were clearly below those of the state labor force. For estimates of the gap, see p. 415 and Appendix O.

[3] On the wage reform see CIA, *An Evaluation of the Soviet Wage Reform 1956–1962,* August 1963; Chapman, *Problems of Communism,* September–October 1964, pp. 76–78; Schroeder, *Soviet Studies,* January 1966, pp. 303–317; Yanowitch, *Slavic Review,* December 1963.

[4] Although cash payments to collective farm members rose by an impressive 44 percent between 1958 and 1964, payments in kind (valued at current retail prices) declined almost 30 percent. Thus, the total earnings bill paid members in money and in kind increased by only 13 percent in six years. (These are estimates by Nimitz for an as yet unpublished study of collective farmer incomes since 1953. Hereafter, this material will be referred to as Nimitz, *Incomes of Collective Farmers.*)

[5] Wage and salary data are officially reported only for personnel of state

Table 9 notes that item 4 includes the statistical discrepancy for the household sector. That is, total outlays are the sum of the various components and total income is identical to total outlays. A residual income entry is then computed as the difference between total income and the sum of all independently estimated income items. Thus, household savings and total outlays are recorded net of additions to cash hoards (balances held outside of the banks). If changes in cash hoards were positive in a given year, household income would, other things being equal, be understated by that amount. On the other hand, if dishoarding took place, total income would be overstated. The statistical discrepancy covers not only omissions but also errors, and it is obviously impossible to distinguish finely between them in this case. Nevertheless, there is some reason to believe that the relatively high level of "other income currently earned; statistical discrepancy" (item 4 of Table 1) in 1960 reflects, at least in part, dishoarding, and that the relatively low 1961–1962 entries partly reflect hoarding.

In May 1960 the government announced its intention to carry through a monetary reform in the first quarter of 1961. With regard to its domestic provisions, the reform involved no more than a simple exchange of 10 old rubles for 1 new ruble, with all prices and wage rates undergoing the same transformation. In the last previous currency exchange, in December 1947, all monetary debt in the hands of households—state bonds, bank deposits,[6] and cash—was depreciated relative to prices and wages; cash exchanges were hardest hit of all.[7] Evidently, memories of the 1947 episode were still fresh and painful in many minds, and fear of possible discrimination against cash holdings apparently induced some dishoarding.[8]

---

farms and subsidiary agricultural enterprises (*NKh 1964,* p. 555). Multiplying the reported average pay by average annual employment (*ibid.,* p. 546) indicates an increase in the wage and salary bill for this agricultural subdivision from 2.94 billion rubles in 1958 to 6.84 billion in 1964. If the structure of incomes in these years is now recalculated, wages and salaries minus this component are found to grow from 49.7 percent of the total in 1958 to 53.9 percent in 1964; the share of income from agriculture, augmented by this component, drops from 25.0 percent in 1958 to 23.7 percent in 1964. The remainder of the state agricultural labor force consists of MTS-RTS and miscellaneous personnel, and their numbers dropped sharply in this period.

[6] Above 300 (new) rubles.

[7] Holzman, *Soviet Taxation,* 1955, p. 232.

[8] See the sources cited by Karcz, in *New Directions in the Soviet Economy,* 1966, p. 439, note 186.

In 1961–1962 the flow was reversed. On this we have the authoritative evidence of Khrushchev himself. At the January 1961 plenum of the Communist Party Central Committee, he warned of possible imbalances between supply and demand in the consumers' goods market.[9] In 1962 he acknowledged that the threat had materialized. Concluding an address to a Central Committee Plenum on March 9, Khrushchev criticized the lag of agricultural output behind the population's needs. "Even with this quantity of output," he declared, "it would be possible to balance supply and demand." However, the state cut taxes, ceased exacting compulsory loans, raised wages, and thereby generated higher levels of demand. Capitalists would not tolerate such an imbalance: they would "immediately inflate prices and would create such conditions under which millions of people would not be able to obtain food." The Soviet state did not do this.[10] On June 2, defending the just-announced increases in retail prices at a meeting of friendship of Soviet and Cuban youth, Khrushchev stated the problem bluntly: "We encountered difficulties arising from the fact that there turned out to be more money in the hands of the population than there were goods produced by our industry and agriculture."[11]

Although on this occasion Khrushchev implied that the retail price increases of June 1962 were intended to sop up consumer purchasing power, it is doubtful that this was in fact the major reason or that the effect was significant. The increases raised the average level of food prices by only 3 percent and the level of prices of all goods by but 2 percent. The aggregate increase in household expenditure siphoned off by the price increase was about 1.8 billion rubles.[12] Perhaps the real motive for the price increases, as Khrushchev himself indicated in an address at the end of June, was to prevent collective farms from buying meat and milk cheap at retail and selling them dear as output to the state at the higher purchase prices introduced at the same time.[13]

Khrushchev's initial warning of a potential inflationary gap had been sounded at the beginning of 1961. In that year disposable household money incomes[14] (that is, after direct taxes and other payments to the

---

[9] *Plenum Tsentral'nogo komiteta . . . 10–18 ianvaria 1961 goda,* p. 524.

[10] Khrushchev, *Stroitel'stvo kommunizma v SSSR i razvitie sel'skogo khoziaistva,* 1963, Volume 7, pp. 471–472.

[11] *Ibid.,* Volume 7, p. 33.

[12] *NKh 1962,* pp. 520, 532.

[13] Khrushchev, *Stroitel'stvo kommunizma . . . ,* 1963, Volume 7, p. 50.

[14] For present purposes, money income is defined as items 1.A, 1.B, 2.A,

state) [15] jumped 9 percent after two years of 4 and less than 6 percent annual increases. The rapid growth of disposable money income was continued in 1962 with an 8 percent increase; in the succeeding two years the increments dropped to around 4 and 5 percent respectively (Tables 1 and 2). No countermeasures from the side of fiscal policy were undertaken. The abrogation of direct income taxes was abruptly halted in 1962, but tax rates were not raised. Neither were the indirect levies, turnover taxes; apart from the two percent increase in prices reluctantly instituted in mid-1962, the state retail price level went virtually unchanged throughout the SYP period. Thus, as growth of output lagged behind increased purchasing power,[16] the fiscal reins were held slack.[17]

The reasoning advanced here has included no reference to the behavior of money savings. Increments to savings deposits, the relevant and most important component of household savings as defined in this study, changed as follows (pp. 379–380):

	1958	*1959*	*1960*	*1961*	*1962*	*1963*	*1964*
Billion rubles	.66	1.34	.86	.78	1.06	1.25	1.71

If those who, in 1960, feared an impending currency repudiation believed that savings would also be discounted, they would most likely have tended to spend rather than save or hoard currency. The decrease

---

2.B, 3.A, 8.E of Table 1, plus 7.5 billion rubles annually of other current money income. The differences between 7.5 billions and the entries in item 4 of Table 1 are assumed to represent errors and omissions on the outlay side and changes in currency holdings. Of course, the assumption is arbitrary but the income categories involved in item 4 are not likely to have changed rapidly, and the movement of disposable income discussed in the text is not very sensitive to alterations in the absolute level of other current money income.

[15] Other payments to the state consist of revenue from lotteries and other state budget revenue "from the population." The latter consist largely of local taxes and fees (see Table C-1). Deduction of lottery revenue from household income to obtain disposable income figures may be questionable but the amounts are small (see p. 382).

[16] Valued at 1958 established prices, real consumption, excluding that of income in kind (Table K-1), increased more rapidly than disposable money income until 1961 when the inequality was sharply reversed. In 1963–1964 the two series moved at roughly the same pace.

[17] In this context the role of monetary policy in the Soviet Union essentially merges into one of fiscal restraint. That is, for given increments of short term lending, the task is to control unplanned leakages into wage distributions but mainly to absorb excess cash in circulation by budgetary measures.

in the savings deposit increment in 1960 is consistent with that hypothesis. On the other hand, there appears to have been no further incentive to shun the savings banks once the currency reform was carried out (in the first quarter of 1961). The continued decline in the savings increment in 1961 also provides no support for a hypothesis of net currency hoarding in that year.

The clearest indication of repressed inflation in the USSR is a marked increase of the price level on the collective farm market, the only more or less free market in the country. This is indeed what occurred from 1960 on: after a four year period of virtual constancy in the market price level, the price index for all urban collective farm market sales jumped 5 percent in 1961, 6 percent in both 1962 and 1963, and rose an additional 3 percent in 1964.[18] The physical volume of sales on the market practically did not change from 1960 to 1962;[19] it declined 10 percent in 1963 and showed no improvement in 1964.[20]

If the 1960–1962 statistical discrepancies do reflect changes in cash holdings, the structure of income origination in those years shown in Table 9 must be modified. Such a recomputation would reduce the shares of all income items except item 4 in 1961–1962 and raise them in 1960. However, it does not seem likely that the patterns discussed earlier in this section would be appreciably altered.

HOUSEHOLD SPENDING PATTERNS

In 1958, as Table 10 indicates, 65 percent of the household's expenditures were directed to purchases for consumption on the retail market. That share grew steadily until 1963, reaching a high of 70 percent. Of this aggregate, a small and generally decreasing proportion represented expenditures on the extravillage farm markets; the overwhelming bulk of purchases were confined to the state-regulated network of state-cooperative trade. The share of outlays on services, although still relatively small, was increasing rapidly. On the other hand, consumption of income in kind and investment absorbed a declining part of the household's ruble expenditure.

Some important factors helping to explain the relative movement of consumption and investment shares are the curtailment of private housing construction after 1959 and restrictions on private livestock holdings. In the summer of 1957, the government announced with considera-

[18] *NKh 1958*, p. 789; below, p. 491.
[19] *NKh 1962*, p. 541.
[20] *NKh 1964*, p. 658.

TABLE 10

STRUCTURE OF HOUSEHOLD OUTLAYS, 1958–1964

(percent)

	1958	1959	1960	1961	1962	1963	1964
1. Retail sales of goods for consumption							
A. State-cooperative trade	60.9	61.9	64.9	65.1	65.5	66.6	65.7
B. Extravillage farm markets	4.5	4.1	3.7	3.8	3.6	3.4	3.3
C. Total	65.4	66.0	68.6	68.9	69.1	70.0	69.0
2. Consumer services							
A. Housing, including imputed rent	1.7	1.7	1.7	1.7	1.7	1.7	1.7
B. Dues	.9	.9	.9	1.0	1.0	1.0	1.0
C. Other	6.6	6.8	7.0	7.5	7.7	7.9	8.1
D. Total	9.3	9.4	9.6	10.3	10.4	10.6	10.8
3. Consumption of income in kind	12.0	11.1	10.1	10.0	9.6	9.1	8.7
4. Other outlays for consumption	3.0	3.1	2.4	2.0	2.7	3.0	3.0
5. Total outlays for consumption	89.7	89.6	90.8	91.2	91.9	92.7	91.5
6. Investment	3.3	3.4	3.1	2.7	2.1	.8	1.6
7. Transfers							
A. Net savings	1.1	1.4	.6	.5	.7	1.2	1.5
B. Direct taxes; other payments to the state	5.8	5.7	5.5	5.6	5.3	5.4	5.4
C. Total	7.0	7.0	6.1	6.1	6.0	6.5	6.9
Total outlays	100.0	100.0	100.0	100.0	100.0	100.0	100.0

Source:
Table 2.

ble fanfare a 10–12 year program to "solve the housing problem." Among the measures announced then were several designed to stimulate private housing construction—larger state credits to individual home-builders, assistance by enterprises to their employees, and so on.[21] At estimate prices the value of private housing investment, excluding construction of summer homes (*dachi*), rose from 2.0 billion rubles in 1957 to 2.7 billion in 1958 and 3.1 billion in 1959.[22] However, as the culmination of an increasingly more indignant campaign against "parasites" and "speculators," governmental encouragement of private urban construction was terminated in the fall of 1960.[23] The volume of private housing floor space completed (except that built on collective farms), which had doubled between 1957 and 1959, declined in each year thereafter; by 1964, construction was down 40 percent from the 1959 peak.[24]

At the inception of the SYP, severe restrictions seemed to be in store for private livestock holdings. The Party Central Committee resolved on December 19, 1958, to have the state farms buy all livestock held privately by their employees within "two to three years." [25] The decree was not fully carried through, although a significant first step was taken in 1959, when holdings of cattle, hogs, and goats by workers and employees (that is, largely state-employed farm households) declined markedly, as did the herds of cattle and goats on private plots in collective farms. Increases in private livestock herds took place in 1961–1962; but by the beginning of 1965, total private holdings were reduced by 2.4 million cows, 1.7 million other cattle, .7 million hogs and 6.0 million sheep and goats.[26] To some extent, of course, these developments stemmed not only from direct state restrictions but also from the dependence of collective farm households on collective farms for fodder supplies in a period of poor crops.

---

[21] *Pravda,* August 2, 1957.

[22] *NKh 1964,* p. 511.

[23] On the charges of parasitism, see "Kto ne rabotaet, tot ne est," *Kommunist,* 1960, No. 14, pp. 13–21. For an economic rationale of the government's change of heart, see Kucherenko's remarks on the results of an opinion poll in *Komsomol'skaia Pravda,* October 8, 1960, translated in the *Current Digest of The Soviet Press,* December 7, 1960, p. 45. Pertinent decrees are summarized in Beermann, *Soviet Studies,* October 1961, p. 201.

[24] *NKh 1964,* p. 604.

[25] See below, p. 420.

[26] *SKh,* pp. 266–269; *NKh 1964,* pp. 353–354.

SOURCES OF PUBLIC SECTOR FINANCE

In computing the structure of public sector incomes, Table 11, total net income is taken gross of subsidized losses, n.e.c. The latter item—consisting of subsidies to procurement organizations and subsidies in connection with the wage reform, as well as to MTS-RTS in 1958–1959—represents extraordinary expenditures that, from a national income accounting standpoint, are properly considered deductions from income. For present purposes, interest in the sources of finance,[27] such an item might more usefully be viewed as an outlay, and it will be so treated here.

Table 11 provides a double view of the structure of public sector incomes, at least for items 1, 2, and 4. The direct translation of Table 3 into percentage terms appears as the B variant of items 1, 2, and 4 in Table 11, along with the latter's items 3, 5, and 6. In the alternative A variants, net income of collective farms and state-cooperative organizations are shown gross of income tax and profits deductions, with a corresponding reduction in the category of budget receipts (item 4). The juxtaposition of A and B variants points up the intrasectoral redistributive functions of the state budget.

Viewed under either variant, collective farm retained incomes represented a continually decreasing share of total public sector revenues. However, inclusion or exclusion of taxes and deductions makes a substantial difference with respect to the pattern of the profit share. Before taxes there was a steady rise in the weight of profits in the total at least until 1962; the decline in 1963 was all but made good in 1964. After taxes, however, the role of profits declined noticeably. This divergence is reflected in the variant behavior of the shares of current budget receipts (item 4). At the same time, depreciation allowances were growing rapidly, with an especially sharp spurt in 1963, the year of introduction of higher amortization norms. Thus, the scope for decentralized financing of public sector outlays was being curtailed as income components more or less subject to centralized redistribution—taxes, deductions from profits, depreciation allowances— [28] were growing more rapidly.

---

[27] Here and throughout this study I deal with a consolidated account of the public sectors. A usual feature of a "sources of finance" analysis, bank lending, is netted out in a consolidated account (except for relations with households). The term "sources of finance" must be understood here in this more restricted sense.

[28] On the degree of centralized control of these allowances, see Campbell,

TABLE 11

STRUCTURE OF PUBLIC SECTOR INCOME, 1958–1964
(percent)

	1958	1959	1960	1961	1962	1963	1964
1. Income of collective farms net of depreciation:							
A. Gross of income tax	4.6	4.7	4.2	3.8	3.7	3.2	3.1
B. Net of income tax	3.3	3.2	2.9	2.8	2.7	2.3	2.3
2. Net profits of state enterprises, nonfarm cooperatives and other organizations							
A. Before income tax and profits deductions	25.4	26.1	27.5	27.8	29.2	27.2	28.5
B. After income tax and profits deductions	7.5	7.3	6.5	5.5	5.7	3.8	4.5
3. Charges to economic enterprises for special funds	4.8	4.8	4.9	5.2	5.2	5.1	4.9
4. Taxes and other payments out of income by economic organizations to the budget [a]							
A. Excluding organization income tax and profits deductions	46.5	45.9	45.1	44.0	42.5	41.6	40.3
B. Including organization income tax and deductions	65.7	66.1	67.4	67.2	66.9	65.9	65.1
5. Depreciation	10.0	10.2	11.0	12.0	12.3	15.5	15.5
6. Transfer receipts							
A. Net savings by households	1.4	1.6	.7	.6	.9	1.3	1.7
B. Direct taxes and other payments by households to the state	7.3	6.7	6.6	6.6	6.3	6.2	6.0
C. Total	8.7	8.3	7.3	7.2	7.2	7.5	7.7
7. Consolidated net income, but gross of subsidized losses, n.e.c.	100.0	100.0	100.0	100.0	100.0	100.0	100.0

Note:

[a] Including net accounting profits from foreign trade.

Source:

Table 3. A variants of items 1, 2, and 4 are computed by deducting tax on income of collective farms, cooperatives and other organizations, as well as on state sector profits, from item 3 of Table 3 and adding them to retained incomes.

Evidently the government became reluctant to countenance further growth of noncentralized investment financed from retained profits. Although noncentralized investment was encouraged in the late 1950s —the volume of such investment grew 2.6 times between 1956 and 1960— [29] restrictions were introduced in 1960. A Council of Ministers decree of June 29, 1960 directed administrative agencies to reexamine the question of decentralized investment and to submit suggestions to Gosplan and the Ministry of Finances by March 1, 1961, "with a view to further decreasing the volume of these investments." [30] The increasing tightness experienced in the supply of investable resources was of course a major factor in the new restrictions. Another was the significantly more rapid growth since 1958 of unfinished construction in noncentralized investment than of unfinished construction in centralized investment.[31] In any event, the volume of noncentralized investment was cut 14 percent in 1961. Some further reduction took place in 1962.[32] In his 1963 budget speech, Garbuzov called for a decrease of noncentralized investment by 350 million rubles in order to "concentrate resources on the state plan." [33] However, instead of a decrease there was actually some increase in 1963 and a considerably larger one in 1964.[34]

A word should be said here about the role of turnover taxes, at one time the mainstay of Soviet public finances. As recently as 1950, pro-

Accounting in Soviet Planning and Management, 1963, pp. 51–52; also, *Finansovo-kreditnyi slovar',* I, 1961, p. 39.

[29] *NKh 1961,* p. 536.

[30] *Zakonodatel'nye akty po voprosam narodnogo khoziaistva SSSR,* 1961, Vol. II, p. 125. See also Riumin in MFI, *Problemy finansovogo planirovaniia,* 1963, pp. 35–36.

[31] Galkin, *Voprosy ritmichnosti i zadela v stroitel'stve,* 1962, p. 70.

[32] NKh 1961, p. 536 and the plan fulfillment report in Pravda, January 26, 1963.

[33] *Izvestiia,* December 11, 1962.

[34] The 1962–1964 yearbooks did not break down state-cooperative investment into its centralized and noncentralized components. Such a breakdown reappears in *NKh 1965* (cf. pp. 528 and 530) and in *Strana sovetov za 50 let* (cf. pp. 199, 201) but in these volumes there has been a change in estimate prices. Moreover, the change appears to affect noncentralized investment more heavily than centralized investment. Thus, for 1960, centralized investment according to *NKh 1961,* p. 536 was 25.7 billion rubles and according to *NKh 1965,* p. 530 it was 25.8 billions; the corresponding figures for noncentralized investment are 5.1 and 4.2 billions. The 1963–1964 changes cited in the text are taken from *NKh 1965* but it should be understood that they are not really comparable to the data for preceding years.

ceeds from the tax accounted for well over half of total public sector revenues;[35] by 1964 this share was down to about 30 percent. In the first part of the 1950s retail price cuts were largely responsible for damping the growth of turnover taxes. Since 1954 the decline in the relative weight of turnover taxes is explained by narrowing of the margin between retail and wholesale prices of consumer goods at the expense of the tax, in an attempt to reduce subsidies to procurement and processing organizations.[36] Over the same period, deductions from profits of state enterprises increased from a tenth to almost one-quarter of total public sector incomes. Together, turnover taxes and profits payments continued to furnish more than half of total revenues.

The patterns discussed here are those relating to public sector incomes, defined in the national product sense. An examination of state budget revenues,[37] the distribution of which is shown in Table 12, shows an analogous decline in the relative importance of turnover taxes and a substantial increase in that of deductions from state sector profits.

PUBLIC SECTOR OUTLAYS

Table 13 displays no startling changes in the structure of public sector outlays. The relative weight of gross fixed investment, far and away the single most important element of public sector outlays, rose still further. So did the share of R&D; those of administration and internal security declined; inventory investment and residual outlays (outlays n.e.c.; statistical discrepancy) fluctuated sharply, defense and transfer payments somewhat less so.

The structure of state budget revenues was presented earlier in connection with incomes of the public sectors. It might be of interest now to show the expenditure side of the state budget, to conclude the discussion of public sector outlays. The relative distribution of major budget expenditures is given in Table 14. Appropriations to the "national economy" consist of investment grants, subsidies, and a variety of operational financing for the various branches of the economy. "Social-cultural measures" embrace education, health care and physical culture, and welfare payments. In addition to the budget appropriation, various

---

[35] *SNIP 1949–1955*, p. 6.

[36] Below, pp. 378–379. The subsidies were reduced by raising wholesale prices.

[37] Budget revenues not entered directly or indirectly in the national income accounts are a variety of miscellaneous revenues from the "socialist sector" deemed to represent transactions on capital account.

TABLE 12
STRUCTURE OF STATE BUDGET REVENUES, 1958–1965
(percent)

	1958	1959	1960	1961	1962	1963	1964	1965
1. From "the socialist economy"								
A. Turnover tax	45.3	42.0	40.6	39.6	39.1	38.6	38.9	37.8
B. Deductions from state enterprise profits	20.1	21.6	24.2	26.6	28.3	28.7	30.4	30.2
C. Income tax on enterprises and organizations	2.5	2.6	2.4	1.6	1.6	1.6	1.4	1.5
D. Social insurance fund charges	4.8	4.8	4.9	5.3	5.2	5.2	5.2	5.4
E. Other	17.1	19.0	18.9	17.9	16.8	17.0	16.2	16.9
F. Total	89.8	90.0	91.0	91.0	91.0	90.9	92.2	91.8
2. From "the population"								
A. Taxes	7.7	7.5	7.3	7.5	7.1	7.0	7.1	7.5
B. Loans	1.6	2.0	1.2	1.0	1.4	1.5	.1	.2
C. Other	.9	.5	.6	.6	.5	.6	.6	.5
D. Total	10.2	10.0	9.0	9.0	9.0	9.1	7.8	8.2
Total revenue	100.0	100.0	100.0	100.0	100.0	100.0	100.0	100.0

Source:
Table C-1.

TABLE 13

Structure of Public Sector Outlays, 1958–1964

(percent)

	1958	1959	1960	1961	1962	1963	1964
1. Communal services, excluding R&D	13.9	13.4	13.8	14.3	13.8	14.1	14.2
2. Administration	1.6	1.3	1.2	1.2	1.1	1.0	.9
3. Gross investment							
A. Fixed capital	44.0	43.8	46.3	47.6	47.0	46.7	46.5
B. Inventories	10.4	11.1	5.4	6.6	5.7	7.4	9.8
C. Total	54.5	54.9	51.7	54.2	52.7	54.1	56.4
4. Other outlays							
A. Defense (budget)	11.9	10.8	10.1	12.3	12.4	12.5	11.0
B. Internal security	2.0	1.8	1.7	1.6	1.5	1.4	1.3
C. R&D	2.7	2.7	2.8	3.1	3.3	3.5	3.6
D. Outlays n.e.c.; statistical discrepancy	.3	2.6	6.3	.3	2.5	1.3	.9
E. Total	16.9	17.8	21.0	17.3	19.6	18.7	16.7
5. Transfer payments	13.1	12.0	12.4	13.0	12.7	12.0	11.7
6. Total outlays	100.0	100.0	100.0	100.0	100.0	100.0	100.0

Source:
Table 4.

TABLE 14

STRUCTURE OF STATE BUDGET EXPENDITURES, 1958–1965

(percent)

	1958	1959	1960	1961	1962	1963	1964	1965
1. National economy	45.2	46.0	46.7	42.7	44.1	44.6	44.0	44.2
2. Social-cultural measures	33.3	32.8	34.1	35.6	35.2	35.6	36.1	37.6
3. Defense	14.6	13.3	12.7	15.2	15.4	15.9	14.4	12.6
4. Administration	1.9	1.6	1.5	1.4	1.3	1.3	1.2	1.3
5. Loan service	.6	1.0	1.0	1.0	1.0	.1	.1	.1
6. Other	4.5	5.3	4.1	4.1	2.9	2.5	4.1	4.3
Total	100.0	100.0	100.0	100.0	100.0	100.0	100.0	100.0

Source:
Table 24.

nonbudget funds are drawn on to finance public sector outlays—retained income, depreciation allowances, and bank credit being the chief other sources. During the SYP period, outlays on the national economy fluctuated as a share of total budget expenditures but continued to be the single most important expenditure item. Social-cultural measures, a close second, expanded their share of the total, whereas loan service and administration outlays declined in relative weight.[38] The explicit allocation to "defense" had a declining share of total expenditures until 1960, then a rising one in 1961–1963, followed by a drop back to the 1960 level by 1965. At a later point it will be necessary to go into further detail on the degree to which military expenditures are concealed in other budget categories, but here it may be sufficient simply to warn that the relative weight of defense shown in Tables 13 and 14 should not be taken at face value.

A SENSITIVITY TEST

The magnitude of public sector incomes, and hence also of public sector outlays and GNP, in 1959–1964 is influenced by an essentially arbitrary decision relating to the proportion of unidentified state budget revenues "from the socialist sector" which can be viewed as income on current account. In this study I have assumed the proportion to be 75 percent; in earlier SNIP studies, the figure used was 50 percent.[39] The sensitivity of the results to the size of this share is tested by repeating the operations performed to this point for alternative shares of 50, 75, and 90 percent and for three years, 1958, 1961, and 1964. The effect of lowering (raising) the share relative to its assumed level of 75 percent is, of course, to reduce (raise) public sector miscellaneous revenues—item 3.E of Table 3, "miscellaneous charges"—and outlays—item 7 of Table 4, "outlays n.e.c.; statistical discrepancy"—as well as the relevant subtotals and totals of Tables 3, 4, 5, and 6. Clearly, the impact is heaviest on the smallest affected entries, the volatile outlays n.e.c. of Tables 4 and 6. However, the absolute values of incomes and outlays at established prices are of less interest to us than their distribution, and our real concern is with the effects of changes in the assumption under discussion on the distributional patterns observed to this point.

---

[38] The sharp decline in the share of loan service outlays in 1963 is explained by the final redemption of the last mass-subscription loan, floated in 1957. See pp. 380–381.

[39] The basis of the choice is discussed below, pp. 367–368.

The details of the test are set out in Appendix M but the results may be briefly summarized as follows:

(1) The absolute values of outlays n.e.c. in 1959–1964 must be treated with considerable reserve. Nevertheless, I think the likely direction of error is down rather than up—that is, the existing entries are more likely to be under- than overestimates.

(2) The absolute values of major public sector aggregates and of GNP are not very sensitive to the choices made.

(3) The distributional patterns of Table 11 and Table 13 are not much affected by alternative assumptions. Although this is considerably less true of Table 13, the most sensitive item again is outlays n.e.c.

On the whole, I would conclude that substantial change in the indicated basic assumption would require no tangible alteration in the discussion of earlier sections of this chapter.

The State Budget and GNP

It is perhaps fitting to close this chapter, whose major subject is the time structure of sectoral accounts, with the results of a calculation emphasizing overall stability of structure. The following tabulation shows the ratio of state budget revenues (expenditures plus budget surplus) to GNP at current established prices in years since the beginning of the First Five Year Plan for which SNIP accounts are available.[40]

1937	38	1955	47
1940	40	1956	46
1944	59	1957	45
1948	52	1958	43
1949	47	1959	43
1950	45	1960	43
1951	47	1961	42
1952	48	1962	42
1953	51	1963	42
1954	50	1964	41

[40] Computed from data in *SNIP 1928–1948*, pp. 10, 14 (1937–1948); *SNIP 1949–1955*, pp. 8, 131 (1949–1955); *SNIP 1956–1958*, pp. 6, 107 (1956–1957); Table 5 and Table C–1 of this study. The series is computed from data that are not quite of the same scope: budget values for 1949–1964 are total reported revenues, whereas for earlier years the values used reflect small adjustments to reported values. For 1948, the difference in scope means a difference of about half a percentage point in the computed ratio of budget to GNP.

GNP and state budget revenues are not entirely in the same universe of discourse. Not all of budget revenue is reflected in GNP—in 1961, the gap amounted to about 5 percent of the former. Whereas revenues from the public sector appear in the SNIP accounts on the current income side of the sectoral balance, revenues from households are entered in household outlays as transfer payments. Apart from their contributions to budget entries, households accounted for almost half of GNP in 1961. Thus, the ratio of budget revenues to GNP is something of a hybrid and little significance can be attached to small changes in its value.

The tabulation displays two rough cycles between 1937 and 1958: in the first, an all-time high of 59 percent is observed for the war year 1944 and a low of 45 percent for 1950; the ratio rose until the year of Stalin's death and then fell uninterruptedly to 1958. It is shown to have declined slightly after 1958, and at 41 percent the 1964 level is the lowest since 1940. Abstracting from the changes during and just after the Second World War, the pattern of the tabulation is in a rough sense a measure of the stability of certain features of Soviet economic organization through the SYP period. Agriculture continued to be dominated by collective farms and the private household plot, operating more independently of the budget than state enterprises; state enterprises, in turn, had the scope of their financial initiative broadened, but not drastically. Hence the perceptible decline in the ratio of budget revenues to GNP, but hence also a steadily maintained level of that ratio at over 40 percent.

For comparison, the corresponding U.S. data for benchmark years are as follows: [41]

1929	4	1950	14
1940	9	1958	16
1944	45	1965	14

Since the Second World War, the degree of structural change, to whatever extent evidenced by this particular indicator, has not been remarkable in the United States either.

---

[41] The numerator is revenues plus deficit, average for the calendar year, from the *World Almanac 1967*, p. 167. GNP figures are the revised estimates shown in U.S. Bureau of the Census, *Long Term Economic Growth 1860–1965*, 1966, pp. 166–167, Series A8.

5

Resource Allocation: National Product at Current Factor Cost

The focus of the previous chapter was on the estimates at current established prices and the analysis of "financial" flows for which such values are appropriate. I come now to consider the shifting pattern of resource allocation, the changes in the final use distribution of total output. To this end, prevailing Soviet prices are deficient in terms of the criteria of the adjusted factor cost standard (AFCS). On the foundation of the critique of Soviet prices set out in Chapter 3, the established-price values of GNP and its component final uses are now recast in an attempt to conform to the requirements of the AFCS. The recasting is performed in two stages. A basic set of AFC values is developed first, incorporating the adjustments for the major divergences from AFCS valuation revealed in Chapter 3—turnover taxes, subsidies, and multiple prices on the retail market (Table 15). Then the sensitivity of the basic series to various alterations is tested: (1) imputation of interest to private sector capital, (2) imputation of depreciation to private sector and government service capital, (3) omission of part of capital repairs, and (4) adjustment for undervaluation of agricultural output. The effect of the latter adjustment should also suggest the impact of imputing agricultural rent, although that imputation is not undertaken explicitly.

The Basic Factor Cost Series

Table J-1 presents a revaluation of GNP by final use, showing three major adjustments. The details are set forth in Appendix J, but the nature of the adjustments may be summarized as follows:

Adjustment for turnover taxes. In outline the procedure is to (1) define categories of final use considered free of tax; (2) apply a nominal tax rate to certain categories as an allowance for tax on petroleum products, gas, and electric power; (3) estimate taxes incident on the materials component of certain services; (4) estimate the tax on household payments for utilities; (5) estimate the tax paid by collective farms; (6) assign the remainder of the tax proceeds to state-cooperative sector retail sales, nonfarm wages in kind, private housing construction, and inventory investment.

Adjustment for subsidies. The subsidies in question are: conventional subsidies;[1] subsidies covering operating losses of state-cooperative housing; accounting subsidies to procurement organizations, occasioned by the increases in procurement prices paid farms and farmers; subsidies to the MTS-RTS; and budget outlays on financing the wage and hour reform of the mid-1950s and early 1960s. Housing subsidies are, of course, confined to one product category. Other subsidies (conventional, MTS-RTS, procurement, and wage) are allocated proportionately among pertinent categories. In computing the incidence of wage subsidies, the first step is to identify the branches of the economy affected and then to allocate the subsidies among the relevant categories of final use.

Adjustment for farm prices. Two considerations are involved in this adjustment, one of which has not been previously discussed: (1) the principle of price uniformity within a given market is considered violated by the divergence of collective farm market from state-cooperative retail prices, especially in 1961–1964; (2) in all years, such a divergence is created by the first two adjustments themselves, which on balance lower state-cooperative retail prices relative to their collective farm market counterparts. Since adjustment for this departure from the AFCS means a reduction in farm incomes, a compounded violation is avoided by raising procurement prices.

Any attempt to make a quantitative appraisal of the reliability of these adjustments would be futile. It is not an easy task to determine margins of error on magnitudes valued at actual established prices, as Chapter 2 demonstrates. At least there, reference could be made to Soviet claims as yardsticks against which my independent estimates could be judged. No such yardsticks exist for the AFC values and they can be attacked only "from within"—that is, with regard to the accuracy or plausibility of particular estimates and assumptions. Whether my

[1] See above, p. 53.

TABLE 15

STRUCTURE OF GNP BY USE AT ESTABLISHED PRICES AND ADJUSTED FACTOR COST, 1958–1964
(percent)

	1958		1959		1960		1961		1962		1963		1964	
	EP	AFC	EP	AFC	EP	AFC	EP	AFC	EP	AFC	EP	AFC	EP	AFC
1. Household outlays for consumption														
A. Retail sales	41.0	32.7	40.2	32.5	41.6	34.1	41.7	34.6	41.7	34.9	41.5	35.0	40.4	34.2
B. Consumer services	5.8	6.5	5.8	6.3	5.8	6.4	6.2	6.8	6.3	6.8	6.3	6.7	6.3	6.8
C. Income in kind	7.5	8.8	6.7	7.8	6.1	7.0	6.1	6.9	5.8	6.6	5.4	6.0	5.1	5.7
D. Other	1.9	2.2	1.9	2.2	1.5	1.7	1.2	1.3	1.7	1.9	1.8	2.0	1.7	2.0
E. Total	56.2	50.2	54.6	48.8	55.0	49.1	55.2	49.6	55.5	50.1	54.9	49.8	53.6	48.7
2. Communal services, excluding R&D	6.7	7.1	6.7	7.0	6.8	7.0	7.1	7.3	6.9	7.1	7.2	7.3	7.3	7.5
3. Government administration	.8	.8	.7	.7	.6	.7	.6	.6	.5	.6	.5	.6	.5	.5
4. Gross investment														
A. Fixed capital	23.2	26.8	23.8	27.4	24.6	28.1	25.3	28.8	24.5	27.8	24.2	27.2	24.9	28.2
B. Inventories	5.0	5.2	5.5	5.5	2.7	2.9	3.3	3.5	2.9	3.1	3.7	4.0	5.1	5.0
C. Total	28.2	32.0	29.3	32.8	27.3	31.0	28.5	32.3	27.4	30.8	27.9	31.2	30.0	33.2
5. R&D	1.3	1.6	1.4	1.6	1.4	1.5	1.6	2.0	1.6	1.9	1.8	2.0	1.8	2.1
6. Internal security	.9	1.2	.9	1.0	.8	.9	.8	1.0	.7	.9	.7	.8	.7	.8
7. Defense														
A. Pay and subsistence	2.6	3.2	2.3	2.8	2.1	2.5	1.9	2.2	2.0	2.3	1.7	2.0	1.5	1.7
B. Other	3.1	3.7	3.0	3.5	2.9	3.3	4.1	4.8	4.1	4.7	4.6	5.2	4.2	4.8
C. Total	5.7	6.9	5.3	6.3	5.0	5.8	6.1	7.0	6.1	7.0	6.4	7.3	5.7	6.5
8. Outlays n.e.c., public sector statistical discrepancy	.1	.2	1.3	1.8	3.1	3.8	.2	.3	1.2	1.6	.7	1.0	.5	.7
GNP	←						100.0							→

Note:
EP = established prices; AFC = adjusted factor cost.

Source:
Computed from Table J-1.

AFC estimates are significantly vulnerable to such an attack the reader will have to judge for himself. The calculations are fully set out in Appendix J.

What difference do the factor cost adjustments make? Table 15 and Fig. 1 show the structure of GNP by use at both established prices (EP) and adjusted factor cost (AFC).

(1) In terms of absolute levels of category shares, the major impact of the adjustments is on retail sales: their share of total output uses declines by roughly one-fifth after adjustment, 8 percentage points at the beginning and 6 points at the end of the period. This, of course, reflects the preponderant weight of turnover taxes on consumer goods production and distribution, as well as the reduction in collective farm market sales effected by the adjustment for farm prices. Because the adjustments raise the shares of household outlays on services and of consumption in kind, the drop in the relative weight of all household consumption is considerably less than that for retail sales alone. These declines are compensated for by share increases in every other final use category in almost all years.[2] The most significant increase is in the weight of gross fixed investment, which rises about 3–4 percentage points.

(2) The trend over time in GNP structure (but still at current prices) is hardly affected by the basic AFC adjustments. At either valuation there is a clear relative decline in household consumption of income in kind; possibly total consumption too was a declining claimant on total resources. Fluctuation characterizes the relative movement of total investment. This is partly because of the instability in the relative weight of inventory investment and partly because of small declines in the share of gross fixed investment in 1962–1963. Through 1961, on the other hand, gross fixed investment was rising slightly faster than GNP. Defense's share in GNP, at least with regard to the explicit budget allocation shown in Table 15, fell through 1960, rose in 1961–1963, and declined in 1964 to a level about that of 1958.[3]

From some aspects of a welfare standpoint, it is useful to lump communal outlays, apart from R&D, with household consumption ex-

---

[2] Stability in 1959 and reduction in 1961 of the weights of inventory investment after adjustment are due to the relatively larger share in these years of a class of inventories in trade and procurement considered to bear relatively higher turnover taxes.

[3] The relation between the announced budget allocation and total military outlays is taken up in Chapter 7.

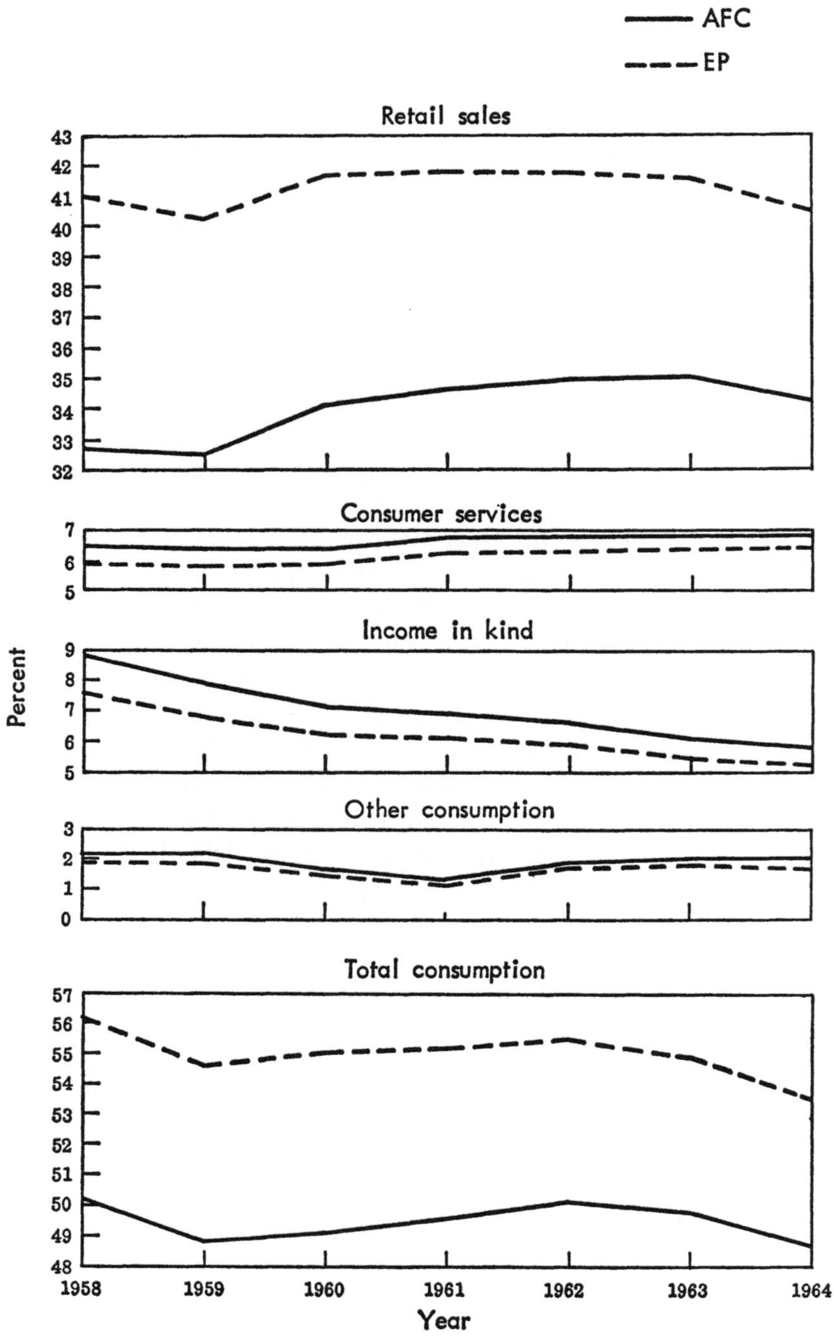

Fig. 1—Structure of GNP by use at EP and basic AFC, 1958-1964 (percent)

Fig. 1—Continued

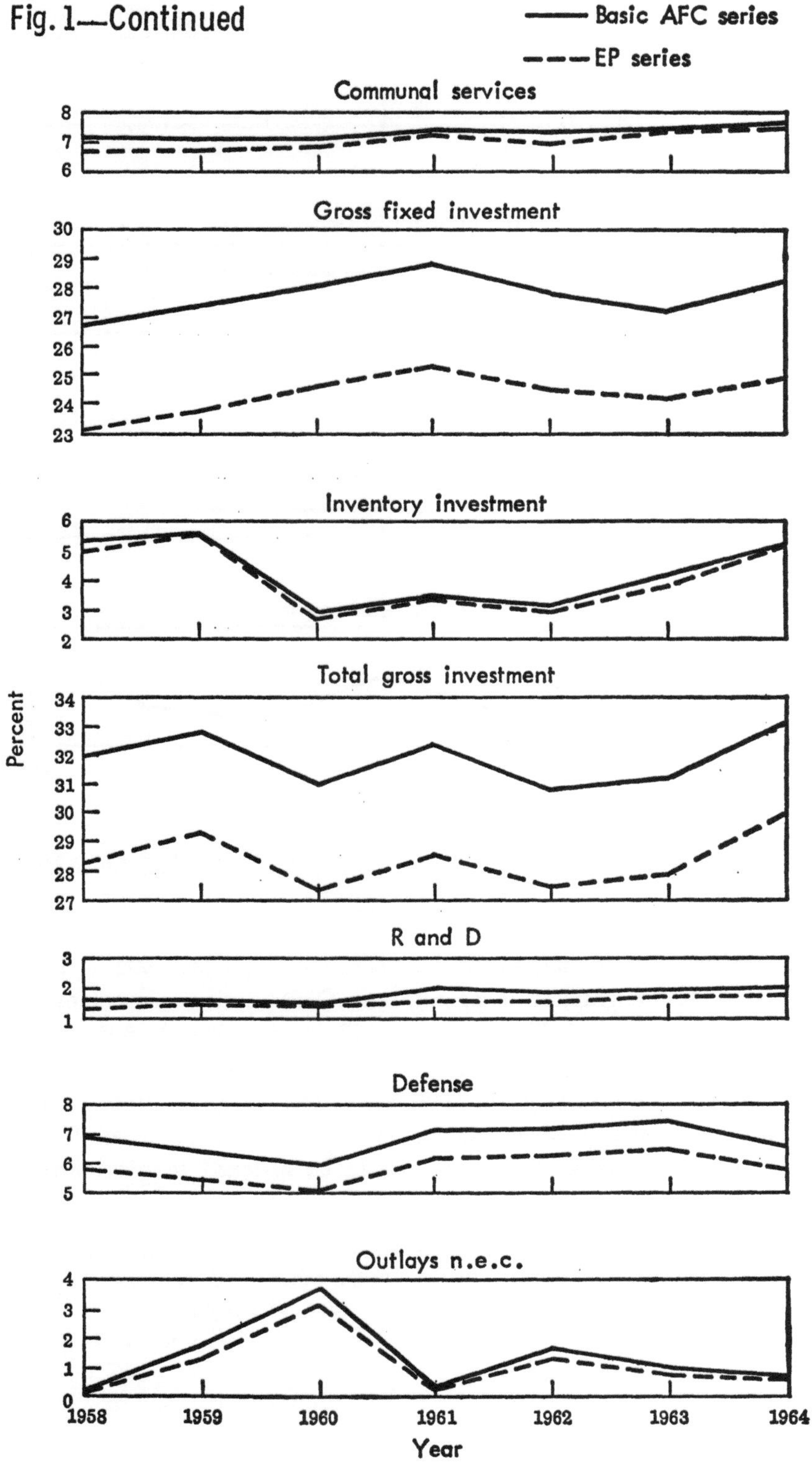

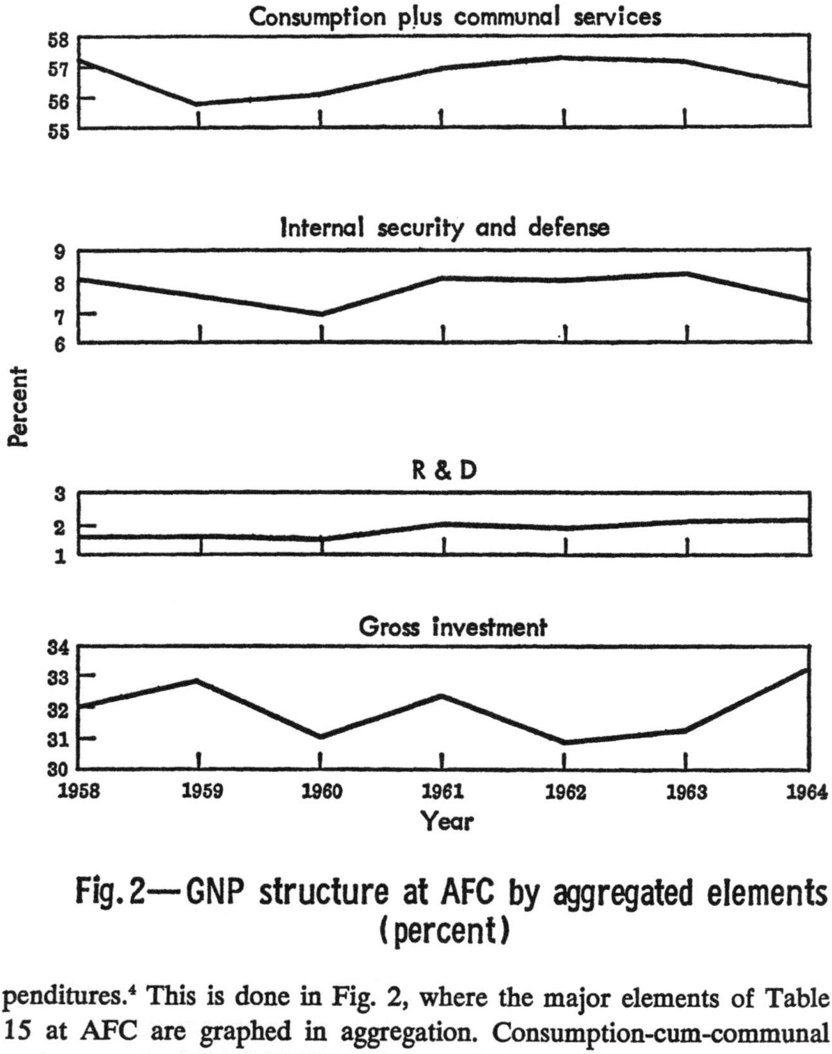

Fig. 2—GNP structure at AFC by aggregated elements (percent)

penditures.[4] This is done in Fig. 2, where the major elements of Table 15 at AFC are graphed in aggregation. Consumption-cum-communal outlays account for 55–57 percent of GNP, internal security and defense for 7–8 percent, and gross investment for 31–33 percent. Figure 2 omits outlays n.e.c., whose share in GNP is relatively large in 1960. If, as I suspect, at least part of the sudden 1960 increase in the absolute and relative increase of outlays n.e.c. should be assigned to gross invest-

[4] A consistent welfare viewpoint of consumption would require revaluation of income in kind at retail prices. On the other hand, only consumption can be treated from this standard so that a structural analysis of GNP from a welfare viewpoint seems awkward at least. See *Real SNIP*, pp. 39, 157 ff.

ment,[5] the latter's relative weight would in all years fall between 32–33 percent. Structural change was not marked in this period and it would be difficult to identify clear time trends in resource allocation by major final uses.

In Chapter 4 I examined the sensitivity of the *ex post* estimates in three selected years—1958, 1961, 1964—to the share of residual state budget revenues considered to be on current account and therefore included in the SNIP accounts. There the tests were restricted to EP values. The same sensitivity test may also be applied to the structural analysis of estimates at basic AFC. Because the method of calculation of factor cost adjustments yields nonsensical results for the 50 percent alternative,[6] the comparison must be restricted to the 75 and 90 percent alternatives. However, the direction of change for the 50 percent relative to the 75 percent alternative, if not the magnitude of the change, is clear *a priori* as well as from an actual calculation for EP values alone. The 50 percent assumption would reduce the share of GNP allocated to "outlays n.e.c." and lowers those of other components. Certainly, as Appendix M shows, going from 75 percent to 90 percent raises the share of outlays n.e.c. and lowers those of other components. For the latter shift, the changes in individual item weights are virtually undetectable except with respect to outlays n.e.c., whose relative weight increases by .7–.9 percentage points at EP and .9–1.2 points at AFC. Total consumption's share is reduced by at most half a point. In general, we can safely ignore this problem in treating Table 15.

Adjustments of the Basic Factor Cost Series

The basic AFC series incorporates adjustments to EP values for turnover taxes, subsidies and farm price divergences. These are the most significant violations of the AFCS. Moreover, Bergson's major AFC series embody adjustments only for these three features of Soviet prices. For the sake of comparability with his core results, it is therefore also advisable to confine the basic AFC series to the three indicated adjust-

[5] See above, pp. 32–33.

[6] For example, "negative" subsidies incident on R&D expenditures. Had I more confidence in the validity of the precise procedure and numerical assumptions of the factor cost adjustments, I would be tempted to use this finding of nonsensical results as support for the greater likelihood of the 75 than the 50 percent assumption.

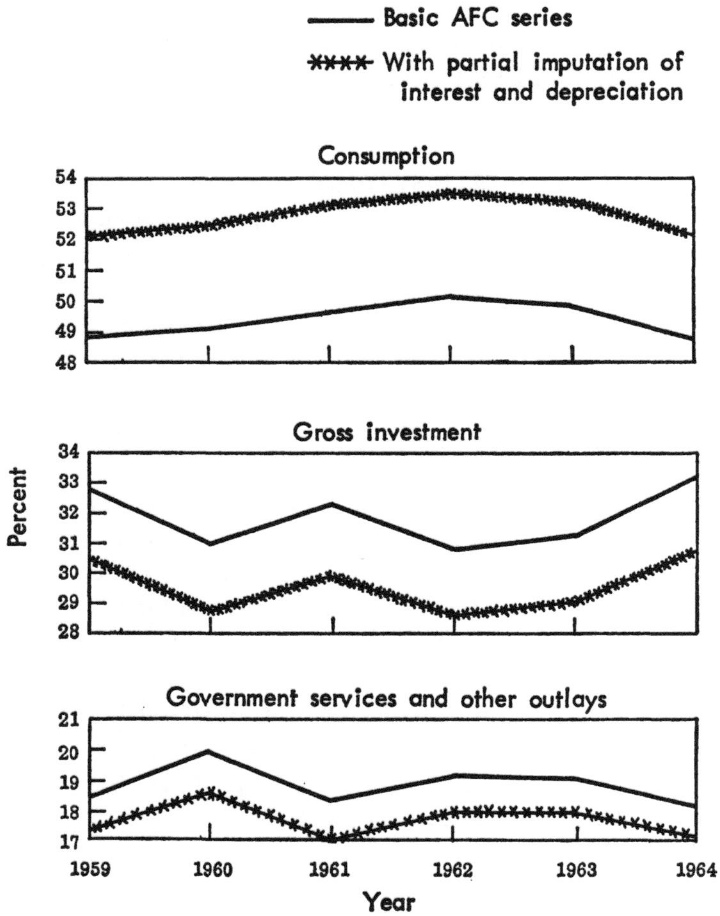

Fig. 3—Effect of partial imputation of interest and depreciation on GNP structure, 1959-1964 (percent)

ments. However, other departures from factor cost pricing noted by Bergson were discussed in Chapter 3, and it is necessary to examine the effect of introducing a number of supplementary adjustments. It is commonly believed that supplementary adjustments, to the degree they are at all significant, widen the gap between EP and AFC values. The following discussion concludes that such a result cannot be taken for granted.

Figure 3 shows the impact on the structure of GNP at AFC of imputing interest on housing and depreciation on both housing and government service capital.[7] An illustrative calculation adduced in Chapter 3 suggested that with certain qualifications actual Soviet profits could be viewed as a reasonable proxy for interest on capital, a factor charge absent from Soviet prices. A major qualification centered on the private sector, for which no profits are recorded in Soviet accounts, and for whose capital imputation of interest would be necessary. The predominant element of private sector capital, accounting for nine-tenths of the total, is housing. Because rentals on state housing are abnormally low in the Soviet Union,[8] we must consider state housing too as requiring separate imputation of interest. In graphing Fig. 3, interest on all housing is imputed at the assumed rate of 10 percent of the average annual value of the stock gross of depreciation.[9]

The discussion in Chapter 3 noted that depreciation is charged by *khozraschet* organizations in the state-cooperative sector and in a relevant sense is computed by collective farms. It is generally acknowledged that Soviet depreciation practice was deficient before the revision of rates in 1963, but I have not considered it worthwhile, in terms of the probable impact of recalculation, to revalue GNP to take account of these criticisms. However, state housing is inadequately or not at all depreciated, and, as may be expected, Soviet depreciation data do not include an imputed charge for private housing.[10] Nor is depreciation

---

[7] In Figs. 3–6 below, the EP and basic AFC series are taken from Table 15 and the series with supplementary adjustments from Table 17, located at the end of this chapter.

[8] See below, pp. 487–488.

[9] In Table 8 profit rates are computed in relation to capital net of wear and tear. Wear-and-tear ratios were officially reported only for the capital census dates and not separately for private housing. If the ratio of net to gross capital were, say, approximately 75 percent in all years of the period, the 10 percent rate imputed on gross capital would be equivalent to one of about 13 percent on net capital.

Strictly, the capital assets on which interest is imputed should be revalued to include that interest and the imputed value should be calculated accordingly. See Moorsteen and Powell, *The Soviet Capital Stock 1928–1962*, 1966, pp. 256–257. Correctly recorded, the imputed interest would be about 10 percent higher than shown in the sources to Table 17. I abstain from this refinement because housing is the only category of capital on which interest is imputed, and the rate of imputation is in any case somewhat arbitrary.

[10] Depreciation on housing is imputed in the Soviet national income accounts and classed with (nonproductive) consumption. The total charges have been reported for the years 1959–1963 (*NKh 1964*, pp. 584–585:

charged on budget organization capital. The organizations involved, which are entirely dependent on the state budget for their financing, are largely engaged in the provision of government services—health and education, administration, R&D, internal security, and defense. Some of the organizations extending these services are *khozraschet* rather than budget entities and hence do charge depreciation. The data are too gross to permit of such a refinement but the problem is of negligible proportions.

For the adjustments of Fig. 3, depreciation is charged on all housing and on all government service capital. The latter is taken to mean, with reference to published statistics, all nonproductive capital except housing and the capital stock in "municipal economy and 'everyday services' (*bytovoe obsluzhivanie*);" it coincides with the residual category "health care, enlightenment, science, art, and other." Presumably, "other" in the residual category embraces administration, internal security, and defense, although this cannot be established with certainty.[11] Straight-line depreciation is assumed and a rate charged representing the reciprocals of estimated service lives of structures.

The effect of the partial imputation of interest and depreciation is gauged in Fig. 3 in terms of a three-class breakdown of GNP—consumption, all gross investment, and government services and other outlays. The third category consists of communal services, administration, R&D, internal security, defense, and outlays n.e.c. The level of aggregation is dictated by the difficulty of allocating imputed depreciation on budget organization capital among component end-uses. Partial imputation raises the share of consumption and lowers the shares of investment and government services, compared with the structure of GNP in the basic AFC series. The increase in consumption's share amounts to about 3½ percentage points and the reduction in the weight of gross investment to a little over 2 points. Imputation of depreciation on government service capital would raise the share of current outlays in this category, but the effect is swamped by the size of the adjustment for housing. For none of the three major use groups is the *trend* in shares affected by the imputations; the direction of change for every

"amortization" charged to personal consumption) and turn out to be roughly twice as large as the imputed values I computed. Presumably, the difference is accounted for by amortization for capital repairs, which my calculation does not take into account.

[11] Becker, *Soviet Military Outlays Since 1955,* July 1964, Appendix A.

category in every year is unaffected, and the magnitude of annual changes is only slightly altered.

In discussion of the problem of Soviet depreciation allowances in Chapter 3, it was acknowledged that major repairs are far more frequently charged to cost in the United States than in the USSR. To the extent that they are so charged, repairs constitute intermediate rather than final product. Bergson wondered aloud "to what extent theoretically sound principles, such as the distinction between asset debits for 'capital repairs' and expense charges for 'current repairs,' are properly observed in practice."[12] Campbell indicates that the distinctions are neither clear nor uniform among branches of industry and that there is some incentive to charge to capital repair funds what are in fact current expenses.[13] Suppose, then, that Soviet investment and GNP are overstated on account of inflation of capitalized repairs. The effect of adjustment for this distortion is tested in Fig. 4; for the test, half of capital repairs are assumed to be current outlays and are deleted from investment and GNP. This adjustment also raises the share of consumption in GNP, as compared with the basic factor cost series, and, of course, it lowers the share of gross fixed investment. The reduction in the weight of fixed investment amounts to about 2 percentage points, half or more of which is absorbed by increases in the consumption share. Here again we observe no alteration in trend with regard to the direction of change in shares and only slight modifications of the size of the annual changes.[14]

The last in this series of supplementary adjustments is for undervaluation of collective farmer incomes relative to earnings elsewhere in the economy. Discussion of this problem in Chapter 3 uncovered a sizable gap in 1958 which widened through 1960 and then began to narrow. Part of the differential was traced to differences in the age-sex-education structure of the collective farm and state sector labor forces. It was therefore concluded that the undervaluation of collective farmer incomes was relatively more significant in the early 1960s than at either the beginning or end of the SYP period. To calculate the effect of revaluing collective farmer incomes it is assumed in Table 17 that the income

---

[12] *Real SNIP*, p. 20.

[13] Campbell, *Accounting in Soviet Planning and Management*, 1963, pp. 78–79, 99.

[14] Within "reasonable" limits, variation in the proportion of capital repairs deleted annually would alter the size of the changes in category shares to a greater degree but would not affect the direction of change.

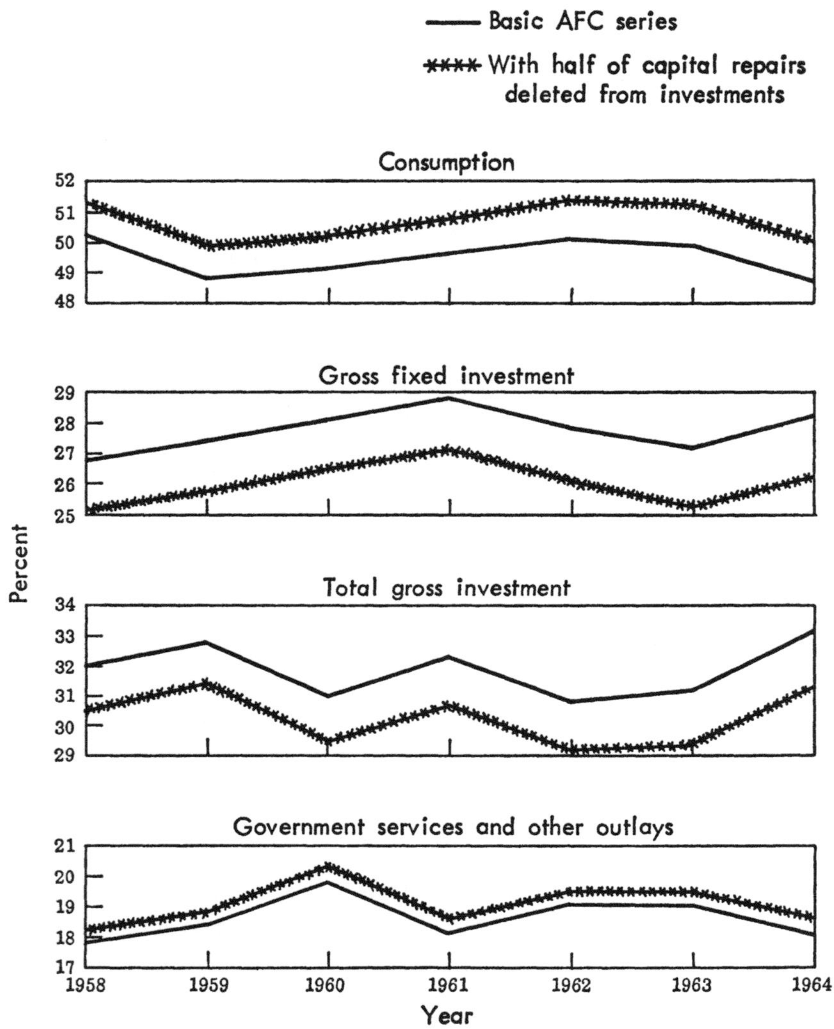

Fig. 4—Effect of deletion of half of capital repairs on GNP structure, 1958-1964 (percent)

differential in 1958 is in fact a measure of relative productivity differences but that anything over that differential constitutes a departure from factor cost pricing. Earnings differentials in subsequent years are then computed from data cited in Appendix O and distributed among end-use categories as explained in the sources to Table 17. The results also appear in Fig. 5 in somewhat more aggregated form.

Of course, the effect of this adjustment too is to raise the share of

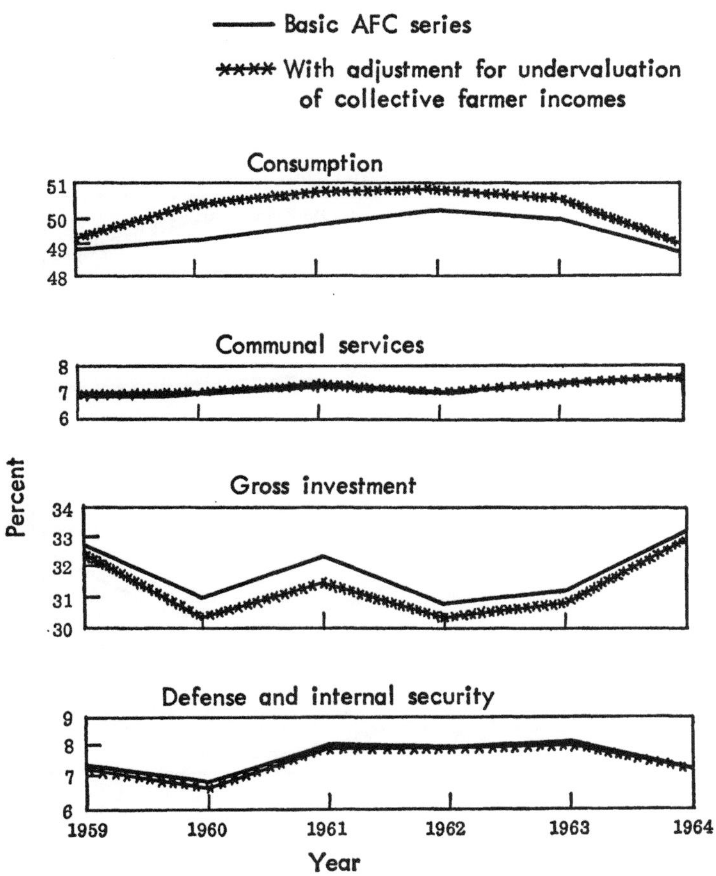

Fig. 5—Effect of revaluing collective farmer incomes on GNP structure, 1959-1964 (percent)

consumption in GNP. Because the understatement of collective farmer earnings is estimated to have been largest in 1960–1961, the increases in consumption's share follow a somewhat bell-shaped curve; the maximum increase is slightly over one percentage point. Investment again is the chief loser with other categories suffering only insignificant loss, if any, in relative weight. No alteration of direction of change in shares is introduced by the adjustment, but the amplitude of annual growth or decline is affected slightly by the bell-curve pattern of increases in consumption's share and decrease in investment's share relative to the basic factor cost series.

Each of the supplementary adjustments discussed here has raised the share of consumption and lowered that of investment. Therefore, com-

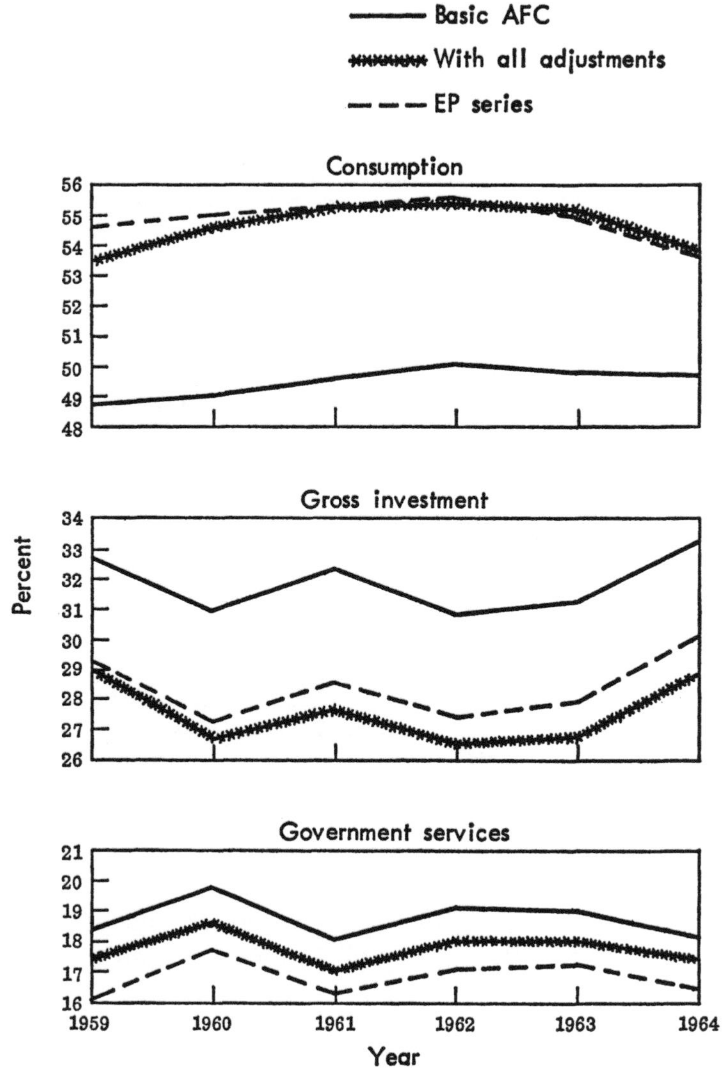

Fig. 6—GNP structure at three alternative valuations, 1959-1964 (percent)

bining all the supplementary adjustments, as in Fig. 6, effects an increase in the weight of consumption of 5 percentage points on the average and a decline in that of investment by about 4 points. As in the individual cases, year-to-year direction of change is unaffected by the combined adjustments.

Figure 6 also shows the use structure of GNP at established prices.

With respect to all three major aggregates, it is striking how close the entries in the EP series are to entries in the series incorporating all the factor cost adjustments, including the supplementary adjustments. Are we to conclude that we have been doubling back on ourselves, that the manifold deficiencies of Soviet prices are miraculously and mutually offsetting? Before we embrace the paradox, it would be well to examine some relevant considerations:

(1) Because of the absence of explicit rent charges in extractive industry, end-use values probably omit a sizable volume of nonagricultural differential rent (Chapter 3). In the absence of appropriate data, there is little to be gained by trying to pinpoint the magnitude and incidence of the understatement, but it may be assumed to bear more heavily on investment, R&D, and defense than on consumption. The absence of a charge for depletion has similar consequences. On the other hand, to the extent that agricultural rent is not reflected in prices and incomes, factor cost values understate consumption approximately in the manner indicated for the undervaluation of collective farmer earnings.

(2) In concluding (in Chapter 3) that actual Soviet profits constituted a reasonable proxy for interest, I noted the absence of profits for private sector capital. Another qualification stated there was that the industrial profit rate was an average of widely disparate component branch rates. The disparity is asymmetrical among branches of industry; profit rates in consumer goods industry are considerably higher than in producer goods industry. To equalize the rates in the two major subcategories in 1964, for example, would require reallocation of an estimated 5 billion rubles of consumer goods profits to producer goods industry. Followed through to end uses,[15] the reallocation would mean a

---

[15] Using a crude procedure based on the 1959 input-output table, as reconstructed by Treml (in *New Directions in the Soviet Economy,* 1966, table facing p. 269). Industrial branches 29–32—textiles, apparel and footwear, food, and industry n.e.c.—are here considered consumer goods branches. All other industrial branches are classified as producer goods. The distribution of final use of the two groups was as follows (percent):

	Consumption	*Government Services*	*Investment*	*Exports—Imports*
Consumer goods	91.4	4.0	10.5	−5.8
Producer goods	23.0	13.6	61.2	2.2

The 5 billion rubles of profits are redistributed in these proportions, yielding a net addition of almost 3 billion rubles to gross investment and the foreign balance and .5 billions to government services, all at the expense of consumption.

decrease of about 1½ to 2 percentage points in the relative weight of consumption in 1964, and an increase of 1½ points in the share of investment, compared with either of the two factor cost series.

Thus, taking into account the overvaluation of consumer goods output on account of arbitrarily high profit rates means, for consumption, increasing slightly the gap between the EP series and that with all factor cost adjustments; for investment, on the other hand, the gap is narrowed. If the "true" values are obtained by combining all adjustments including this last for disparate profit rates in industry, there seems little basis for choice in Fig. 6 between the EP series and that with all supplementary adjustments: for 1964, the EP series is a slightly better approximation to the "true" value with respect to investment, inferior with respect to government services and other outlays, and neither better nor worse with respect to consumption.

(3) It may be argued that the implicit interest rate, represented in proxy by profits, is not high enough for a country whose capital-labor ratio is still so low relative to that of the United States. But the implicit interest rate is in fact higher than it appears because factor incomes in my accounts consist not only of labor incomes, depreciation, and profits, but also of a miscellaneous group of public sector net incomes.[16] If the latter are added to net profits, the sum for 1959–1960 represents 16 percent of net fixed capital and inventories in the public sector on January 1, 1960 instead of the 11 percent indicated in Table 8 for net profits alone. With all subsidies added back (Table J-4), the profit rate rises to 19 percent. To the degree that these miscellaneous public sector net incomes are reflected in product prices, the proxy interest rate is also in effect compounded on capital values. It is unlikely that there is any need to impute a substantially higher interest rate on Soviet capital.

(4) Of all the supplementary adjustments, the most significant by far in its impact on GNP structure is the imputation of interest on all Soviet housing at the rate of 10 percent per year. Is imputation at that rate justified?[17] The rate of return on housing in the United States tends generally to be tangibly lower than the return on nonresidential capital.

---

[16] Items 2.B, 3.E, and 4 of Table 3.

[17] Ten percent is the imputation on gross capital. On net stock values, the computed interest flows represent a rate of perhaps 13 percent, as indicated earlier. The second paragraph of note 9 above also suggests that compounded on capital values the same rates of imputation generate higher interest values.

To the extent that the disparity is explained not by market imperfections but by what Stigler calls "supplements to the average rate of return" [18] (which may be positive or negative—for example, risk premia, psychic income), there may be a case for positing a relatively lower rate of return on Soviet housing in the context of an abstract AFC calculation.

It might be argued that since there is an obvious shortage of housing at existing rental rates in the Soviet Union, the equilibrium rental may be far higher than the going rate, even with per unit subsidies and depreciation added on. But an interest rate of 10 percent implies a net increment to rentals of over 6 rubles per square meter of floor space in 1961, 6 times the average rent paid on state housing.[19] Moreover, the concern here is with a factor cost standard of income valuation, and from this point of view it would be necessary to delete the windfall profits, no matter to whom they accrued, that would show up if rentals were raised to short run equilibrium rates. When one also takes into account the qualitative inferiority of private housing,[20] for which the imputed rent is taken to be equal to paid rent on state housing, there is further ground for doubt that so high an interest return to Soviet housing is justified. A final consideration is that the adjustment for housing losses calculated in Appendix J includes a nominal allowance for profits over operating costs.

How much difference would it make if the imputed interest rate were reduced from 10 percent to, say, 5 percent? The answer is provided for three years of this period in Table 16. Compared with the data based on a 10 percent interest rate, the calculation using a 5 percent rate effects a 1½ point reduction in the share of consumption, of which about one point accrues to investment and the rest to government services. Thus, something like 20–30 percent of the change in consumption and investment shares produced by the three supplementary adjustments com-

---

[18] Stigler, *Capital and Rates of Return in Manufacturing Industries,* 1963, pp. 56–57.

[19] The value of the housing stock at the beginning of 1961 may be estimated at 109 billion rubles (see sources to Table 17) and a 10 percent return would be 10.9 billion rubles. The total stock in physical units is estimated below (pp. 336 and 338) as about 1750 million square meters of floor space. The average rent paid on public housing was 1.05 rubles per square meter of floor space (p. 339).

[20] See, for example, Broner, *Sovremennye problemy zhilishchnogo khoziaistva,* 1961, p. 115; Svetlichnyi, *Kommunist,* No. 6, April 1965 (trans. *Current Digest of the Soviet Press,* June 23, 1965, p. 12).

TABLE 16

STRUCTURE OF GNP BY MAJOR USE GROUP, AT AFC WITH SUPPLEMENTARY ADJUSTMENTS, WITH INTEREST ON HOUSING IMPUTED ALTERNATIVELY AT 10 AND 5 PERCENT, 1959, 1961, 1963

	1959		1961		1963	
	10 Percent	5 Percent	10 Percent	5 Percent	10 Percent	5 Percent
Basic AFC series plus interest and depreciation on housing and depreciation on government service capital						
Consumption	52.1	50.6	53.1	51.6	53.2	51.7
Investment	30.6	31.5	29.9	30.9	29.0	29.9
Government services and other outlays	17.3	17.8	17.0	17.6	17.8	18.4
GNP	100.0	100.0	100.0	100.0	100.0	100.0
Basic AFC series with all supplementary adjustments (interest and depreciation, capital repairs, collective farmer incomes)						
Consumption	53.5	52.1	55.2	53.7	55.1	53.6
Investment	29.0	29.9	27.7	28.6	26.8	27.7
Government services and other outlays	17.5	18.1	17.1	17.6	18.1	18.7
GNP	100.0	100.0	100.0	100.0	100.0	100.0

Sources:
See sources to Table 17, except that entries in columns labelled "5 percent" are calculated with an imputed interest rate on housing of 5 percent instead of 10 percent.

pared with the basic AFC series (compare Tables 15 and 17) is restored by halving the rate of imputed interest on housing; for government services, the effect is greater, half to two-thirds of the change being restored. When the interest rate is reduced, group shares for consumption and government services do tend to diverge from the figures in the EP series, but in two of three test years the contrary is true for investment: with all supplementary adjustments and a 5 percent interest rate, the investment shares in 1961 and 1963 are for practical purposes indistinguishable from the corresponding EP series entries; in 1959, the difference is six-tenths of a point.

What is the upshot of these considerations? The second and fourth suggest that half or more of the increase in the weight of consumption and the reduction in that of investment effected by the supplementary adjustments would be nullified by taking into account the disparity of profit rates in industry and by reducing the imputed interest rate on housing to 5 percent. With respect to government services the two considerations tend to reinforce each other, to increase the gap between AFC and EP valuation. I suspect that adjustment for omitted nonagricultural rent would on balance also penalize consumption to the benefit of investment and government services, but the effects would be partially neutralized by any adjustment for omitted agricultural rent. In short, a judicious answer points to the area between basic AFC and the supplementary series in Fig. 6. Note again that although the EP series lies outside the other two with regard to consumption and government services, it falls between the two for investment. Thus, the final paradox is that after all due consideration the EP series may be a reasonable proxy for the "true" series with respect to investment and possibly for consumption; it seems least appropriate for government services.

These conclusions are unorthodox, and I should emphasize that their validity is sensitive to three factors. The first is the assumption of no significant error in the factor cost adjustments. Second, my supplementary adjustments are to some extent arbitrary—for example, the rate of return imputed to housing, or the assumption of no undervaluation of collective-farmer incomes in 1958. Finally, the conclusions rest on an intuitive appraisal of the effect of some adjustments not actually undertaken, on which, I am sure, there is room for disagreement. It would be laborious in the extreme to attempt to quantify the probable margin of error, and I doubt that usable results would emerge. Here, as at a number of other points in this study, the reader will have to render his own personal judgment.

TABLE 17

Structure of GNP by Major Use Group at AFC with Supplementary Adjustments, 1958–1964 (percent)

	1958	1959	1960	1961	1962	1963	1964
1. Partial imputation of interest and depreciation							
Consumption	n.a.	52.1	52.5	53.1	53.5	53.2	52.1
Gross investment	n.a.	30.6	28.8	29.9	28.6	29.0	30.8
Government services and other outlays	n.a.	17.3	18.6	17.0	17.9	17.8	17.1
2. Deletion of half of capital repairs							
Consumption	51.3	49.9	50.2	50.7	51.3	51.2	50.0
Gross fixed investment	25.1	25.8	26.5	27.1	26.0	25.2	26.2
Total gross investment	30.5	31.4	29.5	30.7	29.2	29.4	31.3
Government services and other outlays	18.2	18.8	20.3	18.6	19.5	19.5	18.6
3. Revaluation of collective farmer incomes							
Consumption	n.a.	49.2	50.3	50.7	50.8	50.5	49.0
Communal services	n.a.	6.9	6.9	7.2	7.0	7.3	7.5
Administration	n.a.	.7	.6	.6	.6	.5	.5
Gross investment	n.a.	32.5	30.3	31.5	30.3	30.8	33.0
R&D	n.a.	1.5	1.5	1.9	1.9	2.0	2.1
Internal security	n.a.	1.0	.9	1.0	.8	.8	.8
Defense	n.a.	6.2	5.7	6.9	7.0	7.2	6.4
Other	n.a.	1.8	3.7	.3	1.6	.9	.7
4. All three supplementary adjustments							
Consumption	n.a.	53.5	54.6	55.2	55.3	55.1	53.7
Gross investment	n.a.	29.0	26.7	27.7	26.6	26.8	28.9
Government services	n.a.	17.5	18.7	17.1	18.1	18.1	17.5

Sources:

1. ***Partial imputation of interest and depreciation.*** Interest on all housing is imputed at the rate of 10 percent of the average annual undepreciated value of the housing stock. Depreciation is imputed on all housing and on government service capital at rates of, respectively, 1.33 and 1.25 percent of the average annual capital values. The rates are reciprocals of assumed service lives of 75 years for housing and 80 years for government service capital, based on data compiled by Moorsteen and Powell, *The Soviet Capital Stock 1928–1962*, 1966, p. 63.

Capital stock values of housing and government service capital (the latter refers to the category in the statistical sources identified as "health care, education, science, art, and other") are calculated from absolute values for 1 January 1964 and 1965 and index numbers for (end-year) 1958, 1960, 1962, 1963, and 1964, in *NKh 1964*, p. 68, and *NKh 1963*, pp. 55–56. Values for 1959 and 1961 are obtained by interpolation rather than from the index series reported in earlier yearbooks because of later revisions of the figures. Index numbers are not reported for the category of government service capital but are estimated on the basis of the absolute data supplied for 1 January 1964 and 1965 as well as for 1960 and 1962 (*NKh 1959*, p. 67, and *NKh 1961*, p. 69). These data show that government service capital was 24 percent as large as housing on 1 January 1960,

TABLE 17 (continued)

27 percent in 1962, 32 percent in 1964, and 35 percent in 1965. The corresponding percentages for 1 January 1959, 1961, and 1963 are assumed to be 22, 25, and 30.

The calculated capital stock values and imputed interest and depreciation are as follows (billion rubles):

	1958	*1959*	*1960*	*1961*	*1962*	*1963*	*1964*
End-year capital stock							
Housing	88	98	109	115	122	128	134
Government service	19	24	27	31	36	41	47
Average annual capital stock							
Housing	..	93	104	112	119	125	131
Government service	..	22	26	29	34	39	44
Imputed flows							
Interest on housing	..	9.30	10.40	11.20	11.90	12.50	13.10
Depreciation							
Housing	..	1.24	1.38	1.49	1.58	1.66	1.74
Government service capital	..	.26	.33	.36	.43	.49	.55

2. *Deletion of half of capital repairs.* The method of calculating the basic AFC series does not directly yield a set of values for capital repairs at AFC. For present purposes, therefore, the following procedure was adopted. The first step is to calculate fixed capital investment by the state-cooperative sector at AFC (I ignore the capital repair component of collective farm gross investment). These values are obtained by subtracting the turnover tax adjustment (Table J-2) from and adding the subsidies adjustment (Table J-4) to values at established prices (p. 387). Fixed investment does not figure in the adjustment for farm prices. AFC values of state-cooperative capital repairs are then computed on the assumption that the proportion of repairs to all fixed investment by the sector is the same at EP as at AFC.

The derived values of fixed capital investment at AFC by the state-cooperative sector and its capital repairs component are as follows (billion rubles):

	1958	*1959*	*1960*	*1961*	*1962*	*1963*	*1964*
State cooperative sector							
Gross fixed investment	30.58	34.33	38.49	41.28	43.90	47.56	51.70
Capital repairs	5.87	6.31	7.05	7.60	8.37	10.02	10.97

3. *Revaluation of collective farmer incomes.*

(a) The amount of understatement of collective farmer earnings is estimated as (billion rubles):

1959	*1960*	*1961*	*1962*	*1963*	*1964*
1.53	4.23	4.36	3.03	2.82	1.52

These figures are calculated from the data presented in Appendix O on the assumption that the earnings gap in 1958 is normal and that gaps larger than this represent understatement of collective farmer income.

(b) The calculated values are distributed among the end-use categories affected by light industry and MTS-procurement subsidies (p. 485) plus extravillage farm market sales, farm income in kind and other outlays for consumption. Allocations are in proportion to values at established prices less turnover tax (Table J-2). The allocation to military subsistence is counted twice, once in terms of income in kind and again as part of the measure of defense services.

4. *All three supplementary adjustments.* Represents combination of partial imputation of interest (housing) and depreciation (housing and government service capital), deletion of half of capital repairs, and adjustment for undervaluation of collective farmer incomes.

6

Growth: National Product at Constant Prices

The estimates of national product at prices of the respective years are now to be revalued at constant prices. As indicated, two alternative weight years are used, 1958 and 1964; output is valued at both established prices and adjusted factor cost. The first section considers the deflated EP and basic factor cost series. Supplementary adjustments, of the kind discussed in Chapter 5, are examined in the second section. Rates of growth of total output are the focus of the chapter, but per capita equivalents are provided in a brief conclusion.

I have relegated the discussion of the derivation of the deflators to Appendix K, but before I embark on the description and analysis of the constant price series, it is necessary to warn the reader of the limitations of these calculations. Because the underlying data are inadequate in quantity and quality, compromises have had to be made and possibly large order uncertainties of interpretation are necessarily introduced. The most important of these is the consequence of the practical impossibility of constructing fully independent deflators for some major components of GNP. Retail sales in the state-cooperative trade network are deflated by the official retail price index. The materials components of government services (including defense) are not deflated at all. New fixed investment by the state cooperative sectors at both current and constant prices appear in these accounts at the same valuation, so-called "comparable" (meaning "constant") estimate prices.

As I have already suggested, independent deflators for the listed components cannot be constructed because the required data are simply absent. A sufficiently large sample of retail prices of consumer goods and services and wholesale and retail prices of producer goods is not available or obtainable, not just for the entire period under review but even for its initial and terminal years. Thus, for example, no wholesale or retail price handbooks of the kind that served as the essential basis for Bergson's real income series have been made available since the few issued in connection with the 1955 wholesale price reforms. Travelers' reports provide fragmentary lists of retail prices chiefly in the Moscow area, but these are hardly the stuff from which to fashion a test of the official retail price indexes. There is evidence of the reliability of the official state retail price index for an earlier period from Janet Chapman's research.[1] Since announced changes in particular retail prices in this period have been relatively few and small, I am not inclined to view the necessity to rely on the official price index as a serious drawback.[2] I think it is a reasonable presumption also that the change in the average level of wholesale prices of producer goods other than investment and military-space hardware was negligible, given the absence of a major price reform between 1955 and 1967 and granted reported changes in cost and productivity in the affected industries. Of course, this does not rule out the possibility of error in particular service series whose material components did experience tangible changes in general price level.

However, my major concern is investment and armaments prices, and the problem seems to me intractable at the current stage. There is an extended discussion in Appendix K of the relation between estimate, current, and constant prices of investment. Unhappily, the subject is shrouded in obscurity, and my tentatively worded conclusion is that "it may be safe to view estimate, current, and constant prices as virtually interchangeable" for construction-installation during these years, but "we cannot be sure that the estimate-price values of equipment do not in fact constitute a current-price series." Judging from American experience alone, I would think it prudent to assume that the Soviet military-space effort also experienced rising costs—although the rapidity of change in product mix in this area makes the measurement of cost particularly tricky—but there is insufficient evidence on which to con-

---

[1] See below, p. 508.

[2] For my purposes that index is deficient in that it is continually changing price weights, so that it is impossible to obtain a value series with price weights of a single year (see Appendix K). Since the index shows little change in this period, perhaps the damage is limited, but one could not be sure short of an independent recalculation.

struct even a crude deflator. Although I see no basis for a reasoned attempt at independent deflation of investment and the materials components of government services, I will attempt later in this chapter to provide a rough indication of the sensitivity of the results to the implicit assumption of no change in general price levels.

Following general practice in this area, I deflate the wage component of major government services (communal services, administration, R&D, but not internal security and defense), in effect assuming no change in productivity.[3] However, the proportion of wages in total outlays of each category is estimated in the initial year and then assumed constant at current prices throughout the period. Thus, "real" outlays on these government services are implicitly held to become more material-intensive with time. There is probably some basis for this with respect to R&D; it is of doubtful validity for communal services and administration.

These empirical problems—and only the outstanding ones have been reviewed here—should also be considered in the light of the discussion in Chapter 3 of the conceptual problem of valuation, highlighting the complexity of establishing unambiguous, meaningful theoretical standards. In short, with the instruments at our disposal, there must inevitably be some fuzziness in perception of Soviet economic growth in this period. That sense can be heightened only by several additional considerations raised in the body of this chapter that imply numerous alternative ways to measure that growth. After Gerschenkron and Bergson this can no longer be surprising, though the plethora of results continues to be burdensome. But these are the facts of life: national output is an abstraction, not a real physical entity. In any environment, it poses fundamental problems of definition, which in turn give rise to multiple alternative ways of measurement. The particular vagaries of Soviet statistics necessarily add to the burden of both writer and reader.

Growth of EP and Basic AFC Series

INDEXES OF GROWTH

In index form, the results of revaluing the current, established-price estimates at 1958 prices are shown in the first four columns of Table 18. For the sake of completeness, indexes of "other outlays for consump-

[3] Per man hour. In industry the number of hours worked annually declined. If this was also true in government services, the deflation of wages does allow for an increase in output per man.

TABLE 18

INDEXES OF FINAL USE OF GNP AT 1958 PRICES—ESTABLISHED PRICES AND BASIC ADJUSTED FACTOR COST, 1959–1964
(1958 = 100)

	1958 EP						1958 AFC					
	1959	1960	1961	1962	1963	1964	1959	1960	1961	1962	1963	1964
1. Retail sales												
A. State-cooperative trade	108	120	124	133	140	146						
B. Extravillage farm markets	108	98	102	94	89	84						
C. Total	108	118	123	130	136	142	108	118	123	130	136	142
2. Consumer services												
A. Housing	105	111	115	120	125	130						
B. Dues	102	109	114	118	123	129						
C. Other services	108	116	129	142	153	165						
D. Total	107	114	125	136	145	155	107	114	124	135	144	154
3. Consumption in kind												
A. Farm income in kind	98	95	95	87	84	86						
B. Nonfarm wages in kind	110	120	130	140	150	160						
C. Military subsistence	96	91	87	97	90	82						
D. Total	99	95	95	90	87	89	98	95	94	90	87	88
4. Other outlays for consumption	103	84	67	99	110	112						
5. Total consumption	106	113	117	124	130	135	106	112	116	122	127	133
6. Communal services	108	116	123	127	138	147						
7. Administration	93	90	87	86	83	83						

TABLE 18 (continued)

	1958 EP						1958 AFC					
	1959	1960	1961	1962	1963	1964	1959	1960	1961	1962	1963	1964
8. Gross fixed investment												
A. Households	108	105	94	74	32	61	107	105	94	73	29	61
B. State-cooperative	111	124	133	142	154	167						
C. Collective farms	102	96	102	108	104	108	103	97	104	109	105	109
D. Total	110	120	127	133	139	153	110	121	128	134	140	154
9. Inventory investment												
A. State-cooperative	121	58	73	67	97	136						
B. Collective farms	80	70	93	108	115	125						
C. Total	119	59	74	69	98	135	118	59	75	70	98	135
10. Total gross investment	111	109	118	122	132	149	111	111	119	123	133	151
11. R&D	114	124	141	158	180	196						
12. Internal security	100	100	100	100	100	100						
13. Defense	100	99	125	136	150	143	100	99	124	135	149	142
14. Outlays n.e.c.; public sector statistical discrepancy	943	2430	130	1048	613	465						
GNP	109	115	118	126	133	141	109	116	118	126	133	141

Sources:
Table K-1. Omitted index numbers at 1958 AFC are by definition identical to corresponding index numbers at 1958 EP.

tion" and of the public sector's "outlays n.e.c.; statistical discrepancy" have been included. However, the index of a statistical discrepancy has no simple interpretation, and the observed trend of these outlay categories will generally not be of concern.

Ultimately, I am interested in obtaining measures of change in production potential. For that purpose a valuation of final output at adjusted factor cost is required. Indexes of such values in terms of 1958 prices are presented in the second half of Table 18. The underlying values, $\sum_u V_{58}Q_i$, were computed, following Bergson[4] as

$$\sum_u V_{58}Q_{58} \frac{\sum_u P_{58}Q_i}{\sum_u P_{58}Q_{58}}$$

That is, for any use category u of national output in year i, a 1958 AFC (value-added) weighted entry, $\sum_u V_{58}Q_i$, is obtained as the product of the basic AFC estimate for 1958 itself, $\sum_u V_{58}Q_{58}$, multiplied by the quantity index of u at 1958 established prices, $\sum_u P_{58}Q_i/\sum_u P_{58}Q_{58}$. This procedure is algebraically correct only if

$$\frac{\sum_u P_{58}Q_i}{\sum_u P_{58}Q_{58}} = \frac{\sum_u V_{58}Q_i}{\sum_u V_{58}Q_{58}} \tag{1}$$

Some implications of this anomaly are set out later in this chapter. For the moment I merely note that the index numbers $\sum_u P_{58}Q_i/\sum_u P_{58}Q_{58}$ are computed from columns 1–7 of Table K-1, while values of $\sum_u V_{58}Q_{58}$ are taken from Tables J-1, J-2, J-4, and J-5. Subtotals in columns 8-14 of Table K-1 are obtained as sums of components and not by deflating subtotals at current prices. The EP and AFC indexes can also be viewed in the left half of Fig. 7, graphed on semi-logarithmic scale.

Whether measured at established prices or at factor cost, a number of end-use categories suffered declines in real values over the period of concern: extravillage farm market sales, consumption of income in kind (except for nonfarm wages in kind), and household fixed investment. The most extensive total growth was experienced by R&D outlays, followed by state-cooperative gross fixed investment and household outlays on "other services." Over the six-year period, retail purchases in

---

[4] *Real SNIP*, p. 128.

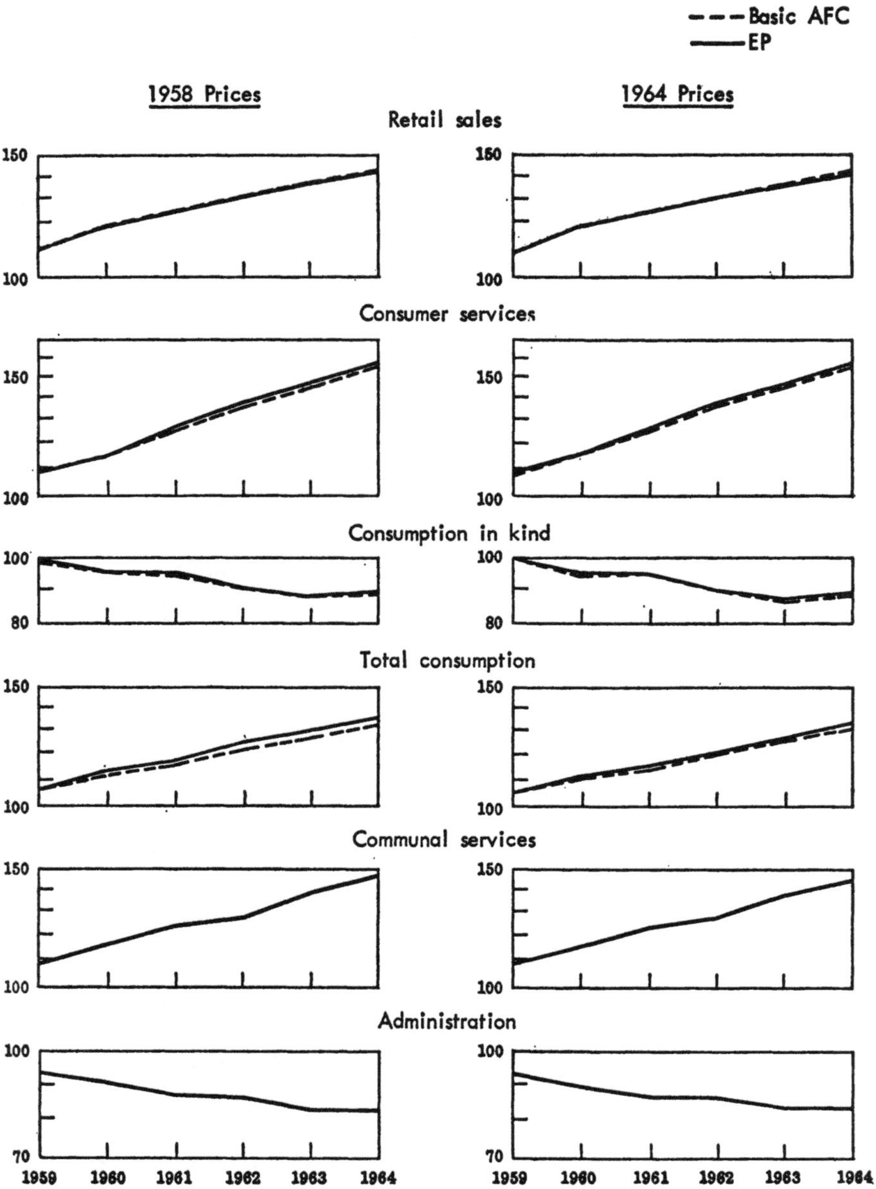

Fig. 7—Indexes of final use of GNP at 1958 and 1964 prices EP and basic AFC, 1959-1964 (1958 = 100)

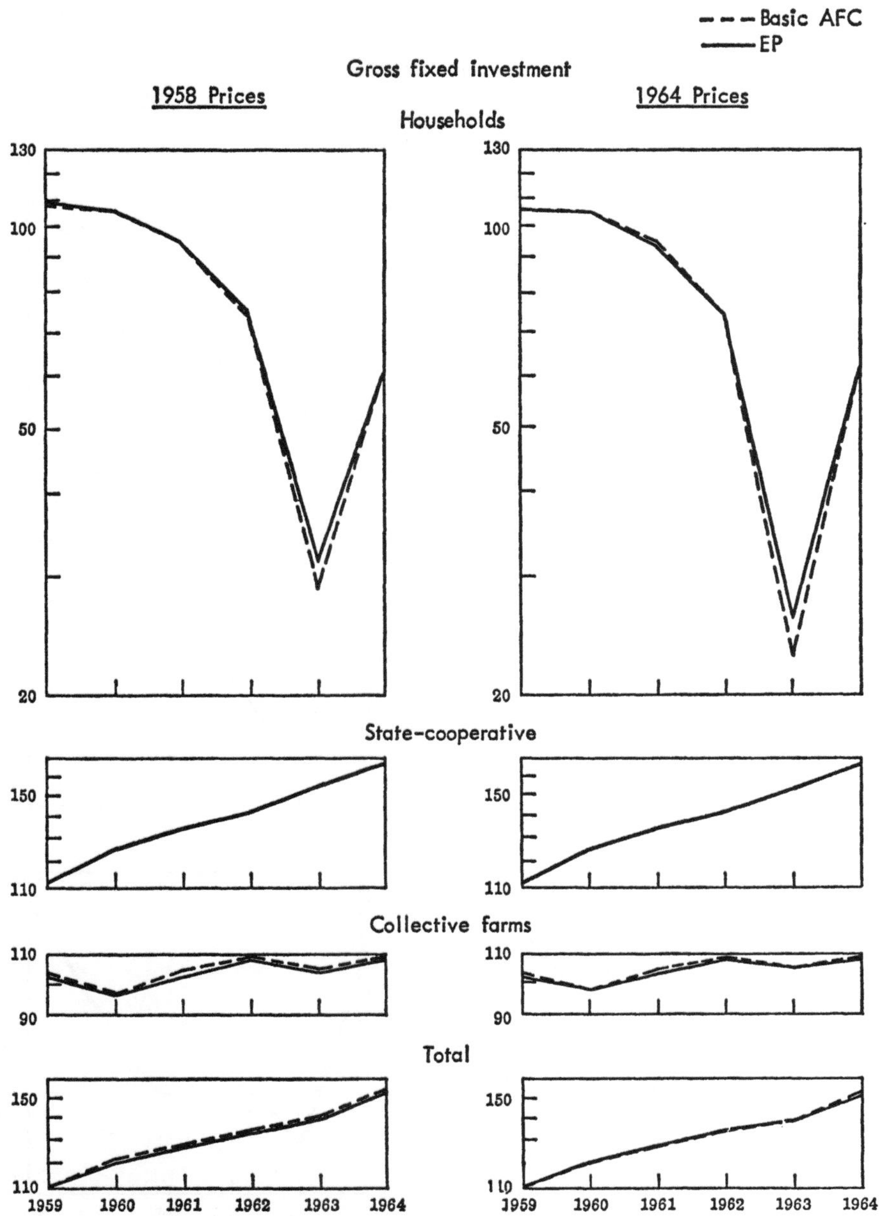

Fig. 7—Continued

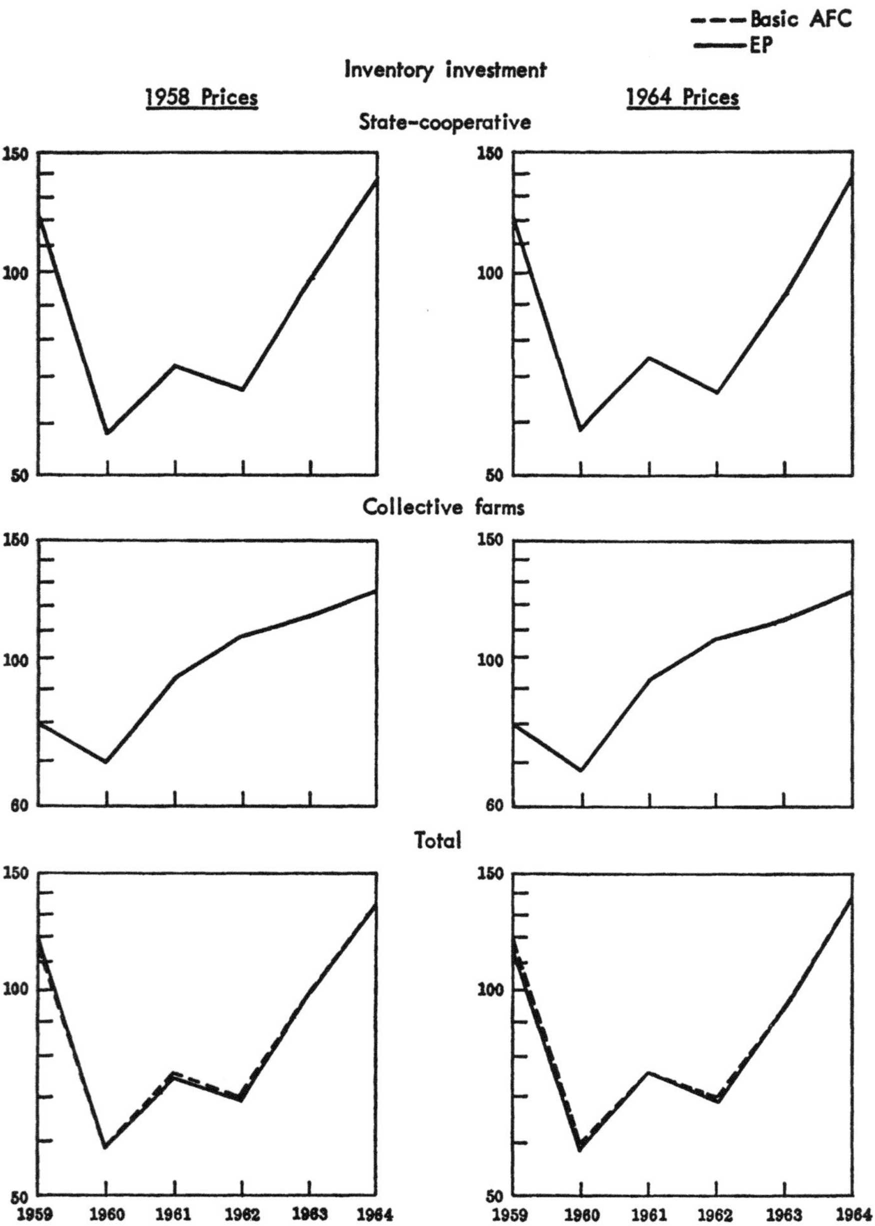

Fig. 7—Continued

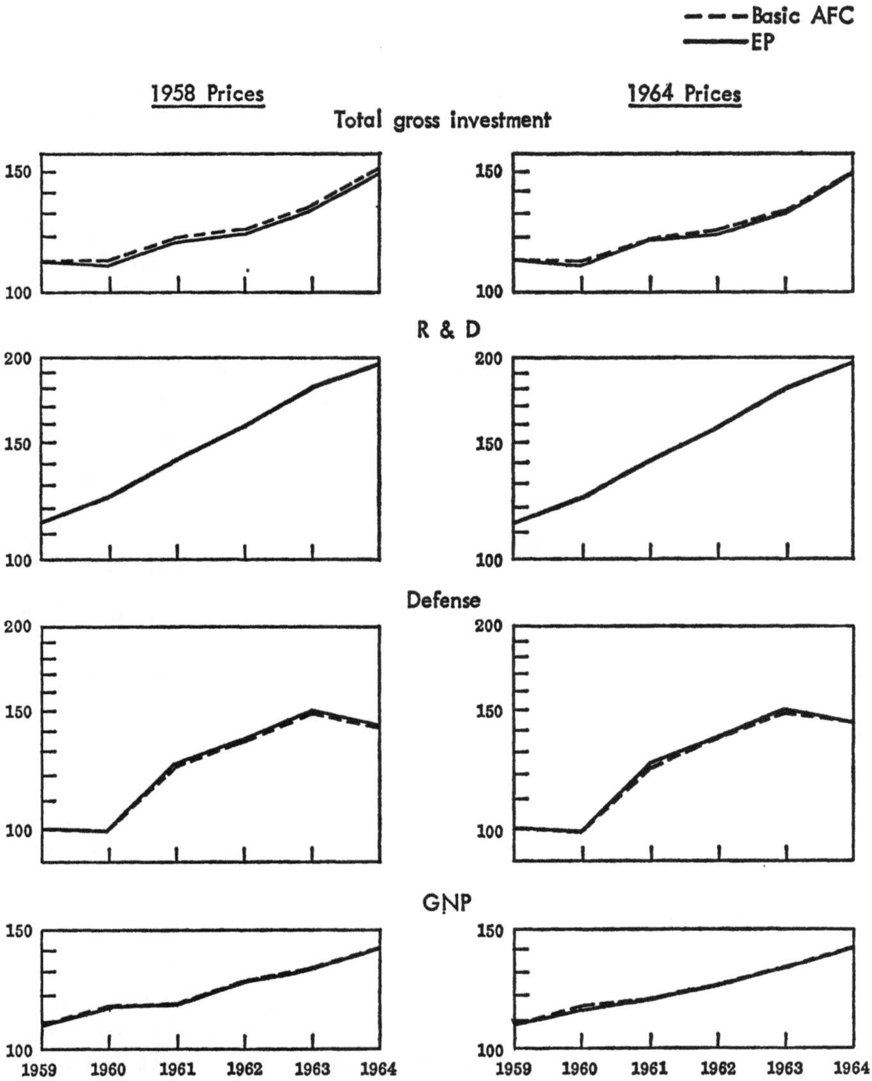

Fig. 7—Continued

state-cooperative stores, communal services, and defense expenditures grew slightly more than total output. State-cooperative inventory investment can only be characterized as fluctuating within wide limits, whereas internal security outlays are unchanged by assumption. Until 1963 the growth of total consumption kept pace with that of total gross investment, the decline in inventory accumulation braking the growth of fixed capital investment, while farm market sales and consumption in kind were a drag on consumer services and state-cooperative retail sales. In 1964, however, sharp increases in inventory investment provided an additional boost to the sustained growth of fixed investment.

The differences between indexes at EP and AFC are only partly measured in these calculations, because the "deflators" for component end uses in both sets of calculations are EP indexes—EP price indexes in the former case, EP-weighted quantity indexes in the latter. In consequence, comparison of indexes in EP and AFC valuations are possible only for use-category aggregations. That is, the AFC indexes in fact use AFC values only as weights to combine EP subindexes. For the 11 aggregates where comparison may be made, the divergences are small but generally in the expected direction—expected, in view of the observed results of basic factor cost adjustments of current-price values. Thus, the use of 1958 values as base-year intergroup weights tends to reduce the real growth of consumption and raise that of fixed investment. At current prices, the basic factor cost adjustments raise the share of pay and subsistence in defense outlays (Table 15). Because the value of pay and subsistence is estimated to have declined (while that of other defense outlays increased), the growth of all defense is slightly smaller at 1958 AFC than at 1958 EP.

Are the indexes of Table 18 sensitive to the choice of the particular weight year? Given the brevity of the time span covered and the absence of general price reforms, we should expect a negative answer to this question. Unfortunately, my data do not permit a rigorous test of the hypothesis. I am able to compute alternative-weighted (that is, with either 1958 or 1964 weights) deflators only for extravillage farm market sales, consumption and investment of farm income in kind, state-cooperative inventory investment, and outlays n.e.c. The sum of the listed expenditures is 12–14 percent of GNP at EP in either 1958 or 1964. Therefore, unless extraordinary price changes occurred in the categories for which alternative-weighted deflators were computed, recalculation at GNP at 1964 EP should yield little difference in the indexes of the affected components or in the index of GNP as a whole. The indexes at 1964 prices are reproduced in Table K-3, and they are also shown graphically in the right hand columns of Fig. 7. Predictably, the change of weight year makes little difference with respect to the level and trend of sectoral index numbers. For collective farm fixed investment, the shift to 1964 prices raises the index numbers in a number of years. Generally, however, the weights of the later year tend to damp the indexes.[5] Either way, the alterations are by and large slight.[6]

Insofar as the smallness of the changes is predictable as a consequence of inadequate information from which to construct alternative-weighted deflators, the question of the degree of index number relativity to weight year changes in this period must remain open. On the other hand, the relative invariance to change of weight year also reflects known or estimated stability of prices for a number of categories of goods and services—consumer outlays on housing and other services, nonfarm wages in kind, the materials component of government expenditures on health, education, and general administration—which account for about 8 percent of GNP at EP in 1958 or 1964.[7] In sum, roughly one-fifth of national product in the base years consists of end uses for which either alternative-weighted deflators cannot be computed or the deflators would be roughly the same with alternative weights because price changes are estimated as minimal. For this reason, I shall frequently exhibit results at both 1958 and 1964 prices. It should be understood, then, that the differences between the two sets of results are predictable but not necessarily to be dismissed.

AVERAGE ANNUAL RATES OF GROWTH

In Table 19 the changes in end-use values over the period as a whole are viewed in terms of conventionally defined compound annual growth rates. These are the rates (r) implied by initial (X_1) and terminal year (X_n) values:

$$X_1(1+r)^{n-1} = X_n \qquad (2)$$

Compared with the data at established prices, values at AFC effect a change in growth rates of at most 2 or 3 tenths of a percentage point; the

[5] With the conspicuous exception of state-cooperative inventory investment in 1963. The reversal is due to change in the structure of stock increments by type and branch (Table L-4), resulting in a substantial narrowing of the gap between the value of total increments at 1958 and 1964 prices.

[6] Again the apparent exception relates to 1963, this time with respect to household fixed investment as well as state-cooperative inventory investment. For the former, there is a six-point difference in the 1963 index numbers which is explained by the fact that higher 1964 livestock prices accentuate the disinvestment in kind in 1963.

[7] Calculated from Tables J-2, K-1, and K-2.

TABLE 19

AVERAGE ANNUAL GROWTH RATES OF FINAL USE OF GNP AT 1958 AND 1964 PRICES, EP AND BASIC AFC, 1958–1964

(percent)

	1958 Prices		1964 Prices	
	EP	AFC	EP	AFC
1. Retail sales of goods for consumption	6.0	6.0	5.9	6.0
2. Consumer services	7.6	7.4	7.5	7.3
3. Consumption in kind	−1.9	−2.1	−2.2	−2.3
4. Total consumption	5.2	4.8	4.9	4.7
5. Communal services	6.6	[a]	6.6	[a]
6. Administration	−3.0	[a]	−3.0	[a]
7. Gross investment				
A. Fixed capital	7.3	7.4	7.2	7.3
B. Inventories	5.2	5.1	5.5	5.5
C. Total	6.9	7.1	6.9	7.0
8. R&D	11.9	[a]	11.9	[a]
9. Internal security	0	[a]	0	[a]
10. Defense	6.2	6.0	6.2	6.1
GNP	5.9	5.9	5.8	5.8

Note:

[a] By the method of computation used, omitted entries at AFC are formally identical to corresponding entries at EP.

Sources:

Computed from Tables K–1 and K–2 where the growth rate is the conventionally defined compounded rate r, implied by initial and terminal year values

$$X_1 (1 + r)^{n-1} = X_n$$

In the table, r values are multiplied by 100 and expressed as percentages.

apparent exception of a decline by 4 tenths of a point at 1958 prices for consumption is due to rounding error in both EP and AFC rates of increase. As we should expect, the rate of growth of total output is unaffected by the change in valuation at either 1958 or 1964 prices. The change of weight year from 1958 to 1964 generally reduces the rate of growth by one or two tenths of a point.

An interesting exception to the latter generalization is provided by inventory investment, whose rate of growth at 1964 prices is visibly higher than at 1958 prices. This difference is entirely the consequence of a higher index number in 1964 at 1964 than at 1958 prices.[8] Of course, this is the inevitable result of the way in which growth rates are defined in Table 19. A glance at Tables 18 and K-3 shows that in 1960–1963, the level of state-cooperative inventory investment, valued at either set

[8] Table 19 and Table K-3.

of prices, was far below the 1958 level, yet the rate of growth computed in the manner indicated is 5.2 or 5.6 percent per year. At such rates of increase applied to the initial year levels, the cumulated sum of inventory increments in 1959–1964 would have been 30–40 percent greater than the actual sum of these increments.

The situation outlined reminds us again how misleading a view of growth the conventional measure may provide for a period in which annual output increments fluctuate. This problem has received systematic examination by Pesek who suggests two alternative measures that do take into account the observations of intervening years.[9] The simpler of these alternatives is the rate of growth $\bar{r}$ at which the initial year output compounded yields a series of values equal to the sum of the actual outputs in the period:

$$X_1 + X_1(1+\bar{r}) + X_1(1+\bar{r})^2 + \cdots + X_1(1+\bar{r})^{n-1} = \sum_{i=1}^{n} X_i \qquad (3)$$

which reduces to

$$\frac{(1+\bar{r})^{n-1}}{\bar{r}} = \frac{\sum_{i=1}^{n} X_i}{X_1} \qquad (4)$$

According to Pesek, this formula suffers from the defect that "the selection of the base period $[X_1]$ is arbitrary."[10] To circumvent the difficulty he recommends an alternative in which both the rate of growth and a fictitious base year, $\hat{X}_1$, are computed such that two constraints are satisfied: first, as before, the sum of the estimated outputs during the period be equal to the sum of the actual outputs; second, that the sum of the squared absolute deviations between actual and estimated outputs be minimized. That is, the rate of growth $\hat{r}$ satisfies the requirements:

---

[9] Pesek, *Economic Development and Cultural Change,* April 1961, pp. 295–315. In addition to the recommended alternatives, Pesek considers and rejects two other methods of fitting exponential growth curves to time-series data—the least squares and Glover's method. He rejects the least squares method on the grounds that the practical requirement to use logarithms rather than the observed values directly implies an economically meaningless requirement for equality of the *product* of actual outputs with the *product* of the estimated outputs; simultaneously it fails to satisfy the requirement he views as critical—that the *sum* of estimated outputs be equal to the *sum* of actual outputs. Glover's technique implies a restriction that also appears to have no economic rationale (pp. 301–303).

[10] *Ibid.*, p. 305.

$$\hat{X}_1 + \hat{X}_1(1+\hat{r}) + \hat{X}_1(1+\hat{r})^2 + \cdots + \hat{X}_1(1+\hat{r})^{n-1} = \sum_{i=1}^{n} X_1 \qquad (5)$$

$$\sum_{i=1}^{n} [\hat{X}_1(1+\hat{r})^{i-1} - X_i]^2 = \min \qquad (6)$$

When (6) is differentiated with respect to $\hat{X}_1$ and the derivative set equal to zero, the fictitious base year value emerges as

$$\hat{X}_1 = \sum_{i=1}^{n} X_i(1+\hat{r})^{i-1} \Big/ \sum_{i=1}^{n} (1+\hat{r})^{2(i-1)} \qquad (7)$$

Substituting (7) in (4) yields the formula for $\hat{r}$ as

$$\frac{(1+\hat{r})^n + 1}{\hat{r}+2} = \sum_{i=1}^{n} X_i(1+\hat{r})^{i-1} \Big/ \sum_{i=1}^{n} X_i \qquad (8)$$

How much difference it makes to take account of fluctuations in a time series intervening between initial and terminal years is illustrated for one series in Fig. 8. There observed values of total inventory investment at 1958 factor cost are graphed along with the estimated values obtained by fitting the three different growth curves. The uppermost line links observed initial and terminal points; because all intervening values except that for 1959 are smaller in magnitude, the line $r = 5.1\%$ lies above the 1960–1963 observations. The dotted line also uses the initial observed value as starting point, but since this curve satisfies the requirement that the sums of observed and estimated values be equal, it describes a negative rate of growth. Finally, the dashed line traces an average growth pattern bound to neither initial nor terminal observed values, satisfies the same requirement as the dotted line and an additional one minimizing the sum of squared absolute deviations between observed and estimated values; in consequence, the average growth rate is positive and sizable.

How shall we interpret these sharply divergent fitted growth patterns? Evidently, r tells us what would have happened if growth had been at a constant rate beginning at the observed initial point and ending at the observed terminal value. Since this is almost never the case, the usefulness of r in such a case depends on the meaningfulness of the observed initial and terminal points and the justification for ignoring the behavior of the series at intermediate points. Under an equally artificial assumption r could equal $\hat{r}$, if the deviations of the observed from the estimated values are uniformly distributed around the line connecting initial and

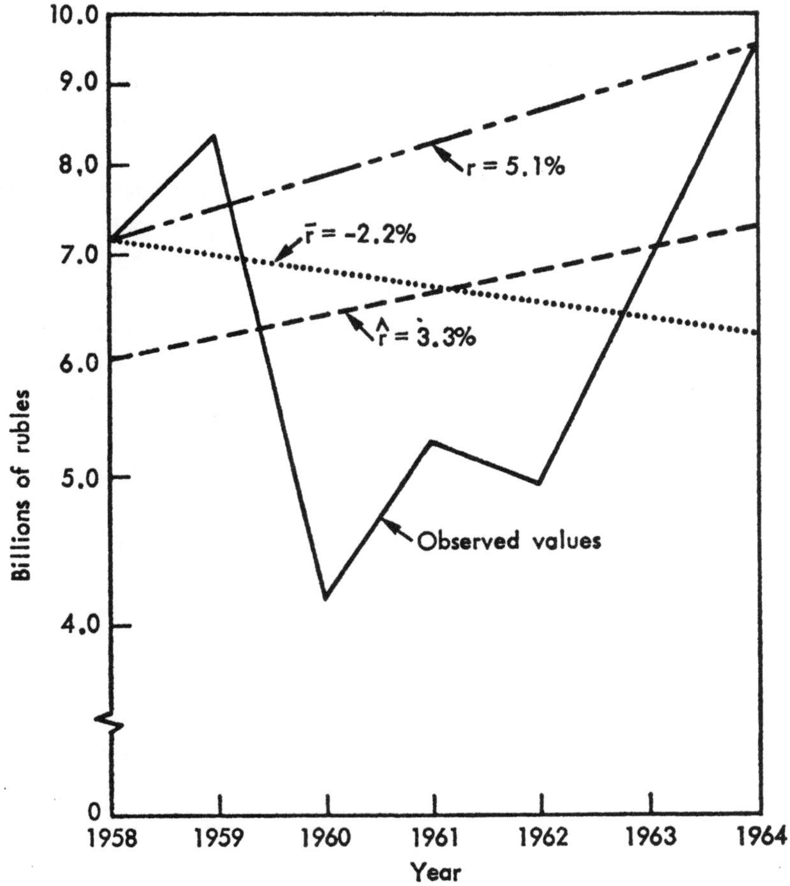

Fig. 8—Values and alternative rates of growth of total inventory investment at 1958 AFC

terminal year values. On the other hand, both $\bar{r}$ and $\hat{r}$ define patterns of growth that reproduce the cumulative actual value of output—what would have happened if growth had been at a constant rate sufficient to insure that the economy obtained all the output during the period of concern that it in fact did obtain.

I find Pesek's argument on the desirability of satisfying a constraint such as (3) or (5) compelling, especially with respect to longer periods of time. On grounds of principle, he opts for $\hat{r}$ rather than $\bar{r}$. The base year of my computations, 1958, is far from arbitrary, being the base year of the SYP. Considering that targets were set in direct or indirect linkage to quantities in that year, it seems legitimate to inquire what is the rate of growth that when projected on the base year of the Plan yields a series whose sum is equal to the sum of observed outputs. So defined, however, the rate of growth is imbedded in the context of the SYP and receives its only acceptable interpretation in terms of plan-fulfillment comparisons.

In the remainder of this chapter I will present growth rates calculated for various concepts of output but, for the most part, only in the $\hat{r}$ formulation. The superiority of Pesek's recommended alternatives to the conventional geometric average of output indexes (for that is what r represents)[11] seems self-evident to me, and r values of the time series of this study will be generally ignored in the rest of this chapter. However, I have computed and will display when required relevant growth rates in the r version in Chapters 10 and 11 to facilitate comparisons with growth rates calculated by others for this and past periods, in most of which the r formulation is used exclusively. When I come to examine the SYP growth targets and the degree of their implementation (Chapter 9), I shall want to calculate growth rates in the $\bar{r}$ formulation as well.[12]

Rates of growth of GNP and its components, computed by formula (8), are displayed in Table 20 for the four valuations that define my basic end-use series. Internal security and outlays n.e.c. are omitted from the table: growth of the former at established prices was defined to be zero; on the latter, the rate of growth of a residual cannot be easily interpreted,[13] and the series values fluctuate violently. For reasons al-

---

[11] $$r = \left[\left(\frac{X_2}{X_1}\right)\left(\frac{X_3}{X_2}\right)\cdots\left(\frac{X_n}{X_{n-1}}\right)\right]^{\frac{1}{n-1}} - 1 = \left(\frac{X_n}{X_1}\right)^{\frac{1}{n-1}} - 1\,.$$

[12] The value of the expression $\frac{(1+\bar{r})^n - 1}{\bar{r}}$ for some values of $\bar{r}$ and n can be found in financial tables showing the amount of an annuity of 1 at compound interest. No such tabulations exist for $\hat{r}$. Here both sets of growth rates were computed by Newton's method. That is, with the functions of $\bar{r}$ and $\hat{r}$ in (4) and (8) set equal to zero, they were evaluated for the range $-.15$ to $+.20$, the approximate real, non-zero roots identified, and Newton's method applied to yield the value of $\bar{r}$ and $\hat{r}$ for values of the relevant function $< |\ .000005\ |$. For aid in developing the computer programs, I am grateful to RAND colleagues Mario Juncosa, Ernest Scheuer, and Sidney Winter. Shirley Marks patiently guided me through the intricacies of RAND's JOSS computer system. Thanks are also due to Nancy Jacobsen who performed the extensive calculation of this chapter on JOSS.

[13] This difficulty is shared in part by item 4, "other outlays for consumption."

TABLE 20
AVERAGE ANNUAL GROWTH RATES ($\hat{r}$) OF SELECTED END USES OF GNP, AT 1958 AND 1964 PRICES, 1958–1964
(percent)

	1958 Prices		1964 Prices	
	EP	AFC	EP	AFC
1. Retail sales				
A. State-cooperative trade	6.4	6.4	6.4	6.4
B. Extravillage farm markets	−3.3	−3.3	−3.6	−3.6
C. Total	5.8	5.8	5.7	5.8
2. Consumer services				
A. Housing	4.4	4.4	4.4	4.4
B. Dues	4.4	[a]	4.4	[a]
C. Other services	9.0	9.0	9.0	9.0
D. Total	7.8	7.6	7.7	7.5
3. Consumption in kind				
A. Farm income in kind	−3.0	[a]	−3.2	[a]
B. Nonfarm wages in kind	8.0	8.0	8.0	7.9
C. Military subsistence	−2.3	−2.3	−2.3	−2.3
D. Total	−2.3	−2.5	−2.5	−2.6
4. Other outlays for consumption	2.5	[a]	2.5	[a]
5. Total consumption	5.1	4.8	4.9	4.6
6. Communal services	6.4	6.4	6.3	6.3
7. Administration	−2.9	−2.9	−2.9	−2.9
8. Gross investment				
A. Fixed capital				
(1) Households	−11.9	−12.3	−12.5	−12.7
(2) State-cooperative	8.5	8.5	8.5	8.5
(3) Collective farms	1.4	1.4	1.4	1.5
(4) Total	6.7	6.8	6.6	6.7
B. Inventories				
(1) State-cooperative	3.0	3.0	2.9	2.9
(2) Collective farms	7.1	7.2	7.2	7.1
(3) Total	3.2	3.3	3.2	3.3
C. Total gross investment	6.2	6.4	6.2	6.3
9. Research and development	12.0	12.0	12.1	12.1
10. Defense	8.1	8.0	8.1	8.0
GNP	5.6	5.5	5.4	5.4

Notes:
[a] Values of these outlays are the same at AFC as at EP.
In the table, $\hat{r}$ values are multiplied by 100 and expressed as percentages.
Sources:
Computed from Tables K-1 and K-2.

ready set out, the rates of growth are not visibly sensitive to either change of weight year or to valuation at factor cost rather than at EP.

Propelled by rapid increases in retail sales at state-cooperative outlets and in outlays on "other services," and despite actual declines in the real value of purchases on farm markets and farm income in kind, household consumption grew over the period as a whole by about 5 percent per year;[14] government expenditures on health and education services increased at an annual rate 1 to 1½ points higher. This is also the approximate pace of increase of all gross investment with fixed investment growing at a slightly faster tempo. Rates of growth of both R&D and defense are high, that for defense reflecting the rapid increase in explicit defense expenditures from 1961. GNP growth rates at 5½ percent fall between those of consumption and all investment.

At the beginning of this chapter I underscored the serious gap in our knowledge of Soviet price changes as related to state-cooperative fixed investment and military-space hardware. Suppose that the entries in the accounts at present represent price-inflated values. How seriously overstated could the real rate of growth of GNP be? Assume that state-cooperative fixed investment, and "other defense," items 8.A(2) and 11.B in Tables K-1 and K-2, in fact constitute figures at current prices, the level of which may have risen between 1958 and 1964 by from 10 to 30

---

[14] A possibly interesting accompaniment to the material on growth of consumption presented here is a calculation of real household income changes. For this purpose I define four alternative concepts of income: (1) all household income as shown in Table 1; (2) The same, except that "other current income" is standardized at 7.50 billion rubles a year (see Chapter 4, note 14); (3) Disposable income, representing household income (1) less direct taxes and other payments to the state (items 8.B and 8.C of Table 2); (4) Disposable income, except that "other current" income is standardized as in (2). Income at current prices is then deflated by a cost of living (COL) index compiled from deflators indicated in Appendix K and with alternative 1958 and 1964 established-price expenditure weights (including investment as well as consumption).

The results are as follows ($\hat{r}$ growth rates in percent):

	Income deflated by COL index with	
	1958 weights	*1964 weights*
(1) All income	4.5	4.8
(2) Same, with standardized "other current income"	4.6	4.9
(3) Disposable income	4.6	4.9
(4) Same, with standardized "other current income"	4.7	4.9

The range of growth rates of real household income is 4.5–4.9 percent per year, at or slightly below the figures for consumption. Such a result would be expected, considering the low relative weight of investment in household expenditures and the retarded growth of investment outlays at current prices.

percent. Then the effect on GNP growth rates can be illustrated by the following matrixes of *r* rates for GNP at 1958 prices.

Rates of growth, r, *of GNP at 1958 prices in 1958–1964*

		EP			AFC		
		If investment price level rose by (%)					
		10	20	30	10	20	30
If "other defense" price level rose by (%)	10	5.5	5.1	4.9	5.4	5.0	4.7
	20	5.4	5.1	4.8	5.3	5.0	4.6
	30	5.0	5.0	4.8	5.3	4.9	4.6

The *r* value of GNP before these hypothetical deflations is 5.9 percent in each case. The maximum effect of deflating both state-cooperative fixed investment and "other defense" by 30 percent—most probably, an outer bound—is a decline in the *r* rate of growth by a little over 1 percentage point. The effect on $\hat{r}$ rates of growth evidently would depend on the time-pattern of the presumed price increases.

In Chapters 4 and 5, I attempted to test the sensitivity of the relevant estimates to alterations in the share of residual budget revenues assumed to be on current account. That test is now applied to the constant price values of GNP in 1959. 1961, and 1964 (Table 21); the details are again relegated to Appendix M. For reasons explained in Chapter 5,[15] the test for constant AFC values compares only the 75 percent alternatives, omitting calculations implied by the 50 percent alternative. Since the test applies only to three separate years, the alternative rates of growth can be computed only in the *r* formulation.

As Table 21 shows, it doesn't seem to make much difference to the rate of growth of GNP, at least in the *r* formulation and for this limited test, whether the share of residual budget outlays included in GNP *in each of the three years* is 50, 75, or 90 percent (columns 1–3). However, if that share varies, the range of possible growth rates is enlarged, as indicated for EP valuations in columns 4 and 5. For the entire period, 1958–1964, the range at EP is increased from 5.7–5.9 percent to 5.4–6.2 percent. In previous applications of the test I have expressed my skepticism on the likelihood of the 50 percent alternative. If I am right, the probable range is apt to be more like that of the AFC entries in columns 4–5, restricted to combinations of the 75 and 90 percent alternatives, than like that of the EP entries. My guess is that the GNP growth rates for the period as a whole are subject to a margin of error, *on this account alone,* of plus or minus less than half a percentage

[15] See above, p. 101.

TABLE 21

SENSITIVITY OF AVERAGE ANNUAL GROWTH RATE (r) OF GNP TO ALTERATIONS IN THE INCLUDED SHARE OF RESIDUAL BUDGET REVENUES, 1958, 1961, 1964
(percent)

	Percent of Residual Budget Revenues Included in SNIP				
				Combinations Yielding Extreme Values of r	
	50	75	90	Minimum	Maximum
	(1)	(2)	(3)	(4)	(5)
1958–1961					
At 1958 prices					
EP	5.6	5.8	5.9	5.0	6.5
AFC	..	5.6	5.8	(5.4)	(6.1)
At 1964 prices					
EP	5.4	5.6	5.7	4.8	6.3
AFC	..	5.5	5.7	(5.2)	(6.0)
1961–1964					
At 1958 prices					
EP	6.1	6.0	6.0	5.2	6.9
AFC	..	6.2	6.1	(5.7)	(6.5)
At 1964 prices					
EP	6.0	5.9	5.9	5.1	6.8
AFC	..	6.0	5.9	(5.6)	(6.4)
1958–1964					
At 1958 prices					
EP	5.8	5.9	5.9	5.5	6.2
AFC	..	5.9	5.9	(5.8)	(6.1)
At 1964 prices					
EP	5.7	5.8	5.8	5.4	6.1
AFC	..	5.8	5.8	(5.6)	(6.0)

Note:
For each time segment the maximum at EP is computed from values assuming 50 percent in the initial year and 90 percent in the terminal year, the minimum at EP from values assuming 90 percent in the initial year and 50 percent in the terminal year. At AFC, only 75 percent and 90 percent values are used, and the entries in columns 4 and 5 at AFC are set in parentheses to call attention to the difference.
Sources:
Rates of growth for the 75 percent assumption are computed from Tables K-1 and K-2. Others are computed from Table M-4.

point. Quite obviously, the corresponding margin of error on the growth rate of outlays n.e.c. is very much larger.

A number of comparisons have been made so far between computations at EP and AFC, with AFC values computed as indicated at the very beginning of the section—that is, as projections of a base year value by price-weighted quantity indexes. It was also indicated there that the procedure is deficient in principle, in that it requires the assumption of the equality of a price-weighted quantity index with a value-added-weighted quantity index in order that the translation from current to constant AFC values be algebraically valid. However, the difficulty does not end there. Given the practical impossibility of computing indexes in terms of AFC, the projection of base year values conceivably could be obtained with various indexes, each of which yields an improper result, in the sense that it requires an assumption analogous to equation (1) to render the translation valid. In particular, the quantity index could be one with a weight year other than the base year. Whether such an index is preferable to the base-year-weighted index is an empirical question: which is a better approximation to the index with value-added weights? Of course, I have no way of making such a test and simply assume the superiority of the base-year-weighted quantity index.

The desired constant AFC values can be obtained not only by projection but also by deflation. I call the former Method I and the latter Method II. Method II has properties as awkward as those of Method I: it requires the assumption of equality of price indexes with value-added indexes; the deflation conceivably could be performed with price indexes whose weight year is different from the year of the current AFC value to be deflated. Here too I merely assume the inferiority of the latter situation, and to obtain the deflated values at 1958 or 1964 AFC the formulas used are, respectively,

$$\sum_u V_i Q_i \frac{\sum_u P_{58} Q_i}{\sum_u P_i Q_i}$$

$$\sum_u V_i Q_i \frac{\sum_u P_{64} Q_i}{\sum_u P_i Q_i}$$

Two questions then arise: (1) What is the likely direction of difference in the results of calculation by the alternative method? (2) Is there any basis for preference between the two? Taking up the questions in order, it turns out that Method II applied to my data can be expected to yield a higher rate of growth of state-cooperative retail sales at both 1958 and 1964 prices (and for the same reasons); considering the high relative weight of the item in the total, it may be presumed that the conclusion holds for GNP as well.[16]

Table 22 compares average annual growth rates for GNP end uses at AFC computed by both methods. As expected the results for all elements of GNP except retail sales are hardly affected by the substitution of Method II for Method I. Again according to expectation, the results for retail sales—hence for consumption—are more sensitive to the test.

---

[16] Consider the relation between Methods I and II in yielding the index $\frac{\Sigma V_{58} Q_i}{\Sigma V_{58} Q_{58}}$ (for simplicity, I omit the category designation, u). That is, we ask whether

$$\left[\frac{\Sigma V_{58} Q_{58}}{\Sigma V_{58} Q_{58}} \cdot \frac{\Sigma P_{58} Q_i}{\Sigma P_{58} Q_{58}}\right] \gtrless \left[\frac{\Sigma V_i Q_i}{\Sigma V_{58} Q_{58}} \cdot \frac{\Sigma P_{58} Q_i}{\Sigma P_i Q_i}\right] \tag{9}$$

Transform the left side of (9) by multiplying by the identity $\frac{\Sigma P_i Q_i}{\Sigma P_i Q_i}$. Then the question is whether

$$\left[\frac{\Sigma V_{58} Q_{58}}{\Sigma V_{58} Q_{58}} \cdot \frac{\Sigma P_i Q_i}{\Sigma P_{58} Q_{58}} \cdot \frac{\Sigma P_{58} Q_i}{\Sigma P_i Q_i}\right] \gtrless \left[\frac{\Sigma V_i Q_i}{\Sigma V_{58} Q_{58}} \cdot \frac{\Sigma P_{58} Q_i}{\Sigma P_i Q_i}\right] \tag{10}$$

or, whether

$$\left[\frac{\Sigma P_i Q_i}{\Sigma P_{58} Q_{58}} \cdot \frac{\Sigma P_{58} Q_i}{\Sigma P_i Q_i}\right] \gtrless \left[\frac{\Sigma V_i Q_i}{\Sigma V_{58} Q_{58}} \cdot \frac{\Sigma P_{58} Q_i}{\Sigma P_i Q_i}\right] \tag{11}$$

The answer depends on whether

$$\frac{\Sigma P_i Q_i}{\Sigma P_{58} Q_{58}} \gtrless \frac{\Sigma V_i Q_i}{\Sigma V_{58} Q_{58}} \tag{12}$$

The following tabulation compares the left and right hand sides of (12) for state-cooperative retail sales:

	1958	*1959*	*1960*	*1961*	*1962*	*1963*	*1964*
$\frac{\Sigma P_i Q_i}{\Sigma P_{58} Q_{58}}$	1.00	1.07	1.18	1.22	1.32	1.40	1.46
$\frac{\Sigma V_i Q_i}{\Sigma P_{58} Q_{58}}$	1.00	1.10	1.24	1.30	1.43	1.54	1.61
Ratio of second to first row	1.00	1.03	1.05	1.07	1.08	1.10	1.10

Thus the right side of (12) is larger than the left for retail sales, and the relative margin increases through 1963. On the other hand, the margin of difference for other end uses of GNP is zero or small. The same reasoning and direction of inequality holds for the series at 1964 prices.

TABLE 22

AVERAGE ANNUAL GROWTH RATES ($\hat{r}$) OF FINAL USE OF GNP, 1958–1964, WITH ALTERNATIVE METHODS (I AND II) OF COMPUTING CONSTANT-PRICE AFC VALUES
(percent)

	1958 AFC		1964 AFC	
	I	II	I	II
1. Consumption				
A. Retail sales	5.8	7.4	5.8	7.2
B. Services	7.6	7.5	7.5	7.5
C. Income in kind	−2.5	−2.4	−2.6	−2.7
D. Total	4.8	5.9	4.6	5.6
2. Communal services	6.4	6.1	6.3	6.1
3. Administration	−2.9	−2.9	−2.9	−2.9
4. Gross investment				
A. Fixed capital	6.8	6.8	6.7	6.7
B. Inventories	3.3	3.5	3.3	3.7
C. Total	6.4	6.4	6.3	6.3
5. R&D	12.0	12.0	12.1	11.9
6. Defense	8.0	7.8	8.0	7.8[a]
GNP	5.5	6.0	5.4	5.9

Note:
[a] By Method II, this is identical to the rate of growth at 1958 AFC.
Sources:
Method I: Table 20. Method II: Computed from Table K-4.

Rates of increase of retail sales are raised by 1½ points, those for consumption by about 1. Consequently, the rates of growth of GNP are raised by roughly half a percentage point. It is important to point out that the effect of Method II in pushing up growth rates is sensitive to the time-structure of my factor cost adjustments, and the latter are admittedly crude.

I cannot see any logical basis for choosing between the two methods. Those who feel more comfortable with comparisons between price-weighted and value-added weighted quantity indexes on the one hand, the equality of which is necessary for the validity of Method I, than with comparisons between price indexes and quantity-weighted value added indexes on the other, the equality of which is necessary for the validity of Method II, will prefer Method I. Given the practical difficulties of constructing an index of value added, and therefore of testing the validity of the assumptions for Method II, perhaps I is to be preferred on pragmatic grounds alone.

GNP at Constant Factor Cost: Supplementary Adjustments

In Chapter 5 the basic factor cost series at current prices were subjected to a number of supplementary adjustments—partial imputation of interest and depreciation, deletion of half of capital repairs, revaluation of collective farmer incomes. These adjustments are now imposed on the constant price data calculated by Method I. The results are viewed in terms of average annual rates of growth in Table 23 to avoid burdening the reader with annual indexes in several variants.

Table 23 shows that the partial imputations of interest and depreciation and the revaluation of collective-farmer incomes tend to raise rates of growth; the deletion of half of state-cooperative sector capital repairs operates in the reverse direction. Most significant, in terms of the size of the increments to the rate of growth, is the effect of the first adjustment on housing. In combination, the first and fourth adjustments dominate, raising rates of growth of consumption and GNP. Adjustment 1 is more powerful than adjustment 4 in its effect on consumption. The combined adjustments depress the growth rate of gross fixed and total gross investment. Finally, we note that the adjustments do not alter the general relation between magnitudes at 1958 and 1964 prices.

Although it does not belong among the supplementary adjustments, one additional operation should be performed on the basic GNP series. At a number of earlier points, I referred to the extreme volatility of outlays n.e.c. and the public sector statistical discrepancy. I speculated that the wide fluctuations in this series may have something to do with changes in the accounting of government stocks. However, this category is extremely sensitive, as also noted before, to error in the estimate of residual public sector incomes, which in turn were estimated by an essentially arbitrary procedure. Therefore, it is appropriate to consider the sensitivity of GNP rates of growth to the magnitude and growth of outlays n.e.c. (for brevity, I will not continually repeat; "public sector statistical discrepancy"). In the tabulation below, $\hat{r}$ rates are shown for GNP in the basic series less outlays n.e.c.:

	1958 prices		*1964 prices*	
	EP	*AFC*	*EP*	*AFC*
GNP, basic series	5.6	5.5	5.4	5.4
GNP less outlays n.e.c.	5.7	5.7	5.5	5.5

Deletion of outlays n.e.c. results in a slight increase of $\hat{r}$.

TABLE 23

AVERAGE ANNUAL RATES OF GROWTH ($\hat{r}$) OF SELECTED END USES AT AFC, BASIC SERIES AND WITH SUPPLEMENTARY ADJUSTMENTS, 1958–1964
(percent)

	1958 AFC		1964 AFC	
	Basic Series	Supplementary Adjustments	Basic Series	Supplementary Adjustments
Adjustment 1				
Housing	4.4	6.9	4.4	6.9
All consumer services	7.6	7.5	7.5	7.4
Total consumption	4.8	5.1	4.6	5.0
GNP	5.5	5.6	5.4	5.5
Adjustment 2				
Government services and other outlays	5.8	5.9	5.9	6.0
GNP	5.5	5.5	5.4	5.4
Adjustment 3				
State-cooperative fixed investment	8.5	8.4	8.5	8.4
All gross fixed investment	6.8	6.5	6.7	6.4
Total gross investment	6.4	6.1	6.3	6.0
GNP	5.5	5.4	5.4	5.3
Adjustment 4				
Total consumption	4.8	4.8	4.6	4.7
Communal services	6.4	6.4	6.3	6.3
All gross fixed investment	6.8	6.8	6.7	6.7
Inventory investment	3.3	3.4	3.3	3.1
Total gross investment	6.4	6.4	6.3	6.3
Defense	8.0	7.9	8.0	8.0
GNP	5.5	5.5	5.4	5.4
Adjustments 1–4				
Total consumption	4.8	5.1	4.6	5.0
All gross fixed investment	6.8	6.5	6.7	6.4
Total gross investment	6.4	6.1	6.3	6.0
Government services and other outlays	5.8	5.9	5.9	6.0
GNP	5.5	5.6	5.4	5.4
Adjustments 1–4, but with housing interest at 5 percent				
Total consumption	4.8	5.0	4.6	4.9
GNP	5.5	5.5	5.4	5.4

TABLE 23 (continued)

Sources:

Basic series. Computed from Tables K-1 and K-2.

Supplementary adjustments

Adjustments 1 and 2. Imputation of interest and depreciation on all housing and of depreciation on government service capital. See sources for Table 17. Values of the adjustments for 1958 not previously estimated are computed on the assumption that the 1958 average annual capital stock values of housing and government service capital were 84 and 20 billion rubles respectively (that is, assuming a 10 percent increase in the 1958 stock).

Adjustment 3. Deletion of half of capital repairs. State-cooperative sector capital repairs at current AFC are estimated in the sources to Table 17. Constant AFC series are obtained by applying 1958 and 1964 EP indexes to the current AFC values for, respectively, 1958 and 1964. For the EP indexes, see p. 513. Half of the resulting values are then deducted from state-cooperative fixed investment, all gross fixed investment, total gross investment, and GNP.

Adjustment 4. Revaluation of collective farmer incomes. The total size of the adjustments at current prices and their allocation by category are shown in the sources to Table 17. Adjustments incident on consumption and communal services are deflated by the implicit deflator for the particular end-use category. Thus the adjustment incident on consumption is deflated by the ratio of consumption values at current AFC (Table J-1) to those at 1958 or 1964 AFC (Tables K-1 and K-2). For adjustments incident on other categories, deflation is either not called for or can be safely ignored because of the small size of the changes involved.

Performing the same operation on GNP after the four supplementary adjustments, the following results emerge: [17]

	1958 AFC	*1964 AFC*
GNP after four supplementary adjustments with housing interest at 10 percent	5.6	5.4
The same, less outlays n.e.c.	5.7	5.6
GNP after four supplementary adjustments with housing interest at 5 percent	5.5	5.4
The same, less outlays n.e.c.	5.7	5.5

The effect of deleting outlays n.e.c. from GNP after the supplementary adjustments is the same as before supplementary adjustments. Again the changes are negligible.

The discussion of the effect of supplementary adjustments on the real rate of growth of output has dealt entirely with constant AFC values calculated according to Method I. I will not encumber this already intricate exposition by duplicating the entire set of calculations for the Method II formula, but it might be of interest to examine the effect of

[17] The implicit assumption involved in subtracting outlays n.e.c. from GNP after supplementary adjustments is that the supplementary adjustments incident on the category "government services and other outlays" are in fact incident only on government services.

using Method II in three cases: first, GNP with and without outlays n.e.c.; second, GNP after four supplementary adjustments but with housing interest imputed at 5 percent; third, the same, excluding outlays n.e.c. The tabulation below shows the comparison with the results obtained using Method I (percent):

	Method	*1958 AFC*	*1964 AFC*
GNP	I	5.5	5.4
	II	6.0	5.9
GNP excluding outlays n.e.c.	I	5.7	5.5
	II	6.2	6.0
GNP with four supplementary adjustments; housing interest at 5 percent	I	5.5	5.4
	II	6.0	5.9
The same, excluding outlays n.e.c.	I	5.7	5.5
	II	6.2	6.0

The calculations indicate that:

(1) Method II everywhere raises the calculated rate of growth.

(2) Within either the Method I or Method II set of calculations, $\hat{r}$ is relatively insensitive to the deletion of outlays n.e.c., or the supplementary adjustments, or a combination of the two.

(3) Again, the results are relatively insensitive to change in the weight year, but this is as always an expected result.

(4) The range of $\hat{r}$ growth rates is narrow (percent):

Method I	5.4–5.7
Method II	5.9–6.2

Calculation of growth by Method II rather than by Method I merely shifts the range upward but does not affect its width.

Rates of Growth, 1958–1964: Summary

The preceding sections have presented and commented upon a broad spectrum of calculations of the average rate of growth of Soviet GNP and its components. The range of growth rates for major end-use categories may be tabulated as follows (percent): [18]

[18] No growth rates are presented for the category "government services and other outlays" as the category figures in only one adjustment and the effects seem negligible. Nor have I included the rates obtained by the deletion of outlays n.e.c. from GNP. As already indicated, the latter operation effected a change in the rate of growth of GNP of no more than two tenths of a point.

	Basic Series: EP and AFC	*AFC with Supplementary Adjustments*
Consumption	4.6–5.1	4.7–5.1
Communal services	6.3–6.4	6.3–6.4
Gross fixed investment	6.6–6.8	6.4–6.8
Inventory investment	3.2–3.3	3.1–3.4
Total gross investment	6.2–6.4	6.0–6.4
R&D	12.0–12.1	n.a.
Defense	8.0–8.1	7.9–8.0
GNP	5.4–5.6	5.3–5.6

This tabulation, in which AFC growth rates are computed by Method I, indicates that (1) within each use category, the range is small, half a percentage point or less; (2) supplementary adjustments are negligible in their effect on the range of growth rates.

The factor cost adjustment and deflation procedures of this study leave room for considerable improvement, a point made repeatedly in the discussion. It is impossible to specify the net size of all the estimating errors or to predict what additional variation in growth rates would be introduced if the required raw data were available. But the possibility of error in the level of the calculated growth rates and of substantial additional dispersion in rates should be borne in mind. In particular, it has been shown that: (1) calculation of constant AFC values by Method II raises growth rates of consumption by a point or more and those of GNP by about half a point; (2) if significant price inflation occurred in state-cooperative investment and in the military-space program, the *r* rate of GNP may be overstated by margins from half to slightly more than a percentage point; (3) if the share of miscellaneous budget revenues that is an entry on current account varied during this period, the *r* rate of growth of GNP may be overstated by perhaps half a percentage point.

Growth Per Capita

The rates of growth discussed in this chapter relate exclusively to total output. It may be useful to record the per capita equivalents. For this purpose I use the following average annual population series: [19]

	1958	*1959*	*1960*	*1961*	*1962*	*1963*	*1964*
Millions	206.8	210.5	214.2	218.0	221.5	224.7	227.7

[19] *NKh 1964*, p. 7, and *VS*, 1963, No. 8, p. 91.

The tabulation below presents $\hat{r}$ rates of growth per capita of GNP and household consumption at the four basic valuations, at AFC with all supplementary adjustments (housing interest at 5 percent), and at AFC computed by Method II. I also show the rates of growth of GNP per head under Method I and with all supplementary adjustments but with outlays n.e.c. deleted in all years (percent):

	1958 Prices	*1964 Prices*
GNP		
EP	3.9	3.7
AFC	3.8	3.7
AFC, Method II	4.4	4.2
AFC, Method I, all supplementary adjustments	3.8	3.7
Same, except delete outlays n.e.c.	4.0	3.9
Consumption		
EP	3.4	3.2
AFC	3.1	3.0
AFC, Supplementary adjustments	3.4	3.3
AFC, Method II	4.2	3.9

Except for the Method II results, per capita average growth rates of GNP fall in the range of 3.7–4.0 percent, compared with the rates for total output of 5.3–5.6 percent; the corresponding pairing for consumption is 3.0–3.4 and 4.6–5.1 percent.[20] Method II calculation of AFC, of course, raises the rates of growth. All of the qualifications attached to the total rates of growth discussed in this chapter necessarily apply to the per capita rates with equivalent force.

[20] The per capita equivalents of the real income growth rates presented in note 14 above are 2.8–3.0 percent with 1958 weights in the COL index and 3.1–3.3 percent with 1964 weights.

7

Military Outlays

After the discussion of the growth of GNP and its major components in Chapter 6, it would be useful now to examine at closer range the relative and absolute growth of a major nonconsumption element, military expenditures. The question posed is natural, indeed obvious. Unfortunately, the answer is far from being so. The reader should have no illusions that a Rosetta stone is about to be unveiled. Although the following pages explore a number of alternative paths to determining the level and trend of military expenditures, no usable quantifications emerge. Ultimately, I am constrained to frame a highly qualified conclusion largely in terms of the material developed in earlier chapters. The reader interested only in my estimate of the "numbers" will find them on pp. 163–164. But perhaps it may prove of some use to explore systematically what we know and do not know about Soviet military outlays from published sources. Such a survey has not previously appeared in print.[1]

No one will be surprised to learn that the Soviet government attempts to conceal the size, structure, and financing of its military activities. Military secrecy is a contemporary hallmark of national sovereignty, and it is the rare government that is prepared to dispense information freely on its military establishment. But neither will it surprise anyone to learn that the Soviet government is rather more adept than most at the task of concealment. Although information on economic activity generally began to be released with relative liberality in the mid-1950s, there has been no substantive change in the policy with respect to military activities.[2]

---

[1] This chapter revises my previous attempt to fill this gap, *Soviet Military Outlays Since 1955,* July 1964. On the same subject see also the references cited in note 12 below.

[2] In 1960, Khrushchev revealed the total size of the Soviet armed forces in

Today, as under Stalin, Soviet military expenditures are made known by announcement of nothing more than a single number, total so-called "defense" expenditures. Discussion in the Soviet open literature provides not an iota of explicit amplification.

In principle, the restriction would not necessarily constitute an insuperable obstacle to the inquiry set here. This is not a study of military policy or of military resource allocation, and a time series for aggregate military expenditures would suffice for my purposes. The critical question is whether the series for total "defense" expenditures is the desired indicator? What does "defense" cover?

The Scope of "Defense"

Soviet financial sources are notably reluctant to enter into details with respect to the content of the defense appropriation. The typical description is brief and cryptic. One of the meatier discussions in an authoritative two-volume financial encyclopedia declares that:

> The basic financial plan of the [Soviet] Armed Forces is the annual estimate [3] of the USSR Ministry of Defense. The following expenditures are carried out through the estimate: payment for the supply of arms and combat equipment, fuel, food, personal equipment (*veshchevoe imushchestvo*), and other material values and services; financing of capital investment, repair of arms, combat equipment and military equipment (*voennoe imushchestvo*), combat and political training, maintenance and support (*khoziaistvenno-bytovoe ustroistvo*) of troops; payment of money allowances to personnel of the army and navy, and others.[4]

A recent financial text provides more detail in an organizational as well as functional definition. The passage is cited below in full:

> Resources for the national defense are appropriated according to the estimate of the USSR Ministry of Defense and are directed to the maintenance of land forces, the Navy and the Air Force, air defense forces, rear echelons and supply organizations of all parts of the armed forces and types

---

a number of years (*Pravda,* January 15, 1960). On the other hand, Soviet sources no longer report expenditures on their internal security forces, as they did in the 1940s.

[3] The Russian term for the arrangements under which budget organizations are financed is *v smetnom poriadke:* literally, "by the estimate system," the estimate referring to an agency's program, detailing its estimated requirements for financing and regulating actual expenditures. See Aleksandrov, ed., *Gosudarstvennyi biudzhet SSSR,* 1965, p. 303.

[4] *Finansovo-kreditnyi slovar',* 1964, II, pp. 477–478.

of troops. The Ministry of Defense controls a number of economic organizations and industrial enterprises.

The USSR Ministry of Defense estimates provide for expenditures on: payment by the army, air force, and navy for arms, munitions, equipment (*vooruzhenie, boepripasy, tekhnika*), fuels and lubricants, as well as food, personal equipment and other articles required for combat and political training and combat readiness of troops; maintenance and support of military units; maintenance of military schools (Suvorov and Nakhimov schools, secondary and higher educational institutions and military academies), hospital networks, other medical institutions and sanatoria, officers' homes, clubs, sport structures, etc.; money allowances to servicemen, earnings of workers and employees of military units and formations; financing capital investment and industrial enterprises of the USSR Ministry of Defense.[5]

This passage, written by A. M. Aleksandrov, is the longest and most explicit on the subject available. Nevertheless, it obscures almost as much as it illuminates. The opening paragraph suggests that all military needs are covered by the defense appropriation, but the particularization in the second paragraph is far from complete. Although military pay and subsistence, operation, maintenance, and procurement are specified as objects of defense appropriation, no mention is made of military stockpiling, civil defense, and foreign military aid.[6] The most conspicuous omission is R&D, research and development (or, in the customary fuller American designation, RDT&E—research, development, testing, and evaluation). Soviet sources of the 1950s listed the maintenance of scientific research institutions as an element of "defense." Such references have been absent in comparable works of the 1960s.[7] However, a recent editorial in the military newspaper, listing agencies over which the Ministry of Defense has authority, includes R&D institutions.[8] In this connection, note also the absence of reference by Aleksandrov to either space activities or nuclear weapon programs.

---

[5] Aleksandrov, ed., *Gosudarstvennyi biudzhet SSSR,* 1965, pp. 382–383. This passage, which is attributed to Aleksandrov himself (p. 2), bears a strong resemblance to an earlier but briefer discussion (attributed to Abroskin) in Allakhverdian, ed., *Finansy SSSR,* 1962, p. 310. Presumably, discussion of this sensitive subject is carefully controlled, and standardized phraseology is a traditional bulwark against breach of security. The first (1961) edition of the Aleksandrov work omits all mention of defense.

[6] From a national income viewpoint, the material component of foreign military aid is of interest only to the extent that it is a disposition of current output.

[7] *The Soviet Financial System,* 1968, p. 175.

[8] *Krasnaia zvezda,* May 25, 1967, p. 1.

To what extent he included military construction and investment in the armaments industry[9] is also unclear. A Soviet source has reported capital construction and capital repair of military buildings and structures as an article of defense expenditures.[10] Aleksandrov speaks of "financing capital investment and industrial enterprises of the USSR Ministry of Defense." The phrase is open to varied interpretation: "investment" may refer to outlays on military facilities or on industrial enterprises; "industrial enterprises" may refer to a sizable portion of armaments production or to a few arsenals and repair plants. It has been noted that a 1958 source spoke of "defense" financing "industrial repair enterprises" rather than "industrial enterprises."[11] Whether the change in wording signifies an actual change in coverage is conjectural.

To sum up, "defense" expenditures appear to fall short of encompassing all military outlays. Precisely what the announced budget outlays do cover, however, is not clear. The Soviet sources cited suggest that "defense" embraces at least military pay and subsistence, operations and maintenance, and probably military construction and repair. All the sources state or imply inclusion of military procurement; some of them also indicate the presence of R&D outlays. Finally, the sources are silent on the score of internal security forces, including the militarized border guards. By naming only the Army, Navy, and Air Force, they tend to suggest exclusion of internal security forces from those encompassed by the Ministry of Defense estimate.

Military Outlays in Other Budget Categories

If "defense" is not all-inclusive, what are the sources of finance and the magnitude of the excluded military outlays? This question is obviously critical in an attempt to trace the growth of total Soviet military expenditures, and it has naturally been the focus of attention in a number of previous studies.[12] Table 24 provides a distribution of state budget

[9] With the exception of non-military space programs and investment in armaments industry by the private sector, the listed activities or items of expenditure, beginning with pay and subsistence, make up the category of "national defense" in the U.S. Federal Budget.

[10] Cited in *The Soviet Financial System,* 1968, p. 176.

[11] *Ibid.*, p. 175.

[12] CIA: *The 1960 Soviet Budget,* November 1960, pp. 13–14, 21, 29–30, 35–37; *The Soviet Budget for 1961,* July 1961, pp. 10–13, 23–27; *The Soviet Budget for 1962,* pp. 4, 12–15, 23–24; Godaire, in *Dimensions of Soviet Economic Power,* 1962, pp. 36–38. The question is also treated at some

resources by major expenditure, where known, including the surplus over total outlays. Official data are available enabling further breakdown of expenditures on social-cultural measures to at least one additional sublevel, and in some instances further. This is not the case for any of the other entries, although some Western estimates have been made for a few items.[13] A number of categories in Table 24 have been suggested as repositories of military expenditures: 1.A., industry and construction; 1.G., other; 2.A., education; and 6. other.[14] They will be examined briefly in turn.

It is reasonably clear that budget-financed investment in military production facilities is channeled through the appropriation to the "national economy," and hence, most likely, through the appropriation to the budget division, "industry." Judging by official organization charts, most if not all of the arms industry is administratively subordinate to industrial agencies, not to the Ministry of Defense.[15] The expenditure classification of the Soviet budget, reported in Soviet sources, identifies the defense appropriation as an allocation to the USSR Ministry of Defense. Presumably, only expenditures by that agency comprise "defense."[16] Investment grants to economic ministries, committees, or councils of the national economy are financed from the budget category

---

length in Becker, *Soviet Military Outlays Since 1955,* July 1964, portions of which are drawn on here.

[13] Planned magnitudes of budgetary allocations, including investment by branch of the economy, are frequently announced in the annual budget speeches before the Supreme Soviet and in articles by the Minister of Finance in *PKh* or *FinSSSR*.

[14] Becker, *Soviet Military Outlays Since 1955,* July 1964, pp. 23–24, suggests the possibility that military outlays were also included in budget expenditures on health care after 1953. However, the data on which this hypothesis rests are not available for years later than 1957.

[15] *The Soviet Financial System,* 1968, Ch. 2. In the U.S. accounts, only investment in government enterprises would be included in national security. Other investment in armaments industry would be entered under private investment.

[16] *Ibid.,* p. 68. See also p. 176: "No procedure that would mitigate this presumption has been encountered in Soviet financial practice, such as awarding a budget grant or credit to one agency for subsequent unilateral transfer to another agency." However, on p. 70, the same study declares that top level agencies may receive budget appropriations from more than one category: for example, an education ministry receiving both a "social-cultural" appropriation and an allocation from "administration." Whether or how this affects the Ministry of Defense is not known.

TABLE 24

USSR STATE BUDGET EXPENDITURES, SURPLUS, AND TOTAL REVENUES, 1958–1965
(billion rubles)

	1958	1959	1960	1961	1962	1963	1964	1965
1. National economy								
A. Industry and construction	13.67	14.88	15.59	15.81	15.36	17.29	18.87	20.99
B. MTS-RTS	1.41	.11	.07	—	—	—	—	—
C. Agriculture and procurement [a]	2.59 [b]	3.41 [b]	4.68	6.10	7.53	7.80	8.67	6.77
D. Trade	2.03	3.21	3.59	1.77	1.75	2.16	1.79	2.27
E. Transportation-communication	2.41	2.69	2.81	2.67	2.75	2.72	2.77	2.27
F. Housing-communal economy	1.90	2.75	3.21	3.65	3.85	3.97	3.80	4.23
G. Other	5.01 [c]	5.33 [c]	4.16	2.57	4.98	4.86	4.71	7.83
H. Total	29.03	32.37	34.12	32.57	36.22	38.80	40.60	44.92
2. Social-cultural measures								
A. Education	8.60	9.41	10.31 [d]	11.33	12.43	13.71	15.10	17.51
B. Health care and physical culture	4.11	4.46	4.84 [d]	5.01	4.94	5.26	5.66	6.67
C. Social assistance	5.73	6.07	6.48	7.15	7.67	8.13	8.58	9.05
D. Social insurance	2.44	2.67	2.81	3.21	3.44	3.41	3.50	4.04
E. Aid to mothers	.53	.50	.50	.49	.48	.47	.47	.46
F. Social assistance fund for collective farmers	n.a.	n.a.	n.a.	n.a.	n.a.	n.a.	n.a.	.44
G. Total	21.42	23.12	24.94	27.19	28.97	30.97	33.31	38.16
3. Defense	9.36	9.37	9.30	11.59	12.64	13.87	13.28	12.78
4. Administration	1.20	1.12	1.09	1.08	1.09	1.09	1.11	1.28
5. Loan service	.37	.69	.7	.8	.8	.1	.1	.1
6. Other	2.90	3.73	3.0	3.1	2.4	2.2	3.8	4.4
7. Total expenditures	64.28	70.40	73.13	76.31	82.15	87.00	92.23	101.62
8. Surplus	2.96	3.62	3.95	1.74	2.15	2.54	2.17	.70
9. Total revenues	67.24	74.01	77.08	78.05	84.31	89.54	94.41	102.32

Notes.

[a] In *Gosbiudzhet II*, figures for agriculture and procurement in 1960–1964 are footnoted as including supplements from the union budget to cover deficiencies in own working capital. Figures for 1950, 1955, and 1965 in the same source are not so identified nor are any of the corresponding figures in *Gosbiudzhet I.*

[b] Excluding procurement.

[c] Including procurement.

[d] The 1960 figure for education in *Gosbiudzhet II* is 17.3 million rubles smaller and the health figure correspondingly larger than the relevant figures in *Gosbiudzhet I.* Evidently, a minor reclassification of outlays took place after the publication of *Gosbiudzhet I*, shifting some education expenditures to the health care category.

Sources:

Except for item 5, data are taken directly from *Gosbiudzhet I*, pp. 5, 18–19, and *Gosbiudzhet II*, pp. 8, 20–21. Entries for item 5 are from *NKh 1959*, p. 801, *NKh 1962*, p. 635, and *NKh 1964*, p. 770; the figure for 1965 is a guess. Items 1.G and 6 are calculated as residuals, subtracting the sums of components from the relevant totals "national economy." It seems safe to conclude that this is the case for military production facilities, too.[17]

The "industry and construction" item of Table 24 has aroused interest for another reason. CIA budget studies have drawn attention to the large residuals left unexplained by subtraction from that item of budget outlays on industry and construction for fixed investment, expansion of working capital, subsidies, and the like. That is, appropriations to industry and construction may encompass not only investment in arms factories but also other outlays of a military nature—procurement or operational expenditures. Some of the activities involved may be in the nuclear weapons program. This is thought to be the true function of the Ministry of Medium Machinebuilding, with nonmilitary nuclear matters the responsibility of the State Committee for Utilization of Atomic Energy.[18] Both agencies are beneficiaries of "national economy" financing.

Suspicion has also fallen on a second residual, the "national economy" residual—item 1.G. in Table 24—aroused by indications in Soviet sources that the "national economy" allocation finances additions to "state material reserves." These reserves are known to include armaments—[19] according to one writer, "means of defense of a special nature." [20] The national economy residual probably includes subsidies

---

[17] See also *Real SNIP,* p. 23. Note that construction of defense industry plants is the function of an identified element of the Ukrainian Ministry of Construction. *The Soviet Financial System,* 1968, p. 21.

[18] Kramish, *Atomic Energy in the Soviet Union,* 1959, pp. 176–179. After Khrushchev's 1957 industrial reorganization, the Ministry of Medium Machinebuilding became a State Committee, whether with the same or reduced administrative competence is not clear. After Khrushchev's removal and the demise of the *sovnarkhozy,* the ministries were revived. See *The Soviet Financial System,* 1968, pp. 6, 9. Under Khrushchev, the Chairman of the State Committee of Medium Machinebuilding had the rank of Minister of the USSR, but his counterpart in the State Committee for Utilization of Atomic Energy did not. *Ekon.gazeta,* January 4, 1964, p. 34.

[19] CIA, *The 1960 Soviet Budget,* November 1960, pp. 14, 25–30. The clearest statement in the Soviet sources seems to be in Bachurin, ed., *Finansy i kredit SSSR,* 2nd ed., 1958, p. 148. "Expenditures on financing the national economy also include outlays on the formation of state material reserves for industrial, agricultural, transport, food, defense and other purposes." For a similar but less concise statement, see Lavrov, ed., *Finansy i kredit SSSR,* 1964, p. 215. On the military component of state reserves, see also *Bol'shaia sovetskaia entsiklopediia,* 2nd ed., 1955, Vol. 36, p. 265.

[20] Bor, *Voprosy metodologii planovogo balansa narodnogo khoziaistvo SSSR,* 1960, p. 311.

for agricultural procurement to cover the difference between the constantly rising level of prices paid farms and farmers and the relatively constant level of prices paid by trade and light industry.[21] Procurement subsidies have been estimated as ranging between a high of 3.40 billion rubles in 1958 and a low of 1.00 billions in 1961, with 1963 and 1964 levels exceeding two billions.[22] Net of these estimated values, the national economy residual is reduced to the following rounded levels (billion rubles):

1958	1.0	1961	1.6	1964	2.6
1959	2.0	1962	3.3		
1960	1.9	1963	2.6		

Order of magnitude estimates of additions to state reserves can be framed from published statistics on NMP, as is done in Table 25.[23] Item 2.B(4) there represents a residual series consisting of the increment of collective farm unfinished construction, private sector agricultural inventories, and state reserves. If the first two components of the residual may be reasonably assumed to be small, the level and trend of the series would approximate those of the increments to state reserves. The series is characterized by considerable fluctuations. However, we may defer this problem for the moment to note that with the sole exception of 1959, the annual additions to state stockpiles, if such they are, considerably exceed the estimated national economy residuals. Perhaps the allocations to particular branches (industry, agriculture) within the national economy appropriations serve as additional sources of finance for stockpiling. Yet, there may be another explanation for the gap between estimated increments to reserves and the national economy residuals. It is possible that "additions to reserves," as was hinted earlier, is in part a euphemism for military hardware procurement. There is some evidence to support this contention, which will be introduced in the next section. If this is the case, it is also possible that such increments to "reserves" are partly or wholly financed from the defense appropriation. There is,

[21] These subsidies are not included in the reported outlays on agriculture and procurement. This may be seen just from a comparison of two figures for 1960. According to *Gosbiudzhet I*, p. 18, budget outlays on agriculture alone were 4.35 billion rubles; the *Gosbiudzhet II* (p. 20) figure is 4.68 billion rubles and includes outlays on procurement and an allocation from the union budget to cover working capital deficiencies. Procurement subsidies in 1960 were estimated as 2.00 billion rubles.

[22] Below, pp. 373 ff.

[23] Below, p. 159.

moreover, some similiarity between the series, additions to state reserves, and that of "defense" less pay and subsistence,[24] as the following tabulation shows (billion rubles):

	1958	*1959*	*1960*	*1961*	*1962*	*1963*	*1964*
"Defense" less pay and subsistence	5.0	5.1	5.2	7.7	8.3	9.9	9.6
Additions to state reserves, etc.	5.0	1.8	5.7	7.6	9.1	5.7	7.8

The two series diverge substantially in 1959 and 1963; agreement is more or less total in 1950 and 1960–1962. The virtual identity in these three years should not be taken too seriously on general principles, but since the discussion of the scope of "defense" suggested the inclusion of operation and maintenance and possibly also construction and repair, "defense" less pay and subsistence should exceed additions to reserves if the latter were composed wholly of military hardware procurement. The values of pay and subsistence as well as of additions to state reserves used in these calculations are estimates subject to varying and not easily definable margins of error. It cannot be established whether additions to state reserves as computed include civilian as well as military procurement. Thus, even leaving aside the strange gaps in 1959 and 1963 between the two series tabulated above, we may conclude only that the partial agreement noted is suggestive in the light of the supporting definitional evidence.

To return to the examination of particular budget categories, we find that expenditures on education (item 2.A in Table 24) are shown in budget sources as distributed among the following classes: general education; culture and enlightenment; cadre training, of which an important subclass is higher education; science; press; art (including the theater); radio, TV.[25] Major interest centers on the "science" class, the predominant source of finance of R&D in the USSR. Moreover, discussions of science outlays in Soviet sources have frequently stressed the connection to military or space achievements.[26] However, R&D programs are also financed through the national economy appropriation. Evidently, the

---

[24] Computed from Table 6, that is, excluding the estimated "defense" allocation for pensions and allowances.

[25] For example, *Gosbiudzhet I*, pp. 21–22.

[26] Nimitz, *Soviet Expenditures on Scientific Research*, January 1963, pp. 10–14, and *An Addendum to Soviet Expenditures on Scientific Research* (forthcoming).

latter covers some investment in R&D facilities, although investment is an item of expenditure in the science class, too.[27] But current outlays on R&D may also be financed through the national economy allocation. This is suggested by (1) the identification in a 1962 budget classification of the State Committee for Aviation Technology as a recipient of national economy appropriations, (2) the likelihood that there were R&D institutions attached to the Committee [28] and (3) the indication in Soviet sources that R&D of a theoretical nature or of national significance was financed from the budget even if the institution was nominally on *khozraschet*.[29] This point should be borne in mind in considering the scope and magnitude of the industry-construction and national economy residuals, discussed above.

The caution applies not only to these residuals but to one relating to budget outlays on science. Analyzing an official distribution of these outlays by article of expenditure (wages, repair, etc.) for 1950–1957,[30] Nimitz noticed that whereas the sum of the items virtually exhausted the indicated republican budget total, it fell far short of doing so with respect to the union budget total: 75 percent of the union budget total in 1957 was unidentified. She concluded that the omissions, approximately 60 percent of all budget (union and republican) outlays on science, represented the expenditures of entire institutions, presumed engaged in industrial R&D, in which military-space projects must be prominent.[31] Such distributions continue to be published for republican budget but, unfortunately, not for union budget outlays.[32]

The final possible repository of military outlays to be considered here is item 6 of Table 24, which I have called the "budgetary expenditure residual." As the Committee of State Security (KGB) and Ministries for

---

[27] See below, pp. 408–409.

[28] *The Soviet Financial System*, 1968, p. 70.

[29] See Bashin, *Planirovanie nauchno-issledovatel'skikh i opytno-konstruktorskikh rabot*, 1966, p. 7.

[30] *Raskhody*, pp. 42, 58–60.

[31] Nimitz, *Soviet Expenditures on Scientific Research*, January 1963, pp. 14–15. In the decade 1955–1965, annual relative increases in union budget science outlays exceeded those of the republican budget in seven of the ten years, and usually by substantial margins. *Gosbiudzhet I*, p. 51, and *Gosbiudzhet II*, p. 53. A likely explanation of the reverse situation, which prevailed in 1957–1959, is the administrative transfer of a number of R&D agencies to republican control. Nimitz, *Soviet Expenditures on Scientific Research*, January 1963, pp. 18–19.

[32] *Gosbiudzhet I*, p. 86, and *Gosbiudzhet II*, p. 88.

Protection of Public Order (MOOP) are accorded a separate place in the budgetary classification, distinct from other top level administration,[33] it is clear that the budgetary expenditure residual covers, among other things, the expenditures of the internal security forces.[34] I have estimated internal security expenditures at 1.5 billion rubles annually. If the estimate is reasonably accurate, the residual shrinks to between 1 and 2 billion rubles in 1958–1964. Some part of this is accounted for by a variety of small outlays of a nonmilitary character,[35] and the size of the ultimate residual, net of all identified components, could hardly be much larger than a billion rubles.

Contemporary Soviet sources claim that the annual surplus of expenditures over revenues is used to "amplify the loan resources of Gosbank." [36] There is no evidence that the surplus is earmarked for particular purposes, although as I indicated earlier the precise function of the budgetary surplus is unclear.[37]

Military Outlays in the NMP Accounts

I alluded earlier to the possible location of military procurement expenditures in "additions to state reserves," an end-use component of utilized NMP. Perhaps some further clues to the identification of unannounced military outlays may be gleaned from a more systematic examination of the official NMP data and definitions. Of course, it is not to be expected that Soviet sources would be less reticent on the score of the classification of military outlays in NMP categories than they are with respect to their classification in budget expenditures.

In his 1948 book on the Soviet economy during World War II, Voznesenskii distributed national income in 1940, 1942–1943 into three classes, as follows (percent): [38]

---

[33] *The Soviet Financial System,* 1968, p. 68.

[34] It is not known whether construction for these forces is financed from the same budget category or from the national economy appropriation. With respect to an earlier period, see *SNIP 1940–1948,* p. 199; *Real SNIP,* p. 361.

[35] *The Soviet Financial System,* 1968, pp. 76–77.

[36] *Finansovo-kreditnyi slovar' II,* p. 233. See also Lavrov, ed., *Finansy i kredit SSSR,* 1964, p. 216.

[37] See above, p. 33; also below, note 54.

[38] Voznesenskii, *Voennaia ekonomika SSSR v period otechestvennoi voiny,* 1948, pp. 65, 67.

	1940	*1942*	*1943*
Consumption	74	67	61
Accumulation	19	4	7
War expenditures, excluding personal consumption of the armed forces	7	29	32
	100	100	100

All references since then to the postwar structure of NMP by use have omitted Voznesenskii's third category, and the official data for utilized NMP show it consisting only of consumption and accumulation. Has the bulk of military outlays been excluded from utilized NMP or have they been redistributed among consumption and accumulation?

Somewhat ambiguous references in Soviet sources supporting the first alternative can be cited. For example, the well-known writer on national income, B. Plyshevskii, alludes to changes in the rate of military spending during the SYP period in terms of "other expenditures, not entering directly into the composition of accumulation and consumption funds." [39] One implication of Plyshevskii's remarks is that military outlays are part of produced NMP but are deducted in computing utilized NMP. This seems highly unlikely: (1) the numerical value of this difference in the period 1958–1964 fluctuated between about 1–3 billion rubles; [40] (2) the yearbooks explain this difference as representing the foreign trade balance and material losses not charged to cost.[41]

If military outlays are included in produced NMP, and there is no reason to believe that this is untrue of at least the material expenditure component, the next assumption to be examined is that they are classi-

---

[39] Plyshevskii, *Natsional'nyi dokhod SSSR za 20 let,* 1964, p. 163.

[40] *NKh 1964,* pp. 575, 578; *VS,* 1966, No. 4, p. 96.

[41] *NKh 1964,* p. 578. Admittedly, the yearbooks have equivocated on the deduction of the foreign trade balance from produced NMP. Thus, *NKh 1960* (p. 154) and *NKh 1961* (p. 599) define the difference between produced and utilized NMP as losses alone; *NKh 1962* (p. 483) and *NKh 1963* (p. 503) add "undistributed expenditures"; *NKh 1964* and *NKh 1965* (p. 592) convert this term to the "foreign trade balance." It seems a fair inference that "undistributed expenditures" and the "foreign trade balance" are synonymous. Was the foreign trade balance also deducted in the data reported in the 1960 and 1961 yearbooks? Possibly, but the retrospective corrections in the 1961 yearbook of 1959 and 1960 data for utilized NMP (sources as cited above) may be evidence to the contrary.

fied with consumption and accumulation in the use distribution. In the official data, consumption consists of three subcategories: personal consumption of households; material outlays in institutions servicing households; and material outlays in science and administration. The second major category of use, dubbed "accumulation and other expenditures," is further distributed between the increment in fixed capital and the increment in "material working capital and reserves" (*material'nye oborotnye sredstva i rezervy*). The yearbooks define "accumulation," apart from net fixed capital formation, as "the increment of material working capital (stocks of raw materials, materials, fuel, finished output, balances of commodities in trade (*ostatki tovarov v torgovle*), stocks of agricultural products, unfinished capital investment, and so forth), the increment of state material reserves, the increment of personal (*lichnye*) stocks of agricultural products held by the population."

The logic of Soviet national accounting and scattered source references suggest the following: (1) Military pay and earnings of civilians employed in military programs should be excluded entirely as payment for nonproductive services. (2) Military subsistence and the material component of current maintenance of the military establishment (including R&D) should be an element of consumption.[42] (3) It is possible that military construction is treated as equivalent to civilian investment and, net of depreciation, is included in the fixed capital component of accumulation, although this is far from certain. (4) As suggested earlier, part or all of procurement of military hardware may be accounted for in additions to state reserves.

To test these interpretations, I attempt in Table 25 to flesh out the skeletal distributions of NMP by use that are available from Soviet sources. In Table 25, the two institutional components of consumption are not distinguished because of uncertainty on the distribution between them of depreciation on nonproductive capital except housing. Otherwise, Table 25 follows the form of the official distribution faithfully. Military pay is omitted entirely from Table 25 but subsistence is part of income in kind under personal consumption. What about current mate-

---

[42] Sobol', *Ocherki po voprosam balansa narodnogo khoziaistva,* 1960, p. 160; Kuleshov, *Sotsialisticheskoe vosproizvodstvo,* 1961, p. 45; Petrov, ed., *Kurs ekonomicheskoi statistiki,* 1961, pp. 389, 414; Maier and Krylov, *Planirovanie narodnogo potreblenie v SSSR,* 1964, p. 15; Eremina and Marshalova, *Statistika truda,* 1965, p. 223; Korovkin and Kirichenko, *PKh,* 1965, No. 9, p. 23; Eidel'man, *Mezhotraslevoi balans obshchestvennogo produkta,* 1966, p. 157.

rial purchases of the military establishment, military construction, and hardware procurement? If the estimates of other components are reasonably accurate, the only possible locations are the consumption fund residual, item 1.B(4), net investment and the increment of unfinished construction, and the accumulation fund residual, item 2.B(4).

The consumption fund residuals in 1958–1964 are not very illuminating, unfortunately. The figures for item 1.B(4)(c) are small and show no tendency to increase after 1960. Granted the estimated material

TABLE 25

NET MATERIAL PRODUCT BY USE, 1958–1964
(billion rubles)

	1958	1959	1960	1961	1962	1963	1964
1. Consumption fund							
A. Personal consumption of households							
(1) State-cooperative retail trade	60.33	64.47	71.13	73.41	79.64	84.29	88.18
(2) Utilities	.69	.77	.87	.98	1.09	1.23	1.35
(3) "Industrial" services	.50	.60	.70	.80	.90	1.00	1.10
(4) Extravillage farm markets	4.43	4.23	4.00	4.31	4.36	4.29	4.42
(5) Income in kind	11.93	11.52	11.10	11.32	11.72	11.50	11.71
(6) "Other outlays for consumption"	3.00	3.19	2.66	2.21	3.34	3.81	4.00
(7) Farm income in kind valuation adjustment	.40	.40	.50	.51	.53	.46	.63
(8) Depreciation on housing	2.7	2.83	2.97	3.16	3.45	3.72	4.1
(9) Total	84.0	88.00	93.93	96.70	105.03	110.30	115.5
B. Material outlays in organizations servicing households, in science and administration							
(1) Education (excluding science), health care and other communal services	3.25	3.50	3.74	4.04	4.23	4.66	5.09
(2) Housing, transportation and communication, other public sector services for consumption	2.15	2.37	2.62	2.96	3.33	3.60	3.96
(3) Depreciation on nonproductive capital excluding housing	1.70	2.09	2.53	2.92	3.31	3.83	4.25
(4) Other							
(a) Science and administration	.86	.91	.98	1.09	1.21	1.36	1.48
(b) Residual	.1	.39	.72	.40	.44	.33	.1
(c) Total	1.0	1.30	1.70	1.49	1.65	1.69	1.6
(5) Total	8.1	9.26	10.59	11.41	12.52	13.78	14.9
C. Total consumption fund	92.1	97.26	104.52	108.11	117.55	124.08	130.4

TABLE 25 (continued)

2. Accumulation fund							
A. Net increase of fixed capital	21.8	22.8	25.3	25.3	28.4	28.2	28.9
B. Net increase of inventories and reserves							
(1) Public sector inventory investment	7.90	9.41	4.80	6.06	5.74	7.97	11.63
(2) State-cooperative increment of unfinished construction	−.12	1.54	2.34	3.43	1.34	.10	.85
(3) Increment of warehouse stocks of equipment requiring installation	—	.10	.18	.52	.40	.33	.13
(4) Other: increment of collective farm unfinished construction, private agricultural stocks and state reserves	5.0	1.8	5.7	7.6	9.1	5.7	7.8
(5) Total	12.8	12.8	13.0	17.6	16.6	14.1	20.4
C. Total accumulation fund	34.6	35.6	38.3	42.9	45.0	42.3	49.3
3. Net material product utilized	126.7	132.9	142.8	151.0	162.5	166.4	179.7

Sources:

1. *Consumption fund.*

A. *Personal consumption.* Entries for items (1), (4), (5), (6) are taken from Table 6. Sources of other figures are as follows:

(2) *Utilities.* Below, p. 354.

(3) *"Industrial" services.* Below, p. 359. The 1958 figure is estimated from the 1959–1964 series.

(7) *Income in kind adjustment.* For the rationale, methodology, and 1959–1963 values, see p. 358. Values for 1958 and 1964 were computed as indicated there.

(8) *Depreciation on housing.* Entries for 1959–1963 are taken directly from *NKh 1964*, pp. 584–585, and the 1958 and 1964 figures are estimated from the 1959–1963 data.

(9) *Total.* 1958, 1964: *VS*, 1966, No. 4, p. 96. 1959–1963: *NKh 1964*, pp. 584–585.

1.B. *Material outlays in organizations, etc.*

(1) *Education (excluding science), health, etc.* Appendix Table J-2, items 2.C (1) (b), 2.C (2) (b) and 6.B.

(2) *Housing, etc.* Material outlays in housing are estimated on the assumption that they account for 25 percent of actual current outlays on socialized housing. Current outlays are calculated as the product of the unit outlay including subsidy (1.58 rubles per square meter of floor space) and the housing stock (pp. 487–488 and 339). The figures for other components of this item are derived from sources explained on p. 486 and using the data of Table J-2.

(3) *Depreciation on nonproductive capital excluding housing.* See sources for item 1.A. (8) above.

(4) *Other.*

(a) *Science and administration.* Table J-2, items 7.B and 8.B.

(b) *Residual.* Item 1.B(4)(c) less item 1.B(4)(a).

(c) *Total.* Item 1.B(5) less the sum of items 1.B(1) through 1.B(3).

(5) *Total.* See sources to item 1.A(9) above.

1.C. *Total consumption fund.* See sources to item 1.A(9) above.

2. *Accumulation fund.*

Figures for items 2.A, 2.B(5) and 2.C are taken from *VS*, 1966, No. 4, p. 96; those for items 2.B(1) and 2.B(3) from pp. 387, 392; those for items 2.B(2) from *NKh 1961*, p. 523, *NKh 1962*, p. 439, *NKh 1963*, p. 461 and *NKh 1964*, p. 523.

In all years, item 2.B(4) is calculated as a residual, the difference between item 2.B(5) and the sum of items 2.B(1)–2.B(3).

3. *Net material product utilized.* The sum of items 1.C and 2.C.

component of science and administration (item 1.B(4)(a)), the ultimate residual, item 1.B(4)(b), increases sharply in the first two years and declines thereafter. As already mentioned, the NMP distributions in the yearbooks divide category 1.B into outlays in "organizations servicing households" and in "science and administration," with depreciation included in both subcategories. These data may be compared with the figures from Table 25 as follows (billion rubles):

	1958	*1959*	*1960*	*1961*	*1962*	*1963*	*1964*
Material outlays in organization servicing households [43]	6.4	7.2	8.2	8.7	9.5	10.4	11.1
Of which:							
Items 1.B (1) and (2) of Table 25	5.4	5.9	6.4	7.0	7.6	8.3	9.1
Other	1.0	1.3	1.8	1.7	1.9	2.1	2.0
Material outlays in science and administration	1.7	2.1	2.4	2.7	3.0	3.4	3.8
Of which:							
Item 1.B (4) (c) of Table 25	1.0	1.3	1.7	1.5	1.7	1.7	1.6
Other	.7	.8	.7	1.2	1.3	1.7	2.2

The differences in the tabulation labelled "other" presumably represent depreciation, but the time patterns of these residuals do not inspire complete confidence, especially in the middle years of the period. Possibly, there is some depreciation by *khozraschet* organizations that has crept into items 1.B(1), (2), and (4) of Table 25 in varying proportions over the years, but the impact of this double-counting is difficult to gauge. At any rate, if the Table 25 estimates are even approximately correct, residual amounts available for the current material expenditures of the military establishment, apart from R&D costs, are surprisingly small.

Turning now to item 2.B(4) of Table 25, these entries may be taken as roughly indicative of the level and trend of additions to state reserves, on the seemingly plausible assumption that annual increments of both collective farm unfinished construction and private agricultural stocks are small.[44] It is clear from Soviet sources, as already indicated, that state reserves have some kind of military component. There is some evidence that this is not just "means of defense of a special nature," in Bor's euphemism, but generally hardware procurement. A recent statistical text by Riabushkin declares, in discussing Soviet official data:

---

[43] *NKh 1964,* p. 578; *NKh 1965,* p. 592.

[44] The increment of collective farm unfinished construction amounted to .08 billion rubles in 1959 and .02 billions in 1960 (Alekseeva and Voronin, *Nakoplenie i razvitie kolkhoznoi sobstvennosti,* 1963, pp. 58–59). There is no information on private inventories.

"Everything connected with consumption by the army—food, uniforms—enters into consumption, whereas the increment of armaments [*voennie sredstva, vooruzhenie*] and so on can be attributed only to accumulation."[45] Another source implies that the additions to reserves include "expenditures on arms" (*predmety vooruzheniia*).[46] The logic of a comparative calculation of NMP and "final product" by Eidel'man also points to the incorporation of hardware procurement in the accumulation category.[47]

But if it seems reasonably certain that military procurement is a component of additions to state reserves, it is still not clear how large is the relative weight of one in the other. The values of item 2.B(4) fluctuate considerably; particularly puzzling is the very low figure for 1959 compared with that for 1958 and later years. But of course the major problem is uncertainty about the level and trend of nonmilitary stockpiling.[48]

---

[45] Riabushkin, *Ekonomicheskaia statistika,* 1966, p. 176.

[46] Katz, *Proizvoditel'nost' truda v SSSR i glavnykh kapitalisticheskikh stranakh,* 1964, p. 52.

[47] Eidel'man, *Ekonomika i matematicheskie metody,* 1967, No. 4, pp. 533–534. For the economy as a whole, the difference between NMP produced and final product is ascribed to depreciation. As indicated earlier, produced NMP is larger than NMP utilized by material losses and the foreign trade balance. But part of the final product is also used for "defense needs." Therefore such outlays must be included in NMP utilized. Eidel'man defines "accumulation" as fixed capital and inventory investment plus additions to consumption stocks and reserves. The published NMP breakdowns provide exactly the same definition for "accumulation" but the figures are reported for "accumulation and other expenditures." What I have identified as the increment to state reserves, collective farm unfinished construction, and household agricultural stocks may therefore include "other"—namely, military—expenditures.

The comparison discussed here is similar to one appearing in Eidel'man's earlier book, *Mezhotraslevoi balans obshchestvennogo produkta,* 1966, pp. 293 ff.

On the evidence presented, perhaps we may understand Plyshevskii's linking of military outlays to "other expenditures, not entering directly into the composition of accumulation and consumption funds" (above, p. 157) as an allusion to the classification of the major military component, hardware procurement, in additions to reserves.

[48] In Becker, *Soviet Military Outlays Since 1955,* June 1964, pp. 58–60, I speculated on the possible magnitude of stockpiling of grain and Cuban sugar. I also noted there that state reserves may include gold and foreign exchange. If so, the annual increments may have been negative during much of this period. See below, pp. 397–398.

"Defense" Versus Military Outlays

If the reader has been following along this survey of distinctly unpromising terrain, it will have become clear that any general conclusions drawn must be hesitant and qualified. There is little doubt that Soviet military outlays are not coextensive with the announced budget expenditures on defense. The latter undoubtedly exclude outlays of the internal security forces and the bulk of investment in arms production. This is probably true of R&D as well. For the rest, there is some evidence that other military outlays are financed from the national economy appropriations; because we know little about the composition of the budget expenditure residual, it too has come under suspicion.[49]

Obviously, these imprecise indications cannot be easily quantified. The national economy and budget expenditure residuals, net of procurement subsidies but gross of internal security outlays, run 4–6 billion rubles annually; the industry and construction residual accounts for possibly as much again.[50] If the 60 percent relation between unidentified union budget and total budget outlays on science which Nimitz found for the middle 1950s persisted into the 1960s, the unidentified union outlays would have risen from 1 billion rubles in 1958 to 2.4 billions in 1964 (Table D-2). Thus, leaving out of account the financing of investment in munitions production, the residuals turned up provide roughly 10–15 billion rubles of sources of additional military outlays over and above the identified defense outlay. The fraction of the indicated range that is in fact an appropriate estimate of concealed military outlays cannot be determined from the information on the budget residuals alone. Nor can

---

However, one must resist the temptation to assume that the listed commodities and little else comprise all of state reserves. Even more mundane items may have some weight in the total. A Soviet book on input-output shows a hypothetical balance of vegetable oil, with 1.7 percent of total resources and 2.7 percent of total utilization stemming from or directed to state reserves (Burshtein and Gusev, *Chto takoe mezhotraslevoi balans,* 1963, p. 59).

[49] A minor additional source of understatement of military outlays is connected with social welfare payments. Except for pensions and grants to officers financed from "defense," these payments to servicemen and their families are made through the budget divisions shown as items 2.C and 2.D in Table 24. *The Soviet Financial System,* 1968, pp. 176.

[50] Based on CIA estimates for the late 1950s and early 1960s. See *The Soviet Budget for 1961,* June 1961, p. 27, and *The Soviet Budget for 1962,* November 1962, p. 24.

we draw much help from the reconstruction of the NMP use distribution. The implication of my discussion is that apart from military subsistence, construction, and R&D, material outlays in this distribution can be associated with residuals totalling 5–15 billion rubles in 1958–1964. These residuals in turn can be associated with the budget allocation to defense or with any of the other budget residuals discussed.

Whatever concealed military outlays there are in the budget expenditure, national economy, and industry and construction residuals can find their reflection in my accounts only in the public sector expenditures on internal security and on outlays n.e.c.[51] Except in 1960, the sum of these two items varies between 2–4 billion rubles, considerably below the estimated value of the indicated budget residuals. Suppose that I have underestimated outlays n.e.c. by underestimating the share of miscellaneous budget revenues rightfully entered in the SNIP accounts. On the assumption that the correct proportion to be entered is not 75 percent but 90 percent, outlays n.e.c. would be augmented by one billion rubles in 1958 and by 2 billions in 1964.[52] Thus, again with the exception of 1960, it is possible to find 3–5 billion rubles of SNIP outlays to match, say, 6–12 billion rubles of budget residuals. Since outlays n.e.c. are believed to include some civilian investment and operational outlays,[53] the magnitude of military expenditures concealed therein is not likely to be large.

At established prices, the explicit defense outlay absorbed between 5.0 (1960) and 6.4 (1963) percent of total GNP, as I have estimated it (Table 15). Addition of internal security outlays, although in fact only the portion devoted to the militarized forces should be added, would raise that share by about a point, as would perhaps addition of the appropriate component of R&D outlays. Thus, without accounting for either investment in military production and military facilities or the military component of outlays n.e.c., the estimate of the share of total resources devoted to military purposes is raised by roughly 2 percentage points. Incorporation of expenditures concealed in outlays n.e.c. could not raise the relative weight of military outlay above one-tenth of total

---

[51] R&D expenditures financed from sources other than the budget allocation earmarked for science but reported in total science expenditures would be incorporated in my R&D series. "Outlays n.e.c." should be understood, again, to include the public sector statistical discrepancy.

[52] Cf. Tables 3 and M-1.

[53] Below, pp. 395 ff.

resources. In the present state of our information, it seems perilous to venture beyond these sketchy conclusions and attempt to trace year to year changes in the military's claim on aggregate output. Our ignorance of price behavior in the military sphere is an additional reason to forswear an attempt to estimate as well the *real* growth of military outlays.

A Concluding Reflection

It is regrettable that so little concrete can be said on this subject, but what little has been said may also be wide of the mark. The hunt for residuals is pursued with enthusiasm by many; it arouses the sporting instinct. In the process, the identity of the quarry is frequently forgotten. The search for concealed military expenditures in budget categories other than "defense" is after all predicated on a simple assumption: what is revealed is identified and therefore innocuous; what is not revealed is mysterious and suspicious.[54] At times it is recognized that the second clause is not always valid, that not all residuals are concealments; some are simply collections of miscellany. The validity of the first clause of the assumption is less frequently questioned.

I am not referring here to the famous question of falsification by keeping two sets of books, one for operational purposes and the other for the outside world. Bergson, I think, has long since disposed of that issue.[55] More significant is the manifold complexity of Soviet government accounting and how little we know about it. Even in the United States, where information on military expenditures is dispensed with open-handed largesse relative to the state of information in the USSR, impor-

[54] On occasion, the passion of the chase is so strong that the rules of the game are completely ignored. Sosnovy (*Foreign Affairs,* April 1964, pp. 492–493) finds concealed expenditures in the budgetary surplus of revenue over expenditure. He declares: "It can be assumed that half that surplus is used for espionage, the financing of Communist parties in other countries, and other subversive activities in all vulnerable parts of the world." I have already indicated (p. 33) that some mystery attaches to the nature of the budgetary surplus. But Sosnovy makes no attempt to grapple with this question and adduces no evidence in support of his claim. There are other dubious assertions in this article, including the claims that defense industry absorbs 29.0 percent of the budget appropriation to industry and construction and that the budgetary expenditure residual finances additions to reserves (p. 490). Neither of these claims is documented.

[55] See *SNIP 1937,* pp. 6–9.

tant operations can and have been kept secret: for examples we need turn only to the concealed budgets of the CIA and the NSA. There is no question of two sets of books here, only of imperfectly understood accounting relations. It should be sobering to recognize that our understanding of Soviet counterparts is considerably less advanced.[56]

---

[56] Anyone familiar with my earlier paper on this subject, *Soviet Military Outlays Since 1955,* June 1964, will perceive that I have become less sanguine than I was then about the prospects of deriving total Soviet military outlays from an exercise in hunting residuals. Paradoxically, I owe part of this increased bearishness to the painstaking and detailed exposition of the authors of *The Soviet Financial System,* 1968. Their effort has notably advanced the state of our knowledge, but it has simultaneously impressed me with the size of the gaps yet remaining. However, I do not know whether the authors of *The Soviet Financial System* share my skepticism of the fruitfulness of the residuals approach to estimating Soviet military expenditures.

8

Investment, Capital, and Output

The material presented in Chapters 5 and 6 dealt with the structure and growth of Soviet output in general terms. In Chapter 7 I attempted a close range view of a major nonconsumption end use, military outlays. This chapter undertakes a more detailed analysis of the other and quantitatively more important nonconsumption end use, investment. The analysis proceeds under two broad headings: first, the sectoral structure and growth of investment; second, the relation between aggregate investment and capital on one hand, and output on the other, in terms of both current and constant prices. No pretense to complete coverage of the topic is intended; investment and capital in the SYP period could well be the subject of a separate volume and much of what such a treatment would encompass is properly outside my terms of reference. I restrict myself instead to a discussion of aspects of the question that seem to have a more direct relation to the core content of the present study.[1]

Sectoral Distribution and Growth of Investment

As a basic source for a discussion of investment patterns in the SYP period, Table 26 presents various elements of gross and net fixed capital investment by sector. Figures are presented for 1965S as well as for 1958–1964, but only the latter will be discussed here; the 1965S estimates are treated in Chapter 9. Item 1 reproduces the investment estimates used in the current EP series of this study (Table 6). For the state-cooperative sector, this includes gross new investment (item 2.A of

---

[1] For a comprehensive treatment of Soviet capital formation and its relation to growth of output since 1928 see Moorsteen and Powell, *The Soviet Capital Stock 1928–1962*, 1966.

TABLE 26

GROSS AND NET FIXED CAPITAL INVESTMENT, 1958–1964 AND 1965S
(billion rubles except percent in row 10.C)

	1958	1965S	1959	1960	1961	1962	1963	1964
1. SNIP gross fixed investment at "current" prices								
A. State-cooperative	30.35	54.2	33.71	37.93	40.78	43.50	47.30	51.40
B. Collective farms	3.04	6.2	3.33	3.20	3.20	3.43	3.39	3.60
C. Private housing and livestock	3.30	3.5	3.52	3.42	3.09	2.50	.95	2.11
D. Total	36.69	63.9	40.56	44.55	47.07	49.43	51.64	57.11
2. Gross new investment, at "constant" estimate prices								
A. State-cooperative	24.52	44.5	27.41	30.80	32.75	34.81	37.01	40.37
B. Collective farms	2.84	5.9	3.53	3.17	3.16	3.27	3.42	3.91
C. Private housing	2.65	3.5	3.05	2.74	2.37	2.07	1.79	1.66
D. Total	30.01	53.9	33.99	36.71	38.28	40.15	42.22	45.94
3. Gross new capital increments, at "constant" estimate prices								
A. State-cooperative	23.77	43.2	25.16	28.06	28.73	32.75	36.22	38.69
B. Collective farms	2.6	5.4	3.4	2.8	2.7	3.2	3.3	3.6
C. Private housing	2.7	3.5	3.1	2.7	2.4	2.0	1.8	1.7
D. Total	29.1	52.1	31.7	33.6	33.8	38.0	41.3	44.0
4. Capital repairs at current prices								
A. State-cooperative	5.83	9.7	6.20	6.95	7.51	8.29	9.96	10.90
B. Collective farms	.38	.8	.68	.70	.66	.63	.62	.7
C. Private housing	.70	.9	.73	.75	.77	.79	.80	.82
D. Total	6.91	11.4	7.61	8.40	8.94	9.71	11.38	12.4
5. Gross new increments plus capital repairs								
A. State-cooperative	29.60	52.9	31.36	35.01	36.24	41.04	46.18	49.59
B. Collective farms	3.0	6.2	4.1	3.5	3.4	3.8	3.9	4.3
C. Private housing	3.4	4.4	3.8	3.5	3.2	2.8	2.6	2.5
D. Total	36.0	63.5	39.3	42.0	42.8	47.6	52.7	56.4
6. Depreciation at book values								
A. State-cooperative	9.2	16.6	10.5	12.0	13.6	15.0	19.7	21.6
B. Collective farms	.9	1.8	1.1	1.0	1.1	1.3	1.6	1.7
C. Private housing	1.4	1.9	1.5	1.5	1.5	1.6	1.6	1.6
D. Total	11.5	20.3	13.1	14.5	16.2	17.9	22.9	24.9
7. Gross new increments plus capital repairs less depreciation								
A. State-cooperative	20.4	36.3	20.9	23.0	22.6	26.0	26.5	28.0
B. Collective farms	2.1	4.4	3.0	2.5	2.3	2.5	2.3	2.6
C. Private housing	2.0	2.5	2.3	2.0	1.7	1.2	1.0	.9
D. Total	24.5	43.2	26.2	27.5	26.6	29.7	29.8	31.5

TABLE 26 (continued)

8. Residual book value of all capital retirements	1.1	..	1.7	1.1	1.2	1.8	1.2	1.2
9. Accidental losses, all sectors	1.0	..	1.0	1.0	1.0	1.0	1.0	1.0
10. Aggregate net investment, current prices								
A. Row 7.D less rows 8 and 9	22.4	..	23.5	25.4	24.4	26.9	27.6	29.3
B. Official data	21.8	..	22.8	25.3	28.4	28.4	28.2	28.9
C. Difference between rows 10.A and 10.B as percent of 10.B	+3	..	+3	0	−16	−5	−2	+1
D. Estimate for 1965S		40						

Source: Appendix P.

Table 26), plus capital repairs and changes in warehouse stocks of equipment requiring installation. Collective farm investment entries in row 1.B derive from money expenditures, whereas the series in 2.B represents official data at estimate prices.

Data on investment by the state-cooperative sectors are defined as being gross of acquisitions of draft livestock, but net of "acquisitions and formation of basic herds." [2] I interpret this to mean that the data exclude (1) purchases of productive livestock and (2) capital outlays on rearing either productive or draft livestock. With respect to collective farm data, the source cited declares that the data exclude "expenditures on acquisition of livestock and formation of basic herds." I take this phrase to mean that livestock outlays are totally excluded from the reported data on collective farm investment at estimate prices. The inference is that the only livestock investment included in the official figures is acquisition of draft livestock by the state-cooperative sectors.

Gross new capital increments (the Russian term is *vvod v deistvie osnovnykh fondov*) differ from gross new investment in the exclusion of both the increment of unfinished construction and of minor expenditures not yielding additional "basic funds." The major component is the former: numerically it accounted for the predominant part of the difference between new investment and new increments in the SYP period, except in 1958 and 1963, years when the increment of unfinished construction was negative or at a positive level less than a billion rubles.[3]

[2] *NKh 1964*, pp. 511, 822.

[3] For unfinished construction values, see *NKh 1964*, p. 522. These are not necessarily at the same prices as either new investment or increments.

The sources do not say explicitly that livestock investment is excluded from reported gross increments; neither do they show livestock as included.[4] However, given the close numerical relation between gross increments and new investment, it seems reasonable to infer that the coverage of new investment data is applicable to the gross increment data as well.

Depreciation in the table consists of both actual amortization allowances charged to cost and imputed weat and tear. The imputations are Soviet-made, inferred from Soviet data, and probably computed on a straight line formula. State-cooperative depreciation increases sharply in 1963 when amortization norms were raised. Book value of retirements is the residual depreciated value of an asset at the moment of retirement after deducting scrapping costs or adding net sales proceeds. Presumably, the residual may be positive or negative, but because of historically inadequate Soviet depreciation rates and rising asset prices (at least until 1950), it has tended on balance to be positive. The entry for accidental capital losses refers to losses not foreseen and therefore not part of the normal capital consumption allowance, amortization. In Soviet accounting such losses are charged to net income.

Throughout the preceding portions of this study I have focused on gross magnitudes—gross investment, gross national product. Discussion of net investment and net national product have doubtless been conspicuous by their absence. I need hardly add that diffidence on this score is occasioned by uncertainty on the meaning and adequacy of Soviet capital consumption allowances, not to speak of the familiar but still thorny theoretical problem of measuring capital consumption. The display of net investment series in Table 26 does not signify any resolution of these doubts but is justified by two considerations: first, the possibility —at least in principle, although, as will become clear shortly, not in practice—of using net investment series and their components to test or clarify official measurements; second, to test, if only roughly, the sensitivity of conclusions on growth, sectoral distribution, and investment-output rates to the distinction between net and gross magnitudes.

The choice of the particular forms of gross and net investment represented in Table 26 also requires some explanation. Soviet national accounting views changes in the capital stock in two different ways. The approaches differ in terms of both treatment of capital consumption and basis of valuation. Capital stock changes in the first method are defined as net investment, where depreciation, the residual book value of retire-

[4] *Ibid.*, p. 821.

ments, and accidental losses (all at original cost) are deducted from the sum of gross new capital increments plus capital repairs[5] (at current prices). Alternatively, changes in the stock may be computed at constant prices and gross of depreciation, with the full value of retirements and accidental losses deducted from gross new capital increments.[6] Official indexes of capital growth, both those published before the capital census and revaluation of January 1, 1960 and those published subsequently,[7] were computed from values gross of depreciation—that is, calculations of the second type. However, values of net investment reported in the yearbooks are exclusively of the first type and are shown as channels of utilization of NMP.[8]

Since the yearbooks have reported the absolute values of fixed capital for particular years, we could in principle infer annual increments from these data and the reported indexes. Unfortunately, the succeeding yearbooks have frequently incorporated changes in coverage or valuation without providing a complete retrospective time series. The effect may be gauged from the following tabulation of the available data on indexes of the total stock (including livestock) at the end of the year. The tabulation is arranged by yearbook in chronological order, with the yearbooks grouped to highlight the discrete changes.

	Indexes, 1940 = 100								
Yearbook Group[9]	*1950*	*1958*	*1959*	*1960*	*1961*	*1962*	*1963*	*1964*	*1965*
I	119	..	241	264	288				
II	..	219	246	269	293	320			
III	118	224	..	275	..	324	354	383	413
IV	117	242	..	289	..	..	..	403	437

[5] Strictly, capital increments originating from repairs, rather than gross capital repairs including unfinished repairs.

[6] Sobol', *Ocherki po voprosam balansa narodnogo khoziaistva,* 1960, pp. 166, 172–173, 210–211, 220–223. Sobol' was chief of the Central Statistical Administration's Department of the National Economic Balance. See also Morozova, *Balans narodnogo khoziaistva i metody ego postroeniia,* 1961, p. 91; Petrov, ed., *Kurs ekonomicheskoi statistiki,* 3rd edition, 1961, pp. 422–427.

[7] *NKh 1958,* pp. 58–59, on one hand; on the other, starting with *NKh 1959* (pp. 66–67) and continuing through each succeeding yearbook in greater or lesser detail.

[8] On the definitional and numerical relations between the two types of capital increments, see the addendum at the end of this chapter.

[9] I: *NKh 1959,* p. 66; *NKh 1960,* p. 85; *NKh 1961,* p. 68. II: *Tsifry 1962,* p. 33; *NKh 1962,* p. 53; *Tsifry 1963,* p. 31. III: *NKh 1963,* p. 55; *NKh 1964,* p. 68; *Tsifry 1965,* p. 27. IV: *NKh 1965,* p. 64.

To return to Table 26, the elements of that table then correspond or are related to elements of both types of Soviet calculations of capital changes. To some extent, therefore, the separate elements of Table 26 may be used to build up totals that should correspond relatively well to the official data and may therefore serve as checks on the latter. However, the coexistence of the two types of calculations in the table is precarious. The table heading does not, for example, identify the prices at which investment is valued. In fact there are several sets of prices underlying the data: new investment and capital increments reported in official sources are said to be valued at "comparable" prices representing July 1, 1955 estimate prices with minor adjustments introduced in 1956, 1958, and 1959.[10] Capital repairs, it is believed, are expressed in current prices; depreciation as well, presumably, as book value of retirements and capital losses are valued at original cost.[11] The residual book values of retirements represent the inheritance of different periods during which very substantial price changes occurred. Of course, this constitutes as

---

[10] *NKh 1964,* p. 507, note 1.

[11] In theory, depreciation was calculated on the new values of capital from 1960 on. In fact, it is not all clear that this was done. Thus, annual state-cooperative amortization allowances, in terms of absolute values and percentage increases, were as follows (p. 379):

	1958	*1959*	*1960*	*1961*	*1962*
Billion rubles	7.06	7.94	9.10	10.21	11.30
Percent increase over previous year		12	15	12	11

Now the census and revaluation of January 1960 had resulted in an increase in value of 12.4 percent for the inventoried capital, an aggregate essentially identical to that category of state-cooperative capital for which amortization allowances are computed (*NKh 1959,* pp. 65, 72–73). Hence, in addition to the effect of real capital formation in 1960, the 1960 increment in amortization allowances should reflect the increased valuation base. The actual increase was 15 percent compared with 12 percent in 1959 and 1961; according to *NKh 1962,* p. 53, total fixed capital (including the slower growing capital of collective farms and the private sector) rose 9 percent in 1960.

It is true that the amortization data are taken from a post-1960 source, and we cannot make a direct check on the possibility that the data for 1958–1959 were not revised to take account of the post-1959 capital value. However, a pre-1960 source (Bunich, *VE,* 1959, No. 9, p. 3) cites a 1957 figure for allowances of 6.34 billion rubles and a 1959 plan figure of 8.1 billion rubles. These seem to be consistent with the 1958–1959 figures shown at the beginning of this note.

much a mark against the Central Statistical Administration's accounts as against Table 26. Regrettably, the yearbooks do not report gross investment at current prices, or capital repairs, depreciation, and the like at constant prices.

This is not the only methodological deficiency of Table 26. There are also gaps in coverage apart from the indicated exclusion of most livestock investment. Private sector production structures and investment by fishing cooperatives are omitted, although the latter item is small, only 26 million rubles in 1958.[12] Private *dacha* (summer residence) construction is not included in the official statistics of the value of private housing investment[13] nor, presumably, in the reported value of housing construction in physical units. It is not known whether *dacha* construction is independently estimated by the CSA for the national balances.

For these reasons it should not be surprising that Table 26 is unable to replicate exactly the official aggregate net investment series. But by the same token, it seems doubtful that we can in fact test the accuracy of the official series by building up comparable totals, and we must instead consider the usefulness of the building blocks in the light of the agreement or lack of agreement between official and reconstructed totals. For seven of the eight years in the series the margin of difference is tolerable, within ±5 percent of the official figures, although changes in sign and magnitude of the relative difference make the reconstructed totals somewhat misleading guides to the annual changes in the official series. However, the data for 1961 provide an obvious special case: the reconstructed total is 4 billion rubles or 16 percent short of the official total.

I know of no explanatory evidence bearing directly on this anomaly for 1961, but the considerable amount of information that has emerged in connection with the Soviet input-output table for 1959 may be scrutinized for aid in clarifying the sources of the other differences shown in row 10.C. Unhappily, this information is inconclusive.[14] It

---

[12] *Kapstroi*, pp. 40, 152.

[13] *Ibid.*, p. 8.

[14] (1) The foreign trade balance in 1959 has been reported as an import surplus of 3.8 billion (domestic) rubles, the difference between 9.1 billions of imports and 5.3 billions of exports. (Efimov and Berri, *Metody planirovaniia mezhotraslevykh proportsii*, 1965, pp. 96–97. These figures also appear in Treml's reconstruction of the table in *New Directions in the Soviet Economy*, 1966, facing p. 269.) The margin between produced and utilized NMP, recently defined as "replacement of losses and the foreign trade balance" (*NKh 1965*, p. 592; see also above, p. 157, note 41) was 3.3 billion

rubles in 1959. (Compare *NKh 1965*, p. 589 and *VS*, 1966, No. 4, p. 96.) By subtraction, replacement of losses is a staggering 7.1 billion rubles. In principle, this figure includes the value of inventories lost as well as of fixed capital. Nevertheless, the figure is uncomfortably larger than the 1.0 billion rubles entered in Table 26, "uncomfortably" if only because it implies a more than 5 billion ruble understatement of the 1959 entry in row 7.D. I cannot explain this paradox, but it is impossible to accept the 7 billion ruble figure as a reasonable estimate of capital losses.

(2) Efimov and Berri also provide a figure for the value of "amortization" on productive capital, including the residual book value of retirements, 9.5 billion rubles. This should be conceptually equivalent to the sum of depreciation and the residual value of retirements in Table 26, less the value of depreciation on nonproductive capital (reported as 4.9 billion rubles, *NKh 1964*, p. 584). The value of this expression is 9.9 billion rubles, or but 4 percent greater than the Efimov-Berri figure.

(3) Eidel'man cites data from which we may infer a rough distribution of net fixed investment by sector, excluding investment in livestock. This distribution may be compared with that of Table 26 and the official total as follows (billion rubles):

	Official total	*Eidel'man data*	*Table 26 values*
State-cooperative	..	19.0	19.2
Collective farms	..	2.2	3.0
Private:			
Productive	..	.1	..
Nonproductive	..	1.7	2.3
All sectors	22.8	23.0	24.5

The Eidel'man data are taken from his *Mezhotraslevoi balans obshchestvennogo produkta*, 1966. I converted his relative breakdowns of productive, nonproductive, and total investment, p. 171, into absolute distributions on the basis of the indications that net investment in the state sector in 1959 was 19.3 billion rubles, of which 12.0 was in productive and 7.3 in nonproductive components (p. 172), and that aggregate net investment by all sectors was distributed between productive and nonproductive components in the proportions 60:40 (pp. 171–172). The Table 26 values refer to item 7, except that the residual book value of retirements is subtracted from the state-cooperative entry in row 7.A for comparability with the Eidel'man data.

If the Eidel'man distribution is consistent with the official total, (a) livestock investment (assuming no other differences) must have been −.2 billion rubles, (b) the Table 26 collective farm and private housing investment entries are considerably overstated, unless accidental capital losses originated exclusively in private and collective farm capital. (Whatever the truth of the latter condition—and, as indicated below, it seems highly unlikely—the approximate consistency of the totals in the three columns implies that capital losses could not have been as high as 7 billion rubles.)

cannot identify the reliable and unreliable elements of Table 26 and it provides no clue to the reasons for the downturn of the reconstructed net investment series in 1961. In the absence of any other information—for example, pointing to a significant increase in investment prices in 1961—I will disregard the 1961 anomaly turned up by Table 26. Fortunately, the discussion in the remainder of this chapter is not particularly sensitive to the issue.

Trends in the sectoral structure of investment of this period may be seen in Table 27, which translates Table 26 into percentage distributions. Such breakdowns are shown for SNIP gross investment, gross new investment, gross new increments, capital repairs, depreciation, and a proxy for net investment—gross increments plus capital repairs less depreciation. The precise magnitude of the time changes varies slightly, but a general pattern is manifest for all the indicated elements of gross and net investment. With a relative weight in the total at or above the 80 percent level in 1958, state-cooperative sector investment assumed an increasingly more dominant role, reaching roughly 90 percent in 1964. That growth was, of course, achieved at the expense of both collective and private sector investment, chiefly the latter.

The discussion up to now has focused on the data of Table 26 which unavoidably commingles series at current prices with those at allegedly constant estimate prices. Table 26 also deals only with fixed investment. At this point it may be useful to reintroduce the SNIP estimates at "constant" prices and to include all gross investment series as well. In presenting these data I remind the reader of the discussion at the beginning of Chapter 6 regarding the limitations of my deflation of investment. The implication of that discussion for present purposes is that the sectoral structure of gross fixed investment at either 1958 EP or 1964 EP cannot diverge substantially from the pattern traced by the corresponding series in Table 26.

Although livestock investment is difficult to estimate (see my discussion of private sector investment in livestock, pp. 304–307), it is hardly credible that overall investment was negative in a year when horse and goat counts declined but herds of cattle, hogs, and sheep and flocks of poultry were enlarged (*NKh 1962*, pp. 302, 307). As to the second implication, it seems likely that most of the capital losses refer to state-cooperative capital, the predominant element in the national stock. The overstatement would then have to be traced to (a) price differences between reported data at estimate prices and the current-price data presumably used by Eidel'man, (b) overstatement of capital repairs, (c) understatement of depreciation, or combinations of these factors.

TABLE 27
STRUCTURE OF GROSS AND NET FIXED CAPITAL INVESTMENT BY SECTOR, 1958–1964
(percent)

	1958	1959	1960	1961	1962	1963	1964
1. SNIP gross investment							
A. State-cooperative	82.7	83.1	85.1	86.6	88.0	91.6	90.0
B. Collective farms	8.3	8.2	7.2	6.8	6.9	6.6	6.3
C. Private housing and livestock	9.0	8.7	7.8	6.6	5.1	1.8	3.7
2. Gross new investment							
A. State-cooperative	81.7	80.6	83.9	85.6	86.7	87.7	87.9
B. Collective farms	9.5	10.4	8.6	8.3	8.1	8.1	8.5
C. Private housing	8.8	9.0	7.5	6.2	5.2	4.2	3.6
3. Gross new increments							
A. State-cooperative	81.8	79.5	83.6	84.9	86.3	87.7	88.0
B. Collective farms	8.9	10.7	8.3	8.0	8.4	8.0	8.2
C. Private housing	9.3	9.8	8.0	7.1	5.3	4.4	3.9
4. Capital repairs							
A. State-cooperative	84.4	81.5	82.7	84.0	85.4	87.5	87.9
B. Collective farms	5.5	8.9	8.3	7.4	6.5	5.4	5.6
C. Private housing	10.1	9.6	8.9	8.6	8.1	7.0	6.5
5. Depreciation							
A. State-cooperative	80.0	80.2	82.8	84.0	83.8	86.0	86.7
B. Collective farms	7.8	8.4	6.9	6.8	7.3	7.0	6.8
C. Private housing	11.3	11.5	10.3	9.3	8.9	7.0	6.4
6. Gross increments plus capital repairs less depreciation							
A. State-cooperative	83.3	79.8	83.6	85.0	87.5	88.9	88.9
B. Collective farms	8.6	11.5	9.1	8.6	8.4	7.7	8.3
C. Private housing	8.2	8.8	7.3	6.4	4.0	3.4	2.9

Note: In each column and for each item, A., B., and C. entries total 100 percent.
Source: Computed from Table 26.

This is, of course, borne out by comparison of Table 27 with Fig. 9, the latter showing sectoral distribution of the constant-price SNIP investment series at four basic valuations. Figure 9 also bears on the patterns of all gross investment. The rapid expansion of the state-cooperative sectoral share at the expense of the relative weights of investment by collective farms and the private sector is sharply outlined with respect to both fixed and all gross investment. Sensitivity to weight year is not, and by virtue of the characteristics of the deflation procedure, cannot be marked. Nor do we observe sensitivity to factor cost adjustments. With regard to state-cooperative investment, valuation at 1964

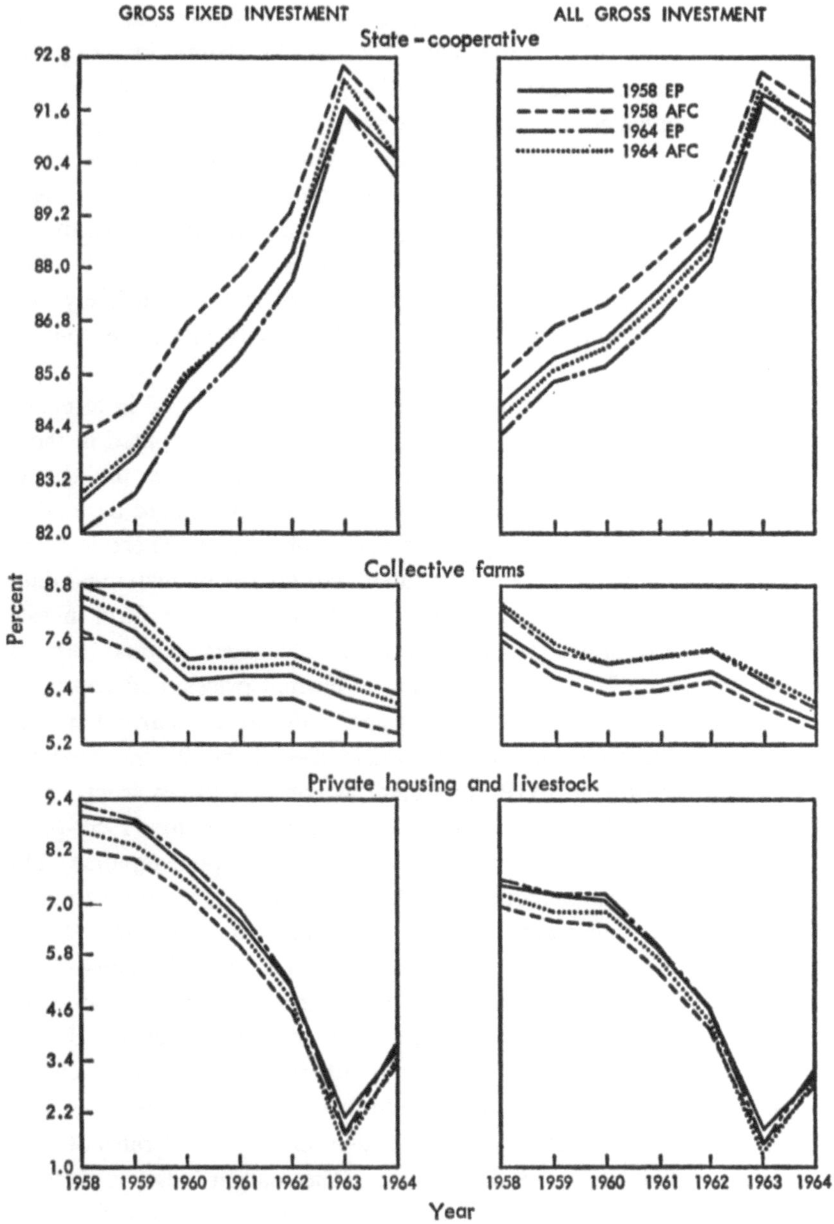

Fig. 9—Sectoral distribution of investment at constant prices, basic series, 1958 - 1964 (percent)

Source: Tables K-1 and K-2.

prices lowers the shares relative to valuation at 1958 prices; adjustments of EP values tend, on the other hand, to raise the shares. Precisely the reverse is true of investment by collective farms and the private sector. However, as indicated, the changes are generally small; more important, the shifts in valuation do not alter either the direction of change or its approximate amplitude. Possibly, somewhat more distinct changes might become evident with a more thoroughgoing deflation, altering the investment price relationship between the sectors. But the weight of state-cooperative investment is preponderant, and it does not seem likely that changes in the observed patterns could substantially affect the conclusions drawn above.

The gross and net investment patterns can also be viewed in terms of rates of growth, as in Table 28. Rates of growth are computed in the $\hat{r}$ formula, on the reasoning set out in Chapter 6. However, the results reflect an unavoidable conglomerate of valuations and should be treated with a correspondingly appropriate measure of reserve. There is some basis for treating the gross new investment and gross new increment data in Table 26 as constant price values,[15] but SNIP collective farm investment values are drawn from current-price balances, capital repairs (except to private housing) are valued at current prices, and depreciation at a combination of original cost and constant and current prices. As a partial corrective for these inconsistencies, Table 28 incorporates (1) rates of growth of SNIP investment at constant prices from Table 20, (2) a crude deflation of public sector capital repairs to a 1958-price basis (deflation is unnecessary for private housing capital repairs), and (3) adjustment of state-cooperative depreciation in 1958–1962 to conform to the new higher amortization norms introduced in 1963. These adjustments do not eliminate all the inconsistencies of valuation—there remains the question of the compatibility of gross increment time-series valued at estimate prices with capital repairs at 1958 prices and depreciation at a heterogeneous valuation—but an important obstacle to drawing inferences on real growth should thereby be eliminated.

Gross investment by the state-cooperative sector grew at rates of 8 or 9 percent; capital repairs, a point higher. The margin between sectoral growth rates is gaping,[16] with private investment, except for capital

---

[15] See the discussion on investment-price changes in Appendix K.

[16] For collective farms the differences between growth rates under item 1 and those under items 2–5 is explained by the differences between SNIP estimates and the reported data in official sources.

TABLE 28

AVERAGE ANNUAL RATES OF GROWTH ($\hat{r}$) OF GROSS AND NET FIXED INVESTMENT, 1958–1964
(percent)

	State-Cooperative	Collective Farms	Private Sector [a]	Total
1. SNIP gross fixed investment				
1958 EP	8.5	1.4	−11.9	6.7
1958 AFC	8.5	1.4	−12.3	6.8
1964 EP	8.5	1.4	−12.5	6.6
1964 AFC	8.5	1.5	−12.7	6.7
2. Gross new investment	8.1	3.4	−8.8	6.5
3. Gross new increments	8.8	3.8	−9.0	7.1
4. Capital repairs, deflated	10.3	4.7	2.5	9.2
5. Gross new increments plus deflated capital repairs	9.1	4.1	−6.4	7.6
6. Depreciation [b]	13.0	11.5	2.1	11.9
7. Gross increments plus deflated capital repairs, less depreciation [b]	6.6	0.6	−13.7	4.6
8. Total net investment at current prices				
A. Reconstructed	..	..	..	4.3
B. Official	..	..	..	4.8

Notes:

[a] For SNIP gross fixed investment, housing plus livestock; for other rows, housing only.

[b] State-cooperative values in 1958–1962 are adjusted for new norms introduced in 1963.

Sources:

Row 1. Table 20.

Others. Computed from Table 26 with the following adjustments:

Row 4. The state-cooperative series at 1958 prices is taken from Table K-1. Collective farm repairs at current prices (from Table 26) have their material component deflated, with the aid of the estimated index of farm investment prices (below, p. 521). It is assumed that material outlays accounted for half of the total at current prices except in 1959 and 1960, when, because of sharp increases in prices, the materials share is assumed to have been 60 percent. Private housing repairs need not be deflated, as they are estimated in proportion to the growth of the physical stock.

Row 6. The introduction of new norms in 1963 raised depreciation in that year, on this account alone, by 2.3 billion rubles (*NKh 1963*, p. 501). It is assumed that this figure relates to the state-cooperative sectors alone and it implies a 17 percent increase in amortization allowances (below, p. 379). Therefore, depreciation figures in Table 26 for 1958–1962 are increased by 17 percent of the amortization allowances in the relevant years.

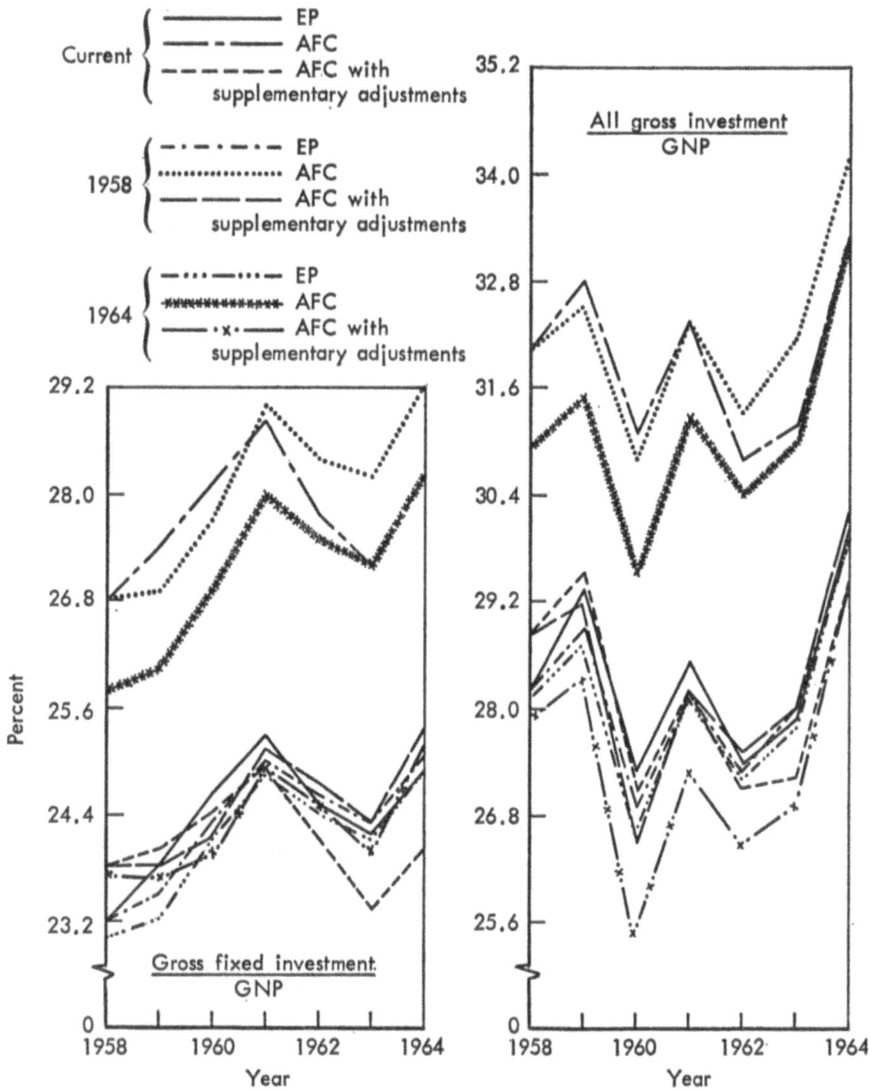

Fig. 10—The rate of gross investment at current and constant prices, 1958-1964

Sources: Table 15; Sources to Tables 16, 17, 23, K-1, and K-2.

repairs, declining precipitously. The implications with respect to government resource allocation policy are too obvious to require explicit statement.

Rates of growth of net investment in the public sectors are generally considerably below those for gross magnitudes, owing to the relatively high rates of increase of depreciation. This is the major reason for the comparatively low growth rates of aggregate net investment, item 8 of Table 28. (The poor record of private housing investment plays a role, but the overwhelming sectoral weight belongs to the public sectors.) The explanation of this phenomenon is, in part, one already advanced by Moorsteen and Powell: [17] the depreciation growth rate reflects the rate of change of the capital stock and the latter rate adjusts itself to the rate of change of investment only with some lag. But it is necessary to reckon with the distinction between investment net of retirements and investment net of depreciation. To repeat, it is the latter with which I am concerned in this section.

The significance of the finding is much less clear than the result itself. It is the meaningfulness of the depreciation rates that is at issue. Does straight-line depreciation make any technical or economic sense as an allowance for obsolescence or physical wear and tear? If it does, the high rate of growth of the gross capital stock (net of retirements)—some 8 or 9 percent per year,[18] in conjunction with the sharply lower rate of growth of net investment, which signifies an approaching decline in the rate of growth of the net capital stock, foreshadows a "retirement crisis." There is independent evidence of a Soviet policy of postponing retirements and making do with extensive capital repair. The latter point is attested to by the impressive public sector figures in row 4 of Table 28, and Soviet sources have been critical of what they consider to have been an inadequate rate of fixed capital retirements.[19] But if the appropriate depreciation model resembles the "one-hoss-shay," the rates of growth of net investment in Table 28 are understated, perhaps considerably.

Investment and Output

THE RATE OF INVESTMENT

Alternative views of the annual share of aggregate output devoted to investment are portrayed in Figs. 10 and 11. The focus of interest is on

---

[17] Moorsteen and Powell, *The Soviet Capital Stock 1928–1962*, 1966, pp. 329–340.

[18] Computed from the indexes shown above, p. 171.

[19] Kamenitzer, *VE*, 1965, No. 8, pp. 10–11, cites a number of examples illustrating the tendency of cumulated repair expenditures to exceed by far the replacement cost of a piece of equipment.

Fig. 10 and rates of gross investment.[20] Reasons for both the neglect of net aggregates throughout this study and their restricted appearance in this chapter were discussed in the previous section. Net investment rates are computed from official data with utilized NMP as denominator and from my estimates with a net national product denominator. Other differences between the two sets of ratios will be noted shortly. Rates of gross investment are shown for fixed investment alone and for all gross investment, at current and constant prices, and at alternative valuations within these categories.[21]

Whether in relation to gross or net investment, gross or net aggregate output, it is clear that it is impossible to speak of *the* rate of investment at a point in time. That conclusion was evident in Chapter 5; Figs. 10 and 11 add the further variety of net rates and, for gross rates, valuation at constant as well as current prices, to underscore the necessity of consistent valuations and product definitions. Valuation at basic factor cost, constant or current, raises the general level of investment shares markedly above that of EP rates. Supplementary adjustments, on the other hand, force the rates down again, and the movement of these ratios is only occasionally and marginally distinguished from that of EP ratios. This finding holds for both gross fixed and all gross investment rates. Again, the insignificant differences between trends at 1958 and at 1964 prices are predictable from the nature of the deflation procedure.

If Fig. 10 draws attention to level differences originating in differences of valuation, it is nevertheless characterized by some important regularities. At all valuations the general pattern is the same within each of the two broad categories of gross investment rates. Rates of gross fixed investment on a rising curve reach a peak in 1961, decline to 1963, and move up again in 1964. In all cases the terminal points are higher than the initial points; with respect to the series at constant prices, the terminal marks are higher than the 1961 levels as well. On the average, the rate of gross fixed investment may have risen slightly: the value of $\hat{r}$ is positive except for fixed investment at current AFC with supplementary adjustments; no value of $\hat{r}$ exceeds ± 1.5 percent.

---

[20] In computing rates of investment at AFC with supplementary adjustments, I have averaged rates where housing interest is imputed at either 5 or 10 percent. Figure 11 is found on p. 185.

[21] Although rates of investment are calculated for EP values, only the AFC calculations bear on resource allocation in terms of the theory outlined in Chapter 3.

At current factor cost, as was noted in Chapter 5, the rate of gross fixed investment exhibited little apparent trend. At constant prices there was an evident but small increase over the period. It should be clear by now that such a finding must be interpreted with caution. If the rate of investment is roughly stable at current prices and rising at constant prices this must be because investment prices are rising less rapidly or falling more rapidly than those of other final expenditures and of GNP as a whole.[22] In my calculations such a finding is the automatic consequence of assuming identity of current and constant new investment prices in the state-cooperative sector. To the extent that investment prices did in fact rise rather than remain stable as assumed, the divergence in trends of the rates of investment would be reduced or indeed the direction of difference reversed altogether. Since I cannot resolve the uncertainties surrounding the movement of investment prices, I am unable to specify whether and to what degree the divergence in trend of the rate of investment at different valuations is reliable. However, whatever changes overall did take place are small in magnitude. In Chapter 6 I speculated on the possible impact on *r* rates of growth of GNP of error in the state-cooperative fixed investment estimates. The maximum error postulated there implies a decline in the rate of fixed investment at 1958 EP or AFC of about 2 percentage points instead of the rise, as now computed, of roughly the same magnitude.

The sharp fluctuations of inventory investment make it equally difficult to phrase a simple conclusion with respect to the rate of all gross investment. The $\hat{r}$ rate of growth is negative for calculations at current factor cost, with or without supplementary adjustments, but positive at constant prices. As before the magnitude of the measured growth is small, less than 1 percent. Here, it is also necessary to bear in mind earlier discussion of the movement of public sector outlays n.e.c., particularly in 1959–1961, the implication of which is that the apparent changes in the rate of all investment, especially in 1959–1961, may not be reliable. To repeat, it may be best to view the rates of all gross investment in conjunction with other major elements of nonconsumption. But if we consider only all investment plus outlays n.e.c., as a proportion of GNP, the findings with respect to the average rate of growth are an echo of those outlined above: on the average, a decline at

---

[22] This is the explanation Bergson advanced to resolve the paradox of roughly equal rates of investment in 1928 and 1937 at current prices despite an intervening period of intensive industrialization.

current factor cost and an increase at constant prices; in all cases, however, the changes fall below 1 percentage point. That rates of investment changed so little in the SYP period is of course the most important conclusion to be drawn from this discussion, but I must defer further consideration of the significance of this result to Chapter 11.

There are some important incomparabilities in the net investment series of Fig. 11. The distinction between the solid and dashed line series in Fig. 11 is not just a matter of the different denominators but also of different numerators. This is apparent for the all net investment rates where the official data numerators include additions to state reserves and private sector inventories, as well as the public sector inventories represented in the numerators of the SNIP ratios.[23] But for both categories of net rates the numerators differ in degree of "netness." The capital consumption allowances of the official data include imputed depreciation on nonproductive capital in (largely) non-*khozraschet* organizations and imputed depreciation on private housing, as well as the residual undepreciated value of retirements and accidental damage to or loss of capital;[24] none of these elements is included in the SNIP depreciation series. Nor is the gross aggregate, from which capital consumption is deducted, the same in both series. The official data use gross new increments plus capital repairs; the corresponding SNIP series is gross new investment plus capital repairs and warehouse stocks of equipment requiring installations. The approximate differences may be gauged by comparing rows 1.D and 5.D of Table 26, although the comparison is further complicated by minor differences in coverage and valuation.

Whether because of these methodological deficiencies or in spite of them, the patterns of SNIP and official net investment rates are not too dissimilar. The movement of SNIP net fixed investment rates is paralleled by that of the official data series in all years except 1964; the changes for all net investment are in the same direction from 1960 on. Owing to the presumably greater value of SNIP compared with official net fixed investment, the SNIP rate of fixed investment is consistently higher than the corresponding official data rate. Official accumulation adds more to net fixed investment than does SNIP all net investment, and therefore the relative positions are inverted in the top half of Fig. 11, with SNIP all net investment rates lower than the rates calculated

[23] Warehouse stocks of equipment requiring installation are presumed incorporated in the inventories and reserves component of "accumulation."

[24] See the sources to item 6.A and 6.C of Table 26.

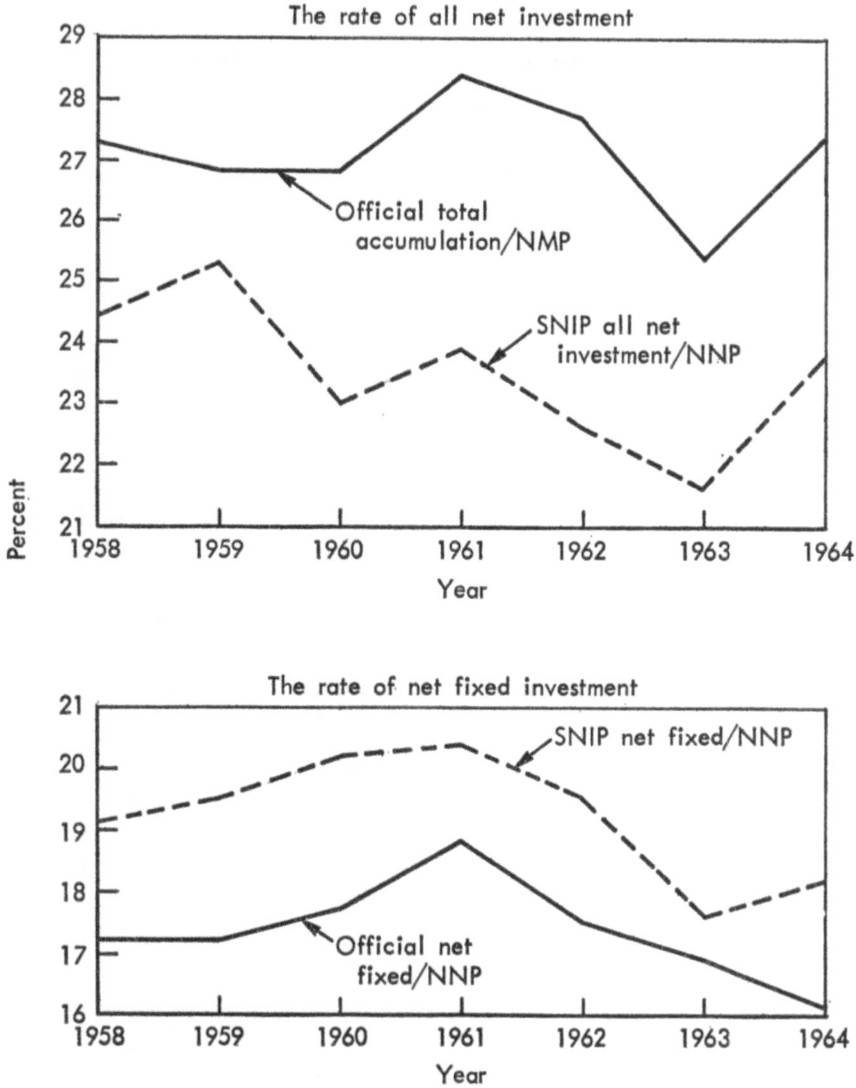

Fig. 11—The rate of net investment at current prices, 1958-1964

Sources: Tables 5 and 6; VS, 1966, No.4, p.96.

from official data. At the same time the absolute value of the gap between the two series tends to increase. Finally, the average rate of growth of the rate of net investment in all four series is small but clearly negative.

The foregoing comparison of rates of investment computed from the SNIP series with those implied by the official NMP accounts suggests a few interesting conclusions.

(1) The direction of change in the rate of net fixed investment looks about the same in the two series, although the absolute size of the rates diverge tangibly.

(2) For all net investment the gap between absolute levels is larger and the series do not always move in tandem.

(3) There is no gross counterpart in official data to my estimates of the rate of gross investment, and the emergent patterns are more complex, in part owing to alternative computations, than those presented by the net investment series.

(4) These findings point up both the opportunities and the dangers of viewing Soviet resource allocation policy through the prism of a system of accounts alien to the system. On one hand, there are valid insights realizable through an analysis of implicit policy choices. On the other hand, it has never been clear to what extent the rate of investment is an explicit policy variable in Soviet planning; but in any case, surely the context is not our Western notion of national accounting but rather material product. As a telescope focused on that distant object, explicit resource allocation policy, Western national income accounts are not necessarily a reliable instrument.[25]

CAPITAL-OUTPUT RATIOS

Of the two concepts of capital stock changes outlined at the beginning of (and defined in detail in the addendum to) this chapter, only one, capital net of retirements, is represented in the official Soviet sources. Earlier I pointed out that succeeding editions of the statistical yearbooks have introduced retrospective changes in the capital stock indexes so that a consistent set is not available for the SYP period.[26] Nevertheless,

[25] Possibly the services excluded from net material product are somehow introduced into the policy equation. Soviet planning and policy literature, however, leaves the clear impression that "accumulation" and its relation to material product are the foci of development models.

[26] See above, p. 171.

year to year changes in the various series, where comparisons are possible, do seem roughly comparable, so that it is possible to estimate the average annual rate of growth in the official indexes as about 9–10 percent.

The capital stock net of depreciation can be crudely estimated from annual net investment flows and data from the capital census and revaluation of January 1, 1960. As of that date, it was officially reported, the nation's capital stock at replacement cost in terms of estimate prices was appraised at 296.5 billion rubles, of which 75 percent, or about 222 billions, was value net of wear and tear.[27] Subtracting reported net investment in 1958 and 1959, 44.6 billion rubles (at current prices but assumed approximately equal to estimate prices), leaves an estimated net capital stock value for January 1, 1958 of about 177 billion rubles. Addition of the annual net investment totals, at current prices, yields the following hybrid capital stock series (billion rubles):

	1958	*1959*	*1960*	*1961*	*1962*	*1963*	*1964*	*1965*
January 1	177	199	222	247	272	300	328	357
Average annual	188	211	235	260	286	314	343	

The annual relative increments in this series do not differ tangibly from those of the official gross capital stock data, and the average rate of growth ($\hat{r}$) of the former series is better than 10 percent. This is about double the rate of growth of official net investment itself[28] or of the estimated proxy (Table 28). On the other hand, gross investment developed at rates of 7 or 8 percent per year. Since the pace of increase of aggregate output may be variously gauged as 5½–6 percent (Table 40), an actual increase in aggregate capital-output ratios shows up relative to the estimated gross investment series, the official gross capital stock indexes, and the hybrid net capital stock series, but not to net investment itself.

The foregoing has related entirely to fixed capital-output ratios. My calculations do not yield estimates of inventories but only of inventory increments. These fluctuated sharply over the period in question, but in

[27] *NKh 1959*, pp. 67, 75. The figure of 75 percent applies strictly to capital that underwent revaluation on that date, two-thirds of the total. Of the omitted one-third, collective farm capital accounted for about 60 percent and the revaluation of collective farm capital two years later showed a wear-and-tear rate of about 29 percent (*NKh 1961*, pp. 420, 425).

[28] Illustrating once again the ability of a stock to lag far behind the flow.

any case the average rate of growth is below that of aggregate output in any of the variants I have estimated.[29] Certainly, the inventory investment-output ratio declined; there is, however, no inference that can be drawn from this with regard to the inventory-output ratio.[30]

---

[29] See Table 20 and pp. 140–143.

[30] Moorsteen and Powell's calculations do provide separate inventory estimates, and their data suggest an increase in the ratio of total inventories (average annual) to either GNP or NNP, all at 1937 factor cost, of about 15 percent over the period of interest to me. The increase is not monotonic but seems unmistakable. Since Moorsteen and Powell estimate agricultural inventories by projecting on agricultural output, it is advisable to look at the ratio of nonagricultural inventories to nonagricultural product. Roughly the same finding holds here as well. Incidentally, their aggregate inventory *investment*-output ratio also declines. Moorsteen and Powell, *The Soviet Capital Stock 1928–1962,* 1966, Tables T-24, T-44, and T-47; *Supplement I,* 1968 (see Chapter 10, note 11), Tables T-24-X, T-44-X, and T-47-X.

Addendum to Chapter 8

Relationships Between the Two Methods of Calculating Fixed Capital Increments

In this addendum I first set out the definitional relations between net investment at current prices and the increments in the gross capital stock series. I then proceed to estimate the difference between corresponding entries in the two series from component values and compare the results with actual differences implied by the official data.

Let $\dot{K}_G$ = capital stock increment gross of depreciation but net of retirements and losses

$\dot{K}_N$ = investment net of capital consumption

I = gross new capital increments

W_F, W_B = capital withdrawals at full value or depreciated book value

L_F, L_B = capital losses at full value or depreciated book value

D_R, D_C = depreciation allowances earmarked for replacement or capital repair

C_D, C_O = capital repair outlays financed from depreciation allowances or from other sources

It is assumed that $D_C = C_D$.

Then

$$\dot{K}_G = I - (W_F + L_F) \tag{1}$$

$$\dot{K}_N = I + C_D + C_O - (D_R + D_C + W_B + L_B) \tag{2}$$

Definition (2) may be simplified to

$$\dot{K}_N = I + C_O - (D_R + W_B + L_B) \tag{2a}$$

The difference between the two methods of measuring capital stock changes is

$$\dot{K}_G - \dot{K}_N = (D_R + W_B + L_B) - (W_F + L_F) - C_O \qquad (3)$$

that is, the difference between the respective capital consumption terms, with the further minor deduction of capital repairs financed from sources other than depreciation allowances.

Now define $\alpha = W_F/W_B$ and $\beta = L_F/L_B$—that is, ratios of full cost to depreciated cost of, respectively, withdrawals and losses. Ignoring C_O for the moment, (3) can be represented as

$$\dot{K}_G - \dot{K}_N = D_R - [(\alpha\text{-}1)W_B + (\beta\text{-}1)L_B] \qquad (4)$$

As α and β approach unity $(\dot{K}_G - \dot{K}_N)$ approaches the value of D_R. The larger α and β, the larger is the expression in brackets and the smaller (algebraically) is $(\dot{K}_G - \dot{K}_N)$.

Under what conditions will α and β approach unity closely? This will happen if (1) the rate of withdrawal (for obsolescence?) is sharply increased without a concomitant reduction in estimated service life in the depreciation formula, and (2) W_F is valued at replacement cost and W_B at original cost in a period of falling investment prices. On the other hand, $(\dot{K}_G - \dot{K}_N)$ can be zero or negative under some combination of (3) large accidental capital damage; (4) high rate of withdrawals of relatively undepreciated assets of high estimated longevities; (5) W_B is valued at original cost and W_F at some form of contemporary cost in a period of rising prices. The further deduction of C_O is an additional factor contributing to the same result. Conditions (1) and (4) are not inconceivable in the future although they have not been true of the recent past. Our understanding of the movement of investment prices is clouded, as already indicated, but condition (2) does not seem to accord with what we do know. Thus, α and β are unlikely to be close to 1. Of course, condition (3) is unpredictable and losses may be presumed to have fluctuated randomly in the past. Eidel'man presents data indicating $D_R > \alpha W_B$ as a general tendency;[31] certainly, then, $D_R >$ $(\alpha\text{-}1)$ W_B. However, further subtraction of $(\beta\text{-}1)L_B$ and of C_O should mean relatively small positive or perhaps even negative values of $(\dot{K}_G = \dot{K}_N)$.

Let us now turn to the data and see how they conform to expectations. The data may be tabulated as follows (billion rubles):[32]

---

[31] Eidel'man, *Mezhotraslevoi balans obshchestvennogo produkta,* 1966, p. 208, and discussion on pp. 209–210.

[32] (1) Values of D_R are estimated as 40 percent of total depreciation shown in Table 26 for 1958–1962 and 45 percent in 1963–1964. The share of amortization allowances in the state-cooperative sector earmarked for

Year	D_R (1)	W_B (2)	L_B (3)	W_F (4)	L_F (5)	C_O (6)	Computed $(\dot{K}_G - \dot{K}_N)$ (7)	Actual $\dot{K}_G$ (8)	Actual $\dot{K}_N$ (9)	Actual $(\dot{K}_G - \dot{K}_N)$ (10)
1958	4.6	1.2	1.0	3.5	2.0	1.6	−.3	..	21.8	..
1959	5.2	1.9	1.0	5.4	2.0	1.3	−.6	62	22.8	14
1960	5.8	1.2	1.0	3.4	2.0	1.5	1.1		25.3	
1961	6.5	1.3	1.0	3.9	2.0	1.5	1.4	61	28.4	4
1962	7.2	2.0	1.0	5.6	2.0	1.7	.9		28.4	
1963	10.3	1.3	1.0	6.0	2.0	2.0	2.6	36	28.2	8
1964	11.2	1.3	1.0	6.0	2.0	2.1	3.4	36	28.9	7

Of the four sets of comparisons that can be made between computed and actual $(\dot{K}_G - \dot{K}_N)$—1959–1960, 1961–1962, 1963, and 1964, the computed value is badly understated in the first, reasonably close to the actual in the second, and an indifferent approximation in the third and fourth. As the margin of error on the estimates in columns (1)–(5) is quite high, the gap showing up in the third and fourth comparisons is not overly disturbing, but that of the first comparison is very much larger. It seems clear that the anomaly is confined to 1959, for the 1960 value of $\dot{K}_G$ can be set at approximately 27 or 28 billion rubles.[33] The

replacement in 1958–1962 averaged about 40 percent; in 1963 and 1964 the share was increased to 48 or 49 percent (*NKh 1962,* p. 634; *NKh 1963,* p. 653; *NKh 1964,* p. 769).

(2) Row 8, Table 26, state sector withdrawals, inflated by 10 percent to cover other sectors.

(3) Row 9, Table 26. Notional allowance.

(4) State-cooperative withdrawals in 1958–1962 at full original cost from Eidel'man, *Mezhotraslevoi balans obshchestvennogo produkta,* 1966, p. 208, inflated by 10 percent as the estimated margin between original and replacement cost (*NKh 1959,* p. 73), further increased by 10 percent as a notional allowance for withdrawals of collective farm capital and private housing. 1963–1964: arbitrary.

(5) Twice the value in column (3). The ratio of column (4) to column (6) values for 1958–1962 averages 2.9. For losses the ratio may be expected to be lower.

(7) The difference between total capital repairs (p. 387) and amortization allowances earmarked for repair (see sources to column (1)).

(8) Differences of values computed by applying indexes of yearbook group III shown above, p. 171, to January 1, 1965 total stock value of 471 billion rubles (*NKh 1964,* p. 68).

(9) Row 10.B, Table 26.

[33] Computed from the January 1, 1960 total value (*NKh 1959,* p. 67) and the indexes of Group I on p. 171, above, or from the January 1, 1962 value (*Tsifry 1962,* p. 31) and the indexes of Group II.

fault probably lies with the 1959 value of $\dot{K}_G$: in a detailed examination of the 1960 capital census data, Norman Kaplan has concluded that the 1959 increment absorbs the entire statistical discrepancy in the revised post-census series from 1928 to 1960.[34]

With account taken of the likely 1960 value of $\dot{K}_G$, there may be some tendency to increase of $(\dot{K}_G - \dot{K}_N)$ displayed in the above tabulation. For 1963 and 1964 this can probably be ascribed to the disproportionate increase in D_R occasioned by the introduction of new amortization norms in 1963. However, the impact of that event must have progressively dissipated, and the further course of the investment differences depends on the factors indicated earlier.

---

[34] From an unpublished manuscript, cited with the author's kind permission.

9

1965S: The SYP and Its Implementation

Up to this point, the presentation and analysis of findings have been confined to the accounts for 1958–1964. To conclude Part II, I now wish to comment in some detail on the accounts for 1965S. I remind the reader that (1) these represent translations of the targets for the terminal year of the Seven Year Plan, as originally conceived and drawn up in 1958–1959, into the SNIP framework; (2) the primary purpose of this calculation was to furnish a systematic view of Soviet economic policy embodied in the Plan and how that policy was affected by the course of events. To the latter end, the 1965S estimates are everywhere juxtaposed to those for 1958, the base year of the SYP, and 1964, the last year of the period under review.

Sectoral Incomes and Outlays

HOUSEHOLDS

The relevant data are set forth in Table 29. On the income side, two elements of wages and salaries, bonuses not included in the wage and salary bill and wages in kind, have been grouped with other income currently earned. This was done to facilitate comparison of 1958 and 1964 with 1965S data; for the latter year the two income components were estimated together. Of the six categories of income listed in Table 29, four display decreased shares of the total in 1965S as compared with 1958: agricultural income (excluding wages and salaries), military pay

TABLE 29
STRUCTURE OF HOUSEHOLD INCOMES AND OUTLAYS, 1958, 1965S, AND 1964
(percent)

	1958	1965S	1964
A. Incomes			
1. Worker and employee wage and salary bill	52.7	56.7	59.0
2. Net income of households from agriculture (excluding wages and salaries of state employed farm labor)	22.0	18.7	18.6
3. Military pay and subsistence	4.1	2.9	2.5
4. Bonuses not included in wage and salary bill; wages in kind; other income currently earned [a]	8.8	7.8	8.0
5. Imputed rent and imputed value of owner-supplied building services	2.3	2.1	1.5
6. Transfer receipts	10.0	11.7	10.3
7. Total income	100.0	100.0	100.0
B. Outlays			
1. Retail sales of goods for consumption			
A. State-cooperative trade	60.9	66.1	65.7
B. Extravillage farm markets	4.5	.. [b]	3.3
C. Total	65.4	..	69.0
2. Consumer services			
A. Housing, including imputed rent	1.7	1.7	1.7
B. Dues	.9	.9	1.0
C. Other	6.6	9.4	8.1
D. Total	9.3	12.0	10.8
3. Consumption of income in kind	12.0	15.2 [c] (rows 3 and 4)	8.7
4. Other outlays for consumption	3.0		3.0
5. Total outlays for consumption	89.7	93.3	91.5
6. Investment	3.3	2.5	1.6
7. Transfers			
A. Net savings	1.1	1.6	1.5
B. Direct taxes; other payments to the state	5.8	2.7	5.4
C. Total	7.0	4.3	6.9
Total outlays	100.0	100.0	100.0

Notes:

[a] Includes statistical discrepancy for household sector in 1958 and 1964. The statistical discrepancy in 1965S is recorded on the outlay side.

[b] Not separately estimated but included with consumption of income in kind and other outlays for consumption.

[c] Including extravillage farm market sales and the statistical discrepancy for the household sector account. In 1958 and 1964 the statistical discrepancy is recorded on the income side of the household account.

Sources:

Tables 1 and 2.

and subsistence, imputed incomes, and all other current incomes.[1] Only the relative weights of wages and salaries and of transfer incomes were to increase. The largest changes in shares are those of wages and salaries and of agricultural incomes; the 4 percentage point increase of the first is almost balanced by a three point decrease of the second.

It is not difficult to see in this pattern a reflection of consciously sought directions of change in Soviet social-economic organization. The SYP provided for a significant sectoral restructuring of agricultural output and incomes.[2] The 70 percent growth of gross agricultural output called for in the Control Figures was probably to be attained with the aid of a more than 2.5-fold increase in the volume of state farm production but an increase of private sector output of no more than one-seventh. The conjunction of announced output and productivity targets indicates a planned transfer of manpower out of collective farms with a probable increase in state farm employment. Therefore, although real income per collective farmer was supposed to increase by 40 percent and the average wage and salary by 26 percent, the share of worker and employee earnings was to increase from 53 to 57 percent, whereas that of agricultural income was to decline from 22 to 19 percent.[3]

One of the main paths in the transition to "full communism," the proclaimed general goal of the SYP, was a rapid increase in the so-called "social funds of consumption" (*obshchestvennye fondy potrebleniia*). A major element of these funds is public sector transfer outlays. Payments to households from the social funds, realized and imputed, were to grow by more than two-thirds during the SYP period. In contrast, the

---

[1] Since a statistical discrepancy is included in the 1958 but excluded in the 1965S entry for item 4, the decrease shown may be illusory.

[2] See Appendix E.

[3] The estimates of agricultural output changes developed in Appendix E (pp. 416, 421, 425–426) imply a planned change in the sector of origin structure of farm output. In 1958, 37 percent of the total originated in the private sector, with the state sector contributing only about a sixth and collective farms somewhat less than one-half. In 1965S state farms would be contributing about as large a share as in the private sector, one-quarter, the other half of all output originating on collective farms. By way of comparison, Johnson and Kahan (in *Comparisons of the United States and Soviet Economies,* 1959, p. 207) estimated the 1950 shares as 54 percent for collective farms, 7 percent for state farms, and 39 percent for the private sector.

estimates of total household income in Table 1 imply an increase of 42 percent in the seven years.

In the large, the income structure actually obtained during the SYP period followed the Plan's pattern. Thus, the wage and salary bill became more clearly the dominant element of household income, accounting for 59 percent of the total in 1964 against 53 percent in 1958. In this respect, expectations were exceeded. However, the desired aggregate result was obtained in a manner contrary to that expected. The SYP provided for a 54 percent increase in the wage and salary bill, compounded of a 22 percent increase in the number of workers and employees and a 26 percent growth of average wages and salaries. A 54 percent increase in wages and salaries was attained, even a year earlier than foreseen (Table 9), but in the interim employment had risen 34 percent and average compensation only 15 percent.[4] As indicated earlier, part of the substantial gain in employment levels represented only a bookkeeping change—transformation of collective into state farmers and of members of producers' cooperatives into state wage and salary earners.[5] The same phenomenon also helps account for the drop in the share of incomes, excluding wages and salaries, originating in agriculture.

In the utilization of these incomes, Part B of Table 29, the SYP provided for an increasing share to be devoted to consumption at the expense of investment and transfer outlays. The 1965S estimates allow for no farm investment in kind, bearing in mind the Party's intended imminent dissolution of private livestock herds on state farms and the unconcealed desire to do the same on collective farms in the not too distant future.[6] Indeed, net disinvestment rather than zero investment may be a more reasonable guess for 1965S. The SYP allowed for an extensive program of private housing construction but evidently phased so that the peak annual level of construction was to antedate the terminal Plan year.[7]

By present estimates, transfer outlays were slated for an absolute as well as relative decline, as a consequence of the proposed abrogation of direct taxes on the urban population.[8] On the other hand, the projected

---

[4] See pp. 295 and 415–416. For this calculation the 1958 figures are taken net of earnings by members of producer cooperatives.

[5] See above, p. 75.

[6] See below, pp. 420–421.

[7] See below, pp. 437–438.

[8] In his speech to the 21st Congress on January 27, 1959, Khrushchev declared the tax reform impending but the details not yet worked out. They

1958–1965S increase in household net savings, the other major component of transfer outlays, was 100 percent. This figure is more appropriately linked to the increase in household outlays on "other services," also 100 percent, since the 1965S expenditure levels for both categories were derived as residuals in the process of estimating "real income" (Soviet-definition) in 1965S.

A planned doubling of the 1958 level of net savings in seven years is not as surprising as it may first appear. Soviet households have long exhibited an extremely low propensity to save. In the wake of the 1957 decision to discontinue compulsory bond subscriptions, savings accounted for only 1.4 percent of household disposable cash income in 1958 and were 70 percent smaller in that year than in 1956.[9] A doubling of the 1958 level would have left the flow of savings, albeit voluntary rather than compulsory, still 40 percent smaller than in 1956 and still accounting for less than 2 percent of disposable money income.[10]

The largest anticipated SYP change in the structure of household outlays is better than a 5 percentage point increase in the proportion spent in the state-cooperative retail trade network. By these estimates, four-fifths of consumption in 1965S was to originate in state-cooperative retail sales and in "other services," compared with three-quarters in 1958. Correspondingly, the combined share of rent, dues, income in kind, market purchases, and other consumption outlays would be reduced from one-quarter to one-fifth. The share of total household expenditures allocated to consumption did rise after 1958, although the 1964 level was not quite that envisioned for 1965S.[11] But if the SYP contemplated raising consumption's weight at the expense of both invest-

---

were made public 15 months later in a speech to the Supreme Soviet (*Pravda*, May 6, 1960).

[9] Table 2 and *SNIP 1956–1958*, p. 3.

[10] In computing disposable money income, it is necessary to deduct income in kind and imputed incomes from the total. For 1965S farm income in kind was not separately estimated (Appendix E). It is here estimated as 10 billion rubles, compared with 10.57 billions in 1958. The latter figure is 49 percent of item 2.D of Table 1. For 1965S, the corresponding ratio should be considerably smaller, in view of the intended encroachments on private livestock and the tendency to increasing monetization of farm income. Ten billion rubles of farm income in kind is 38 percent of the 1965S entry for item 2.D in Table 1. Military subsistence in 1965S is assumed at the 1958 level (see pp. 426–427) and wages in kind, arbitrarily, at 1.0 billion rubles. For the data on taxes and other payments to the state, see Table G-3.

[11] That level was in fact attained in 1963 (Table 10), but as a consequence of a sharp drop in farm investment in kind, in turn related to the crop failure in that year.

ment and transfer outlays, the actual increase in relative outlays on consumption was attained wholly at the expense of investment. In the event, transfer outlays remained as significant in household spending at the end of the SYP period as at the beginning. In large part this was the consequence of the constraints placed on private housing construction and private investment in livestock, which were discussed in Chapter 4.

An additional factor of some importance was a turnabout in tax policy. A Supreme Soviet Decree of May 8, 1960 had provided for the complete abrogation of direct taxes by the end of 1965S in gradual stages.[12] The program of tax reduction was "temporarily" suspended in September 1962, in the wake of financial difficulties that also required increases in retail prices earlier that year (more on this below). Not until 1967 did the government resume cutting direct taxes, and proceeds in 1965 were almost 50 percent greater than in 1958.[13]

If the share of household outlays on consumption increased after 1958, this was because of increases in only two components, sales in state-cooperative retail trade and "other services," and obtained despite relative declines in several expenditure categories. The two-thirds share of total outlays intended to be absorbed by state-cooperative retail sales was attained by the early 1960s (Table 10). On the other hand, the proportion of the household's ruble finding its way to the farm markets (extravillage or intravillage), reflected in consumption in kind, or spent on other outlays for consumption, declined almost without interruption to the level estimated as the 1965S objective. Thus, the state was implementing its objective of further monetizing peasant consumption and of channeling an even greater proportion of household consumption outlays to the regulated state-cooperative retail trade outlet, away from the relatively free farm markets.

Outlays on housing services (paid and imputed rent) remained unchanged as a proportion of the total, despite the retardation of state construction and the severe restrictions on private housing. Indeed, the absolute value of all rent in 1964 represented 92 percent of the estimated SYP goal. At least two factors help explain this paradox. First, the rent estimates of this study are directly proportional to the estimated size of the housing stock. Because of the weight of the initial stock, the

---

[12] See below, pp. 454–455.

[13] Net savings displayed an erratic course in these years for reasons that may have something to do with changes in currency holdings (see above, pp. 78–81). However, by 1964 total net savings were at the 2 billion ruble level, virtually the sum estimated as the 1965S goal (Table 1).

degree of fulfillment of a stock goal will be higher, other things being equal, than that of a construction target. Second, the 1965S targets are estimated on the basis of the stock data available to planners when the SYP was formulated. For urban housing, these data turned out later to be erroneous, in terms of both the total and the division between private and public sectors.[14]

PUBLIC SECTOR INCOMES

As in the consideration of the *ex post* estimates in Chapter 4, public sector incomes in Table 30 are computed gross of subsidized losses, n.e.c., and the relative distribution is viewed with retained incomes both

TABLE 30

STRUCTURE OF PUBLIC SECTOR INCOME, 1958, 1965S, AND 1964 (percent)

	1958	1965S	1964
1. Income of collective farms net of depreciation:			
A. Before income tax	4.6	5.0	3.1
B. After income tax	3.3	3.9	2.3
2. Net profits of state enterprises, nonfarm cooperatives and other organizations			
A. Before income tax and profits deductions	25.4	33.3	28.5
B. After income tax and profits deductions	7.5	8.9	4.5
3. Charges to economic enterprises for special funds	4.8	4.1	4.9
4. Taxes and other payments out of income by economic organizations to the budget [a]			
A. Excluding organization income tax and profits deductions	46.5	42.8	40.3
B. Including organization income tax and deductions	65.7	68.4	65.1
5. Depreciation	10.0	10.4	15.5
6. Transfer receipts			
A. Net savings by households	1.4	1.6	1.7
B. Direct taxes and other payments by households to the state	7.3	2.7	6.0
C. Total	8.7	4.3	7.7
7. Consolidated net income, but gross of subsidized losses, n.e.c.	100.0	100.0	100.0

Note:

[a] Including net accounting profits from foreign trade.

Sources:

Table 3, with adjustments for A variants of items 1, 2, and 4 in 1958 and 1964 as explained in the sources to Table 11. For 1965S, the relevant amounts are given in Table G-3; deductions from state sector profits in 1965S are assumed at a level of 33 billion rubles—that is, the midpoint of the range shown in Table G-2, although slightly lower than the 34.2 billion rubles derived on p. 447.

[14] Cf. *NKh 1958*, p. 641; and *NKh 1960*, p. 613. See below, p. 430.

gross (variant A) and net (variant B) of income taxes or other deductions to the budget. Similarly, budget revenues in item 4 are shown excluding and including income tax and profits deductions. Apart from its usefulness as a reflection of redistributive aspects of budget policy, the A variant is of additional interest here. The estimate of profits deductions in 1965S is even more fragile than that of total state-cooperative profits in that year, hence it is useful to look at the envisioned changes in the share of profits before as well as after deductions to the budget.

Consider items 2, 4, and 6. Under the A variant we note a striking planned rise of 8 points in the net, pretax profits share by 1965S. Excluding profits deductions and income tax on farms and cooperatives, current budget receipts were to sustain an almost 4 point decline in their relative weight. On the other hand, net profits after taxes and deductions show only a one point increase, compared with 8 points of variant A, and budget receipts a 3 point increase instead of a 4 point decline. Thus, the proportion of profits in total income was to rise sharply during the SYP period but so was the part deducted by the budget. It is the latter change that largely compensates for the more than 4 point expected drop in the share of transfer receipts from households, made up of a slight increase in the share of savings with an almost 5 point decrease in the share of taxes and other payments to the state. As previously indicated, the declining weight of the latter item is a reflection of the SYP program to curtail and eventually abolish direct taxes on households. All these SYP intended changes continue a pattern manifested in the middle 1950s—reduced significance of household taxes and savings, sharply increased importance of deductions from state sector profits, and declining relative weight of turnover taxes.[15]

To what extent were these expectations realized? Viewed under either variant, collective farm incomes provided a decreased instead of an increased share of total public sector revenues. On the other hand, receipts from households were almost as important in 1964 as in 1958, largely because of the indefinite suspension in 1962 of the programmed abrogation of direct taxes. Before or after taxes and deductions, profits were supposed to supply an increasing share of total incomes. For profits before taxes, this did indeed occur. After taxes, however, the role of profits declined noticeably. The other side of this coin is a corresponding divergence in the variant shares of current budget receipts (item 4).

---

[15] *The Soviet Financial System*, 1968, pp. 87–89.

Excluding taxes on and deductions from profits, other payments to the budget decreased considerably, even more than the SYP is believed to have contemplated. Gross of taxes and deductions from profits, current budget receipts were supposed to increase but on balance did not.

Thus the redistributive mechanism of state finances played a considerably more important role in 1959–1964 than had been contemplated. The conclusion is underscored when we consider the spurt in the relative weight of depreciation allowances, bearing in mind the extent to which these allowances are in fact controlled by the central plan.[16] The unexpectedly large increase in the contribution of depreciation allowances to public sector income, the consequence of the decision to raise sharply the norms of depreciation in 1963, partly explains the relatively poor showing of state-cooperative retained net profits, before or after tax. With depreciation included, the shares of retained net profits in 1964 are seen as in fact exceeding the correspondingly calculated 1965S goals.[17] The fact remains, however, that depreciation allowances are of restricted availability to the enterprise; and from the point of view of the trends in decentralized financing, the decline relative to plan and base level in retained net income after tax is a significant index of the constraints imposed from the center. Another way of looking at the same development is to lump depreciation with budget revenues from organizations: from that angle, the budget's access to current income generated in the public sectors in 1964 exceeded the SYP expectations for 1965S.

PUBLIC SECTOR OUTLAYS

Table 31, presenting the structure of public sector outlays, is startling. Comparing 1958 and 1965S, the relative weights of communal services (excluding science), administration, gross investment, military pay and subsistence, and transfer outlays—indeed, of all items except item 4.F —are shown as declining; the share of item 4.F in Table 31—defense, internal security, R&D, and outlays n.e.c.—is shown growing by about 8 points, 10 points if pay and subsistence are excluded. The increase in total public sector outlays (Table 4) is 82 percent, but the increase for item 4.F of Table 31 is 263 percent!

---

[16] See Chapter 4, note 28.

[17] However, though the average annual rate of growth of state sector net profits (before deductions to the budget and gross of certain incentive payments to households) was a respectable 10.5 percent (below, p. 363), the SYP had apparently expected an annual average rate in excess of 13 percent (below, pp. 444–445).

TABLE 31

STRUCTURE OF PUBLIC SECTOR OUTLAYS, 1958, 1965S, AND 1964
(percent)

	1958	1965S	1964
1. Communal services, excluding R&D	13.9	13.3	14.2
2. Administration	1.6	1.1	.9
3. Gross investment			
A. Fixed capital	44.0	43.8	46.5
B. Inventories	10.4	5.3	9.8
C. Total	54.5	49.1	56.4
4. Other outlays			
A. Military pay and subsistence	5.4	3.0	2.9
B. Other defense (budget)	6.5	..	8.1
C. Internal security	2.0	..	1.3
D. R&D	2.7	..	3.6
E. Outlays n.e.c.; statistical discrepancy	.3	..	.9
F. Total	16.9	24.6	16.7
5. Transfer payments	13.1	12.0	11.7
6. Total outlays	100.0	100.0	100.0

Sources:
Table 4, except that the breakdown of defense outlays is computed from Table 1.

Realized outlays present a different pattern. True, by 1964, expenditures on administration, inventory investment, pay and subsistence, and transfers to households were relatively less important than in 1958; for three of these four categories, the 1964 entries closely resemble the 1965S goals. But whereas the SYP apparently expected a decline in the share of gross investment in total outlays and a whopping increase in that of item 4's miscellany, no net change in the relative weight of item 4.F is observed in 1964; gross investment in fact increased somewhat faster than total outlays.

If we could be confident of the results, the size of the changes in relative weight of items 3 and 4, in conjunction with the divergence between these changes *ex ante* and *ex post,* would comprise one of the most piquant findings resulting from the calculations of this study. As an outlay residual, item 4.F (and all of item 4 except 4.A in 1965S) is extremely sensitive to errors in the estimation of all other public sector outlays and of total public sector incomes. The estimate of total public sector incomes in 1965S, in turn, is an interpretation of cryptic statements by official Soviet sources with regard to the size of aggregate budget revenues in 1965S. As incorporated in these accounts and *relative to those official statements,* the revenue total may be off by five billion rubles either way. The impact of this margin of error on the

1965S accounts as a whole is discussed in detail in Appendix M, but here it should be noted that the probable margin of error on "other outlays" in 1965S in Table 31 is 3 percentage points. The major compensating change of roughly 2 percentage points would affect the share of gross fixed investment. If I have seriously misinterpreted the official statements, or if they are materially in error, the margin of error on my estimates is correspondingly greater.

There is some additional evidence on the credibility of the sharp increase in the public sector residual which rests on an attempt to reconstruct NMP by use in 1965S. The evidence is discussed in Appendix Q but is tenuous and suggests only that there may be some basis for believing that "other outlays" were to increase sizably; by how much is not clear.

It should not be concluded that the value of "other outlays" represents *in toto* an earmarked allocation for military expenditures and R&D. The category also includes the public sector statistical discrepancy and with respect to 1965S may possibly include a contingency fund. The annual state budgets have traditionally incorporated such an allowance, the "Reserves of the Council of Ministers," which are usually expended through the budget category "national economy." For a plan covering as long a period of time as seven years, a contingency fund makes obvious sense. If such a reserve was allowed for, a part of the 1958–1965S increase of "other outlays" may have been intended for other categories, the most likely being investment. To that extent, and apart from offsetting errors, the share of gross investment in 1965S may be substantially understated. The point will be taken up again later.

The sharpness of the indicated drop in the share of inventory investment between 1958 and 1965S may also be more apparent than real, because the 1958 figure may be overstated whereas the 1965S value may be understated.[18] Yet for the share of inventory investment to remain unchanged, the absolute value in 1965S would have to be over 14 billion rubles, or virtually twice the estimate adopted. Such a result seems unlikely on the evidence, and some decline in the relative weight of inventory investment between 1958 and 1965S seems a reasonable bet.

SECTORAL DISTRIBUTION OF GNP

Perhaps one other structural comparison may be of interest. Table 32 compares the shares of households and the public sectors in GNP, by

[18] See below, pp. 394, 466–467.

TABLE 32

CONTRIBUTION OF HOUSEHOLDS AND PUBLIC SECTORS TO GNP, 1958, 1965S, AND 1964
(percent)

	1958	1965S	1964
Incomes			
Households	56.4	48.6	52.5
Public sectors	43.6	51.4	47.5
GNP	100.0	100.0	100.0
Outlays			
Households	58.3	52.7	54.5
Public sectors	41.7	47.3	45.5
GNP	100.0	100.0	100.0

Source:
Table 5.

both incomes and outlays, and thus represents a relative distribution of the two halves of Table 5. Its usefulness consists in summarizing some of the interesting trends implicitly or explicitly treated in previous sections of this chapter. Table 32 says, in brief, that the SYP contemplated a sharply increased role for the public sectors in the generation and utilization of the national product; simultaneously, net transfers to households were to be increased absolutely and relatively.

Ex post the direction of change was generally that postulated by the SYP, but the magnitude of the changes was not as large as expected, especially with respect to incomes. By 1964 the public sectors still accounted for less than half of GNP, earned or expended, and in relative terms, the extent of net transfer from the public sectors to households was no greater in 1964 than in 1958.

Resource Allocation at Current Prices

Table 32 leads us directly to the question of resource allocation under the SYP. Discussion of this subject, as Chapter 3 was at some pains to point out, requires a factor cost valuation of national product flows. Unfortunately, data gaps precluded a systematic attempt to convert 1965S EP into AFC values. Given the diminishing relative importance of turnover taxes in the SYP, a major source of distortion in Soviet price relations was to be weakened. The lengthy discussion in Chapter 5 also suggests that an EP series may bear more directly on resource allocation, understood in terms of production potential schedules or Bergson's "feasibility loci," than is commonly imagined. If that is true, it may be permissible to compare the SYP resource allocation targets, explicit or implicit, in EP terms with the EP and AFC data developed for 1958 and 1964. The uncertainties besetting such a comparison will not be repeated but should be borne in mind.

When we come to consider the SYP projected changes in the end-use structure of GNP as a whole (Table 33), the pattern is somewhat different from what would be expected by merely conjoining Tables 29 and 31. In the framework of just household expenditures, consumption was to rise in relative weight. Within GNP, the share of consumption was to drop 5 points. If public sector investment was to account for virtually the same proportion of total public sector expenditures in

TABLE 33

STRUCTURE OF GROSS NATIONAL PRODUCT BY USE AT EP, 1958, 1965S, AND 1964 (percent)

	1958	1965S	1964
1. Retail sales of goods for consumption in the state-cooperative trade network	38.2	36.3	38.5
2. Consumer services	5.8	6.6	6.3
3. Consumption of income in kind; extravillage farm market sales; other outlays for consumption	12.2	8.3 [a]	8.8
4. Total household outlays for consumption	56.2	51.3	53.6
5. Communal services, excluding R&D	6.7	7.1	7.3
6. Government administration	.8	.6	.5
7. Gross investment			
A. In fixed capital			
(1) By households	2.1	1.4	0.9
(2) By public sectors	21.1	23.6	24.0
(3) Total	23.2	24.9	24.9
B. In inventories	5.0	2.8	5.1
C. Total	28.2	27.8	30.0
8. Other outlays			
A. Military pay and subsistence	2.6	1.6	1.5
B. Other defense (budget)	3.1	..	4.2
C. Internal security	.9	..	.7
D. R&D	1.3	..	1.8
E. Outlays n.e.c.; public sector statistical discrepancy	.1	..	.5
F. Total	8.1	13.2	8.6
Gross national product	100.0	100.0	100.0

Note:
[a] Includes statistical discrepancy for the household sector.

Source:
Table 6.

1965S as in 1958, its share of GNP was to rise by 2½ points. Within household consumption, the structure of household outlays shows a larger absolute gain in the share of retail store purchases compared with the gain in the share of services. In the structure of GNP, retail purchases account for a declining part of the whole and services a slight gain.[19] Inventory investment's claim on the total is again less in 1965S than in 1958, but naturally the decline is not as sharp as when viewed on the screen of public sector outlays alone. By the same token, the translation to a larger denominator, the projected mushrooming of the share of the residual item appears less spectacular.

Table 33 points at some substantial alterations in the structure of gross fixed investment. These hints can be made explicit in Table 34 which looks at breakdowns for various forms of fixed investment. In all cases, SYP targets implied increasing relative importance of the public sectors at the expense of private housing. This conclusion can be broadened to cover the entire private sector, as there is no question that private agricultural investment was to diminish in relative if not also in absolute size. The actual course of events was somewhat different from the SYP blueprint. Private housing did indeed absorb a smaller share of investment resources, but the shrinkage in its share was considerably greater than anticipated, as was true also of private housing and livestock together. Moreover, although the role of collective farm investment was supposed to be augmented, it was in fact diminished. The beneficiary, of course, was the state-cooperative sector, which by the end of the SYP period accounted for 88 percent of gross or net investment (90 percent of SNIP gross investment), compared with 82–84 percent at the beginning of the period. With respect to SNIP gross investment, gross new investment or gross new increments, the collective farm share in every year (Table 27) fell short not just of the 1965S target but also

[19] It will be readily seen that these divergences are explained by two factors: first, differential relations between the percent increase in the absolute values of particular expenditures and of the total with which the items are being compared. Thus, purchases in retail stores show a 55 percent increase and consumer services 84 percent; the increase in total household outlays is 42 percent but in GNP 62 percent. Second, the smaller the share of any item in a total, the smaller the *absolute* increase in that share necessary to produce a given *relative* increase. Thus, with respect to household outlays, a less than three point increase in the share of consumer services means a greater relative increase than the more than five point increase in the weight of retail store purchases.

TABLE 34
STRUCTURE OF GROSS AND NET FIXED CAPITAL INVESTMENT BY SECTOR, 1958, 1965S, AND 1964
(percent)

	1958	1965S	1964
1. SNIP gross investment			
A. State-cooperative	82.7	84.8	90.0
B. Collective farms	8.3	9.7	6.3
C. Private housing and livestock	9.0	5.5	3.7
2. Gross new investment			
A. State-cooperative	81.7	82.6	87.9
B. Collective farms	9.5	10.9	8.5
C. Private housing	8.8	6.5	3.6
3. Gross new increments			
A. State-cooperative	81.8	82.9	88.0
B. Collective farms	8.9	10.4	8.2
C. Private housing	9.3	6.7	3.9
4. Capital repairs			
A. State-cooperative	84.4	85.1	87.9
B. Collective farms	5.5	7.0	5.6
C. Private housing	10.1	7.9	6.5
5. Depreciation			
A. State-cooperative	80.0	81.8	86.7
B. Collective farms	7.8	8.9	6.8
C. Private housing	11.3	9.4	6.4
6. Gross increments plus capital repairs less depreciation			
A. State-cooperative	83.3	84.0	88.9
B. Collective farms	8.6	10.2	8.3
C. Private housing	8.2	5.8	2.9

Note:
In each column and for each item, A., B., and C. entries total 100 percent.
Source:
Computed from Table 26.

of the initial year, 1958, level. Private housing absorbed but 3 or 4 percent of gross or net investment in 1964 (6 percent in terms of imputed capital repairs) compared with 8–9 percent in 1958 (capital repairs, 10 percent).

The most significant issue of Table 33 is that of overall resource allocation. On its own terms, apart from a comparison with prior outlay breakdowns, the structure of GNP by end use indicates that the SYP seemed to have provided for a notable cut in the claim of consumption on the total—and this is true even if communal services excluding science are grouped with household outlays on consumption—in favor of nonconsumption outlays. Since a relative decline is estimated for administration and inventory investment, the restructuring appears to have provided a dramatic spurt in the combined share of gross fixed investment and "other outlays." For the reasons already set forth, it is probably advisable to treat these two items as one.

But the latter question must be treated more systematically. Did the SYP attempt to raise the rate of investment or of nonconsumption more generally? How far was that effort realized? Table 33 provides equivocal answers and perhaps the best way to demonstrate that is to calculate shares in GNP of several alternative aggregates, as follows (percent):

	1958	*1965S*	*1964*
Public sector fixed investment	21.1	23.6	24.0
All fixed investment	23.2	24.9	24.9
All public sector investment	26.1	26.4	29.1
All investment	28.2	27.8	30.0
Other outlays plus:			
Public sector fixed investment	29.2	36.8	32.7
All fixed investment	31.3	38.2	33.6
All public sector investment	34.2	39.6	37.8
All investment	36.3	41.0	38.7

With the single exception of all investment, rates of investment and of nonconsumption were expected to increase under the SYP, the former by small margins, the latter by 5–8 percentage points. The 1964 rates are in all cases higher than in 1958 but within a narrower margin of 2–4 points. Comparing expected with realized increments, we find that for rates of investment the changes were positive in three of four cases (zero in the case of all fixed investment) but for the other aggregates shortfalls were the rule, by 2–5 percentage points. Thus, the SYP did not expect large order changes in the rate of investment and was not disappointed in this regard.[20] On the other hand, large increases were expected for alternatively defined rates of investment plus other outlays; instead shortfalls were obtained. Any further interpretation of these findings would have to be based on a surer grasp of the meaning of the 1965S residual than the information at hand allows.[21]

---

[20] See above, p. 181 ff.

[21] Incidentally, the patterns noted are not sensitive to alterations either in the share of residual budget revenues entered in the SNIP accounts or to the estimated size of total budget revenues in 1965S. The sensitivity of the *ex post* estimates to the former test was discussed in connection with Table 15 and found generally not significant. The same conclusion holds also for the sensitivity test of the 1965S data. The inclusion (deletion) of 5 billion rubles in budget revenues ultimately implies small decreases (increases) in consumption's share of GNP as well as in those of gross investment; the

SYP Growth Objectives and Their Fulfillment

So far this chapter has dealt with structural relations in the 1965S accounts and at current prices. I turn now to the subject of growth and of output valued at constant prices.

Indexes and the rates of growth [22] implied by the indexes have been computed for major use categories of GNP in 1958 and 1965S and are shown in Table 35. The calculations are performed on GNP components at 1958 prices and, of course, at established prices. With respect to nonlabor charges, 1965S prices are assumed to differ from 1958 prices only by the small planned decline in retail prices. In addition, household outlays on dues and expenditures on communal services and administration have been deflated by increases in average wages and salaries, announced or estimated in this study. Deflation for wage increases cannot be attempted for R&D and internal security, as these items are inextricable from the residual category in 1965S. Given the limited scope of price changes under the SYP, some of the ensuing discussion is deducible from material of previous sections of this chapter.

Table 35 indicates an average rate of growth of GNP implied by the 1965S index number of 7.2 percent per year. The SYP rate of growth of consumption is one percentage point smaller and that of gross fixed investment one point larger. The estimated decrease in inventory invest-

---

offsetting increase (decrease) in "other outlays" is less than 2 points (Table M-5). These changes do not affect the conclusions drawn above with respect to plan and fulfillment.

[22] In the following discussion, rates of growth of 1965S relative to 1958 are computed by the conventional r formula. Realized rates of growth in 1958–1964 are presented in terms of $\bar{r}$ *and* $\hat{r}$. For the definitions and general rationale the reader should refer back to Chapter 6. One additional comment needs to be made here on the *ex ante* rates. With the single exception of private housing construction, where it appears that the growth curve was expected to peak in 1960 (see below, p. 438), I have no evidence that the SYP provided for varying annual growth rates of different expenditure categories. Most likely this was in fact contemplated for at least some items; the evidence is simply absent. I am therefore constrained to assume that *ex ante* average growth rates are constant annually. Under that assumption r is identical to $\bar{r}$ and $\hat{r}$.

Inasmuch as the realized annual relative increments are not constant, r is an inappropriate *ex post* measurement formula. To measure the implementation of the 1965S targets, whose reference point is 1958, $\bar{r}$ seems to be called for, while $\hat{r}$ is entirely independent of the values of the base year.

TABLE 35
INDEXES AND RATES OF GROWTH OF GNP BY END USE AT 1958 EP, PLAN AND FULFILLMENT
(percent)

	1965S Index Numbers 1958 = 100	Average Annual Rates of Growth		
		Ex Ante	1958–1964	
		$r \equiv \hat{r} \equiv \bar{r}$	$\hat{r}$	$\bar{r}$
1. Consumption	153	6.3	5.1	5.5
2. Communal services	149	5.8	6.4	6.8
3. Administration	100	0	−2.9	−4.0
4. Gross investment				
A. Fixed capital				
(1) Households	106	0.8	−11.9	−6.7
(2) Public sector				
(a) State-cooperative	178	8.6	8.5	9.4
(b) Collective farm	207	10.9	1.4	0.9
(c) Total	181	8.8	8.0	8.7
(3) Total	174	8.2	6.7	7.6
B. Inventories	92	−1.1	3.2	−2.3
C. Total	160	6.9	6.2	6.1
5. Other outlays				
A. Military pay and subsistence	100	0	−2.3	−2.8
B. Other defense, internal security, R&D, outlays n.e.c.; statistical discrepancy	343	19.2	9.1	14.5
C. Total	263	14.8	6.5	10.0
GNP	163	7.2	5.6	6.1

Sources:

1965S index numbers. Calculated from Table 6 and p. 464 with the following adjustments for price changes:

(1) Five billion rubles are added to the 1965S figures for retail sales, representing the difference between sales at 1965S and 1958 prices (*NKh 1958*, p. 103).

(2) Outlays on dues are deflated by the planned 26 percent increase in average wages and salaries (p. 415).

(3) Assuming the same distribution of communal service outlays between wage and nonwage costs in 1965S as in 1958 (Table J-2), 73 percent, wage charges are deflated by an assumed 25 percent increase in average wages and salaries.

(4) Deflated administration expenditures are assumed to be equal to outlays in 1958—that is, after allowing for the assumed 25 percent increase in average earnings, increases in material expenditures are ignored (see p. 464).

(5) Total outlays on consumption and GNP in 1965S are adjusted accordingly.

1958–1964 rates of growth. Computed from Table 20 and Table K-1.

ment by 1965S drags the rate of growth of all investment down a little below the average for GNP as a whole. Growth of total "other outlays" between 1958 and 1965S is indicated at the unusually high rate of 15 percent per year.

How well did these growth objectives, explicit and implicit, fare in the course of the SYP period? Or, since underfulfillment of the Plan is the general assumption, how far short did actual results fall? At first glance, the answer of Table 35 is, surprisingly, not much, in essential respects. Some striking shortfalls do appear in the sphere of fixed investment. Not only did private sector investment decline sharply but the rate of growth of collective farm investment was only nominal, in striking contrast to the 11 percent expected annual rate of increase. However, state-cooperative sector investment expanded more rapidly than planned or anticipated ($\bar{r}$ measuring fulfillment), and the aggregate fixed investment $\bar{r}$ value is not far below the Plan level.[23] The rate of growth of consumption *ex post* is no more than a percentage point below the *ex ante* level, and communal services developed more rapidly than expected. The greater than foreseen decline in administration and in inventory investment (again, using $\bar{r}$ for 1958–1964) may be reasonably viewed as overfulfillment rather than underfulfillment. That is, Soviet policy clearly aims at a reduction of administrative expenditures but is also intent on reducing inventory-output ratios.[24] The rate of growth of total "other outlays" failed to reach 15 percent but managed a highly respectable $\bar{r}$ value of 10 percent. Overall, the actual rate of growth of GNP at 6 percent was only 1 point below the *ex ante* rate of 7.2 percent.

For reasons already made clear, it may be more appropriate to consider the implicit target for "other outlays" in conjunction with public sector investment. The corresponding rates of growth are as follows (percent):

	SYP	*1958–1964*	
	$r \equiv \hat{r} \equiv \bar{r}$	$\hat{r}$	$\bar{r}$
Other outlays	14.8	6.5	10.0
Other outlays plus			
public sector fixed investment	9.0	7.6	9.1
all public sector investment	7.8	7.1	7.7

Measured at $\bar{r}$ the SYP average growth targets for other outlays plus public sector investment, fixed or fixed and inventory, appear to have been precisely implemented. In the preceding section, I noted that targets for the share of resources allocated to "other outlays" plus investment were underfulfilled by varying margins. Is there a contradiction between the two sets of findings? A small part of the answer may be

[23] This is a reflection of the predominant weight of the state-cooperative sectors in fixed investment, a share which, as we have already seen, grew still further over the SYP period.

[24] See Moorsteen and Powell, *The Soviet Capital Stock 1928–1962*, 1966, p. 231.

found in the difference between measuring rates of investment, broadly or narrowly defined, at current and at constant prices. Thus, the gaps between 1964 and 1965S shares of other outlays plus investment in GNP are slightly narrowed, relative to those shown in the previous section, when the calculation is at 1958 prices.[25] Compared to the corresponding rates at current prices, the 1965S rates at 1958 prices are all slightly decreased and several of those for 1964 are increased. This is the consequence of the relatively large increase in the share of consumption in 1965S brought about by the allowance for the intended retail price decrease and, for 1964, of the comparatively greater degree of deflation of elements of GNP other than investment and "other outlays."

A more complex problem is posed by the difference between $\dot{r}$ and $\hat{r}$ growth rates. This difference is relatively small for public sector fixed investment and even for all public sector investment (6.9 and 7.4 percent respectively). But for outlays n.e.c. alone, the gap is enormous: $\dot{r} = +70.1$ percent; $\hat{r} = -3.4$ percent. The reasons are self-evident: the very small 1958 value relative to subsequent annual entries and the sharp fluctuations in the series. Naturally, the gulf between $\dot{r}$ and $\hat{r}$ rates for outlays n.e.c. must expand the growth rate differences for investment when the latter is added to outlays n.e.c. Since I cannot separate outlays n.e.c. from "other outlays" in 1965S, I cannot test the impact on these plan-fulfillment calculations of deleting outlays n.e.c. But because of the volatility of these expenditures and the extreme sensitivity of their $\dot{r}$ measure to the 1958 value, it would be well to keep in view the $\hat{r}$ rates of growth of "other outlays" and of "other outlays" plus investment in considering the degree of attainment of the estimated 1965S targets. From that point of view, a more notable shortfall from the SYP is indicated in Table 35.

There is also the problem of the margin of error on "other outlays," to which I have referred at a number of points throughout this study. Granted a margin of 5 billion rubles on the 1965S data, the SYP growth rate of GNP could be in the range 6.9–7.7 percent. The *ex post* data have been tested only for three years, so I cannot compute alternative $\dot{r}$ and $\hat{r}$ growth rates. Assuming that the proportion of public sector residual revenues entered on current account was not 75 percent and was different in 1958 than in 1964 (see Appendix M), the range of r rates for 1958–1964 is 5.5–6.2 percent (Table 21). The consequent

[25] The 1965S ratios are developed from the data underlying Table 35; those for 1964 are computed from Table K-1.

range of underfulfillment of the average SYP growth rate is 10–30 percent. However, the margin of error on "other outlays" itself is far greater: the range of SYP expected growth rates is 3.0–19.6 percent and the *r* range for 1964 relative to 1958 is from −5.7 to +11.8 percent. Hence, the degree of implementation of the "other outlays" growth rate target extends from about −130 percent to +300 percent. Addition of all public sector investment, as expected, diminishes the range but still leaves an uncomfortably wide margin: the SYP growth rate is 5.9–10.7 percent, the 1958–1964 *r* rate is 3.8–8.7 percent, implying a degree of fulfillment from −64 percent (3.8 compared with 10.7) to 147 (8.7 compared with 5.9) percent.[26]

It appears safe to assume that the pace of GNP increase actually achieved in 1958–1964 was below that expected for the SYP. However, it is dangerous to make an unqualified statement about the relation between SYP and fulfillment of the rate of growth of expenditures on what we might label as the priority elements of nonconsumption, "other outlays" plus public sector investment.

Finally, the implementation record of the SYP also appears less favorable when viewed on a per capita basis. Total consumption, as we have seen, rose in 1959–1964 at an average rate of only a point or less behind the target rate, 5.1 or 5.5 instead of 6.2 percent. However, the realized growth rate of per capita consumption fell farther behind plan. Soviet planners in 1958–1959 apparently expected a population rate of increase of about 1.2 percent per year.[27] With that rate the 6.2 percent average annual growth target for total consumption was equivalent to a per capita rate of 4.9 percent. But the planners miscalculated: by 1964 there were over 5 million more mouths to feed than they had expected.[28]

[26] SYP estimates explained in the sources to Table 35 are recomputed ±5 billion rubles. The value of outlays n.e.c. at current prices in 1958 is either −1.51 or 1.27 billion rubles and in 1964 either −2.12 or 3.06 billions (Table M-1) as alternatives to the existing estimate. The 1964 values are deflated by the same procedure used in Appendix K to −2.05 and 2.96 billion rubles. Other 1964 values at 1958 prices as required are taken from Table K-1.

[27] A 1965S average annual population estimate of 225.4 millions is obtained by applying to the 1958 average, 206.8 millions (above, p. 144), the expected relative increase, 9 percent, cited by both Bor, *Voprosy metodologii planovogo balansa narodnogo khoziaistva SSSR*, 1960, p. 293; and Belik, *Natsional'nyi dokhod SSSR v semiletke*, 1959, p. 25.

[28] The planners' error was, in fact, greater than is implied, inasmuch as they had also failed to anticipate the extent of rural emigration. By 1963 the urban population was 12 million larger and the rural population 7 million

Consumption per head grew during 1959–1964 at 3.4 or 3.7 percent per year, a rate 25–30 percent below original expectations.

Similarly, the underfulfillment of GNP was larger per head than for aggregate outlays. For the latter, the realized rate was 15–20 percent below plan; on a per capita basis, actual results fell a quarter or a third short of the target, 3.9 ($\hat{r}$) or 4.3 ($\bar{r}$), instead of 5.9 percent.

Capital, Investment and Output

Table 36 assembles the data on rates of growth of capital, investment, and aggregate output, available both *ex ante* and *ex post.*

None of the SYP official documents—the Khrushchev reports or the Control Figures—makes any reference to capital stock changes, in either of the two definitions set out in Chapter 8 and its addendum. Nor does it seem possible to speculate about the level of retirements expected in 1965S. I am constrained, therefore, to deal only with the first concept of capital growth, that involving net investment. Unfortunately, neither the structure nor the total size of the capital stock corresponding to this concept is known for any recent year. However, based on data from the capital census and revaluation of January 1, 1960 and reported net investment at current prices, I have estimated a crude net capital stock series.[29] The entry for January 1, 1958 is about 177 billion rubles. If one may assume a constant annual rate of growth during the SYP period, the base and terminal year levels of net investment of 21.8 and 40 billion rubles (Table 26), respectively, imply a cumulative seven-year total of 219.5 billions. Thus, the following estimated values may be set down:

---

smaller than had been expected. Tiukov and Lokshin, *Sovetskaia torgovlia v period perekhoda k kommunizmu,* 1964, p. 151. Cited by Karcz, in *New Directions in the Soviet Economy,* 1966, p. 386, note 4.

Incidentally, in 1960 the Foreign Manpower Research Office of the U.S. Bureau of the Census estimated the total Soviet population in 1965S as 231.0 millions (cited in CIA, *Labor Supply and Employment in the USSR 1950–1965,* October 1960, pp. 16, 26) or 2.5 percent above the Soviet projection and less than two-tenths of a point below the actual average population in 1965 of 230.6 millions (*NKh 1965,* p. 7). The American estimate implied an average annual rate of growth to 1965S of 1.6 percent, compared with the Soviet-expected 1.2 percent, and hence a rate of increase of per capita consumption of 4.5 instead of 4.9 percent. The attained rate was lower than either figure.

[29] See above, p. 187.

	Billion rubles
Stock, 1/1/58	177
Net investment, 1958	21.8
Net investment, 1965S	40
Net investment cumulative total, SYP expected	219.5
Stock, 1/1/66S	418.3
Stock, 1/1/65S	378.3

If growth of the capital stock is measured between the beginning of 1958 and the beginning of 1965S, the implied increase is 114 percent; measured instead over the SYP period itself, the increase is 110 percent. These aggregate changes imply, correspondingly, average rates of

TABLE 36

AVERAGE ANNUAL RATE OF GROWTH OF FIXED CAPITAL, FIXED INVESTMENT, AND AGGREGATE OUTPUT, EX ANTE AND EX POST

(percent)

	SYP expected [a]	1958–1964 realized	
	$r \equiv \bar{r} \equiv \hat{r}$	$\bar{r}$	$\hat{r}$
Capital and investment			
1. Net capital stock at current prices	11	11.2	10.6
2. SNIP gross fixed investment	8.2	7.6	6.7
3. Gross new investment [b] at constant estimate prices	8.7	7.9	6.5
4. Gross new increments [b] at constant estimate prices	8.7	7.0	7.1
5. Capital repairs, deflated	7.4	8.6	9.2
6. Gross new increments [b] plus deflated capital repairs	8.4	7.3	7.6
7. Gross new increments [b] plus deflated capital repairs less depreciation	8.4	4.3	4.6
8. Reported net investment at current prices	9	6.2	4.8
Aggregate output			
9. GNP at 1958 EP	7.2	6.1	5.6
10. NMP utilized at 1958 EP	7.1–7.3	6.3	6.0

Notes:

[a] The underlying values are estimated or presumed to be at 1958 prices.

[b] Excluding livestock investment.

Sources:

Row 1. See text. Computed between 1/1/58 and 1/1/65.

Rows 2, 9. Table 35.

Rows 3–4, 6–8. Computed from Table 26. The SYP rate compares row 10.D with the 1958 entry in row 10.B of Table 26.

Row 5. SYP expected: computed from Table 26. 1958–1964. See sources to row 4 of Table 28.

Row 10. SYP expected: computed from Table Q-1. 1958–1964: Table 40 and the sources thereto.

growth of about 11 percent per year. Investment was apparently scheduled to increase less rapidly but not by very much; the largest margin of difference is relative to capital repairs. Whether defined as GNP or NMP, output was slated to increase at rates below those of either the capital stock or investment. It seems reasonably clear that the SYP intended or expected rising aggregate fixed capital-output ratios. It goes without saying that the addition of "other outlays" to investment strongly reinforces this conclusion. Whether the same would be true for outlays n.e.c. alone is not determinable.

The gross pattern of implementation does not look substantially different in the $\bar{r}$ and $\hat{r}$ frameworks. In the former, the proxy net investment series (row 7) and in the latter, both proxy and reported net investment (rows 7 and 8), are the sole exceptions to the finding that growth rates for capital and investment exceeded those of aggregate output. This is a finding discussed at some length in Chapter 8. Of particular interest here is the question of the degree of implementation. For the most part, $\bar{r}$ values of capital, investment, and output exceed the corresponding $\hat{r}$ rates. Thus, implementation appears more favorable from an $\bar{r}$ viewpoint, and since arbitrariness of the initial year values is not a significant issue in Table 36, $\bar{r}$ has a valid claim to superior standing in the set of comparisons. The net capital-output ratio is shown as increasing more than expected, but deflation of the net investment increments might upset this finding. Possibly, the gross investment-output ratios also rose relative to plan; for the relation of net investment to output the reverse is clearly true, especially after allowance for deflation of the reported net investment series.

Table 36 focuses exclusively on fixed capital numerators. I have speculated that the SYP intended an average annual growth of state-cooperative inventories of about 6 or 7 percent (Appendix H). My total inventory investment estimate for 1965S is below that of 1958. Hence, the SYP inventory-output ratio is estimated more or less constant, while inventory investment-output ratios were, by these estimates, to decline. Because of the sharp fluctuations in inventory investment, the *ex post* rates of growth of inventory investment in different formulations diverge sharply, but in any case are below those of output in either variant.[80] The realized inventory investment-output ratio thus declined; whether more or less than expected is indeterminate.

---

[80] See p. 467 and Tables 35 and 36.

Part III

Comparisons and Implications

10

Comparisons with Other Calculations

The presentation of findings has been completed and I now want to appraise them against those of other calculations, Soviet and non-Soviet. However, the field of comparisons is constricted: as there is no counterpart to my 1965S estimates, only the 1958–1964 accounts can be considered; with respect to the latter neither the official Soviet data nor the available Western reconstructions offers exact parallels to the material of the present study. Where comparisons are possible at all, they will necessarily be drawn between only partly comparable entities.

Structure of Final Use

Soviet statistical yearbooks report the final use distribution of NMP in current prices between consumption and "accumulation and other expenditures." Such data were discussed in Chapter 7 and the extensive differences with the SNIP accounts brought out. The Soviet data are, of course, valued at prevailing prices; this is true of the calculations of growth at constant prices as well. A number of Soviet economists have experimented with revaluations according to a variety of theoretical criteria, but the official data do not report such revaluations. These are, in any case, considerably removed from the logic and motivation of the AFCS.

I stated in Chapter 1 that the material of the present study makes up the only independent reconstruction of Soviet national accounts for the period in question. There exist alternative estimates of growth of national output but only scattered computations of the structure of resource use. The available data are presented in Table 37 juxtaposed to my estimates at basic AFC, but the degree of comparability is so limited that little significance can be attached to the indicated differences.

TABLE 37
ALTERNATIVE DISTRIBUTIONS OF GNP BY END USE, 1960 AND 1964
(percent)

	1960		1964		
	Cohn [a]	Becker [b]	ACDA [c]	Cohn [a]	Becker [b]
1. Household consumption	47.1	49.1	..	46.5	48.7
2. Communal services, excluding R&D	10.1 (rows 2–3)	8.6 (rows 2–3)	9.3 [f]	9.4	7.5
3. Administration [d]				2.3	1.3
4. Gross investment					
A. Fixed capital [e]	31.3	29.6	..	28.9	30.3
B. Inventories	1.3	2.9	..	1.6	5.0
C. Total	32.6	32.5	..	30.5	35.3
5. Defense	10.2	5.8	10.0–13.3	11.3	6.5
6. Other	—	3.8	0.2 [g]	—	.7
GNP	100.0	100.0		100.0	100.0

Notes:
[a] At factor cost.
[b] At basic AFC.
[c] At "dollar equivalents."
[d] Including internal security.
[e] Including R&D.
[f] May include R&D.
[g] Foreign economic aid.

Sources:
Cohn 1960. Dimensions of Soviet Economic Power, 1962, p. 72. Cohn is not specific about the scope of the end-use categories in his table, and it is only my presumption (based on Bornstein's classification, which serves as Cohn's benchmark) that internal security is included with administration and R&D with gross fixed investment. I have not attempted to replicate Cohn's calculations.
Cohn 1964. New Directions in the Soviet Economy, 1966, p. 129.
ACDA. "Worldwide Defense Expenditures and Selected Economic Data, 1964," cited in *Bulletin of Atomic Scientists*, September, 1966, pp. 44, 46.
Becker. Table 15.

The periodic reviews of the Soviet economy published under the auspices of the Joint Economic Committee of the U.S. Congress (identified hereafter as JEC studies) have included estimates of the growth of Soviet GNP calculated by origin rather than from end use. The compiler of these estimates, Stanley Cohn, has also computed the end-use structure of Soviet GNP in two years of the period under consideration, 1960 and 1964.[1] For neither of these years is his calculation directly comparable to mine. In both years Cohn's results represent an extension of 1955 end-use weights, originally estimated by Morris Bornstein, to 1960 and 1964 by means of selected time series.

Bornstein's calculation differs considerably from those of the SNIP accounts, past and present, in terms of the scope of individual end uses, but comparability is impaired by other differences in methodology. Bornstein valued farm income in kind at an average of state retail and collective farm market prices; the SNIP series uses average realized farm prices. He viewed miscellaneous state budget revenues as largely indirect taxes on public sector output and hence deducted them along with turnover taxes in his factor cost adjustment. He did not make an adjustment in retail sales and procurement prices for the retail price divergence caused by adjustment for indirect taxes and subsidies incident on retail sales.[2]

The end use indexes applied to Bornstein's 1955 distribution are drawn from various sources, and some of these indexes will be discussed later in this chapter, but several features of the indexes make it difficult to interpret a direct comparison of Cohn's end-use breakdowns with mine. For example, the 1960 structure relies on a time-series for investment that combines fixed capital investment at constant prices with a series for inventory investment derived as a constant proportion of net industrial output and trade turnover. The 1964 distribution employs some earlier calculations of mine to extend the 1955 defense component and to aid in reflating an index of private consumption, calculations that are superseded by the present study. Inventory investment in 1964 is computed as the product of such investment in 1955 and a 1964/1955 ratio of state-cooperative stocks.

The partial breakdown for 1964 identified as "ACDA" is a published estimate of the U.S. Arms Control and Disarmament Agency, valued in "U.S. dollar equivalents." No details of the calculation are provided.

The striking differences in Table 37 between my estimates and the others are in the defense share of GNP. My estimates are factor cost adjustments of the explicit state budget allocation, whereas Cohn and (presumably) ACDA have attempted to include concealed military expenditures as well. Apart from my earlier remarks on the methodol-

---

[1] *Dimensions of Soviet Economic Power,* 1962, p. 72; and *New Directions in the Soviet Economy,* 1966, p. 129.

[2] Bornstein *et al., Soviet National Accounts for 1955,* 1961, pp. 68–69, 75.

ogy of the Cohn estimates and the absence of information on the basis of the ACDA figures, I need only refer to my discussion in Chapter 7. My conclusion there was, first, that possibly I had underestimated the magnitude of public sector outlays n.e.c. as a consequence of underestimating the share of residual public sector revenues appropriately entered on current account; and second, that including internal security outlays but excluding investment in armaments industry, the military's share of GNP appeared to be a maximum of about one-tenth. However, the similarity between the latter figure and the Cohn-ACDA numbers in Table 37 provides neither vindication of their estimates nor support for my Chapter 7 conclusion. Differences in the methodology of the various calculations are, or in the case of ACDA may be, too large to permit either conclusion.

In the remainder of this chapter I focus on growth calculations, that is, those at constant prices. My estimates are compared with the official Soviet data and with some non-Soviet studies. Here too, the comparison is not of strictly similar products. There has been no other published attempt to deflate end-use values in recent years.[3] In the alternative American estimates of consumption growth discussed below, national accounts may serve only as a source for group weights. All the calculations shown in Table 39 and discussed later on in this chapter relate to GNP computed by branch of origin. Except for the official Soviet indexes, these calculations represent aggregations of heterogeneous branch indexes weighted by base-year income.

Consumption

The JEC studies have provided indexes of consumption, generally per capita but also more recently in aggregate, for various years and in varying detail. Findings from the three most recent JEC studies are compared with mine and with official Soviet data in Table 38; the comparison is in terms of annual growth rates in both r and $\hat{r}$ formulations.

The JEC 1964 and 1965 series appear anonymously, but David Bronson and Barbara Severin are identified as the authors of the JEC 1966 section on consumption from which the 1966 series have been taken. It is clear that essentially the same methodology underlies all three series in the top half of the table. The JEC 1964 series, on which

[3] The Moorsteen-Powell investment calculations are a special case discussed below.

TABLE 38

ALTERNATIVE ESTIMATES OF GROWTH OF AGGREGATE CONSUMPTION, ANNUAL PERCENT GROWTH RATES, 1958–1964

	1959	1960	1961	1962	1963	1964	1958–1964 average[a]	
							r	$\hat{r}$
JEC 1964	7.0	3.9	3.3	5.0	..	..	n.a.	n.a.
JEC 1965	4	6	4	5	3	..	n.a.	n.a.
JEC 1966	5.0	4.9	4.1	5.2	2.0	3.5	4.1	4.1
Becker: 1958 EP	5.9	6.2	3.4	4.6	4.3	4.4	4.8	4.6
1964 EP	5.8	5.8	3.1	4.5	4.1	4.4	4.6	4.5
							1959–1963 average[a]	
							r	$\hat{r}$
Official Soviet	..	8	3	6	3	..	5.0–5.2	4.9
JEC 1966, adjusted	..	5	4	6	2	..	3.9–4.1	4.1
Becker, 1958 EP, modified	..	7.1	3.6	5.8	4.5	..	5.2	5.0

Note:

[a] My computations throughout. For definitions of r and $\hat{r}$ see pp. 127 ff.

Sources:

JEC 1964. Computed from an index of total consumption per capita on a 1955 base, from *Annual Economic Indicators for the USSR*, 1964, p. 37, multiplied by an index of average annual population, from *NKh 1964*, p. 7 and *VS*, 1963, No. 8, p. 91.

JEC 1965. Computed from an index of total consumption per capita on a 1955 base, from *Current Economic Indicators for the USSR*, 1965, p. 119, multiplied by the population index, as above.

JEC 1966. Computed from an index of aggregate total consumption on a 1950 base, from *New Directions in the Soviet Economy*, 1966, p. 521.

Becker, 1958 and 1964 EP. Computed from an aggregation of household outlays on consumption and communal services (excluding R&D). For comparability with the JEC data, outlays on dues are deducted and net consumption of farm income in kind is revalued at adjusted collective farm market prices, as an approximation to the JEC valuation at retail prices. The adjustment to collective farm market prices consists in a discount to the value of consumption in kind (net of production expenses) at 1958 or 1964 prices, represented by the ratio of collective farm market to state retail prices in either weight year (p. 490). The underlying data for these series are taken from Tables A-2, K-1, and K-2; on the deflation of household production expenses, see p. 510).

Official Soviet. Computed from *NKh 1964*, p. 589 (total nonproductive consumption excluding amortization at "comparable prices").

JEC 1966, adjusted. *New Directions in the Soviet Economy*, 1966, p. 523: "adjusted to approximate the coverage of the official index through the exclusion of rent expenditures on services and on salaries in health and education."

Becker, 1958 EP, modified. Computed from an aggregation of household outlays on consumption and government services (excluding "defense"). For comparability with the official data, the series excludes the wage component of services, calculated as indicated in the sources for my reconstruction of NMP produced, Table 40 below. No attempt is made to estimate the current material outlay component of "defense" expenditures, presumably included in Soviet "consumption" data (see above, p. 158). Farm consumption in kind is adjusted by the amounts shown in Table 25. Except as indicated above, the underlying data are from Table K-1.

there is the least supplementary information, is said to be an average of subindexes for food products, nonfood goods, and services, weighted 61.4 percent, 23.3 percent, and 15.3 percent, respectively. These are also the weights used in the JEC 1965 and 1966 series.[4] The methodology underlying the JEC 1965 subindexes is identified as that of a 1962 JEC contribution by Rachel Golden.[5] Golden's methodological notes, in turn, differ little from those provided by Bronson and Severin for the 1966 series. The only notable exception is that the JEC 1962 services subindex is largely derived from values at 1958 prices, whereas the corresponding JEC 1966 subindex is based on 1955 expenditures moved by volume indicators. There appear to be small differences in the scope of coverage among the JEC studies as well: the sample for the JEC 1966 durables subindex, for example, includes musical instruments, which were not explicitly included in the JEC 1962 sample; the food products sample is said to embrace 25 products in the 1962 study and 20 products in the 1966 study. Apart from the exception noted, all the JEC consumption series may be characterized briefly as 1955 expenditure weights moved by volume indicators. The latter are production indexes in the case of foods and beverages, soft goods, and consumer durables; a variety of other indicators are used for the services subindex. Thus, the JEC series are not derived from national income accounts and in this sense are conceptually different from mine.

In the early years of the period under review, there are considerable differences among the JEC studies with respect to the calculated rates of growth, as shown in Table 38. The annual rates of growth range between 4 and 7 percent for 1959 and 4 and 6 percent for 1960. Differences in subsequent years are considerably smaller or nonexistent. The JEC studies do not comment on these changes in the consumption indexes, and we can only assume some connection with the differences in scope and methods outlined above. Annual increases in my estimated series vary on either side of those computed for the JEC reports but tend to be higher than the Bronson-Severin rates. In terms of the latter comparison, the largest gap shows up in 1963 where my estimate is 2 points higher. For the six-year period as a whole, the average annual

[4] For the 1965 series this is stated explicitly in the source. On the JEC 1966 weights see note 6, below.

[5] *Dimensions of Soviet Economic Power*, 1962, p. 360. I have not reproduced the JEC 1962 calculations because they are shown in the source only as annual averages for 1951–1955, 1956–1961, 1956–1958, and 1959–1961.

rate of growth in my series is roughly half a percentage point greater than that computed for the JEC series.

It might be useful to pinpoint the outlay categories responsible for these observed differences. Bronson and Severin cite their subindexes for soft goods, consumer durables, foods and beverages, and services; the subindex of services has component subindexes of personal services and of health and education. The subindexes for goods may be combined and compared with indexes computed from my data [6] as follows (annual percentage changes):

	1959	*1960*	*1961*	*1962*	*1963*	*1964*	*Average (r) 1958–1964*
Goods							
Bronson-Severin	5.4	4.8	3.9	5.1	1.4	2.9	3.9
Becker, 1958 EP	5.5	5.9	2.4	4.4	3.4	3.8	4.1
Personal services							
Bronson-Severin	8.2	8.0	6.5	8.1	6.0	6.7	7.2
Becker, 1958 EP	7.2	7.3	9.5	9.3	6.8	7.4	8.1
Health and education							
Bronson-Severin	4.8	7.0	6.6	4.7	6.4	6.1	6.0
Becker, 1958 EP	7.9	7.5	6.4	2.8	9.0	6.2	6.4

In comparisons of the component series, too, the annual relative increases in my estimates tend to be higher—4 of 6 observations in each set—than those in Bronson and Severin's. Agreement between our respective calculations is greatest for goods, where the average annual rates of growth are essentially the same. Because of the preponderant weight of goods in both calculations (Bronson and Severin, 84.7 percent; Becker, 82.3 percent), the 2 point goods margin in 1963 is largely responsible for the slightly larger overall consumption margin in that year appearing in Table 38. But by the same token, the close agreement of the two goods series assures the relatively small divergences found in Table 38. The margin of difference in average growth rates is greater for personal services than for health and education, but in both categories it is a percentage point or less.

---

[6] The Bronson and Severin weights, kindly supplied by the authors, are .2022 for soft goods, .0308 for consumer durables, .614 for foods and beverages, and .153 for services. My index of goods consumption is obtained from the consumption total, as indicated in the sources to Table 38, less communal services and household outlays on rent and other services.

In the 1964 yearbook the Central Statistical Administration published a detailed distribution of "consumption" by product group at current prices for the years 1959–1963 and a series of indexes at "comparable prices" [7] for the same commodity classification. Annual changes in the official index for all "consumption" excluding depreciation on nonproductive capital are shown in the sixth row of Table 38. The following row is taken directly from Bronson and Severin and represents an attempt on their part to match the official series in scope and methodology. My "modified" series in the last row of Table 38 is similarly designed—that is, in essence to exclude the wage component of services. There is evidently complete agreement among these last three series for 1962; Bronson and Severin's adjusted data are closer than mine to the official in 1963, whereas the reverse is true for 1960. Measured by the $\hat{r}$ formulation, the average annual rate of growth of the Bronson-Severin adjusted series is almost a percentage point below that of the official series; there is almost no gap between my estimates and the official series in this respect.

Bronson and Severin explain the divergence of their results from the official series as due in part to the lag of sales of animal products behind their production. By implication, Bronson and Severin appear to accept the official index as a reliable standard. If this is so, my modified 1958 EP series provides a good approximation to the growth of "consumption," defined in the official sense, in the period 1959–1963, except for the overstatement in 1963. Since my consumption totals at current prices are explicitly reconciled with the official data,[8] whatever divergences appear between my modified 1958 EP series and the official index must be due to one or more of the following: (1) errors in the reconciliation at current prices; (2) differences between the official and my series in the deflation of current-price values; (3) differences in the respective series' estimates of the material component of government services. On the first, there is nothing I can add here to the discussion in Appendix B. The second does not seem applicable, as the implicit price

[7] According to Eidel'man, *Ekonomika i matematicheskie metody*, 1967, No. 4, p. 537, these are 1959 prices. This is also the implication of multiplying the reported subindexes for foods, nonfood goods, and depreciation on nonproductive capital by their respective shares in the total for 1959: the calculation yields an index of total consumption including depreciation that precisely replicates the reported index in 1960–1961 and departs from the reported index in 1962–1963 by only one percentage point.

[8] See below, pp. 357–359.

deflators of consumption excluding depreciation derivable from the official data match mine almost exactly:

Ratios of indexes of current-price values to indexes of constant-price values

	1959	*1960*	*1961*	*1962*	*1963*
Soviet	100	99	100	102	103
Becker, modified series	100	99.8	99.6	102.2	102.9

My guess is that the third factor is the source of the few divergences observed.[9]

Investment

Gross investment in my accounts consists of two elements: fixed investment by state-cooperative, collective farm, and household sectors; and inventory investment by the state-cooperative and collective farm sectors. For the major component of fixed investment, at both current and constant prices, new investment by the state-cooperative sectors, and private housing construction, I use official data valued at "comparable" estimate prices. Collective farm fixed investment, on the other hand, is derived from farm reports on cash incomes allocated to investment and is conceptually distinct from the official data at estimate prices. My inventory investment series again derives either from collective farm accounts or official data on working capital held in the state-cooperative sector. No official data are available on inventory investment at (average annual) current or constant prices, whereas I have attempted an involved deflation procedure (following Bergson) to arrive at such values. This brief recapitulation of the methodology of my investment estimates indicates that there is neither point to, nor scope for, comparisons with official data.

The only non-Soviet independent calculation of investment now available is that by Richard Moorsteen and Raymond Powell. Their data may be briefly characterized as follows:

(1) Fixed investment embraces increments of construction, installation, and equipment; investment in livestock is separately estimated. Capital repairs to structures and equipment are included with investment in construction and equipment. Valuation is at three sets of prevailing

[9] There may be a relation here to a difficulty discussed on p. 118, arising from my method of deflating wages in government services.

prices—1928, 1937, and 1950—of which only the latter two are used for the 1960s. Investment in construction is estimated by means of an index of material inputs to construction, whereas the post-1956 equipment series is an extrapolation of the 1956 figure by the corresponding official Soviet series at "constant" estimate prices. The growth of investment in installation is assumed to be intermediate between the growth of investment in construction and that of equipment acquisitions. Moorsteen and Powell do not estimate the value of activities constituting "other investment" in the official series. Thus, the Moorsteen-Powell fixed capital data are narrower in coverage than my figures in their exclusion of livestock and "other investment." In addition two other differences must be noted: (a) Acquisitions of equipment requiring installation are treated as inventories in their study but as fixed investment in mine; (b) My collective farm fixed investment estimates represent money income allocated to the investment fund, whereas in the Moorsteen-Powell series collective farm investment is on the same basis as investment by other sectors.

(2) The Moorsteen-Powell inventory investment series is derived from deflated values of nonagricultural inventories held by the state-cooperative sectors plus agricultural inventories projected on agricultural output. My estimates are derived from deflated values of all inventories held by the state-cooperative sector and the allocation of collective farm cash income to increments of working capital. As indicated, inventory investment according to Moorsteen and Powell includes equipment requiring installation, which appears in my data as fixed investment. Increments of immature livestock are grouped with inventory investment in my series but form part of their separate estimates of livestock investment. Finally, they exclude from inventory investment, as I do not, "expenditures of future periods" in construction.[10]

I have outlined the considerable conceptual differences between the Moorsteen-Powell data and my own. There are also differences of a procedural order with regard to inventory investment. I noted that the Moorsteen-Powell computations use three sets of weights but only 1937 and 1950 prices for the 1960s. There is considerable similarity though not identity of the deflators in our respective computations, but inasmuch as these differ somewhat in the sector-product breakdown of inventories at current prices to which the deflators are applied, there must inevitably be some divergence in the constant-price results on this

[10] On the meaning of this term and my reasons for considering this item an element of inventories, see below, p. 393.

account alone. Moorsteen and Powell also revalue their estimates at constant factor cost, but their method of factor cost adjustment differs substantially from mine.[11]

Despite the differences in concept and procedure noted, there may be some interest in comparing the results of our respective calculations. Such a comparison, in terms of indexes and $\hat{r}$ average annual rates of growth, is provided in Table 39. For simplicity I have used only my 1958 price series; the 1964 EP and AFC results differ only marginally from the 1958 price data. For the period as a whole, the results of our respective fixed as well as all gross investment calculations look very much alike; overall increase and average annual rates of growth are separated by small margins. This is not true of inventory investment where the Moorsteen-Powell series show no increase on the average, compared with the 3 percent growth rate of my series, and substantially different index numbers in 1964 compared with those of my series.

That the Moorsteen-Powell and my fixed investment estimates are near look-alikes is not surprising. In both cases the state-cooperative equipment components reflect the official data. Although independently constructed, the Moorsteen-Powell construction-installation series is also not far removed, especially in the later years of the period, from the official data, as the following tabulation shows:[12]

	Indexes, 1958 = 100						*Average annual rate of growth* ($\hat{r}$)
	1959	*1960*	*1961*	*1962*	*1963*	*1964*	
Moorsteen-Powell, 1950 prices	111	119	124	128	132	137	4.8
Official, "comparable" estimate prices	115	125	127	128	131	140	4.6

[11] Moorsteen and Powell, *The Soviet Capital Stock 1928–1962,* 1966 and *Supplement I,* 1968. The latter, a pamphlet written by Moorsteen, Powell, and myself, was intended primarily as an updating of the major series of the book. My contribution was supplied within the conceptual framework of the original study by Moorsteen and Powell, which is obviously distinct from that of the present one. Although there are topics of common interest to both Moorsteen-Powell (including *Supplement I*) and the present work, I view the two studies as essentially complementary rather than competitive.

[12] Moorsteen-Powell data are computed from Table A-4 of their book and Table A-4-X of *Supplement I.* The data underlying the official series represent the sum of state-cooperative construction-installation plus private housing construction (*NKh 1964,* pp. 511–512) and the collective farm component. For 1958–1963 the latter is taken from *VS,* 1964, No. 5, p. 92. The 1964 figure is projected on the 1963 figure by the relative increase in collective farm investment at estimate prices (*NKh 1964,* p. 522).

TABLE 39

COMPARISONS OF INDEXES AND AVERAGE RATES OF GROWTH FOR MOORSTEEN-POWELL AND BECKER ESTIMATES OF GROSS INVESTMENT, 1958–1964

	Indexes, 1958 = 100						Average annual rate of growth ($\hat{r}$) (percent)
	1959	1960	1961	1962	1963	1964	
Fixed Investment							
Moorsteen-Powell [a]							
1937 prices	110	118	126	137	146	159	7.8
1950 prices	110	117	125	134	142	153	7.1
Becker							
1958 EP	110	120	127	133	139	153	6.7
1958 AFC	110	121	128	134	140	154	6.8
Inventory Investment							
Moorsteen-Powell [a]							
1937 factor cost	94	62	61	47	69	115	0.0
1950 factor cost	95	56	70	54	77	113	0.0
Becker							
1958 EP	119	59	74	69	98	135	3.2
1958 AFC	118	59	75	70	98	135	3.3
All Gross Investment							
Moorsteen-Powell [b]							
1937 prices	106	105	113	118	125	149	6.4
1950 prices	107	105	115	119	124	145	5.8
Becker							
1958 EP	111	109	118	122	132	149	6.2
1958 AFC	111	111	119	123	133	151	6.4

Notes:
[a] Excluding livestock.
[b] Including livestock.

Sources:
Moorsteen-Powell. The Soviet Capital Stock 1928–1962, 1966, Tables T-44 and T-46; *Supplement I*, 1968, Tables T-44-X and T-46-X.
Becker. Tables 18 and 20.

The relevance of this last comparison to the central issue, differences between the Moorsteen-Powell and my series, is only somewhat attenuated by the fact that my collective farm investment figures are not derived from the official series at estimate prices. Because of the predominant weight of fixed investment in all gross investment, our respective all gross investment estimates on balance should also resemble each other. It is clear then that our series differ on year to year changes while arriving at similar overall and average growth levels.

Inventory investment is a strong exception to this generalization. Possibly, some role is to be assigned to the difference between 1950 and

1958 prices, especially as they affect agricultural inventories. But the major divergence can be traced to a single year, 1959. If the Moorsteen-Powell index number for the series at 1950 factor cost were, say, 115 instead of 95 and all other entries in the series were projected on that figure in proportion to the existing series, the revised figures would compare more closely to mine. Roughly the same outcome would be achieved if I raised my 1958 inventory investment figure to a level 5 percent above that of 1959, as in the Moorsteen-Powell series:

	Indexes, 1958 = 100						*Average annual rate of growth (r̂) (percent)*
	1959	*1960*	*1961*	*1962*	*1963*	*1964*	
Revised Moorsteen-Powell	115	68	84	65	93	136	2.6
Becker, 1958 AFC	118	59	75	70	98	135	3.3
Original Moorsteen-Powell	95	56	70	54	77	113	0.0
Revised Becker, 1958 AFC	95	48	60	56	79	109	0.0

The probable major source of the difference in our respective (original) index numbers for 1959 is not the 1959 but the 1958 investment value. Except for inventories held in agriculture, Moorsteen-Powell and I alike begin with the detailed official distribution of assets held by branch at current prices as reported in the statistical yearbooks. Such data are available for January 1, 1956, 1959, and thereafter annually. Because of the absence of official data for January 1, 1958, I arrived at an estimate for 1958 somewhat arbitrarily; Moorsteen and Powell have filled in the gap by a variety of estimating procedures. Moreover, in all years they project inventories in agriculture on an independent estimate of agricultural output, whereas I rely in the first instance on the official data for inventories in state agriculture and add allocations by collective farms to their working capital funds.

Conceivably, I have underestimated inventory investment in 1958, although an overestimate by Moorsteen and Powell for that year or a combination of the two are also admissible hypotheses. If I have underestimated inventory investment in 1958, the rates of growth of all gross investment are overstated: taking 1958 AFC as an example, the maximum margin (using the Moorsteen-Powell figures as the baseline) would be four-tenths of a point in the $\hat{r}$ and 1.2 percentage points in the $\bar{r}$

formulations.[13] Under the existing procedure the rate of growth of GNP would be unaffected; only the value of outlays n.e.c. would have to change. Since that change would be to a negative value of 1.37 billion rubles, it is at least possible that residual public sector revenues (item 3.E of Table 3), which directly influence the value of outlays n.e.c., have been understated. If that is true GNP in 1958 would have to be raised, but the rate of growth at 1958 AFC in the existing series would be overstated by a maximum of one-tenth of a point in the $\hat{r}$ and four-tenths of a point in the $\bar{r}$ formulations.

Aggregate Output

Table 40 sets out indexes on a 1958 base and annual rates of growth of aggregate output as measured in official Soviet computations, my own estimates, and those of two other American studies. To the best of my knowledge, the Moorsteen-Powell and Cohn series are the only other independent calculations that have been published. Only my estimates are derived from deflated values of end uses; the other calculations are weighted averages of branch of origin indexes.

Net material product series of two kinds are shown in Table 40.[14] Indexes of *produced* NMP have been a regular feature of Soviet yearbooks since their first reappearance in 1955 after almost twenty years of statistical repression. Produced NMP is a branch of origin calculation in which depreciation and intermediate material purchases are deducted from gross material product in the particular branch. Values of *utilized* NMP at current prices have been published regularly beginning with the 1960 yearbooks, but an index at constant prices was introduced only in the 1965 yearbook. The price weights are apparently those of 1958.[15]

---

[13] The $\bar{r}$ values are included here for their relevance to the plan-fulfillment comparisons of Chapter 9.

[14] Recently the Soviet statistical yearbooks have been reporting indexes of gross material product (GMP) as well. GMP differs from NMP by the inclusion not only of depreciation on "productive" capital but also of intermediate "productive" output. Indexes of GMP, omitted from Table 40, move closely with those of produced NMP.

[15] According to the methodological notes at the back of the yearbooks, the weights of the NMP indexes are 1956 prices for the years 1956–1958 and 1958 prices for entries from 1959 on (*NKh 1965*, p. 813). I understand this to refer only to a series embracing both pre- and post-1958 figures; the indexes with 1958 base reproduced in Table 40 most probably are derived

Alongside my estimates of GNP, I also show a reconstructed produced NMP series. This is derived from my estimates of GNP at 1958 EP by a series of adjustments (described in full in the sources to Table 40) intended to yield measurements conceptually equivalent to the official series. Apart from deduction of certain services, the reconciliation process requires the deduction of deflated depreciation of "productive" capital and a slight upward revision in the SNIP valuation of farm consumption in kind.

Three sets of GNP estimates by Stanley Cohn are identified in Table 40 by the year of the JEC report in which they appeared. The weights of the 1964 series are in the main Bornstein's estimates of national income by branch of origin at factor cost in 1955, with the addition of an imputed rental return to superior land; both the 1965 and 1966 series employ 1959 originating-branch weights, but between his latter two JEC contributions Cohn substantially revised the weights. Cohn's aggregate indexes are weighted averages of indexes for industry, construction, agriculture, transportation, communication, "commerce,"[16] and services. In all cases his index of construction is derived from official investment data, but the indexes of industrial and agricultural production are independently estimated by various JEC contributors. For his transportation and communications indexes in the JEC 1965 and 1966 series, Cohn relied on Kaplan's estimates,[17] whereas the 1964 series had used railroad ton-kilometers and officially reported communications revenue (or output?) values. Indexes of "commerce" and services are essentially employment series, boosted in the 1965 and 1966 contribu-

---

from 1958 price weighted series. At least, this can be shown to be true of produced NMP, for which the 1964 and 1965 yearbooks cite absolute values at current and at "comparable" prices. The 1958 entries are identical in both series, and the 1958-based index that can be computed from the absolute values at "comparable prices" is identical to the published index. (*Ibid.*, p. 589; *NKh 1964*, p. 575. The rates of growth of official produced NMP in the second half of Table 40 are calculated from the absolute value series.)

[16] Trade, procurement, and supply-sales. The JEC 1964 series was based on trade activity alone.

[17] Kaplan, *Soviet Transport and Communications: Output Indexes,* 1928–1962, November 1964, and Supplement, November 1965. The Supplement extends the series through 1963. Cohn estimated 1964 links on the basis of increases in freight volume and communications employment adjusted for the relationship of these indicators in 1958–1962 to Kaplan's series.

TABLE 40

ALTERNATIVE ESTIMATES OF GROWTH OF AGGREGATE SOVIET OUTPUT, 1958–1964

	1959	1960	1961	1962	1963	1964	Average, 1958–1964	
	A. Indexes: 1958 = 100							
Official Soviet: NMP								
Produced	108	116	124	131	136	149		
Utilized	106	115	121	128	132	144		
Cohn: GNP								
JEC 1964	104	109	116	119	..	..		
JEC 1965	104	109	117	122	125	..		
JEC 1966	105	110	117	123	126	136		
Moorsteen-Powell								
GNP	106	113	120	127	131	141		
NNP	106	112	118	125	128	137		
Becker								
NMP produced	109	116	118	125	131	141		
GNP								
1958 AFC	109	116	118	126	133	141		
1964 AFC	109	115	118	125	131	140		
AFC Method II, 1958 AFC	110	117	121	129	137	145		
AFC Method I, 1958 AFC								
With 4 supplementary adjustments [a]	110	120	122	129	135	142		
Same, excluding outlays n.e.c.	108	114	122	127	134	141		
AFC Method II, 1958 AFC								
With 4 supplementary adjustments [a]	111	121	125	132	139	146		
Same, excluding outlays n.e.c.	109	117	125	130	138	145		
	B. Annual rates of growth, percent						$\hat{r}$	r
Official Soviet: NMP								
Produced	7.5	7.7	6.8	5.7	4.1	9.3	6.5	6.8
Utilized	6	8	5–6	5–6	3–4	9	6.0	6.3
Cohn: GNP								
JEC 1964	3.9	5.0	6.5	2.2	..	..	n.a.	n.a.
JEC 1965	4.2	4.9	6.8	4.3	2.6	..	n.a.	n.a.
JEC 1966	4.9	5.2	6.2	5.1	2.6	7.9	5.2	5.3
Moorsteen-Powell								
GNP	6.3	5.8	6.4	5.8	3.5	7.6	5.7	5.9
NNP	5.9	5.4	5.9	5.3	2.8	7.4	5.3	5.4
Becker								
NMP produced	8.6	6.4	2.3	5.8	5.3	6.8	5.4	5.8
GNP								
1958 AFC	9.2	6.7	1.2	7.0	5.2	6.3	5.5	5.9
1964 AFC	8.8	6.1	1.8	6.5	5.0	6.6	5.4	5.8

TABLE 40 (continued)

	1959	1960	1961	1962	1963	1964	Average, 1959–1964	
							p	*r*
AFC Method II, 1958 AFC	9.6	6.9	3.4	6.7	5.9	5.8	6.0	6.4
AFC Method I, 1958 AFC								
With 4 supplementary adjustments [a]	10.4	8.6	1.4	5.9	4.7	5.4	5.5	6.0
Same, excluding outlays n.e.c.	8.4	5.5	6.2	4.2	5.6	5.8	5.6	5.9
AFC Method II, 1958 AFC								
With 4 supplementary adjustments [a]	10.9	8.8	3.5	5.7	5.4	5.0	6.0	6.5
Same, excluding outlays n.e.c.	9.2	6.7	7.1	4.3	6.0	5.3	6.1	6.4

Note:

[a] Housing interest is imputed at the rate of 5 percent.

Sources:

Official Soviet: NMP. *NKh 1964*, p. 575; *NKh 1965*, pp. 59, 589.

Cohn. 1964: *Annual Economic Indicators for the USSR*, 1964, p. 93. 1965: *Current Economic Indicators for the USSR*, 1965, p. 12. 1966: *New Directions in the Soviet Economy*, 1966, p. 104.

Moorsteen-Powell. The Soviet Capital Stock 1928–1962, 1966, Table T-47, and *Supplement I*, Table T-47X.

Becker.

NMP produced. Represents GNP at 1958 EP (Table K-1) plus a valuation adjustment for farm consumption in kind less the wage component of services and less capital consumption. For the valuation adjustment, see Table 25; deflation is not attempted since the adjustments are small.

For ease in calculation, the deduction of the wage component of services is handled as follows. First, the following service categories (Table K-1) are deducted in full: consumer services, communal services, R&D, administration, internal security, and military pay and subsistence. Household outlays on utilities and "industrial services" are added back, as is the materials component of household and government expenditures on services excluding "defense" (Tables 25 and J-2; these expenditures are not deflated in Appendix K).

The capital consumption deduction represents total depreciation on productive and nonproductive capital, plus the book value of retirements, less depreciation of nonproductive capital (the latter item viewed in Soviet accounting as an element of consumption). Figures for book value of retirements in all years and for depreciation in 1958–1962 are taken directly from Table 26 and the sources thereto. The 1963 and 1964 figures for depreciation shown there are deflated for the increase in depreciation norms instituted in 1963. For nonproductive depreciation, an implicit deflator is computed from the data in *NKh 1964*, pp. 584–585, 589. The 1963 figure for total depreciation in Table 26 is deflated on the indications in *NKh 1963*, p. 501, that the increase in norms meant a net decrease in produced NMP of 2.3 billion rubles. At current prices, my estimate of the 1963 depreciation deduction is 22.9 billion rubles of total depreciation, plus 1.2 billions of retirements at book value, less 7.55 billion rubles of depreciation of nonproductive capital. Deflated, the latter figure reduces to 7.3 billion rubles. Given these data, deflated total depreciation in 1963 is by subtraction 20.3 billion rubles, or 88.6 percent of the current price figure. This deflator is then applied to the 1964 current price figure for total depreciation given in Table 26.

GNP. Tables K-1, K-2, K-4, and the sources to Table 23.

tions by an assumed average annual productivity growth factor of .7 percent.[18]

The Moorsteen-Powell indexes differ from the other branch-of-origin computations in several major respects. To begin with, the weights are Bergson's price and income weights from a relatively remote base year, 1937, and GNP is obtained by adding straight-line depreciation to NNP. There are additional differences in the derivation of branch indexes. The agricultural index is an extension and recomputation at 1937 average realized prices of the Johnson-Kahan gross agricultural output series,[19] adjusted for changes in herds. For industrial output, the Kaplan-Moorsteen index of industrial output[20] was extended to 1966, using investment in machinery as a proxy for 1950–1966 machinery production. Munitions output is estimated from the explicit state budget allocation to defense after deducting estimated pay and subsistence. The construction index is one of material inputs at 1937 prices, including capital repairs. Transportation and communication are represented by the simple sum of ton and passenger kilometers of transport by all carriers. Retail sales to households (excluding intravillage farm market sales), restaurant sales, and retail sales to institutions make up the series for trade. An independent computation of the average annual gross value of the housing stock provides a measure of housing services. Indexes of finance, health, education, and administration are constructed from employment data without a productivity "boost." The real value of personal services (domestic and barbers), repair services, and custom work is assumed unchanged at the 1928 level.

The Moorsteen-Powell indexes cannot be weighed in the same balance as the other calculations. Their original rationale was the need to interpolate and extrapolate Bergson's calculations for benchmark years

> to provide a context in which to explore, quite provisionally, some implications of the capital stock estimates. [The national product series] are not among the primary findings of this study and . . . many important questions concerning their reliability must go unanswered. The justification for the use

[18] The index of services incorporated in the JEC 1966 series is itself a weighted aggregate of employment in subsectors with estimated costs as weights.

[19] Johnson and Kahan, in *Comparisons of United States and Soviet Economies,* 1959, Part I, pp. 201–237.

[20] Kaplan and Moorsteen, *American Economic Review,* June 1960, pp. 295–318.

made of them derives essentially from their relation to the Bergson calculations.[21]

The extension of the series to 1966 should be similarly understood.

Finally, my GNP calculations are reproduced in abbreviated form. To avoid burdening the reader with the full range of results yielded by the conceivable combinations of my calculations, I have restricted the number of series to eight and, with one exception, to calculations at 1958 AFC. Not much loss of information is involved, as the alternative computations do not yield substantially different results. The four supplementary adjustments, it will be recalled, involve imputation of interest and depreciation on housing and government service capital, deletion of half of capital repairs, and revaluation of collective farmer incomes. For this purpose, housing interest is imputed at 5 percent.

Inspection of the figures entered in Table 40 suggests the following patterns:

(1) Overall growth from 1958 through 1964 displayed by the official data is greater than in any other series except those of my estimates using Method II to calculate constant factor cost. The smallest growth is shown by Cohn's 1966 and the Moorsteen-Powell NMP series. The 1964 index numbers of most of my calculations fall somewhere in between. In terms of average annual growth rates measured by the $\hat{r}$ formula, the finding is broadly similar. Cohn's JEC 1966 estimates imply an average rate of increase of 5.2 percent, compared with a Moorsteen-Powell series rate of 5.7 percent for GNP (5.3 percent for NNP) and with a range of 5.4–5.6 percent for my basic series and Method I calculations. The rate of growth of the (official) utilized NMP series is equivalent to that of my Method II calculations but is smaller by half a point than the growth rate of (official) produced NMP. The latter, in turn, exceeds all the averages from my calculations. My attempted replication of produced NMP yields an average rate of increase falling short of that implied by the official series by about one percentage point, due largely to the relatively low increase shown in my estimates for 1961.

(2) There are substantial differences among the various series in terms of relative annual changes. The range of percentage changes in output among the official and American indexes, if one excludes Cohn's JEC

---

[21] Moorsteen and Powell, *The Soviet Capital Stock 1928–1962*, 1966, pp. 619–620.

1964 series, is 3 percentage points in 1962 and 1963, 4 in 1960 and 1964, but 6 and 7 points in 1961 and 1959, respectively. My computed 1959 growth rates are visibly higher than those of the Cohn, Moorsteen-Powell, and even official series. The reverse is true for 1961 when the change in my series is computed from values including outlays n.e.c.; their deduction leads to close correspondence of the percentage changes in all the series in that year.

Considering the diversity of results relating to the pace of Soviet output in the 1930s,[22] Table 40 portrays a remarkably narrow range of disagreement on either the overall increase between 1958 and 1964 or the average annual rate of growth. For all series, Soviet and non-Soviet, the range of $\hat{r}$ growth rates is 5.2–6.5 percent and among the non-Soviet calculations 5.2–6.1 percent. There is, as indicated, considerably greater variation in estimates of annual changes, and I view the results of my calculations for the period as a whole with much greater confidence than the annual increments, absolute or relative; the year to year changes are sensitive to the fluctuations in outlays n.e.c., a series whose reliability is low.

In this connection, Table 40 suggests the possibility that outlays n.e.c. are understated in 1961. The impression is reinforced by recalling that there is no serious gap between (1) the JEC and my consumption growth estimates, (2) my modified consumption series at constant prices and that of the official data (Table 38) or (3) between the Moorsteen-Powell and my investment index numbers for 1960–1961 (Table 39). But the impact of understatement of outlays n.e.c. should not be exaggerated. Raising their value in 1961 alone—say, so that the relative increase of GNP at 1958 AFC in 1961 were 4.0 instead of 1.2 percent—has no discernible effect on the rate of growth at $\hat{r}$ to one-tenth of a percentage point. If my estimates of the 1959 relative increase are also in error, this may have something to do with the value of outlays n.e.c. in 1958–1959 but may reflect as well an underestimate of inventory investment in 1958. The latter possibility was discussed in the previous section on investment.

Sources of Divergences in Table 40

The comparison of the growth indexes and rates of change assembled in Table 40 suggests both a measure of agreement and visible disparities in

---

[22] See Chapter 11 of *Real SNIP*.

the results of the various calculations. Since the array of series present a wide spectrum of approaches to the measurement of aggregate output, perhaps the observed dispersion of results is only a consequence of such methodological diversity. However, this cannot be taken for granted, and it will be necessary to examine the question in some detail.

Before turning attention to such an analysis, it is appropriate to ask whether the explanation of at least some of the differences observed should not be simply error in my calculations. Certainly, these are subject to varying margins of error for reasons that have been set forth at length in the text as well as the appendixes of this study. With regard to the annual relative changes cited in Table 40, it is apparent that my calculations are frequently sensitive in particular to the size of outlays n.e.c.[23] which, in turn, are critically affected by a rather arbitrary decision on the proportion of residual budget revenues to be included in the SNIP public sector income account. I have considered the possibility that outlays n.e.c. are understated in 1958 and 1961, although I have also indicated that adjustment for the errors would have no impact on the overall growth and would barely affect the average rate of growth.

The latter could be overstated on other grounds—inadequate allowance for price inflation, particularly with respect to investment and armaments. An illustrative calculation in Chapter 6 disclosed that if both state-cooperative investment and "other defense" prices rose by as much as 30 percent, the *r* rate of growth of GNP at 1958 EP would be exaggerated by a little more than one percentage point. But it seems to me that this is an outer bound and that the likely margin of error is smaller. Indeed, the pure deflation error may be in the other direction, if we are to believe the Central Statistical Administration. Compare the implicit price deflators (relation of current to constant-price values) of the official produced NMP series with those of my estimated reconstruction (in percent):[24]

	1959	*1960*	*1961*	*1962*	*1963*	*1964*
Official	99.2	98.0	96.8	98.6	97.2	95.5
Reconstructed	99.4	99.5	99.2	101.2	100.3	101.1

[23] The sensitivity is greater for AFC series, with or without supplementary adjustment, than for EP series, because the basic factor cost adjustments raise the absolute and relative size of outlays n.e.c. in all years.

[24] The source for the official series is *NKh 1965*, p. 589. The deflators for the reconstructed series are derived by repeating the procedure described in the sources to Table 40 for data at current prices and comparing these values with the series at 1958 EP.

With the exception of a slight "bump" in 1962, the official series implies a continuous decline in the average price level of material product, whereas my reconstruction indicates a slight overall price increase for the period as a whole. In a previous section of this chapter, I showed that the implicit price deflator of the official consumption data is identical to that of my modified estimates. If the two sets of consumption and NMP data are mutually consistent, the official data reflect a substantial decline in the average price level of "accumulation and other expenditure."

BRANCH INDEXES

The differences between my results and those of the other series shown in Table 40 probably are not attributable solely to error in my current-price estimates or in their deflation. Indeed, the variations among the non-Soviet indexes other than mine are also substantial. Part of the explanation of the divergences revealed in Table 40 certainly relates to differences in weights and branch indexes among the GNP indexes computed by branch of origin. For industry and agriculture, the various non-Soviet indexes are compared with each other and with official Soviet claims in Table 41.[25]

To begin with industrial output, the table shows considerable disagreement among the various series in terms of computed year to year percentage changes. Annual percentage changes in the official gross output series are higher than those in the JEC 1966 series in all of the 10 years covered, with the margin of difference varying between ½ and 1½ percentage points. Entries in the JEC 1966 series are higher than in those of the other JEC or the CIA indexes except in 1956–1957. Rates of change computed from the Moorsteen-Powell civilian index, in turn, vary appreciably in a number of years from those of the other series, Soviet or non-Soviet.

In interpreting these comparisons, it is necessary to take account of significant conceptual and procedural differences among the series presented. The official Soviet gross output index is defined as the sum of enterprise outputs at 1955 enterprise prices net of turnover tax and excludes only intra-enterprise consumption (with minor exceptions).

[25] The index of industrial output underlying Soviet NMP calculations is of course net output. But a net output index is not regularly published. As the GMP series approximates the NMP, there is also reason for independent interest in the official gross industrial production index.

TABLE 41
SOVIET AND NON-SOVIET ESTIMATES OF ANNUAL INCREASES IN INDUSTRIAL AND AGRICULTURAL OUTPUT, 1956–1965
(percent)

	1956	1957	1958	1959	1960	1961	1962	1963	1964	1965
Industrial output										
Official Soviet										
Gross	11	10	10.3	11.4	9.5	9.1	9.7	8.1	7.3	8.7
Net	..	..	..	..	8	10	..	..	7	..
JEC 1966	9.5	9.1	9.8	10.2	7.8	7.9	8.2	6.9	6.8	7.2
JEC 1965	..	..	..	8.5	6.8	7.1	7.8	6.6	..	..
JEC 1964	..	..	..	8.6	6.3	6.7	7.2	..	..	..
CIA 1963	10.8	10.6	9.1	8.6	6.3	6.6	..	..	..	..
Moorsteen-Powell										
Civilian industries	11.8	8.9	9.8	7.9	5.4	6.1	6.4	6.3	6.8	6.9
Munitions industries	3	3	4	1	8	22	11	4	−2	1
All industry	11	8	9	7	6	7	7	6	6	6
Agricultural output										
Official Soviet										
Gross	13.0	3.8	10.0	0.4	2.3	3.0	1.2	−7.5	14.4	2.0
Net	..	..	..	..	3	3	..	..	19	..
Marketed	18	−2	17	4.0	2.4	4.2	6.4	..	..	..
JEC 1966	12	0	10	−4	1	9	−1	−5	11	1
JEC 1965	..	..	10.4	−5.1	0.5	8.6	−1.2	−5.1	..	..
JEC 1964	..	..	..	−4.0	2.8	8.2	−5.0	..	..	..
JEC 1962	13	0	13	−6	4	5	..	..	..	..
Moorsteen-Powell	15.2	0.1	10.7	1.0	1.3	3.9	.6	−9.6	15.7	2.7

Sources:

Official Soviet. Gross industrial and agricultural output: *NKh 1965*, pp. 121–122, 260. Net industrial and agricultural output: *NKh 1960*, p. 153; *NKh 1961*, p. 598; *NKh 1963*, p. 502; and *NKh 1964*, p. 577. Marketed output: *NKh 1961*, p. 296; and *NKh 1962*, pp. 230–231.

JEC 1966. New Directions in the Soviet Economy, 1966, pp. 282 (industry), and 346 (agriculture).

JEC 1965. Current Economic Indicators for the USSR, June 1965, pp. 50 (industrial output), and 20 (agricultural output).

JEC 1964. Annual Economic Indicators for the USSR, 1964, p. 37 (industrial output), and pp. 32 and 93 (agricultural output).

CIA 1963. Index of Civilian Industrial Production in the USSR, 1950–1961, September 1963, p. 1.

JEC 1962. R. Greenslade and P. Wallace; and J. Willett, both in *Dimensions of Soviet Economic Power*, 1962, pp. 120 and 98.

Moorsteen-Powell. Table P-1 (*The Soviet Capital Stock 1928–1962*, 1966), and Table P-1-X (*Supplement I*).

Indexes of industrial output net of materials purchased and depreciation are not regularly published in the USSR; the three entries in the table are obtained from sporadic yearbook comparisons of NMP by branch at current prices with indexes at constant prices. The JEC 1964–1965 series are apparently extensions of the CIA index,[26] and these three are distinguished in two important respects from the JEC 1966 index. All four series represent aggregations of commodity-group indexes with intragroup price weights and intergroup value added weights. The JEC 1966 index substitutes 1960 value added for the 1955 weights used in the other three and includes an explicit capital charge, absent previously. Second, whereas the CIA and JEC 1964–1965 series were intended to cover only civilian industrial production and estimated machinery output in the same way as they did output of other branches, the JEC 1966 index incorporates the official Soviet gross index of machine building and metal working at a discount, to adjust for presumed biases in the official index. Since it is believed that the official index covers military as well as civilian output, the JEC 1966 index is in principle an index of all industrial output.

As indicated earlier, the Moorsteen-Powell civilian industrial output index is an extension of the Kaplan-Moorsteen index, which, in turn, is an approximation to a net output index using a mixture of price and wage-bill weights drawn from 1950. The extension differs from the original in the use of an adjusted index of investment in machinery and equipment as a post-1950 proxy for an index of their production. Munitions output is derived from the state budget "defense" appropriation after subtracting pay and subsistence. Moorsteen and Powell do not present an index of all industrial output; the series shown in Table 41 was calculated using their 1937 income-originating weights.

In their 1962 JEC discussion of the pattern of industrial production, Greenslade and Wallace suggested a lag of armaments production behind civilian industry in the middle 1950s and then an acceleration of arms output after 1957.[27] If the hypothesis is accepted, a comprehensive index including armaments would have grown slower than one of civilian production alone in 1956 and 1957 but should have grown faster thereafter. The JEC 1966 and CIA 1963 indexes do in fact display such a pattern. Whether this factor alone accounts for the differences between the two series cannot be determined short of an intensive analysis, including revaluation of one with the weights of another. It is clear that

---

[26] The line of descent is actually to the Greenslade-Wallace index in *Dimensions of Soviet Economic Power,* 1962, p. 120. The latter is virtually identical to the CIA index.

[27] *Dimensions of Soviet Economic Power,* 1962, pp. 122–123.

the hypothesis cannot explain the differences between the CIA-JEC civilian production indexes and the Moorsteen-Powell extension of the Kaplan-Moorsteen civilian output index.

My estimates of GNP are, of course, derived from the side of use rather than origin. In terms of the commodity structure of such a calculation, the implied industrial output series is neither gross nor net but final output, in the strict national income sense. That is, viewed in the frame of an input-output table for a single year, the required data would be neither a total column (row) sum (gross output), nor the sum of value added in the southwest quadrant (net output), but the sum of the northeast quandrant's final demand entries in the row distribution. The elements of a time series would be supplied by several tables valued at constant prices. None of the series arranged in Table 41 is of the required variety, and it is conceivable that were it available it would display marked differences in annual changes compared with the other series. At least one factor tending to generate such divergences would be a different ratio of armaments to civilian goods in final output than in either net or gross output.[28]

The rationale for independent calculation of Soviet industrial output is the belief that the Soviet gross value of output index is deficient in concept and procedure. This long-standing Western distaste for the Soviet index is grounded on a rejection in principle of gross value weights and on the suspicion that (1) new products are introduced into the index at improper, high prices of initial model production, and (2) as a "gross-gross" index, it is upwardly biased because of growing specialization, hence disaggregation of production units and an increase in the level of double counting.[29] There may well be some evidence of the first infraction,[30] and if changes in industrial classification do take

---

[28] The only example of an index remotely resembling that required is one by Powell appearing in Bergson and Kuznets, eds., *Economic Trends in the Soviet Union,* 1963. Powell describes his index as "final from the viewpoint of industry, although in part intermediate for the economy as a whole" (p. 155)—that is, only sales to industry itself are excluded. The terminal year of this index is 1958. In the three years 1956–1958, the implied annual increases in the index at 1950 prices (p. 178) are 13, 8, and 13 percent, compared with the JEC 1966 figures of 10, 9, and 10 percent.

[29] For example, see Noren, in *New Directions in the Soviet Economy,* 1966, p. 277.

[30] See my comments on the wholesale price index of machinery and metal working in Appendix K.

place, there may be a bias on the second account as well, although it cannot be assumed *a priori* that net disaggregation is the rule.[31]

Suppose, however, that the pricing of new products is appropriate (or that there is no new product pricing problem) and that the index is computed from a time series with a consistent industrial classification. Is the gross value of output index still likely to be biased? Domar has compared four types of production indexes: the "pure" Soviet (with constant classification), denoted S; a true value added (net output index), V; an approximation to the latter in which, for lack of data, intracategory weights are prices instead of value added, H; and a "final product" index, F (where "final" means with respect to industry, not the economy as a whole).[32] H is, of course, the prototype of all the non-Soviet indexes in Table 41. Domar finds: In principle the S index is biased, but so is H; applied to alternative sets of U.S. input-output tables, S, H, and F are close together and far apart from V, with H a poor approximation for V, though a good one for F. Domar concludes that the result of the contest between S and H is a draw.[33]

Table 41 indicates that in the three years for which the comparison can be made, the gap between official Soviet net and gross industrial output increments is relatively small. This is a necessary but not sufficient condition to conclude that the double counting of intermediate output in the Soviet gross index is of minor significance. The net increment figures may be preliminary results, subject to later revision, and we still know little about Soviet methods of computing net output. In principle and practice, it would seem that the case against the Soviet gross industrial production index is not yet conclusive. By the same token, granted the relative completeness of information available to the Central Statistical Administration, the case for the independent indexes is weakened.

The JEC contributions have taken a more skeptical attitude to reported Soviet agricultural output data in physical units than they have toward the corresponding industrial production figures, and all of the

---

[31] Liberman strongly suggests that this is in fact the case. See his comments, ostensibly directed to a Soviet book on U.S. growth but possibly bearing on Soviet indexes as well, in *Mirovaia ekonomika i mezhdunarodnye otnosheniia,* 1967, No. 12, p. 142.

[32] That is, it is apparently identical in concept to the Powell index cited in note 28, above.

[33] Domar, *Quarterly Journal of Economics,* May 1967, pp. 169–188.

JEC indexes embody substantial and varying discounts of the official output claims with respect to major products—grain, meat, and milk, in particular. Not surprisingly, these series show correspondingly substantial differences in computed annual growth rates from those of the official indexes. On the hypothesis that the official Soviet indexes are padded, the differences between the JEC and the Soviet indexes are generally in the expected direction. The major and surprising exception occurs in the year 1961. For that year the Russians claim only a 3 percent increase in net and gross output; the JEC estimates are almost twice or three times as high. The divergences between the official Soviet and JEC 1964–1965 indexes were not discussed, but it is apparent from the comments attendant on the JEC 1966 estimate that the explanation of the 1961 anomaly is largely in differential discounting of official grain statistics—25 percent in 1960 compared with 14 percent in 1961. Although the official data claim an increase of grain output (excluding immature corn) in 1961 of only 4 percent, the JEC 1966 series implies growth in that year by 18 percent.[34] There seems to be considerable agreement among Western analysts on the deficiencies of Soviet agricultural output statistics after 1958, and I can provide no independent judgment on these matters. On the other hand, my estimates of consumption in kind imply that the accepted discounts to official claims of grain output may be overstated.[35] As was to be expected, the Moorsteen-Powell index, using reported physical output data, runs close to the official gross index.

There seems to be no need to compare the various indexes for other branches. I should, however, remind the reader that Cohn's JEC 1965 and 1966 indexes of services are employment series incorporating an assumed average annual labor productivity growth factor [36] derived from U.S. data, whereas in my series the estimated labor component of a number of service categories is deflated by an index of earnings. Agreement of the growth patterns of our respective indexes, under these circumstances, would be only coincidental. I know of no basis to judge whether productivity in Soviet services increased, or if so, by how much.

---

[34] *New Directions in the Soviet Economy,* 1966, p. 369.

[35] See below, p. 326 and the discussion preceding it.

[36] Except for the subindexes of housing and municipal (Cohn uses the term "communal") services in the 1966 JEC series. The housing subindex is said to be based on estimates of housing space by Bronson and Severin; the derivation of the municipal services index is not explained.

THE WEIGHTS

I come now to consideration of the weight systems reflected in the indexes of Table 40. There is one conclusion that we may draw, I think, from the outset. It seems unlikely that significant differences among the various series, the Moorsteen-Powell data aside, arise purely from differences in weight years. The weight years of the Soviet, Cohn, and my estimates are close together, and structural change intervening could not have been large enough to cause radical changes in weights. The direction of whatever change did take place cannot be predicted *a priori:* the divergence of the 1964 from the 1958 series in my calculations yields no implication regarding the corresponding values at 1955, 1957, or 1959 prices.

The Moorsteen-Powell series, because they reflect 1937 weights, present a special case. For price weights of 1928, 1937 and 1950, the work of Bergson and Moorsteen indicated that index number relativity is a major problem only with respect to the prewar period. According to Bergson, GNP calculated by use at 1937 factor cost grew between 1950 and 1955 at the same rate as GNP measured at 1950 factor cost.[37] However, it is not clear *a priori* that index number relativity is insignificant when the weight year is changed to 1955 or later, because of the substantial changes in agricultural pricing introduced after Stalin's death. In particular, post-1955 prices might be expected to depress the index of aggregate output in the SYP period relative to one calculated with 1950 prices, as higher agricultural prices are applied to a slowly growing branch of production and industrial output is weighted by prices lower than in 1950.

Table 42 compares the weight systems underlying the output estimates under consideration. The Moorsteen-Powell weights are essentially Bergson's estimates of labor incomes originating in 1937. The 1955 value added weights of Cohn's 1962 and 1964 JEC contributions are based on the 1955 national accounts compiled by Morris Bornstein. However, for the 1964 JEC report, Cohn adjusted the Bornstein results in a number of ways, chiefly by imputing agricultural rent at the rate of 40 percent of agricultural labor incomes, the same coefficient Bergson used for his illustrative calculations.[38] Partly in response to criticism by Nove focused on the imputation of a high rate of agricultural rent in the

---

[37] *Real SNIP,* p. 217.
[38] *Ibid.,* p. 138.

TABLE 42
ORIGINATING BRANCH WEIGHTS OF ALTERNATIVE INDEXES OF NATIONAL OUTPUT
(percent of total output or income originated)

	Weight Year	Industry	Agriculture	Construction	Transportation and Communication	Trade	Services
Official Soviet NMP	1958	50.2	24.1	9.5	4.4[a]	11.8[b]	n.a.
Cohn:							
JEC 1966	1959	30.9	28.8	9.8	8.0	5.3	17.2
JEC 1965	1959	31.0	29.2	10.6	7.8	4.5	16.9
JEC 1964 adjusted	1955	30.6	33.2	6.0	6.8	3.7	19.7
JEC 1964	1955	30.3	36.2	8.8	5.9	3.9	14.9
JEC 1962	1955	31.3	27.1	5.3	5.0	5.0	26.3
Moorsteen-Powell	1937	32.2	31.0	5.2	8.3	5.1	18.1

Notes:
[a] Excluding passenger transportation and communication for nonproductive use.
[b] Including miscellaneous material production branches.

Sources:
Official Soviet NMP. NKh 1964, pp. 67, 577. The implied percentages for NMP in *NKh 1965*, p. 591, differ very slightly from those shown here.
JEC 1966. Cohn, *Derivation of 1959 Value-Added Weights . . .* , 1965, p. 20.
JEC 1965. Current Economic Indicators for the USSR, pp. 20–21. Some obvious misprints in the text have been corrected here.
JEC 1964 adjusted. Cohn, *Soviet Studies*, January 1965, p. 307.
JEC 1964. Annual Economic Indicators for the USSR, 1964, p. 93.
JEC 1962. Bornstein *et al.*, *Soviet National Accounts for 1955*, 1961, p. 84, is the source cited by Cohn, *Dimensions of Soviet Economic Power*, 1962, p. 75.
Moorsteen-Powell. The Soviet Capital Stock 1928–1962, 1966, Table P-1.

absence of imputed returns to capital,[39] Cohn revised his 1955 weights, as shown in the row labeled "JEC 1964 adjusted." Land rent in this set of weights is imputed at the same rate as before but interest and depreciation are added for the first time. Interest is imputed separately for nonresidential fixed capital and housing, at rates of 8 percent and 3 percent, respectively, derived from American experience; interest on inventories is not imputed. The depreciation charges are said to represent the combined official charges for amortization and capital repair.[40]

Cohn's JEC 1966 weights, apart from shifting the weight year from

[39] Nove, *Soviet Studies,* July 1964, pp. 18–19.
[40] In his rebuttal of Nove's critique (*Soviet Studies,* January 1965), Cohn also amplifies the procedures underlying his JEC 1964 calculations.

1955 to 1959, incorporate two departures from his JEC 1964 adjusted set: First,

> the evident recognition, at least in part, that some factor payment to superior land has been recognized since 1955, leads the author to conclude that the adjustment for agricultural rent should be smaller than the estimate of rent as 40 percent of labor income that was adopted in the construction of 1955 agricultural income.[41]

Therefore, he revised his rent imputation downward to a rate of 20 percent.[42] Second, imputed interest previously charged only on fixed capital is extended to inventories as well. On the other hand, the 8 percent return is now restricted to nonservice stocks, rather than nonresidential capital, and the 3 percent return is applied not only to housing but to stocks in all services.

For all the distinctions outlined, there is scant difference among the non-Soviet systems in the figures of Table 42 with regard to the relative weight of industry; the range is 1.9 percentage points, or 6 percent of the lowest estimate. On the other hand, the variation in the estimated size of the agricultural weight is more extensive absolutely and relatively. The adjustment of Bornstein's original 1955 weighting system (JEC 1962), chiefly by imputing land rent, raises the agricultural weight by 9 percentage points or by one-third. Cohn's later adjustments continually reduce the weight, finally to a level only 1.7 points above his original starting point. Given the slow growth of agricultural output during these years, the Cohn series including imputed rent would tend to constrict the rate of growth of aggregate output relative to rates computed with other weight systems. In this regard, the Moorsteen-Powell estimate is relatively neutral. Of course, the Soviet weights are the most buoyant, emphasizing industrial growth and de-emphasizing agricultural stagnation. There are not inconsiderable differences in estimated weights for the remaining branches as well, but the effects on the aggregate growth rate must be of lesser consequence.

But the issue of central interest to me is the relation between the differences in the weight systems and the disparities in growth evidenced by my estimates compared with the Soviet and other non-Soviet series. I

---

[41] Cohn, *Derivation of 1959 Value-Added Weights . . .*, April 1966, p. 19.

[42] The imputation is expressed as 13 percent of all agricultural factor incomes, derived from Griliches' work on U.S. agriculture production functions, but works out to 20 percent of agricultural labor incomes in the USSR.

must, therefore, make explicit the differences between my weights and those of the other calculations. Factor incomes in my basic factor cost series consist of labor incomes, depreciation, profits, and other public sector net incomes. Supplementary adjustments add imputed interest and depreciation on housing, imputed depreciation on government service capital, and a supplement to collective farmer incomes.[43] The Soviet weights, of course, omit incomes generated in service activity considered nonproductive; the NMP series, additionally, omits depreciation on productive capital. Depreciation is excluded from the Moorsteen-Powell weights, which consist only of labor incomes, but is added to NNP to obtain GNP. Cohn's latest factor income shares differ from mine not only in his imputation of rent but in several other major respects as well:

(1) Farm income in kind is valued at average realized farm prices in my calculations but at an average of retail and extravillage farm market prices (less trade markup and turnover taxes) in Cohn's. His estimate for 1959 at 12.22 billion rubles is 22 percent larger than mine (9.99 billions).

(2) Cohn makes no explicit adjustment for procurement subsidies and it is not clear whether they are correctly reflected in his weights. Except for agriculture and services his estimates of wages and wage supplements are derived from official data on net income originating by branch after deducting profits and turnover tax as appropriate. I do not know how the Central Statistical Administration treats procurement subsidies in its national accounts, but assuming they are included in net income[44] it is at least possible that they are entered in net income of agriculture or procurement. In the latter case Cohn's estimate of labor income in procurement would be considerably overstated. Only if the CSA classed procurement subsidies with net income originating in industry would their reflection in Cohn's weights be comparable to their classification in my estimates.

(3) Cohn deducts net profits and imputes interest. My basic factor cost series includes gross profits on the assumption that they are a reasonable proxy for interest and makes no separate interest imputations. However, supplementary adjustments (and their evaluation) take into account the undervaluation of housing (by imputing interest) and

[43] The deletion of half of state-cooperative capital repairs would mean a reduction in all categories of the corresponding factor incomes.

[44] Procurement subsidies are not among the deductions from gross to obtain net profits.

the distorted structure of profits by major industry groups. On the other hand, I make no attempt to impute interest on the capital of government services provided by budget organizations that do not earn profits.

(4) Cohn charges depreciation generally at the amortization rate (including allowance for capital repair) recorded by *khozraschet* organizations.[45] Depreciation on service capital is imputed at a rate derived from the share of depreciation in value added by services in the United States. My basic factor cost series undervalues housing depreciation and makes no allowance for depreciation on the capital of budget organizations, but a supplementary adjustment imputes depreciation on housing and government service capital at a rate derived from estimated service lives of buildings and structures. Cohn's estimate of depreciation in the services branch during the single year 1959 (3.3 billion rubles) is 2.2 times as large as my estimate of depreciation on housing and government service capital.

(5) One of the supplementary adjustments to my basic factor cost series increases collective farmer incomes in compensation for a shortfall from incomes of labor of comparable qualification employed elsewhere in the economy. This adjustment is absent from Cohn's calculations.

(6) Cohn does not impute, as I do, a return to the construction labor supplied by prospective owners of private housing.

(7) By implication Cohn views a number of public sector charges—for worker training and research, budget income from forestry, local taxes and fees, and the like—as indirect taxes. On the other hand, to the extent that these items are included in official data as net income, Cohn's method of estimation of income originating in most branches of the economy must result in overstating the labor income residual.

I cannot provide an alternative set of factor incomes by branch of origin to compare with Cohn's, but a comparison of the income aggregates is possible, as shown in Table 43. Two income distributions for 1959 are compiled from my calculations, one at basic AFC and the other with supplementary adjustments but without deletion of capital repairs. (The latter would require unknown cuts in almost all categories

[45] The figures are taken from Treml's reconstruction of the 1959 input-output table (*The 1959 Soviet Intersectoral Flow Table,* 1964, Vol. I, p. 72). In that table collective farm depreciation is probably recorded from farm accounts and hence valued at state farm rates.

TABLE 43
ALTERNATIVE CALCULATIONS OF GNP IN 1959 BY TYPE OF INCOME AT FACTOR COST

	Billion Rubles			Percent of Total		
		Becker			Becker	
	Cohn JEC 1966	Basic AFC	Supplementary Adjustments	Cohn JEC 1966	Basic AFC	Supplementary Adjustments
	(1)	(2)	(3)	(4)	(5)	(6)
1. Labor income						
A. Wages and supplements [a]	80.1	85.60	..	59.6	57.7	..
B. Income in kind [b]	13.6	11.44	..	10.1	7.7	..
C. Total	93.7	97.04	98.60	69.7	65.4	63.2
2. Profits and interest						
A. Profits	—	42.30	42.30	—	28.5	27.1
B. Interest	23.0	—	4.60	17.1	—	2.9
C. Total	23.0	42.30	46.90	17.1	28.5	30.1
3. Depreciation	12.8	9.00	10.50	9.5	6.1	6.7
4. Agricultural rent	5.0	—	—	3.7	—	—
Total	134.5	148.34	156.00	100.0	100.0	100.0

Notes:

[a] Cohn figures presumably, and Becker figures certainly, include wages in kind.

[b] Excluding wages in kind.

Sources:

Cohn. Derivation of 1959 Value-Added Weights . . ., 1965, p. 20.

Becker.

Basic AFC. Labor income: Total income currently earned from Table 1 plus enterprise social security payments (Table 3). Profits: This is the sum of consolidated total charges against current product of the public sector, net of depreciation and less turnover taxes and enterprise social security payments (Table 3) plus gross subsidies (Table J-4). Depreciation: Table 3.

Supplementary adjustments. Basic AFC plus adjustment for undervaluation of collective farmer incomes, imputation of interest and depreciation on housing, and imputation of depreciation on government service capital (sources to Table 17). Interest on housing is imputed at the rate of 5 percent.

of income.) For the supplementary adjustments in Table 43, housing interest is imputed at 5 percent. The farm price adjustment is negligible in aggregate and is therefore ignored here. With or without supplementary adjustment, profits are broadened to include all net income of the public sector except turnover taxes and enterprise social security payments, the latter entered as wage supplements for comparability with the Cohn data.

It is evident that Cohn's estimates of income generated are substantially different from mine—in total, by component, and in relative distribution. The value of wage income in his calculation is 5½ billion rubles lower than mine, but his estimate of income in kind is higher than mine. Including the imputations with respect to housing and government service capital, my depreciation figure is somewhat below his. The most important differences in Table 43 relate to profits, interest, and rent. On the issue of rent, there seems to be little to add to the comments in Chapter 3: Not all rent is retained on the farm, and by failing to impute an explicit rental charge I undoubtedly understate its weight in the total; on the other hand, it has seemed to me that Cohn takes insufficient account of the degree to which agricultural pricing policy favored fertile regions and penalized the relatively poorly endowed. As for profits and interest, my total in column 3 is more than twice as large as Cohn's imputed interest. The relative margin would be reduced to 60 percent if other public sector net incomes except profits (and the taxes on them) were subtracted from my total. Including these miscellaneous public sector net incomes,[46] the total of profits and interest amounts to 19 percent of the sum of net fixed capital and inventories at the end of 1959,[47] compared with the 9 percent implied by Cohn's imputed interest; net of the miscellaneous incomes, my total would come to 15 percent of the same stock.[48]

It may be legitimately argued, I think, that the relation of some of the miscellaneous incomes—for example, the price differentials on agricultural machinery, or local taxes and fees—to turnover taxes is that of a distinction without a real difference.[49] But under the conditions of Soviet price formation the same is true of profits *per se*. In my AFC calculations, profits are retained as a proxy for interest, and the relevant question then becomes, what is the "appropriate" rate of return to impute to Soviet capital in 1959? It does not seem possible to provide an unequivocal answer to that question. Cohn's imputations are based on

---

[46] The incomes in question are items 2.B, 3.E, and 4 of Table 3.

[47] See Table 8 above.

[48] All the percentages cited are overstated inasmuch as Table 8 understates the total capital stock by excluding state stockpiles.

In principle, imputed interest should be compounded in the values of the capital assets to which it relates. Cohn and I are both derelict in this respect, but since my imputation is only on housing, the error is inconsequential. For Cohn's calculations the omission may be important.

[49] One of this miscellaneous group—forest revenues from stumpage fees—can be viewed as an element of nonagricultural rent. Possibly we might also consider charges on oil and gas production for geological prospecting as a surrogate for a depletion allowance.

U.S. market rates and have no lesser but also no greater claim to appropriateness than that. In the end, our sharply divergent profits-interest shares must simply be viewed as alternative fixes on an elusive magnitude.

CONCLUSION

The fundamental difference between my estimates of the growth of aggregate output and all the others shown in Table 40 is that mine are derived by deflating final expenditure whereas the others are weighted sums of branch of origin output indexes. I have repeatedly acknowledged that my estimates may be in error from a variety of sources, particularly as regards year to year changes. But it is not clear to me that the calculations from the side of origin are necessarily more reliable. On both sides there are data obstacles of nontrivial magnitude. With respect to my estimates the issues are largely two: comprehensiveness of coverage due to gaps in information on miscellaneous public sector incomes and outlays; the reliability of the deflation procedure in view of uncertainties on price trends in investment and military activities. Among the alternative non-Soviet calculations there are, as we have seen, substantial differences in method and concept with regard to both weights and branch indexes (explicit or implied). All of them have chosen to reject, to greater or lesser degree, the Soviet indexes of industrial and agricultural output in favor of independently calculated substitutes based on limited production samples. Because of data gaps, each of the alternative studies is forced to procedural compromises in the choice and calculation of weight systems. Other questions of appropriate procedure, not necessarily connected to the problems of information flow, have also been raised in previous sections.

I would not wish to have to justify the accuracy of my estimates of annual increments in real total product or its components. Granted the problems besetting the other non-Soviet studies, I doubt that much more authority can be imputed to the year to year changes in their series. As for the official Soviet indexes, we still know too little about their makeup to judge their reliability for the period of concern here. For the period as a whole there is considerably more agreement on the size of the total growth and its average rate of change. Considering the methodological diversity of the various series in Table 40, this happy outcome must be in part fortuitous.

It is hardly necessary to add that it would be an illusion to view the problem as one of determining *the* rate of growth, true and unique. The relativism of index number measurements in terms of concept and procedure, whether from the side of origin or use, is by now a truism, although one that is frequently overlooked in the glare of public discussion. The GNP series developed in this study and relating to a brief six-year span imply a range of rates of growth for a variety of different valuations. For consumers of national income statistics, *caveat emptor* is still an appropriate motto.

11

Intertemporal and International Comparisons

The comparisons cited in the chapter title are of two kinds. First, and conceptually the more reliable of the two, is a comparison with past SNIP calculations—primarily the constant price estimates of Bergson, but including also current price calculations by Hoeffding and Nimitz. A second set of comparisons is with contemporaneous output growth and structure in several leading noncommunist states. The validity of these comparisons is attenuated by methodological differences for which adjustments are difficult to perform.

Soviet Economic Growth Since 1950

I choose 1950 as a formal baseline because 1950–1955 is the latest time segment covered by Bergson's calculations. In some cases it is feasible and perhaps useful to move back to 1948 as a starting point, although results for the extended period may be biased because of the possibility that economic changes in 1948 and 1949 still bore the imprint of "recovery" from World War II and its aftermath. The rate of growth under consideration is that of GNP and its components. I make no attempt to develop intertemporal comparisons of changes in productivity. The calculations of this study do not provide the required input series, and it is best to refer the reader to the work of Moorsteen and Powell, cited earlier on a number of occasions, for a comprehensive treatment of this subject. My national product estimates differ from those compiled by Moorsteen and Powell, as explained in Chapter 10,

TABLE 44

AVERAGE ANNUAL RATES OF GROWTH OF GNP AND MAJOR END-USE COMPONENTS, SELECTED PERIODS, 1948–1964 (percent)

	Weight	Bergson				Becker	
		1948–1955		1950–1955		1958–1964	
	Year	r	r̂	r	r̂	r	r̂
1. Consumption							
Basic series							
EP	1937; 1958	12.8	12.0	9.5	10.2	5.2	5.1
	1950; 1964	13.0	12.3	9.8	10.7	4.9	4.8
AFC	1937; 1958	11.3	10.6	8.7	9.3	4.8	4.7
	1950; 1964	11.4	10.8	9.0	9.7	4.7	4.6
Supplementary adjustments [a]	1958	←n.a.→				5.3	5.0
	1964					5.1	4.9
2. Communal services, including R&D							
Basic series							
EP	1937; 1958	2.2	2.8	4.2	4.4	6.6	7.4
	1950; 1964	2.0	2.6	4.1	4.3	6.6	7.3
AFC	1937; 1958	2.6	3.1	4.2	4.4	[b]	7.5
	1950; 1964	2.6	3.1	4.1	4.3	[b]	7.4
3. Gross fixed investment							
Basic series							
EP	1937; 1958	14.2	12.5	11.0	11.1	7.3	6.7
	1950; 1964	14.2	12.3	10.8	10.7	7.2	6.6
AFC	1937; 1958	14.2	12.5	11.0	11.1	7.4	6.8
	1950; 1964	14.2	12.3	10.8	10.7	7.3	6.7
Supplementary adjustments [c]	1958	←n.a.→				7.2	6.5
	1964					7.1	6.4
4. All gross investment plus outlays n.e.c.							
Basic series							
EP	1937; 1958	8.0	6.3(6.7)	8.4	5.4(6.0)	6.9	5.8
	1950; 1964	8.4	6.5(6.9)	8.3	5.4(5.9)	6.9	5.7
AFC	1937; 1958	8.7	7.3(7.6)	8.5	6.4(6.8)	7.1	5.8
	1950; 1964	9.3	7.8(8.1)	8.6	6.7(7.0)	7.0	5.8
Supplementary adjustments [c]	1958	←n.a.→				7.2	5.5
	1964					7.1	5.4
5. Defense							
Basic series							
EP	1937; 1958	6.3	6.7	7.9	6.1	6.2	8.1
	1950; 1964	6.6	7.1	7.7 [e]	5.7	6.2	8.1
AFC	1937; 1958	6.2	6.6	7.9	6.1	6.0	8.0
	1950; 1964	6.7	7.2	7.7 [e]	6.0	6.1	8.0
Supplementary adjustments [d]	1958	←n.a.→				6.1	7.9
	1964					6.1	8.0

TABLE 44 (continued)

6. GNP							
Basic series							
EP	1937; 1958	9.2	8.8(8.8)	8.2	7.8(7.9)	5.9	5.6
	1950; 1964	9.4	8.9(9.0)	8.2	7.9(8.0)	5.8	5.4
AFC	1937; 1958	8.1	7.8(7.9)	7.6	7.0(7.2)	5.9	5.5
	1950; 1964	8.4	8.0(8.1)	7.6	7.2(7.3)	5.8	5.4
Basic AFC, excluding outlays n.e.c.	1958					5.8	5.7
	1964					5.7	5.5
Supplementary adjustments[a]	1958	n.a.				6.0	5.5
	1964					5.9	5.4
Supplementary adjustments,[a] excluding outlays n.e.c.	1958					5.9	5.7
	1964					5.8	5.5

Notes:
[a] Adjustments 1–4, with housing interest at 5 percent.
[b] Identical to EP rates.
[c] Adjustments 3–4 alone apply.
[d] Adjustment 4 alone applies.
[e] See note 4, below.
For the definition of r and $\hat{r}$, see pp. 127 ff.

Sources:
Bergson: 1937 EP and AFC; 1950 EP. Computed from *Real SNIP*, pp. 301–303. *1950 AFC.* Bergson does not provide annual data at 1950 AFC as he does for the other valuations. I have reconstructed the required series as the products of indexes at 1950 EP, calculated from Table 84 on p. 302 of *Real SNIP*, and corresponding values in 1950 at 1950 AFC, from Table 30 on p. 150. The pattern of aggregation is not the same on p. 150 as on p. 302, necessitating both special computations and one compromise. On the latter, it should be noted that my reconstruction of total retail sales at 1950 AFC is not the sum of components but the product of the corresponding EP index and the 1950 AFC value. The same is true of household outlays on services, although for this category the level of aggregation is the same in both source tables. Indexes of labor and nonlabor inputs to communal services, military services and munitions (components of "defense"), livestock investment, investment in trade and "other" inventories, and "other" investment were computed from indications in the relevant appendixes—D, E, and G—of *Real SNIP*. Evidently my reconstructed 1950 AFC series is not far off the mark; at least it yields an r value identical to that cited by Bergson (Table 52, p. 217). The agreement also holds for consumption, communal services, and all gross investment; defense is an exception, signalled by note e.
Becker: Tables 20, 23, and p. 142; or computed from the series discussed there.

but probably not enough to affect the general conclusions on productivity changes drawn by them.

The essential data are assembled in Table 44, showing rates of growth for GNP and five major components—household outlays on consumption, communal services including R&D, gross fixed investment, all gross investment plus outlays n.e.c., and defense (the budget appropriation, net of pensions). Amalgamation of gross investment and outlays n.e.c. is necessary for comparability with Bergson's category of all gross investment; this is also the reason for including R&D in communal service outlays. A number of other minor differences in coverage between Bergson's and my series could not be easily rectified and should be noted here:

(1) Bergson's consumption data do not explicitly include non-farm wages in kind.

(2) My basic AFC estimates include an estimated subsidy to housing. An even larger housing subsidy is included in Bergson's "adjusted market price" valuation of consumption but not in his basic series shown in my Table 38 above.

(3) Bergson's 1950 factor cost series omit the adjustment for farm prices "because of its unimportance."

(4) My estimates include, as Bergson's do not, a charge for labor services provided by prospective owners in private housing construction.[1]

The differences listed above can have no substantial impact on the validity of the comparisons to be drawn. There are, however, two more serious impediments to comparability of Bergson's and my estimates discussed in Chapter 6—my reliance on the official index of state retail prices as a deflator of state-cooperative retail sales and on official data as both current and constant price series for state-cooperative fixed investment and defense. I believe that my consumption estimates do not err tangibly on this account, and their average rate of growth differs little from the independent JEC estimates cited in Chapter 10. My fixed investment and defense entries may be overstated, especially in regard to the equipment and military hardware components; I would doubt that the error is severe.[2]

The second problem of comparability in Table 44 is the absence of uniform sets of price weights between the periods 1948–1955 and 1958–1964. Table 44 juxtaposes rates of growth for Bergson's series at

---

[1] *Real SNIP*, pp. 166, 148, 383.

[2] The Moorsteen-Powell index of investment in construction and installation corresponds fairly well to the official index; their index of investment in equipment for this period is in fact the official one (above, pp. 227–228). My review of the evidence in Appendix K also pinpoints equipment acquisition as the area of possibly significant price increases. On the other hand, official Soviet data imply a decline in the average level of investment and defense hardware prices (above, p. 240).

1937 prices with those of mine at 1958 prices and Bergson's series at 1950 prices with mine at 1964 prices. Of course, there is little justification other than convenience for such a procedure, and the comments on the data below are in fact based on ranges drawn from all the elements of a single GNP category simultaneously. This still does not dispose of the uncertainty introduced by heterogeneous price weights. I suggested in Chapter 10 that although Bergson's results were not especially sensitive to change of weight year from 1937 to 1950, the shift to prices of 1955 or a later year might make a more substantial difference because of the decline in industrial and the increase in agricultural prices relative to 1950. Therefore, in the few cases where trends are not unmistakable, the conclusions drawn from table 44 must necessarily be fuzzy.

Rates of growth in r and $\hat{r}$ formulations are compared as appropriate for three periods—1948–1955, 1950–1955, and 1958–1964. I can see no reason to introduce $\bar{r}$ calculations for the period 1948–1955—that is, to provide an analytical justification for 1948 as the base year. There is almost as little reason to do so for 1950, despite its identity as the base year of the Fifth Five Year Plan, in view of the doubtful meaningfulness of the official economic periodization based on the Five Year Plans.[3] Bergson, of course, made no estimates for the year 1955-plan and intended no plan-fulfillment comparison. Therefore, it seems most appropriate to omit $\bar{r}$ calculations entirely. All computations at AFC are those of Method I; Bergson did not use Method II at all.

Bergson's data are shown at four valuations, combinations of EP and AFC at 1937 and 1950 prices. He confined his presentation of postwar growth rates to the r formulation relating to AFC values for the benchmark years 1950 and 1955. However, the other entries in Table 44 could be computed directly from supplemental tables of annual data presented at the back of his book or indirectly by tracing through the appendix notes.[4] Bergson's "composite" indexes for this period are

---

[3] See Jasny, *Soviet Industrialization 1928–1952,* 1961, especially Chapter 1; also Jasny, *Essays on the Soviet Economy,* 1962.

[4] For the 1950–1955 period, insignificant discrepancies between the r rates of growth cited by Bergson and rates computed directly or indirectly from his annual series were encountered for consumption at 1937 and 1950 AFC. However, a more substantial discrepancy turned up with respect to defense. According to Bergson, the rate of growth of defense outlays was 7.9 percent at 1937 AFC and 7.2 percent at 1950 AFC (*Real SNIP,* p. 217). Calculation of r at 1937 AFC directly from the annual data (p. 303) confirms the figure of 7.9 percent; but the value of r at 1950 AFC, calculated from a series that had to be reconstructed, is 7.7 percent. If my reconstruction is

identical to the 1950-price indexes. Figures for gross investment and GNP enclosed in parentheses are calculated from a Bergson series that allows an alternative entry for inventory investment in 1954.

Table 44 omits government administration and internal security outlays which were declining almost uninterruptedly throughout this 15-year period. Otherwise, major GNP components exhibit positive and generally substantial rates of increase in each of the subperiods examined. For one of the GNP components, communal services including R&D, it is evident that the rate of growth was higher in the early 1950s than in the late 1940s, and higher still in the SYP period; these changes are unlikely to be affected by revaluation at prices of a later year. On the other hand, significant and striking retardation is evident in the growth of household outlays on consumption and of gross fixed investment. If consumption $\hat{r}$ growth rates were about 11–12 percent during 1948–1955 and 9–10 percent when the first two years are dropped, they are only 5 percent in 1958–1964. The rate of change of gross fixed investment declines from 12 or 12½ percent to 11 and finally to 6½–7 percent. Revaluation at a single set of prices could make a difference but probably not enough to affect the sign of the inequalities.

The trend of rates of change is not so clear with respect to the remaining two components of GNP, items 4 and 5, where the absence of homogeneous weights may be significant. Measurement at $\hat{r}$ suggests some falloff in the rate of increase of all gross investment plus outlays n.e.c., equivalent to Bergson's total gross investment, in 1950–1955 against 1948–1949, but little in 1958–1964 compared to 1950–1955. This conclusion also holds for the apparent movement of the rate of growth of defense outlays, confined to the narrow range of 6–8 percent. As for total GNP itself, the ostensible trend is again downward. The margin of about 2–3 points between 1950–1955 and 1958–1964 might be augmented under revaluation at 1950 AFC but diminished by a shift to 1958 or 1964 AFC.

To the question of whether there has been a retardation in the postwar rate of growth it is then necessary to give an affirmative but qualified reply. The slowdown in the pace of advance of consumption and fixed investment is unmistakable. On the other hand and equally

---

faulty, the error originates in a reconstructed index of outlays at EP, as that index yields an r value of 7.7 percent compared with the 7.2 percent implied by the annual series on p. 302 of *Real SNIP*. For the sake of consistency, the figures for the 1950 EP and AFC series in Table 44 of the present study are computed from my reconstructions.

clearly, expenditure on communal services was accelerating. Growth of defense and all gross investment including outlays n.e.c. may or may not have slowed down. Aggregate output is heavily influenced by consumption and gross fixed investment, and we find some downturn from 7–9 percent in the earlier subperiods to 5–6 percent for the basic series in 1958–1964. Whether that margin would hold up could depend on whether earlier or later year prices served as weights throughout, but the occurrence of some deceleration would undoubtedly be confirmed. Bergson does not provide annual data for a category comparable to my GNP with supplementary adjustments. He does cite index numbers for benchmark years at 1937 EP, AFC, and AFC with further adjustment.[5] The 1950–1955 overall percentage changes seem to be insensitive to the adjustments, but this reflects directly only on the r rates of growth; possibly, the $\hat{r}$ rates are no farther off than is shown in Table 44.

The conclusion that the rate of aggregate Soviet growth turned down between the 1950s and early 1960s will, of course, occasion no surprise.[6] It is generally accepted by Western students, and even Soviet leaders have publicly acknowledged the fact. Nor has there been much dispute outside of the USSR on the approximate magnitude of the slowdown. For example, the Moorsteen-Powell calculations imply an $\hat{r}$ rate of growth of 7.6 percent for 1950–1955 and 5.7 percent for 1958–1964. Cohn's r rate of growth for 1958–1964 of 5.3 percent is compared with one of 7.1 percent for 1950–1958. Surprisingly, the official Soviet claims for NMP imply an even sharper downturn, from 11.2 percent in 1950–1955, or 10.8 percent in 1950–1957 and 1950–1958, to 6.5 percent in 1958–1964, all in terms of $\hat{r}$.[7] Although the conclusion is not novel, it is useful to have it framed in terms of an intertemporally consistent set of GNP accounts by end use (previous comparisons have all related to output measured by branch of origin) and to note that the margin of retardation may be subject to some index number relativity.

In the light of the comparisons drawn from Table 44 and against the background of Table 35, it appears that the SYP itself anticipated or provided for some reduction in overall growth relative to the 1950s, but planners got more than they bargained for. If the conclusion is a

[5] *Real SNIP*, p. 140.

[6] Since the rate of population change was virtually the same in 1950–1955 as in 1958–1964, 1.7 percent (*NKh 1964*, p. 7, and *VS*, 1963, No. 8, p. 91), aggregate and per capita comparisons yield the same inferences.

[7] See the sources to Table 40.

qualified one with respect to GNP, it stands out clearly with regard to consumption and gross fixed investment; it does not hold, however, for communal services (including R&D outlays). Nominal defense expenditures may be viewed as having grown more rapidly in 1958–1964 than in 1950–1955, but it is possible that the Plan had an even more ambitious target in view. This seems the more likely in relation to the collection of expenditures consisting of defense, internal security, R&D, and outlays n.e.c., but a direct comparison with changes in previous periods is not possible.

International Growth Comparisons, 1950–1964

There can be no intention here of anything like a systematic comparison of Soviet growth with that in other countries. I restrict myself instead to a brief presentation of rates of increase of GNP and two major components—household consumption and gross fixed investment—for several noncommunist countries and groupings thereof. The choice of countries is dictated partly by availability of data and motivated, for the rest, by the frequency of their appearance in just such comparisons. The calculations relate to the intervals 1950–1955 and 1958–1964—that is, the major periods of the Soviet comparisons in Table 44. Again, these intervals are convenient in terms of data availability, but their primary justification is that they obviate the necessity of determining "appropriate" initial and terminal points. Evidently, these considerations also make it incumbent upon us to stay within the confines of $\hat{r}$ calculations.

The data compiled in Table 45 are computed from Organization for Economic Cooperation and Development (OECD) sources, in which national product concepts are drawn from the Standardized System of National Accounts adopted in 1958 by its predecessor organization, the Organization for European Economic Corporation (OEEC). There are, of course, differences between the OECD and the SNIP systems of national accounting, but they are not significant enough either to warrant detailed discussion here or, I believe, to disqualify the limited comparisons to be drawn with the corresponding Soviet magnitudes.[8]

[8] A general notion of the differences may be gauged from a schematic reconciliation of U.S. Department of Commerce data with the OECD accounts for the United States in the single year 1960, since the SNIP system is a modified version of the Commerce Department accounts. See OECD, *Statistics of National Accounts 1950–1961*, 1964, pp. 279–282.

TABLE 45

AVERAGE ANNUAL RATES OF GROWTH ($\hat{r}$) OF CONSUMPTION, FIXED INVESTMENT, AND GNP IN SELECTED NONCOMMUNIST COUNTRIES AT MARKET PRICES, 1950–1955 AND 1958–1964 (percent)

	GNP		Consumption		Fixed Investment	
	1950–1955 [a]	1958–1964 [b]	1950–1955 [a]	1958–1964 [b]	1950–1955 [a]	1958–1964 [b]
United States	3.6	4.2	3.3	4.0	3.2	3.8
Canada	4.1	4.4	4.8	4.2	4.8	2.0
Japan	..	12.0	..	8.4	..	18.1
France	4.2	5.5	4.6	5.6	3.9	7.8
Germany	8.7 [c]	5.6 [c]	8.1 [c]	5.5 [c]	13.5 [c]	9.0 [d]
Italy	5.8	6.3	4.6	7.0	9.2	7.7
United Kingdom	2.7	3.6	2.3	3.3	5.6	6.4
OECD, Europe only [e]	4.8	5.2	4.2	5.0	7.4	7.9
EEC [e]	5.9	5.6	5.3	5.7	8.4	7.8

Notes:

[a] At 1954 prices.

[b] At 1958 prices.

[c] Excluding the Saar and West Berlin. Computed from a series incorporating the Saar and West Berlin from 1960, $\hat{r}$ = 6.5 percent for GNP and 6.6 percent for consumption in 1958–1964.

[d] Including the Saar and West Berlin from 1960 on.

[e] Computed from dollar series based on 1958 exchange rates. OECD, Europe includes, in addition to the listed countries, Austria, Belgium, Denmark, Greece, Iceland, Ireland, Luxembourg, The Netherlands, Norway, Portugal, Spain, Sweden, Switzerland, Turkey. Belgium, Luxembourg, France, Germany, Italy and The Netherlands constitute the EEC.

Sources:

1950–1955, except Japan: OECD, *Statistics of National Accounts 1950–1961*, 1964, pp. 40, 44, 74, 90, 98, 130, 196, 206. 1958–1964: OECD, *National Accounts Statistics, 1955–1964*, March 1966, pp. 4, 5, 13, 17, 19, 27, 35, 67, 75, 107, 171.

Rates of growth are computed in Table 45 for consumption, total fixed investment and GNP, all at market prices. In a number of cases factor cost values are available for GNP, but not for consumption or investment. With few exceptions, rates of growth of GNP at factor cost coincide with or are close to corresponding rates at market prices.[9] For simplicity's sake, the factor cost alternatives have been omitted from Table 45.

In the first five years of the 1950s there were few to rival Soviet rates of growth. With a rate of increase of 8 percent, only Germany approached the 9–10 percent rates of change of Soviet consumption

[9] The largest differences observed from the sources cited were of four-tenths of a percentage point for Canada in 1958–1964 and Italy in 1950–1955.

(Table 44). German fixed investment and GNP appear to have risen at even more rapid rates than Soviet, 13.5 and 8.7 percent compared with about 11 and 7–8 percent, but the nearest other competition was the Italian rate of growth at 9 percent for investment and 6 percent for GNP. The comparison for 1958–1964 yields a different conclusion. Owing to Soviet growth retardation and European acceleration, the Soviet figures are easily matched or bettered: for consumption and GNP, by France, Germany, Italy, all European OECD and the EEC; for investment, by the same countries and even the United Kingdom. The extraordinary rates of growth achieved by Japan in this period, of course, far surpass the Soviet levels in this or indeed in the previous period under consideration. In the growthmanship race, the Soviet Union lost its lead position during the SYP period, retreating to the middle of the pack.

Longer Period Comparisons of Soviet GNP Structure

Completion of the estimates for 1958–1964 means the availability of an unbroken annual series at current prices for 17 years, beginning with 1948. Measured at current adjusted factor cost, changes in resource allocation during this period may be viewed in Fig. 12.[10] Because the pre-1958 components do not separate them out, R&D has been included with communal services, and other outlays n.e.c. (including the statistical discrepancy) with gross investment. The Bergson-Heymann-Nimitz series do not adjust for undervalued collective farmer incomes, impute capital charges, or deduct capital repairs; for the sake of comparability I use my basic series alone. I have already referred to minor differences in coverage and methodology between Bergson's and my basic series, but one other change, possibly of some significance, must be brought up here. Throughout the SNIP series, the public sector statistical discrepancy is entered on the outlay side and is sensitive to the basically arbitrary decision on the proportion of public sector miscellaneous revenues to be considered a charge on current account. In previous

[10] The estimates for 1948 are by Bergson and Heymann (*SNIP 1940–1948*), as revised in *SNIP 1928–1948;* those for 1949–1955 represent established price values compiled by Hoeffding and Nimitz (SNIP 1949–1955) adjusted to a factor cost basis by Nimitz (*SNIP 1956–1958*, pp. 16–17), and slightly revised by Bergson; estimates for 1956–1958 are by Nimitz (*ibid.*). A SNIP estimate of gross fixed investment in 1948 is not available.

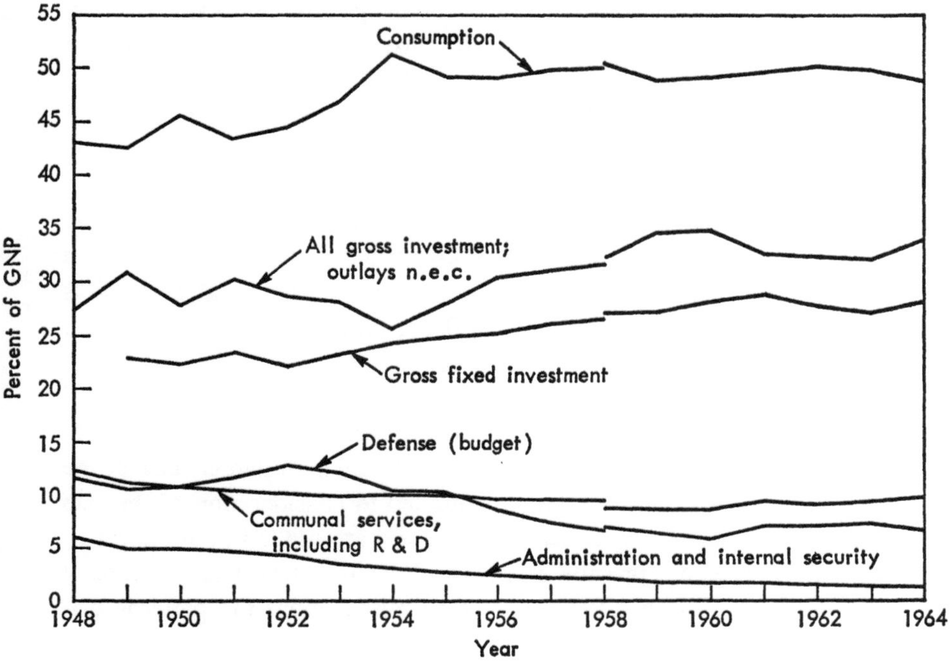

Sources:
1948-1958: Real SNIP, p.245; SNIP 1956-1958, p.17.
1958-1964: Table 15.

Fig. 12—Structure of GNP by use at current AFC, 1948-1964

SNIP studies that proportion was set at half; as indicated, it is three-quarters in the present estimates. The change is not likely to have affected the rates of growth of Table 44 but may be of consequence in consideration of changes in resource allocation.[11]

The 17-year record traced in Fig. 12 shows a peak level of 51 percent in consumption's share of GNP reached in 1954 (Malenkov's New Course?). However, the subsequent dip is shallow, and it is probably

[11] I should add that Bergson's adjustment for subsidies to procurement includes a revaluation of farm income in kind. Such a revaluation has been considered unnecessary for subsequent years on the ground that subsidies to procurement were no longer subsidies to agriculture but to consumer goods industry. This difference between the components of the 17-year series is properly viewed not as a break in the uniformity of methodology but as a reflection of the changing pattern of agricultural pricing.

justifiable to think of consumption maintaining a relatively steady claim since 1954 of half of total output. Gross fixed investment seems to have risen slowly but steadily from 1952 to 1961, with a slight dip (1½ points) in 1962–1963. All gross investment (including the residual public sector outlays) was subject to greater fluctuation, especially in the earlier period, but rose steeply between 1954 and 1959. After its Korean War peak, the explicit defense share of total resources declined steadily until 1960, from a high of 12.7 to a low of 5.8 percent; the increase in 1961–1963 is relatively small. The weight of communal services is virtually unchanged from about 1950 on, and that for administration and internal security is steadily declining.

Since the question of the magnitude and movement of the share of total resources devoted to investment has been of focal importance in discussion of Soviet growth, it may be worth taking a closer look at the rate of investment. My discussion is limited to consideration of the rate of gross investment—gross investment as a share of GNP, both at AFC; *Real SNIP* does not provide estimates of net investment to accompany the gross series. Two questions may be raised about the patterns displayed in Fig. 12: (1) Are the conclusions sensitive to supplementary adjustment of the AFC values? (2) Did such transformations in relative prices take place during these two decades that the change in rates of investment at current AFC is substantially different from real rates of growth of numerator and denominator?

Supplementary adjustments in Bergson's calculation apparently made little difference. In mine they tend to neutralize the effect of the basic factor cost adjustments. The impact of supplementary adjustments on the fixed investment share of GNP is to convert a slight positive average ($\hat{r}$) rate of growth at current AFC to a slight negative one. With or without supplementary adjustments, the rate of all gross investment excluding outlays n.e.c. shows a declining average movement.[12]

The second question cannot be answered definitely with available data, although I suspect the response should be a qualified negative. Figure 13 graphs the rate of gross investment in two variants and at both current and constant AFC—1950 AFC for the Bergson data and 1958 or 1964 AFC for mine. There is a three year gap in the middle 1950s in the constant price data and, in addition, a shift in price weights between the two subperiods 1948–1955 and 1958–1964. I have already alluded

[12] See pp. 182–184 and Fig. 10.

to the latter problem in commenting on Table 44. The issue here is the difference between rates of investment at current and constant prices. Figure 13 indicates that there is not much difference in pattern between the two within the two subperiods. Possibly, revaluation of the 1950–1955 data at 1958 AFC would diminish the steepness of the rise in the rate of investment. By the same token, the alternative revaluation of SYP data at 1950 AFC might produce a perceptible though probably small increase in rates of investment.[13]

I conclude that there was a sustained spurt in the rate of fixed investment in the 1950s. Fluctuations in inventory investment in 1958–1964 tended to depress the rate of investment. The addition of outlays n.e.c. acts in the opposite direction, but the scope of this category is not homogeneous over time, an important break being introduced, as indicated, in 1958. At any rate, whether some further increase in rates of investment, at either definition, was obtained in the SYP period, there was an unmistakable relative stabilization in comparison with the movement of the earlier period.

The problem of the scope and magnitude of outlays n.e.c. again raises the question of the relative weight of total military outlays and their growth over time, a question that proved so intractable in Chapter 7. The undeflated explicit defense outlay remained relatively constant in 1959–1960 at the 1958 level, and then rose sharply in 1961–1963 (Tables 18 and K-3). The GNP share for defense at current AFC behaves similarly, declining through 1960 and then rising in 1961–1963 to a little over 7 percent (Table 15). A small downturn is observed for 1964. Of course, it is hardly likely that this is an adequate account of the movement of total military expenditures in this period. The existence of concealed military outlays seems a safe assumption but, as Chapter 7 was at pains to point out, the relative size and growth of the concealed expenditures cannot be determined from published data, except in the grossest terms. I concluded there that the total military effort could not have absorbed more than about a tenth of Soviet resources during the SYP period, and one may reasonably assume that the period increase in relative weight was confined to a few percent of GNP.

Here, as in Chapters 5, 8, and 9, I have emphasized the relatively

[13] Figure 13 shows rates of investment at 1964 AFC paralleling those at 1958 AFC though at a somewhat lower absolute level. But the shift of weights is only partial (p. 126), and the reliability of this pattern is therefore open to question.

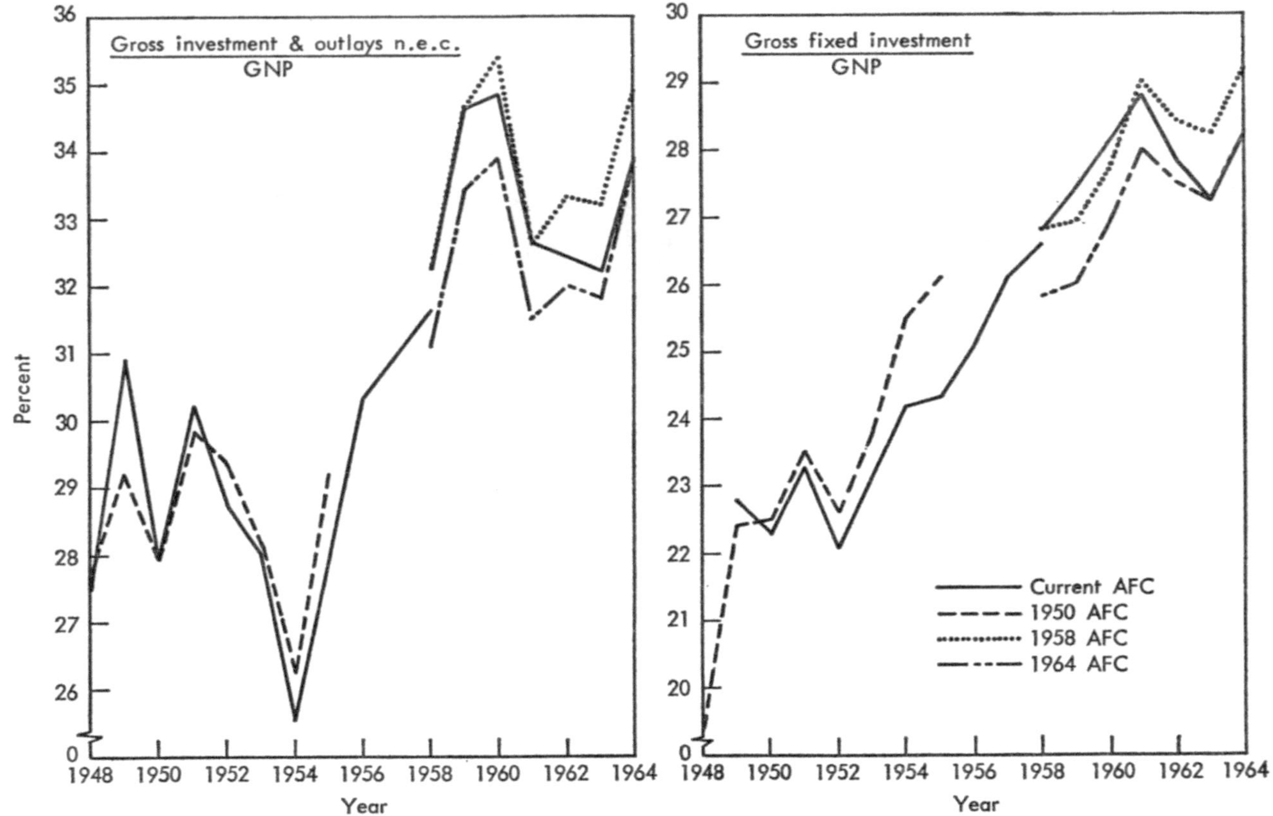

Fig. 13—The rate of gross investment at current and constant AFC, 1948-1964 (percent)

Sources: Real SNIP, p.245; SNIP 1956-1958, p.17; Sources to Table 44; Tables 15, K-1 and K-2.

TABLE 46
CONSUMPTION VERSUS MILITARY OUTLAYS, R&D, AND INVESTMENT: SHARES OF GNP AT CURRENT AFC IN SELECTED YEARS, 1937–1964
(percent)

	1937	1940	1950	1955	1958	1960	1962	1963	1964
1. Consumption plus communal services, excluding R&D	63	60	55	58	57	56	57	57	56
2. Defense (budget), R&D, gross investment, outlays n.e.c., and statistical discrepancy	34	36	40	39–40	41	42	41	42	43
Of which:									
Defense (budget)	8	16	11	10	7	6	7	7	7
Gross investment, outlays n.e.c., and statistical discrepancy	26	19	28	28	32	35	32	32	34

Sources:
1937–1955. *Real SNIP*, p. 237, except that R&D has been separately estimated, subtracted from communal outlays, and added to defense and gross investment. The estimate of the share of R&D is based on Nimitz, *Soviet Expenditures on Scientific Research*, January 1963, pp. 40–41 (absolute outlays on R&D); *Real SNIP*, pp. 128, 149 (GNP at AFC in 1937 and 1950); *SNIP 1928–1948*, p. 32 (GNP at AFC in 1940); *SNIP 1956–1958*, p.153 (GNP at AFC in 1955).
1958–1964. Table 15.

small changes in the pattern of resource allocation during the SYP period. It may be of some interest to view recent trends in the rate of investment and military outlays in a longer historical sweep. Table 46 contrasts the shares in GNP of consumption, including communal outlays net of R&D, and an aggregate consisting of explicit defense outlays, R&D, gross investment, residual public sector outlays and the statistical discrepancy, for benchmark years of Bergson's study [14] and five years of the SYP period. It is a remarkable pattern that Table 46 reveals. Consumption's share of GNP declined considerably between 1937 and 1950 and never regained the prewar levels. The weight of defense outlays in 1958–1964 was at or below the 1937 level, having receded from the peaks of 1940–1955. Sharply down in 1940, the share of gross investment including outlays n.e.c. rebounded by 1950 to exceed the 1940 mark and attained even higher ground between 1955 and 1960.

[14] Data for 1928 are omitted because of the revolutionary institutional and price transformations of the Soviet economy during the first two Five Year Plans. For the period 1928–1937, rates of investment and defense differ sharply at alternative valuations.

The combined claim of R&D, defense and augmented investment was raised after the war to over 40 percent of GNP. Through more than a quarter century of turbulent development, interrupted by a shattering war and preceded by a decade of frenzied industrialization, the Soviet government managed to raise and thereafter sustain at a high level the fraction of output devoted to economic and military growth.

Resource Allocation in Noncommunist Countries, 1950–1964

The nature of that achievement is perhaps better appreciated when compared with the structure of output utilization in some leading noncommunist countries, as set down in Table 47. I need hardly warn the reader again of the imperfect comparability of these national account data with my own—in particular, the juxtaposition of noncommunist accounts at market prices with SNIP accounts at factor cost—but I believe that the former suffice for the broadly phrased conclusions to be drawn.

When we compare the pattern of resource allocation in some of the advanced noncommunist countries, as displayed in Table 47, with that of the USSR, some striking differences emerge. By and large more than three-fifths of GNP in the major noncommunist countries is devoted to private consumption. Only Japan with 52–53 percent in 1960 and 1964 and Germany with 56–58 percent in three of the four years fall below this mark. If the OECD accounts at market prices are reasonably comparable to those of the USSR at factor cost, even the Japanese figures might exceed the average Soviet share since 1954. This comparison, of course, ignores the role of state supported welfare expenditures, which varies from country to country. Exclusive of R&D, communal outlays claimed only about 7 percent of Soviet aggregate outlays. An exact counterpart of such a category is not available for the noncommunist countries, but we do know that in 1960 current government expenditure other than on defense accounted for probably over 5 percent of national product in Japan and 10 percent in the EEC and the European OECD countries.[15] It does not seem likely that, in terms of

[15] The OECD sources do not provide a breakdown of Japanese government expenditure, as they do for most other countries, between "civil" and "defense." In 1960, 8.6 percent of Japanese GNP was allocated to government expenditure; presumably, the overwhelming share was for nonmilitary purposes.

TABLE 47

STRUCTURE OF GNP AT CURRENT MARKET PRICES BY MAJOR USE IN SELECTED NONCOMMUNIST COUNTRIES, 1950, 1955, 1960, 1964
(percent)

	Canada	United States	Japan	France [a]	Germany [b]	Italy	United Kingdom	OECD Europe [c]	EEC [c]
Private consumption									
1950	67	68	61	67	64	71	71	70	68
1955	64	63	61	67	58	67	68	66	64
1960	65	64	53	64	57	61	66	63	61
1964	63	63	52	64	56	61	65	62	60
Defense									
1950	3	5	..	6	5	..	6	5	5
1955	7	10	..	5	3	..	8	5	4
1960	5	9	..	5	3	..	6	4	4
1964	4	8	..	4	4	..	6	4	5
Gross domestic fixed capital formation									
1950	22	17	17	16	19	17	13	16	17
1955	23	17	18	18	23	20	15	18	20
1960	23	16	31	19	24	22	16	20	21
1964	23	17	34	21	26	21	18	22	23
Total investment, including change in stocks									
1950	24	20	25	19	23	19	11	18	21
1955	23	19	26	19	26	21	16	20	22
1960	24	17	36	21	27	24	18	22	24
1964	24	17	39	23	28	22	19	24	25

Notes:

[a] Data for 1960 and 1964 are from a new revised series, not strictly comparable to those for 1950 and 1955.

[b] Excluding Saar in 1950 and 1955; inclusion or exclusion of Saar does not affect the 1960 figures; including the Saar and West Berlin in 1964.

[c] European currency values converted to dollars at current exchange rates.

Sources:

1950, Japan: U.N., *Statistical Yearbook, 1965*, 1966, p. 549. 1950, 1955, 1960 (except Japan): OECD, *Statistics of National Accounts 1950–1961*, 1964, pp. 39, 43, 74, 90, 98, 130, 196, 206. 1955, 1960, and 1964 for Japan and 1964 for all others: OECD, *National Accounts Statistics 1955–1964*, March 1966, pp. 11, 15, 18, 26, 34, 66, 74, 106, 170.

output allocation at *current domestic prices,* taking account of differential relative emphasis on government welfare measures would affect the general conclusion: apart from Japan, the leading noncommunist countries devote a larger—often substantially larger—proportion of their annual product to consumption than does the USSR.

The relative claim of (explicit) defense in the USSR is not much different from that in the United Kingdom and somewhat higher than in France or Germany. Considering all Soviet military outlays, however, and on the assumption that concealment is a significant problem only in the USSR, it seems likely that only the United States rivals the USSR in terms of the percentage weight in total output. With respect to rates of gross fixed investment,[16] only Germany and Japan appear to be in a class with the USSR. Particularly noteworthy are the extraordinarily high Japanese rates of all gross investment during the first part of the 1960s, which may well exceed comparable Soviet rates. High Japanese and German investment rates are the obverse of low consumption and defense shares of GNP, a pattern only somewhat less apparent with regard to France and Italy, or, indeed, the two general European groupings.

Soviet Capital-Output Ratios, 1950–1964

There is only an imperfect correlation for the noncommunist countries in my sample between national consumption and investment-GNP proportions and relative rates of growth, as a glance back at Table 45 suffices to indicate.[17] It certainly has not been true for the USSR. The missing link, of course, is the effectiveness of investment—incremental output-capital ratios. For other purposes, average ratios are of interest too; the following review encompasses both types.

At the end of Chapter 9, I concluded that the SYP intended or expected rising aggregate fixed capital-output ratios. Whereas output was to grow at 7 percent per year, gross or net fixed investment was to increase at 8–9 percent and the net capital stock at 11 percent. Though there was an apparent downward shift in the key magnitudes, the *ex post* data suggest that the direction of change was the expected one. Growth of output at 6 percent per year was slower than that of gross investment

[16] Fixed and all gross investment include government investment.

[17] See also U.N., *Some Factors in Economic Growth in Europe During the 1950s,* 1964, pp. 17–18.

(7–8 percent), the net capital stock at current prices (11 percent), or the gross capital stock (about 9–10 percent in the *r* formulation); the pace of only net investment fell below that of output.[18]

Earlier in the present chapter, I compared rates of growth of GNP components as computed by Bergson and myself. I noted that growth rates for fixed investment were declining in the three periods under consideration—1948–1955, 1950–1955, 1958–1964. But this was also true of GNP, and the rates of increase of fixed investment were in each case higher than that of output. It would be useless to introduce data on the net capital stock computed as before, for the annual increments derive from official net investment at current prices, and in the 1950s price changes were substantial. Between the end of 1950 and the end of 1958, the gross capital stock, valued at allegedly constant prices, rose by 90 or 107 percent, depending on the yearbook series chosen, for an implied annual *r* value of 8.4 or 9.5 percent. Bergson roughly estimated the growth rate of GNP by origin in 1956–1958 as 7 percent, so that for the entire 1950–1958 interval the rate was about the same as in 1950–1955. Here too, then, the implication is of rising capital-output ratios, average and marginal.

Strong supporting evidence is supplied by Moorsteen and Powell. At 1937 factor cost, the average ratio of total net capital (including inventories and livestock) to GNP rose in every year between 1950 and 1966 except 1955, in which a small decline is observed; the overall increase amounts to 40 percent. The incremental ratio fluctuates but also shows a rising tendency from less than 2 to about 3–4.[19] When the numerator is confined to net fixed investment (including livestock) the upward movement in the average ratio is monotonic, from 1.3 to 2.1, implying an overall increase of three-fifths. Again, the incremental ratio displays considerable instability, but a three year overlapping moving average shows substantial and almost uninterrupted increase in the early 1960s with a dropoff thereafter.[20]

---

[18] Table 36 and pp. 171, 187. The meaningfulness of the net investment series is questionable on two grounds: (1) Use of current price instead of constant-price data; (2) the validity of straightline depreciation (p. 181). The series growth rate may be overestimated on the first count but significantly underestimated on the second.

[19] Tables T-53 and T-54 in Moorsteen and Powell, *The Soviet Capital Stock 1928–1962,* 1966, and Tables T-53-X and T-54-X in *Supplement I,* 1968.

[20] Computed from Tables T-25, T-47, and their extensions. *Ibid.*

The phenomenon of rising aggregate capital-output ratios is not new to the Soviet Union, which witnessed a substantial rise in the pre-World War II period as well.[21] What is new is the concurrence of high but apparently stabilizing investment rates, rising capital-output ratios, and retardation in the rate of overall growth. The clear dilemma such a conjunction of forces presents to the Soviet leadership has been noted and discussed extensively elsewhere: either raise the rate of investment still further or attempt to lower the incremental capital-output ratios, if high growth rates are to be sustained. The current movement to economic reform is certainly viewed in the USSR as an attempt to resolve that dilemma. Whether it will succeed is another matter, but that is a question outside the limits of this study.

---

[21] *Ibid.*, pp. 252–253. See also Bergson, in Bergson and Kuznets, eds., *Economic Trends in the Soviet Union,* 1963, Table I.1, p. 4.

12

Summary and Conclusions

The exposition of the findings of this study has now been completed; my results have been compared with those of others for the same period; some comparisons have been drawn with Bergson's results for the 1948–1955 period as well as with relevant international experience since 1950. It now remains but to set out some concluding comments on the period of direct concern to this study.

Summary of Findings

Before proceeding, it might be useful to summarize the salient points of the study to this point, grouped below under four major headings.

THE VALUATION PROBLEM

So long as the student of Soviet macroeconomics is content to confine his analysis to financial flows, he may successfully operate in the medium of prevailing Soviet prices. But as soon as he decides to probe issues of growth, resource allocation, standards of living, he must confront the dual problem of the conceptual framework of analysis and the compatibility of that framework with the raw data at his disposal. This study has been concerned very largely with the structure and growth of the Soviet economy, viewed in terms of Bergson's modification of the production potential standard of national income valuation. That conceptual apparatus was applied in an attempt to establish the degree of suitability of Soviet relative prices in the SYP period as weights in the aggregation of physical outputs. In partial compensation for the distortions of the Soviet price system, several major adjustments to the values of established prices, essentially the same as those underlying Bergon's factor cost estimates, were carried through. Together with the original data at

EP, these AFC values form the basic series of this study's concern. In addition, supplementary adjustments were undertaken to observe the effect of attempts to correct for other inadequacies of Soviet prices.

At current prices the basic factor cost adjustments have, as Bergson observed for other periods, a marked effect in reducing the ostensible share of consumption in GNP and in increasing that of investment. However, supplementary adjustments operate in the reverse direction. With allowance for the likely impact of adjustments not undertaken—for example, imputation of nonagricultural differential rent, one may conclude that (1) with appropriate valuation, the share of consumption in GNP would fall somewhere between the levels indicated by the basic AFC and the series with supplementary adjustments; (2) the EP series is a reasonable approximation to the desired series for investment and perhaps also for consumption, but not for all other outlays considered as a group. These conclusions depart from those drawn by Bergson with respect to an earlier period, but because of intervening changes in the price system my findings have no necessary bearing on his.

Divergences between EP and basic AFC values at constant prices tend to be small but in the directions suggested by analysis of the current-price data—reducing the increment of consumption and raising that of investment. Changes effected by the supplementary adjustments are generally also predictable and small, raising rates of growth of consumption, lowering those of investment; since these alterations are offsetting, the overall rate of growth, that of GNP, is unaffected. So it remains, even after deduction of public sector residual outlays, a series subject to a high margin of error. The growth calculations are only marginally sensitive to shift in price weights, but the result is predictable from (1) known or estimated stability of prices in a number of end-use categories, and (2) my inability, because of inadequate information, to compute alternative-weighted price deflators for more than a fraction of total output. For consumption and to a lesser extent for GNP as a whole, the estimates are more sensitive to the method of computing constant AFC, whether by projection of a base year AFC value (Method I) or by deflation of annual AFC values (Method II), but the result is linked to the particular time pattern of the factor cost adjustments at current prices.

MEASUREMENT OF THE RATE OF GROWTH

Three distinct formulations of an average annual rate of growth are discussed in this book, designated r, $\bar{r}$, and $\hat{r}$. The first is the conventional geometric average of output indexes—in effect, the compounded rate implied by initial and terminal years alone. Except as a supplementary aid for comparison with results of other studies, r is rejected in favor of the other two, which have the advantage of taking account of fluctuations between initial and terminal years by requiring equality of the sum of the estimated with the sum of the observed values. The initial year is also the base year of $\bar{r}$ calculations, but the formula for $\hat{r}$ chooses a fictitious base year so as to minimize the sum of the squared absolute deviations of estimated from observed values. Because of the sensitivity of $\bar{r}$ to initial year values, the formula has been used only for comparisons of plan and implementation in Chapter 9, where the initial year takes on independent significance as the base of SYP targets. Thus, $\hat{r}$ is the fundamental growth formula of this study.

SECTORAL INCOMES AND OUTLAYS

The SYP provided for a radical restructuring of the sectoral origination of agricultural output and incomes, primarily in favor of the state sector and at the expense of the private sector. In consequence, the distribution of household incomes was to be altered to increase still further the dominant share of wages and salaries and to decrease the weight of agricultural incomes excluding or including wages and salaries. Expectations were exceeded in the sense of an even larger 1964 share for all wages and salaries than that hoped for in 1965S, but the change was obtained less by relative increase in wages and more by increases (actual and accounting) in the size of the state labor force. It was also expected that in the household outlay budget, the proportion devoted to consumption would rise and that of investment and transfers (taxes and savings) fall. In the event, the increased weight of consumption was attained wholly at the expense of investment, as the government felt obliged abruptly to discontinue a program of tax reduction. The environment in which that decision was taken was one of imbalance in the consumer goods market with symptoms of considerable repressed inflation.

These conditions are also reflected in the contrast between *ex ante* and *ex post* patterns of financing public sector expenditures. The SYP apparently allowed for increasing relative weights of retained incomes and profits as well as of income and profit taxes; the share of transfer payments from households and of depreciation allowances, it is estimated, were to decrease. In actuality, the regime put a brake on the growth of retained profits, transfers were maintained at comparatively high levels, and a far more important place was taken by depreciation allowances, for which norms were sharply raised in 1963, than appeared to have been contemplated originally. The redistributive mechanism of state finances played a considerably greater role *ex post* than is shown by the *ex ante* accounts. The intended disposition of public sector revenues, according to my estimates, shows a startling reallocation in favor of "other outlays" (defense, R&D, internal security, outlays n.e.c., and the public sector statistical discrepancy) with a relative decline in every other outlay category. As it turned out, the increase in other outlays was considerably less, and that in gross investment greater than expected. However, it is possible that part of the hoped for growth in other outlays was actually earmarked for expansion of the capital stock. I return to this problem below.

STRUCTURE AND GROWTH OF THE ECONOMY

The pattern of resource allocation during the years of the SYP period assumes somewhat varying aspects at different valuations, but by and large radical change is not the hallmark of the *ex post* data. At basic AFC, current or constant, the rate of gross fixed investment shows a positive average rate of change; supplementary adjustments, however, change the sign. In any case, the margins are small. The rate of all gross investment is characterized by great fluctuations, reflecting the instability of inventory investment. Here too the sign of the average rate of change is not clear but the magnitudes are small. At current AFC with all supplementary adjustments, the curve traced by consumption's share in GNP, from 50 percent in 1958 to 55 percent in 1960–1963, is somewhat concave to the origin, owing in considerable part to the assumption that the relation of collective farmer incomes to earnings of workers of comparable skill elsewhere may be taken at par in 1958; between 1959 and 1964 there is no net change and the gap between intervening high and low is two points. Not much change was observed for the relative weight of communal services. As for the burden of military expenditures, only dim outlines can be recognized through the fog of Soviet secrecy. I have ventured the conclusion that not much more than a tenth of total output was allocated to the military and that changes over the SYP period were confined to a few percentage points of GNP.

In the absence of extensive price changes or possibly also because of imperfect deflation, the comparative stability of the pattern of resource allocation is the obverse of considerable bunching in rates of growth of major GNP components. Excluding the measurements of AFC by Method II, annual rates of increase come to about 5 percent for consumption; 6 for communal services; 6½ to 7 for gross fixed investment; 6 to 6½ for all gross investment; and about 8 for (explicit) defense. Only R&D outlays advanced at a markedly different pace, 12 percent per year. The rate of growth of GNP as a whole is calculated at about 5½ percent.

The revealed patterns in a number of respects depart from the regime's preferences, at least to the extent the latter may be judged from the estimated 1965S GNP accounts. If the Plan seemed to call for a considerable restructuring of output disposition in favor of fixed investment and other nonconsumption expenditures (military, R&D, etc.) at the expense of household outlays on consumption, the reallocation achieved was only partial: the desired increase in fixed investment's share was attained, but neither the drop in the rate of consumption nor the spurt in other outlays materialized to the degree expected.

With the exception of communal services and state-cooperative fixed investment, growth objectives of the Plan for major GNP elements were also underfulfilled, although perhaps by not quite as much as seems commonly believed. Attained average annual rates of growth fell short of the estimated targets by roughly one percentage point for consumption and 1½ points for GNP. Goals for household and collective farm investment were missed by huge margins. The rate of growth of "other outlays" was high but substantially below what had apparently been expected. Whether the estimated target for what I have called the priority elements of nonconsumption—public sector investment plus other outlays—was fulfilled depends on the growth formula used. Since the planners had underestimated the expected population increase the gap between plan and fulfillment is larger on a per capita basis than in aggregate: a quarter to a third below plan for consumption and GNP per capita compared with the roughly 15–20 percent shortfalls for the aggregate counterparts.

As is by now generally agreed, Soviet rates of growth suffered a retardation between the early 1950s and the middle 1960s. The conclusion appears unmistakable with respect to consumption and fixed investment and is most likely true of GNP as well. Growth of communal services, on the other hand, was accelerating, and the change for all gross investment plus outlays n.e.c. is ambiguous. To a considerable extent retardation was built into the SYP—certainly, with respect to consumption and fixed investment, probably, for "other outlays," possibly, in regard to GNP—but the slowdown appears to have been greater than expected.

The Soviet economy seems to have encountered almost continuously rising capital-output ratios, including the early 1950s. Against this background and that of the upward trend in the rate of investment during the 1950s, it is interesting to note that the SYP intended or expected further increases in the aggregate fixed capital-output ratio. This did happen, although the change took place with lower values in numerator and denominator than had been anticipated. Capital-output ratios continued to increase but in an environment of retardation in the pace of economic growth coupled with relative stabilization of the rate of investment.

The Growth of Production Potential

Given the theoretical and methodological considerations as well as the statistical findings summarized above, what conclusions can be drawn about the growth of Soviet production potential from 1958 to 1964?

According to the theoretical principles reviewed at the end of Chapter 3, the presumption that production possibilities schedules are concave to the origin implies a preference for measurement by given-year weighted quantity indexes if the objective is to obtain a series measuring potential changes in terms of a constant mix. Such a series might be subject to greater index number bias than one generated by a base-year weighted quantity index which would be measuring production potential in terms of a continually changing basket of goods and services. As it turned out, the data at my disposal are inadequate to yield consistent indexes of either type. In view of the empirical difficulties, the explicit goal was base-year weighted indexes with two alternative weight-years, 1958 and 1964. The computed indexes depart from these guidelines, to a degree difficult to appraise. The actual indexes must, of course, diverge from pure given-year-weighted quantity indexes, but I would not venture to suggest whether the gap is wider here than with respect to the ostensible objectives, base-year-weighted series. In considerable part because of an inability to construct alternative weighted deflators, the measurements of this study reveal relative insensitivity of the results to alteration of the weight year from 1958 to 1964. What little change can be observed is generally of a reduction in growth.

Two questions may then be posed: (1) Can the actual observations be taken as a reliable reading on the measurements that would have been obtained with pure base-year or pure given-year-weighted quantity indexes? (2) How shall we interpret the reduction in growth generally observed in moving the weight year from 1958 to 1964? The answer to the second question in part depends on the answer to the first, for if we may not draw any inferences on the behavior of the pure indexes from the movement of the computed indexes, it cannot be assumed that the observed lower growth yielded by 1964-price-weighted measurements is meaningful.

The dependence may become clearer if we reexamine the meaning of the phenomenon of Paasche quantity index numbers lower than those of Laspeyres. Such an outcome may eventuate from a pattern of aggregate growth in which goods and services whose production expands more rapidly than the average are also cheapening relative to the prices of other components of output; or, put another way, from a pattern of growth such that goods and services whose output is expanding comparatively slowly are also becoming relatively more expensive. I have assumed that investment and armaments prices remained relatively stable during the SYP period in contrast to the known small increase in retail prices and substantial growth of agricultural prices as well as of wages in services. Given the more rapid growth of investment and "defense" excluding pay and subsistence than of consumption and government services, the natural consequence is a lower aggregate Paasche than Laspeyres index number. On the other hand, I have also expressed reservations on the reliability of the official indications of investment-price stability and of the assumption of unchanged prices for military hardware. To the extent that these reservations are justified, a factor generating the observed difference in growth with alternative weight years would be attenuated.

The sharp structural transformations that are the foundation of the well-known Gerschenkron hypothesis (a special form of the index number divergence under discussion here) occurred in the Soviet Union before 1937. Bergson's calculations relating to post-1937 years, with price weights of a year no later than 1950, show little index number relativity. There was no general revision of nonagricultural prices between 1955 and 1967, but agricultural prices were generally on the rise throughout that period. The pattern of index number relativity found in this study (and the relation of SYP changes to those of the early 1950s) is therefore sensitive to the reluctant assumption of relative constancy in prices of investment goods and military hardware. By the same token, the reliability of the computed indexes relative to the pure base or given-year standards is similarly in question, although here other factors, deriving from various data gaps, play a contributing if minor role.

The Seven Year Plan in Retrospect

I come now to some final reflections on the SYP and its implementation. The word "reflections" is used advisedly: The findings of this study constitute the basis for the following remarks, but I have ventured beyond the strict boundaries of national income accounts in order to try to gain a broader policy perspective on the results of my research.

THE SYP AS PLAN

The attempt to view the SYP targets through the prism of national income accounting was motivated by the hope of providing a more ordered view of Soviet economic policy in this period. But given the 1965S accounts it may be useful to ask first whether they shed additional light on the SYP *qua* plan, apart from its implications for economic policy? Do the 1965S accounts provide evidence on a number of characteristics of the SYP, in particular, on the degree of *articulation, comprehensiveness,* and *consistency?* By *articulation* I mean the identification of explicit links between income and product flows; *comprehensiveness* refers to the scope and detail of the articulation;[1] *consistency* to the absence of tangible contradictions not explainable as statistical discrepancies.

The process of casting the available information on 1965S into the mold of national income accounts provides little independent evidence on the comprehensiveness and degree of articulation of the SYP. The basic Plan documents available to us—the approved Control Figures and Khrushchev's speeches to the 21st Party Congress—are merely skeleton plans. Additional information was extracted from official or unofficial sources, and the accounts were balanced with the aid of liberal applications of assumptions and presumptive logic. This does not necessarily mean that a comprehensive and well articulated plan did not exist, although there are some grounds for such an assertion, some of which will be introduced shortly. The point is that the question cannot be settled on the basis of the internal evidence of my accounts alone.

Supposing that the estimates derived from semiofficial or unofficial sources are in fact *bona fide* SYP artifacts, there still remains the

---

[1] Vernon defines comprehensiveness in a manner similar to my notion of articulation, as an explicit statement of targets with quantitative tracing out of paths between targets and necessary inputs. Vernon, *Economic Journal,* March 1966, p. 56.

problem of my assumptions, deductions, and inferences. Do they too have "real" antecedents in the undisclosed parts of the SYP? On the reply to this question hangs the answer to the query on the consistency of the Plan. I found no clear contradictions in the data underlying account entries, although in a few cases the ambiguity of Soviet sources may have allowed for an interpretation artificially resolving a real inconsistency. Obviously, the dimensions of this problem cannot be easily assessed. To these generalizations there is one important possible exception—the magnitude of the public sector residual, other outlays, in 1965S. To balance the public sector account in 1965S, given the estimates of incomes and of other expenditures, requires a value of other outlays implying an extraordinarily large increase over the corresponding 1958 level. The interpretation of that increase is discussed at some length below.

PLAN AND FULFILLMENT

Important goals of the SYP were not met; some others were, or the shortfalls were small. Was the SYP a clear failure or a near miss? Evidently, this is in one sense an index number problem with a solution sensitive to the choice of weights, the ranking of targets in order of "importance." A more important consideration, discussed in Chapter 1, is the function of a perspective plan in Soviet planning and the predictive expectations to which a perspective plan may be reasonably held. I was at some pains to suggest that the requirement for realism must be understood, first, in terms of the information available at the time of plan formulation; and second, as constrained by other objectives, such as flexibility, mobilizing effort, and so on. I have maintained that the perspective plan must be evaluated essentially in terms of the fidelity of its reflection of planners' and policy makers' judgments. An assessment of the plan's realism would require an understanding of what it set out to do and tracing the interaction with changing information, preferences, and policies. This book is not directly a study of economic policy but of national income. Interest here is restricted to the policy implications of the national income accounts, and I have largely ignored such obviously relevant considerations as the assumptions underlying agricultural policy, where the most conspicuous apparent underfulfillment occurred.

The SYP has been examined in the framework of a set of national income and product accounts. Comparison of the 1965S targets with attained levels in the base year, 1958, was the instrument used to derive first level inferences on plan objectives and more general implications about economic policy orientation. At a late point in the analysis, I referred to a hazard of this methodology inherent in the use of a perspective, GNP *à la* AFCS, alien to Soviet planners and policy makers. Although the analysis of resource allocation and growth must proceed with the awareness that the framers of policy perceived and decided within a different accounting system,[2] not to speak of their particular development model, the implications of these decisions from an admittedly superimposed viewpoint are potentially interesting nevertheless. They are interesting first, for the same reason and to the same degree that analysis *ex post* from that viewpoint is, deriving from the rationale of the theory of national income measurement. Moreover, Soviet planners are not unmindful of the deficiencies of their price system, although they have differed sharply on the remedial measures required. An instrument designed to adjust for distortions in the object of examination, albeit of foreign manufacture, may yield insights not totally unlike those arrived at by thoughtful Soviet observers intent on giving a "truer" picture of the economic processes in operations.

I believe this a reasonable justification for the form of this study's discussion of economic policy in the SYP. Nevertheless, the most intriguing and the most serious problem of interpretation of SYP policy is one for which the questions of product boundaries and valuation standards are not significant obstacles to understanding. The issue in question is the extraordinary relative and absolute increase in "other outlays" estimated as expected between 1958 and 1965S. That the above-mentioned methodological problems are not at issue is clear: (1) the problem is treated in the SNIP accounts at EP; and (2) there is evidence of very large increases in residuals linked to "other outlays" appearing in a distribution of NMP (Table Q-1). How, then, shall we interpret the surprising finding? Four possible explanations may be listed:

(1) My estimates are substantially in error. The error would be a consequence of underestimating other elements of public sector outlays or of overestimating public sector revenues, particularly budget revenues. I have explored this question in Appendix M and tested the sensitivity of the results to alternative assumptions with respect to the

[2] The problem is of considerably less significance with regard to sectoral incomes and outlays at prevailing prices.

size of budget revenues. The absolute size of other outlays (items 4, 5, 6, and 7 of Table 4) in 1965S is altered by ±15 percent, reducing (increasing) the growth over the 1958 level from about 160 percent to 120 (200) percent. Even at the reduced level, this is a very substantial change indeed, double the 63 percent increase of GNP (Table 35). Assuming that the error lies in overestimating rather than underestimating public sector revenues, could the error be still larger than indicated? Perhaps, considering also the possibilities of error in estimates of other public sector outlays. But there seems to be no reason to assume the existence of systematic unidirectional bias in the major outlay components; only the target for inventory investment appears "low."

(2) The increase in "other outlays" covers as large or even larger growth in military expenditures. On the assumption that the SYP did not contemplate a marked expansion of internal security activities, the increment in R&D, explicit defense, and outlays n.e.c. would have been greater than that of the total. Conceivably, the military expenditure part of the three components was slated for rapid rise. But is this a plausible interpretation? Evidence on this point must be adduced from outside the framework of my national income accounts—for example, the literature of debate on issues of military policy. This is not the place to attempt to analyze that debate, but the major secondary sources do not give the impression that an intensive rearmament drive was under way or contemplated in this period.[3]

(3) Respectable increases in civilian R&D and military outlays were planned, but "other outlays" in 1965S allowed for a large contingency fund, possibly to be considered as a reserve for investment. In his address to the 21st Party Congress, Khrushchev declared that the SYP could be easily fulfilled and overfulfilled. Perhaps this is evidence supporting the hypothesis of a large explicit contingency fund. But what was the nature of this reserve? Was it incorporated in sectoral and branch output programs and intended to reflect real commodity and labor flows? Did the planned rate of growth of NMP take account of the increment of output obtainable from the investment reserve? If not, is it likely that Khrushchev would have been satisfied with so "soft" a plan given (a) the evident decrease in rates of growth embodied in the SYP and (b) his unrelenting emphasis on the "time factor," on catching up

[3] I refer primarily to the work of Wolfe, especially his *Soviet Strategy at the Crossroads*, 1964. See also Horelick and Rush, *Strategic Power and Soviet Foreign Policy*, 1966.

with and surpassing levels of output in the capitalist world? Or was much of the reserve no more than a financial wraith?

(4) The latter question suggests the possibility that the extraordinary size of "other outlays" in 1965S represents a mixture of real intended growth and a financial illusion, reflecting an unsuccessful meshing of physical and financial planning. Such imperfect linkage could easily have been the consequence of the relatively undeveloped state of Soviet planning processes. Let us take two characteristics as examples, of which the first concerns the coordination of plan and budget. The annual plan is complemented by an annual budget, but there is no evidence that perspective plans are similarly accompanied. What evidence exists that specific numbers relate to the budget in 1965S is frequently expressed in a form consistent with the hypothesis that the figures were implications drawn from the Plan rather than explicitly set goals. Extensive Soviet experimentation with input-output models largely postdated the drafting of the SYP. Even recently, in a relatively advanced stage of their experience with such models, it appears to have been impossible to transit accurately from value to physical-unit tables and vice versa. The achievement of such transferability is still a goal on the agenda of contemporary research.[4]

The SYP was notable as the first perspective plan to have made use at some stage of an *ex ante* macroeconomic balance.[5] Such a balance is

---

[4] Kossov, *Ekon.gazeta,* December 1967, p. 16. See also Isaev, in Nemchinov, ed., *Primenenie matematiki v ekonomicheskikh issledovaniiakh,* Vol. 3, 1965, p. 244.

[5] My interest here is in the balance as an accounting form. Precisely how the SYP balance was arrived at, the model, is not known. Bor and Notkin (*VE,* 1961, No. 5, pp. 37–39) have described three alternative approaches (the rate of investment and capital-output ratios; employment and labor productivity; consumption and output of Divisions I and II) but did not link them to a particular balance. In 1958 Kaser believed that with the SYP the USSR had "reverted to overall 'rate-of-growth' programming, variants for which were then tested before sector plans were elaborated." Several years later he decided "this view seems to have echoed aspiration rather than actuality." He concluded: "There was not, and there still is not, a long term macro-economic plan." (Kaser, in Grossman, ed., *Value and Plan,* 1960, pp. 215–217, and *Soviet Studies,* October 1962, p. 113 and p. 128, note 9.) The Poles have distinguished between two alternative methods: postulating an aggregate growth rate from which sectoral implications are derived, or building up the aggregate growth rate from projection of sectoral capacities. The second was rejected because it would allegedly "tend to create surpluses

comprehensive in its coverage, but this is not true of the state plan itself which covers intrastate sector flows and only the relations between the state and other sectors. Activities within the cooperative, collective farm, or private sectors are reflected in the *ex ante* balance but no plan objectives are framed for them. Moreover, with relation to the internal operation of these sectors, there was no provision for the flow of objectives, information, and counterplans up and down the administrative hierarchy, a process which is supposedly essential to the concretization and elaboration of the state plan. In short, for non-state intrasector activity there was incomplete formal protection against abstract planning.[6]

The fact is, of course, that even for the state sector the elaboration of the SYP was aborted at an early stage. Evidently nothing beyond the Control Figures was produced. In the careful wording of one writer, "the elaboration of the SYP for 1959–1965 by enterprise was not carried through at that time to its conclusion." [7] Not the least of the SYP's methodological problems was that its aggregates were only incompletely aggregated from the bottom of the hierarchy up, but largely created at the top.

Incomplete linkages between physical and financial flows and the truncation of the process of plan formulation are factors that may be expected to facilitate a divorce of goals from reality. Whether for these or other reasons, the degree of fulfillment of the Plan fell considerably short of 100 percent in many cases, as we have seen. The relative and absolute growth of "other outlays" was below the estimated target level, by a margin varying with the measure of growth used. The Plan was underfulfilled with respect to rates of growth of GNP and consumption. More outstanding divergences were the drastic cutbacks in collective

---

and deficits in an uncoordinated manner" (Chandra, *Soviet Studies*, January 1967, p. 301). Perhaps the Soviet penchant for planning "from inherited proportions," in the phraseology of the now frequently cited critique, was indeed the basis for the SYP planning model and led to the results feared by the Poles. The remedy for such imbalance was in iteration of the planning process, in feedback. As will be indicated shortly, the feedback process was truncated.

[6] Bor, in AN SSSR, *Uchenye zapiski po statistike*, 1959, Vol. IV, p. 50.

[7] Levitskii, in Goncharenko *et al.*, *Nepreryvnost' v planirovanii i pokazateli gosudarstvennogo plana*, 1962, p. 55. The two previous five year plans were no more completely elaborated. See Jasny, *Essays on the Soviet Economy*, 1962, p. 245 ff.

farm investment and private housing construction. On the other hand, rates of growth of communal services and state-cooperative fixed investment were at or above target levels, and the state did succeed in maintaining a high rate of aggregate investment throughout the period.

The most significant setback to Soviet economic policy in the SYP period would appear to have been the failure to secure what Khrushchev had viewed as the "root problem of the forthcoming seven-year period —the problem of a maximal gain of time in the economic competition of socialism with capitalism." For Khrushchev that "gain of time" meant realization of a long-standing Soviet dream of "overtaking and surpassing" the advanced capitalist states, a decisive step to ultimate victory over the capitalist world. It meant stunning the uncommitted world with the brilliance of Soviet achievement while luring them with appropriately distributed economic aid. Undoubtedly it had a military dimension too, although the data are, as we have seen, difficult to interpret. In short, it was "A Plan to Shake the World," as a contemporary Soviet newspaper headline marveled.

Some successes were recorded, but the hope of a "maximal gain of time" faded. Output in several noncommunist states picked up while USSR agriculture stagnated, and Soviet per capita consumption grew at a pace a quarter to a third slower than planned. Soviet strategic inferiority was made humiliatingly plain in the Cuba confrontation in October 1962. Although the rate of investment remained high, capital-output ratios rose more rapidly but aggregate growth rates less rapidly than anticipated. Soviet planners too, like their less experienced brethren in developing countries, "often mistake the shadow of investment for the substance of production." [8]

The accepted, semi-official explanation of the retardation of Soviet growth through 1965 makes reference to one set of objective factors— the harvest failures of 1963 and 1965 and the "sharpening of the international situation . . . in recent years," requiring additional military expenditures. For the rest the critique is interestingly un-Marxian, a catalog of subjective errors: imperfections of planning and administration, incomplete utilization of material and moral incentives, "a subjectivist approach to the solution of a number of economic problems, arbitrary alterations in proportions, disdain for scientific conclusions, undervaluation of the operation of objective economic laws of socialism

[8] Singer, *Economic Development and Cultural Change,* April 1967, p. 371.

and of *khozraschet* methods of economic management." For good measure, the indictment also throws in "miscalculations and premature actions (*zabeganie vpered*) that reacted negatively on national economic proportions and production effectiveness." [9]

Khrushchev had tried to force the acceptance of a reversal of Lenin's dictum on the superiority of politics over economics, resorting even to the "discovery" of an unpublished Lenin work in which economics was enthroned over politics.[10] The failures of the SYP may be viewed as both political and economic. Soviet writers have devoted a great deal of attention to the problem of rising capital-output ratios, and in large part the blame has been laid at the door of investment planning.[11] Without attempting to probe so large and complex a subject in a few words, the deficiencies of investment planning can yet be summarily phrased as a failure to compare alternatives appropriately. The planning process is not geared to force the consideration of enough alternatives correctly weighed relative to each other. From this point of view, the root of Soviet difficulties, of the retardation of growth, was economic in its classic essence—a matter of incorrect use of means to given ends.

On the other hand, the SYP bespeaks an inability to distinguish conflicting objectives, a failing more political, or perhaps psychological. The SYP is a child of the mid-1950s, reflecting both the successes and failures of that period. It has to be viewed against the background of the initial successes in reviving agriculture and their consequent effect of reinforcing Khrushchev's unbounded faith in management as the key to the solution of all problems; of the Malenkov–Khrushchev contest for power, in which Khrushchev successfully used the weapon of the priority of heavy over light industry to dispose of Malenkov, only to proclaim his own fidelity to consumer interests; of the initial political successes in wooing the developing countries and in exploiting Soviet space achievements for political ends. These successes may have strengthened the sense of euphoria that already seemed natural to Khrushchev and induced the impression that refined ordering of objectives was useless pedantry.

Optimism was especially rampant in the abortive Sixth Five Year

---

[9] *Ekonomicheskii ezhegodnik, god 1966,* 1967, p. 11.

[10] Linden, *Khrushchev and the Soviet Leadership 1957–1964,* 1966, p. 149.

[11] For example, see Sominskii, *Kommunist,* 1964, No. 10, pp. 78–80. There is a vast and growing literature on the "effectiveness" of investment.

Plan, but its very demise and the general lowering of sights thereby made necessary might have induced a more careful weighing of alternative or incompatible objectives. In fact, that general lowering of sights may itself have contributed to the bombast with which the SYP was launched. For Khrushchev had the difficult task of selling a plan with reduced rates of growth of key series relative to realized rates of the 1950s and the rates of the short-lived Sixth FYP. His boast to "overtake and surpass the United States" was doubtless partly due to misplaced confidence that the American economy would stagnate, but it is difficult to escape the conclusion that another reason was his desire to soft pedal the apparent deceleration of Soviet growth. Perhaps, too, as has been suggested,[12] he sought to provide a stimulus to increased effort, hoping thereby to overfulfill minimum objectives. In this he would be counting less on commodity reserves than on his traditional guidelights of organization and Bolshevik will.

What I am suggesting here is that the "maximum gain of time" was not so much a fundamental aspect of the SYP as a basic feature of the Khrushchev *modus operandi.* Though the theme of "overtake and surpass" was muted as agricultural difficulties began to multiply, the restlessness and sense of time pressure, the tendency to view problems in their organizational dimensions, remained characteristic of Khrushchev's style, not the least so in the field of agricultural policy. As Robert Conquest once suggested, Khrushchev was at least a convinced activist.

The debate, such as it was, as to which was to be accorded priority, politics or economics, has usually been linked with the 1962 scheme for Party reform or with issues arising out of the Sino-Soviet dispute. I am tempted to see in it as well as reflection of a fundamental antinomy in the Khrushchevian character and economic policy. By antinomy I mean the literal dictionary definition of a "contradiction between two principles each taken to be true, or a contradiction between inferences correctly drawn from such principles." Khrushchev believed in both dicta: the classical Leninist, that politics takes primacy over economics, and the revisionist heresy that economics must dictate to politics. This, it seems to me, is one reason why the apologetics for the Khrushchevian reinterpretation of the Lenin slogan sound so labored.[13]

Khrushchev had blown a fresh wind through the stale atmosphere of Soviet agriculture by explicit recognition of the critical significance of

[12] Grossman, *Problems of Communism,* May–June, 1959, p. 3.

[13] See, for example, Glezerman, *Kommunist,* 1963, No. 7, pp. 30–40.

price and income incentives. In conversation with Hubert Humphrey in 1958 he deprecated the Chinese communes because "you can't get production without incentives." Yet the SYP provided for an annual rate of growth of average earnings in the state labor force of a little over 3 percent, predicated increases in collective farmer peasant incomes entirely on increases in their own productivity with no increases in prices even for unprofitable livestock products, and gave advance notice of intention to whittle down the private sector severely. The Plan provided for extraordinary expansion of collective farm investment, but just as the draft Control Figures were being discussed throughout the country, an unpublished decree sharply raised the prices of agricultural machinery and spare parts to state and collective farms, and the decision was taken to curtail production of farm machinery.[14]

If his belief in the priority of economics over politics was not absolute neither was his faith in the converse principle. Khrushchev sought to break the hegemony of the West and to that end menacingly rattled sputniks and rockets (to some extent phantom). Yet he would not yield to his military lobby and divert resources from economic construction to securing the reality as well as the illusion of world power; he clung to a strategic doctrine of minimum deterrence even after the emptiness of his boasts of world wide power was made embarrassingly clear.

In this sense as in a number of others that I pointed to earlier, Khrushchev and his economic policy have struck me as transitional types—backward looking in the emphasis on political organization and the hortatory function of plan goals, still tolerant of a planning process that depended on buffer sectors (collective farms, private housing, consumption generally) to bear the brunt of unfolding imbalances; forward looking in the increasing dissatisfaction with "inherited proportions," that is with traditional patterns of resource allocation. Kosygin is reported to have said on a visit to Paris that "any isolation finds expression sooner or later in a retardation of growth and loss of power."[15] The remark would not have been inimical to Khrushchev, under whose regime the importance of "learning from the capitalists" was given renewed emphasis and concrete expression.

Thus, the SYP period reflects the main lines of Khrushchevian economic policy: maintenance of a high rate of investment; acceptance of

---

[14] See below, p. 385; also Karcz, in *New Directions in the Soviet Economy*, 1966, pp. 402–403.

[15] Ullman, *L'Express* (Paris), December 12, 1966.

moderate growth of consumption; continuing effort to obtain military power and international influence on the cheap. There were disappointments in both levels of growth and the associated patterns of resource allocation. They were evidently failures of intelligence, both economic and political. Embedded in the Plan, they originated in the system, to be sure, but also in the character of the directing force during this period of Soviet economic history, Nikita Khrushchev.

Appendixes

A

Sources to Table 1: 1958-1964

1. *Wages and salaries, farm and nonfarm.*

A. *Worker and employee wage and salary bill.* Computed as follows:

	1958	*1959*	*1960*	*1961*	*1962*	*1963*	*1964*
Average annual number of workers and employees (millions)	55.9	57.9	62.03	65.86	68.30	70.53	73.26
Average annual money wage and salary (rubles)	933.6	948.0	961.2	1000.8	1034.4	1051.2	1081.2
Worker and employee wage and salary bill (billion rubles)	52.19	54.89	59.62	65.91	70.65	74.14	79.21

The sources are *NKh 1962,* pp. 452–453 and *NKh 1964,* p. 546 for employment and *NKh 1964,* p. 555 for average compensation. The product of the two series yields the wage and salary bill. The employment figures for 1958 and 1959 include members of the producer cooperatives, which were absorbed into the state sector in 1960. The inclusion is necessary for the sake of comparability with the average compensation series which appears to cover the producer cooperatives (at least, this is my interpretation of the footnote on p. 555 of *NKh 1964*). TsSU computes the average wage and salary as the quotient of the wage and salary bill divided by the number employed; the description of the employment denominator appears to match the definition of the average annual number of workers and employees (*NKh 1964,* pp. 823–824).

The employment statistics are believed to include labor hired by collective farms (Nimitz, *Farm Employment in the Soviet Union, 1928–1963,* November 1965, p. 134). Presumably the average wage and salary data also include these hired laborers.

B. *Bonuses not included in wage and salary bill.* These are assumed equal to the cash payments to households from enterprise and cooperative incentive funds (below, pp. 363–365). That such bonuses are not included in the wage and salary bill is clearly indicated in the Soviet sources: e.g., *Statisticheskii slovar',* 1965, p. 149; Kats, *Ocherki statistiki truda,* 1960, p. 70.

C. *Wages in kind.* Some in kind payments are included in the wage and salary bill, but those provided in accordance with legislation on worker health and safety (special clothing, special foods) are not. See Kats, *Ocherki statistiki truda,* 1960, p. 70; Eremina and Mashalova, *Statistiki truda,* 1965, p. 167. My estimates are based on a statement by V. Grishin, head of the trade unions, that more than 700 million rubles were to be spent in 1963 on the free distribution of work clothing; this represented an increase of 27 percent over the level of 1959 (*Pravda,* October 29, 1963, p. 5).

2. *Net income of households from agriculture, excluding wages and salaries of state employed farm labor.*

A. *Money payments by collective farms.* Obtained as follows (billion rubles):

	1958	*1959*	*1960*	*1961*	*1962*	*1963*	*1964*
Payments to members							
From general farm incomes	4.75	4.49	4.66	5.19	5.84	6.34	7.43
From investment funds	.21	.20	.19	.20	.21	.22	.21
From cultural and social funds	.04	.07	.09	.12	.15	.17	.23
Total	5.00	4.76	4.94	5.51	6.20	6.73	7.87

These are estimates compiled by Nimitz for an as yet unpublished study of collective farmer incomes since 1953. I shall refer to this material hereafter as Nimitz, *Incomes of Collective Farmers.* The figure for payments from general farm incomes may be overstated by as much as .3 billion rubles (*ibid.*). Payments to hired labor are believed included in the wage and salary bill.

B. *Net income from sales of farm products.* Computed as follows (billion rubles):

	1958	1959	1960	1961	1962	1963	1964
Gross income from							
Sales to state-cooperative procurement	2.51	2.96	2.88	2.61	3.88	4.64	3.6
Extravillage collective farm market sales	4.12	3.88	3.64	3.93	4.02	3.91	3.98
Total	6.63	6.84	6.52	6.54	7.90	8.55	7.6
Less: money expenses of production	.41	.51	.54	.50	.55	.63	.59
Equals: net income from sales	6.22	6.33	5.98	6.04	7.35	7.92	7.0

Gross income is derived in Table A-1 as a residual by subtracting collective farm receipts for each type of sale from total receipts of farms and households together. The cash expenses of producing all private sector output, marketed and nonmarketed, are initially estimated as follows (billion rubles):

	1958	1959	1960	1961	1962	1963	1964
Collective farm market charges							
Market-use fee	.10	.10	.10	.10	.10	.10	.10
Fees for other market services	.02	.02	.02	.02	.02	.02	.02
Purchases from collective farms							
Goods	.04	.05	.09	.09	.10	.10	.13
Services	.40	.40	.40	.40	.40	.50	.50
Purchases from state-cooperative sector	.50	.70	.75	.65	.65	.65	.65
Total	1.06	1.27	1.36	1.26	1.27	1.37	1.40

The market use fee (*razovyi sbor*) is levied on all sellers for each day's use of a trading place on the market. Fees vary from a high of one ruble for sales from a truck to 10–20 kopecks for sales "by hand" and from trays. Forty percent of the proceeds are deposited in the budget, 60 percent are used for the upkeep of markets (Allakhverdian, ed., *Finansy SSSR,* 1962, p. 252). In the period 1958–1964, budget income from the market use fee was 44–49 million rubles annually (*Gosbiudzet I* and *II,* pp. 68 and 70, respectively). Thus, total market use fee proceeds were on the average about 120 million rubles. Households accounted for about 90 percent of market sales (Table A–1) but possibly for a slightly smaller share of the total market use fee revenue.

Fees are also charged for other market services—cutting meat, renting scales, renting trade clothing and implements, storage, etc. RSFSR markets in 1959 received 40 million rubles from these fees as well as the market use fee (Vasil'ev *et al., Ekonomika torgovli,* 1962, p. 176). Since RSFSR budget revenues from the market use fee were 21 million rubles in 1959 (*Gosbiudzhet I,* p. 99), all proceeds from the fee in the RSFSR must have been 53 millions. Evidently, the 40 million ruble figure refers to the sum of market services and only part of the market use fee, possibly the part kept by the markets. In that case, market services alone accounted for 8 million rubles (40 – [53 – 21] = 8). Total budget revenue from the market use fee was 2.25 times as high as that received from the RSFSR alone (*ibid.,* pp. 68, 99). Assuming that this is also true of market service fees, the total would have been 18 million rubles, of which possibly 15 million or more originated with households.

Collective farmers purchase feed from collective farms on the so-called "intracollective farm market." Data supplied by Morozov (*Trudoden', den'gi i torgovli na sele,* 1965) indicate that farms sold 13 million rubles worth of hay and straw to households in 1960 and 16 millions in 1963 (absolute values of all intracollective farm market sales from pp. 265 and 267 multiplied by shares of hay and straw sales on p. 270). But in addition, in these two years, farmers bought 144 and 202 million rubles of grain from the farms, some part of which was intended for feed. Arbitrarily, I assume half of grain purchases in 1960 were purchases of feed. Because of the crop failure in 1963, I assume that a larger share of purchases in that year were for food. Hence household purchases of grain feed, hay and straw are set at 85 million rubles in 1960 and 100 millions in 1963. Figures for 1959 and 1961–1962 are estimates loosely based on the physical volume of grain sales to households on the intracollective farm market (*ibid.,* p. 265). The 1958 and 1964 figures are arbitrary estimates.

Morozov's figures indicate a very sharp rise in grain sales to households during a period in which private livestock operations were subject to restriction if not harassment from the state. Nevertheless, other evidence suggests that it is permissible to use the series as an indicator of the trend in feed sales: (1) Expansion of consumer cooperative baking facilities by 1965 is said to have insured 70 percent of the bread requirements of the rural population compared with 40 percent in 1958 (A. Balashov, in *Sovetskaia potrebitel'skaia kooperatsiia,* 1966, No. 3, p. 31). (2) The Morozov data, which serve as the basis for my estimates, exclude not only sales by state farms to their households but also sales on collective farms that use the labor day exclusively for wage accounting (Morozov, *Trudoden', den'gi i torgovli na sele,* 1965, pp.

266, 274–275). Thus, any overestimation of the fodder component of the reported sales of grain would tend to be compensated for by omission of state farm sales and those on collective farms with labor day accounting.

Production services purchased by households from farms include plowing of private plots with farm draft power, use of farm transportation, milling of grain, and veterinary and stud services (*Vestnik Moskovskogo universiteta,* 1958, No. 3, p. 10; *VS,* 1958, No. 6, p. 14; cited in *SNIP 1956–1958,* p. 25). The value of these services is estimated as approximately half of collective farm income other than from sales of crops and livestock products (*NKh 1962,* p. 342; *NKh 1963,* p. 346; *NKh 1964,* p. 400).

Purchases from the state-cooperative sector are estimated on the basis of changes in the unspecified residual of consumer cooperative retail sales of nonfood goods. Retail trade in rural areas is largely in the hands of the consumer cooperatives, from whom households purchase a variety of producer goods—seed, feed, fertilizer, tools, and the like. These sales are most likely contained within the unspecified residual of sales of nonfood goods. The values of the residual changed as follows (billion rubles; sources are *NKh 1960,* p. 695 and *Sovtorg II,* p. 82):

1958	.54	1962	.70
1959	.79	1963	.71
1960	.83		

Data are not available for 1961 or 1964. The 1958 figure is net of .57 billion rubles of sales to collective farms of gasoline, trucks and some other types of producer goods; after 1958 sales of these articles to farms were no longer included in retail trade (*NKh 1959,* p. 629, note).

It seems likely, however, that these figures do not include fodder, for in an official distribution of retail purchases by nonhouseholds (*VS,* 1961, No. 6, p. 96) fodder is shown with foods. My final estimates allow for both this omission and the inclusion in the cited residuals of goods other than producer goods purchased by households. The 1964 figure is an arbitrary estimate.

Total money production expenses are then distributed between incomes from sales and consumption in kind (p. 301) in proportion to the respective levels of gross income; investment in kind is small enough to ignore for these purposes. I have taken no account of the cost of production services rendered by households to private sector producers. Data from a sample study of collective farm households in 1959 show that the number of hours worked by all members of farm households for private citizens was a little over one percent as much as time devoted to work for the collective farm or on the private plot. Of the hours worked for private citizens, 73 percent was performed by ablebodied farmers and 27 percent by the overaged, disabled, and juveniles (Vasilenko, *Puti preodoleniia sezonnosti truda v kolkhozakh,* 1963, as compiled and calculated by Nimitz, *Farm Employment in the Soviet Union, 1928–1963,* November 1965, p. 86). Suppose work for private citizens is valued at the same rate as work for the collective farm or on the plot —the proportion of nonablebodied man hours in work for private citizens is higher than in work for the farm but lower than in work on the plot. On the assumption that collective farmers account for 90 percent of private sector gross marketings and 60 percent of its nonmarketed gross output (see below, p. 423), collective farmer earnings from farm and plot in 1959 would amount to 12.8 billion rubles. Hence, earnings of collective farmers from work for other households would be on the order of 150 million rubles. Part of these earnings may reflect building rather than agricultural services and are properly considered elsewhere (Appendix B, item 6.A). Moreover, earnings may be paid in kind as well as in cash; in kind payments deducted as production costs would have to be added back as income in kind. For these reasons, and in view of the relatively small magnitudes involved, I do not attempt to deduct payments to households for productive services.

An alternative series of estimates of net household income from sales, compiled by Krueger (cited in *New Directions in the Soviet Economy,* 1966, p. 526), may be compared with my series as follows (billion rubles):

	1958	*1959*	*1960*	*1961*	*1962*	*1963*	*1964*
Krueger	5.77	6.32	5.95	6.26	7.69	8.53	7.82
Becker	6.22	6.33	5.98	6.04	7.35	7.92	7.0
Percent difference Krueger compared to Becker estimates	−7	0	−1	4	5	8	11

Krueger's 1963 and 1964 figures are close to or virtually identical to my estimates of *gross* household income from sales; in earlier years the ratio of the former to the latter series increases from .87 in 1958 to .98 in 1962. No information is available on the derivation of Krueger's estimates other than that they are "based on total private sales as reported" in the statistical yearbooks (*ibid.,* p. 527).

C. *Net farm income in kind.* The sum of investment and consumption in kind, as follows (billion rubles):

	1958	*1959*	*1960*	*1961*	*1962*	*1963*	*1964*
Consumption in kind	10.57	10.28	9.94	10.12	10.27	10.13	10.48
Less: cash production expenses	.65	.76	.82	.76	.72	.74	.81
Equals: net consumption in kind	9.92	9.52	9.12	9.36	9.55	9.39	9.67
Investment in kind	.65	.47	.68	.72	.43	−.84	.45
Net farm income in kind	10.57	9.99	9.80	10.08	9.98	8.55	10.12

Consumption in kind is estimated from a detailed calculation in Table A-2 for seven farm products—grain, potatoes, vegetables, meat, milk, eggs, and fruits and berries. The first step in the procedure is to derive an estimate of consumption in kind in physical units by subtracting "urban" marketings, consisting primarily of state procurements (deliveries by the state sector, purchases from collective farms and households) and extravillage farm market sales (for definition see Table A-1, source for item 2), and nonmarketed production use (seed and feed) from total gross output. The residual so obtained is then valued at the average realized price of urban marketings, derived by valuing each type of marketing at the appropriate price and dividing the sum of the values by the sum of the quantities.

The sum of the residual values for the seven products, as shown in part H, Summary, of Table A–2, is (million rubles):

1958	*1959*	*1960*	*1961*	*1962*	*1963*	*1964*
10,567	10,279	9,942	10,117	10,268	10,127	10,476

In making the extrapolation from these partial estimates to estimates of total farm consumption in kind, the following considerations are relevant:

(a) The calculation of average realized prices takes no account of sales (not labor-day distributions) by collective farms to collective farmers (the intracollective farm market). These sales, which were insignificant before 1960, take place at a variety of prices—purchase, retail, collective farm market, cost, or any other. For grain and potatoes, the average price level in intracollective farm market sales is higher than that of state purchases but lower than the price level in extravillage market sales; for vegetables, meat, milk, and eggs, the price level of sales in all the channels of urban marketings is higher than in the intracollective farm market (Morozov, *VE*, 1963, No. 8, pp. 146, 148).

(b) Because of the absence of information, Table A-2 takes no account of changes in inventories. Hopefully, no systematic bias is thereby introduced.

(c) Because of the unavailability of estimates of post-harvest, on-farm losses, the residuals for all products except grain and fruits and berries are gross of spoilage and other losses.

(d) The nonmarketed residuals of vegetables in Table A-2 include output utilized for feed in the private sector, since information gaps prevented the estimation (and subtraction from total output) of this category of production use.

(e) Apart from other grounds for skepticism, the method used by the statistical authorities to estimate private sector output, which relies heavily on consumer budget studies, suggests the need for caution in accepting Soviet farm output claims. (See articles by Kahan and Richter in Laird, ed., *Soviet Agricultural and Peasant Affairs,* 1963, pp. 153–156, 167–168.) Nevertheless, even if one is justified in assuming an upward bias in the output data, it seems difficult to say whether there was any change in the degree of bias during this period. Perhaps there was a greater incentive to inflate in the years after 1958. One of the presumed important sources of bias in the output data for milk, inclusion of milk sucked by calves, may be neutralized in Table A-2 by a deduction for feed use of milk that seems large enough to cover the statistically offending component.

(f) Consumption of the seven products mentioned does not exhaust consumption in kind but must come close to doing so; the only notable omissions would seem to be sunflower seed and melons. Nimitz estimated that consumption of six of the seven products in the present calculation—that is, excluding fruits and berries—accounted for 87 percent of total farm consumption in kind in 1955 (*SNIP 1956–1958,* pp. 27–28).

It seems likely, then, that (a) total consumption in kind is greater than consumption of just the seven products treated, but also (b) the estimate of the value of consumption in kind of these products is overstated. There is evidence that for 1959 at least, under and overstatement are mutually offsetting:

In Appendix B, the sources for item 5 refer to detailed data on the product distribution of consumption published in *NKh 1964.* For 1959 there is also available a breakdown of household consumption of food products by channels of distribution and for most of the product categories of the *NKh 1964* data (Eidel'man, *Mezhotraslevoi balans obshchestvennogo produkta,* 1966, pp. 160–161). Entries are identified for (a) bread and bread products, macaroni, (b) flour and groats, (c) industrially processed meat and products, (d) industrially processed milk and products, (e) crops and (f) livestock products not undergoing industrial processing. Comparison with the *NKh 1964* data shows omission from the Eidel'man data of fish and fish products, sugar, and "other food industry" products. Two of the channels of distribution listed are "received for labor on collective farms and from own economies" and "received in kind from state farms and subsidiary state enterprises." The total of the identified entries for these two channels is 10,873 million rubles. It seems unlikely that there are significant elements of consumption in kind in the categories for which Eidel'man omitted entries. Indirect confirmation of this supposition appears as follows:

(1) On p. 157 of the same work, Eidel'man declares that 13.5 percent of household consumption in 1959 represented products received for labor days earned on collective farms and from the private plot and 4.2 percent represented products purchased on the farm market. Since total household consumption was 88.0 billion rubles (*NKh 1964,* p. 584; the figure includes amortization of 2.83 billion rubles), consumption of products received for labor days and from the plot comes to 11.88 billion and purchases on the market 3.70 billion rubles.

(2) However, the data on pp. 160–161 of Eidel'man's book sum to 10.84 billion rubles for consumption of income in kind (excluding payments in kind by the state sector) and 4.76 billion rubles for consumption of products purchased on the farm market, extravillage and intravillage. The two sets of figures seem inconsistent. On the other hand, the sum of the components is almost exactly the same in both sets, 15.58 vs. 15.60 billion rubles.

(3) This finding suggests the following reconciliation: the first set of data on p. 157 relates to (a) income from the plot or earned from labor days gross of the amount later sold on the farm market and in (b) sales on the market other than of products from source (a). Conversely, the second set of data relates to consumption of income in kind net of sales on the market and to consumption of all products obtained from the market.

(4) A corollary of this reconciliation is that the figure for consumption of income in kind from the second set of data (10.87 billion rubles) is more or less global in scope.

Eidel'man's income in kind data most probably reflect a different valuation procedure from mine—average prices realized in sales by collective farms and households alone (see his p. 135). Revalued on this basis, my estimate of consumption in kind in 1959 is raised by about .4 billion rubles to 10.7 billions or within 2 percent of Eidel'man's figure.

Thus, understatement and overstatement in my estimates for 1959 appear mutually offsetting. Since it is difficult to ascertain the magnitude of either error in any other year, or whether the relative size of either error changed during the period under review, it is assumed that understatement and overstatement are mutually offsetting in all years.

Only the deduction of money expenses of production remains. Total cash expenses in the production of marketed as well as nonmarketed output are estimated under item 1.B above. The totals are allocated between incomes from sales and consumption in kind in proportion to the respective gross values. For this purpose, investment in kind is small enough to be ignored.

Investment in kind. Computed as follows:

	1958	*1959*	*1960*	*1961*	*1962*	*1963*	*1964*
Increase in private herds, million tons, live weight	0.9	0.7	1.0	1.0	0.5	−1.0	0.5
Average price of meat realized in all marketings, rubles per ton of live weight	717	668	679	718	861	843	892
Value of increase in private herds, billion rubles	.65	.47	.68	.72	.43	−.84	.45

The herd-weight increases for 1958–1960 are computed as residuals from data in *NKh 1960,* p. 462, showing meat output in live weight with and without herd increments for all sectors, the state sector and collective farms. For 1961, only the slaughter weight increments are given in *NKh 1961,* p. 391; the private sector increment is converted to a live weight figure using a factor of 1.6, the average ratio of live weight to slaughter weight increments in the previous five years.

No data on weight increments, either in slaughter or live weight terms, have been included in subsequent yearbooks. The figures for 1962–1964 are guesses based on the figures for previous years and agricultural conditions in the three final years of the period. For average prices, see Table A-2, part D.

The statistical yearbooks also report numbers of animals at the beginning of the year by sector. A comparison of changes in private sector herd numbers, computed from these data (*SKh,* pp. 266–269, and *NKh 1962,* pp. 303–304), with the indicated official figures for private sector herd-weight increments, is disquieting:

	Changes in Number of Animals (thousands)				Herd-weight Increment (million tons)
Year	*Cows*	*Other Cattle*	*Hogs*	*Sheep and Goats*	
1958	+750	−777	+462	+2347	+.9
1959	−1411	−2831	−1324	−1191	+.7
1960	−800	−1132	+1582	−1170	+1.0
1961	−60	+904	+1909	+1318	+1.0

In 1960, herds of all the major livestock categories except hogs declined in number, yet an aggregate herd-weight increment of one million tons is reported. In 1959, indeed, numbers declined in all categories, but a positive herd-weight increment somehow still emerges. True, the herd-weight increments are subject to a significant margin of error, plus or minus about 40 percent in 1959, owing to their calculation as residuals from data rounded off to one decimal place. However, rounding error cannot fully explain the apparent inconsistency between the two sets of data; indeed, the real difference could be larger than indicated. Nevertheless, in the absence of data on numbers and weights of minor livestock holdings and of average weight changes for major categories, it is necessary to accept the aggregate weight increments despite misgivings on their reliability.

There are also available data on the capital stock from which we may calculate the values of agricultural capital, including livestock, held in the private sector. The calculation is as follows (billion rubles):

	1958	*1959*	*1960*	*1961*	*1962*	*1963*	*1964*
Productive fixed capital in agriculture, including livestock, at end of year, gross of depreciation, at constant prices:							
All sectors	38.7	41.7	44.3	47.3	52.2	56.4	62.0
Less: public sector	31.5	34.0	36.8	40.0	44.6	49.2	54.7
Equals: private sector	7.2	7.7	7.5	7.3	7.6	7.2	7.3

Public sector agricultural capital is reported directly (*NKh 1964,* p. 258). Agricultural capital in all sectors is computed from the absolute value reported for end-1964 (*ibid.,* p. 68) and indexes on a 1940 base (*ibid.; NKh 1963,* p. 55; *NKh 1962,* p. 53; *Tsifry 1962,* p. 33). Since the end-1964, all-sectors figure is probably preliminary, and later revisions of index numbers of that year generally seem to be in a downward direction, private sector capital may be viewed as unchanged from end-1960 to end-1961. According to the yearbooks, the all-sector values are at constant prices—those of the 1 January 1960 census and revaluation for the state sector and those of the 1 January 1962 revaluation for collective farms (*NKh 1964*, p. 800). Nothing is said on the basis for valuation of private sector capital.

[According to *NKh 1965*, pp. 812–813, estimates in that volume of private sector capital were raised to include private orchards. A comparison of the series on public sector agricultural capital in *NKh 1965*, p. 271 with the corresponding series in *NKh 1964*, p. 258 shows declines of .7 billion rubles for end-1958, .2 billions for 1959, 1960 and 1962, .1 billions for 1961, but 1.1 billions for 1963 and 2.7 billions for 1964. Are these declines due entirely to the indicated broadening of coverage of private sector capital estimates? It seems highly unlikely that private sector investment in orchards jumped to levels of almost 1 billion rubles in 1963 and 1½ billions in 1964.]

Now compare the changes in private sector capital with the value of the private sector herd-weight increment. For this purpose I value annual herd-weight increments at alternative average prices of 500 or 1000 rubles per ton (cf. prices in Table A-2). As indicated, I do not know the prices at which private capital is valued in the official capital statistics, but the indicated range seems broad enough to encompass likely alternatives. The comparison is as follows (billion rubles):

	1959	*1960*	*1961*	*1962*	*1963*	*1964*
Increment of private sector capital	.5	−.2	0	.1	−.4	.1
Value of private sector herd-weight increment						
Average price 500 rubles per ton	.35	.5	.5	.25	−.5	.25
Average price 1000 rubles per ton	.7	1.0	1.0	.5	−1.0	.5
Difference between increment of capital stock and value of herd-weight increment, with increment valued at						
500 rubles per ton	.15	−.7	−.5	−.15	.1	−1.5
1000 rubles per ton	−.2	−1.2	−1.0	−.4	.6	−.4

Eidel'man, *Mezhotraslevoi balans obshchestvennogo produkta,* 1966, p. 171, implies a level of net productive investment, excluding livestock, by the private sector of .1 billion rubles in 1959.

Given the capital stock increments, the implication of these estimates of the value of herd-weight increments is virtually continuous net disinvestment (net, that is, of retirements) after 1959 in other private sector agricultural capital (mostly, structures). Over this period, there were large net decreases in number of cows, hogs, and sheep and goats held in the private sector; a small increase in the number of other cattle was registered. Possibly, there was a simultaneous decrease in the structures serving livestock. Obviously, this information does not substantiate the computed changes in other private sector capital nor thereby confirm my estimates of private sector livestock investment, but the various sets of data are not obviously inconsistent.

3. *Income of armed forces.*

Average pay of 690 rubles and subsistence of 400 rubles per man per year estimated for 1958 (*SNIP 1956–1958,* p. 33) are assumed constant through 1964. In January 1960, Khrushchev indicated that he expected the demobilization of 1.2 million men to effect savings of 1.6 to 1.7 billion rubles, or 1333–1417 rubles per man (*Pravda,* January 15, 1960, p. 4). The pay and subsistence per man used here totals 1090 rubles. However, Khrushchev's figure probably includes some operation and maintenance costs in addition to pay and subsistence.

Force levels are estimated as follows:

(1) Khrushchev announced the size of the armed forces at the beginning of 1960 as 3,623,000 (*ibid.*). A planned 300,000 man reduction during 1958, announced at the beginning of the year (*Pravda,* January 7, 1958) is assumed to have been carried out during the course of the year. No change appears to have taken place during 1959.

(2) In his January 1960 speech, Khrushchev announced plans for demobilization to a level of 2.4 million by the end of 1961. In July 1961, further demobilization was suspended. In August of the same year, demobilization of the draft class whose service had been completed was partially deferred and a new class was mobilized at its regular time in the fall. The Institute for Strategic Studies (*The Military Balance 1962–1963,* November 1962, p. 2) estimated that 600,000 men had been demobilized by July 1, 1961 and at the end of the year the armed forces numbered 3,800,000. I assume a January 1961 level of 3.3 million men.

(3) According to the Institute, the class whose demobilization was partially deferred in August 1961 began to be released from service in the spring of 1962, and by the fall the armed forces numbered 3.6 million.

(4) In *The Military Balance 1963–1964* (November 1963, p. 3), the Institute estimated a reduction in military manpower of 300,000 between October 1962 and October 1963.

(5) In December 1963 (*Pravda,* December 15, 1963, p. 3) Khrush-

chev linked a possible further decrease in the size of the armed forces to a planned cut in the defense budget for 1964 by 600 million rubles. Since his January 1960 speech indicated that demobilization reduced defense costs 1375 rubles per man (averaging the range shown above), it is assumed that demobilization of 400,000 men was planned for 1964.

(6) Marshall V. D. Sokolovskii stated that the armed forces numbered 2,423,000 at the beginning of 1965 (*New York Times,* February 18, 1965, p. 6), or precisely the end-1961 target in Khrushchev's 1960 speech. The Institute for Strategic Studies is frankly skeptical (*The Military Balance, 1965–1966,* November 1965, p. 2) and estimates 3,150,000 for October 1965. This represents a decline of 150,000 from the level estimated for October 1964 (*The Military Balance 1964–1965,* November 1964, p. 3). I assume a January 1965 level of 2,900,000—that is, realization of Khrushchev's planned demobilization of 400,000 men.

Thus I estimate force levels at the different dates as follows (millions):

	1958	*1959*	*1960*	*1961*	*1962*	*1963*	*1964*	*1965*
January 1	3.92	3.62	3.62	3.30	3.80	3.53	3.30	2.90
July 1				3.00				
October 1					3.60	3.30		
Average annual	3.77	3.62	3.46	3.28	3.67	3.39	3.10	

4. *Other income currently earned; statistical discrepancy.*

This item is computed as a residual, the difference between total income, item 9 and the sum of all other income, items 1–3, 5–6, and 8. In principle this category includes the following components: (i) business travel allowances and expenditures; (ii) earnings of households from sales to households of goods and services; (iii) earnings of members of fishing cooperatives. Possibly also included are earnings of the militia and internal security troops, salaries of Communist Party officials, and payments to prison labor (see Chapman, *Real Wages in Soviet Russia Since 1928,* 1963, p. 111). Note, however, that in its distribution of average wages by branch of the economy, *NKh 1964,* (pp. 555–556) lists as one of the branches "apparatus of the organs of state and economic administration, administrative organs of cooperative and social organizations."

The value of these components in 1959 may be very roughly estimated as follows:

(1) Business travel allowances amounted to over 1.2 billion rubles in 1960 (*Ekon.gazeta,* April 6, 1961, p. 3), and I assume a 1959 level of 1 billion.

(2) I estimate the value of private sector consumption services in 1959 as .77 billion rubles (below, p. 351; as noted there, the figure may be an understatement). To this must be added earnings from private sector production and building services; the former were estimated earlier as about 150 million rubles in 1959 (above, p. 300), the latter were estimated by Nimitz as about 400 million in the same year (*SNIP 1956–1958,* p. 66). Finally, the value of intrahousehold goods sales must also be added. This component I estimate as about 1 billion rubles: Intravillage market sales in 1959 amounted to a minimum 1.32 billion rubles (Eidel'man, *Mezhotraslevoi balans obshchestvennogo produkta,* pp. 160–161), of which only about .11 billion can be ascribed to sales by collective farms to collective farmers (Nimitz, *Incomes of Collective Farmers*) and perhaps another .20–.30 billion to sales by state farms to their personnel (Morozov, *Trudoden', den'gi i torgovli na sele,* p. 275).

(3) Earnings of members of fishing cooperatives are estimated at .1 billion rubles, the product of 200,000 households and assumed average earnings in 1959 of 475 rubles, half the average wage and salary.

The sum of these crude estimates is 2.5 billion rubles. If we were to add earnings of the militia and security troops, Communist Party salaries and payments to prison labor, the result would surely exceed 3 billions. However, even this total falls short of the residual value for 1961, 6 billion rubles, which is by far the smallest figure in the series; entries in other years exceed the 1961 figure by 1–5 billion rubles. The explanation of the largest of these margins must be in one or more of the following factors: (1) underestimation of previously identified money incomes—money payments by collective farms, income from sales of farm products, wages and salaries, earnings of cooperative artisans, military pay, and transfer receipts; (2) overestimation of money outlays; (3) omission of other, yet unidentified components of money income; and (4) omission of changes in household currency holdings. Overestimation of money outlays seems doubtful, in view of (1) the control totals provided by official Soviet data on total consumption (Appendix B, item 5), (2) the small size of private sector fixed capital investment as estimated here (above, p. 304 and below, p. 360), (3) the omission of private sector inventory investment (4) the omission from my estimates of transfer outlays of certain taxes and charges paid by households but considered revenues "from the socialist sector" (see Appendix C, item 3.E). If underestimation of identified and omission of unidentified incomes can also be assumed small, the pattern of change of the residual would reflect substantial movements in household cash balances.

5. *Imputed net rent of owner-occupied dwellings.*

Appendix B, sources for item 2.A.

6. *Imputed value of owner-supplied building services.*

Appendix B, sources for item 6.A.

7. *Total incomes currently earned.*

The sum of items 1 through 6.

8. *Transfer receipts.*

Appendix D, sources for item 9.

9. *Total income.*

Equal to total outlays (Table B, item 9).

TABLE A-1

RECEIPTS OF COLLECTIVE FARMS AND HOUSEHOLDS FROM EXTRAVILLAGE MARKETINGS OF AGRICULTURAL PRODUCTS

(billion rubles)

	1958	1959	1960	1961	1962	1963	1964
1. Sales to state and cooperative procurement agencies							
A. By collective farms in existence at end of year	10.85	11.42	10.88	11.52	13.14	13.75	15.3
B. By collective farms converted to state farms during the year [a]	.05	.11	.40	.37	.06	.06	.1
C. By households	2.51	2.96	2.88	2.61	3.88	4.64	3.6
D. Total	13.41	14.49	14.16	14.50	17.08	18.45	18.97
2. Extravillage market sales							
A. Collective farm market proper							
(1) By collective farms	.35	.41	.47	.57	.56	.57	.62
(2) By households	3.70	3.42	3.23	3.36	3.32	3.22	3.24
(3) Total	4.05	3.83	3.70	3.93	3.88	3.79	3.86
B. Sales to consumer cooperatives							
(1) By collective farms	.39	.37	.29	.28	.25	.28	.30
(2) By households	.40	.42	.34	.45	.57	.56	.60
(3) Total	.79	.79	.63	.73	.82	.84	.90
C. Total	4.84	4.62	4.33	4.66	4.70	4.63	4.76

Note:

[a] For convenience, the adjustment for all types of sales made by collective farms converted to state farms during the year is attributed to procurement sales alone.

Sources:

Items 1.C, 2.A(2), and 2.B(2) are obtained as residuals, by subtracting other components from the indicated totals.

1. *Sales to procurement agencies.*

A. *By farms in existence at end of year. NKh 1962*, p. 342; *NKh 1963*, p. 346; *NKh 1964*, p. 400.

B. *By farms converted to state farms during year.* The necessity to estimate sales by converted farms arises because it is believed that reported total sales to procurement, item 1.D of this table, include receipts by converted farms (see discussion below).

Each entry represents the product of estimated income of converted collective farms in the given year and the share of income deriving from sales to procurement organizations or on the market. The income estimates were obtained as follows (billion rubles; only the minimum data necessary for the present calculation are shown):

TABLE A-1 (continued)

	1957	*1958*	*1959*	*1960*	*1961*	*1962*	*1963*	*1964*
(1) Income of comparable aggregate of farms in being at the end of								
1957	9.52							
1958	9.45	13.20						
1959		12.98	13.68					
1960			12.87	13.34				
1961				12.62	13.57			
1962					13.46	15.24		
1963						15.12	16.01	
1964							15.8	17.9
(2) Income of converted farms in year before conversion	.07	.22	.81	.72	.11	.12	.2	
(3) Income of converted farms in year of conversion		.05	.12	.42	.39	.06	.06	.1

Sources for entries under (1) are *NKh 1958*, p. 498; *NKh 1959*, p. 427; *NKh* 1960, p. 496; *NKh 1961*, p. 436; *NKh 1962*, p. 342; *NKh 1963*, p. 346; *NKh 1964*, p. 400. Entries under (2) are obtained as the difference between entries for the indicated year under (1). Figures in row (3) are obtained on the assumption that first, on the average, income of converted farms during the year of conversion was increasing over the previous year's level by the same percentage margin as the increase for farms not converted (computed from consecutive year entries in each row under (1)) and second, that converted farms received only half the income they would have received in that year as collective farms had they not been converted. Finally, income from sales to procurement or on the market is assumed to have been 95 percent of all income of converted farms, roughly the same as for farms in being throughout the year (*NKh 1962*, p. 342; *NKh 1964*, p. 400).

The estimating procedure just described is obviously contrived. It ignores the fact that conversions took place at varying times during the year and affected farms that were generally poorer than the average in some years and richer in others. Moreover, it relies on official data which have been criticized by Grushetskii (*ESKh*, 1965, No. 3, pp. 90–93) as inaccurate and misleading. Grushetskii is referring to Central Statistical Administration estimates of collective farm money income for comparable aggregates of farms, and he claims that these are estimates obtained by "deflating" the series of income of farms in being at the end of the year by changes in the number of farm households (*kolkhoznyi dvor*). According to Grushetskii, this is not a reliable indicator: for example it results in significantly understating the change in money income between 1953 and 1962 for a comparable farm aggregate. Grushetskii advises the alternative use of agricultural land as a deflator, but whether this would provide a more accurate income series for my purposes is not clear. Evidently, then, my estimates of receipts from sales to procurement by converted farms are crude. Correspondingly, my estimates of household receipts may be in error. Whether there is any systematic bias introduced is not apparent.

D. *Total. NKh 1959*, p. 325; *NKh 1964*, p. 257. The source reference is to payments to collective farms, collective farmers, workers and employees for output sold to the state and to cooperative and state trading organizations. Two questions of scope arise: (1) Are sales to consumer cooperatives at market prices included? Probably not, because the value of such sales alone is large enough to exhaust the sum of payments for output sold to cooperative and state trading organizations, without allowance for sales to these organizations at controlled prices. (2) Are sales by converted collective farms included? Probably, if only because similar data for 1956 and 1957 (*NKh 1959*, pp. 325, 427) imply an improbably large increase in residual household sales in 1957, a year of large scale

TABLE A-1 (continued)

conversions, unless sales by converted farms are included in the reported totals (see *SNIP 1956–1958*, pp. 23–24).

2. *Extravillage market sales.*

The data cover sales on the "extravillage collective farm market," as defined in the official statistical handbooks: "sales of agricultural products by collective farms, collective farmers, and other elements of the population possessing a subsidiary farm plot, to workers, employees, and organizations at prices determined in the market. . . . Sales of goods among collective farms and collective farmers represent intravillage market turnover, which does not enter into the turnover of the extravillage collective farm market." (*NKh 1965*, pp. 843–844; definitions in earlier yearbooks are identical or virtually so with the one quoted.) I call this same aggregate "extravillage market sales" and distinguish two components—sales to consumer cooperatives at market prices and sales on the collective farm market proper.

A. *Collective farm market.* (1) *By collective farms.* Derived as the sum of sales on markets in the 251-city network that provides the basic sampling area for Soviet market statistics, plus sales on other urban collective farm markets, as follows (million rubles):

	1958	*1959*	*1960*	*1961*	*1962*	*1963*	*1964*
Sales on markets of 251 cities	169	140	122	78	64	66	69
Sales on other urban markets	178	268	351	489	498	500	555
	347	408	473	567	562	566	624

Sales on markets of 251 cities. The value of sales of all products in the network of 251 large cities in 1950 was 1948.0 million rubles (*Sovtorg I*, p. 188). It is assumed that sales of livestock are included. Corresponding values for 1958–1964 are obtained by applying to that figure a value index obtained by multiplying together official price and quantity indexes (*NKh 1962*, pp. 542–543; *NKh 1964*, pp. 658–659; indexes in the former source, with base year 1952, are linked to those of the latter source, with base year 1950, through common-year links). Sales by collective farms are then obtained as the product of these values and reported collective farm shares in sales on these markets; shares for 1958, 1960, 1962, and 1963 are given in *Sovtorg II*, p. 278; the 1961 share is cited by Egereva (*Balans proizvodstva i raspredeleniia produktsii sel'skogo khoziaistva*, 1963, pp. 97–98); the 1959 share is estimated by interpolation; the 1964 share is assumed the same as in 1963. The calculation is shown below:

	1958	*1959*	*1960*	*1961*	*1962*	*1963*	*1964*
Value index, sales in 251 cities, 1950 = 100	147	128	118	118	126	121	126
Calculated value of sales in 251 cities (million rubles)	2,864	2,493	2,299	2,299	2,454	2,357	2,454
Share of collective farms in these sales (percent)	5.9	5.6	5.3	3.4	2.6	2.8	2.8
Value of collective farm sales in 251 cities (million rubles)	169	140	122	78	64	66	69

Sales on other urban markets. The first step is to estimate sales in 1962 as the implication of estimates of incomes of collective farms and the private sector from sales in collective farm market trade:

(1) According to Nazarov (*Kolkhoznaia torgovlia*, 1964, p. 32), in 1962 collective farms and the private sector received 22.3 billion rubles from sales to the state and on the market, of which "almost" 5.3 billion rubles came from sales on the market. The difference between these two figures, 17.0 billion rubles, almost exactly corresponds to the officially reported sum of incomes received by collective farms and households from sales to state and cooperative organizations (row 1-D, this table). It is, therefore, assumed that 5.3 billion rubles cover all incomes by farms and households from sales on the market, including intravillage, and that "almost 5.3" billions are actually 5.25 billions.

TABLE A-1 (continued)

(2) If the assumption is valid, the following breakdown of total market sales in 1962 can be derived (billion rubles):

	Total	Collective Farms	Households
Total market sales	5.25	1.23	4.02
Less: Sales to consumer cooperatives	.82	.25	.57
Sales on 251 city markets	2.45	.06	2.39
Equals: Sales on small-city and village markets	1.98	.92	1.06
Of which: Sales on small-city markets	1.43		
Sales on village markets	.55		

Total market sales by collective farms are from *NKh 1963*, p. 346 (sales *v poriadke kolkhoznoi torgovli*, which presumably, though not explicitly, cover all market sales). For sales to consumer cooperatives see item 2.B(2) of this table. Total and collective farm sales on the 251 city markets were estimated above. Sales by farms and households on the small-city markets are derived as the difference between total extravillage collective farm market sales of 3.88 billion rubles, item 2.A(3) of this table, and total sales on the 251 city markets of 2.45 billions.

(3) In 1962 collective farms sold to collective farmers .39 billion rubles of agricultural products (Nimitz, *Incomes of Collective Farmers*). Collective farm sales on village markets include, in addition, sales to other collective farms (and to other households?), but these sales must be relatively small (see Morozov, *VE*, 1963, No. 8, p. 145). If all collective farm sales on the village market totaled .39 billion rubles, collective farm sales on the small-city markets would be .53 billion rubles. Since the former figure is an underestimate of intravillage sales, I reduce the latter figure to .50 billion rubles.

(4) This figure represents 35 percent of total sales on the small-city collective farm markets in 1962. At first glance, this seems high, because from other data a corresponding share for 1957 of 13 percent is indicated.

(a) According to Morozov (*VE*, 1962, No. 2, p. 63), 7 percent of sales on urban collective farm markets in 1957 and 5.3 percent in 1960 consisted of sales by collective farms. The cited 1960 share clearly applies to sales in the network of 251 large cities (*Sovtorg II*, p. 278). The 1957 figure is, presumably, of the same nature.

(b) Ignatov (*Puti razvitiia kolkhoznoi torgovli*, 1959, p. 89) provides an absolute figure for sales by households on the extravillage farm market in 1957—3.63 billion rubles. Since the total sales were officially reported as 3.96 billions (*NKh 1959*, p. 708), Ignatov implies a collective farm share in total sales of 8.3 percent, or .33 billion rubles. Ignatov does not indicate how the 3.63 billion rubles figure was calculated; it may represent an extrapolation from a 251-city sample value (Karcz, *American Economic Review*, June 1964, pp. 318–320). It is assumed that a true global value is involved, hence that .33 billion rubles represents collective farm sales in all extravillage markets in 1957.

(c) Given the 1955 value of all sales in markets of the 251 cities, 3.023 billion rubles (*Sovtorg I*, p. 188) and a 1955-based value index of sales (*NKh 1959*, pp. 713–714), the 1957 value of sales on markets of the 251 cities may be computed as 2.68 billion rubles. Given further the value of all extravillage market sales in 1957, 3.96 billion rubles, and the collective farm shares in 251-city market sales, 7.0 percent, the value of all sales on small-city markets is determined as 1.27 billion rubles and the part originated by collective farms as .14 billions, or 11 percent.

Could the weight of collective farms in small-city market sales have risen so rapidly, from 11 percent in 1957 to 35 percent in 1962? Nazarov strongly implies an affirmative answer: ". . . In conditions of a general decline in trade turnover of collective farm market trade, sales of farm products by collective farms on the market have, on the contrary, grown, especially in such products as milk and milk products, eggs, and potatoes" (p. 46). ". . . The share [of collective farms] in general market turnover increases uninterruptedly" (p. 47). "It is true that accounting data on the volume of agricultural products brought to market in the 251 cities show a tendency to decline in the role of collective farms in collective farm market trade. But the predominant part of this

TABLE A-1 (continued)

produce is sold by the farms not on these markets but on the markets of other cities" (p. 77). ". . . The bulk of the surplus of [collective farm] marketed output is sold in smaller cities and worker settlements" (p. 78).

On the evidence of Nazarov's testimony, it is estimated that the share of collective farms in small-city market sales grew steadily from 11 percent in 1957 to 35 percent in 1962. The 1962 share is assumed unchanged in 1963 and 1964. The percentages are then applied to the values of all sales in the small-city markets to yield the values of collective farm sales in these markets in 1958–1964, as follows (million rubles, except where otherwise stated):

	1958	*1959*	*1960*	*1961*	*1962*	*1963*	*1964*
Total extravillage collective farm market sales	4,050	3,831	3,702	3,929	3,877	3,788	4,041
Less: all sales on 251-city markets	2,864	2,493	2,299	2,299	2,454	2,357	2,454
Equals: all sales on small-city markets	1,186	1,338	1,403	1,630	1,423	1,431	1,587
Share of collective farms in small-city market sales (percent)	15	20	25	30	35	35	35
Value of collective farm sales on small-city markets	178	268	351	489	498	500	555

The function of Table A-1 is to provide a series for household gross receipts from sales. There is another way to derive gross household receipts from sales on the extravillage market, and the results conflict with those shown in this table. The alternative method is to subtract all market sales by collective farms from the sum of total extravillage market sales by farms and households plus collective farm intravillage market sales. The two series are compared as follows (billion rubles):

	1958	*1959*	*1960*	*1961*	*1962*	*1963*	*1964*
Total extravillage market sales (item 2.C, this table)	4.84	4.62	4.33	4.66	4.70	4.63	4.76
Add: collective farm intravillage market sales	.05	.11	.26	.35	.39	.47	.61
Less: all market sales by collective farms	1.55	1.45	1.50	1.19	1.23	1.22	1.60
Equals: household extravillage market sales	3.34	3.28	3.09	3.82	3.86	3.88	3.77
Compare: sum of items 2.A(2) and 2.B(2), this table	4.10	3.84	3.57	3.81	3.89	3.78	3.84

Collective farm intravillage market sales are in fact estimates of collective farm sales to collective farmers, as compiled by Nimitz (*Incomes of Collective Farmers*), except that the 1958 figure is my estimate based on her data for subsequent years. All market sales by collective farms are reported in *NKh 1962*, p. 342 and *NKh 1964*, p. 400. The row marked "household extravillage market sales," therefore, is understated by the value of collective farm sales on village markets other than to collective farmers. Thus, the direction of the difference between the last two rows of the tabulation is the expected one in all years except 1961 and 1963. However, the magnitude of the difference may be too large in 1958–1960 and too small in 1962. Because we know very little about intravillage trade among collective farms, it is impossible to resolve this conflict.

3. *Total.*

NKh 1962, p. 540; *NKh 1964*, p. 657; *NKh 1965*, p. 665.

B. *Sales to consumer cooperatives.* Transactions here are of two kinds, commission sales and "purchases at local prices." The latter refers to the system of procurements by consumer cooperatives set up under the decree of February 20, 1959, "On cooperative trade in agricultural products in cities and urban settlements" and subsequently altered in the decree of February 25, 1961, "On the improvement of the organization of sales of collective farms' and collective farmers' surplus agricultural products." (For discussion of these decrees see Morozov, *VE*, 1962, No. 2.)

TABLE A-1 (continued)

From 1953 through 1958, sales on commission by the consumer cooperatives were the only other channel for urban disposition of agricultural production at the more or less unregulated prices of the collective farm markets. The 1959 decree, cited above, authorized the cooperatives to procure "surplus" agricultural output from collective farms and households at prices no higher than state procurement prices. The output was to be sold in urban outlets at state retail prices. Because of the restrictive conditions of the 1959 decree, the volume of these procurements was only 20 million rubles in 1959 and 75 million in 1960 (*ibid.*, p. 64). To stimulate somewhat more rapid expansion of these procurements, the cooperatives were authorized under the 1961 decree to negotiate purchase prices with the producers and to sell at market prices. From 1961 on, cooperative purchases at local prices are supposedly obtained largely from households and commission purchases largely from collective farms.

(1) *By collective farms.* Computed as the product of total receipts from sales to cooperatives (item 2.B(3) of this table) and collective farm shares of total receipts.

Collective farm shares are obtained as follows: From physical unit data in *Sovtorg II*, pp. 86–87, we may compute the share of output originating in collective farms in 15 product groups received by the cooperatives in 1958, 1960, and 1962. The same source also gives the value of sales by the cooperatives in these years for the same 15 product groups plus two minor categories; the minor categories account for 5 percent or less of total sales. (Resales of sugar are excluded from consideration.) If the percentages calculated from physical units of output received by cooperatives are applied to the value of sales by cooperatives and the products summed, the implied average shares of cooperative sales originating in disposition of collective farms are 49.7 percent in 1958, 45.1 percent in 1960, and 30.6 percent in 1962. The missing percentages are estimated by interpolation as 47.4 in 1959, 37.9 in 1961, and for 1963 and 1964 I assume a one-third share.

(3) *Total.* 1958–1961: *NKh 1962*, p. 540.

1962: Total market sales by cooperatives, excluding markup, rose from 734 million rubles in 1961 to 1391 million in 1962 (*ibid.*). However, the same source shows market sales by cooperatives including commission (excluding sugar sales) as having grown from 856 million in 1961 to 958 million rubles in 1962 (p. 522). If the relative markup remained the same as in 1961, the value of the markup included in the 958 million rubles would have been 137 million rubles. Hence, 570 million rubles of the total shown on p. 540 of *NKh 1962* probably represents a reclassification of sales previously entered elsewhere. This is confirmed on p. 688 of the yearbook, where it is indicated that up to 1962 consumer cooperative purchases for restaurants were not included in market trade because they were made at procurement prices. Since 1962, such purchases are made at prices reached by agreement with the sellers and therefore are included henceforth with market trade.

Should the newly added half billion rubles of sales be added here? The issue is whether in 1962 these sales were no longer included in the reported totals of items 1.A and 1.D of this table. This seems highly unlikely: incomes of collective farms and households from sales to the state increased from 13.82 billion rubles in 1961 to 15.62 billion in 1962, or by 13 percent; income from sales to cooperative and state trading organizations rose from 0.67 to 1.43 billion rubles or by 113 percent (*ibid.*, p. 240). The negative conclusion also seems applicable to collective farm incomes alone: income from sales to state and cooperative agencies increased 14 percent while income from sales in collective farm market trade rose only 3 percent (*ibid.*, p. 342).

Therefore, total receipts in 1962 are estimated as .82 billion rubles (958 million rubles less markup of 137 million rubles).

1963 and 1964: Sales by consumer cooperatives at market prices including commission, but apparently excluding the purchases for restaurants reclassified in 1962, came to 978.1 million rubles in 1963 and 1046.7 millions in 1964 (*NKh 1964*, p. 631, and *NKh 1965*, p. 637; compare with p. 657 and p. 665 of these two sources, respectively). A markup of 14 percent, the same as in 1961, is again assumed.

C. *Total.* The sum of items 2.A(3) and 2.B(3).

TABLE A-2

ESTIMATION OF FARM CONSUMPTION IN KIND, 1958–1964

A. GRAIN[a]

	1958			1959			1960			1961			1962			1963			1964		
	Q	P	V	Q	P	V	Q	P	V	Q	P	V	Q	P	V	Q	P	V	Q	P	V
1. Gross output																					
A. Official[b]	134.7			119.5			125.5			130.8			140.2			107.5			152.1		
B. Adjusted[c]	115.8			94.7			96.5			110.5			110.9			91.3			123.6		
2. Marketings (excluding intravillage)																					
A. State farm deliveries[d]	21.7	44.3	961	17.5	44.3	775	20.3	44.3	899	22.4	60	1344	25.8	60	1548	18.5	60	1110	36.2	60	2172
B. Purchases from collective farms and households[d]	34.9	64.0	2234	29.2	65	1898	26.5	67	1776	29.7	74	2198	30.9	80	2472	26.3	86	2262	32.1	85	2729
C. Extravillage collective farm market sales	2.5	225.3	568	2.4	198.6	477	2.2	206.2	452	1.8	219.0	403	1.7	224.0	388	1.1	281	309	1.3	335	436
D. Other[e]	3.3			4.1			5.1			3.7			3.7			2.5			4.5		
E. Total	62.4	63.7	3763	53.2	64.2	3150	54.1	63.8	3127	57.6	73.2	3945	62.1	75.5	4408	48.4	80.2	3681	74.1	76.7	5337
3. Nonmarket utilization																					
A. Household output; *kolkhoz* distributions and sales to households, less household sales on extravillage farm markets	19.5			16.2			13.0			13.5			12.7			8.8			12.4		
B. Remainder: public sector seed, feed, and waste; errors and omissions	33.9			25.3			29.4			39.4			36.1			34.1			37.1		
C. Total	53.4			41.5			42.4			52.9			48.8			42.9			49.5		
4. Farm household consumption	9	63.7	573	9	64.2	578	8	63.8	510	6	73.2	439	4	75.5	302	3	80.2	241	4	76.7	307

Notes:

Q = million tons; P = rubles per ton; V = million rubles.

[a] Excluding immature corn.

[b] Weight of grain in combine bunkers, gross of cleaning and drying losses.

[c] Estimated barn weight net of cleaning and drying losses.

[d] Accounting weight (reflects discounts for substandard quality).

[e] Includes difference between physical weight and accounting weight of deliveries and procurements.

TABLE A-2 (continued)

B. POTATOES

	1958			1959			1960			1961			1962			1963			1964		
	Q	P	V	Q	P	V	Q	P	V	Q	P	V	Q	P	V	Q	P	V	Q	P	V
1. Gross output	86.5			86.6			84.4			84.3			69.7			71.8			93.6		
2. Marketings (excluding intravillage)																					
A. State farm deliveries	0.7	62.2	44	1.2	62	74	1.8	62	112	2.1	62	130	1.5	62	93	2.1	70	147	3.2	70	224
B. Purchases from collective farms and households	6.3	41.9	264	5.6	44	246	5.3	47	249	4.9	47	230	4.1	49	201	5.9	72	425	7.9	72	569
C. Extravillage collective farm market sales	6.5	138.5	895	6.3	131.4	829	5.7	142.8	813	5.7	127.1	718	5.3	149.9	794	4.7	183	860	5.1	171	872
D. Other	.6			.6			.9			.9			.5			—			.4		
E. Total	14.1	89.1	1203	13.7	87.7	1149	13.7	91.7	1174	13.6	84.9	1078	11.4	99.8	1088	12.7	112.8	1432	16.6	102.8	1665
3. Nonmarket utilization																					
A. Seed	19.0			19.0			18.2			17.8			17.4			17.0			17.0		
B. Feed	40.0			40.0			41.0			41.0			33.0			34.0			44.0		
C. Remainder	13.4	89.1	1194	13.9	87.7	1219	11.5	91.7	1055	11.9	84.9	1010	7.9	99.8	788	8.1	112.8	914	16.0	102.8	1645
D. Total	72.4			72.9			70.7			70.7			58.3			59.1			77.0		

C. VEGETABLES

	1958			1959			1960			1961			1962			1963			1964		
	Q	P	V	Q	P	V	Q	P	V	Q	P	V	Q	P	V	Q	P	V	Q	P	V
1. Gross output	14.9			14.8			16.6			16.2			16.0			15.2			19.5		
2. Marketings (excluding intravillage)																					
A. State farm deliveries	1.2	89	107	1.7	89	151	2.4	89	214	2.7	89	240	2.9	89	258	3.6	89	320	4.5	89	401
B. Purchases from collective farms and households	3:0	78	234	2.8	78	218	2.7	86	232	2.8	86	241	3.0	75	225	2.8	75	210	3.4	75	255
C. Extravillage collective farm market sales	2.0	193.6	383	1.7	215.6	356	1.6	181.9	287	1.3	190.7	250	1.4	214.2	304	1.4	227	318	1.4	231	323
D. Other	.9			1.1			1.3			1.4			1.5			.6			1.1		
E. Total	7.1	116.8	724	7.3	116.9	725	8.0	109.4	733	8.2	107.5	731	8.8	107.8	787	8.4	108.7	848	10.4	105.3	979
3. Nonmarket utilization																					
A. Feed in socialized sector	1.0			1.0			1.1			1.1			1.1			1.0			1.7		
B. Remainder	6.8	116.8	794	6.5	116.9	760	7.5	109.4	821	6.9	107.5	742	6.1	107.8	658	5.8	108.7	630	7.4	105.3	779
C. Total	7.8			7.5			8.6			8.0			7.2			6.8			9.1		

Note:
Q = million tons.
P = rubles per ton.
V = million rubles.

TABLE A-2 (continued)

D. MEAT

	1958			1959			1960			1961			1962			1963			1964		
	Q	P	V	Q	P	V	Q	P	V	Q	P	V	Q	P	V	Q	P	V	Q	P	V
1. Gross output [a]	12.3			14.2			14.0			13.9			15.2			16.3			13.3		
2. Marketings (excluding intravillage)																					
A. State farm deliveries	1.5	625	938	2.0	625	1250	2.5	625	1563	2.9	671	1946	3.3	750	2475	3.9	750	2925	3.5	750	2625
B. Purchases from collective farms and households	4.2	617	2591	5.5	642	3531	5.4	642	3467	4.4	671	2952	5.3	833	4415	5.4	833	4498	4.8	833	3998
C. Extravillage collective farm market sales	.9	1306.5	1202	1.2	855.0	1026	1.0	1051.0	1009	1.2	1040.5	1207	1.4	1208.5	1716	1.2	1187	1424	1.1	1481	1629
D. Other	.9			.9			.8			.7			.9			1.4			.2		
E. Total	7.5	716.8	4731	9.6	667.5	5807	9.7	678.5	6039	9.2	718.2	6105	10.9	860.6	8606	11.9	842.6	8847	9.6	877.9	8252
3. Nonmarket utilization	4.8	716.8	3441	4.6	667.5	3071	4.3	678.5	2918	4.7	718.2	3376	4.3	860.6	3701	4.4	842.6	3707	3.7	877.9	3248

Notes:

Q = million tons (live weight).

P = rubles per ton (live weight).

V = million rubles.

[a] Net of increment of livestock herds.

TABLE A-2 (continued)

E. MILK[a]

	1958			1959			1960			1961			1962			1963			1964		
	Q	P	V	Q	P	V	Q	P	V	Q	P	V	Q	P	V	Q	P	V	Q	P	V
1. Gross output	58.7			61.7			61.7			62.6			63.9			61.2			63.3		
2. Marketings (excluding intravillage)																					
A. State farm deliveries	5.0	111.5	558	6.1	112	683	8.4	113	949	9.7	114	1106	10.6	128	1357	10.9	142	1548	12.5	142	1775
B. Purchases from collective farms and households	17.1	113.0	1932	18.9	117	2211	17.9	118	2112	17.8	118	2100	18.6	122	2269	17.7	122	2159	18.9	122	2306
C. Extravillage collective farm market sales	2.1	231.8	480	1.9	241.9	469	1.9	239.4	445	1.8	259.6	472	1.9	279.7	526	1.6	291	466	1.6	314	502
D. Other	1.2			1.3			.9			1.7			1.4			1.1			1.2		
E. Total	25.4	122.7	2970	28.2	125.0	3363	29.1	124.3	3506	31.0	125.5	3678	32.5	133.5	4152	31.3	138.2	4173	34.2	138.9	4583
3. Nonmarket utilization																					
A. Feed	8.2			8.5			8.7			9.0			9.4			9.7			9.8		
B. Remainder	25.1	122.7	3080	25.0	125.0	3125	23.9	124.3	2971	22.6	125.5	2836	22.0	133.5	2937	20.2	138.2	2792	19.3	138.9	2681
C. Total	33.3			33.5			32.6			31.6			31.4			29.9			29.1		

Notes:
Q = million tons.
P = rubles per ton.
V = million rubles.
[a] Including milk products in terms of milk equivalent.

TABLE A-2 (continued)

F. EGGS

	1958			1959			1960			1961			1962			1963			1964		
	Q	P	V	Q	P	V	Q	P	V	Q	P	V	Q	P	V	Q	P	V	Q	P	V
1. Gross output	23.0			25.6			27.4			29.3			30.1			28.5			26.7		
2. Marketings (excluding intravillage)																					
A. State farm deliveries	1.1	71.4	79	1.4	71.4	100	1.9	71.4	136	2.4	70	168	2.9	80	232	3.1	80	248	3.5	80	280
B. Purchases from collective farms and households	3.4	61.7	210	4.3	59	254	4.6	60	276	5.0	60	300	5.6	70	392	5.5	70	385	4.8	70	336
C. Extravillage collective farm market sales	3.1	104.0	318	3.1	103.0	320	3.2	105.1	333	3.2	111.2	359	3.2	113.2	360	2.5	120	300	2.4	131	314
D. Other	.4			.5			.8			.8			.6			.7			.6		
E. Total	8.0	79.9	607	9.3	76.6	674	10.5	76.8	745	11.4	78.0	827	12.3	84.1	984	11.8	84.1	933	11.3	86.9	930
3. Nonmarket utilization																					
A. For production	2.3			2.4			2.5			2.6			2.7			2.5			2.2		
B. Remainder	12.7	79.9	1015	13.9	76.6	1065	14.4	76.8	1106	15.3	78.0	1193	15.1	84.1	1270	14.2	84.1	1194	13.2	86.9	1147
C. Total	15.0			16.3			16.9			17.9			17.8			16.7			15.4		

Note:
Q = billion units.
P = rubles per thousand units.
V = million rubles.

G. FRUITS[a] AND BERRIES

	1958			1959			1960			1961			1962			1963			1964		
	Q	P	V	Q	P	V	Q	P	V	Q	P	V	Q	P	V	Q	P	V	Q	P	V
1. Gross output	4846			4951			4942			5050			5978			6411			6866		
2. Marketings (excluding intravillage)																					
A. All procurements	1900	339	644	1922	316	607	1951	307	599	2325	316	735	2937	316	928	3061	316	967	3415	316	1079
B. Extravillage collective farm market sales	1475	670	988	1556	670	1043	1215	653	793	1110	784	870	1191	789	940	1394	731	1019	1377	696	958
C. Other marketings by the public sector[b]	500			500			500			500			500			500			500		
D. Total	3875	484	1632	3978	474	1650	3666	440	1392	3935	467	1605	4628	453	1868	4955	446	1986	5292	425	2037
3. Nonmarket utilization	971	484	470	973	474	461	1276	440	561	1115	467	521	1350	453	612	1456	446	649	1574	425	669

Notes:
Q = thousand tons.
P = rubles per ton.
V = million rubles.
[a] Including grapes but excluding melons.
[b] Including on-farm losses.

TABLE A-2 (continued)

H. SUMMARY[a]
(million rubles)

Product	1958	1959	1960	1961	1962	1963	1964
Grain	573	578	510	439	302	241	307
Potatoes	1,194	1,219	1,055	1,010	788	914	1,645
Vegetables	794	760	821	742	658	630	779
Meat	3,441	3,071	2,918	3,376	3,701	3,707	3,248
Milk	3,080	3,125	2,971	2,836	2,937	2,792	2,681
Eggs	1,015	1,065	1,106	1,193	1,270	1,194	1,147
Fruits and berries	470	461	561	521	612	649	669
Total, seven products	10,567	10,279	9,942	10,117	10,268	10,127	10,476

Note:
[a] Values for item 4 (grain), 3.C (potatoes), 3.B (vegetables, milk, eggs), and 3 (meat, fruits and berries) in parts A-G of this table.
Sources:
Quantities
Official gross output. All products except meat: NKh 1962, pp. 234–235, 297; *NKh 1963*, p. 273; *NKh 1964*, pp. 249, 251, 336. *Meat.* 1958–1960: *NKh 1960*, p. 378. 1961–1964: meat output in terms of slaughter weight (*NKh 1964*, p. 251) is converted to a live weight equivalent using a coefficient of 1.6. This is the coefficient implied for 1957, 1958, average 1954–1958, 1959, and 1960 in *NKh 1960*, p. 378.

Adjusted gross output of grain. The sum of estimates by the U.S. Department of Agriculture for 5 major grains (wheat, rye, barley, oats, corn for grain), plus output of minor grains as reported. The USDA estimates are from *Current Economic Indicators for the USSR*, 1965, p. 61; and *The USSR and Eastern Europe Agricultural Situation*, March 1966, p. 5. The Soviet data are from *NKh 1962*, pp. 234–235 and *NKh 1964*, p. 249.

For comparison, two other estimated output series may be cited—one by Kahan (Laird, ed., *Soviet Agricultural and Peasant Affairs*, 1963, p. 149) and the other by Diamond in *New Directions in the Soviet Economy*, 1966, p. 369):

	Million Tons						
	1958	*1959*	*1960*	*1961*	*1962*	*1963*	*1964*
Kahan	121.2	107.6	112.9	117.7[a]	126.2[a]	96.8[a]	136.9[a]
USDA for major grains, official data for minor grains	115.8	94.7	96.5	110.5	110.9	91.3	123.6
Diamond	119.0	95.7	93.0	109.5	109.0	92.0	120.0

[a] My calculation, assuming the same 10 percent rate of discount of official data as Kahan employed for 1958–1960.

Kahan's 1958–1960 estimate of the discounts required to be applied to the official claims on account of moisture and weed infestation—a flat 10 percent—is criticized by Richter as "somewhat mechanical." Her preferred approach is to estimate yields per hectare by type of grain on the basis of a variety of data on growing conditions. Both the USDA and the Diamond estimates are derived in such a manner (Laird, ed., *Soviet Agricultural and Peasant Affairs*, 1963, pp. 165–166; *New Directions in the Soviet Economy*, 1966, p. 369). The Diamond series differs only marginally from that adopted here.

State sector deliveries. NKh 1962, p. 358 (grain, meat, milk, and eggs, 1958–1962); pp. 240, 273, 291 (potatoes and vegetables, 1958–1962—the product of state sector shares applied to total procurements). *NKh 1963*, p. 359 (grain, meat, milk, and eggs,

TABLE A-2 (continued)

1963). *NKh 1964*, pp. 256, 318, 321, 324, 368, 370, 371 (potatoes and vegetables, 1963, grain, potatoes, vegetables, meat, milk, and eggs, 1964—the product of state sector shares applied to total procurements).

Purchases from farms and households. Total procurements (deliveries and purchases), as reported in the yearbooks, less state sector deliveries.

All procurements of fruits and berries. 1958, 1960, 1962–1964: *NKh 1964*, p. 255. The available data for 1959 and 1961 exclude berries (*NKh 1962*, p. 239). Judging from the quantities of berries procured in 1958, 1960, and 1962—12, 16, and 28 thousand tons, respectively, the corresponding volumes in 1959 and 1961 may be estimated as 14 and 22 thousand tons, respectively.

Extravillage market sales (except fruits and berries). 1958–1962: Karcz, January 1965, mimeographed supplement to his article in *American Economic Review*, June 1964. 1963–1964: Obtained by applying official quantity indexes to 1962 levels. The quantity indexes are taken from *Sovtorg II*, p. 259; *NKh 1963*, p. 547; and *NKh 1964*, p. 658.

Extravillage market sales and other marketings of fruits and berries. Because so little information is available, the estimating procedure is roundabout. I first estimate retained output in 1962 directly, proceed to collective farm market sales and other marketings in that year, and then complete the series for other years.

1962: According to R. S. Nazarov, (*Kolkhoznaia torgovlia*, 1964, pp. 55–56) approximately half the gross output of fruits and berries in the private sector is marketed. Nazarov's data on private sector output apparently exclude grapes (cf. his p. 53 with *NKh 1961*, p. 379) but it seems reasonable to assume that the 50 percent marketing ratio applies to grapes as well. Private sector output in 1962 was 2,721 thousand tons (*NKh 1962*, p. 297). Thus, private sector output not marketed may be estimated as about 1,350 thousand tons. Collective farmers do not receive fruits as labor-day distributions, and sales by farms to farmers appear to be small enough, if they occur at all, to have been omitted from V. Morozov's discussion of the intravillage market (*VE*, 1963, No. 8). Therefore, 1,350 thousand tons is assumed to constitute the entire volume of retained fruits and berries in 1962.

In the same year, 579 thousand tons of fresh and dry fruits and berries were sold on the collective farm markets of the 251 large cities that serve as the sample for Soviet market statistics (*Sovtorg II*, p. 267). The figure evidently does not include sales by consumer cooperatives at market prices (cf. *ibid.*, pp. 268–269 with pp. 271–274). In 1962, collective farms accounted for 1.3 percent of all sales of "fruit" on the markets of the 251-city network (*ibid.*, p. 278). Assuming that here too sales by consumer cooperatives are excluded and that "fruit" is shorthand for fruits and berries, the distribution of sales in these markets is 8 thousand tons by collective farms and 571 thousand tons by households. The consumer cooperatives received for sale at market prices 80 thousand tons of fruits, berries, and melons from collective farms, and 95 thousand tons from households (*ibid.*, pp. 86–87). To exclude melons, not included in other parts of my fruit and berry balance, I reduce sales to consumer cooperatives by, say, 20 percent. Hence, without allowance for sales on collective farm markets of the smaller cities and towns, we can account for extravillage market sales of 719 thousand tons, of which 72 represent collective farm and 647 thousand tons represent household sales.

Having accounted for 5,006 thousand tons of output in procurements, extravillage large city market sales and output retained by households, there remain 972 thousand tons of gross output to be distributed among other marketings by the public sector, on-farm spoilage in the public sector, and extravillage market sales (in small cities and towns) by both public and private sector. Clearly the distribution must be largely conjectural.

However, the residual to be distributed can be reduced somewhat further. So far 1,997 thousand tons of private sector output have been accounted for in extravillage market sales and retentions, leaving 724 thousand tons to be distributed among sales to state procurement and on the market in small towns. It is likely that private sector sales to procurement would have been considerably below 724 thousand tons, for Nazarov strongly implies that private sector marketings were predominantly through extravillage market trade. Therefore, of the 1,371 thousand tons of private sector marketings,

TABLE A-2 (continued)

it is unlikely that more than 500 thousand tons were sold to procurement organs, with 871 thousand tons going to all extravillage market channels.

At the maximum then, there remain 748 thousand tons for spoilage, other marketings, and extravillage market sales in small towns by the public sector. Of this residual, 500 thousand tons is allowed for spoilage and other marketings by the public sector, leaving 248 thousand tons of extravillage market sales to be added to the previously computed 72 thousand tons by the public sector and the 871 thousand tons of private sector sales on these markets.

1958–1961, 1963–1964: Extravillage market sales are estimated from the 1962 figure and the official volume index of sales on all extravillage markets. (As framework for the index I use *NKh 1964*, p. 658 and *NKh 1965*, p. 665. Gaps in 1959, 1961, and 1963 are filled in from *NKh 1962*, p. 541 and *Sovtorg II*, p. 259.) The official index apparently includes sales by consumer cooperatives at market prices: compare Nazarov, p. 29 and *NKh 1962*, p. 541.) It is assumed that the category "fruit" in the index data is shorthand for fruits and berries. Other marketings (including spoilage) are assumed constant throughout at 500 thousand tons.

Other marketings (except fruits and berries). Total marketings less identified components.

Total marketings. All products except meat, and fruits and berries. NKh 1962, p. 233, *NKh 1964*, p. 253. *Meat.* 1958–1961: *NKh 1961*, p. 299. 1962–1964: total marketings in terms of slaughter weight (*NKh 1964*, p. 253) are converted to a live weight equivalent using coefficients derived from data on procurements in those years (*ibid.*, p. 255). *Fruits and berries.* The sum of components.

Nonmarket utilization. The total for all products is obtained as the difference between official gross output (adjusted, in the case of grain) and total marketings. Where calculated, the "remainder" is the difference between total nonmarket utilization and the sum of identified components.

Grain.

Household output; kolkhoz distributions and sales to households; less household sales on extravillage farm markets. Computed as follows:

	1958	*1959*	*1960*	*1961*	*1962*	*1963*	*1964*
Household output	3.1	2.4	2.5	2.5	2.4	2.1	1.5
Kolkhoz distributions and sales	18.4	15.4	11.5	11.7	11.0	7.1	11.4
Subtotal	21.5	17.8	14.0	14.2	13.4	9.2	12.9
Less: household sales on extravillage farm markets	2.0	1.6	1.0	.7	.7	.4	.5
Total	19.5	16.2	13.0	13.5	12.7	8.4	12.4

Household output (excluding immature grain). Figures for 1958–1959, 1961 and 1962 are obtained as the difference between output for all sectors and output by collective farms and state enterprises (*SKh*, pp. 202–207; *NKh 1961*, pp. 300–301; *NKh 1962*, pp. 234–235). Figures for 1960 and 1963–1964 are obtained by applying the private sector share of output to the totals for all sectors (*NKh 1964*, pp. 249, 252).

Kolkhoz distributions and sales. Nimitz, *Incomes of Collective Farmers.*

Household sales on extravillage farm markets. The share of households in sales of grain and grain products is over 90 percent in the farm markets of the 251 cities comprised by the official market sample (*Sovtorg II*, p. 278). However, sales by all sellers in the 251 cities accounted for only a small fraction of total sales in all extravillage markets: e.g., whereas Karcz estimated 2.2 million tons of grain sold on the extravillage market in 1960, data for sales by farms and households on the 251-city markets indicate disposal of 275 thousand tons of grain, 56 thousand tons of flour and 31 thousand tons of groats (*Sovtorg II*, p. 267). Moreover, as indicated earlier, the share of collective farms in rural market sales is much higher than in sales on the large city markets (above, pp. 314–315)

TABLE A-2 (continued)

Egereva (*Balans proizvodstva i raspredeleniia produktsii sel'skogo khoziaistva*, 1963, p. 56) compares 1959 and 1960 values of output from the private plot plus labor-day payments with the value of sales on the collective farm market for a number of products, including grain. Assuming that Egereva's reference is to the extravillage farm market—this appears to be the context of the discussion—and that prices in all cases are those on the market (none of these crucial pieces of information is given in the source), her values of private sector sales of grain may be compared directly with those estimated by Karcz (appearing in this table as item 2.C in the value column).

	1959	*1960*
Egereva, million rubles	310.4	198.9
Karcz, million rubles	477	452
Egereva value as percent of Karcz estimate	65	44

Accordingly, for 1959 and 1960, 65 and 44 percent, or 1.6 and 1.0 million tons, respectively, of marketings in extravillage collective farm market trade are considered to have originated from households. For 1958, this allowance is estimated arbitrarily as 2 million tons; for other years I assume a household share at 40 percent of all sales in physical units.

Remainder: public sector seed, feed, and waste; errors and omissions. The figures seem low, especially those for 1959–1960. Very crude estimates of grain utilization for seed and feed in the public sector may be obtained as follows (million tons):

	1958	*1959*	*1960*	*1961*	*1962*	*1963*	*1964*
Seed	17	16	16	17	19	16	19
Feed	20	20	20	20	20	20	20
	37	36	36	37	39	36	39

The estimate of seed requirements assumes a seeding rate of 1.58 centners per hectare (Laird, ed., *Soviet Agricultural and Peasant Affairs*, 1963, p. 150). Using reported figures on the area sown to grain, excluding corn harvested in the milk-wax stage (including the private sector, but the resulting error is slight for present purposes—*NKh 1962*, p. 247; *NKh 1964*, p. 267), total seed requirements are computed as follows (million tons):

1958	*1959*	*1960*	*1961*	*1962*	*1963*	*1964*
19.20	18.09	18.26	19.32	20.33	20.54	21.06

From these amounts it is necessary to deduct seed loans repaid to the government out of regular procurements. The amounts have been estimated by Nimitz (*Soviet Government Grain Procurements, Dispositions, and Stocks, 1940, 1945–1963*, November 1964, p. 58) as 2.2 million tons in 1958, a minimum of 2 million tons in 1959–1962, and 4 million tons in 1963. For 1964 I assume a figure of two million tons. Morozov (*Trudoden', den'gi i torgovli na sele*, 1965, p. 50) cites a figure reported at the March 1965 Plenum of the Party Central Committee: in 1962 the government sold 1,373,000 tons of seed grain to collective and state farms and about 2 million tons were requested in 1965.

The estimate of feed use is based on a statement by Lemeshev (*VE*, 1962, No. 6, p. 7) that on the average in 1956–1958 and 1959–1961, 19.4 and 21.2 million tons of non-marketed grain were utilized for feed in the public sector. I assume annual feed use of 20 million tons throughout this period.

Thus, the residual figures, item 3.B of this appendix table, fall short of these crude estimates of seed and feed requirements in every year except 1961; the largest discrepancies occur in 1959–1960 and amount to 11 and 7 million tons, respectively. Note that the seed figures for the 1960s may be underestimates: Studenkova, *Metodika ischisleniia sebestoimosti . . .* , 1965, p. 25) cites collective farm expenditure of 14.5 million tons of grain (excluding corn) for seed in 1962. In that year collective farms

TABLE A-2 (continued)

sowed 60.2 million hectares to grain excluding corn (*NKh 1962*, pp. 254–255). Thus, the implied seeding rate is 2.41 centners per hectare, 53 percent higher than the rate used here. If state farms were equally prodigal with seed, the total public sector seed (based on sown area data in *ibid.*) and feed requirements would have been about 49 million tons in 1962, 13 million tons greater than my residual. Possibly my adjusted gross output figures, based on USDA estimates, overstate the deductions required to be applied to Soviet official data. (For additional evidence of high seeding rates see the sources cited by Johnson, in the *American Economic Review, Proceedings*, May 1966, p. 152).

Potatoes. Seed. These are estimates based on 1960 physical-unit potato balances given in percentage terms for the whole economy and for the three sectors separately by Egereva (*Balans proizvodstva i raspredeleniia produktsii sel'skogo khoziaistva*, 1963, p. 58). Unfortunately, there are a number of puzzling features about Egereva's balance: for example, inclusion of distributions to households by collective farms in the availability side of the balance for the economy as a whole, inconsistency between these distributions and either the comparable item in the household's availability section or the apparently identically defined distribution items. There are other inconsistencies for which no explanation is supplied. (For a sharply critical Soviet review of this book, see *VS*, 1964, No. 6, pp. 67–70.) However, the major outlines of the balance seem consistent with the official statistics on production and procurements.

Translating the percentage figures of the balance into absolute data by means of the reported total output in 1960, I obtain 18.2 million tons as the seed use of potatoes in 1960. Given an area sown to potatoes of 9.1 million hectares in 1960 (*NKh 1962*, p. 248), the implied seeding rate is two tons per hectare. This rate is applied to the reported sown areas in 1958–1959 and 1961–1964 (*ibid.*, and *NKh 1964*, p. 268), as follows:

	1958	*1959*	*1960*	*1961*	*1962*	*1963*	*1964*
Sown area (million hectares)	9.5	9.5	9.1	8.9	8.7	8.5	8.5
Seed requirements (million tons)	19.0	19.0	18.2	17.8	17.4	17.0	17.0

Feed. Egereva's balance implies a figure of 31.6 million tons of potatoes used for feed in 1960. However, Vintaikin states (*ESKh*, 1963, No. 8, p. 17), that "more than 40 million tons of potatoes were fed to livestock in the country as a whole in 1960, according to data of the Central Statistical Administration." The Vintaikin reference seems the more authoritative. "More than 40" is taken to mean, arbitrarily, 41 million tons. Feed utilization is estimated as 40 million tons in both 1958 and 1959, and as 41 million tons in 1961. Feed use is assumed to have declined in 1962 and increased thereafter approximately in proportion to changes in output.

Remainder. The apparent declines in consumption in 1960 and in 1962 may be too abrupt. Sample budget data for the RSFSR indicate that consumption of potatoes per head by collective farm families declined 2 percent from 1959 to 1960, rose slightly in 1961 and dropped again by 2 percent in 1962 (*NKh RSFSR 1959; 1960; 1961; 1962;* pp. 485, 456, 502, 476, respectively). Possibly, seed and feed requirements have been overestimated in some years. However, failing additional information, there seems little basis for adjustment of the remainders.

Vegetables. Feed in socialized sector. "In 1961, 1,208 thousand tons of vegetables and food melons, or 20 percent of the total volume of their procurements in the country, were fed to livestock on collective and state farms." (Alisov, *Kommunist*, No. 15, October 1963, p. 94.) The corresponding figures for 1964 and 1965 have been reported as "about" 1.8 and 1.3 million tons, out of gross production in the public sector of 12 and "less than" 10.5 million tons (*Pravda*, August 6, 1966, p. 2). Since public sector production of vegetables alone in 1964 was at least 11.8 million tons (*NKh 1964*, pp. 249 and 252), the proportion of melons in the totals cited above must be small, say no more than 5 percent. Therefore, public sector feed use of vegetables is estimated as 1.1 million

TABLE A-2 (continued)

tons in 1961 and 1.7 millions in 1964. Estimates for other years take into account differences in the level of total gross output.

Milk. Feed. The 1960 figure is obtained by translating a relative balance in Egereva (*Balans proizvodstva i raspredeleniia produktsii sel'skogo khoziaistva*, 1963, p. 59) into absolute terms using official output data as the key. This figure seems large enough to be presumed to cover milk sucked by calves (Laird, ed., *Soviet Agricultural and Peasant Affairs*, 1963, p. 155 and pp. 315–316, note 40). Estimates for other years are obtained by moving the 1960 figure backward and forward in time in proportion to the officially reported herds of cows in all sectors (*NKh 1964*, p. 352).

Eggs. Production use. The 1958 figure, an estimate by Nimitz (*SNIP 1956–1958*, p. 45), is increased in subsequent years in proportion to the increase in the total poultry flock (*SKh*, p. 322; *NKh 1962*, p. 307; *NKh 1964*, p. 360; *NKh 1965*, p. 375).

Meat and milk. Diamond estimates total output 6–15 percent lower than official claims (*New Directions in the Soviet Economy*, 1966, p. 370). If these discounts are accepted my estimates of nonmarket utilization are correspondingly overstated.

Farm household consumption of grain. These figures represent estimates of grain milled into flour and groats on the farm, obtained by converting Nimitz's estimates of rural milling of flour and groats to grain equivalent, assuming an extraction rate of 95 percent for flour and 80 percent for groats. The Nimitz data are taken from her *Soviet Government Grain Procurements, Dispositions, and Stocks, 1940, 1945–1963*, November 1964, p. 89; her 1963 and 1964 estimates of flour output at rural mills are reduced from 8.7 and 8 to 7 and 5 million tons, respectively, as *NKh 1964*, p. 226 shows total USSR flour output in those years of 36 and 34 tons, compared with her figures of 37.3 and 38 millions.

If these estimates are subtracted from entries under item 3.A of this table (household output, distributions and sales to households, less household sales on the extravillage market), the remainder, conceptually, should embrace seed, feed, and waste in the private sector. The data are as follows (million tons):

	1958	*1959*	*1960*	*1961*	*1962*	*1963*	*1964*
(1) Item 3.A	19.5	16.2	13.0	13.5	12.6	8.8	12.4
(2) Grain equivalent of rural grain milled into flour and groats	13	14	13	11	9	8	6
(3) Difference, (1) less (2)	7	2	0	3	4	1	6

A zero entry in row (3) of the tabulation is obviously impossible; entries for 1959 and 1963 are certainly and those for 1961 and 1962 are probably too low. Total concentrates fed to livestock in the private sector, according to official data, fluctuated between 15 and 18 million tons in 1958–1964 (*NKh 1961*, p. 410; *NKh 1964*, p. 377). These concentrates consist mainly of grain, including byproducts, and oil cake (Nimitz, *Soviet Government Grain Procurements, Dispositions, and Stocks, 1940, 1945–1963*, November 1964, p. 101). Possibly 250,000 tons of grain were required for seed in 1958 with lesser amounts thereafter (sown area in *NKh 1964*, p. 272, multiplied by a seeding rate of 1.58 centners per hectare).

It is clear that row (2) overstates household consumption from non-marketed output because it includes flour and groats sold by households on the extravillage farm market and consumption through public catering on collective and state farms, a form of utilization included under marketing. I previously estimated (p. 324) that the peak level of household sales of all grain on the collective farm market was 2 million tons in 1958. Of this probably less than half was in the form of flour and groats (the share was considerably smaller in the 251 large city markets—*Sovtorg II*, p. 267). In 1959 collective farms produced, presumably for public catering and sales on the market, 1.6 million tons of flour, .1 million tons of groats and .04 million tons of baked bread (Sigov, *Razdelenie truda v sel'skom khoziaistve*, 1963, p. 252, note). Presumably, state farm output was somewhat larger. Note, however, that item 1.D of this table, other marketings, which includes this component as well as decentralized deliveries by state farms and the differ-

TABLE A-2 (continued)

ence between physical and accounting weight for both deliveries and purchases, varies between 3 and 5 million tons in the period under consideration.

As a crude guess I suspect that entries in row (2) are overstated and those in row (3) are understated by a maximum of 4–5 million tons. I assume the margin is 4 million tons in 1958 and 5 millions in 1959–1963. For 1964 I assume the same level of consumption as in 1962.

Prices

The required information is average revenues per unit. Such data are available for 1958 but not for later years. Data after 1958 generally refer to an average price structure. However, the difference from average unit revenues may be expected to be small: compare pp. 306 and 311 of Zverev, *Natsional'nyi dokhod i finansy SSSR*, 1961; see also Borkhunov, *VS*, 1965, No. 1, p. 76.

Purchases: all products except meat, fruits and berries.

1958: Zverev, *Natsional'nyi dokhod i finansy SSSR*, 1961, pp. 306 (vegetables; average price) and 311 (grain, potatoes, milk, and eggs; unit revenues). The grain unit revenue refers to the accounting weight of purchases, as required for consistency with the data on quantity of deliveries and purchases (*NKh 1964*, p. 295). For other years, sources are as follows:

Grain. 1959–1961. Stoliarov, *O tsenakh i tsenoobrazovanii v SSSR*, 2nd ed., 1963, pp. 84, 86. 1962: The average purchase price of grain excluding corn, given in Studenkova, *Metodika ischisleniia sebestoimosti . . .* , 1965, p. 29 and Khlebnikov, *VS*, 1965, No. 5, p. 20. 1963: Khlebnikov, *ESKh*, 1965, No. 11, p. 39. The reference is again to grain excluding corn. 1964: No direct information on 1964 prices is available but there were no significant changes in that year anyhow. With the recovery of grain yields in the eastern regions, discounts for moisture and weeds are likely to have been relatively more important in 1964 than in the previous year.

Potatoes. 1959–1960: Stoliarov, *O tsenakh i tsenoobrazovanii v SSSR*, 1963, p. 84. 1961: Assumed the same as in 1960. A price index given by Stoliarov (*ibid.*, p. 106), which is evidently an official index (compare with *SKh*, p. 117) indicates no change in average potato prices in 1961. 1962. Studenkova, *Metodika ischisleniia sebestoimosti . . .* , 1965, p. 29 and Khlebnikov, *VS*, 1965, No. 5, p. 20. 1963: Khlebnikov, *ESKh*, 1965, No. 11, p. 39; also, Gumerov, *FinSSSR*, 1965, No. 8, p. 8. 1964: Assumed the same as in 1963. According to Belousov and Petrakov (*VE*, 1965, No. 11, p. 146), there were no changes in purchase prices of sugar beets, potatoes, raw cotton and tobacco after 1963.

Vegetables. 1959: Assumed the same as in 1958. 1960: Khlebnikov, *VE*, 1962, No. 7, p. 53. 1961: Assumed the same as in 1960. 1962: Studenkova, *Metodika ischisleniia sebestoimosti . . .* , 1965, p. 29. 1963: Khrushchev in *Pravda*, March 7, 1964, p. 1. Note that the 1962–1963 price at 75 rubles per ton is lower than the 1960 price, 86 rubles, and even below the 1958 price, 78 rubles. This seems strange. Possibly, the explanation may be found in changes in the product-mix. 1964: Assumed the same as in 1963.

Milk. 1959–1960. Stoliarov, *O tsenakh i tsenoobrazovanii v SSSR*, 1963, p. 84. 1961: Assumed the same as in 1960. 1962: Studenkova, *Metodika ischisleniia sebestoimosti . . .* , 1965, p. 29 and Khlebnikov, *VS*, 1965, No. 5, p. 21. 1963: Khrushchev, in *Pravda*, March 7, 1964, p. 1; also Khlebnikov, *ESKh*, 1965, No. 11, p. 39. 1964: Assumed the same as in 1963.

Eggs. 1959–1960. Stoliarov, *O tsenakh i tsenoobrazovanii v SSSR*, 1963, p. 84. 1961: Assumed the same as in 1960. 1962: Studenkova, *Metodika ischisleniia sebestoimosti . . .* , 1965, p. 29. 1963: Khrushchev, in *Pravda*, March 7, 1964, p. 1. 1964: Assumed the same as in 1963.

Deliveries: all products except meat, fruits, and berries.

1958: Zverev, *Natsional'nyi dokhod i finansy SSSR*, 1961, pp. 306 and 311. For other years, estimates are derived as follows: Delivery prices of vegetables are assumed unchanged through 1964, those of potatoes through 1962, and grain prices through 1960. There is no evidence of price changes for potatoes and vegetables before 1962. When in 1961 a number of delivery prices were raised, it was explicitly indicated that prices of

TABLE A-2 (continued)

hogs, blooded cattle, cotton, vegetables, potatoes, tea, and milk were not changed (except milk in the Baltic and Belorussian republics). See Pakhomov, *Sovkhoznoe proizvodstvo*, 1961, No. 4, p. 6. The 1958 delivery price of vegetables was high enough to insure a margin over cost through 1964 and this was true of potatoes through 1961. (For state farm costs see Studenkova, *Metodika ischisleniia sebestoimosti . . .* , 1965, p. 101, and *NKh 1964*, pp. 412–413). We know that delivery prices of potatoes were raised in 1963 (*Zakupki sel'skokhoziaistvennykh produktov*, 1963, No. 10, p. 26; cited in Karcz, *A Compendium of Soviet Farm Prices in 1961*, 1964, p. 108; it is not certain that the prices referred to are all-union prices). I assume a level just sufficient to cover 1962 average costs of 69.3 rubles (Studenkova, *Metodika ischisleniia sebestoimosti . . .* , 1965, p. 101); the 1964 price is assumed the same as in 1963. According to Karcz (*A Compendium of Soviet Farm Prices in 1961*, 1964, p. 77), state farms sold potatoes and vegetables directly to wholesale or retail state-cooperative organizations and were paid local state retail prices less retail margin, procurement and storage costs.

In 1961 the delivery prices of a number of products were set at the level of purchase prices. Among these products were buckwheat, rice, peas and other legumes, and eggs (Pakhomov, *Sovkhoznoe proizvodstvo*, 1961, No. 4, pp. 5–6). Since buckwheat, rice, and peas and other legumes are of relatively minor weight in grain deliveries, the 1958–1960 delivery price for grain would seem to require only a token increase in 1961. Apparently, however, soft wheat prices were raised too, at least in several regions (Semenov, *Khoziaistvennyi raschet i finansy sovkhozov*, 1964, p. 32). According to Kondrashev (*Tsena i khoziaistvennyi raschet*, 1961, p. 36), grain delivery prices in 1961 were to be 78 percent of purchase prices. In a later work, Kondrashev places grain delivery prices at 85 percent of the purchase price level (*Tsena i stoimost' v sotsialisticheskom khoziaistve*, 1963, p. 308). The figure accepted here is 80 percent of the purchase price. The 1961 price is assumed unchanged through 1964.

In his 1961 book (p. 36), Kondrashev indicated that delivery prices of milk were to be the same as purchase prices. Evidently, this was not carried out, as his 1963 reference omits any mention of milk. Moreover, as previously indicated, milk prices in 1961 were changed in only a few regions of the country. Stoliarov, *O tsenakh i tsenoobrazovanii v SSSR*, 1963, in a breakdown of the elements of the retail price of butter, indicates the cost to and losses by state farms incurred in the sale of milk to the state per pound of butter sold at retail (p. 188). His data imply delivery prices of 112 rubles per ton in 1959, 114 rubles in 1961 and 142 rubles in 1962, after June 1. (For this calculation, I use data on state farm unit costs from Studenkova, *Metodika ischisleniia sebestoimosti . . .* , 1965, p. 103, to obtain from Stoliarov's cost of milk used per ton of butter the implied input coefficient and thereby to transform losses per unit of butter to a price per unit of milk. It is assumed that Studenkova's and Stoliarov's data are mutually consistent.) Apparently, the 1958 price remained virtually unchanged in 1959. Stoliarov suggests that the 1961 price was about the same as in 1960; I assume an average of the 1961 and 1959 prices. My 1962 price is similarly an average of the 1961 and post-June 1, 1962 prices. Prices in 1963 and 1964 are the post-June 1, 1962 price. (Note that this still means operation at a loss for state farms: average costs in 1964 were 181 rubles per ton—*NKh 1964*, pp. 412–413.)

As indicated, delivery prices of eggs in 1961 were set at purchase price levels, but in 1958 delivery prices of eggs were substantially higher than purchase prices. The 1961 average purchase price, as estimated, is at about the 1958 level. Consequently, setting the average delivery price equal to the purchase price in 1961 means a reduction in the delivery price of 15 percent from the 1958 level. However, Karcz (*A Compendium of Soviet Farm Prices in 1961*, 1964, pp. 76–77) indicates that only eggs delivered directly to procurement points were sold at purchase prices; eggs delivered to retail organizations were paid for at full retail prices or at the retail price less the trade margin. My estimates take that factor into account.

In *VE*, 1966, No. 11, p. 38, Pankova cites 1964 and 1965 delivery prices for a variety of products. I have not used these prices because of doubts on the score of the coverage of her data aroused by cost figures she supplies. Pankova's cost figures differ in unex-

TABLE A-2 (continued)

plained ways from those reported in *NKh 1964*, pp. 412–413 and *NKh 1965*, pp. 428–429. Possibly she deals with a less than global aggregate of farms. In any case, substitution of Pankova's 1964 prices would yield a value of deliveries for five products—that is, excluding meat, fruits and berries—about 10 percent less than obtained with my estimates. The substitution would evidently make little difference for average realized prices and total consumption in kind in 1964.

Purchase prices: meat. Prices for 1960–1962 represent unit values obtained as quotients of collective farm incomes from sales of cattle and poultry to state and cooperative organizations divided by purchases (in tons of live weight) from collective farms (*NKh 1962*, pp. 314 and 343). Prices for 1958 and 1959 are estimated on the basis of a price index for livestock excluding poultry, given by Stoliarov (*O tsenakh i tsenoobrazovanii v SSSR*, 1963, p. 106), and the 1960 unit value. Since the 1960 average purchase price for poultry is very little different from that for 1958 (cf. Zverev, *Natsional'nyi dokhod i finansy SSSR*, 1961, p. 306 and *NKh 1961*, p. 426, note), the 5 percent increase in 1959 and less than 1 percent increase in 1960 shown by the Stoliarov price index are reduced to 4 percent in 1959 and zero in 1960. Prices in 1963 and 1964 are assumed unchanged at the 1962 level (compare Khlebnikov, *VS*, 1965, No. 5, p. 21, and *ESKh*, 1965, No. 11, p. 39).

Delivery prices: meat. In the absence of unit values of meat deliveries from the state sector, average prices are estimated as follows:

1958. Average delivery prices for cattle, hogs, sheep and goats, and poultry are known (Zverev, *Natsional'nyi dokhod i finansy SSSR*, 1961, pp. 306, 311), as are the volume of production of various meats in slaughter weight, distributed by sectors of agriculture (*SKh*, pp. 334–335). If the structure of deliveries in live weight was equivalent to the structure of output in slaughter weight, these sets of data may be combined to obtain an implied average weighted delivery price of 650 rubles per ton. The result is probably not too far off the mark, considering that the same calculation for collective farms yields a weighted average price that is within 3 percentage points of the previously computed unit value of purchases from collective farms. On this basis, the 1958 delivery price for meat is estimated as 625 rubles per ton.

1959–1961. Effective January 1, 1961, delivery prices of all livestock except hogs and blooded cattle were set at the same level as purchase prices (Pakhomov, *Sovkhoznoe proizvodstvo*, 1961, No. 4, pp. 5–6). Semenov (*Khoziaistvennyi raschet i finansy sovkhozov*, 1964, p. 33), in discussing the June 1962 price changes, in which delivery prices of livestock were generally set 10 percent below purchase prices, states the percentage increase in both purchase and delivery prices of cattle, hogs, and poultry. The implication of these data is that 1961 delivery prices of cattle were slightly below purchase prices, whereas for hogs and poultry delivery prices were slightly higher than purchase prices. Therefore, the average delivery price of meat in 1961 is estimated equal to the average purchase price.

Average delivery prices in 1959 and 1960 are assumed unchanged from the 1958 level. Average prices paid for state farm deliveries of cattle may be estimated as 421 rubles per ton in 1960 and 630 rubles per ton in 1961. (Estimated from the following data for the indicated years in Stoliarov, *O tsenakh i tsenoobrazovanii v SSSR*, 1963, pp. 184–185: payments in rubles per centner to state farms for their share of cattle expended on the production of a centner of beef; the average yield of beef per unit of weight of cattle processed; distribution of processed cattle by origin—collective farms, state farms, and so forth.) Thus, prices paid state farms for cattle rose by only 2 percent between 1958 (see Zverev, *Natsional'nyi dokhod i finansy SSSR*, 1961, p. 311) and 1960 and by 50 percent in 1961 alone.

1962. The sweeping livestock price change of June 1, 1962 set delivery prices of livestock at a level 10 percent below prices paid collective farms and collective farmers (*Pravda*, June 1, 1962, p. 1). Therefore, the average delivery price of meat is estimated as 90 percent of the average purchase price. The implied 1961–1962 increase in the average delivery price is 12 percent. According to Semenov (*Khoziaistvennyi raschet i finansy sovkhozov*, 1964, p. 33), in 1962 delivery prices of cattle were raised 26 percent, hogs 13 percent, and poultry 35 percent.

1963–1964. Prices are assumed unchanged from the 1962 level.

Purchase and delivery prices: fruits and berries. Prices in 1958–1961 are computed by

TABLE A-2 (continued)

applying an index of purchase prices alone (Stoliarov, *O tsenakh i tsenoobrazovanii v SSSR*, 1963, p. 106) to an estimated 1962 price. It is assumed that state farm delivery prices moved proportionally to purchase prices in that period. Prices in 1963 and 1964 are assumed unchanged at the 1962 level.

The 1962 price is obtained as follows:

(1) In that year collective farms and households received 520 million rubles from sales of "fruit" to the state (*NKh 1964*, p. 257). "Fruit" explicitly includes grapes and citrus fruit; it is not clear whether berries are also included but I assume they are.

(2) This figure is to be divided by the volume of purchases from collective farms and households in physical units. These two sectors accounted for 70.7 percent of the procurements of non-citrus tree fruit (*semechkovye kostochkovye plody*) and 61.2 percent of the total for grapes (Bolgov *et al.*, *Ekonomika sotsialisticheskogo sel'skogo khoziaistva*, 1965, p. 450). Given total procurements of 909 thousand tons of non-citrus tree fruit and 1964 thousand tons of grapes (*NKh 1964*, p. 255), purchases from collective farms and households are calculated as 1845 thousand tons. This figure, of course, excludes berries as well as citrus fruit, total procurements of which amounted to 64 thousand tons in 1962. It is assumed that collective farms and households accounted for two-thirds of the omitted volume, raising fruit purchases from these two sectors to 1888 thousand tons.

(3) Hence, the average value of fruit purchases from collective farms and households was 275 rubles per ton. Average prices received by state farms were probably higher; whereas collective farms received 266 rubles per ton of grapes sold in 1961, state farms received 306 rubles, or 15 percent more (Badir'ian, ed., *Ekonomika, organizatsiia i planirovanie sel'skokhoziaistvennogo proizvodstva*, 1963, p. 287). I therefore raise the 1962 average price to 316 rubles.

Extravillage farm market prices. Average prices in 1958–1962 for all products except fruits and berries are from Karcz's January 1965 mimeographed supplement to his *American Economic Review* article. Prices of fruits and berries in 1959–1962 are obtained from the application of the official price index (*Sovtorg II*, p. 266) to an estimated average 1958 price, derived as follows:

The unit value of commission sales of fruits, berries, and melons was 483 rubles per ton (*ibid.*, pp. 86–87). According to *NKh 1960*, p. 718, in 101 cities commission prices in that year were 82 percent of collective farm market prices for all products, 71 percent for potatoes, 69 percent for vegetables, and 74 percent for fresh apples. It is assumed that the collective farm market price in 1958 was 700 rubles per ton; the commission price for fruits and berries is assumed to have been 500 rubles per ton. These prices are averaged in the proportion 6:1. (Of the 1400 thousand tons of extravillage market sales, somewhat more than 200 thousand tons represent dispositions of fruits and berries to cooperatives for sales at market prices—*Sovtorg II*, pp. 86–87.)

Prices of all products in 1963 and 1964 are obtained by applying to the 1962 price an official price index of transactions in the 251-city market sample (*NKh 1962*, p. 543 and *NKh 1964*, p. 659; indexes in the former source, with base year 1952, are linked to those of the latter source, with base year 1950, through links for the common year, 1960). Unfortunately, none of the 1963–1965 yearbooks reported all-union price indexes by commodity. Index numbers for 1963 in this series were reported in *Sovtorg II*, p. 266, but these figures may not be reliable, judging from the extensive changes in the 1963 *quantity* index numbers made between publication of *Sovtorg II* (p. 259) and *NKh 1963* (p. 547).

Price of total marketings: all products. Computed as unit value quotients of total marketed quantities divided by total marketed values, net of "other" marketings.

Price of remainder of nonmarket utilization or of "final estimate": all products. Price is average unit value of all marketings.

Values

For purchases and deliveries as well as the nonmarketed remainder (or "final estimate"), obtained as the product of price times quantity. The value of total marketings is the sum of components. Values of extravillage sales for 1958–1962 are taken from the mimeographed appendix to Karcz's *American Economic Review* article; those for 1963–1964 are obtained as the product of price times quantity sold.

B

Sources to Table 2: 1958-1964

1. *Retail sales of goods for consumption.*

A. *State-cooperative trade.* Derived as follows (billion rubles):

	1958	*1959*	*1960*	*1961*	*1962*	*1963*	*1964*
State-cooperative retail sales	67.72	71.92	78.56	81.08	87.30	91.69	96.36
Less:							
Sales by consumer cooperatives at market prices	.87	.87	.75	.86	.96	.98	1.05
Services	.80	.88	.96	.98	1.06	1.15	1.32
Sales to institutions							
Noncash sales	4.77	4.72	4.69	4.88	4.68	4.49	5.01
Cash sales	.18	.18	.18	.19	.18	.17	.19
Producer goods sold to farm households	.30	.25	.25	.20	.20	.20	.20
Building materials sold to households for construction	.47	.55	.60	.56	.58	.41	.41
Equals:							
Sales to households for consumption	60.33	64.47	71.13	73.41	79.64	84.29	88.18

The source for total state-cooperative retail sales, services, and noncash sales to institutions, 1958–1963, is *Sovtorg II*, pp. 40, 54, and 56. The 1964 figure for all sales is from *NKh 1965*, p. 631. Sales to institutions in 1964 are reported to have been 5.2 percent of total state-cooperative retail sales (Nikitin, in *Sovetskaia torgovlia*, 1966, No. 6, p. 35). The data on sales to institutions refer to transactions implemented with deposit money. In addition, a small volume of institutional purchases is paid for with currency. In the year extending from the fourth quarter of 1959 through the third quarter of 1960, cash sales came to 180 million rubles, or 3.6 percent of noncash sales (Titel'baum, *VS,* 1961, No. 10, p. 57). A 1965 source (Borisov, *Balans denezhnykh dokhodov i raskhodov naseleniia,* 1965, p. 58) declares that "at present" such cash purchases do not exceed 200 million rubles, or a little more than 0.2 percent of retail trade turnover. My estimates are based on these indications.

Cooperative sales at market prices (included below under item 1.B) are taken from *NKh 1962,* p. 511 (1958–1962), *NKh 1964,* p. 631 (1963), and *NKh 1965,* p. 637 (1964). The yearbooks present two series for cooperative sales at market prices (for example: *NKh 1961,* pp. 641 and 664; *NKh 1965,* pp. 637 and 665). Up to 1962 these differed only in the inclusion or exclusion of trade markup. However, from 1962 on the scope of the series excluding markup has been enlarged to embrace purchases of agricultural products by the cooperatives for use by the public catering network (*NKh 1962,* p. 688 and *NKh 1965,* p. 844; also compare the two series in *NKh 1965* as indicated above and in *NKh 1962,* pp. 522 and 540). Consumer cooperative sales at market prices are also included in reported state-cooperative retail sales; the series involved is that including markup but net of the post-1961 extension in coverage (see *Sovtorg II,* p. 57).

The deduction for services included in the retail trade totals represents receipts by artisans for custom-made shoes and clothing as well as for a variety of repair and cleaning services. As these receipts include the value of materials provided by the artisans (*Sovtorg II,* p. 486), their full value overstates the deduction required. The degree of overstatement is not known. Artisan receipts in 1964 have not been reported; they are estimated here from a reported volume of operations valued at 1 July 1955 prices, 1,102 million rubles (*NKh 1965,* p. 598). In previous years the ratio of receipts to volume was as follows (*NKh 1962,* p. 491; *NKh 1964,* p. 594; *Sovtorg II,* p. 54):

1959	1.44
1960	1.37
1961	1.31
1962	1.22
1963	1.23

For 1964 I assume a ratio of 1.2.

Sales of producer goods (excluding building materials) to farm households in 1958 were estimated as 0.3 billion rubles in *SNIP*

1956–1958 (p. 26), partly on the basis of data on residual consumer ual declined 29 percent in 1959, increased 5 percent in 1960 (*NKh 1960,* p. 695), dropped 16 percent in the two years 1961–1962, and increased 1 percent in 1963 (*Sovtorg II,* p. 82). The deductions entered above for 1959–1963 are estimated on the basis of these data. The 1964 estimate is a guess.

The value of building materials sold to households for construction is estimated as 40 percent of the total value of sales of window glass and other building materials in state-cooperative retail trade (*NKh 1961,* p. 640; *Sovtorg II,* p. 65; *NKh 1964,* p. 630). According to *VS,* 1961, No. 6, p. 96, sales to institutions in the period October 1959-September 1960 amounted to .89 billion rubles or 60 percent of total retail sales of these commodities. This implies household purchases in that period of .59 billion rubles.

Retail sales data include the value of goods distributed as winnings in the state lottery. However, goods account for only 19 percent of total winnings, in turn representing 50 percent of sales of tickets (Borisov, *Balans denezhnykh dokhodov i raskhodov naseleniia,* 1965, p. 51). Thus in 1960, for example, based on receipts net of winnings of .14 billion rubles (below, p. 382), in kind winnings amounted to .03 billions. The amounts seem small enough to ignore safely.

B. *Extravillage farm markets.* Derived as follows (billion rubles):

	1958	*1959*	*1960*	*1961*	*1962*	*1963*	*1964*
Collective farm market sales	4.05	3.83	3.70	3.93	3.88	3.79	3.86
Consumer cooperative sales at market prices (including commission)	.87	.87	.75	.86	.96	.98	1.05
Total extravillage market sales	4.92	4.70	4.45	4.79	4.84	4.77	4.91
Less: Sales to institutions	.49	.47	.45	.48	.48	.48	.49
Equals: Sales to households	4.43	4.23	4.00	4.31	4.36	4.29	4.42

Collective farm market sales are from *NKh 1962,* p. 540, *NKh 1964,* p. 657, and *NKh 1965,* p. 665. For consumer cooperative sales, see item 1.A above. Sales to institutions are assumed to account for 10 percent of total extravillage market sales: sales to institutions in the period October 1959-September 1960 came to .456 billion rubles (Titel'baum, *VS,* 1961, No. 10, p. 63).

Household outlays in the intravillage market are covered in item 4, "other outlays for consumption."

2. *Consumer services.*

A. *Housing (including imputed rent)*. Computed as follows:

	1958	*1959*	*1960*	*1961*	*1962*	*1963*	*1964*
Money rent on socialized housing	.61	.66	.71	.76	.82	.88	.93
Imputed rent on private housing							
Collective farm	.50	.52	.53	.54	.55	.56	.57
Other	.60	.62	.65	.67	.69	.70	.72
Total	1.10	1.14	1.18	1.21	1.24	1.26	1.29
Total	1.71	1.80	1.89	1.97	2.06	2.14	2.22

The estimates are obtained as the product of the average annual stock of housing and the average rental on state housing, 1.5 rubles per square meter of living space per year. According to Gol'tsman (*Ekonomika kommunal'nogo khoziaistva uslugi, tarify,* 1966, p. 71), this was the average in 1959–1962 on a range of 1.47–1.56 rubles. Earlier sources put the average rental slightly lower, at 1.46 rubles (Broner, *Sovremennye problemy zhilishchnogo khoziaistva,* 1961, p. 178; Kapustin, ed., *Obshchestvennye fondy i rost blagosostoianiia naroda v SSSR,* 1962, p. 156).

The average annual housing stocks estimated here contain a sizable element of guesswork. The statistical yearbooks report the stock of housing only in "cities and in settlements of urban type." By some indications (*Bol'shaia sovetskaia entsiklopedia,* 2nd ed., Vol. 34, p. 233; and Vol. 35, p. 451) "settlements of urban type" would appear to exclude only collective farms. However, recent data indicate that the housing stock statistics exclude not only collective farm housing—built by farms, farmers, or "rural intelligentsia"—but also noncollective farm housing, socialized and private, in rural areas (compare pp. 605, 610, 611 of *NKh 1964*). Unfortunately, there is very little basis for estimating the noncollective farm rural stock. My procedure is simply to guess at the missing stock figures for a base year, 1959—being guided by the per capita housing availability in urban areas and the relation between urban and rural rates of new construction over the 6 year period, 1959–1964 (*NKh 1965,* p. 610)—and to move the base year stocks with data on new construction, allowing for an annual rate of withdrawal of 0.7 percent. The latter is the actual average rate for all urban housing in 1959–1965 (withdrawals from *NKh 1965,* p. 616; stocks at the end of the previous year from *NKh 1962,* p. 499, *NKh 1964,* p. 610, and *NKh 1965,* p. 615).

For private housing, new construction in rural areas as a percent of construction in urban areas rose from 77 percent in 1959 to 90 percent in 1961 and then dropped to 76 percent in 1964; for socialized housing the relation rose to 30 percent in 1961 from the low of 22 percent in 1959, declined to 26 in 1962, rose to 27 in 1963 and dropped back to 22 in 1964. I estimate the stock of socialized rural housing at the beginning of 1959 as one-fifth of the socialized urban stock, or 100 million square meters of floor space; the corresponding estimate for private rural housing is 250 million square meters, three-quarters of the private urban stock. The urban population of 100 millions at the beginning of 1959 had at its disposal a housing stock of 832 million square meters. For 46.2 million rural dwellers outside of collective farms a stock of 350 million square meters means a per capita availability of 7.6 square meters, compared with the urban dweller's 8.3. (Population data are taken from TsSU, *Itogi vsesoiuznyi perepisi . . . , SSSR,* 1962, pp. 90–91.) The comparison seems reasonable.

Calculation of the stock figures for other years proceeds, on the basis described, as follows (million square meters of floor space):

	1958	*1959*	*1960*	*1961*	*1962*	*1963*	*1964*	*1965*
Socialized, urban and rural								
Stock on 1 January	557.2	600	649.3	700.6	752.3	806.8	863.1	916.0
New construction	46.7	53.5	55.8	56.6	59.8	61.9	58.9	
Withdrawals	3.9	4.2	4.5	4.9	5.3	5.6	6.0	
Private, urban and rural								
Stock on 1 January	561.4	582	605.1	627.9	647.1	663.3	676.1	687.6
New construction	24.5	27.2	27.0	23.6	20.7	17.4	16.2	
Withdrawals	3.9	4.1	4.2	4.4	4.5	4.6	4.7	

The distinction between private and socialized in these data is not completely clear owing to the uncertain classification of the stock of housing built by the so-called "housing construction cooperatives." Although these cooperatives are in fact engaged in private construction, the new housing erected by them is classed with socialized housing in the new construction statistics. Whether this is also true of the stock data is not known. Since the housing cooperatives were of little importance before 1964–1965—new construction levels were 70,000 square meters in 1958, 1.8 million in 1963, and 7.5 million planned for 1965 (*Ekon. gazeta,* January 15, 1962, p. 30; *Kommunist,* No. 6, April 1965, p. 44), I have not attempted to separate out the new housing volumes constructed by them from those built by the state-cooperative sector.

I am also constrained to guess at the stock of collective farm housing. After the census and revaluation of capital in existence on 1 January 1962, collective farms (agricultural and fishing artels alike) and inter-collective farm organizations were revealed to have 859 million rubles of housing, valued at replacement cost (*NKh 1961,* p. 421). New housing constructed by the state-cooperative sector is valued in the investment statistics at about 90 rubles per square meter (cf. value data on p. 515 with physical unit data on p. 605 of *NKh 1964*). At that unit value, the collective farm housing stock amounts to about 9.5 million square meters. Clearly, this represents only a small fraction of the total stock of housing on collective farms.

It may be noted in passing that the statistical yearbooks record no housing investment by collective farms before 1961. This may be seen as follows: The statistical yearbooks provide distributions of investment by branch of the economy, for all sectors and for the state-cooperative sector alone. The difference between branch values in the two distributions, of course, measures investment by collective farms and households. If we subtract all investment by collective farms (including fishing cooperatives) from the sum of investment by farms and households, the remainder should be private sector investment. The calculation is shown as follows (million rubles):

	1958	*1959*	*1960*	*1961*	*1962*	*1963*	*1964*
Collective farm and private sector investment [1]	5497	6579	5910	5524	5342	5204	5564
Less: collective farm investment [2]	2843	3526	3166	3155	3274	3416	3909
Equals: private sector investment	2654	3053	2744	2369	2068	1788	1655

[1] *NKh 1962*, pp. 434 and 435; *NKh 1964*, pp. 513 and 515.

[2] *NKh 1964*, p. 517. That this series includes investment by fishing cooperatives is shown by comparison with *Kapstroi*, p. 40.

The computed value of private sector investment is identical to the difference between investment by all sectors in housing and investment in housing by the state-cooperative sector alone, but only until 1961. In that year the computed value of private sector investment is smaller by 30 million rubles; it is smaller by 31 million rubles in 1962, 32 million rubles in 1963, and 50 millions in 1964. Evidently, this margin represents investment by collective farms in housing. Before 1961 this category of collective farm investment was either not counted or included with private sector investment.

At any rate, collective farm housing must be largely privately owned. If there are 7.6 square meters per capita in rural areas outside of collective farms, perhaps an appropriate assumption for collective farmers should be slightly lower, say 6.5. For 62.3 million collective farmers in rural areas at the beginning of 1959, this would mean a housing stock of about 400 million square meters.

With regard to new housing constructed on collective farms, the statistical yearbooks report only the number of dwellings built (in *NKh 1965,* p. 611, the number of apartments, too). For non-collective farm housing, private and socialized, the yearbooks indicate an average size of a little over 40 square meters per apartment (*NKh 1965,* p. 611). The average may be smaller on collective farms, say 30 square meters. (See Smirnov, in *Nekotorye ekonomicheskie problemy povysheniia effektivnosti proizvodstva,* 1966, p. 224; also Kats, *Proizvoditel'nost' truda v SSSR i glavnykh kapitalisticheskikh stranakh,* 1964, p. 55, note 1.) I follow *SNIP 1956–1958* (p. 56) in assuming that half the new construction is for replacement. Thus, collective farm housing in the years of concern may be estimated as follows (million square meters; I ignore here the effects of conversion of collective to state farms):

	1958	*1959*	*1960*	*1961*	*1962*	*1963*	*1964*	*1965*
Stock on 1 January	389.4	400	412.0	421.2	428.7	435.2	441.2	446.9
New construction [3]	21.2	24.1	18.5	15.0	13.0	12.1	11.5	
Withdrawals	10.6	12.1	9.3	7.5	6.5	6.1	5.8	

Academician Strumilin placed the stock of rural housing in 1959 (apparently, the beginning of the year) at 430 million square meters (*Oktiabr',* 1960, No. 3; translated in *Current Digest of the Soviet Press,*

[3] Number of dwellings (*NKh 1962*, p. 502; *NKh 1965*, p. 610) times average size of 30 square meters per dwelling.

May 11, 1960, p. 12). Since he relates this figure to a rural population of 107 millions, it is clear that Strumilin had in mind not just collective farm housing but all rural housing. My estimate for all rural housing is 750 million square meters (400 million collective farm, 100 million socialized and 250 private non-collective farm), or about 75 percent higher than Strumilin's figure. In private discussion with Western visitors, some Soviet economists have scoffed at Strumilin's estimate. Since it implies a per capita housing allowance of 3.5 square meters of living space (4 square meters of floor space) per person, about that available to the urban population of Communist China at about the same time (Chao, *The Journal of Asian Studies,* May 1966, p. 382), Strumilin's estimate appears to merit the skepticism expressed. Possibly he was referring to housing of collective farms only.

I now combine estimates to show *average* annual housing stocks in the private and state-cooperative sectors (housing owned by collective farms is implicitly part of the private sector's stock), as follows (million square meters):

	1958	*1959*	*1960*	*1961*	*1962*	*1963*	*1964*
State-cooperative sector	579	625	675	726	780	835	890
Private sector							
Collective farm	395	406	417	425	432	438	444
Other	572	594	617	638	655	670	682

These data relate to square meters of floor space whereas the unit rental is expressed per square meter of living space. According to Broner, *Sovremennye problemy zhilishchnogo khoziaistva,* 1961 (pp. 91, 99) and Kapustin, ed., *Obshchestvennye fondy i rost blagosostoianiia naroda v SSSR,* 1962 (p. 159), living space accounts for 70 percent of floor space in socialized housing. (Golt'sman, *Ekonomika kommunal'nogo khoziaistva uslugi, tarify,* 1966, p. 75, uses a much lower coefficient of 57 percent, but this seems unlikely; her discussion is also confused by an inconsistency between the coefficient and the results obtained with it.) It is assumed this applies to private noncollective farm housing as well. Again I follow *SNIP 1956–1958* (pp. 56–57) in assuming that living space accounts for 85 percent of floor space in collective farm housing. Thus, for all housing except that on collective farms, the rental rate applied is 1.05 rubles per square meter of floor space (70 percent of 1.5); the imputed rental rate for collective farm housing is 1.275 rubles per square meter of floor space (85 percent of 1.5).

I emphasize again that the estimates of the annual housing stock in physical units are obtained by the liberal use of assumptions and guesses. On the other hand, the absolute values of the estimated rent, paid or imputed, are relatively low, and significant error in these estimates is not likely to have much impact on the household income and outlay accounts as a whole.

B. *Trade union and other dues.* Derived as follows (billion rubles):

	1958	*1959*	*1960*	*1961*	*1962*	*1963*	*1964*
Trade unions	.48	.50	.55	.61	.65	.68	.73
Communist Party	.23	.24	.26	.29	.31	.34	.37
Other organizations	.20	.20	.21	.22	.23	.24	.25
Total	.91	.94	1.02	1.12	1.19	1.26	1.35

Trade union dues are estimated as increasing from the 1958 level of .48 billion rubles (*SNIP 1956–1958,* p. 57) in proportion to the increase in the worker and employee wage and salary bill (above, p. 295).

Communist Party dues are estimated as 1.5 percent of members' wages, assumed to be, on the average, double the average wage and salary of workers and employees (*SNIP 1956–1958,* p. 58). Hence, the average dues paid by a Communist Party member may be calculated as 3 percent of the average wage and salary of workers and employees, as follows (rubles):

	1958	*1959*	*1960*	*1961*	*1962*	*1963*	*1964*
Average wage of workers and employees	933.6	948.0	961.2	1000.8	1034.4	1051.2	1081.2
Dues paid per Communist Party member	28.01	28.44	28.84	30.02	31.03	31.54	32.44

The average annual number of party members is estimated from reported numbers of full and candidate members at the beginning of the year, as follows (thousands):

	1958	*1959*	*1960*	*1961*	*1962*	*1963*	*1964*	*1965*
Members on January 1	7,843	8,239	8,709	9,276	9,891	10,387	11,022	11,758
Average annual membership	8,041	8,474	8,993	9,584	10,139	10,705	11,390	

The source of the January membership data is *Partiinaia zhizn':* 1962, No. 1, p. 44, and 1965, No. 10, p. 8.

Dues paid to other organizations (Communist Youth League, DOSAAF, and so on) are arbitrarily estimated as growing from .20 billion rubles in 1958 to .25 billions in 1964.

C. *Other services.* Since information on these outlays has always been scarce, estimates are necessarily somewhat conjectural. Those derived in this study are based largely on pathbreaking distributions for 1958 and 1960 compiled by the staff of the Gosplan Economic Research Institute and set out by Agabab'ian in Maier and Krylov, eds., *Planirovanie narodnogo potreblenie v SSSR,* 1964, p. 104, and on a distribution taken to relate to 1962 by Sukharevskii, in *VE,* 1964, No. 10, pp. 3–4 and 7. Unfortunately, the Soviet authors provide almost no discussion of the methodology and coverage of their estimates. The necessity to infer the essentials from fragmentary evidence explains the length of the discussion below.

The Agabab'ian distribution, labeled "volume of services in values by branch" and "at current prices" is as follows (million rubles):

	1958	*1960*
Education	5,866	7,196
Health care	4,094	5,740
Housing (*zhilishchnoe khoziaistvo*)	2,400	2,901
Municipal services (*kommunal'nye uslugi*)	493	616
Art (*iskusstvo*)	1,014	1,047
Communications serving the population	600	900
Passenger transport	2,764	3,358
Other personal services	1,627	1,717
Cultural services by collective farms	108	130
Total	18,966	23,605

In the article cited, Sukharevskii presents a relative distribution of services by type and a value figure for the total of such services of "about" 35 billion rubles, but no indication of the year to which the data refer. However, in another article in *Izvestiia,* September 25, 1964, p. 5, Sukharevskii specifies 1962 as the year applicable to a total of "more than" 35 billion rubles. The relative distribution in the *VE* article may still refer to another year, as there are minor differences between the two articles in the stated breakdown by major groups. According to the *VE* article, 53.4 percent of the total represents services of a material nature (trade, housing and so forth); according to the *Izvestiia* article that proportion is "about" 56 percent. Possibly the *VE* distribution refers to 1963. However, it is not likely that significant error will be introduced by assuming it applicable to 1962 as well.

Translated from percentages to absolute values, Sukharevskii's distribution, designated as the volume of services provided by branches serving the population directly, is shown in column (3) below. In the journal article Sukharevskii also indicates the proportions of each type of service that are provided free or are charged for. These proportions, multiplied by the column (3) values, yield the values in columns (1) and (2).

	Billion Rubles		
	Free	*Paid*	*Total*
	(1)	(2)	(3)
1. Education	8.7	.5	9.2
2. Health care and physical culture	5.0	.3	5.3
3. Social assistance (*obespechenie*)	.2	—	.2
4. Radio and television	.2	—	.2
5. Places of entertainment	—	1.2	1.2
6. Upkeep of cultural and everyday service (*kul'turno-bytovye*) institutions by enterprise funds	.2	—	.2
Subtotal 1–6	14.3	2.0	16.3
7. Housing	2.8	.8	3.6
8. Municipal-everyday services (*kommunal'no-bytovoe obsluzhivanie*)	—	1.1	1.1
Subtotal 7–8	2.8	1.9	4.7
9. Trade and restaurants (trade surcharges)	—	8.2	8.2
10. Communications serving nonproductive branches	—	1.3	1.3
11. Passenger transport	—	4.5	4.5
Subtotal 9–11	—	14.0	14.0
Total	17.1	17.9	35.0

The indicated subtotals, which appear as percentages in Sukharevskii's article, are computed here for a specific reason. Sukharevskii's table showing the division of each type of service into free and paid shares also serves as a test of the hypothesis that his percentage breakdown of all services, free and paid, refers to 1962. If in fact all data refer to 1962, multiplication of subtotal values in column (3) by the shares of free and paid services of these groupings given by Sukharevskii's table should yield the same values as are shown in columns (1) and (2), now obtained as the sums of the indicated components. Such an outcome is obtained with the subtotal for 1–6 and for the grand total; it is not obtained with the subtotal for 7–8. The test is not applicable to the 9–11 subtotal. It is clear, however, that the incompatibility for the 7–8 subtotal is explained by an error in the underlying percentage data given by Sukharevskii:

	Percent of Grand Total of All Services, Free and Paid	*Percent of Each Type*	
		Free	*Paid*
7. Housing	10.3	79	21
8. Municipal-everyday services	3.0	—	100
Subtotal 7–8	13.3	50	50

If the figures for items 7 and 8 are correct, the subtotals for these items are wrong: the correct distribution of the subtotal of 13.3 percent would be in the ratio 61:39. The alternative hypothesis, that the division of housing services is in error (it is safe to assume that there are no free municipal services), is rejected for reasons explained later in the discussion.

Let us now compare the Agabab'ian and Sukharevskii distributions directly:

(1) Education and health care are categories in both distributions, except that physical culture is part of the identification in Sukharevskii's tables. It seems likely that in both distributions coverage is similar for education: the implied increases between 1958–1960 and 1960–1962 are roughly similar, and on the assumption that outlays on science, art, and some other minor subcategories are excluded from consideration, the levels and implied rates of growth of the reported values are not inconsistent with available data on state expenditures (see *NKh 1962*, pp. 637–638). Agabab'ian's data probably include outlays on broadcasting, separated out by Sukharevskii. The case of health care is less clear: Sukharevskii's 1962 figure is lower than Agabab'ian's 1960 figure (incorporation of the social assistance outlay for 1962 would not affect the comparison), whereas the 1958–1960 increase is a whopping 40 percent. Neither change seems consistent with available data on health care and physical culture outlays.

(2) According to official data (*NKh 1962*, p. 381), passenger traffic on all forms of common carrier transport, measured in passenger-kilometers, rose 17 percent in 1959–1960 and 19 percent in 1961–1962. The implied increases of the values in the two distributions are 21 and

32 percent. Possibly, structural changes in passenger transportation account for the differences between the two sets of growth rates. The values in the two distributions for communications serving the population (nonproductive branches according to Sukharevskii) are difficult to reconcile with the official value series for output of all communications (*NKh 1962,* p. 422). The ratio of the Agabab'ian-Sukharevskii to the official values is .51 in 1958, .67 in 1960, and .81 in 1962. If the two series are consistent, these ratios imply abandonment of the Central Statistical Administration rule-of-thumb, assigning two-thirds of communications output to the nonproductive sphere (Riabushkin, in *Voprosy ekonomicheskoi statistiki,* 1958, pp. 52, 55). However, if communication services to nonhouseholds were subtracted from Sukharevskii's figure, which presumably includes such a component, the resulting value would look more reasonable, relative to both the Agabab'ian 1960 figure and the official series. Agabab'ian's figures in any case would seem to be rough estimates, judging from the rounding off of these numbers relative to that of other figures in his table.

(3) In the two distributions the implied increases in outlays on housing are 21 percent between 1958 and 1960 and 24 percent in the second period. Since the socialized housing stock rose by 17 and 16 percent in the two periods, and the private stock by even smaller margins (above, p. 339), increases in outlay per unit of housing space are implied, which in 1961–1962 are of a substantial nature. According to Agabab'ian, "housing" includes depreciation of socialized housing along with other current material and wage outlays. Did Sukharevskii use a higher depreciation rate, in line with the general revision of depreciation rates introduced into the economy in 1963?

More likely, the differences have something to do with the two categories of municipal services—utilities, and the so-called "everyday services" (*bytovoe obsluzhivanie*). The coverage of the latter term is rarely specified, but it appears to include baths, laundries, barber and beauty shops, repair shops, cleaning and dyeing establishments, tailor and seamstress workshops, ticket agencies, and the like. It apparently does not include entertainment, communication, and transportation.

In the Agabab'ian table we find a category called *kommunal'nye uslugi;* Sukharevskii's table refers to *kommunal'no-bytovoe obsluzhivanie.* Considering these two categories as one, we find that Sukharevskii's 1962 figure is 83 percent larger than Agabab'ian's 1960 figure, whereas the increase in the previous two years was 25 percent. Smirnitskii's *Russian-English Dictionary,* 3rd ed., defines *kommunal'nye uslugi* as "public utilities." The term is employed in the same sense by a number of Soviet writers (for example, Oldak, *Ekonomicheskie problemy povysheniia urovnia zhizni,* 1963, p. 15). Moreover, Agabab'ian declares that

> . . . the volume of outlays of the sphere of personal services (*lichnye uslugi*) excludes expenditures of workshops for sewing and repair of clothing and footwear, everyday-service combines (the portion representing industrial activity), cleaning and dyeing shops, workshops for repair of cultural and household goods (*predmety kul'turno-bytovogo nazacheniia*), and so forth. Although many of these institutions are administered by municipalities or by the recently formed administrations for everyday service of the population, they belong to the productive sphere by the nature of their activity, since here labor is materialized in corresponding means of consumption.

There is, therefore, a strong presumption that Agabab'ian's *kommunal'nye uslugi* includes only utilities. The rest of "everyday" services (those not excluded in his table) may possibly be found in the category of "other personal services."

Sukharevskii indicates that in 1964 outlays on "everyday" services of an industrial nature—and as examples he cites to-order production of clothing and footwear, and repair of household articles—were planned to be slightly over 1 billion rubles, or twice as large as expenditures on "everyday" services of a nonindustrial nature—examples of which are baths, laundries, and barbershops (p. 9). Hence, his valuation of communal-everyday services, inferred to be 1.1 billion rubles in 1962, would appear to encompass both industrial and nonindustrial everyday services. This figure is too low. An article by Bobrovnikov of Gosplan in *Nedelia* (28 June—4 July 1964, p. 2) implies a 1962 level of expenditure on all everyday services of 1.3 billion rubles.

[This figure was obtained as follows: Bobrovnikov declares that per capita output of services in 1963 was 6.29 rubles. Given an average annual population level of 224.7 million (*NKh 1964,* p. 7) aggregate output in 1963 was 1.413 billion rubles. Bobrovnikov also indicates that aggregate output of everyday services was to be 3.610 billion rubles in 1964–1965, which was 33.2 percent larger than in 1962–1963. The implied 1962–1963 cumulated total is therefore 2.710 billion rubles, and subtracting 1.413 billions yields a 1962 level of 1.297 billion rubles.]

But where are outlays on utilities in Sukharevskii's distribution? If by municipal-everyday services he means all industrial and nonindustrial everyday services, outlays on utilities must be included with those on housing. This implies that the distribution of housing outlays in 1962 between paid and free services is incorrect: the paid component seems to be large enough to cover only rental payments on socialized housing (see above p. 335). Suppose outlays on utilities rose to .7 billion rubles in 1962, or roughly 15–20 percent over Agabab'ian's 1960 level (whose series implies a 25 percent increase between 1958 and 1960). Given rent payments of .82 billion rubles, paid outlays on housing including utilities in 1962 would amount to 1.5 billion rubles; uncompensated state outlays would be 2.1 billion rubles. If "municipal-everyday services" remain unchanged, the division between free and paid services would be in the ratio 58:42 for housing, 45:55 for the subtotal of items 7–8 (housing and "municipal-everyday services") and 47:53 for the grand total of Sukharevskii's table.

This hypothesis, therefore, carries the awkward implication that there are three errors in Sukharevskii's data on the proportions of free and paid services. To avoid this embarrassment, we must have recourse to an alternative hypothesis. Suppose there is no error in Sukharevskii's breakdown of housing outlays. Hence, the amount of paid outlays is too small to include utilities payments (in addition to rent on socialized housing), and they are either excluded altogether from his table or included in municipal-everyday services. If the latter is the case, roughly .4 billion rubles of the total of 1.1 billions for municipal-everyday services consists of expenditures other than on utilities, presumably the nonindustrial everyday services. Thus, the implication of the alternative hypothesis is that Sukharevskii excluded outlays on either utilities or industrial everyday services.

What would be the rationale for these exclusions? Exclusion of industrial everyday services would have had a precedent in Agabab'ian's procedure. His explanation, it will be recalled, was that industrial everyday services were in fact not services but productive activities yielding material values. But then this is also true of electricity, gas, and water supply, which are in fact classified as industrial output (Volodarskii, *Statistika promyshlennosti i voprosy planirovaniia,* 1958, pp. 269, 275). However, what Agabab'ian appears to be after is a measure of aggregate consumption of goods and services by the population, representing the sum of the "population's fund of consumption in the national income" and the volume of services (p. 105). Since the industrial everyday services are included in retail trade but outlays on utilities are not, it would seem reasonable for him to omit the first component but not the second.

Sukharevskii's procedure may be the same but for slightly different reasons. Among the services he includes trade and catering, but enters only the trade margin. Since the industrial everyday services are included with retail trade, avoidance of double counting would require their omission from the municipal service category. Judging from the reported values of costs and profits in trade (*Sovtorg II*, pp. 147, 154) the derived value for the 1962 trade margin is global in scope.

Agabab'ian's estimates of payments for utilities, if such they are, appear to be on the low side. Thus, CIA has estimated outlays on utilities in 1955 as .64 billion rubles (*A Comparison of Consumption in the USSR and the US*, January 1964, p. 13), or 30 percent more than Agabab'ian's figure for 1958. His estimates are 20 and 13 percent less than my estimates of money rent on socialized housing. It is possible that the ratio of utility to rent payments should be larger: According to Broner (*Sovremennye problemy zhilishchnogo khoziaistva*, 1961, p. 208), at a recent but unspecified date household outlays on utilities per unit of living space were 230 percent of the unit rental charge in the RSFSR. However, it is not clear whether the comparison embraces all non*kolkhoz* housing, only socialized housing, or even just socialized housing appropriately equipped. Data for 1964, to be introduced shortly, also indicate that Agabab'ian's utilities estimates are too low. Nevertheless, it remains the only reasonable explanation of the differences between his data and those of Sukharevskii that the former's figures for *kommunal'nye uslugi* are outlays on utilities.

(4) It seems highly unlikely that by "art" Agabab'ian means only admission to museums, many of which make no charge, and the purchase of art objects. If his figures do include movie and theater attendance, the two-year growth seems very small relative to official data on attendance (*NKh 1962*, pp. 601–602). On the other hand, the fact that proceeds from the amusements tax barely increased between 1958 and 1960 (Table C-1, sources for item 1.G(1)) may be evidence in support of Agabab'ian's figures. The Sukharevskii entertainment figure for 1962 is (excluding radio and television) 20 percent larger than Agabab'ian's 1960 figure, whereas in that period theater and movie attendance rose by only 9 percent, and proceeds from the amusements tax by only 5 percent. Again, for lack of other data, we must accept these despite the misgivings they arouse.

It is assumed that outlays on radio and television, separated out by Sukharevskii, are included with education by Agabab'ian. That is at any rate the budget category from which radio and television outlays would be financed.

(5) Apart from nonindustrial everyday services—say, roughly .3 billion rubles around 1960—what is the content of Agabab'ian's "other personal services"? The label is misleading, for "personal services" is

used at several points as a description of all the items in his table. Evidently, this is merely Agabab'ian's catchall category. No counterpart exists in the Sukharevskii distribution, it will be noticed, and possibly this provides a clue to the nature of these miscellaneous outlays.

Among household outlays on services not yet identified are payments to nursery schools and kindergartens for child care, to Pioneer camps, sanitoriums, rest homes, and other recreational facilities (such as alpine camps). Upper limits on charges to parents for nursery schools and kindergartens may be established from official data showing expenditures on these institutions financed both from payments by parents and from other nonbudget funds (*Gosbiudzhet I,* pp. 87, 92; *Gosbiudzhet II,* pp. 89, 94). These outlays were as follows (million rubles):

	1958	*1959*	*1960*	*1961*	*1962*	*1963*	*1964*
Kindergartens	173	197	269	280	335	390	487
Nursery schools	64	74	94	88	94	95	106

State budget outlays on kindergartens are financed from the appropriation to "education," those on nurseries from the appropriation to "health care." I have inferred from Sukharevskii's data payments by households for educational services of .5 billion rubles and for health care services, .3 billion rubles. It seems a fair inference that these include household payments for, respectively, kindergartens and nursery schools (budget outlays on nursery schools are classified under "health care"). Presumably, the remainder of Sukharevskii's .5 billion rubles of outlays for education covers household payments for children's meals in expanded-day schools and for general maintenance of children in boarding schools (Aleksandrov, *Gosudarstvennyi biudzhet SSR,* 1961, pp. 358–361). As for Pioneer camps, sanitoriums, rest homes, and other recreational facilities, outlays on these services are possibly to be found under the rubrics of health or entertainment or both in Sukharevskii's distribution.

Hence, it is conceivable that Agabab'ian's "other personal services" includes household payments for state educational, health, and recreational services, which Sukharevskii classified directly under these headings. However, the absence in Sukharevskii's distribution of a counterpart could also be explained by his exclusion and Agabab'ian's inclusion of private sector services (private medical, dental, domestic, and artisan services) under the heading "other personal services." Possibly, both explanations would apply. Although Agabab'ian's discussion of his estimates seems to imply a concern with intersectoral transactions alone, the numbers suggest that private sector services are included: Deduct nonindustrial everyday services of, say, .2 billion rubles in 1958 and .3 billion in 1960 from Agabab'ian's "other personal services" and add to the remainders his estimates of outlays on "art." The resulting figures for 1958 and 1960 may be compared with the sum of paid outlays on education, health care and physical culture, and entertainment, derived from the Sukharevskii data for 1962:

Year	*Billion Rubles*
1958	2.4
1960	2.4
1962	2.0

The derived pattern seems quite improbable. Even if Agabab'ian classified outlays on kindergartens, nurseries, and so forth with "other personal services," and on the assumption that Sukharevskii did not omit them, something else is contained in the mysterious box labeled "other personal services." Since it seems difficult to think of any significant public sector services omitted from consideration, it is assumed that Agabab'ian did include private sector services.

If "entertainment" in the Sukharevskii distribution omits no recreational activities not included with health care, it seems unlikely that "art" in Agabab'ian's table is substantially understated: the latter's 1960 figure is, allowing for rounding, possibly no more than 10 percent below the 1962 figure. It is, therefore, assumed that the figures for "art" and "entertainment" are a mutually consistent series representing outlays on recreation.

A preliminary estimate of the value of "other services" in all years may now be set out as follows (billion rubles):

	1958	*1959*	*1960*	*1961*	*1962*	*1963*	*1964*
Education, health, and physical culture	.66	.69	.73	.76	.80	.84	.88
Entertainment and culture	1.01	1.03	1.05	1.12	1.20	1.25	1.30
Transportation	2.21	2.45	2.69	3.14	3.60	3.89	4.20
Communication	.60	.75	.90	1.00	1.10	1.18	1.27
Utilities	.49	.55	.62	.70	.78	.88	.99
Other public sector services for consumption	.84	.93	1.04	1.16	1.30	1.41	1.62
Private sector services	.75	.77	.78	.80	.81	.83	.84
Total	6.56	7.17	7.81	8.68	9.59	10.28	11.10

The 1962 figure for household outlays on education, health, and physical culture is that derived from the Sukharevskii data. It is estimated for other years on the arbitrary assumption of a 5 percent rate of growth in these outlays. Entertainment and culture outlays in 1958, 1960, and 1962 are the Agabab'ian-Sukharevskii values, with 1959 and 1961 entries obtained by interpolation. Figures for 1963 and 1964 are computed on the assumption of a 4.4 percent annual growth rate, the average rate in 1958–1962.

The Agabab'ian-Sukharevskii figures on passenger transport probably include business travel expenses, whereas most of the corresponding business communication expenditures are probably excluded from their figures. At least this seems a reasonable inference from Soviet national income practice which, in pursuit of the distinction between productive and nonproductive activity, separates freight transportation and communication services for production from passenger transportation and communication services for households (*NKh 1962,* p. 664; Sobol', *Ocherki po voprosam balansa narodnogo khoziaistva,* 1960, pp. 150–151). Thus, the Agabab'ian values of communication services can be accepted without change; both his and Sukharevskii's figures for passenger transportation need adjustment. Since Sukharevskii explicitly indicates inclusion of communication services to nonproductive branches of the economy as well as presumably to households, some adjustment of his figure is also necessary.

Travel allowances in 1960 came to over 1.2 billion rubles (*Ekon. gazeta,* April 6, 1961, p. 3), of which, arbitrarily, half is assumed to represent transportation costs. Agabab'ian's figure for the value of passenger transport services in 1960, 3358 million rubles, is therefore reduced to 2.8 billion rubles, or 82 percent of the original figure. My estimates of passenger transportation services to households in 1958, 1960, and 1962 are obtained by taking 80 percent of the original Agabab'ian-Sukharevskii figures. The 1959 and 1961 entries for transportation are obtained by simple interpolation.

These estimates imply an annual rate of growth between 1958 and 1962 of 13.0 percent, whereas the rate of growth of all passenger transportation turnover in physical units was lower, 11.8 percent (*NKh 1964,* p. 433). In the two years 1963–1964, the turnover series shows a growth of 6.8 percent per year. I therefore estimate outlays on transportation as having grown at 8 percent per year.

As indicated earlier (p. 344), Sukharevskii's figure for communications is 81 percent of the official figure for total output of communications in 1962; the corresponding ratios using Agabab'ian's estimates are

.51 in 1958 and .67 in 1960. It is assumed that the appropriate ratio for 1962 is .7. The 1959 and 1961 entries are then obtained by interpolation. Figures for 1963 and 1964 are 70 percent of the reported output of communications (*NKh 1964*, p. 500).

Entries for utilities in 1958 and 1960 are Agabab'ian's values of municipal services. The 1959 figure is obtained by interpolation and the 1961–1964 figures on the assumption of an unchanged rate of growth, 12.5 percent. Official data show household outlays on electric power, heat energy, and "products of the gas industry" at current prices rising at a rate of 11 percent per year between 1959 and 1963 (*NKh 1964*, pp. 580–581).

By "other public sector services for consumption" are meant the "everyday services," industrial as well as nonindustrial. For this category I use the Bobrovnikov estimates for 1962 and 1963 previously cited. The 1959 figure is implied in an article by Roze (in Bunich, ed., *Ekonomicheskaia rabota v finansovo-kreditnoi sisteme*, 1965, p. 305), who declares that the 1963 level of over 1.4 billion rubles was 52 percent greater than in 1959. Entries for 1960–1961 are interpolated between those of 1959 and 1962. Figures for 1958 and 1964 assume annual changes in proportion to increases in, respectively, artisan receipts (the industrial component) at current prices (*Sovtorg II*, p. 54) and the volume of the industrial component at 1955 prices (*NKh 1964*, p. 594). Possibly, the estimates overstate the value of services performed for households: the figures may include services to institutions (*Izvestiia*, September 4, 1964, p. 3) and materials supplied by artisans (see above, p. 333).

The values of private sector services in 1958 and 1960 are initially estimated as Agabab'ian's "other personal services," less nonindustrial everyday services and indicated outlays on education, health, and physical culture. The resulting figures are .77 billion rubles in 1958 and .69 billion in 1960. It is arbitrarily assumed that the 1958 value was .75 billion rubles and that outlays increased at 2 percent per year.

These figures may be too low. A Soviet source (Sarkisian, *VE*, 1966, No. 6, p. 80) discloses that whereas one-quarter of the urban population's outlays (in 1964?) on clothing and footwear made to order (including repair) were with individual artisans, the proportion for the rural population was two-thirds. Assuming that for the country as a whole, the private sector's share was at least 30 percent and no more than 40 percent, and given receipts by state sector enterprises in 1963 from such sales of 881 million rubles (*Sovtorg II*, pp. 54, 486, including materials supplied by the enterprise), private sector receipts could have been about .4–.6 billion rubles. (It is clear that the upper limit on the private sector share nationally must be near 40 percent, because above that point the proportion of total national receipts, private and state, accounted for by urban sales recedes below 60 percent. From all the evidence the urban ratio is significantly greater than half: in 1964 the urban share of the state sector value of industrial services was 83 percent, according to *NKh 1964,* p. 595.) Allowance for services of private professionals, builders, domestic servants, and artisans other than those discussed above, should raise these figures by a relatively substantial amount.

A recent discussion of the balance of household money incomes and outlays by Borisov (*Balans denezhnykh dokhodov i raskhodov naseleniia,* 1965, p. 69) discloses the percent distribution of outlays on services in 1964. Translated into percentage terms, my 1964 estimates may be compared with Borisov's information as follows:

Borisov			*Becker*	
	Percent of Total	*Percent of Total Excluding "Other"*		*Percent of Total*
Rent and utilities	24.9	25.5	Rent and utilities	19.5
Everyday services	4.6	4.7	Everyday services	3.0
Children's institutions	6.7	6.9	Education, health and physical culture	8.9
Sanitoria and rest homes	2.4	2.5		
Movies, theaters and other entertainment	10.8	11.0	Entertainment	13.2
Transportation	41.9	42.8	Transportation	42.6
Communication	6.5	6.6	Communication	12.9
Other	2.2			
	100.0	100.0		100.0

For the purposes of the comparison I have added my estimate of paid rent (p. 335) to that of utilities and omitted the estimate of private sector services; Borisov is clearly dealing only with relations between households and the public sector. Following Borisov I have also omitted the industrial everyday services included in retail trade (p. 332). There is as yet no counterpart for Borisov's "other" component, which is said (p. 73) to consist "chiefly of payments for production services in connection with the processing of agricultural products in state and cooperative enterprises." Also included are payments to collective farms for repair and erection of buildings, for the use of collective farm transport, tuition fees in self-financing courses (i.e., stenography, foreign languages), and lawyer's fees.

With two exceptions, my distribution closely parallels Borisov's. The exceptions are the first and last items, rent and utilities, and communications. Borisov's allowance for rent and utilities exceeds mine by 6 percentage points, but his communications entry is smaller than mine by about the same margin. Part of the first-named gap can be explained by Borisov's inclusion in rent and utilities of expenditures on hotels and inns (p. 70), which in my distribution might be included with entertainment. Nevertheless, it is likely that my estimates understate utilities. As for communication, I have evidently failed to deduct a sufficiently large allowance for communication services to nonproductive users other than households.

These comments reflect comparison of absolute as well as relative levels. Justification may be found in another piece of information supplied by Borisov, that outlays on the services he identified represent about a tenth of all money income of households. Net of intrahousehold sector exchanges, household money outlays in 1964 implied by my estimates adds up to 117.34 billion rubles. (This is the sum of 92.60 billion rubles of retail sales, .93 billion rubles of paid rent, 1.35 billions of dues, 10.26 billions other services (p. 349), 2.00 billions other outlays for consumption (pp. 357–358), .92 billions cash outlays on private housing construction (p. 361), and 9.28 billions transfer payments (pp. 379–382). My tentative estimate of "other services," net of intrahousehold services but gross of money rent, at 11.19 billion rubles represents 9.5 percent of the indicated money income total. The addition of Borisov's miscellaneous component would raise the ratio slightly.

On this basis it seems reasonable to tailor my 1964 estimates to Borisov's form, with the following adjustments:

(1) Total outlays, excluding private sector services and, for the moment, Borisov's miscellaneous component, are calculated dividing my estimate of transportation outlays by their share in Borisov's distribution. The figure resulting is 9.81 billion rubles.

(2) Education, health, and physical culture outlays as well as those on communication are obtained as the products of the shares in Borisov's distribution (for, in the former case, children's institutions, sanitoriums and rest homes, and in the latter case, communication) and the indicated total.

(3) Computed in the same way, rent and utilities amount to 2.50 billion rubles compared to the original figure of 1.92 billions; the new and old figures for entertainment are, respectively, 1.08 and 1.30 billion rubles. I retain the original entertainment estimate and, on the assumption that the difference between old and new figures relates to hotel and inn outlays, deduct that margin from the new rent and utilities figure to get a final estimate for that category of 2.28 billions. Original estimates for utilities in 1958–1963 are raised by 40 percent, or roughly the margin between the new 1964 utilities figure and the original estimate.

(4) I retain my original estimate for everyday services, industrial as well as nonindustrial. The latter component, recomputed in the manner described in (2) and (3) above, would amount to .46 billion rubles, implying an industrial component of 1.16 billions, compared with the inferred figure of 1.32 billions for artisan receipts (p. 332). As indicated, the value of the artisans' receipts includes some materials supplied by them. It is not known whether the indicated difference of .16 billion rubles is an accurate estimate of the value of materials supplied.

(5) Figures for 1963, obtained by interpolation, are adjusted accordingly.

(6) Figures for communications in all years are reduced: the computed 1964 figure is 36 percent of the official value of communications output in 1964 (*NKh 1964*, p. 500), and I arbitrarily assume the same relation in all years.

(7) Borisov's "other" component, which should amount to about .2 billion rubles, is ignored because probably only an insignificant part consists of services for consumption.

Thus, my final estimates of "other services" are as follows (billion rubles):

	1958	*1959*	*1960*	*1961*	*1962*	*1963*	*1964*
Education, health and physical culture	.66	.69	.73	.76	.80	.85	.92
Entertainment and culture	1.01	1.03	1.05	1.12	1.20	1.25	1.30
Transportation	2.21	2.45	2.69	3.14	3.60	3.89	4.20
Communication	.42	.45	.49	.52	.56	.60	.65
Utilities	.69	.77	.87	.98	1.09	1.23	1.35
Other public sector services for consumption	.84	.93	1.04	1.16	1.30	1.41	1.62
Private sector services	.75	.77	.78	.80	.81	.83	.84
Total	6.58	7.09	7.65	8.48	9.36	10.06	10.88

A rough check on the accuracy of my 1960 estimate is provided by a gross breakdown of the consumers' budget in 1960 (Belik, *PKh,* 1962, No. 1, pp. 10–11, and Maier, *Zarabotnaia plata v period perekhoda k kommunizmu,* 1963, pp. 105–106). According to these sources, services accounted for 9 percent of household outlays on goods and services in that year (transfer payments and organization dues are apparently excluded). By my estimate, "other services" plus paid rent are 8.8 percent of household outlays for consumption in 1960, excluding imputed rent and dues but including consumption of income in kind. With investment included in the denominator, the calculated relation drops to 8.5 percent. If I add outlays on hired building services to the numerator and omit owner-supplied building labor from the denominator (p. 361), the relation is increased to 9.2 percent.

After the accounts at established prices were completed and at a point too late to incorporate any revisions, a new book on Soviet services became available: Turetskii, ed., *Razvitie uslug i printsipy tsenoobrazovaniia na bytovye uslugi,* 1966. On the whole, what little quantitative information is provided in this collection of symposium papers does not seem to be clearly at variance with the estimates set out above. The relevant new information is as follows (page references are to the Turetskii volume cited):

(1) A distribution of the volume of services in 1964 financed by both state budget and household outlays is estimated by Turetskii (p. 14):

	Billion rubles
1. Retail trade	6.4
2. Public catering	1.7
3. Passenger transport (including municipal) and communications serving the population	5.9
4. Education, health care, and other social-cultural outlays, from state budget and other sources (excluding outlays on science and outlays on investment and capital repair)	18.7
Of which: entertainment	1.2
resort passes (*oplata putevok*) and payments to children's institutions	1.0

	Billion rubles
5. Housing-municipal and everyday services (excluding municipal transport)	4.3
Of which: utilities	1.3
repair of articles and custom production of clothing	1.0
6. State outlays on housing maintenance, not covered by rent	2.1
Total	39.1

Turetskii's transport-communications figure is one billion rubles higher than mine. His figures for the two components under item 4 are close to my estimates for education, health care, entertainment, and culture. The utilities figure virtually coincides with mine and that for repair and custom production is consistent with my estimate of other public sector services for consumption. As Turetskii provides no backup detail, it is difficult to evaluate his estimates further.

(2) S. G. Stoliarov reports (p. 49) that the volume of industrial "everyday" services rose 21 percent in the single year 1965 to a level of 1292 million rubles at 1955 wholesale prices. The corresponding figures for non-industrial services were 23 percent and 702.5 million rubles at current wholesale prices. Stoliarov's industrial figures conflict slightly with those given in *NKh 1965,* p. 598: 1102 million rubles for 1964 and 1330 millions for 1965. The data seem consistent with my 1964 estimate of other public services for consumption.

(3) According to Kosiachenko (p. 73), "the volume of services of an industrial type performed by everyday service enterprises increased 75 percent from (*s*) 1959 through (*po*) 1964." This statement probably refers to the increment in the series reported in the statistical yearbooks, specifically *NKh 1964,* p. 594. The 1964 figure in that series was revised upward in *NKh 1965,* p. 598.

(4) Azar (p. 169) cites data on per capita outlays on transportation which can be translated into aggregate expenditures using official population statistics (*NKh 1965,* p. 7). The results are as follows (billion rubles): 1960, 2.4; 1963, 3.4; 1964–1965, 4–5. The title of Azar's paper refers to interurban transportation, but his 1964–1965 per capita estimate is labeled "expenditures on the services of all forms of social transportation." The numbers derived from Azar's per capita data for 1960 and 1963 are 12–13 percent smaller than my estimates. As noted

earlier, Turetskii's 1964 figure for transportation-communication, at 5.9 billion rubles, is one billion rubles higher than my estimate; the transportation component of Turetskii's figure may also be higher than Azar's figure for 1964–1965. Azar, too, provides no further explanation of his estimates, and it is therefore impossible to determine the reasons for the divergences.

3. *Consumption of income in kind.*

A. *Net farm income in kind.* Appendix A, sources for item 2.C.

B. *Nonfarm wages in kind.* Appendix A, item 1.C.

C. *Military subsistence.* Appendix A, item 3.B.

4. *Other outlays for consumption.*

This category covers mainly sales in the intravillage farm market—transactions among collective farms and farmers, sales by state farms to their employees, and the like. Data cited by Eidel'man (*Mezhotraslevoi balans obshchestvennogo produkta,* 1966, pp. 160–161) suggest a minimum value for intravillage market sales in 1959 of 1.3 billion rubles. Also included here are purchases of goods from individual artisans and possibly, too, subsistence of the internal security forces. Presumably, the value of individual artisan services appears in entries under item 2.C above, "other services," although as suggested in the discussion there, contributions from the private sector may be understated. For the years 1959–1963 the values entered for "other outlays for consumption" represent the difference between "total consumption," item 5, and the sum of items 1.C., 2.D., and 3.D. Thus, this category also includes errors in the component consumption estimates. Figures for 1958 and 1964 are derived by reconciliation of my consumption estimates with the official aggregates allowing for depreciation on housing and an adjusted valuation of farm income in kind. On the latter see immediately below. See also Table 25.

5. *Total outlays for consumption.*

1958 and 1964: the sum of items 1.C., 2.D., 3.D and 4.

1959–1963: *NKh 1964,* pp. 580–585, provides relatively detailed data by major product aggregates for 1959–1963 on value of (1) consumption by households and (2) "material outlays in institutions servicing the population, in scientific institutions, and administration." Thus, the data represent a product breakdown of the official estimates of consumption as an end-use of net material product, except that science and administration are aggregated with "institutions servicing the population." By source of consumption, the household outlays cover sales in state-cooperative retail trade, extravillage and intravillage farm markets, income in kind, outlays on utilities and on "industrial" services (see above, p. 345) provided by non-coop artisans, subsistence for "persons on government support" (*lits sostoiashchikh na gosudarstvennom obespechenii*), and depreciation of housing; retail sales to institutions, household purchases of nonconsumption goods and of secondhand goods are, of course, excluded (Eidel'man, *Mezhotraslevoi balans obshchestvennogo produkta,* 1966, pp. 157–158).

The Soviet data (throughout the following discussion I consider the Soviet consumption totals net of depreciation) differ in scope from my estimates of household outlays on consumption in the following ways:

(1) The Soviet data exclude the values of certain services—rent (paid and imputed), trade union and other dues, and most of "other services;"

(2) The Soviet data exclude household purchases of producer goods, except construction materials for current repair, according to Eidel'man (*ibid.,* p. 158). He is not clear on whether the values of income in kind are estimated gross or net of the money expenses of producing private sector output. However, another reliable source (Petrov, *Kurs ekonomicheskoi statistiki,* 1961, p. 399) states unequivocally that production expenses are netted out;

(3) Income in kind in the Soviet series is probably valued at average prices realized in sales by collective farms and households (Eidel'man, *Mezhotraslevoi balans obshchestvennogo produkta,* 1966, p. 135) rather than at average prices realized in all transactions, including state sector delivery prices, as is my procedure. Since delivery prices tended to be below purchase prices and were certainly below market prices, my estimates of income in kind should be lower than those included in the reported consumption data. A recalculation of consumption of farm income in kind in 1959 at average prices realized in just sales of collective farms and households raises the aggregate value for the seven products considered by 400 million rubles.

I use the reported data on consumption to establish a series for "total outlays for consumption," as follows (billion rubles):

	1959	*1960*	*1961*	*1962*	*1963*
Reported Soviet total household outlays on consumption, excluding depreciation on housing	85.18	90.96	93.54	101.58	106.58
Less: adjustment for valuation of farm income in kind	.40	.50	.51	.53	.46

Add: services omitted in Soviet data					
Rent, paid and imputed	1.80	1.89	1.97	2.06	2.14
Trade union and other dues	.94	1.02	1.12	1.19	1.26
All "other services," excluding utilities and "industrial everyday" services	5.72	6.08	6.70	7.37	7.83
Equals: total outlays for consumption	93.24	99.45	102.82	111.67	117.35

The adjustment for valuation of income in kind, as indicated, represents the difference between valuation at average prices realized in all transactions and valuation at average prices realized by collective farms and households (Table A-2). Delivery prices and quantities for fruits and berries are aggregated with purchase equivalents in Table A-2. To disaggregate them for present purposes, it is assumed that purchase prices are 95 percent of the combined purchase and delivery price; the corresponding proportion for quantities sold is assumed to be 70 percent. These proportions are based on data for 1961–1962 cited in Badir'ian, ed., *Ekonomika, organizatsiia . . .* , 1963, pp. 274, 282, 287; and Bolgov *et al., Ekonomika sotsialisticheskogo . . .* , 1965, p. 450.

Calculation of the part of "other services" added to the reported official totals proceeds as follows. Household outlays on utilities and "industrial everyday" services need not be added because as productive services they are included in the Soviet data. From various indications appearing in the discussion of "other services" (pp. 344–354), the "nonindustrial" component of "everyday" services was estimated as .3 billion rubles in 1960, .4 billion in 1962 and .5 billion in 1964. Estimates for other years are interpolated, and the "industrial" component is then obtained by subtraction from the series "other public sector services for consumption." The calculation is as follows (billion rubles):

	1959	*1960*	*1961*	*1962*	*1963*
Total "other services"	7.09	7.65	8.48	9.36	10.06
Less: utilities	.77	.87	.98	1.09	1.23
Less: "industrial everyday" services	.60	.70	.80	.90	1.00
	5.72	6.08	6.70	7.37	7.83

For lack of information no adjustment is attempted for outlays on construction materials included in the Soviet consumption data.

6. *Investment.*

A. *Private housing construction.* Obtained as follows (million rubles):

	1958	*1959*	*1960*	*1961*	*1962*	*1963*	*1964*
Total investment, all sectors	30,012	33,986	36,705	38,271	40,150	42,214	45,938
Less: total investment, state-cooperative sector	24,515	27,407	30,795	32,747	34,808	37,010	40,374
Less: collective farm investment	2,843	3,526	3,166	3,155	3,274	3,416	3,909
Equals: private sector investment	2,654	3,053	2,744	2,369	2,068	1,788	1,655

The sources are *NKh 1962*, pp. 434–435 and *NKh 1964*, pp. 513, 515, 517. That the computed residuals cover only private housing investment is clear from the correspondence of the 1958–1960 figures with explicit private housing investment values reported in *Kapstroi*, p. 188.

Presumably, investment here too is valued at estimate prices. The implied unit value of private housing construction, using construction volumes in physical units as estimated above (p. 339), is about two-thirds of the implied unit value of state-cooperative sector construction (above, p. 337). The direction of the inequality is clearly correct; whether this is also true of its magnitude is not so evident. If there is any upward bias in the official figures, with respect to the desired valuation for this account, it would tend to be offset by the omission from the official data of expenditures on the construction of private *dachi* and on repairs (*Kapstroi*, pp. 8, 188).

For purposes of estimating the value of labor investment in kind in construction of private housing (item 6 of Table 1), it is assumed that (1) materials account for one-third and labor two-thirds of the value of private housing construction, and (2) payment for hired building services accounts for one-third, and the value of unpaid labor supplied by prospective owners for two-thirds, of the labor component of private housing investment.

In terms of the accounting concepts employed in construction, the relation between outlays on materials and on "basic" wages is roughly 3:1 in costs of all construction-installation (*NKh 1962*, p. 447) and even more heavily in favor of materials in mass construction of state housing (Kuperman, *Oborotnye sredstva i proizvodstvennye zapasy stroitel'nykh organizatsii*, 1964, p. 30). However, the share of all expenditures on labor, no matter where classified, is closer to 40 percent of the total cost of construction-installation. Private housing construction is clearly labor-intensive, involving little presite fabrication and scarcely any machinery. It would seem a reasonable guess that the proportion of labor expenditure would be far higher here than in state construction generally.

The second assumption is based merely on evidence from Soviet sources that labor supplied by prospective owners themselves is the major source of building services.

The calculation is as follows (million rubles):

	1958	*1959*	*1960*	*1961*	*1962*	*1963*	*1964*
Value of private housing construction	2,654	3,053	2,744	2,369	2,068	1,788	1,655
Building materials	884	1,017	914	789	689	595	551
Labor	1,770	2,036	1,830	1,580	1,379	1,193	1,104
Hired	589	678	609	526	459	397	368
Owner-supplied	1,181	1,358	1,221	1,054	920	796	736

Under item 1.A of this appendix I estimated a series of household outlays on building materials purchased in the state-cooperative retail trade network. Figures in that series lie roughly between one-half and four-fifths of the figures for all private sector outlays on building materials developed here from the official investment data. The remainder presumably represents purchases from collective farms and state enterprises. This structure does not seem unreasonable. As for labor services, Nimitz estimated the value of hired building services provided by the private sector in 1958 as .34 billion rubles (*SNIP 1956–1958,* pp. 64–66), or almost 60 percent of the figure estimated here. The remainder presumably represents the value of services supplied by collective farms and enterprises. Again, this does not seem unreasonable.

B. *Farm investment in kind.* Appendix A, sources for item 2.C.

7. *Total outlays for consumption and investment.*

The sum of items 5 and 6.

8. *Transfer outlays.*

Appendix C, item 9.

9. *Total outlays.*

The sum of items 7 and 8.

C

Sources to Table 3: 1958-1964

1. *Net income retained by economic organizations.*

A. *Retained income of collective farms.* Obtained as follows (billion rubles):

	1958	*1959*	*1960*	*1961*	*1962*	*1963*	*1964*
Money income allocated to							
Investment fund	3.04	3.33	3.20	3.20	3.43	3.39	3.60
Less: Depreciation	.90	1.06	1.04	1.09	1.29	1.57	1.66
Working capital fund	.40	.33	.29	.37	.45	.49	.55
Cultural fund	.12	.25	.17	.17	.20	.21	.24
	2.66	2.85	2.62	2.65	2.79	2.52	2.73

As explained in Chapter 2, only money incomes and outlays of collective farms are reflected in these accounts. Incomes of fishing cooperatives are not included for lack of data.

Gross allocations to the various collective funds are estimates compiled by Nimitz (*Incomes of Collective Farmers*); for 1964 Nimitz supplies only the sum of allocations to the working capital, cultural, and pension fund. This total is here distributed among its components on the assumption that component increases over the 1963 level were the same as the overall increase. For 1958, the allocation to the cultural fund cited by Nimitz is .17 billion rubles but it includes an allocation to the pension fund as well. The latter is estimated here as .05 billion rubles, judging from values for later years supplied by Nimitz.

Collective farms do not make actual deductions from incomes for deposit in an earmarked amortization fund, as do *khozraschet* enterprises, but simply compute depreciation as an accounting category. Thus for collective farms retained income in fact includes depreciation. However, if depreciation as Soviet state enterprises calculate it is used as the distinction between gross and net national product—and this has been traditional in SNIP studies—then collective farm depreciation should be deducted here and added to item 7. For derivation of the depreciation figures, see item 7 below.

B. *Retained net profits of state enterprises.* Derived as follows (billion rubles):

	1958	*1959*	*1960*	*1961*	*1962*	*1963*	*1964*
Net profits	18.70	21.46	23.86	26.13	29.82	29.84	34.01
Less: deductions to budget	13.62	15.94	18.73	20.80	23.86	25.70	28.73
Less: payments to households	.50	.57	.55	.67	.64	.60	.82
Equals: retained net profits	4.58	4.95	4.58	4.66	5.32	3.54	4.66

Total net profits are from *NKh 1959,* p. 799, *NKh 1962,* p. 627, and *NKh 1964,* p. 747. The 1960 figure represents the official datum less an estimated .51 billion rubles of profits earned by the producer cooperatives before their incorporation into the state sector in October 1960. See Table C-1, sources for item 1.D(2).

Although these data include in principle some outlays unrelated to production, it seems doubtful that the actual distortion is very serious. See Appendix I.

Deductions to the budget are computed net of changes in the volume of deductions paid in the current year from the previous year's profits, as follows (billion rubles):

	1958	*1959*	*1960*	*1961*	*1962*	*1963*	*1964*
(1) Total deductions to the budget	13.54	15.96	18.63	20.74	23.86	25.70	28.73
(2) Deductions from previous year's profits	.17	.25	.23	.3+	.4	..	..
(3) Annual change in (2)	–.08	.02	–.10	–.1	0	0	0
(4) Row (1) less row (3)	13.62	15.94	18.73	20.8	23.86	25.70	28.73

Total deductions to the budget are from *Gosbiudzhet I,* p. 7 and *Gosbiudzhet II,* p. 10. Deductions from previous year's profits are planned figures, assumed to equal realized values, and are generally computed as the difference between total deductions and deductions from current profits (all planned). Sources are as follows: *Pravda,* December 20, 1957, p. 5, and Zverev, *PKh,* 1957, No. 12, p. 18 (1958); *Izvestiia,* October 28, 1959, p. 5, and Zverev, *PKh,* 1959, No. 1, p. 12 (1959); Garbuzov, *PKh,* 1959, No. 12, p. 6 (1960); Lavrov, *PKh,* 1962, No. 2, pp. 40, 42 (1962). For 1961 plan, Garbuzov's report (in *Izvestiia,* December 21, 1960, p. 4) that while all profits would reach 30.2 billion rubles and total deductions 20.5 billions, retained profits would exceed 10 billions, is taken to mean that deductions from the previous year's profits would exceed .3 billions. In the absence of data for 1963 and 1964, it is assumed no net change occurred in those years.

The estimates of payments to households are derived from data showing expenditures from, and end-year balances of, incentive funds maintained by state enterprises and organizations (*NKh 1962,* pp. 629–630; *NKh 1963,* pp. 648–649; *NKh 1964,* pp. 764–765). From these data we may compute the annual allocation to these funds. Expenditures from these funds are made for a variety of purposes, only some of which represent direct payments to households. The relevant categories and the computed allocations are as follows (million rubles):

	1959	*1960*	*1961*	*1962*	*1963*	*1964*
Allocation to						
Enterprise fund						
For individual premiums, improvement of services, rest home and sanitorium leaves, and extraordinary assistance to personnel	313	285	243	338	333	395
Consumer goods fund						
For premiums and services (*kul'turno-bytovye nuzhdy*)	20	10	12	12	4	16
Individual premiums from socialist competition awards	91	91	81	82	86	101
Premium fund for construction	19	14	13	14	54	92
For premiums earned for creation and introduction of new technology	49	65	138	49	77	134
Other funds	496	453	610	641	423	576
Total	988	918	1097	1136	977	1314

"Other funds" consist mainly of funds of agricultural enterprises for production purposes and premiums, and, up to 1960, of funds of the former industrial cooperatives. For discussion of sources and dispositions of the incentive funds, see *Ekon.gazeta,* August 15, 1964, pp. 21–26.

It is clear that in the above listing, part of the allocations to the enterprise funds, the consumer goods fund, and "other funds" represents transfer payments and payments not directly to households—in sum, something other than a factor payment. Since information is lacking for a further breakdown of the data, it is arbitrarily estimated that only half of the listed allocations to the enterprise fund, consumer goods fund, and "other funds" represents a factor payment. The figure for 1958 is an arbitrary estimate.

C. *Retained profits of nonfarm cooperatives.* Calculated as follows (billion rubles):

	1958	*1959*	*1960*	*1961*	*1962*	*1963*	*1964*
Net profits	1.41	1.51	1.33	.66	.78	.83	.88
Less: income tax	.46	.49	.44	.23	.27	.29	.31
payments to households	.05	.10	.04	.07	.09	.02	.02
Equals: retained profits	.90	.92	.85	.36	.42	.52	.55

For derivation of profits and income tax figures, see Table C-1, sources for item 1.D(2).

Allocations to all incentive funds by consumer cooperatives were as follows (million rubles):

1959	95	1962	128
1960	44	1963	31
1961	108	1964	35

Sources are *NKh 1962,* p. 628; *NKh 1963,* p. 648; *NKh 1964,* p. 764.

These figures require adjustment in both directions: allocations by producer cooperatives (until their transformation in 1960) are omitted while allocations for expenditures other than premiums are included. For 1959 and 1960 it is assumed that these are offsetting, and the reported totals for consumer cooperatives are used without adjustment. For 1961–1964, two-thirds of the reported figure is assumed to represent allocation for premiums. The 1958 figure is an arbitrary estimate.

D. *Retained profits of other organizations.* Calculated as follows (billion rubles):

	1958	*1959*	*1960*	*1961*	*1962*	*1963*	*1964*
Net profits	.68	.68	.76	.28	.16	.24	.24
Less: income tax	.17	.17	.19	.07	.04	.06	.06
Equals: retained profits	.51	.51	.57	.21	.12	.18	.18

Net profits are computed as four times income tax proceeds (Table C-1, item 1.D(3)). These organizations, largely voluntary societies, pay a flat 25 percent of their taxable profit to the budget (Miroshchenko, ed., *Gosudarstvennye dokhody,* 1964, p. 181). Thus, the computed net profits figures are understated on this score and hence also the retained profits figures. Since the tax figures are computed as residuals and are subject to a considerable relative margin of error, the profits figures suffer from this additional drawback.

No data on transfers to households from these organizations are available.

2. *Charges to economic enterprises for special funds.*

A. *Social-insurance budget.* Table C-1, item 1.E. The computed entries include social insurance payments by budget institutions. The magnitude of the consequent overstatement of current enterprise incomes has been estimated by Nancy Nimitz as possibly .3–.4 billion rubles a year in the mid-1950s (*SNIP 1956–1958,* p. 83).

B. *Training of workers; research.* Derived as follows (billion rubles):

	1958	*1959*	*1960*	*1961*	*1962*	*1963*	*1964*
Training of workers	.20	.25	.25	.25	.30	.30	.30
Research	.32	.42	.48	.55	.65	.70	.70
Total	.52	.67	.73	.80	.95	1.00	1.00

The 1958 figures are taken from *SNIP 1956–1958,* p. 84. The estimates of outlays on training in 1959–1964 are arbitrary. For research, the 1959 figure assumes realized outlays to have been equal to plan (*ibid.,* p. 85). The 1960–1964 figures represent half the difference between reported total outlays on "science" from all sources and the budget allocation to "science" (Table D-2); the independently obtained estimate of research outlays charged to cost in 1959 is almost exactly half the indicated difference in that year. This difference includes enterprise outlays and, possibly, other budget outlays on R&D (Nimitz, *Soviet Expenditures on Scientific Research,* January 1963, pp. 10–12).

3. *Taxes and other payments out of incomes by economic organizations to budget.*

A and B. *Tax on income of collective farms, nonfarm cooperatives, and other organizations.* Table C-1, item 1.D.

C. *Deductions from profits of state enterprises.* Computed as follows (billion rubles):

	1958	*1959*	*1960*	*1961*	*1962*	*1963*	*1964*
Deductions net of changes in current year payments from previous year's profits	13.62	15.94	18.73	20.80	23.86	25.70	28.73
Less: Personal insurance premiums net of indemnities	.05	.06	.08	.10	.12	.15	.18
	13.57	15.88	18.65	20.70	23.74	25.55	28.55

Entries in the first row of this tabulation are discussed above in the sources for item 1.B. Personal insurance premiums are estimated below, in the sources for item 9.A. Premiums are deducted here to avoid double counting. Gosstrakh, the state insurance organization, turns over a major part of its receipts to the budget in the form of deductions from profits. (Compare indemnities paid collective farms, cooperatives, and households with the total annual premium income as shown in Zverev, *Natsional'nyi dokhod i finansy SSSR,* 1961, pp. 256, 258, 261.) Strictly, only a corresponding portion of personal insurance premiums should be deducted here, but the overstatement involved in deducting the total value is small enough to ignore.

D. *Turnover tax.* Table C-1, item 1.A.

E. *Miscellaneous charges.* Computed as follows (billion rubles):

	1958	*1959*	*1960*	*1961*	*1962*	*1963*	*1964*
Forest income	.23	.23	.24	.25	.26	.26	.25
Local taxes and fees	.73	.78	.42	.44	.44	.43	.45
Rental income from property of local soviets	.13	.12	.12	.12	.13	.13	.14
Price differentials on agricultural machinery and parts	.04	1.56	1.87	1.10	1.04	1.13	1.28
Other revenues	5.21	6.59	7.30	8.73	8.75	9.57	9.71
Total	6.34	9.28	9.95	10.64	10.62	11.52	11.83

Except for other revenues, the figures are taken directly from Table C-1, items 1.F, 1.G(1)–1.G(3).

Previous SNIP practice, admittedly an arbitrary expedient, has been to consider only half the value of income from local Soviet property and of residual revenues "from the socialist economy" (item 1.G(6) of Table C-1) a charge against current product. (See *SNIP 1940–1948,* pp. 173–174, pp. 207–210; *SNIP 1928–1948,* p. 101; *SNIP 1949–1955,* pp. 129–130, 134; *SNIP 1956–1958,* pp. 87–88.) Since the first named item is identified in recent contemporary sources as *rental* income, there seems little basis in this study to exclude half the annual proceeds as representing capital transfers. More important but also more troublesome is the increasingly large "socialist economy" residual, reaching almost 13 billion rubles in 1963 and 1964. The composition of this category is only partly known. The following listing is based on *The Soviet Financial System,* 1968, Ch. VI, Section C, and on Gel'rud and Iakovleva, *Albom nagliadnykh posobii po kursu "Gosudarstvennyi biudzhet,"* 1963, p. 8:

(1) *Special purpose funds,* of which known components are (a)

profits of local industry (part or all?) expended for investment in local industry and for education and health, (b) deductions from compulsory property insurance used to finance property protection measures, (c) highway construction and maintenance fund, financed by a 2 percent deduction from the gross income of automotive transport organizations, (d) funds for repair of urban housing originating in rental receipts of apartment house managements, (e) a markup on radio and television products, beginning January 1, 1962, to finance broadcasting, and replacing radio and TV subscription fees, (f) a charge for geological prospecting work deducted from petroleum and gas prices;

(2) Receipts of budgetary institutions;

(3) Customs duties;

(4) Sale of unclaimed or confiscated property;

(5) Fees for: automotive inspection; registration of trademarks; inspection of weights and measures; fishing licenses; judicial, arbitration and notary services;

(6) Amounts recovered from pilferage and from illegal price changes, overdue obligations paid, fines, etc.

In this listing only items (4) and (6) embrace incomes clearly not on current account. Possibly some small part of the receipts of budgetary institutions also derive from capital transactions. Also, it would be obviously preferable to enter net rather than gross incomes (e.g., item b of the special purpose funds). But these seem minor obstacles to accepting the listed items as valid entries in the accounts.

For the rest, the composition of the residual is unknown, although CIA (*The Soviet Budget for 1960,* November 1960, p. 60) has speculated that the residual may also include the value of sales from state reserves as well as repayments of foreign aid extended by the USSR. Possibly also included are unexpended budget funds carried over from previous years. (Data for the 1950s shown in *SNIP 1949–1955,* p. 131, suggest that carryover funds account for less than 1 percent of budget revenues, or less than a billion rubles in the period under study.) Unless the unknown elements account for a substantial share of the residual and consist largely of noncurrent transactions (e.g., state reserve receipts from sales of commodities produced in prior years or carryover funds) it appears doubtful that there is justification in writing off half the residual as not representing charges to current product. The decision as to what part of the residual should be so considered must still be quite arbitrary, of course. My expedient is to assign three-quarters of the residual in each year to current charges.

4. *Net accounting profits of foreign trade organizations.*
Estimated as follows (billion rubles):

	1958	*1959*	*1960*
Accounting profits on imports	1.62	1.88	2.09
Accounting losses on exports	1.50	1.90	1.95
Net accounting profits	.12	(−).02	.14

By dint of rigid exchange controls, a state monopoly of foreign trade, and administered internal prices, the Soviet domestic economy has been kept well insulated from external price influence. The level and structure of Soviet internal prices have been in no necessary relation to those of the world market. In its trade with Bloc and non-Bloc countries alike, the USSR relied on gold or convertible currencies and so-called "world market" prices, converted to rubles at the official and arbitrary rates of exchange. Before 1961 the official exchange rate overvalued the ruble in terms of purchasing power parities; domestic prices were higher than the "world market" prices converted to rubles at the official rates. Therefore, sales of imports to domestic enterprises created accounting profits and purchases from domestic producers for export brought on accounting losses to the foreign trade corporations.

In the first quarter of 1961, the USSR carried through a currency reform and exchange rate change which represented a substantial devaluation of the ruble for other than tourist expenditures. (See Bornstein, *American Economic Review,* March 1961, pp. 117–123.) In discussing the reform and revaluation Soviet leaders claimed that at the new rates the average level of internal wholesale prices would be "basically" equal to that of the world market (Minister of Finance Garbuzov in *Pravda,* November 15, 1960, p. 2; see also his article in *Kommunist,* No. 1, 1961, p. 62).

In his speech on the 1961 planned budget, on the eve of the revaluation of the ruble, Garbuzov apparently recalculated the 1960 plan figures for purposes of comparison with the 1961 budget. The difference between the revised and original figures for planned revenues in 1960 was 2.09 billion rubles and for planned expenditure, 1.95 billion. It appears likely that these differences represent the accounting profits and losses on imports and exports, respectively, planned for 1960, categories that presumably were eliminated by the 1961 revaluation of the ruble. (For detailed discussion, see CIA, *The Soviet Budget for 1961,* June 1961, pp. 3, 21.)

Planned and realized losses are assumed equal in 1960. Estimates of profits and losses in 1958 and 1959 are obtained by extending the 1960 figures back in time in proportion to changes in the value of imports and exports, respectively (*NKh 1961,* p. 668). It is not known whether such profits and losses continued after 1960.

The implicit assumption in these estimates is that foreign trade accounting profits are a category of Soviet budget revenues separate from the deductions from enterprise profits. CIA, on the other hand, treated the accounting profits as part of enterprise profits subject to ordinary deduction to the budget (CIA, *The Soviet Budget for 1961,* June 1961, p. 13. This appears to represent a change of view: cf. CIA, *The 1960 Soviet Budget,* November 1960, p. 60). CIA's judgment was evidently based on the virtual identity of 1961 planned profits deductions with those of 1960, unadjusted for the estimated accounting profits on imports. Evidence of a contrary sort, supporting my treatment, has appeared since the publication of the CIA estimates:

(1) Customs duties have been described recently as the most important revenue in a group of miscellaneous revenues which is explicitly said to include state fees (*gosudarstvennaia poshlina*—90 million rubles in 1960) and collective farm payments to a new centralized social security fund (planned 1965 level, 1 billion rubles). (Alexandrov, ed., *Gosudarstvennyi biudzhet SSSR,* 2nd edition, 1965, p. 148; cited in *The Soviet Financial System,* 1968, p. 163, note 228.) If customs duties exceed 1 billion rubles (i.e., the value of collective farm payments to the social security fund), the term may include the accounting profits. An incidental corollary is that accounting profits were significant after 1961 as well as before.

(2) In a branch of origin distribution of budget revenues from profits deductions, *Gosbiudzhet II* (p. 10), leaves a substantial volume unidentified—.75 billion rubles in 1955, 1.78 billions in 1960, and 3.43 billions in 1964. The listed originating branches are industry and construction, agriculture including procurement (*ibid.,* p. 6), transportation, communications, housing and municipal economy, and trade. Thus, the unidentified residual presumably originated in supply and sales, foreign trade, and miscellaneous branches of the economy. If foreign trade accounting profits are included in profits deductions, as the CIA argues, they must be found in the unidentified residual; the deductions listed for "trade" are less than a billion rubles. However, the cited estimate of foreign trade accounting profits in 1960 is .31 billion rubles larger than the residual in that year.

5. *Allowance for subsidized losses, n.e.c.*
Estimated as follows (billion rubles):

	1958	*1959*	*1960*	*1961*	*1962*	*1963*	*1964*
Operating losses of MTS/RTS	—	(–).10[a]	.05	—	—	—	—
Budget subsidization of the wage reform	.20	.75	.90	1.15	1.00	.10	.20
Subsidies to agricultural procurement	3.40	2.65	2.00	1.00	1.70	2.25	2.10
Total	3.60	3.30	2.95	2.15	2.70	2.35	2.30

[a] Surplus

No allowance is necessary for ordinary operating losses of *khozraschet* enterprises and organizations, which are supposed to be netted out in the official net profits data used in item 1.B above (p. 363). The same conclusion should apply to losses of state housing, whether operated by the local soviets or by enterprises, *sovnarkhozy,* or ministries. Profits and losses of "enterprise" housing (as we may refer to state housing not operated by local soviets) are supposed to be reflected in the accounts of the parent unit. The difficulty is that the methods of financing operating losses in enterprise housing are far from uniform. Generally, losses are said to be covered by reallocation of profits from municipal enterprises of the *sovnarkhoz* or of profits from sale of output. However, enterprises of the coal, peat, and timber industries are empowered to charge housing losses against costs of production. In construction, planned housing losses form part of overhead costs (Birman *et al., Finansy predpriiatii i otraslei narodnogo khoziaistva,* 1960, p. 537, note). By definition, also, the profits data take no account of housing operated as budget organizations; all incomes and outlays of such organization appear in the state budget. However, this exception to the general rule of *khozraschet* operation seems small enough to ignore (*ibid.,* pp. 522, 540).

Operating losses of MTS/RTS. Incomes of these budget organizations (until 1960) and budget appropriations to them were as follows (billion rubles; data from *Gosbiudzhet I,* pp. 8, 18):

	1958	*1959*	*1960*
MTS/RTS incomes	.97	.18	—
Budget appropriations	1.41	.11	.07

Appropriations cover grants for investment as well as operating subsidies. Evidently there was a net operating deficit in 1960 and a net surplus in 1959; the sign of the difference in 1958 can only be guessed at. It is assumed that investment grants account for only a third of the appropriation; the net balance for 1958 is assumed to be zero.

Budget subsidization of the wage reform. Two developments are of concern here—increases in minimum wage rates and the wage reform proper, involving changes in the wage and salary system. Minimum wage rates were raised at the beginning of 1957, before our period of interest, and in 1959–1962 at enterprises transferred to new wage scales under the wage reform proper. The reform of the wage and salary system also resulted in changes in average wages, and both developments necessitated considerable budgetary aid to enterprises. According to *Ekon. gazeta* of August 24, 1963, p. 23, budget subsidies for wage regulation in the previous five years totaled about 4 billion rubles. Presumably, the period involved is 1958 through 1962. The following additional information on budget wage subsidies in the indicated years is available:

(1) In 1956–1958 about one billion rubles were expended on wage regulation and an additional 2.2 billion rubles were allocated for this purpose in 1959–1960, according to Figurnov (*Real'naia zarabotnaia plata . . .*, 1960 p. 147). Figurnov does not indicate whether these figures refer to budget subsidies alone or also include enterprise expenditures. Moreover, since the book was completed in early 1960 at the latest, his 1959–1960 figure must be at least partly a planned figure.

(2) The planned budget subsidy in 1960 was 1.1 billion rubles while enterprise outlays were to be .3 billion rubles. The planned subsidy or the total planned expenditure on wage regulation in 1960, it is not clear which, approximately equaled state expenditures for this purpose in the three years 1957–1959. (Garbuzov, *PKh,* 1959, No. 12, pp. 14–15).

(3) The planned expenditure on the wage reform in 1961, from all sources, was to be "almost" 2 billion rubles, "approximately twice as much" as in 1960; the budget share of the 1961 planned total is not given (Garbuzov, *Pravda,* December 21, 1960, p. 4). The implication of this statement by Garbuzov is that realized outlays in 1960 were somewhat less than the planned 1.4 billion rubles, possibly little more than one billion rubles.

From this incomplete information the following conclusions are drawn:

(1) The budget subsidy in 1958 is likely to have been small, judging from the figures supplied by Figurnov and on the assumption that the heaviest outlay was likely to have been associated with the increase in minimum wages in 1957. Beyond this, the estimate for 1958 is necessarily arbitrary.

(2) Figurnov's total for 1959–1960 is taken to represent a planned volume in both years from all sources and, in conjunction with Garbuzov's statement, to imply a 1959 planned figure of 1.1 billion rubles. As the wage reform was somewhat slow in getting started and the realized expenditure in 1960 was apparently below the planned figure, the 1959 realized outlay from the budget is set at .75 billion rubles.

(3) If the 1960 realized expenditure including enterprise outlays was little more than one billion rubles, the budget subsidy alone is estimated at .9 billion.

(4) It is assumed that of the close to 2 billion rubles planned outlay in 1961, 1.5 billion was to come from the budget. Given the control total of 4 billion rubles for the period 1958–1962 and the foregoing estimates, a residual of 2.15 billion rubles remains to be allocated between 1961 and 1962. The average wage rose somewhat faster in 1961 than in 1962 (4.0 percent compared with 3.5 percent). On this basis it is assumed that the budget subsidy was larger in 1961 than in 1962. Beyond this, the estimates for 1961–1962 are necessarily arbitrary.

The next extension of the wage reform came in the fall of 1964 with a program intended to stretch over 1965 (*Pravda,* July 14, 1964). This extension covered trade, health, education, and municipal and other services and was also intended to raise minimum wages. The major impact was to occur in 1965, since (1) only the Far North was to be affected during October of 1964 and (2) during November and December only employees of health and education were to have their wages changed. After Khrushchev's overthrow, the new regime decided to speed up the reform and in its 1965 budget plan scheduled a budget subsidy of 890 million rubles for raising minimum wages on January 1 and to increase wages in trade, municipal economy and some other services (excluding health and education) (*Pravda,* December 10, 1964, p. 5). It appears, then, that the budget subsidy in 1964, if any, must have been small. My estimates for 1963 and 1964 are guesses taking these indications into account.

Subsidies to agricultural procurement. Obtained as follows (billion rubles):

	1958	*1959*	*1960*	*1961*	*1962*	*1963*	*1964*
Subsidies on meat and milk procurement	1.20	1.85	1.70	.90	1.00	1.25	1.10
Subsidies on other procurement	2.20	.80	.30	.10	.70	1.00	1.00
Total	3.40	2.65	2.00	1.00	1.70	2.25	2.10

Subsidies to procurement organizations have been necessitated by periodic increases in prices paid to farmers which have not been matched by increases in prices charged to industry processing agricultural products. Nimitz estimated the cost to the budget in 1958 of procurement price increases in that and earlier years as 3.4 billion rubles (*SNIP 1956–1958,* pp. 90–94).

Subsidies on meat and milk procurement may be partially estimated on the basis of data for 1959–1962 showing the unit value of subsidies of beef and butter produced and sold by the state, presented by Stoliarov (*O tsenakh i tsenoobrazovanii v SSSR,* 1963, pp. 184, 188):

	1959		*1960*		*1961*		*1962*		*1963*	*1964*
	beef	*butter*	*beef*	*butter*	*beef*	*butter*	*beef*	*butter*	*beef*	*beef*
Subsidy per ton, rubles	..	481	597	..	383	34	433	17	475	450
Production, thousand tons	1922	721	2000	737	1680	781	2027	830	2371	2160
Total subsidy, billion rubles	..	.35	1.19	..	.64	.03	.88	.01	1.13	.97

For 1962, subsidies per ton represent simple averages of the reported subsidy after June 1, 1962 and of the 1961 average annual subsidy. Stoliarov indicated that no subsidy on account of butter production was necessary after June 1962. The beef subsidy prevailing in the second half of 1962, 482 rubles per ton, is arbitrarily assumed to have been reduced to the indicated levels in 1963 and 1964. Production data for all years refer to beef and veal; the sources are *NKh 1962,* pp. 205, 207, and *NKh 1964,* p. 228.

In an apologia for the June 1962 retail price increases, Gritskov declared that in 1961 "the meat industry sustained losses of 680 million rubles" and the loss to budget on account of butter production reached approximately 200 million rubles (*Kommunist,* 1962, No. 9, pp. 43–44). Neither of these figures is easy to interpret in the present context:

(1) To begin with, there is little to indicate that the meat industry was unprofitable in 1961; Stoliarov made clear that the industry earned a profit and that the "losses" involved accounts with the procurement organizations. It is, therefore, assumed that Gritskov had in mind subsidies to these organizations.

(2) When unit prices and costs for milk and butter cited by Gritskov

are compared with those shown by Stoliarov it appears that Gritskov lumped subsidies to procurement organizations with losses by state farms on deliveries to the state.

(3) On the other hand, Gritskov's figure for meat subsidies seems too low. Thus, he cited state expenditures on procurement, processing and sales of beef as 1386 rubles per ton, on the average in 1961, while the retail price was 1108 rubles per ton. According to Stoliarov, 1108 rubles per ton was the retail price in 1960, and it rose 29 rubles in 1961; state expenditures per unit were 1449 rubles in 1960 and 1536 rubles in 1961. Since Stoliarov's cost figures are net of the value of by-products and profits of procurement, processing and sales organizations, but gross of state farm losses on deliveries to the state, there is considerable room for difference in the coverage of the two sets of data, and perhaps both writers were in fact discussing the 1961 price structure. But if subsidies on account of beef alone were 640 million rubles, the total for all meat production should have been considerably more than 680 million rubles. The gap between state costs and retail price for pork, Gritskov declares (p. 43), was 116 rubles per ton in 1961. Pork production reached 1506 thousand tons in that year; therefore, the aggregate shortfall for pork was 175 million rubles. If Gritskov's data understate the true pork subsidy to procurement organizations to the degree that his figures for the beef price structure understate the apparent beef subsidy, the total subsidy for pork production in 1961 must have reached roughly 250 million rubles.

Kondrashev stated (*Tsena i stoimost' v sotsialisticheskom khoziaistve,* 1963, p. 283) that the state incurred a loss of 37 rubles per centner of poultry meat produced and sold at retail. Neither the date nor the scope of the loss is clear. The context suggests that the intended date is the latter half of 1958 or possibly 1959. Whether the cited loss is gross or net of production losses in state farms or turnover taxes levied on meat sales is not indicated. For these various possible combinations, Stoliarov's figures for state losses on beef sales in 1960 indicate a range of 2.6:1. By analogy, the unit loss on poultry sales could fall anywhere between approximately 15 and 100 rubles per centner. With 1958/1959 production at about 125 thousand tons (*NKh 1962,* p. 205) the overall loss in the period from the middle of 1958 to the middle of 1959 could have been between roughly 20–125 million rubles.

In the next paragraph, however, Kondrashev declared that total losses by procurement organizations were "over" 500 million rubles. The figure is far too large for losses on poultry sales alone and seems much too small for losses on all meat sales. Possibly, the figure represents cumulated losses on poultry sales through 1962. In that case, the accounting loss on poultry sales charged to procurement organizations might have been about 50 rubles per centner; in aggregate these losses would have amounted to some 50 million rubles in 1958 and close to 100 million rubles by 1960.

To allow for subsidies on meat other than beef, based on the information developed above, total subsidies on meat and milk are estimated as .90 billion rubles in 1961 and 1.00 billion rubles in 1962. Meat subsidies in 1963 and 1964 are estimated from the data on p. 374.

Subsidies for milk procurement in 1960 may be taken as approximately equal to those in 1961. Turnover taxes were eliminated from the price structure of the dairy industry after 1959 (see *Zakonodatel'nye akty po voprosam narodnogo khoziaistva SSSR,* I, pp. 4-3-414). Stoliarov (*O tsenakh i tsenoobrazovanii v SSSR,* 1963, p. 188) indicated that the 1960 price structure was similar to that of 1961.

The figure of 1.70 billion rubles of meat and milk subsidies in 1960 allows for a volume of subsidies on procurement of meats other than beef estimated on the basis of the 1961 estimate and the relation between beef subsidies in the two years.

Procurement prices of cattle were almost the same in 1959 as in 1960 and about 5 percent lower in 1958 (*ibid.,* p. 106). All other things equal, this would suggest that the unit beef subsidy in 1960 was the same as in 1959 and slightly higher than in 1958. Given output of beef and pork in 1959 of 1922 and 1354 thousand tons, respectively, and assuming unit subsidies the same in 1959 as in 1960, aggregate subsidies on meat may be roughly estimated as 1.5–1.6 billion rubles.

Approximately the same result can be obtained by another route. Income earned by collective farms and households from sales of livestock to the state was 3.555 billion rubles in 1959 (*SKh,* p. 118). If we revalue this sum in terms of 1957 prices by means of a procurement price index (*ibid.,* p. 117), the difference between the computed and the given value is 1.305 billion rubles. To this must be added an allowance for the incremental costs to the state of purchasing output formerly delivered in kind to the MTS. For all agricultural products this addition to state costs was estimated as a billion rubles in 1958 (*SNIP 1956–1958,* p. 94). Considering the relative weight of meat subsidies in the aggregate for all products, and the fact that the full impact of the 1958 price changes was not felt until 1959, total subsidies for meat procurement in the latter year could easily have been 1.5 billion rubles.

It is also reassuring that a similar calculation for milk suggests a total milk procurement subsidy in 1959 exceeding .30 billion rubles; the figure derived from the Stoliarov data is .35 billion rubles.

Meat and milk subsidies in 1958 are estimated from Nimitz's calculations described in *SNIP 1956–1958,* p. 94: partial reproduction of her calculations suggests 70 percent as the share of meat and milk subsidies in the preliminary total that includes, in addition, grain and eggs.

Subsidies on other procurement. Of the 3.4 billion rubles of subsidies estimated for 1958 by Nimitz, 1.2 billion rubles, by my estimate, consist of subsidies on meat and milk procurement; 2.2 billion rubles remain for subsidies on other products—chiefly, grain, cotton, sugar beets, wool, and eggs. For these products, deflation of the 1959–1962 procurement bills in the same manner as performed for the 1958 bill (*SNIP 1956–1958,* pp. 93–94) indicates relative increases, compared with the 1958 value, in the growth of the procurement bill due to the 1958 price changes alone of the following magnitude: 1959, 5 percent; 1960, 4 percent; 1961, 20 percent; 1962, 44 percent. These would imply subsidies of 2.3 billion rubles in 1959, 2.3 billion in 1960, 2.6 billion in 1961, and 3.2 billion in 1962.

[Inputs into the calculation, procurement bills at current prices and price indexes with 1955 or 1957 as base year, were obtained as follows: (a) Procurement bills for 1959 are given in *SKh,* p. 118. For other years, values were computed as the product of procurement from collective farms and households multiplied by average prices. For grain and eggs, quantities and prices are taken from Table A-2. Quantities of cotton, sugar beets, and wool procured are derived by subtracting state sector deliveries from total procurements (*NKh 1962,* pp. 240, 281, 290, 317, 358; for sugar beets the state sector share given on p. 245 is multiplied by total procurements on p. 290). Prices of cotton and wool in 1960 are taken from Khlebnikov, *VE,* 1962, No. 7, p. 53, and that for sugar beets in both 1960 and 1961 from Stoliarov, *O tsenakh i tsenoobrazovanii v SSSR,* 1963, p. 86. Cotton prices are assumed unchanged in 1961 and 2 percent higher in 1962 (the average price of all technical crops increased by that margin in 1962); the 1960 average price of wool is extended to 1961 and 1962 by means of the official price index; and the price of sugar beets in 1962 is estimated as lying between the 1961 and 1963 prices (the latter given in *Pravda,* March 7, 1964, p. 1). (b) Price indexes are directly or indirectly taken from *SKh,* p. 117 and Stoliarov, *O tsenakh i tsenoobrazovanii v SSSR,* 1963, p. 106. The index link between 1960 and earlier years for cotton and sugar beets, necessitated by Stoliarov's aggregation of all technical crops, is obtained by comparison of 1960 with 1958 prices (the latter taken from Zverev, *Natsional'nyi dokhod i finansy SSSR,* 1961, pp. 306, 311, and Stoliarov, *O tsenakh i tsenoobrazovanii v SSSR,* 1963, p. 79).]

It is, however, difficult to estimate procurement subsidies on the basis of these data because there appear to have been a number of changes in wholesale prices of food products during 1959–1961. Given relative stability of retail prices (*NKh 1962,* p. 533), wholesale price changes for consumer goods may occur by altering turnover tax rates. Thus, the 1959 planned budget did not take into account a prospective change in wholesale prices of grain products, fodder, and oil seed when it called for turnover tax proceeds of 33.24 billion rubles. *Zasedaniia Verkhovnogo soveta SSSR . . . ,* 1959, pp. 16, 601. Actual collections in that year were 31.07 billion rubles (Table C-1, item 1.A). The 1960 planned level of tax receipts was 31.71 billion rubles (*Izvestiia,* October 28, 1959, p. 5), or just 2 percent over the realized 1959 level, suggesting that further wholesale price adjustments were contemplated. The realized value in 1960 was even slightly below plan, 31.34 billions. In 1961, actual proceeds declined again, by .42 billion rubles.

The impact of reduction of turnover taxes appears to have been particularly great with respect to meat and milk products, which by 1961 were no longer subject to taxation. The loss of turnover tax proceeds from sales of meat and milk alone may have amounted to a billion rubles: According to Kondrashev (*Tsena i khoziaistvennyi raschet,* 1961, p. 80), .3 billion rubles of turnover tax on meat production were liquidated in 1959; the tax rates on beef and butter shown by Stoliarov (*O tsenakh i tsenoobrazovanii v SSSR,* 1963, pp. 184–188) when multiplied by 1960 production levels yield an additional 600 million rubles.

Nevertheless, the reduction of turnover taxes encompassed more than just the meat and dairy industries. Lack of additional information, however, necessitates guessing. It seems possible that subsidies on procurement of products other than meat and milk were affected by reduction of perhaps 2 billion rubles of turnover taxes by 1961. The major reduction was probably effected in 1959. These subsidies are, therefore, estimated as .8 billion rubles in 1959, .3 billion in 1960, .1 billion in 1961, and .7 billion in 1962. The partial recouping of losses by the government in the form of increases in retail prices in 1962 affected largely meat and dairy products. (The total increase in retail prices came to 1.450 billion rubles, according to Stoliarov, *O tsenakh i tsenoobrazovanii v SSSR,* 1963, p. 101; revaluation of 1962 meat and dairy sales in 1961 prices—*NKh 1962,* pp. 520 and 533—indicates that most of this sum represents increases in prices of meat and dairy products.)

In 1963, procurement and delivery prices of cotton, sugar beets and potatoes were raised, as were procurement prices of beans (*Zakupki sel'skokhoziaistvennykh produktov,* 1963, No. 4, p. 3; 1963, No. 5, p. 10; 1963, No. 10, pp. 26 and 68, cited in Karcz, *A Compendium of Soviet Farm Prices in 1961,* 1964, pp. 105, 107–108). No further changes of significance took place before 1965. At the same time there appears to have been little change in the turnover tax margin between enterprise and industry wholesale prices in the food industry (*NKh 1963,* pp. 136–137; *NKh 1964,* pp. 154–155). My crude estimate is based on these developments.

6. *Consolidated total charges against current product, net of depreciation.*

The sum of items 1–5.

7. *Depreciation.*

Computed as follows (billion rubles):

	1958	*1959*	*1960*	*1961*	*1962*	*1963*	*1964*
Collective farms	.90	1.06	1.04	1.09	1.29	1.57	1.66
State-cooperative	7.06	7.94	9.10	10.21	11.30	15.55	17.05
Total	7.96	9.00	10.14	11.30	12.59	17.12	18.71

Collective farms. 1958–1961: Alekseeva and Voronin, *Nakoplenie i razvitie kolkhoznoi sobstvennosti,* 1963, p. 67. 1962–1964: Estimates compiled by Sally Anderson for an unpublished paper on collective farm accounts. Her estimates are based on information chiefly in Kassirov, *Planovye pokazateli i khozraschetnye stimuly,* 1965, p. 211, and Lukanina, *Rol' kredita v formirovanii osnovnykh sredstv kolkhozov,* 1965, p. 26.

These estimates omit depreciation in fishing and inter-collective farm organizations. (For indication that the latter compute their own amortization allowances see Loza, *VE,* 1960, No. 3, p. 141.) However, the omissions must be insignificant: if amortization is computed at 6 percent of the value of the capital stock excluding productive livestock, the size of the capital stock in fishing cooperatives and inter-collective farm organizations on January 1, 1962 (*NKh 1961,* p. 420) implies amortization in 1962 of .03 billion rubles.

Other public sector. NKh 1962, p. 634; *NKh 1963,* p. 653; *NKh 1964,* p. 769.

8. *Consolidated total charges against current product.*

The sum of items 6 and 7.

9. *Transfer receipts.*

A. *Net savings of households.* Derived as follows (billion rubles):

	1958	*1959*	*1960*	*1961*	*1962*	*1963*	*1964*
Increment in savings deposits	.66	1.34	.86	.78	1.06	1.25	1.71
Net bond purchases	.40	.01	(−).29	(−).31	(−).29	.07	.11
Personal insurance premiums	.05	.06	.08	.10	.12	.15	.18
Total	1.11	1.41	.65	.57	.89	1.47	2.00

Increment in savings deposits. The 1958 figure is from *NKh 1958,* p. 915, and includes only deposits in savings banks; all other entries (from *NKh 1962,* p. 492; *NKh 1963,* p. 509; *NKh 1964,* p. 595), include deposits in the State Bank as well. (The annual change in State Bank savings deposits was but 20 million rubles in 1961 and less than 10 million rubles in other years of the period.)

Net bond purchases. Obtained as follows (billion rubles):

	1958	*1959*	*1960*	*1961*	*1962*	*1963*	*1964*
Gross bond purchases	.40	.16	.06	.04	.06	.07	.11
Less: debt retirement	—	.15	.35	.35	.35	—	—
Equals: net bond purchases	.40	.01	(−).29	(−).31	(−).29	.07	.11

Gross bond purchases by households are from Table C-1, items 2.B(1) and (2). Purchases by the savings banks, item 2.B(3), are excluded as representing transfers of the annual increment in deposits. After 1963, savings banks no longer bought state bonds and their deposits were treated as part of the lending resources of the State Bank.

Debt retirement is estimated as follows (billion rubles):

	1958	*1959*	*1960*	*1961*	*1962*	*1963*	*1964*
Debt service payments							
To households							
Interest	.04	.05	.05	.05	.05	.01	.01
Debt retirement	—	.15	.35	.35	.35	—	—
Total	.04	.20	.40	.40	.40	.01	.01
To all debt holders	.37	.69	.7	.8	.8	.1	.1

Debt service payments to all debt holders are given in *NKh 1959,* p. 801; *NKh 1962,* p. 635; *NKh 1964,* p. 770. A large share of these outlays is presumably accounted for by payments to savings banks: between 1957 and 1964 they were the major purchasers of state bonds. Total payments to households in 1958 and 1960 are given by Figurnov, *Real'naia zarabotnaia plata . . . ,* 1960, p. 182, and *Stroitel'stvo kommunizma i rost blagosostoianiia naroda,* 1962, p. 49, respectively.

The rest of the figures are estimates based on those just mentioned and an interpretation of the 1957 decree discontinuing issue of mass-subscription bonds (*Pravda,* April 20, 1957, p. 1). In addition to the action cited, the decree also provided for the following: (1) Repayment of principal on all mass-subscription bonds outstanding as of the date of the decree was deferred to 1977–1997; (2) no further lottery drawings on outstanding debt of this type were to take place. In effect, interest payments on pre-decree mass-subscription loans were discontinued; (3) a five-year mass-subscription loan of 1.2 billion rubles was to be floated in 1957 with annual lottery drawings to take place in 1958–1962 and retirement during 1959–1962; (4) the 3 percent lottery loan was to be maintained.

The small sum of interest payments to households in 1958 most probably represents winnings on the 3 percent lottery loan. These were augmented in 1959–1962 by winnings on the 1.2 billion ruble 1957 bond issue; assuming an interest rate of 4 percent, annual distributions on account of the bond issue would have to come to about 50 million rubles.

Personal insurance premiums. Computed as follows (billion rubles):

	1958	*1959*	*1960*	*1961*	*1962*	*1963*	*1964*
Premiums paid by households	.08	.10	.13	.16	.20	.25	.30
Indemnities paid to households	.03	.04	.05	.06	.08	.10	.12
Premiums net of indemnities	.05	.06	.08	.10	.12	.15	.18

Premiums paid by households. 1958: Mar'iakhin in *FinSSSR,* 1960, No. 2, p. 40. 1959–1961: interpolated between the 1958 and 1962 figures. 1962: Premiums paid by households for all voluntary insurance were 237 million rubles in 1962 compared to 106 millions in 1958 (Baranov in *Voprosy gosudarstvennogo strakhovaniia,* 1964, p. 11). A considerably higher rate of growth of personal insurance than of property insurance premiums is assumed because of the retardation of private housing construction. 1963–1964: interpolated between the 1962 figure and a figure for 1965 of 363 million rubles, cited by Pleshkov, in *FinSSSR,* 1966, No. 8, p. 23.

Indemnities paid to households in 1958–1960 are from Zverev, *Natsional'nyi dokhod i finansy SSSR,* 1961, p. 258. Estimates in other years are based on Pleshkov, *FinSSSR,* 1966, No. 8, p. 23, who cites a three year total, 1963–1965, of indemnities paid households for both property and personal insurance of 709 million rubles. On the basis of data shown by Zverev for 1958–1960 I assume that the 1963–1965 total is split roughly equally between indemnities for personal and for property insurance.

B. *Direct taxes.* Table C-1, item 2.A.

C. *Other payments to the state.* Obtained as follows (billion rubles):

	1958	*1959*	*1960*	*1961*	*1962*	*1963*	*1964*
Revenue from lotteries	.31	.13	.14	.13	.14	.15	.17
Other state budget revenue "from the population"	.28	.27	.29	.30	.32	.36	.36
Total	.59	.40	.43	.43	.46	.51	.53

For sources, see Table C-1, items 2.C and 2.D. Figures for proceeds from sale of lottery tickets are apparently net of winnings (Zverev, *Natsional'nyi dokhod i finansy SSSR,* 1961, p. 250).

10. *Consolidated net income.*

The sum of items 8 and 9.

TABLE C-1

STATE BUDGET REVENUES, 1958–1965
(billion rubles)

	1958	1959	1960	1961	1962	1963	1964	1965
1. "From the socialist economy"								
A. Turnover tax	30.45	31.07	31.34	30.92	32.95	34.52	36.69	38.66
B. Profits deductions, state enterprises	13.54	15.96	18.63	20.74	23.86	25.70	28.73	30.87
C. Income of MTS-RTS	.97	.18	—	—	—	—	—	—
D. Income tax on enterprises and organizations								
(1) Collective farms	1.03	1.24	1.21	.93	1.01	1.04	.98	1.16
(2) Cooperatives	.46	.49	.44	.23	.27	.29	.31	.32
(3) Other	.17	.17	.19	.07	.04	.06	.06	.06
(4) Total	1.66	1.90	1.84	1.23	1.32	1.39	1.35	1.54
E. Social insurance fund revenues: charges to enterprises and organizations	3.26	3.58	3.74	4.15	4.41	4.63	4.95	5.56
F. Forest income	.23	.23	.24	.25	.26	.26	.25	.25
G. Other								
(1) Local taxes and fees	.73	.78	.42	.44	.44	.43	.45	.46
(2) Rental income from local Soviet property	.13	.12	.12	.12	.13	.13	.14	.14
(3) Price differentials on agricultural machinery and parts	.04	1.56	1.87	1.10	1.04	1.13	1.28	1.32
(4) Accounting profits on imports	1.62	1.88	2.09	. .	. .	. .	. .	. .
(5) Payments by collective farms for MTS machinery	.83	.55	.10	.10	.10	.10	.10	—
(6) Residual	6.94	8.79	9.73	11.64	11.67	12.76	12.95	15.08
(7) Total	10.29	13.68	14.34	13.70	13.87	14.92	15.04	17.00
H. Total	60.40	66.61	70.14	71.00	76.68	81.41	87.01	93.89
2. "From the population"								
A. State taxes from population	5.19	5.52	5.60	5.83	6.00	6.31	6.75	7.70
B. State loans								
(1) Subscription loans	.32	—	—	—	—	—	—	—
(2) 3% lottery loan	.08	.16	.06	.04	.06	.07	.11	.18
(3) Purchases by savings banks	.66[a]	1.33	.85	.76	1.11	1.24	—	—
(4) Total	1.06	1.49	.91	.80	1.17	1.31	.11	.18
C. Revenue from lotteries	.31	.13	.14	.13	.14	.15	.17	.19
D. Other								
(1) Social insurance fund revenues: other	.05	.05	.05	.06	.06	.07	.07	.08
(2) Residual: local taxes and fees	.23	.22	.24	.24	.26	.29	.29	.29
(3) Total	.28	.27	.29	.30	.32	.36	.36	.37
E. Total	6.83	7.41	6.94	7.05	7.63	8.13	7.39	8.43
3. Total revenues	67.24	74.01	77.08	78.05	84.31	89.54	94.41	102.32

TABLE C-1 (continued)

Note:

[a] Including unspecified residual of 3.4 million rubles.

Sources: Except as indicated below, data are from *Gosbiudzhet I*, pp. 7–9, 67–69, and *Gosbiudzhet II*, pp. 10–11, 70–71.

1.D(2) *Cooperatives.* Calculated as 35 percent of consumer cooperative net profits and 30 percent of producer cooperative profits. Tax rates for consumer cooperatives are a flat 35 percent (Miroshchenko, ed., *Gosudarstvennye dokhody*, 1964, p. 181) and for producer cooperatives before their absorption by state industry in 1960 the rates ranged between 20 and 35 percent (Suchkov *et al.*, *Gosudarstvennye dokhody SSSR*, 1960, pp. 184–185). The calculation proceeds as follows (billion rubles):

	1958	*1959*	*1960*	*1961*	*1962*	*1963*	*1964*	*1965*
Producer cooperatives								
Net profits	.60	.64	.51					
Income tax	.18	.19	.15					
Consumer cooperatives								
Net profits	.81	.87	.82	.66	.78	.83	.88	.90
Income tax	.28	.30	.29	.23	.27	.29	.31	.32
All cooperatives								
Income tax	.46	.49	.44	.23	.27	.29	.31	.32

Net profits of producer and consumer cooperatives in 1958–1959 are given in *NKh 1959*, p. 799. Profits of consumer cooperatives in 1960–1965 are from *NKh 1962*, p. 627, *NKh 1964*, p. 747, and *NKh 1965*, p.757. Producer cooperative profits in 1960 are estimated on the assumption that they were increasing over the previous year's level at the same rate as in 1959. This rate would have yielded total net profits of .68 billion rubles for a full year; since the cooperatives were transferred into state enterprises in October 1960, I assume receipt of three-quarters of the computed figure.

The income tax figures for consumer cooperatives in 1962–1964 are exactly confirmed by Fonarev, *Raspredelenie i ispol'zovanie pribyli potrebitel'skoi kooperatsii*, 1966, p. 141; the source gives no data for 1965.

1.D(3) *Other.* Calculated as a residual, the difference between item 1.D(4) and the sum of items 1.D(1) and 1.D(2).

1.E. *Social insurance fund revenues: charges to enterprises and organizations.* The figures are inferred to be charges to enterprises and organizations, rather than total fund revenues, from a comparison of the *Gosbiudzhet* series with that of *NKh 1959*, p. 800. Figures for 1958 and 1959 from the former source are 98.5 percent and 98.6 percent respectively of those from the latter source. Total fund revenues after 1959, and hence the component not deriving from enterprises and organizations (item 2.D(1)), are assumed to increase in proportion to enterprise and organization charges.

1.G(1) *Local taxes and fees.* These are composed of the following elements (billion rubles):

	1958	*1959*	*1960*	*1961*	*1962*	*1963*	*1964*	*1965*
Building tax and land rent	.42	.47	.14	.15	.16	.17	.18	.18
Amusements tax	.37	.38	.37	.39	.39	.38	.41	.42
Legal fees	.09	.09	.09	.09	.09	.09	.09	.10
Collective farm market tax	.05	.05	.05	.04	.04	.04	.04	.04
Other	.04	.01	.01	.01	.01	.04	.02	.01
Total	.96	1.00	.66	.68	.70	.72	.74	.75

According to *The Soviet Financial System*, 1968, p. 127), the residual item in the above distribution may be identified with fees charged on means of transportation and on urban owners of livestock. These fees evidently would be paid by individuals; the amusements tax is considered to originate in "the socialist economy"; the remaining taxes and fees are presumably paid by individuals and organizations alike.

The estimate of local taxes and fees paid by enterprises and organizations is obtained by subtracting from total local taxes and fees the amounts

TABLE C-1 (continued)

paid by individuals. The latter are identified with residual budget revenues "from the population." See item 2.D(2).

1.G(3) *Price differentials on agricultural machinery and spare parts.* By decree of October 31, 1958, the USSR Council of Ministers revised the procedure for supplying machinery parts to agriculture. At the same time, it ordered an increase in prices paid by farms (apparently both state and collective) of 50 percent for automotive parts and 90 percent for parts for farm machinery and tractors. These increases applied to parts for which so-called "uniform wholesale prices" had been established earlier that year; parts for which uniform wholesale prices did not exist were to have their industry wholesale prices doubled on the average. The difference between old and new prices in all cases was to be appropriated by the budget (*Spravochnik partiinogo rabotnika*, 2nd ed., 1959, pp. 368–369).

Prices of machinery were raised as well. This is implied by the category label in *Gosbiudzhet I* (p. 69) and explicitly stated in other Soviet sources: Alekseeva and Voronin, *Nakoplenie i razvitie kolkhoznoi sobstvennosti*, 1963, p. 42; and Panin, *PKh*, 1964, No. 9, p. 76.

1.G(4) *Accounting profits on imports.* See above, p. 369.

1.G(5) *Payments by collective farms for MTS machinery.* 1958–1959: Garbuzov, *FinSSSR*, 1959, No. 2, p. 16. The figure for 1959 is a planned value. 1960–1964: the total value of former MTS machinery purchased by collective farms is difficult to establish because of varying information in the literature. By the end of 1959 purchases aggregated 1.8 billion rubles, according to *NKh 1959*, p. 437. It does not seem likely that substantial additional acquisitions could have taken place. The grand total may thus be set at 2 billion rubles. According to Nedelin (*FinSSSR*, 1965, No. 5, pp. 14–15), as of January 1, 1965, the remaining debt of collective farms of 120 million rubles was entirely written off. Thus, 1.88 billion rubles had presumably been paid by that date, of which 1.38 in 1958–1959. This leaves .50 billions to be distributed among 1960–1964 and I simply assume a constant annual level of .10 billions.

1.G(6) *Residual.* The difference between item 1.G(7) and the sum of items 1.G(1)–1.G(5).

1.G(7) *Total.* The difference between item 1.H and the sum of items 1.A–1.F.

2.D(1) *Social insurance fund revenues: other.* Represents the difference between the total of such revenues and their major component—charges to enterprises and organizations. See item 1.E.

2.D(2) *Residual: Local taxes and fees.* The difference between items 2.D(3) and 2.D(1).

2.D(3) *Total.* The difference between item 2.E and the sum of items 2.A–2.C.

D

Sources to Table 4: 1958-1964

1. *Communal services.*

A. *Education, excluding science.* Calculated as the difference between current outlays on all education (item 4 of Table D-1) and current outlays on science (item 4 of Table D-2).

B. *Health care and physical culture.* Table D-3, item 3.

C. *Other.* Computed as follows (billion rubles):

	1958	*1959*	*1960*	*1961*	*1962*	*1963*	*1964*
Miscellaneous ("other") expenditures from social insurance funds	.03	.02	.03	.03	.03	.03	.03
Social assistance outlays excluding pensions and allowances	.18	.20	.20	.20	.20	.20	.20
Total	.21	.22	.23	.23	.23	.23	.23

Miscellaneous expenditures from social insurance funds—that is, outlays other than on health care, physical culture, and education—are taken from *NKh 1962*, p. 639 and *NKh 1964*, p. 774. Social assistance outlays excluding pensions and allowances are derived below in the source for item 3 of Table D-4. As transfer payments, pensions and allowances are entered under item 9.A below.

2. *Government administration.*

Gosbiudzhet I, p. 19 and *Gosbiudzhet II*, p. 21.

3. *Gross investment.*

A. *Fixed capital.* Computed as follows (billion rubles):

	1958	*1959*	*1960*	*1961*	*1962*	*1963*	*1964*
Public sector, excluding collective farms							
Capital repairs	5.83	6.20	6.95	7.51	8.29	9.96	10.90
Change in warehouse stocks of equipment requiring installation	—	.10	.18	.52	.40	.33	.13
New investment	24.52	27.41	30.80	32.75	34.81	37.01	40.37
Collective farms: "gross investment"	3.04	3.33	3.20	3.20	3.43	3.39	3.60
Total	33.39	37.04	41.13	43.98	46.93	50.69	55.00

Capital repairs. The 1958 figure is estimated by interpolation between the 1956 level at 5.15 billion rubles (Bunich, in NIFI, *Planirovanie i finansirovanie kapital'nogo remonta osnovnykh fondov,* 1958, p. 5) and the 1959 value of 6.2 billion rubles. The latter figure is obtained by adding a 0.1 billion ruble allowance for the repairs of producer and consumer cooperatives to the 6.1 billion rubles for the state sector reported by Eidel'man (*Mezhotraslevoi balans obshchestvennogo produkta,* 1966, p. 172); repairs by consumer cooperatives alone, financed by amortization allowances, came to 44 million rubles (*NKh 1962,* p. 634). For 1960 I use the planned volume implied by Bunich in *VE,* 1960, No. 10, pp. 48–49, note.

Outlays in 1961–1964 are estimated on the assumption that amortization allowances earmarked for capital repair accounted for 80 percent of total repairs in the state-cooperative sector. The actual ratio for 1959 was 79 percent and for 1960, 78 percent (compare amortization allowances in *NKh 1962,* p. 634 with totals given above). Earmarked allowances in 1961–1964 were as follows (billion rubles):

1961	6.01	(*NKh 1962,* p. 634)
1962	6.63	(*NKh 1963,* p. 653)
1963	7.97	(*NKh 1964,* p. 769)
1964	8.72	

Note that according to Bunich, ed., *Ekonomicheskaia rabota v finansovo-kreditnoi sisteme* (1965, p. 92) capital repairs in 1964 totaled "almost 11 billion rubles." My estimate is 10.9 billions.

Change in warehouse stocks of equipment requiring installation. In Soviet accounting, equipment not requiring installation (*montazh*) is considered part of fixed capital investment as soon as it is received at the warehouse of the construction site. However, equipment requiring installation is not recorded in investment until it is withdrawn from the project warehouse for the purpose of beginning installation. (D'iachkov, *Statistika kapital'nogo stroitel'stva,* 1962, p. 33; Maizel's, *Statistika kapital'nogo stroitel'stva,* 1962, p. 42.) Although the equipment requiring installation is considered part of working capital, that of the construction organization or of the contractee (VPSh, *Ekonomika stroitel'stva,* 1962, pp. 256 and 259), it appears likely that the yearbook data on current assets in fact exclude them. The evidence is of two kinds:

(1) Uninstalled equipment as a component of working capital is classified under "production stocks," as distinguished from "circulating production funds in the process of production." The remaining components of production stocks are structures and members (*stroitel'nye konstruktsii i detali*), basic materials, other materials and fuel, small-valued and short-lived articles. However, a breakdown of production stocks in contract construction at the beginning of 1960 omits uninstalled equipment; production stocks are shown as exhausted by the remaining components (*ibid.,* pp. 256–257 and 259). The indicated distribution is most likely the same as that reported in *NKh 1962,* p. 61. The comparison is as follows (percent).

Ekonomika stroitel'stva		*NKh 1962*	
1. Production stocks		Production stocks	
A. Structures and members	8.5	A. Raw and basic materials and purchased semifabricates	62.6
B. Basic materials	54.0		
C. Small-valued and short-lived articles	15.3	B. Small-valued and short-lived articles	15.2
D. Other materials and fuel	16.1	C. Auxiliary materials	14.6
		D. Other production stocks	1.5
E. Total	93.9	E. Total	93.9
2. Circulating production funds in the process of production		Unfinished production	
A. Unfinished production in construction-installation	5.7	A. Unfinished nonindustrial production	3.5
B. Other outlays in production	0.4	B. Unfinished industrial production and produced semifabricates	0.4
		C. Expenses of future periods	2.2
C. Total	6.1	D. Total	6.1
3. Total circulating production funds	100.0	Total circulating means in material values	100.0

(2) Indebtedness of contract construction to the banks may be obtained from two different distributions reported in the yearbooks—that relating to current liabilities and a separate tabulation of bank loans by

branch of destination. The data may be grouped as follows (million rubles; sources are *NKh 1962,* pp. 56–57, 639–640, and *NKh 1964,* pp. 751, 753, 774–775):

	Values on January 1						
	1959	*1960*	*1961*	*1962*	*1963*	*1964*	*1965*
(1) Indebtedness to banks as current liability	519	744	983	1318	1525	1682	1641
(2) Short-term loans outstanding to construction	1067	1234	1569	2381	3145	3203	3044
(3) Excess of (2) over (1)	548	490	586	1063	1620	1521	1403
(4) Short-term loans outstanding to construction covering stocks of equipment	527	435	528	978	1321	1215	1125

Thus, total short-term loans outstanding to construction exceeded the branch's current indebtedness as shown in the distribution of its liabilities by amounts shown in row (3). In row (4) I show a component of short-term loans outstanding to construction, loans covering stocks of equipment. In the period 1960–1962, row (4) entries are about 90 percent as large as those in row (3); the proportion was 96 percent in 1959 but only 80 percent in 1963–1965. Therefore, it is possible that construction current liabilities exclude their debt to the bank on account of equipment loans and that this in fact largely explains the discrepancies between the two sets of loan data shown in row (3). If equipment loans are omitted from construction liabilities presumably the corresponding assets are also omitted. (This discussion owes much Moorsteen and Powell, *The Soviet Capital Stock, 1928–1962,* 1966, pp. 443–444, 503, 581–582).

Bank loans are not the sole source of finance of stocks of uninstalled machinery—loans account for only about a third of such stocks at construction sites (Podshivalenko, *Ekonomika stroitel'stva,* 1966, No. 1, p. 38), but it seems unlikely that the Central Statistical Administration would have excluded only part of the assets and liabilities relating to this category.

For these reasons, it seems necessary to attempt a separate estimate of changes in stocks of equipment requiring installation. However, estimates of this category of investment are difficult to make. Available data generally emerge not from a summation of enterprise balance sheets but from annual CSA censuses of what is also translated as "uninstalled equipment" (*neustanovlennoe oborudovanie*) but is in fact a broader concept. A more appropriate translation might be "equipment not yet set for operation." That is, all equipment included in the enterprise balance sheet but not in place in the production area of the plant is considered not set for operation. This category includes machinery in the process of being installed in the production area (*Statisticheskii slovar'*, 1965, pp. 354–355). Thus, the category of equipment not yet set for operation consists of machinery in warehouses awaiting installation, machinery in the process of installation, and machinery in warehouses surplus to the enterprise in question (Zel'tser, *VS*, 1963, No. 12, p. 12). Only the first and third components are of interest, of course, but it is frequently difficult to tell to which of these three or the possible totals thereof the available data refer.

My estimates are obtained largely from the following information supplied by Riznik (*VS*, 1965, No. 6, pp. 3–4):

(1) Annual increases in the two relevant components of uninstalled equipment were as follows (percent):

	1961	*1962*	*1963*	*1961–1963 Total*
Equipment awaiting installation	42	21	10	88
Surplus equipment	6	12	27	50
Both components	33	19	13	79

(2) In these three years stocks of uninstalled equipment (excluding machinery in the process of installation, in storage, and in technically required reserves) rose almost 1.3 billion rubles.

(3) At the beginning of 1964, surplus equipment amounted to almost 600 million rubles, representing more than a quarter of the value of all warehouse stocks of equipment.

(4) In 1963 warehouse equipment stocks grew by almost 329 million rubles of which that part intended for use increased 203 millions or 10 percent; surplus equipment increased 126 million rubles or 27 percent.

These indications are sufficient to establish the following tabulation of absolute values (billion rubles):

Type of Equipment Stock	*Stocks at the Beginning of*			
	1961	*1962*	*1963*	*1964*
Awaiting installation	1.19	1.69	2.04	2.24
Surplus	.40	.42	.47	.60
	1.59	2.11	2.51	2.84

However, by my reconstruction, surplus equipment on January 1, 1964 was less than a quarter of the total, rather than the more than a quarter indicated by Riznik. Possibly he intended a comparison not with the sum of the two components but just with the value of equipment awaiting installation.

The series is partially extended with data from another source (Voziakov *et al.*, *FinSSSR*, 1966, No. 6, p. 22), according to which the stock of *neustanovlennoe* equipment came to 2.97 billion rubles on January 1, 1965 compared with 1.41 billions in 1960 (presumably, January 1). Hopefully, these figures refer to the sum of surplus equipment and equipment awaiting installation. Differences between the beginning year totals for 1960–1965 serve as my estimate of changes in the stock of equipment requiring installation for the period 1960–1964. (It is not clear whether all of surplus equipment requires installation. I shall assume that it does, but even if the assumption is wrong the resulting error cannot be very large.) Estimates for 1958–1959 are estimates based on the 1960–1964 figures and increments in the volume of unfinished construction at the beginning of the year (billion rubles; *NKh 1964*, p. 522):

	1958	*1959*	*1960*	*1961*	*1962*	*1963*	*1964*
Increment of unfinished construction	−0.1	1.5	2.4	3.4	1.3	0.1	0.9

I must also point out other information in Soviet sources at variance with that summarized above:

(1) The value of *neustanovlennoe* equipment (apparently exclusive of reserve stocks, equipment in storage, and equipment being shipped) is reported to have increased from 3644 million rubles on January 1, 1962, to 4840 millions on January 1, 1964 (Tikidzhiev and Rubinshtein, *PKh*, 1965, No. 7, p. 39). Presumably, these figures include machinery in the process of installation. If that is the explanation of the difference between these figures and those derived above from Riznik, the implication of juxtaposing the two sets of data is that the stock of equipment in the process of installation rose from 1.53 billion rubles at the beginning of 1962 to 2.00 billions, two years later.

(2) If the two sets of data are compatible, the relative share of each component in the total stock on the two dates was as follows (percent):

Type of Equipment Stock	*January 1, 1962*	*January 1, 1964*
Awaiting installation	46	46
In the process of installation	42	41
Surplus	12	12
Total	100	100

However, from indexes of growth of the three components and their total for 1962 and 1963 presented by Zel'tser (*VS,* 1963, No. 12, p. 12), the relative distribution of the total on January 1, 1962 may be computed as follows: awaiting installation 20 percent; in the process of installation 71 percent; surplus 9 percent.

Zel'tser and Riznik cite the same 1962–1963 indexes of growth for equipment awaiting installation and for surplus equipment. In another article (*PKh,* 1964, No. 8, pp. 51–52) Zel'tser provides growth indexes for the period 1961–1963; those relating to stocks of equipment awaiting installation and to surplus equipment are identical to Riznik's figures. Evidently, Zel'tser's indexes for equipment in the process of installation are not compatible with the Riznik data. Possibly, too, the cited absolute values for January 1, 1962 and 1964 are not compatible with either the Riznik or Zel'tser data. It is not immediately apparent how these contradictions can be resolved.

New investment. NKh 1962, p. 435 and *NKh 1964,* p. 515. These figures are the officially reported values at estimate prices which are alleged to be July 1, 1955 prices, adjusted for "new unit valuations introduced from 1956, the decrease of the norm of overhead expenditures from 1958, and the decrease from 1959 of prices of installing machinery" (*NKh 1964,* p. 507, note). A current-price series is not available, and no attempt is made to estimate one independently for reasons set out in Appendix K (pp. 513 ff.).

Collective farms: "gross investment" represents deductions from money incomes for allocation to the investment fund (p. 362).

Collective farms' internal financing of investment consists of money and in-kind resources. Since the latter are not included on the income side of the public sector balance, they must also be excluded here.

B. *Inventories.* Computed as follows (billion rubles):

	1958	*1959*	*1960*	*1961*	*1962*	*1963*	*1964*
Collective farms	.40	.33	.29	.37	.45	.49	.55
State-cooperative sector	7.50	9.08	4.51	5.69	5.29	7.48	11.08
Total public sector	7.90	9.41	4.80	6.06	5.74	7.97	11.63

Collective farm inventory investment represents allocations to the working capital fund from money incomes (as estimated by Nimitz—see above, p. 362). This procedure is analogous to that employed for collective farm fixed capital investment and the rationale is identical. Much of collective farm inventory investment does not represent outlays from money incomes—i.e., does not have a counterpart entry on the income side of the public sector's account and, hence, cannot be entered here on the outlay side. The estimate of allocations from incomes to the working capital fund, which are here taken to represent inventory investment, may err in the other direction by including increments in financial assets. However, there is reason to believe that allocations to the cultural fund, the third component of retained incomes (in addition to allocations to the investment and working capital funds), may also include some inventory investment (Rumiantseva, *Obshchestvennye fondy kolkhozov,* 1960, p. 24). It is assumed that omission of inventory investment in the form of allocations to the cultural fund offsets investment in financial assets from allocations to the working capital fund.

The statistical yearbooks contain relatively detailed data on working capital (*oborotnye sredstva*) in the state-cooperative sector, subdivided by branch of industry. Current assets are broken down into five categories—stocks of goods and supplies (*tovarno-material'nye tsennosti*); goods shipped and services performed; money and accounts; *debitory,* which consist of a variety of other financial claims; and other assets. To estimate inventories, it is of course necessary to deduct money and accounts as well as *debitory.* I also deduct the residual category of "other assets," the content of which is uncertain but more likely to be claims than material assets. (See the model balance sheet in Shchenkov, *Bukhgalterskii uchet v promyshlennosti,* 1961, pp. 376–383). An error in interpretation here probably will not affect my estimates substantially, since "other assets" account for only half of 1 percent of total current assets.

I exclude, in addition, goods shipped and services performed in construction and transportation-communication as well as expenses of future periods in all branches except construction. In construction and transportation-communication, the first named asset category is believed to consist largely of services; for all other branches of the economy, the corresponding designation is just "goods shipped." Expenses of future periods, a component of the category "stocks of goods and supplies" are deducted everywhere except in construction. According to Moorsteen and Powell, *The Soviet Capital Stock 1928–1962,* 1966 (p. 117), " 'expenses of future periods' appear to be essentially financial assets, though Soviet accounting practice may suggest a contrary interpretation." However, in construction these expenses "consist chiefly of outlays on temporary attachments and structures intended to service the construction site until the completion of operations" (VPSh, *Ekonomika stroitel'stva,* 1962, p. 468).

On this basis, I compute inventories valued at prices of the accounting date. Increments of inventories are valued at average prices of the respective years. The details of the calculation are shown in Appendix L.

The series of reported values on the level and structure of current assets, from which my estimates for 1959–1964 are derived, contains a gap between January 1, 1956 and January 1, 1959, and I am able to estimate inventory investment only for the three years as a whole. Using the procedure indicated, the three-year increment in stocks at current prices is calculated as 19.59 billion rubles. Estimates by Moorsteen and Powell, *The Soviet Capital Stock 1928–1962,* 1966 (pp. 457, 557, 591) suggest that roughly half the three-year overall increase occurred in 1958. For individual branches, the 1958 increment was about half the three-year increase in industry, one-third in state agriculture, half in procurement and almost three-fifths in domestic trade. On the other hand, a time series of sources of financing working capital presented by Zverev (*Natsional'nyi dokhod i finansy SSSR,* 1961, p. 150) shows that only 40 percent of the three year total occurred in 1958. (Zverev's figures evidently depart from the scope or coverage of the official data: his figures for "own and equivalent funds" and bank loans are 5–7 percent below the official figures for the two dates at which comparison is possible; the relative shortfall with respect to *kreditory* is substantially larger, about one-quarter.) Since part of the 1958 increment is also attributable to price changes in that year, I assume a figure of 7.5 billion rubles, or slightly less than 40 percent of the three year increment.

4. *Research and development.*

Table D-2, item 4.

5. *Internal security* (*MVD, KGB*).

The estimates assume continuation of the rate of expenditure in the middle 1950s (see *SNIP 1956–1958,* p. 118, and CIA, *The 1960 Soviet Budget,* November 1960, p. 43). In January 1960 the Ministry of Internal Affairs (MVD) was abolished at the Union level and replaced by republican Ministries for the Preservation of Public Order (MOOP); in that year residual outlays of the budgets of the Union-Republics increased by 651 million rubles over the previous year's level, compared with previous annual increases of 9, 47, 107, and 73 million rubles in the years 1956–1959 (*Gosbiudzhet I,* p. 72). This suggests a 1960 value of outlays on the MOOP of about half a billion rubles. On some evidence, the implied estimate of one billion rubles on the Committee on State Security (KGB) does not appear out of consideration:

(1) Nikolai Galay, an emigré specialist, estimates KGB manpower in 1962 as 350,000–400,000 (cited in Gass, *Commentary,* November 1963, p. 357). Assuming average annual earnings in that year of 1200 rubles, compared with the average for the entire state labor force of

1034 rubles (above, p. 295), direct personnel costs would amount to 420–480 million rubles, leaving roughly a half billion rubles for operation and maintenance, procurement, investment, and other outlays.

(2) The Institute for Strategic Studies estimated the size of Soviet "paramilitary forces"—security and border troops—as about 270,000 in the fall of 1964, reduced from a prior (date unspecified) level of 300,000 (*The Military Balance, 1964–1965,* November 1965, p. 3).

(3) According to the columnist, Victor Riesel, "a high official of the KGB (Soviet Committee of State Security) who defected not too long ago, revealed to FBI Director J. Edgar Hoover that the Russians' external intelligence apparatus has an annual budget of $1.5 billion." (*Los Angeles Times,* May 18, 1964.)

The reliability of this information is not known. Nor is it possible to evaluate a *New York Times* report (November 10, 1967, p. 14) that the KGB "employs 600,000 to one million people inside and outside the Soviet Union, according to Western estimates."

6. *Defense (explicit).*

Obtained as follows (billion rubles):

	1958	*1959*	*1960*	*1961*	*1962*	*1963*	*1964*
Identified budget defense	9.36	9.37	9.30	11.59	12.64	13.87	13.28
Less: Military pensions from defense funds	.30	.30	.30	.30	.30	.30	.30
Equals: Defense net of defense pensions	9.06	9.07	9.00	11.29	12.34	13.57	12.98

Identified budget defense data are from *Gosbiudzhet I,* p. 19 and *Gosbiudzhet II,* p. 21. On military pensions from the defense allocation see below, notes to item 9.A in this appendix, p. 399.

7. *Outlays n.e.c.; statistical discrepancy.*

Calculated as the difference between total outlays (item 10) and the sum of items 1–6 and 9.

Outlays n.e.c. encompass both operating and investment expenditures not elsewhere accounted for. In the former group, the major component is probably the so-called "operational expenditures," certain current budget-financed outlays of *khozraschet* enterprises, relating to: inventions; production rationalization and output of experimental models; maintaining icebreakers; maintaining waterways and hydro-technical installations; land use, forestry, and reclamation measures; animal and plant disease control and other agricultural activities; some geological-prospecting work (*The Soviet Financial System,* 1968, p. 81). Operational expenditures in agriculture alone rose from .4 billion rubles in

1958 to .5 billions in 1960 (*Gosudarstvennyi bank SSSR k xxii s"ezdu KPSS,* 1961, p. 56) and to .8 billions in 1964 plan (Bolgov *et al., Ekonomika sotsialisticheskogo sel'skogo khoziaistva,* 1965, p. 338). Budget outlays on inventories and rationalizations came to .01 billion rubles in 1958 and outlays by industrial enterprises from their own funds for these purposes were .08 billions (Birman *et al., Finansy predpriiatii i otraslei narodnogo khoziaistva,* 1960, p. 109).

Outlays n.e.c. of an investment character include miscellaneous capital outlays not included in the official investment statistics, government stockpiling, procurement of domestic gold production, and the net foreign balance. The available information on these outlays is set out as follows (most of the references given in paragraphs (1)b and (3) below were cited in an unpublished paper by Sally Anderson):

(1) The official data on investment by the state-cooperative sector exclude geological prospecting not connected with a particular investment project, urban planning and construction design, standard construction design, planting forests and forest belts, acquisition and formation of basic livestock herds (*NKh 1964,* pp. 511, 822); outlays for acquisition of draft livestock *are* included in the investment statistics. Indications of the volume of these expenditures are sketchy and frequently inconsistent but suggest annual values on the order of 3 or 4 billion rubles, derived as follows:

(a) Annual values for all the activities indicated plus collective farm outlays on livestock acquisition and formation of basic herds appear to have amounted to something like 5 billion rubles in the early 1960s. The rough indication is inferred from comparison of cumulative investment data, net and gross of these expenditures, as cited in succeeding yearbooks: *Kapstroi,* p. 22; *NKh 1961,* p. 530; *NKh 1962,* p. 429; *NKh 1963,* p. 451; *NKh 1964,* p. 511. Collective farm money outlays on acquisition of livestock came to about a billion rubles in 1960 and 1961 (Alekseeva and Voronin, *Nakoplenie i razvitie kolkhoznoi sobstvennosti,* 1963, p. 105). This, of course, excludes in kind outlays, but the latter were probably considerably smaller than money outlays.

(b) Budget outlays on standard construction design and other design operations whose value is not included in the fixed capital of the enterprises being planned have generally amounted to about 0.25 percent of investment (Nazarov, *PKh,* 1966, No. 7, p. 76). Assuming that the denominator in question is state-cooperative sector gross new investment, the amounts indicated are 60–100 million rubles.

(c) Expenditures on forming basic herds of state farms in 1963–

1965 came to 1.1–1.3 billion rubles (Semenov, *DiK,* 1965, No. 4, p. 39; Bolgov *et al., Ekonomika sotsialisticheskogo sel'skogo khoziaistva,* 1965, p. 339; Semenov, *FinSSSR,* 1965, No. 4, p. 32). These figures probably omit some state sector livestock investment but they may, on the other hand, include some purchases of draft livestock.

(2) Government stockpiling. I refer to additions to central state reserves rather than to ordinary inventories of enterprises and organizations. Estimates of annual increments to stockpiles must be very approximate, but a calculation in Chapter 7 (Table 25, item 2.B(4)) suggests sharply fluctuating levels on the order of 1–10 billion rubles. Whatever else they encompass, state reserves evidently embrace armaments as well. Thus, it is possible that additions to state reserves double count part of explicit defense expenditures, entered under item 6 of Table 4, or perhaps even of R&D outlays, under item 4. (See, however, the detailed discussion of the problem of concealed military outlays, presented in Chapter 7.)

(3) Purchases of domestic gold production. It is known that gold is purchased from the population by Gosbank with budget funds (Nazarkin, *Uchet i operatsionnaia tekhnika v Gosbanke,* 1959, p. 273). Presumably this is also the method of procuring domestic gold output. I assume that subsidies to producers are treated on a par with ordinary subsidies to *khozraschet* enterprises. The official purchase price after 1 January 1961 was set at 1 ruble per gram of pure gold or 1.3 percent higher than the simultaneously set gold content of the ruble, .987412 grains of pure gold (*Denezhnoe obrashchenie i kredit SSSR,* 1965, p. 413). The ruble value of Soviet production may be computed from the Bureau of Mine's estimates of Soviet physical output as follows (*Minerals Yearbook 1964,* Volume I, 1965, pp. 530–531; one troy ounce equals 31.103481 grams):

	1958	*1959*	*1960*	*1961*	*1962*	*1963*	*1964*
Output in million troy ounces	3.6	3.9	4.1	4.4	4.8	5.1	5.6
Output in million rubles	112	121	128	137	149	159	174

It seems a reasonable assumption that changes in the state's gold reserves are an element of the net increment in state reserves discussed above. The following discussion suggests that the changes in gold reserves are negative.

(4) The net foreign balance. The USSR publishes no official information on its balance of payments other than data on merchandise trade

valued at foreign trade rubles. Its merchandise trade balance has been as follows (*Vneshtorg 1959–1963*, p. 11; *Vneshtorg 1965*, p. 10):

	1958	*1959*	*1960*	*1961*	*1962*	*1963*	*1964*	*1965*
Million foreign trade rubles	−47	331	−60	154	518	192	−48	101

These figures may be entirely misleading as to both the magnitude and sign of the balance expressed in domestic prices. In the context of the 1959 input-output table, the merchandise trade balance in domestic prices has been reported as −3.8 billion rubles, the difference between 9.1 billions of imports and 5.3 billions of exports (Efimov and Berri, *Metody planirovaniia mezhotraslevykh proportsii,* 1965, pp. 96–97). The basis for valuation of foreign trade flows in the input-output table has never been made explicit. Treml (*The 1959 Soviet Intersectoral Flow Table,* 1964, I, pp. 29, 56 [note 25]) infers from a Soviet discussion of the 1962 *ex ante* input-output table that the valuation procedure in both 1962 and 1959 tables was identical to that used by the CSA in compiling national accounts—i.e., exports net and imports gross of turnover tax. The procedure seems appropriate for the SNIP accounts as well. If the Efimov-Berri figure is appropriately valued, if the trade balance time-series in foreign trade rubles can be taken as indicative of order of magnitude changes in the balance at domestic prices, it is then possible to speculate that the merchandise balance was chronically and significantly negative in the period under concern. The same conclusion has been prompted by other, indirect evidence—sustained high levels of sales of Soviet gold abroad. Thus, gold sales have been estimated as increasing from levels of $75 million in the late 1940s and early 1950s to $150 million in 1956 and to $200–300 million thereafter, with an extraordinary $500 million registered in 1963. Estimates of sales and of changes in reserves, based on the previously cited Bureau cf Mines estimate of production, are as follows (Bush, *Soviet Studies,* April 1966, p. 491; million dollars):

	1957	*1958*	*1959*	*1960*	*1961*	*1962*	*1963*	*1964*
Sales	260	210	255	210	265	215	560	320
Change in reserves	−137	−84	−118	−66	−111	−47	−381	−124

I assume that the net foreign balance is negative and roughly equal to the value of gold sales abroad. (For further discussion see *Dimensions of Soviet Economic Power,* 1962, pp. 453–455; *New Directions in the Soviet Economy,* 1966, p. 932.)

I cannot summarize the foregoing discussion in a series of numerical totals for the years of the SYP period. If the evidence on operational outlays and the capital expenditures not included in investment statistics indicate sums in the general environs of 5 billion rubles, the fragmentary information on state stockpiling and the balance of payments suggests small positive or even negative entries in the accounts. On balance one should probably not be surprised at the size of the residuals for most years shown in Table 4. However, the 1958 residual is probably too small, possibly reflecting an overstatement of inventory investment in that year (see above, item 3.B). The 1961 residual seems also understated. On the other hand, the residual value for 1960 appears high. Interestingly, the increment in inventories in that year is relatively low. Whether this relation is other than coincidental is not known. Finally, apart from omitted outlays, the residual includes the net effect of errors in all the other estimates of public sector incomes and outlays.

8. *Consolidated total value of goods and services, exclusive of sales to households.*

The sum of items 1–7.

9. *Transfer outlays.*

A. *Pensions and allowances.* Derived as follows (billion rubles):

	1958	*1959*	*1960*	*1961*	*1962*	*1963*	*1964*
Pensions and allowances, excluding those paid from defense funds	8.60	9.15	9.58	10.6	11.3	11.7	12.3
Pensions paid from defense funds	.30	.30	.30	.3	.3	.3	.3
Total	8.90	9.45	9.88	10.9	11.6	12.0	12.6

The first component is from Table D-4, item 3. Pensions paid from defense funds are estimated as .3 billion rubles a year, as in *SNIP 1956–1958,* pp. 119–120.

B. *Stipends.* Some nine-tenths of all stipends are at present financed from the state budget. Budget stipends are appropriated almost entirely through the outlay division "enlightenment" (*prosveshchenie*). In turn, two subdivisions, or outlay chapters (as Soviet accounting terms them), "higher educational institutions" and "specialized secondary educational institutions," account for the major share of "enlightenment" stipends. These relations form the basis for the estimates of total stipends, as follows:

(1) State budget stipends to students in higher educational institu-

tions amounted to 365 million rubles in 1958 and 355 million in 1959 (TsSU, *Vysshee obrazovanie v SSSR,* 1961, pp. 228–229); state budget stipends for specialized secondary students were 214 million rubles in 1957 (*Raskhody,* p. 55), 169 millions in 1959 and 163 millions in both 1960 and 1961 (TsSU, *Srednee spetsial'noe obrazovanie v SSSR,* 1962, p. 113). The 1958 figure is estimated by interpolation as 192 millions.

(2) Outlays on stipends do not appear to be a simple function of all outlays on the particular elements of education nor of the size of the student population, as shown below (stipends and budget outlays in million rubles; other units as indicated):

	1955	*1956*	*1957*	*1958*	*1959*	*1960*	*1961*
Higher education							
State budget stipends	362	376	366	365	355	..	..
All state budget outlays	1021	1072	1111	1141	1152	..	..
Day students enrolled (fall; thousands)	1147	1177	1193	1180	1146	..	..
Stipends per							
Ruble of budget outlays (kopecks)	35	35	33	32	31	..	..
Day student enrolled (rubles)	316	319	307	309	310	..	..
Specialized secondary education							
State budget stipends	246	253	214	..	169	163	163
All state budget outlays	592	619	583	..	523	527	552
Day students enrolled (fall; thousands)	1470	1407	1259	1125	1067	1091	1203
Stipends per							
Ruble of budget outlays (kopecks)	42	41	37	..	32	31	30
Day student enrolled (rubles)	167	180	170	..	158	149	135

Sources of data are TsSU, *Vysshee obrazovanie v SSSR,* 1961, pp. 80, 228–229; *Raskhody,* p. 55; and TsSU, *Srednee spetsial'noe obrazovanie v SSSR,* 1962, pp. 69, 113.

The data indicate a declining share of stipends in budget outlays on either major subcategory as well as a declining average stipend per day student in specialized secondary schools. For purposes of estimating stipends after 1959 or 1961, I assume average stipends of 300 rubles per day student in higher education and 125 rubles per day student in specialized secondary education. Data on enrollments are taken from *NKh 1962*, p. 562 and *NKh 1964*, p. 678. The calculation is as follows:

	1960	*1961*	*1962*	*1963*	*1964*
Day students enrolled in the fall (thousands)					
Higher education	1156	1204	1287	1383	1514
Specialized secondary education			1310	1474	1634
State budget outlays on stipends (million rubles)					
Higher education	347	361	386	415	454
Specialized secondary education			164	184	204

(3) Stipends from the republican budgets to other subcategories—science and unspecified "others"—were 27–30 million rubles in 1956–1958 but roughly 85–100 million rubles in 1959–1964 (*Gosbiudzhet I* (and *II*): the difference between education totals on p. 76 (p. 78) and the sum of identified subcategory stipends on pp. 77, 84 and 85 (pp. 79, 86, 87)).

(4) The following reported and estimated values of budget stipends have now been accumulated (million rubles):

	1958	*1959*	*1960*	*1961*	*1962*	*1963*	*1964*
(a) State budget stipends for							
Higher education	365	355	347	361	386	415	454
Specialized secondary education	192	169	163	163	164	184	204
(b) Republican budget stipends to science and unspecified other subcategories	28	93	84	85	108	86	89
(c) Subtotal, (a) and (b)	585	617	594	609	658	685	747

In 1956 and 1957 the corresponding subtotals accounted for 86 and 88 percent of total budget stipends to all education (*Raskhody*, p. 46). On the assumption of an average ratio of 90 percent after 1957, total budget stipends to education may be estimated as (million rubles):

1958	650	1962	731
1959	686	1963	761
1960	660	1964	830
1961	677		

(5) In 1964 enterprises and organizations furnished 9.6 percent of all stipends (Borisov, *Balans denezhnykh dokhodov i raskhodov naseleniia*, 1965, p. 48). Thus, 1964 stipends paid by nonbudget sources were about 90 million rubles and stipends from all sources about 920

millions. This total is projected back in time in proportion to the changes in the estimated series of budget stipends.

C. *Interest payments to households.* Derived as follows (billion rubles):

	1958	*1959*	*1960*	*1961*	*1962*	*1963*	*1964*
Interest on savings deposits	.21	.23	.26	.28	.31	.33	.37
Interest on bonds	.04	.05	.05	.05	.05	.01	.01
Total	.25	.28	.31	.33	.36	.34	.38

Savings deposits earn interest at the rate of 2 percent (demand, "conditional" and current accounts) or 3 percent (time deposits) annually. In addition, lottery deposits may win amounts calculated on the basis of a 2 percent annual rate (*Finansovo-kreditnyi slovar',* II, p. 252). I assume an average annual interest rate of 2.5 percent and apply it to average annual deposits computed as follows (billion rubles):

	1957	*1958*	*1959*	*1960*	*1961*	*1962*	*1963*	*1964*
Savings deposits								
At end of year	8.06	8.72	10.06	10.91	11.67	12.75	13.99	15.71
Average annual		8.39	9.39	10.48	11.29	12.21	13.37	14.85

Deposits at the end of the year are from *NKh 1959,* p. 810; *NKh 1962,* p. 492; *NKh 1964,* p. 595.

For interest on bonds, see above, p. 380.

Lottery winnings are netted out of the data on sales of tickets and are therefore not included here. See above, p. 382.

D. *Net new bank loans to households. NKh 1959,* p. 807; *NKh 1962,* p. 639; *NKh 1964,* p. 774.

10. *Consolidated total outlays.*

Equals consolidated net income, Table C, item 10.

TABLE D-1

OUTLAYS ON EDUCATION, 1958–1964

(billion rubles)

	1958	1959	1960	1961	1962	1963	1964
1. All outlays on education							
A. State budget	8.60	9.41	10.32	11.35	12.44	13.71	15.10
B. Other	1.84	2.07	2.29	2.6	2.8	3.3	3.7
C. Total	10.44	11.48	12.61	14.0	15.2	17.0	18.8
2. Stipends	.72	.76	.73	.75	.81	.84	.92
3. Capital outlays							
A. New investment	1.31	1.63	1.95	2.09	2.23	2.24	2.47
B. Capital repairs	.44	.48	.53	.59	.64	.71	.78
C. Total	1.75	2.11	2.48	2.68	2.87	2.95	3.25
4. Current outlays, excluding stipends	7.97	8.61	9.40	10.6	11.5	13.2	14.6

Sources:

1. *All outlays on education.*

A. *State budget. NKh 1962*, p. 637; *NKh 1964*, p. 772.

B. *Other.* Item 1.C less item 1.A.

C. *Total. NKh 1960*, p. 848; *NKh 1962*, p. 637; *NKh 1964*, p. 772. According to *Strana sovetov za 50 let*, p. 244, the 1960 total is 13.6 billion rubles. Because of uncertainty as to the scope and reference of this figure, I choose to disregard it. See the detailed discussion on pp. 408–409.

2. *Stipends.*

See above, pp. 399–401.

3. *Capital outlays.*

The available data on investment in education may be compared by source as follows (billion rubles):

	1950	*1953*	*1955*	*1956*	*1957*	*1958*	*Average 1956–1958*	*1960*	*1962*
Finstroi (p. 349):									
All budget investment from division enlightenment, at current prices	.257	..	.337	.421	←		n.a.		→
Raskhody (p. 46):									
Identified budget investment from division enlightenment, at current prices									
Investment	.257	.277	.333	.411	.547	←	n.a.		→
Capital repairs	.168	.175	.202	.232	.264				
Total	.425	.452	.535	.643	.811				
NKh 1958 (p. 905):									
Investment in enlightenment, all state-cooperative									

TABLE D-1 (continued)

	1950	1953	1955	1956	1957	1958	Average 1956–1958	1960	1962
sources, at presumably current prices	.42	.51	.56	.70	.84	←———	n.a.	———→	
VS, 1963, No. 5 (p. 95):									
Investment in institutions of enlightenment and culture, at constant prices									
Collective farms	..	..	..	..	..	..	.297	.361	.295
State-cooperative	..	..	..	..	..	..	.815	1.286	1.630
Total	..	..	..	..	..	..	1.112	1.647	1.925
NKh 1963 (pp. 452, 454) and *NKh 1964* (pp. 514–515):									
Construction of institutions of science, culture, art, enlightment, at constant prices									
Collective farms	.053	..	..	..	..	.311	..	.361	.216
State-cooperative	.382	..	..	..	..	1.320	..	2.100	2.655
Total	.435	..	..	..	..	1.631	..	2.461	2.871

The budget division (*razdel*) enlightenment (*prosveshchenie*) encompasses the following major chapters (*glavi*): general education (*obrazovanie*), cultural-enlightenment work, preparation of cadres (specialized secondary and higher education are the major subcomponents), science, press, art and broadcasting. The *NKh 1958* data refer to enlightenment and mean the entire division, whereas the *VS* table defines institutions of enlightenment (again, *prosveshchenie*) as "schools, higher educational institutions, technicums, children's institutions and the like" and those of culture as "theaters, movies, clubs, houses of culture, and the like;" the later *NKh* provide no detail on coverage. Data in *VS*, *NKh 1963* and *NKh 1964* exclude capital repairs; whether *NKh 1958* figures do so too is not indicated.

What inferences can be drawn from the data?

(1) The *VS* data probably cover the activities of general education, cultural-enlightenment work, and preparation of cadres, from budget and other sources. In referring to science, culture, art, and enlightenment, *NKh 1963* and *NKh 1964* probably cover all, or virtually all, the activities of the entire budget division.

(2) Collective farm outlays in the *VS* series most likely are of the same coverage as in the later *NKh* series; the 1962 figures from *VS* are declared "preliminary" in the source, thus possibly explaining the difference between the collective farm entries for that year in the two series.

(3) To judge by the comparison with *Finstroi*, *Raskhody's* identified investment in education encompasses virtually all such investment—100 percent in 1950, 98.8 percent in 1955 and 97.6 percent in 1956. The total for 1957 might be estimated as about .56

TABLE D-1 (continued)

billion rubles. Such a conclusion seems disturbing for the following reason: In a corresponding functional distribution of budget outlays from the chapter science, *Raskhody* (p. 59) fails to identify large sums, ranging from roughly 40 percent of the total in the early 1950s to 60 percent by 1957. Nimitz (*Soviet Expenditures on Scientific Research*, January 1963, p. 14) has interpreted these omissions as the outlays of whole institutions, which suggests that the investment outlays of these institutions would also be omitted. On the other hand, the *Raskhody* distribution may omit a number of articles of expenditure including above-plan investment, judging from a comparison with a listing of the titles of the articles applicable to budget organizations presented in *The Soviet Financial System*, 1968, Table 5–11, p. 78. However, since *Finstroi* claims to include above-plan investment, it must be small and perhaps accounts for the small difference with the *Raskhody* series.

The value of total investment in science for 1958 and 1960 may be derived independently as follows (million rubles; estimate prices):

	1958	*1960*
Public sector investment in		
Trade, municipal economy, and health care (*Nkh 1963*, p. 452)	2,670	3,461
Less: trade and municipal (*Kapstroi*, p. 187)	2,265	2,946
Equals: health care	405	515
Science, culture, education, and health care (*Kapstroi*, p. 187)	2,001	2,853
Less: health care	405	515
Equals: science, culture, and education	1,596	2,338
Less: culture and education (*VS*, 1963, No. 5, p. 95)	1,300	1,647
Equals: science	296	691

The 1958 figure for investment in culture and education is an estimate derived by averaging the average annual value for 1956–1958 and the annual value for 1959, given in the source.

Identified budget investment from the science chapter was close to 100 million rubles in 1957, according to *Raskhody*. If the corresponding figure for 1958 was 125–150 millions (the budget appropriation to science, current and capital, rose 25 percent in 1958 —*Gosbiudzhet I*, p. 22), 150–175 millions would have come from budget appropriations to the chapter higher education and to the division national economy and from decentralized sources. This does not appear inconceivable.

(4) Do the *NKh 1958* data include or exclude capital repairs?

(a) Assume first that capital repairs are included. Then the small differences between the *NKh 1958* figures and the *Raskhody* totals, apart from the insignificant amount of investment noted as omitted from *Raskhody* by comparison with the data of *Finstroi*, may be due to one of two factors: (i) The *NKh 1958* values are at estimate prices which are higher than current prices, the basis of *Raskhody* valuation. The hypothesized difference between estimate and current price levels appears to be true for state-cooperative construction in the period 1956–1958, but not for the period 1950–1955, judging by official Soviet data (*Kapstroi*, pp. 258–259). However, too little information is available on the scope and reliability of the price and cost indexes for an adequate test of the hypothesis. (ii) Investment in education from other budget divisions and from other state cooperative sources is very small—indeed zero in 1950; for other years the implied figures are .06 billion rubles in 1953, .02 billions in 1955, .06 billions in 1956 and .02 billions in 1957. Yet a footnote in *Raskhody* warns that the figures shown are net of investment by "economic organizations." Moreover, *Finstroi* declares that beyond the sums originating in the specific budget divisions concerned with health and education outlays, "substantial capital investment in construction of social-cultural institutions, carried out by economic organizations, is transmitted through the division 'national economy'."

(b) Suppose the *NKh 1958* figures exclude capital repairs.

If the *NKh 1958* data are at current prices, the implied values of state-cooperative in-

TABLE D-1 (continued)

vestment other than from the budget division enlightenment may be shown as follows (billion rubles):

	1950	*1953*	*1955*	*1956*	*1957*
Total state cooperative investment (*NKh 1958*)	.42	.51	.56	.70	.84
All investment from budget "enlightenment"	.26	.28	.34	.42	.56
	.16	.23	.22	.28	.28

(i) If the *NKh 1958* data are at estimate prices they presumably belong to the same series as the state-cooperative data from the later *NKh*. However, the one-year increase in investment in 1958, implied by joining the two series, is a whopping 57 percent. This is approximately the increase between the first two entries in the later *NKh* series, but the interval here is two years. In the *NKh 1958* series the annual increases are 25 and 20 percent, respectively.

(ii) The assumption that the *NKh 1958* data are at current prices makes better sense in view of the previous indication of a probably higher estimate price level in 1956–1958 compared with current prices. Thus, it would be expected that the 1950 state-cooperative datum from the later *NKh* would be smaller than the corresponding *NKh 1958* figure. However, the indicated difference of 10 percent seems small. On the other hand, it is difficult to believe that the difference between estimate and current prices in 1957–1958 was so large as to explain the 57 percent increase in 1958 between the two series.

The later *NKh* series arouse misgivings on their own account. Thus, the series, "construction of trade and communal enterprises, institutions of science, culture, art, enlightenment and health care" in *NKh 1963* includes 35 million rubles for 1958 and 123 million rubles for 1960 which were classified with investment in Group A industry in *NKh 1962* (p. 435, state-cooperative sectors only).

[Calculated as follows: investment in Group B industry, agriculture, and housing are the same for the two years in both yearbooks. Data for 1962 in *NKh 1962* were preliminary figures and must be omitted from this test. *NKh 1963* separates out the construction industry from other Group A industry investment. The sum of investment in Group A and the construction industries as shown in *NKh 1963* is 257 and 459 million rubles less than investment in Group A industry shown in *NKh 1962* for 1958 and 1960. All of this difference except 35 million rubles in 1958 and 123 millions in 1960 is accounted for by an increase in the investment shown in transport and communication.]

Possibly of greater significance is another question of coverage. The investment tables in the yearbooks make no mention of investment in administrative, internal security, and other military facilities, nor is there any unexplained residual in the distribution that might be attributed to these components. Either administration and military investment is excluded from the reported data or it is concealed within one of the subcategories. A likely place for inclusion would be the subcategories covering nonproductive investment.

I therefore assume that the unusually large increase between 1957 and 1958, comparing *NKh 1958* and the later *NKh* series, is only partly accounted for by growth in education investment and by differences between current and estimate prices; the later *NKh* series are assumed to include the unidentified investment in administration and military facilities. To estimate investment in education I assume a 1958 state-cooperative current-price value of 1.00 billion rubles, equivalent to a 19 percent increase over the 1957 entry in *NKh 1958*, and I move the 1958 value forward in proportion to the later *NKh* series. Investment by collective farms is added as reported. Figures for 1959 and 1961 are estimated by interpolation.

Since *Raskhody* investment figures appear to reflect all budget investment from the division enlightenment, I assume this is the case for capital repairs as well. No further data are available on capital repairs financed from the state budget. However, outlays from the republican budgets are available for later years (*Gosbiudzhet I*, p. 76 and *Gosbiudzhet II*, p. 78). In the last three years for which state budget figures may be compared with republican budget data, the former exceed the latter by 22 percent in 1955,

TABLE D-1 (continued)

19 percent in 1956, and 14 percent in 1957; the margin was 26 percent in 1950. The margin is assumed to have been 14 percent in 1958, implying a capital repairs total for "enlightenment" of 291 million rubles.

I further assume that this figure accounts for two-thirds of all public sector outlays on capital repair of educational capital in that year, or .44 billion rubles. This relation is derived from a comparison of the investment series of *Finstroi* and *Raskhody* with that of *NKh 1958;* the investment ratios are about 60 percent in 1950, 1955 and 1956, and 65 percent in 1957. (In this calculation collective farm repairs may be neglected. Amortization computed on all nonproductive buildings and structures of collective farms totalled 32 million rubles in 1959 and 37 millions in 1960, according to *Effektivnost kapital'nykh vlozhenii v sel'skoe khoziaistvo*, 1963, p. 131; capital repair outlays are always a fraction of annual amortization.)

Official statistics (*NKh 1964*, p. 68) imply an average annual rate of increase in the stock of nonproductive capital other than housing of about 12 percent in the period after 1958. A very small part of nonhousing, nonproductive capital consists of capital in the municipal economy and everyday services (*bytovoe obsluzhivanie*). Educational facilities probably make up a substantial portion of the remainder. Hence, educational capital is likely to have expanded at a rapid rate in this period. It may be assumed that outlays on capital repairs move more or less in proportion to the increase in the capital stock. I therefore project the 1958 estimate of .44 billion rubles at an average annual rate of 10 percent.

Note that similar results would be obtained by projection according to the reported republican budget outlays on enlightenment repairs, which, under my assumption, account for almost 60 percent of total capital repair outlays in 1958. Republican budget outlays grew somewhat faster than 10 percent per year in 1959–1961 and somewhat slower in 1962–1964. For the entire period, the average annual rate of growth is 9.1 percent.

3. *Current outlays, excluding stipends.*

Item 1.C less items 2 and 3.C.

TABLE D-2
OUTLAYS ON SCIENCE, 1958–1964
(billion rubles)

	1958	1959	1960	1961	1962	1963	1964
1. All outlays on science							
A. State budget	1.70	2.00	2.34	2.68	3.01	3.46	3.97
B. Other	.72	.82	.95	1.1	1.3	1.4	1.4
C. Total	2.42	2.82	3.29	3.8	4.3	4.9	5.4
2. Stipends	.02	.02	.03	.03	.03	.04	.04
3. Capital outlays							
A. New investment	.30	.45	.69	.80	.90	1.03	1.13
B. Capital repairs	.04	.04	.05	.05	.06	.06	.07
C. Total	.34	.49	.74	.85	.96	1.09	1.20
4. Current outlays, excluding stipends	2.06	2.31	2.52	2.9	3.3	3.8	4.2

Sources:

1. *All outlays on science.*

A. *State budget. NKh 1962*, p. 638; *NKh 1964*, p. 773.

B. *Other.* Row 1.C less row 1.A. These figures would include not only enterprise outlays from their own funds but also budget funds not designated to science: e.g., R&D outlays financed from the budget division national economy or from the appropriation to higher educational institutions, possibly even from the appropriation to defense. See Nimitz, *Soviet Expenditures on Scientific Research*, January 1963, p. 12; *NKh 1962*, p. 690.

C. *Total.* 1958–1962: *NKh 1960*, p. 848; *NKh 1962*, p. 637. 1963: 1964 Plan goal of 5.2 billion rubles was 5.6 percent greater than 1963 level (*Pravda*, December 17, 1963, p. 6). 1964: 1965 Plan goal of 5.9 billion rubles was 8.7 percent greater than 1964 level (Garbuzov, *FinSSSR*, 1965, No. 1, p. 16).

To what extent do these figures include investment? The yearbook tables have been generally silent on this issue but the notes in the back of the yearbooks (e.g., *NKh 1962*, p. 690); *NKh 1964*, p. 832) seem to be unequivocal in declaring the inclusion of investment. However, the question is raised inferentially in a statement by a reliable observer, Sominskii (*Ekon. gazeta*, 1967, No. 10, p. 7), that 1967 planned total outlays on science of 7.2 billion rubles excluded construction of "scientific institutions and experimental bases." Addition of the latter component would raise the total to about 9 billion rubles. Since the figure of 7.2 billions seems to be in the same series as item 1.C of this table (see Nimitz, *Addendum to Soviet Expenditures on Scientific Research*), the inference to be drawn is that row 1.C excludes construction of "scientific institutions and experimental bases."

To add to the confusion, the statistical volume celebrating the Soviet jubilee (*Strana sovetov za 50 let*, 1967, p. 244) supplies a figure for all outlays on science in 1960, purportedly in the same series as row 1.C. of this table but explicitly inclusive of investment, which is 0.6 billion rubles higher than the figure shown in previous yearbooks. Earlier (p. 405) I derived an independent figure for 1960 investment in science at estimate prices of 691 million rubles, or slightly more than the difference of 0.6 billions just indicated. Are we then to assume that new investment, in part or in whole, is excluded from entries in row 1.C.?

The evidence of *Strana sovetov* is, however, not completely clear on this point. To begin with, the source does not give data for years comparable with those covered by previous yearbooks except for 1960. Even for 1960, the new data are difficult to interpret. Thus, as compared with the corresponding figures from previous yearbooks, *Strana sovetov* indicates a *decrease* in health care and physical culture (from all sources) of 0.2

TABLE D-2 (continued)

billion rubles, exactly matched by an increase in social assistance and social insurance outlays. Not only are expenditures on science increased but so are those on all of the enlightenment. However, the increase in the latter, 1.0 billion rubles, is far short of investment in science, culture, and education in that year, 2.3 billion rubles (p. 405). Possibly, the differences between *Strana sovetov* and previous yearbooks represent reclassifications of certain activities or institutions.

The statistical sources of prior years seem clear enough on the inclusion of construction in reported outlays on science:

(1) In a distribution of budget outlays on science by type of expenditure, the official handbook *Raskhody* (pp. 59–60) shows entries for "capital investment in construction." Such entries are listed in breakdowns of both the union and republican budget totals for the years 1950–1957.

(2) The official handbook *Gosbiudzhet I* (p. 86) provides a comparable breakdown of republican budget outlays for the years 1950, 1955–1960. "Capital investment in construction" is one of the rows and the entries in the row for common years are identical with those published in *Raskhody.*

(3) *Gosbiudzhet II* (p. 88), which covers the years 1950, 1955, 1960–1965, also provides a breakdown of republican budget expenditures on science. The distribution does not list an item called "capital investment in construction" but, instead, one labelled "capital investment according to the state plan"; otherwise the item listing is identical with that in *Gosbiudzhet I.* For common years, the entries in *Gosbiudzhet II* under the indicated rubric differ from the construction entries in *Gosbiudzhet I* by small amounts: 0.9 *million* rubles in 1950, 2.1 millions in 1955, and 1.2 millions in 1960. Similarly small differences appear in comparing other rows of the distribution from the two sources. These differences appear to be explained by a change in classification: outlays on museums and permanent exhibitions, previously included with science, were reclassified as cultural-enlightenment outlays, another component of the budget division enlightenment (*Gosbiudzhet II*, p. 6).

(4) Notes at the back of the statistical yearbook state that the figures for expenditures on social-cultural measures from all sources, of which entries in row 1.C of this table are components, include, among other sources of finance: "outlays on social-cultural measures (including capital investment) of the state budget and the budget of state social insurance; . . . . Capital investment in construction of social-cultural objects from sources of financing the national economy. . . ." (*NKh 1965*, p. 848; also *NKh 1964*, p. 832 and *NKh 1963*, p. 714). The second element of the passage quoted indicates that not only do the figures in row 1.C include investment from the budget appropriation designated to science but also from that designated to the division national economy.

Thus, reported outlays on science from the budget and other sources are explicitly indicated as including investment in construction. Whether a change in coverage took place subsequently is not known. I choose to ignore Sominskii, relying instead on the previous yearbooks' indications of the inclusion of investment. Also, I leave the 1960 figure unchanged until such time as *Strana sovetov*'s series can be reconciled with prior official data.

2. *Stipends.*

Identified stipends in the budget appropriation to science came to 7 million rubles in 1956 and 8 million in 1957, according to *Raskhody*, p. 59. However, a sizable portion of budget outlays on science are omitted in this source's distribution of expenditures by type (see above, p. 405). The difference between the reported figures and my estimate for 1958 is intended to allow for (i) stipends in the unidentified budget outlays, (ii) stipends from nonbudget expenditures on science, if any, and (iii) increases in the level of spending between 1957 and 1958. Estimates for other years assume that stipends were a constant proportion of all outlays on science. See also above, pp. 399–401.

3. *Capital outlays.*

A. *New investment.* The 1958 and 1960 figures are obtained as follows (million rubles):

TABLE D-2 (continued)

	1958	*1960*
Investment in science, culture, education and health care (*Kapstroi*, p. 187)	2001	2853
Less: investment in health care (Table D-3, item 2.A)	405	515
Less: investment in culture and education (*VS*, 1963, No. 5, p. 95)	1300	1647
Equals: investment in science	296	691

The 1958 figure for investment in culture and education is an estimate based on data reported in the indicated source showing average annual values for 1956–1958 and annual values for 1959–1962.

The possibility of inclusion in these figures of investment in administrative and/or military facilities cannot be ruled out. See above, p. 406.

Failing any other basis of projecting the estimated 1958 and 1960 values of investment in science, I assume growth in proportion to total gross outlays. The 1959 figure is obtained by simple interpolation between the 1958 and 1960 figures.

B. *Capital repairs.* Previously (above, p. 405) I estimated that identified budget investment in science in 1958 accounted for roughly half of all investment in science. I now assume this was true for capital repairs as well. Identified budget financing of science capital repairs was 12 million rubles in 1956 and 15 million in 1957 (*Raskhody*, p. 59); I assume 20 millions in 1958. The estimate of all science capital repairs of 40 million rubles in 1958 is projected at an average annual rate of 10 percent, compared to 15 percent for total gross outlays.

4. *Current outlays, excluding stipends.*

Item 1.C less items 2 and 3.C.

TABLE D-3

OUTLAYS ON HEALTH CARE AND PHYSICAL CULTURE, 1958–1964
(billion rubles)

	1958	1959	1960	1961	1962	1963	1964
1. All outlays on health care and physical culture							
A. State budget	4.11	4.46	4.82	4.99	4.95	5.26	5.66
B. Social insurance budget	.32	.32	.35	.33	.38	.40	.41
C. Other	.60	.76	.73	.8	.9	.9	1.1
D. Total	5.03	5.54	5.90	6.1	6.2	6.6	7.2
2. Capital outlays							
A. New investment	.41	.46	.52	.55	.56	.59	.65
B. Capital repairs	.21	.23	.25	.26	.28	.30	.32
C. Total	.62	.69	.77	.81	.84	.89	.97
3. Current outlays	4.41	4.85	5.13	5.3	5.4	5.7	6.2

Sources:

1. *All outlays on health and physical culture.*

A. *State budget. NKh 1962*, p. 638 and *NKh 1964*, p. 773.

B. *Social insurance budget. NKh 1962*, p. 639 and *NKh 1964*, p. 774 (the sum of outlays on sanatoria and on services to children).

C. *Other.* Obtained as the difference between item 1.D and the sum of items 1.A and 1.B.

D. *Total. NKh 1960*, p. 848; *NKh 1962*, p. 637; *NKh 1964*, p. 772.

2. *Capital outlays.*

A. *New investment.* Available data on investment in health care and physical culture are as follows (billion rubles):

	1950	*1953*	*1955*	*1956*	*1957*	*1958*	*1960*
Finstroi (p. 349):							
All budget investment from divisions "health care" and "physical culture" at current prices	.070	..	.121	.151	n.a.	n.a.	n.a.
Raskhody (p. 71):							
Identified budget investment from division "health care," at current prices							
Investment	.067	.070	.095	.114	.155	n.a.	n.a.
Capital repairs	.068	.078	.085	.096	.115	n.a.	n.a.
NKh 1958, p. 905:							
Investment in "health care" and "physical culture," all state-cooperative sources, at presumably current prices	.18	.21	.27	.33	.33	n.a.	n.a.
NKh 1963 (p. 452) and *Kapstroi* (p. 187):							
All public sector at estimate prices:							
Construction of trade and communal enterprises and institutions of health care	..	..	..	..	..	2.670	3.461
Less: construction of trade and communal enterprises	..	..	..	..	..	2.265	2.946
Equals: construction of institutions of health care	..	..	..	..	..	.405	.515

TABLE D-3 (continued)

The *Raskhody* investment series covers a decreasing portion of total state budget outlays from the divisions health care and physical culture, judging by comparison with the *Finstroi* data. The latter series in turn covers somewhat less than half of total state-cooperative outlays as measured by the *NKh 1958* series. The value of all public sector health care investment (at estimate prices) in 1958 is a fifth to a quarter larger than the current-price, state-cooperative value for 1957; the difference does not seem unreasonable. (For discussion of these sources with reference to investment in education, see above, pp. 403–407.)

As the 1958 and 1960 new investment entries I take the indicated estimate-price values. A corresponding value for 1959 of 460 millions is estimated by simple interpolation. These figures represent 8.1, 8.3, and 8.7 percent of item 1.D in 1958, 1959, and 1960, respectively. It is assumed that after 1960 new investment accounted for 9 percent of total outlays on health care and physical culture.

Since the *Raskhody* data cover roughly half of all new investment by the state-cooperative sector, it is likely that the same source's capital repairs figures are similarly understatements of the relevant totals (collective farm repairs are negligible). Thus, all capital repairs in 1957 are estimated as .20 billion rubles. No further data on state budget outlays are available; only republican budget expenditures have been reported (*Gosbiudzhet I*, p. 88 and *Gosbiudzhet II*, p. 90). In 1955–1957, the last three years covered in common by these sources, identified state budget outlays (from the health care division) on capital repairs were 8.1, 6.9, and 4.8 percent greater than the expenditures from republican budgets. The republican budget outlay series grows somewhat erratically after 1957 and at an average annual rate of 6.8 percent between 1958 and 1964, with a 21 percent increase in 1958. I assume an annual growth rate for all public sector repairs of 7 percent.

3. *Current outlays.*

Item 1.D less item 2.C.

TABLE D-4

OUTLAYS ON PENSIONS AND ALLOWANCES, EXCLUDING PENSIONS PAID FROM DEFENSE FUNDS, 1958–1964
(billion rubles)

	1958	1959	1960	1961	1962	1963	1964
1. State budget outlays							
A. Pensions							
(1) From social insurance budget [a]	4.06	4.49	4.95	5.47	5.97	6.47	6.96
(2) From social assistance allocation (net of funds transferred from social insurance budget) [a]	2.25	2.15	2.0	2.2	2.2	2.2	2.3
(3) Total	6.31	6.64	7.0	7.7	8.2	8.7	9.3
B. Allowances (*posobiia*)							
(1) From social insurance budget [b]	1.51	1.75	1.85	2.14	2.28	2.20	2.20
(2) Mothers' allowances	.53	.50	.50	.49	.48	.47	.47
(3) Total	2.04	2.25	2.35	2.63	2.76	2.67	2.67
C. Total	8.35	8.89	9.4	10.3	11.0	11.4	12.0
2. Outlays of enterprises, organizations, cooperatives	.25	.26	.2	.3	.3	.3	.3
3. Total outlays	8.60	9.15	9.58	10.6	11.3	11.7	12.3

Notes:

[a] Part of the social insurance budget appears in the state budget as the allocation to social insurance. The balance is transferred in the budget accounts to social assistance.

[b] Largely, pregnancy, maternity, and temporary disability allowances.

Sources:

1. *State budget outlays.*

A. *Pensions.* (1) *From social insurance budget. NKh 1962*, p. 639, *NKh 1964*, p. 774.

(2) *From social assistance allocation, etc.* Obtained as the difference between item 1.A(3) and 1.A(1).

(3) *Total.* 1958: *SNIP 1956–1958*, p. 130. 1960: *NKh 1960*, p. 848. 1961: *NKh 1961*, p. 765. 1962: *NKh 1962*, p. 639. 1963: *NKh 1963*, p. 658. The 1959 value was estimated as follows: Total pensions including those paid from life insurance funds amounted to 6.68 billion rubles in 1959 (*NKh 1959*, p. 806). It is assumed that pensions from life insurance funds accounted for no more than .04 billion rubles, as compared with an estimated .03 billion in 1958 (*SNIP 1956–1958*, p. 130). For 1964 no budget total is given in the 1964 yearbook. Instead, total outlays on pensions from all sources are reported for the years 1950, 1958, 1960, 1963, and 1964 (*NKh 1964*, p. 772). These totals exceed the entries for item 1.A(3) in this table by .1 billion rubles in 1958, .2 billions in 1960, and .2 billions in 1963. A difference of .2 billions is assumed for 1964.

B. *Allowances.* (1) *From social insurance budget. NKh 1962*, p. 639; *NKh 1964*, p. 774.

(2) *Mothers' allowances. NKh 1962*, p. 638; *NKh 1964*, p. 773.

(3) *Total.* The sum of components.

C. *Total.* The sum of components.

2. *Outlays of enterprises, organizations, cooperatives.*

Obtained as the difference between item 3 and item 1.C.

3. *Total outlays.*

Computed as follows (billion rubles):

	1958	*1959*	*1960*	*1961*	*1962*	*1963*	*1964*
Outlays on social assistance and social insurance from all sources	8.78	9.35	9.78	10.8	11.5	11.9	12.5
Less: social assistance outlays excluding pensions and allowances	.18	.20	.20	.2	.2	.2	.2
Total outlays on pensions and allowances	8.60	9.15	9.58	10.6	11.3	11.7	12.3

TABLE D-4 (continued)

Aggregate outlays from all sources are from *NKh 1960*, p. 848, *NKh 1962*, p. 637, and *NKh 1964*, p. 772. State budget social assistance outlays include some outlays for purposes other than pensions or allowances. These are computed as follows:

	1958	*1959*	*1960*	*1961*	*1962*	*1963*	*1964*
State budget allocations to social assistance, net of funds transferred from the social insurance budget (*NKh 1962*, p. 638; *NKh 1964*, p. 773)	2.43	2.35	2.26	2.39	2.45	2.44	2.48
Less: Pensions from social assistance allocation (item 1.A(2))	2.25	2.15	2.0	2.2	2.2	2.2	2.3
Equals: Social assistance outlays excluding pensions and allowances	.18	.20	.3	.2	.3	.2	.2

The fluctuations in the entries of the final row are doubtless due in considerable part to the rounding of entries in the middle row. Hence, it is assumed that after 1958 the allocations for purposes other than pensions and allowances were a constant .20 billion rubles.

E

Sources to Table 1: 1965S

1. *Wages and salaries, farm and nonfarm.*

A. *Worker and employee wage and salary bill.* The SYP target for the number of workers and employees in 1965S was 66.5 million or 22 percent more than in 1958. According to an English language broadcast of Radio Moscow on November 14, 1958, the monthly average pay of workers and employees in 1965S was planned to be 99 rubles or 26 percent more than in 1958, implying a wage and salary bill in 1965S of 79.0 billion rubles.

To the figure of 79.0 billion rubles, I add an allowance of 1.0 billion rubles for earnings of members of producer cooperatives. The producer cooperatives were absorbed by state industry in 1960, but I assume this was not a SYP objective. Average earnings of artisans in 1958 are assumed to have been 70 percent of the average wage and salary in the state labor force (see *SNIP 1956–1958,* pp. 32, 33, 47). Given the average annual number of workers and employees in 1958 as 54.61 millions, the number of producer cooperative members as 1.3 million (*NKh 1962,* p. 452), and the average wage and salary including earnings of cooperative artisans as 933.6 rubles (above, p. 295), the implied average earnings of cooperative members are 658 rubles per year; the implied value of aggregate cooperative earnings is .86 billion rubles. My 1965S estimate of 1.0 billion rubles is a guess which allows for a small increase in average earnings with no growth in the number employed, or a decline in the number of members with an increase in earnings comparable to that planned for the state labor force.

References to the goal of a 26 percent increase in average pay appeared frequently in Soviet sources. The 1965S absolute average wage has not since been repeated, as far as is known. However, the implied 1958 wage, 77.9–79.2 rubles per month (allowing for rounding of both the 1965S figure and the percentage increase), is within 1 percent of the figure of 78.3 rubles implied by the calculation in the previous paragraph.

2. *Net income of households from agriculture.*

The non-wage and salary categories included here are the same as those listed in Appendix A, except that for lack of information, incomes of independent peasants are ignored in what follows. According to the 1959 census, there were less than 1 percent as many independent peasants as collective farmers (*NKh 1960,* p. 24).

In the absence of any direct information on the 1965S targets for incomes in this category, they have had to be estimated by a lengthy, circuitous process of reasoning centering on two groups of SYP goals, output and productivity targets and the planned increase in real income per collective farmer. The procedure is admittedly hazardous but there seems to be no alternative.

The SYP directed a 70 percent increase in agricultural gross output and productivity increases of 100 percent on collective farms and 60–65 percent on state farms. At 1958 prices, sectoral shares of gross agricultural output in 1958 were as follows (based on unpublished estimates by Nimitz): Collective farms 47.2 percent; state farms and other state agricultural enterprises 15.9 percent; private sector, 36.9 percent. It is not clear whether the value calculations underlying the SYP targets are at 1956 or 1958 prices, since up to 1958 prices of 1956 were used. (See Table 12 of official preliminary SYP data forms, published in *Le Plan Septennal Soviétique,* p. 123.) It is assumed that sectoral shares at 1956 prices would not be substantially different.

Given the 1958 sector shares, the next step is to derive the SYP output increases. These can be estimated only with great difficulty and subject to a considerable margin of error, for they must be inferred from the Plan's productivity targets, unofficial speculations on projected changes in the labor force (collective farms), and incomplete data on state farm delivery targets. The nature of the productivity targets is also unclear. We have not been told whether the denominator of published productivity targets was employment or man-days. Since it appears that the government desired and expected both an increase in the number of days worked per collective farmer on the farm and a decline in collective farm employment, the productivity increase would be larger if based on employment than on man-days worked. I assume that the SYP targets represent output divided by number employed.

Collective farms. Productivity on collective farms was to double by

1965S compared with 1958. The SYP makes clear that employment was expected to decline in this period. For the 1958 level of employment a number of figures are available for an equivalent range of employment concepts. Those most relevant here are the following (Nimitz, *Farm Employment in the Soviet Union, 1928–1963,* November 1965, pp. 112–113):

	Millions
(1) Members of collective farm households who earn income from the farm. Excludes members who do not participate in collective production.	
Ablebodied (males 16–59 and females 16–54)	26.8
All working members, including juveniles 12–15 and overaged	36.8
(2) Number of members—ablebodied, juveniles and overaged—participating in collective production at least one day during peak employment month (July)	31.9
(3) Average annual employment (the average of monthly number of employed, including all who work at least one day a month)—ablebodied juveniles and overaged	24.9

Kotov (*Voprosy truda v semiletnem plane,* 1960, pp. 112–113) estimated that collective farms would need to release three million persons to help satisfy requirements for expansion of the state labor force. Presumably, this number is to be subtracted from the pool of ablebodied in estimate (1) above, if not, indeed, from some larger figure which would include collective farm members who do not engage in collective farm operations at all in the course of the year. At any rate, Kotov's estimate suggests a decline of no more than 11 percent in the size of the collective farm labor force.

Higher estimates of the manpower expected to be released from collective farms are also to be found in Soviet sources. Gol'tsov declared (*Sotsialisticheskii trud,* 1960, No. 5, p. 39): "Calculations show that the planned seven year increase in gross agricultural output, while insuring a doubling of labor productivity [in collective farms], will lead to the release of not less than 15 percent of the work force now utilized on the collective farms." The absolute employment level relevant to this calculation is not indicated, but the reference point seems to be 1959 rather than 1958 (see his article in Shishkin, ed., *Trudovye resursy,* 1961, p. 113).

According to Kirichenko, "since labor productivity on collective farms is to double, approximately, during the course of the Seven Year Plan, the 1965 volume of agricultural operations (*raboty*) could be performed with about four million fewer personnel (*rabotniki*) than were employed on the farms in 1958" (Tsagolov, ed., *Razvitie kolkhoznoi sobstvennosti,* 1961, p. 123). Kirichenko did not indicate how much of a relative decline his estimate implied.

Finally, Academician Strumilin stated that the collective farm productivity target "presupposes" (*predpolagaet*) a release of at least 12 million workers from the collective farms (*VE,* 1960, No. 7, p. 94). I cannot make any sense of this figure.

Some additional light is cast on these fragments by the implied 1965S level of total employment. That is, division of the target for total so-called *vyplaty i l'goty* (roughly, social services and some transfer payments—see below, p. 468), 36 billion rubles, by the planned level of payments per employed, 380 rubles, implies a 1965S employment total of 95 millions. Of this, 66.5 millions are accounted for by the planned number of workers and employees; the remainder, 28.5 millions, presumably consists almost entirely of collective farmers. If the 1958 level of collective farm employment was 3 million men higher, it was 31.5 million; if the 1958 level was to be reduced by 10 percent, it was 31.7 million. A 15 percent decrease signifies a 1958 level of 33.5 million, a 4 million men decrease, an initial level of 32.5 million. On the whole, these calculations suggest that Kotov was closest to the truth.

Given the planned doubling of labor productivity, a decline in employment of 10 percent implies an output increase target of 80 percent —a 15 percent employment decrease, output growth by 70 percent.

State agricultural enterprises. At the December 1958 plenum of the Party Central Committee, Khrushchev declared (*Plenum TsK KPSS 15–19 dekabria 1958 goda,* 1958, p. 52) that the quantity of "basic" farm produce delivered by the state farms in 1965 would be 2 to 2½ times the 1957 level; for sugar beets the corresponding figure was "more than 4 times." The state farms were to be charged with the chief responsibility for supplying potatoes and vegetables to towns and industrial centers. On the basis of 1965S state farm shares in total procurement cited by Khrushchev at the Plenum, the SYP targets for total procurements, and data on state farm deliveries in 1958 (*SKh,* p. 48), the planned increases in state farm deliveries in the 7 years may be estimated as more than 100 percent for wool and milk and 175 percent for meat. While the expected increase in deliveries of grain was small, perhaps 10 percent, the Plan implied that production of grain for use as fodder on the farm was to grow considerably more rapidly.

Direct information on output targets of the state farms for the USSR as a whole is not available, but the planned increases for RSFSR state farms, which probably accounted for considerably more than half the gross output of all USSR state farms in 1958, can be derived from other data (Table E-1).

Output goals for the Ukraine's collective farms and state farms together are available for the four chief livestock products—meat, milk, eggs, and wool. The targets are increases of, respectively, 323, 209, 250, and 66 percent (*ESKh,* 1959, No. 2, p. 31). It is probably safe to assume that the planned production increases for Ukrainian state farms were as large as or larger than those for the republic's collective farms. The combined 1958 output of state farms in the RSFSR and the Ukraine accounted for from three-quarters to nine-tenths of all USSR state farm output of meat, milk, and eggs, and somewhat less than half for wool. (*SKh,* pp. 344–345, 353, 358, 363.)

From all this it seems clear that the Plan called for at least a doubling in state farm output and not unlikely for an increase of 150 percent. Note that a seven-year increase in output of 150 percent in conjunction with a productivity increase of 60–65 percent implies a better than 50 percent growth in employment. Very little has appeared in Soviet sources with regard to state farm employment targets of the SYP. One writer on labor problems, Sonin (*Vosproizvodstvo rabochei sily v SSSR i balans truda,* 1959, p. 341, note 2), foresaw an eventual decline in the state farm labor force but gave no indication when this would take place. The implied sharp growth in employment suggests an even greater growth in the state farm wage bill. Such a development may be inferred from at least one section of the approved Control Figures. Noting the planned 62 percent increase in retail trade, the document declared: "In connection with the more rapid growth of money income of the rural population, trade turnover in the village will also develop at a more rapid rate" (presumably, compared with the national or urban average). It will shortly become clear that this could not have been ascribed to growth of collective farmer incomes. In any event, largely as a consequence of conversion of collective to state farms, employment in state and institutional farms increased 37 percent in just the first two years of the Plan period (*NKh 1960,* p. 636).

Private sector. Having estimated the output increases planned for USSR collective and state farms and given the sectoral shares in 1958, I can now compute the implied projected increase in the output of the private sector. (It is assumed below that the output goal for state farms applied to institutional farms as well. This assumption may be erroneous but cannot affect the results greatly.) The private sector targets implied by alternative output goals for the collective and state farms can be conveniently shown as follows:

Collective Farm Output Increases, Alternative Assumptions (percent)	*Private Sector Implied Output Increase When State Farm Output Increase Is (percent)*	
	100	150
70	57	36
80	44	22

It is inconceivable that Soviet planners expected private sector output to increase by anything like 57 percent. Following Khrushchev's lead, the plenary meeting of The Party's Central Committee resolved on December 19, 1958, to have the state farms buy all livestock held privately by their employees within "two to three years." Although no deadline was set, the state farms were ordered to undertake to "meet in full the requirements of workers and employees in potatoes and vegetables." The plenum concluded that "as a result of implementing these measures, state farm workers and employees will have no need to work on their individual plots . . ." (*Plenum TsK KPSS 15–19 dekabria 1958, goda,* p. 486). The approved Control Figures proclaimed:

> As collective farm production develops in conditions where collective farms become large-scale enterprises, equipped with modern machinery and skilled cadres, the material and everyday needs of collective farms will be increasingly satisfied from the collective economy, and, hence, the private holdings of the collective farmers will gradually lose their significance.

(See also Khrushchev, *Stroitel'stvo kommunizma v SSSR i razvitie sel'skogo khoziaistva,* 1962, III, p. 404.)

There is reason to believe that private sector output was not expected to increase by even as much as 36 percent. The Plan directed a minimum 40 percent increase in real income per collective farm worker, to be attained largely from the collective economy of the farms. If collective farm employment was to decline by 10–15 percent, the aggregate expected increase in real income of collective farmers would be 19–26 percent. Clearly, this Plan goal is inconsistent with a 36 percent increase in real output from collective farmers' plots. Nor does it seem possible to circumvent the difficulty by postulating a lower rate of growth of private output on collective farms, compensated by a higher rate for the plots of workers and employees. The resolution of the December 1958 Party Central Committee Plenum concerning private livestock holdings on state farms is compelling evidence to the contrary. In addition, Lagutin and Skuratov (*VE,* 1959, No. 2, p. 19) implied a lower rate of growth of net output in the SYP from the plots of workers and employees than from those of collective farmers:

> Already in this seven year period there will be an appreciable increase in the share of national income originating in the collective economy of the collective farms and, correspondingly, a decrease in the share originating in the private holdings of collective farmers. There will be a *sharp* decrease in the share of national income originating in the private holdings of workers and employees. (Emphasis added.)

In the light of this evidence (see also Nimitz, *Problems of Communism,* May–June 1965, p. 13), I tentatively set the SYP increase of private sector output at 20 percent, the growth targets for collective farms and the state sector, 80 percent and 150 percent, respectively.

Having estimated the SYP expected increases in value of gross output, I must now make the translation to household incomes. Appendix A provides estimates of all household income from sales of farm products and from income in kind as well as of money payments by collective farms to their member households. I do not estimate separately the incomes of workers, employees and collective farmers from their plots. For this purpose, it might seem helpful to use data provided by Aganbegian (*Povyshenie proizvoditel'nosti truda . . . ,* 1960, pp. 124–126): (1) Collective farmers' income from their plots was almost as large as their income from the farm (presumably in 1958); (2) In 1958, income from plots accounted for about 40 percent of total collective farmer income, including transfer payments and social services; (3) Transfer incomes and social services provided by the government (mostly in the areas of public health and education) amounted to about 4 billion rubles in 1958 or roughly 40 percent of collective farmer income from the farm.

These clues imply the following approximate distribution of collective farm household incomes in 1958 (billions of rubles):

Income from plot	9
Distribution, money and in-kind, by farms	10
Transfer incomes, value of social services	4
	23

According to Nimitz (*Incomes of Collective Farmers*) distributions by collective farms in cash and in kind, with the kind component valued at retail prices, amounted to 8.71 billion rubles in 1958; the sum is 8.96 billions if cash payments to hired labor are included. (In kind payments to hired labor are not known but must have been small.) These figures are somewhat below the 10 billions derived from Aganbegian but consistent with it within the wide margins allowed by the latter's highly rounded benchmark figures. Let us accept the figure of 8.96 billion rubles and return to the Aganbegian statements for a revised estimate of collective farm household income. The value of social services and transfer incomes is set at 40 percent of income from the farm, or 3.60 billion rubles, consistent with Aganbegian's "about 4" billion rubles. The value of income from the plot is then obtained as 40 percent of all collective farmer income, including transfer payments and social services. The adjusted distribution is as follows:

		Billion Rubles	*Percent*
Income from plot		8.37	40.0
Distributions by collective farms		8.96	42.8
Money	5.25		
In kind	3.71		
Total currently earned income		17.33	
Transfer incomes, value of social services		3.60	17.2
		20.93	100.0

At this point Aganbegian's data become suspect, for they imply an abnormally low share of collective farmers' plot income in total household income from private plots:

(1) The 3.71 billion rubles of distribution in kind by farms represent a value at retail prices, of which grain accounted for about 3.1–3.4 billions, or 85–90 percent, and potatoes for an additional few percentage points, or about .15 billion rubles (Nimitz, *Incomes of Collective Farmers*). Scaled down by the relation between average realized farm prices and extravillage farm market prices (as a surrogate for retail prices—Table A-2), these figures reduce to .88–.96 and .10 billion rubles, for a combined total of .98–1.06 billions. If the scale factor for other distributions in kind is the same as that for potatoes (for grain, the margin between retail and average realized farm prices is unusually wide), all distributions in kind valued at averaged realized prices would amount to 1.2–1.3 billion rubles, say, 1.25 billions.

(2) These distributions are most likely consumed (or fed to livestock) rather than sold. Thus, if total household net income in kind valued at average realized prices came to 10.57 billion rubles in 1958, net income in kind originating on the plot may be estimated as at least 9.32 (10.57–1.25) billion rubles, and with the addition of income from

sales (6.22 billions) all net plot income totals at least 15.54 billions. Of course, these figures would be larger, gross of production outlays.

(3) Aganbegian's data imply collective farmer income from the plot of over 8 billion rubles. At best this indicates a 54 percent share for collective farmers' plot income in total incomes from the private plot (8:37 ÷ 15.54); that is, this is so if the 8.37 billion ruble figure includes an in kind component valued at average realized prices. If, as seems more likely, the in kind component is valued at retail prices, the implied share of collective farmers' plot income in total private plot income is much lower. Yet, collective farmers accounted for 75 percent of the sown area in the private sector; 84 percent of the meat, 91 percent of the milk, 92 percent of the eggs, and 97 percent of the wool marketed by the sector; 66 percent of the meat, 64 percent of the milk, 56 percent of the eggs, and 59 percent of the wool produced and not marketed by the sector (*SKh*, pp. 128, 334–337).

In short, the estimate of collective farmer income from the plot derived from the Aganbegian data is far too low. Whether income in kind is valued at average realized or at retail prices, collective farm household plot income is surely not "almost as large" as income from the farm but considerably larger. In consequence, the distribution of household incomes in 1958 must be recast. For the purpose, I assume on the basis of sown area, output and sales data just cited, that 90 percent of net sales by the private sector and 60 percent of its net income in kind originated in collective farm households. If in kind distributions by collective farms are estimated as 1.25 billion rubles at average realized prices and deducted from the collective farmer share of net income in kind, private sector production incomes in 1958 may be broken down as follows (billion rubles; excluding collective farm payments to hired labor):

		Collective Farmers		*Workers and Employees*
Income from collective farm		6.25		
Money	5.00		n.a.	
In kind	1.25			
Income from the plot		10.69		4.85
Money	5.60		.62	
In kind	5.09		4.23	
Total		16.94		4.85

The SYP called for a 40 percent increase in real income per collective farmer. On the assumption of a 10 percent decline in employment, the aggregate increase in real income expected is 26 percent. In Soviet usage, "real income," or "final income," of households in any given year is the sum of actual incomes received, including transfers from the public sector, plus material outlays in "institutions servicing households," less transfer payments of households and their outlays on nonproductive services. (*NKh 1960,* p. 874; Eremina and Marshalova, *Statistika truda,* 1965, pp. 216–218; *Problemy ekonomiki truda,* 1965, pp. 161–162.) Real income in 1958 is, therefore, computed as follows (billion rubles):

Income of collective farmers from the farm and plot	16.94
Transfer incomes	1.00
Material outlays in institutions servicing population	1.25
Less:	
Net savings, direct taxes and other contributions to the state	1.00
Dues to trade unions and other organizations; other nonproductive services	1.93
Real income	16.34

The value of transfer incomes as well as of savings, taxes and other contributions are based on unpublished estimates of J. F. Karcz. Initially, the share of material outlays in institutions servicing households —6.4 billion rubles total (*NKh 1965,* p. 592)—that affects collective farmers is assumed to be 20–40 percent, or 1.3–2.6 billions. If pure transfer incomes (pensions, stipends, interest receipts) were one billion rubles and the value of all transfers and social services enjoyed by collective farmers 3.60 billion rubles, the social service component alone is 2.60 billions. Allowing for services for which households pay in full, hence which do not enter the 3.60 billion ruble figure, on one hand, and the predominance of wages in total costs, on the other, suggests 1.25 billion rubles as an approximately appropriate entry in the tabulation. Collective farmers are assumed to account for one-third of all household outlays on dues (excluding trade union dues—p. 340), .43 billion rubles, and on other nonproductive services, 5.39 billions. Other nonproductive services are taken to be "other services" as computed in Appendix B, exclusive of outlays on utilities and the industrial component of the so-called "everyday" (*bytovye*) services (pp. 354 and 359).

Thus, real income in 1958 came to 16.34 billion rubles by my estimate, and a 26 percent increase implies a 1965S level of 20.59 billion rubles. I make no attempt to estimate the separate 1965S values of transfer incomes, material outlays in service institutions, savings, taxes, contributions, dues and outlays on services. However, these items are roughly offsetting in the calculation of real incomes in 1958 and I assume that this is also true of the 1965S distribution. On this assumption I focus on current incomes alone. The SYP stated that the 40 percent increase in real incomes per collective farmer was to come primarily from the farm. If this is interpreted to mean that at least half of the increase in real income was to represent growth of income from the farm, then no more than 2 billion rubles would consist of increases in other components of real income.

Some small part of this increment represents the value of a projected decrease in public catering prices. The aggregate value of the decline was to be 5.3 billion rubles (*NKh 1958,* p. 103). Since all rural areas accounted for only 17 percent of public catering trade turnover in 1958 (*Sovtorg II,* p. 46), it seems doubtful that more than 10 percent of the value of the price decline was to accrue to collective farmers.

Thus, perhaps 1.5–2.0 billion rubles of the increase in collective farmer real income may be ascribed to income components other than income from the farm and the gain from price decreases in retail trade. If all of this sum represented growth of income from the plot, the implied increase in real plot income is 14–19 percent. Earlier I tentatively estimated the SYP increase of all private sector output as 20 percent and pointed to indications that the rate of growth of plot income in worker and employee households was to be considerably smaller, perhaps even negative. At this point, it seems clear that the projected growth of all private sector output was probably below 20 percent and that the growth of collective farmer plot income alone was probably not expected to be greater than that figure. However, this also suggests that plot income of workers and employees was not expected to decline substantially. I assume, therefore, (1) constancy in the level of worker and employee plot income, and (2) a 20 percent projected increase in the corresponding income of collective farmers. Together, these assumptions imply a 14 percent increase in plot output (billion rubles):

	1958	*1965S*
Collective farmers	10.69	12.8
Workers and employees	4.85	4.9
Total income from plot	15.54	17.7

Finally, I assume an unchanged price level in 1965S relative to 1958. The SYP referred only indirectly to agricultural price changes and then only to price decreases. Demanding economy in resource use from collective and state farms, the Plan declared: "It is on this basis that we shall insure a steady decline in prices of agricultural production and continued improvement of the welfare of the people." Comments in Soviet sources on this aspect of the Plan have not been much more explicit. Recalling suggestions for price reductions on certain commodities made by some central Asian party leaders at the December 1959 Party Central Committee Plenum, Aganbegian (in *Povyshenie Proizvoditel'nost' truda . . .*, p. 116) concluded: "In the future, particularly considering the accelerated growth of labor productivity and the significant decline of the average cost of collective farm output, revisions of agricultural prices will be carried out on a wider scale."

However, if there were to be price decreases during the SYP period, they may have been planned only for technical crops (which figure neither in the in kind distributions of the collective farms nor in the production of the private sector). Thus, 1958 procurement prices for grain, potatoes, and vegetables were only slightly higher than average costs of producing these staples on collective farms. In contrast, the prices of sugar beets, cotton, and flax (and perhaps wool) exceeded production costs by 50 percent or more. On the other hand, prices of most livestock products were below even state farm costs (Zverev, *Natsional'nyi dokhod i finansy SSSR,* 1961, p. 306). It is not inconceivable that price increases were contemplated for livestock products, to be instituted later in the Plan period in order to allow for some further decline in costs. While it would not be surprising that no mention was made in Soviet sources of impending price increases, it would be unjustified here to assume without additional evidence that such a significant change was incorporated in the Plan.

The formation of 1958 and 1965S household incomes in current prices can now be set out as follows (billion rubles):

	1958	*1965S*
Collective farmers' income from the farm	6.25	8.7
Collective farmers' income from the plot	10.69	12.8
Workers and employees' income from the plot	4.85	4.9
	21.79	26.4

3. *Income of armed forces.*

Was the demobilization program announced in 1960 (*Pravda,* January 15, 1960) incorporated in the SYP drawn up 18 months earlier? Were increases in average pay and allowances contemplated in the SYP? One can only speculate. If the range of possible 1965S goals can be assumed to be (1) for armed force levels, 2.4–3.8 million men—the maximum being the 1958 level, the minimum the level projected for 1961–1962 by Khrushchev in his 1960 demobilization program, and (2) for average pay and allowances, from the 1958 level to one 25 percent higher, then total armed force incomes in 1965S would be 2.6–5.2 billion rubles compared to 4.14 billions in 1958. The midpoint of the 1965S range is close to the 1958 level. It seems prudent to assume that the 1965S and 1958 levels of both aggregate military pay and aggregate military subsistence are the same.

4. *Bonuses not included in wage and salary bill; wages in kind; other income currently earned.*

The assumption of a 25 percent gain over the 1958 level, 7.76 billion rubles (cf. with 50+ percent increase in the wage and salary bill), fits in with a calculation of "real income" in 1965S. See below, pp. 435–437.

5. *Imputed net rent.*

Appendix F, sources for item 2.A.

6. *Imputed value of owner-supplied building services.*

An increase over the 1958 level in proportion to the increase in private housing construction, 32 percent (Appendix F, sources for item 6.A), is assumed.

7. *Total income currently earned.*

The sum of items 1–6.

8. *Transfer receipts.*

Appendix H, sources for item 9.

9. *Total income.*

The sum of items 7 and 8.

TABLE E-1

SEVEN YEAR PLAN TARGETS AND 1958 SHARES OF RSFSR STATE FARM OUTPUT OF MAJOR AGRICULTURAL PRODUCTS

	Percent Increase in Gross Output of RSFSR State Farms Between 1958 and 1965S (1)	RSFSR State Farm Output as Percent of USSR State Farm Output in 1958 (2)
Grain	31	55
Sugar beets	300	47
Sunflower seed	50	68 [a]
Potatoes	356	69
Vegetables	420	61
Meat	220	61
Milk	192	67
Wool	123	44
Eggs	240	76

Note:

[a] RSFSR state farm sown areas as percent of USSR state farm sown area.

Sources:

Column (1): reported or calculated from Iurkin, *ESKh*, 1959, No. 3, pp. 43–45. Column (2): absolute 1958 output by RSFSR state farms of grain, potatoes, vegetables, meat, milk, and eggs, and 1958 output by USSR state farms of all products, are taken from *SKh*, pp. 208, 213, 237, 242, 345, 353, 358, 363. RSFSR and USSR state farm sown area of sunflower seed, *ibid.*, p. 171.

F

Sources to Table 2: 1965S

1. *A. Retail sales of goods for consumption in the state-cooperative trade network.*

Obtained as follows (billion rubles):

State-cooperative retail sales, excluding cooperative sales at market prices	103.0
Less:	
Services	1.60
Sales to institutions	7.21
Producers' goods sold to farm households	.34
Building materials sold to households	.62
Equals:	
Retail sales of goods to households for consumption	93.2

The value of state-cooperative retail sales, excluding cooperative market sales, is computed from *NKh 1958,* p. 103, showing index numbers at constant and given year prices as well as the 1958 base value. A planned increase of 100 percent over the 1958 level is assumed for the industrial everyday services included in retail trade data (see below, p. 436). Sales to institutions are estimated as 7 percent of retail sales, excluding cooperative market sales (see above, p. 332). Producers' goods sold to farm households are assumed to increase from the 1958 level of .30 billion rubles in proportion to the increase in private sector agricultural output and income, 14 percent (above, p. 426). Building materials sold to households are assumed to increase from the 1958 level of .47 billion rubles in proportion to the increase in private housing construction, 32 percent (Table 2).

2. *Consumer services.*

A. *Housing (including imputed rent)*. Obtained as the sum of the following components (billion rubles):

Rent on non-collective farm housing		1.79
Rent on state housing	1.07	
Imputed rent on private housing	.72	
Imputed rent on collective farm housing		.63
Total		2.42

Rent on non-collective farm housing. Obtained as the product of a rental rate of 1.05 rubles per square meter of floor space per year (above p. 339), and an estimated stock of non-collective farm housing in 1965S, both private and state-owned, of 1695 million square meters of floor space.

The stock estimate was obtained as follows: At the end of 1958, the housing stock, private and state-owned, in "cities and worker settlements" totaled 781 million square meters of floor space (*NKh 1958,* p. 641: the capital census of January 1, 1960 resulted in a revised official estimate of the size of the housing stock—*NKh 1960,* p. 613, but the SYP housing goals were drafted on the basis of estimates reflected in *NKh 1958*). The SYP called for (1) a 60 percent increase in the housing stock of "cities and worker settlements," (2) 650–660 million square meters of new construction, socialized and private, during 1959–1965 in "cities and worker settlements, settlements of state farms, RTS and timber enterprises (*lespromkhozy*)."

Thus, the urban housing stock was to reach 1250 million square meters of floor space by the end of 1965S. However, the projected 650–660 million square meters of new construction covered rural housing (apart from collective farms) as well as urban housing. This is evident from the fact that the goal is linked in *NKh 1959* (p. 566) to a series that in *NKh 1964* (pp. 604–605) is shown to include a rural component as well. In terms of the non-collective farm stock on January 1, 1959, urban housing accounted for about 70 percent of the total (using the urban total as shown in *NKh 1958* and the rural total of 350 million square meters estimated above, p. 336). I assume that the urban share of new construction was roughly 75 percent, or 500 million square meters (using the midpoint of the range for the announced target). By implication, expected net retirements in the SYP period were to be 31 million square meters (781 + 500 − 1250). (By "net" retirements, I mean net of increments to the urban housing stock from reclassification of rural communities, a factor of some importance in actual events of the period (*NKh 1965*, p. 616).) This volume of expected retirements represents 4 percent of the beginning-period stock. For rural non-collective farm housing I assume 3 percent replacement, or 10 million square meters. Thus, the information available to this point may be summarized as follows:

	Stock 1/1/59	Million Square Meters of Floor Space, Seven-year Cumulated Totals: New Construction	Retirements	Stock 12/31/65S
Urban	781	500	31	1250
Rural	350	155	10	495
	1131	655	41	1745

The 1965S component of the cumulative construction target was planned to be 96 million square meters of floor space (Broner, *Sovremennye problemy zhilishchnogo khoziaistva,* 1961, p. 98). Assuming retirements in that year as, say, 5 million square meters, the planned stock at the end of 1964S would be 1654 million and the average annual stock in 1965S would be 1700 million square meters.

Rent on socialized and imputed rent on private housing (except collective farms). Sixty percent of the total rent, 1.79 billion rubles, is assigned to paid rent on socialized housing and 40 percent to imputed rent on private housing. These proportions are estimated starting from the sectoral structure of the stock on 1 January 1959, the share of socialized in the total new construction target, about ⅔ (*ibid.*, p. 98) and allocation of retirements according to the beginning period stock structure. (Shown as 50:50 on p. 336, the January 1959 sectoral ratio is raised to 55:45 in favor of socialized housing to take account of the fact that *NKh 1958* estimated the public sector's share in urban housing higher than did the post-census yearbooks. See below, p. 438.)

Imputed rent, collective farm housing. Obtained as the product of the rental rate of 1.275 rubles per square meter (above, p. 340) and an estimated stock of collective farm housing in 1965S of 498 million square meters of floor space.

The stock estimate was obtained as follows: On p. 338, I estimated the January 1, 1959 stock as 400 million square meters of floor space. The SYP provided for new construction of 7 million dwellings by collective farmers and "rural intelligentsia" in 1959–1965. The average dwelling size is assumed to be 30 square meters, as was done for the 1958–1964 estimates. Therefore, the planned seven year volume of new construction is equivalent to 210 million square meters of floor space.

Since the Plan does not mention the planned increase in the stock of rural housing, it is not possible to estimate expected retirements by the method used for urban housing. For the decade 1949–1958, a rate of retirements approximately equal to, if not higher than, annual new construction may be inferred from a comparison of the stock at the end of 1958 with an estimate by Bergson and Heymann (*SNIP 1940–1948,* p. 132) of the stock in 1948. The Bergson-Heymann estimate was 382 million square meters of living space, equivalent, on the assumption that the ratio of living to floor space in rural housing is 0.85 (above, p. 339) to 450 million square meters of floor space.

It seems doubtful that the SYP contemplated a decrease or even no net increase in the rural housing stock, although, from all accounts, the quality of existing farm housing was so low as to necessitate rapid replacement. On the other hand, since the Plan clearly pointed to a decline in the collective farm population, the ratio of new housing constructed to old housing retired need not have been nearly as high as that implied for other housing in the SYP period, 16:1. Lacking additional information, I assume that retirements were to be half as large as new construction (the same assumption used previously with respect to realized construction—see above, p. 338), or 105 million square meters of floor space. Therefore, the rural housing stock at the end of 1965S is estimated as 505 million square meters of floor space. Gross new construction in 1965S is assumed at a level of one million dwellings (the 1958 realized volume was 706,000—*NKh 1962,* p. 502, and I allow for a pre-1965S peak in construction comparable to that evidently provided for non-collective farm housing—see below, p. 438), or 30 million square meters, and net additions at 15 million square meters. Then, the implied stock at the end of 1965S is 490 million and the average annual stock in 1965S is 498 million square meters of floor space.

B. *Trade union and other dues.* This is the sum of two components (billion rubles):

Trade union dues	.74
Other dues	.54
	1.28

Trade union dues. Estimated as increasing from the 1958 level of .48 billion rubles in proportion to the increase in the worker and employee wage and salary bill (excluding earnings of cooperative artisans), 54 percent.

Other dues. An arbitrary 25 percent increase of the 1958 figure of .43 billion rubles.

C. *Other services.* Services and "net savings" are estimated as residuals in a calculation of "real income" of collective farmers, workers and employees. The calculation proceeds as follows:

(1) The Plan called for increases in average real income of 40 percent for workers and employees and "at least" 40 percent for collective farmers.

(2) The number of workers and employees was to increase from 54.6 to 66.5 millions. Previously I estimated that employment of collective farmers was to be close to 28.5 millions in 1965S and that this represented a 10 percent decline from the 1958 level (above, p. 418). Thus, for both categories of employment together, the planned change was for a 10 percent increase. Golt'sov (in Shishkin, ed., *Trudovye resursy,* 1961, p. 52) estimated a higher figure—an increase of 15.5 percent in the total number of employed (*kolichestvo zaniatykh*). But Golt'sov may have been using a different employment concept: the agricultural component is defined as employment at the peak season (*ibid.,* p. 40); the distribution evidently is of employment at a point in time rather than of annual averages (compare *ibid.,* p. 40 with TsSU, *Itogi vsesoiuznoi perepisi . . . , SSSR,* 1962, p. 104 and *NKh 1962,* p. 451); Golt'sov's distribution implies a 1.6 percent increase in employment in agriculture and forestry (*Trudovye resursy,* pp. 40 and 52), whereas other writers speak of a reduction in agricultural employment (Sitarian, *FinSSSR,* 1959, No. 9, p. 10; Lagutin, *VE,* 1960, No. 11, p. 61). Given (a) the collective farm employment figures for 1958 and 1965S, (b) the estimated employment increase on state farms of 50+ percent (p. 419), and (c) average annual employment in 1958 of 4.6 millions on state farms and subsidiary agricultural enterprises (*NKh 1962,* p. 453), a 2 percent decline in the combined employment of state employees and of collective farmers is implied for 1965S.

Thus, I take the intended increase in aggregate real income of collective farmers, workers and employees over the SYP period as 54 percent, the product of a 10 percent increase in employment and a 40 percent average increase in real incomes.

(3) The next step is to estimate aggregate real income in the base year, 1958 (for the definition of the concept, see above, p. 424). The calculation is as follows (billion rubles):

1. Household income			
A. Wages and salaries,[a] farm and nonfarm		52.38	
B. Net income of households from agriculture, excluding agricultural wages and salaries		21.79	
C. Other income currently earned		7.71	
D. Transfer receipts		9.95	
E. Total			91.83
2. Add: material outlays in institutions servicing population			6.40
3. Subtract:			
A. Net savings		1.11	
B. Direct taxes; other contributions to state		5.78	
C. Household outlays on nonproductive services			
(1) Rent	.61		
(2) Dues to trade unions and other organizations	.91		
(3) Other services	5.39		
(4) Total		6.91	
D. Total			13.80
4. Real income			84.43

[a] Including bonuses and wages in kind.

Item 1.A represents the total shown in Table 1 (item 1.D) less the earnings of members of producers cooperatives estimated in Appendix E (p. 415). Items 1.B, 1.C, and 1.D are taken directly from Table 1, items 3.A, 3.B, and 3.C(2), directly from Table 2. For items 2 and 3.C(1), see above, pp. 424 and 335, respectively. Item 3.C(3) is computed from the data on pp. 354 and 359. Only nonproductive services are entered: that is, outlays on utilities and on the industrial component of everyday services are not.

Thus, the real income of collective farmers and the state labor force in 1958 is estimated as 84.43 billion rubles. Omitted from this total are the incomes of members of producer cooperatives and of the armed forces, summing to 4.97 billion rubles. However, the addition under item 2 and the deductions under item 3 are global; hence, for the intended coverage, the total real income figure is overstated and understated by the amounts of items 2 and 3 applying to the omitted income categories. It does not seem likely that either overstatement or understatement is significant. Thus, if the proportion of incomes spent on transfer payments and service outlays were the same in the omitted group as in the population as a whole, the understatement of real income would amount to about .7 billion rubles. In fact that proportion was probably far lower among artisans and soldiers and hence the amount of understatement of real incomes is likely to be insignificant. Similar reasoning applies to the overstatement relating to item 2.

Real income was to increase during the SYP period by 54 percent, hence to 130.0 billion rubles. Of this amount, 5.3 billion rubles represents the value of a projected decrease in retail prices (*NKh 1958,* p. 103). At prices of 1965S, real income in 1965S was to be 124.7 billion rubles. This total may be distributed as follows:

1. Wage and salary bill, farm and nonfarm	79.0
2. Nonwage and salary agricultural income	26.4
3. Wages in kind; bonuses not included in wage and salary bill; other income currently earned	11.0–13.1
4. Transfer receipts; material outlays in institutions servicing population	27.0
5. Total	143.4–145.5
6. Subtract:	
A. Net savings	?
B. Direct taxes; other contributions to state	3.8
C. Rent	1.1
D. Dues	1.3
E. Other nonproductive services	?
F. Total	18.7–20.8
7. Real income	124.7

For the estimates of items 1 and 2 see Appendix E, pp. 415 and 416–426. An increase of 25–50 percent is assumed for item 3, compared with a 54 percent increase in the wage and salary bill. The combined sum of transfer incomes of households and material outlays in institutions is estimated as increasing over the 1958 level in proportion to the planned growth of the *vyplaty i l'goty* (below, p. 468), 67.4 percent. For items 6.B, 6.C and 6.D see, respectively, pp. 454, 430, and 432.

Two items are left blank—net savings and other nonproductive services. Their combined value, computed as a residual, is 12.5–14.6 billion rubles. Since the corresponding 1958 figure is 6.36 billion rubles, the implied relative growth is 95–128 percent. Is such a target reasonable? That is, is it reasonable to assume that Soviet planners expected so large an increase in the proportion of incomes saved or spent on services?

The level of net savings in 1958 was far below—more than two-thirds—those of the two immediately preceding years (*SNIP 1956–1958,* p. 3). To a considerable extent, the abrupt decline is connected with the abrogation of compulsory loan subscriptions. The 1958 increment in savings deposits was 60 percent below the increment of the previous year but net bond purchases were cut by 75 percent. The last mass-subscription bond issue, floated in 1957, was due to be completely retired by 1962 (*Pravda,* April 20, 1957, p. 1), and it may be assumed that in 1958 Soviet planners did not intend to resume compulsory subscriptions during the SYP period. Since repayment of principal on mass-subscription bonds outstanding at the beginning of 1957 was deferred for twenty years, the difference between gross and net purchases of other bonds during the SYP period would also be reduced. On balance, however, Soviet planners could hardly expect a 1965S level of net bond purchases resembling that of 1956 or 1957 (2.59 and 1.70 billion rubles respectively).

There is no evidence on what volume of bank savings Soviet planners hoped to see in 1965S. If the relation to income was to be the same as in 1957, the increment in bank savings in 1965S would come to about 3 billion rubles. (For this calculation the increment in deposits is related to a 1957 income value corresponding to my 1965S total of 143.4–145.5 billion rubles. The data are from *SNIP 1956–1958,* pp. 2–3; material outlays in institutions servicing the population are assumed to have been 10 percent smaller than in 1958.) If the planners also forecast a 1965S volume of net bond purchases unchanged at the 1958 level of .4 billion rubles, the expected value of net savings could have been over 3 billion rubles or 3 times the 1958 level.

As for the nonproductive other services—household outlays on health, education, entertainment, transportation, communication, and personal services (baths, laundry, barbershop, and so on)—the expectation must certainly have been for rapid increase. The volume of passenger traffic on all forms of transport was scheduled to expand 70 percent —20 percent on railways, 30 percent on internal waterways, 39 percent in maritime transport, 380 percent in automotive transport, and 590 percent in air transport (Rudoi and Lazarenko, *Razvitie transporta i sviazi v SSSR 1959–1965,* 1960, pp. 46–47). There was to be "considerable" improvement in "everyday" (*bytovye*) services, extensive investment in facilities for health, education, physical culture and sports, motion pictures, press, radio and television. Early in 1959 a program for expansion of "everyday" services was announced which provided for a two-thirds increase in volume by 1961, compared with 1958 (*Pravda,* March 13, 1959, p. 2). At the implied average rate of increase, the growth in volume of such "everyday" services over the full seven years would be 227 percent. Given the heavy weight of transportation in nonproductive services (about 40 percent), aggregate growth of close to 100 percent over the SYP period seems likely.

Thus, the evidence does not rule out the possibility that Soviet planners contemplated a doubling or near tripling of the combined total of savings and outlays on nonproductive services. The final estimates for 1965S are obtained by (1) assuming the minimum of the range of values for wages in kind, bonuses, and other money income currently earned, (2) assuming a doubling in both net savings and household outlays on other services, productive and nonproductive. It is hardly necessary to add that these residual estimates of savings and other services are quite sensitive to variations in estimates of the other elements of "real income."

3. *Consumption of income in kind.*

B. *Nonfarm wages in kind.* The 1958 figure is .50 billion rubles. The 1965S figure is set arbitrarily at .75 billion rubles.

C. *Military subsistence.* Appendix E, sources for item 3.

4. *Consumption of farm income in kind; collective farm market sales; other outlays for consumption.*

There is no evidence on the level of collective farm market sales projected for 1965S; nor is there any basis for distinguishing sales from income in kind in household agricultural output and income. To maintain the separation between investment and consumption, I assume zero farm investment in kind in 1965S, bearing in mind the regime's expressed intention to cut into household ownership of livestock. Farm income in kind plus sales to households on collective farm markets are then obtained as a residual, deducting the sum of all other components from total outlays. As a residual, the sum of these two outlay components also includes any errors or omissions—that is, the statistical discrepancy between the household income and outlay accounts.

5. *Total outlays for consumption.*

The sum of items 1–4.

6. *Investment.*

A. *Private housing construction.* This is the sum of 2 billion rubles of investment in the construction of collective farm housing and 1.5 billions in other private housing.

Stroitel'naia gazeta of December 3, 1958 (p. 2) declared that the 7 million dwellings expected to be constructed by collective farms over the SYP period would amount to 15 billion rubles, or 2100 rubles per dwelling. I assume 1965S construction of about 1 million dwellings. This level of construction is suggested by (1) the 802,000 homes built in 1959 (*NKh 1962*, p. 502) and the 1 million dwellings planned to be built in 1960 (*Izvestiia,* 28 October 1959, p. 4), and (2) the planned SYP pattern of growth of other private housing construction (see immediately below).

According to Broner (*Sovremennye problemy zhilishchnogo khozaiastva,* 1961, p. 98) the private sector's share of the targeted 650–660 million square meters of new construction outside of collective farms (see above, pp. 430–431) was about 230 million square meters. Private sector construction was to reach a peak in 1960 and level off to 30 million square meters in 1965S. The unit value of this construction is estimated as 50 rubles, yielding a 1965S aggregate of 1.5 billion rubles.

The average unit value is estimated on the following evidence: (1) Uriupin (*FinSSSR,* 1960, No. 1, p. 14) estimated the 1959 average replacement value, in current wholesale prices, for privately owned urban "structures" as 1600 rubles per household (*khoziaistvo*). This figure is said to have been obtained by adjusting the actual average insured value for price changes. Since insurance for private structures was compulsory, the basic datum of average insured value is presumably comprehensive and accurate. The reliability of the adjustment factor cannot be ascertained. Gladkov (*FinSSSR,* 1960, No. 1, p. 74) stated that in 1959 8.9 million urban households owned "structures." It is assumed that all urban structures were dwellings and that households and dwellings were equivalent. From information available at the time, the stock of private urban housing in 1959 may be estimated as about 280 million square meters of floor space.

[Subsequent to the capital inventory of 1 January 1960, official estimates of the size of the private urban housing stock were increased substantially: compare *NKh 1958*, p. 641 and *NKh 1960*, p. 613. According to the former source, the stock at the end of 1958 totaled 257 million square meters. In 1959, 27.2 million square meters of private urban floor space was completed (*NKh 1959*, p. 566). Retirements in 1959 may be estimated as about four million square meters, judging from the relation between construction and stock in 1957–1958 (*NKh 1958*, pp. 636, 641). Therefore, the 1959 stock is estimated as 280 million square meters on the basis of pre-1960 information.]

These data imply a replacement cost per square meter in 1959 wholesale prices of about 50 rubles.

(2) We can try another approach by way of data on state loans granted for private construction and the floor space completed with the

aid of those loans. In 1958, loans of about .15 billion rubles were granted and 227,000 dwellings with 9.8 million square meters of floor space were completed with this aid (*Stroitel'naia gazeta,* February 11, 1959, p. 4; Zaks and Guterman, *FinSSSR,* 1960, No. 5, p. 70). There is some question here about the definition of the unit of space constructed. The Soviet sources refer to "living space" (*zhilaia ploshchad'*)—a term that ostensibly excludes kitchens, bathrooms, hallways, and so forth, but it is difficult to believe that a true "living space" measure is actually intended since the average size of dwelling built, 43 square meters, is relatively large. According to *NKh 1965,* p. 611, the average size of apartments publicly or privately built in 1958, but excluding construction on collective farms, was 43 square meters of floor space (*obshchaia ploshchad'*). I assume that the earlier Soviet sources really intended a measure of total floor space rather than "living space." These data imply a loan value of 15 rubles per square meter of floor space constructed with the aid of loans. However, the actual total cost was far higher than this figure, since the bank was permitted to lend no more than 50 percent of the estimated cost of construction; the rest had to be supplied by the prospective owner, either in cash or in personal labor. Some exceptions to this rule were permitted—for example, 70 percent mortgages for doctors and teachers, but their weight in the total was probably small. (*Zakondatel'nye akty po voprosam narodnogo khoziaistva SSSR,* II, 1961, pp. 549–550.)

It is likely that the average loan granted covered less than half the estimated construction cost. Apart from the 50 percent of cost limit on loans, there was an absolute-value limit of 700 rubles (again, with some exceptions, such as war disabled workers and employees, doctors, teachers, demobilized and retired officers). Loans granted in 1958 averaged 660.8 rubles per dwelling; the average replacement value of the dwelling in the stock in 1959 was 1600 rubles, as previously cited, or 2.4 times the average 1958 loan value per dwelling. As an estimate of cost per dwelling constructed, 1600 rubles may be an underestimate, for the average size of the dwelling in stock was 30 percent less than that of construction aided by state loans, 32 as compared with 43 square meters. Hence, the true cost should have been at least two-and-a-half times as great as the average loan value, or at least 37.5 rubles per square meter.

Of the total volume of private urban floor space completed in 1958 (24.5 million m^2—*NKh 1958,* p. 636), only 9.8 million square meters was financed even in part from state credits. What was the average value per square meter of the remaining 14.7 million square meters? Occasional reports in the Soviet press provide some ground for the belief that a considerable volume of private housing in the relative luxury class was constructed without the aid of loans. For example, the newspaper *Sovetskaia Rossiia,* September 9, 1960, p. 2 (translated in *Current Digest of Soviet Press,* November 23, 1960, pp. 10–11) reported examples of private homes in Dagestan of up to 170 square meters in size, valued in the tens of thousands of rubles. *Literaturnaia gazeta* on December 20, 1960 disclosed sales of housing plots to individuals in a suburb of Kuibyshev at prices in the thousands of rubles (reported by Paul Wohl in the *Christian Science Monitor,* January 12, 1961, p. 1).

(3) Data supplied by Broner (*Sovremennye problemy zhilishchnogo khoziaistva,* 1961, p. 90) imply an average value of the private urban housing stock on January 1, 1956 of 48.1 rubles per square meter at current prices; the implied value for state and cooperative housing is 76.4 rubles per square meter. At estimate prices the yearbooks show the unit value of state and cooperative housing construction in 1956–1960 was roughly 100 rubles (*NKh 1960,* pp. 594–595, 611). The figure of 100 rubles per square meter is obtained as the quotient of the value of all state and cooperative housing investment divided by the volume of urban state and cooperative housing in physical units completed and brought into use. Since unfinished construction is included in the numerator but not in the denominator of the unit value, the true value at estimate prices per square meter of state and cooperative housing construction is undoubtedly below 100 rubles but probably higher than the figure of 76.4 rubles implied by Broner's data. If the unit values of private housing behave similarly, we may conjecture that the estimate price counterpart of Broner's valuation for private housing should be roughly 50–60 rubles per square meter.

B. *Farm investment in kind.* See sources for item 4, this appendix.

7. *Total outlays for consumption and investment.*

The sum of items 5 and 6.

8. *Transfer outlays.*

Appendix G, sources for item 9.

9. *Total outlays.*

Equal to total income (Table 1, item 9).

G

Sources to Table 3: 1965S

1. *Net income retained by economic organizations.*

A. *Retained income of collective farms.* Obtained as follows (billion rubles; 1958 data from p. 362):

	1958	*1965S*
Allocations to collective funds from money incomes		
Investment fund	3.04	6.2
Cultural fund	.12	1.0
Working capital fund	.40	
Total	3.56	7.2
Less: Depreciation	.90	1.8
	2.66	5.4

The 1965S value of additions to the investment fund assumes a constant annual rate of growth in the Plan period equal to that implied by the collective farm investment target (see below, p. 466): discussion of investment loans to farms is conspicuous by its absence in both the Plan and the commentaries thereon. The estimate of additions to the cultural and working capital funds is arbitrary, except that contemporary Soviet discussion of inventory investment in collective farms suggests the possibility of (and need for) a substantial relative increase. Depreciation is assumed to increase over the 1958 level in proportion to the increase in the allocation to the investment fund.

Since considerable arbitrariness attaches to these estimates it is advisable to see whether they "fit"—that is, within reasonable collective farm total income and outlay control totals. Accordingly I estimate first money income in 1965S and then the distribution of money outlays.

Table G-1 sets out a calculation of collective farm income from sales of 11 major farm products to state procurement. Proceeds from these sales as calculated amount to 16.2 billion rubles at 1958 prices. In 1958 proceeds from sales of the same products accounted for 10.46 billion rubles (sources as indicated in Table G-1) and represented 79 percent of collective farm money income from all sources (*SKh,* p. 64). If this relation carries over to 1965S, collective farm money income in that year from all sources would be about 21 billion rubles.

Almost the same total value can be built up as a minimum on the outlay side, as shown in the following tabulation (billions of rubles; 1958 data from Nimitz, *Incomes of Collective Farmers*):

	1958	*1965S*
Insurance and fees, administrative and production expenses	3.80	5.3–6.8
Allocations to collective funds		
Investment fund	3.04	6.2
Cultural fund	.12	1.0
Working capital fund	.40	
Pensions and allowances	.05	.2
Payments to members	4.75	6.5–8.3
Subtotal	12.17	19.2–22.5
Income tax	1.03	1.4–1.7
Total	13.20	20.6–24.2

The figures for insurance and fees, administrative and production expenses in 1965S assume an increase of 40–80 percent over the 1958 level, as compared with an estimated planned increase in gross output of 80 percent. The minimum figure implies a drop of roughly more than a fifth in costs per unit of gross output. In the light of the overall ambitiousness of collective farm targets and the likelihood of an increase in the weight of double counting in gross output (animal feed is counted twice, once as a crop and again in the value of the livestock), such a decline might well have been programmed. The range of values for payments to members was obtained on the assumption that the share of cash payments in total distributions to members was planned to be no less than in 1958, 79 percent,[1] with a maximum at 100 percent. These percentages, multiplied by the value of total distributions, estimated as 8.7 billion rubles (above, p. 426), and roughly adjusted for wage payments from investment, cultural and social funds (for 1958 values see p. 296), yielded the indicated values. Income taxes are calculated as

[1] 4.75 billion rubles of cash distribution from current income (p. 296) divided by the sum of 4.75 plus 1.25 billion rubles of in kind distributions (p. 423).

7 percent of total incomes (see Table G-3, item 2.B). The 1965S figure for pensions and allowances is arbitrary.

Thus, total cash incomes were estimated as 21 billion rubles and total outlays as 21–24 billion rubles. These figures represent increases over the 1958 level of 56–83 percent. Are they consistent with the previously estimated (above, pp. 416–418) target of an 80 percent increase in collective farm gross output? Consistency implies roughly a 70–110 percent increase in the value of that part of gross output not realized in the form of money income.

[Gross output of collective farms in 1958 has been estimated as 22.9 billion rubles (Egereva, *Ekonomicheskoe obosnovanie struktury* . . . , 1965, p. 158.) With an 80 percent increase, the 1965S value is 41.2 billions. The corresponding money income figures are 13.2 billion rubles in 1958 and 20–24 billions in 1965S. If we may ignore the small amount of money income that does not originate in gross agricultural output, 10 billion rubles in 1958 and 17–21 billions in 1965S remain for gross output not realized in money income.]

Gross output that is not realized in money income may be considered in three categories of disposition—payments in kind to collective farmers, increments to inventories and herds, and seed and feed used as inputs into production during the year. Payments in kind in 1958 are estimated as 1.25 billion rubles, the increment in livestock herds (excluding poultry and horses) on collective farms (*SNIP 1965,* p. 206) as .77 billion rubles, while inventory investment other than in seed and feed (but including livestock considered part of working capital) accounted for an additional 1–1.5 billion rubles. (At current prices, the investment was 2.31 billion rubles (*SNIP 1958–1962,* Part II, p. 190), but probably half of this represented capital gain through price increases.) This leaves roughly 6–7 billion rubles as the value of seed and feed consumed in production during the year or added to stocks. Thus, the value of seed and feed is the predominant element—roughly 60–70 percent—in gross output not realized in money income.

For all agriculture, the SYP provided for at least a doubling of hay output, compared with 1957, at least a quadrupling of silage, and an approximate doubling of potatoes used as feed. The projected increase in grain output was to result in the allocation of 85–90 million tons of concentrated fodder in 1965S (*SKh,* p. 379). The corresponding figure for 1958 is in the area of 40 million tons (31.7 million tons in collective and state farms, according to *Tsifry 1961,* p. 193). As Johnson and Kahan note (*The Soviet Agricultural Program,* 1962, p. 11), "The planned increase in fodder crops [in the SYP] must be substantially greater than 100 percent to be consistent with the livestock goals."

B., C. and D. *Retained profits of state enterprises, nonfarm cooperatives and other organizations.* Retained profits of cooperatives and other organizations are estimated on the basis of an assumed rate of growth of the tax on the incomes of these entities (see Table G-3, sources for item 2.D). Retained profits of state enterprises in 1965S are estimated as roughly twice the 1958 level of 4.58 billion rubles. Assuming a constant annual rate of growth, the SYP target of investment from noncentralized funds (this category of investment bears a close relation to retained profits) implies a 1965S level 110 percent greater than that of 1958 (below, p. 464).

Though these increases appear sizable, there is evidence that they may understate the true planned growth: Table G-2 presents a crude but nevertheless instructive calculation of costs and profits of four branches of the state sector in 1958 and 1965S, showing a 1965S level of 39–53 billion rubles, 2.6–3.5 times that of 1958. A similar increase may also have been planned for state farms and sea and river transport: it was previously estimated that the target increase for state farm output was 150 percent (above pp. 418–419), and we are told that the cost of the basic output of state farms was to decrease by 24 percent (Duginov, *PKh,* 1960, No. 2, p. 83). The Control Figures called for a doubling in maritime cargo transport operations and an increase of 60 percent in inland water freight transport, while sea and river transport costs were also to decline by 24 percent (Rudoi and Lazarenko, *Razvitie transporta i sviazi v SSSR 1959–1965,* 1960, pp. 81, 91).

Total net profits of all state enterprises and nonfarm cooperatives in 1958 came to 20.1 billion rubles (*NKh 1964,* p. 747). The branches listed in Table G-2 accounted in that year for 14.9 billions, or three-quarters of the total. If the profits of the remaining state sector branches and those of cooperatives, amounting to 5.2 billion rubles, were planned to double only, the goal for total net profits in 1965S would have been 49–63 billion rubles. In 1962 Garbuzov, The Minister of Finance, declared that total profits in 1965S were to "exceed" 50 billion rubles (*Ekon.gazeta,* April 23, 1962, p. 9). Since Garbuzov compared this target with a 1955 figure, 12.5 billions, that is almost identical with the 1955 entry in the yearbook net profit series (*NKh 1960,* p. 843), it may be presumed that the 1965S goal also refers to net profits. However, in view of the relatively late date of the statement, April 1962, and the contemporary discussion of a wholesale price reform, originally scheduled to be introduced in 1963 (see Bornstein, *Soviet Studies,* July 1963, pp. 43–52), Garbuzov's 1965S figure may be a revised target. Whether the original target was larger or smaller and by how much is debatable, but I believe my estimate of 1965S total profits is in the right ball park.

Table G-3 derives an estimate of deductions from state enterprise profits to the budget as a residual after deducting other budget revenues. The residual estimate of proceeds from the profits tax is 29–37 billion rubles. In 1958, the profits tax of 13.54 billion rubles siphoned off about 70 percent of all state enterprise net profits, 18.7 billions (p. 363). If this proportion were to remain unchanged, profits deductions of 29–37 billion rubles would imply total state enterprise profits in 1965S of 41–53 billion rubles. The latter result is noteworthy in two respects: (1) adding an allowance of 3 billion rubles of profits by nonfarm cooperatives (retained income plus income tax), the range of total net profits of 44–56 billion rubles is close to the range of total net profits calculated above on the basis of Table G-2, 49–63 billion rubles; (2) the implied level of state enterprise profits net of profits tax, 12–16 billion rubles, is 2.3–3.1 times the 1958 level of 5.2 billions. Thus, the accepted estimate for retained profits of state enterprises, little more than twice the 1958 level, might well be an understatement.

2. *Charges to economic enterprises for special funds.*

A. *Social insurance budget.* Table G-3, item 2.C.

B. *Training of workers; research.* Expenditures remained relatively constant in 1956–1958 (*SNIP 1956–1958,* p. 4) at about .5 billion rubles. The estimate for 1965S allows for an arbitrary one-third increase over the 1958 level.

3. *Taxes and other payments out of income by economic organizations to the budget.*

The 1958 entry in 3.E plus charges to enterprises for the social insurance budget represent 92 percent of state budget revenues from the socialized sector. The same ratio applied to the corresponding 1965S figure, 109 billions (Table G-3), yields 100 billion rubles. Of this total 5.0 billion rubles are entered under item 2.A, enterprise social insurance contributions, leaving a residual of 95 billions for item 3.

Approximately the same value can be obtained by a somewhat different but more involved route, as follows:

In a work published in the summer of 1959, the then Minister of Finance, Zverev, declared that the volume of "money accumulation" in the form of profits, turnover taxes, social insurance funds, deductions from collective farm money incomes for indivisible funds, and other revenues was planned to reach 120–125 billion rubles in 1965S (Zverev, *Khoziaistvennoe razvitie i finansy v semiletke,* 1959, pp. 20, 49). Zverev defined the term "money accumulation" somewhat more carefully in an earlier work as a form of the "net income of society, representing part of the national income" and consisting of "profits, turnover tax, social insurance premia in productive branches, customs revenues, revenues of credit institutions, local taxes on enterprises and organizations, collective farm payments into indivisible funds, etc." (Zverev, *Voprosy natsional'nogo dokhoda i finansov SSSR,* 1958, p. 111.)

The concept "net income of society" in Soviet accounting is reasonably straightforward and denotes the aggregate net material product less payments to labor employed in the productive sphere. There should then be a definable relation between "money accumulation" and the nonhousehold charges against current product of the SNIP accounts. "Money accumulation" would appear to be substantially identical with item 6, "consolidated total charges against current product, net of depreciation," on the income side of the SNIP public sector account—gross, however, of the allowance for subsidized losses n.e.c., item 5.

With regard to the 1965S goal of 120–125 billion rubles, Zverev declared (*Khoziaistvennoe razvitie i finansy v semiletke,* 1959, p. 49): "The vast growth of money accumulation in the current seven year period is the result of the planned increase in production and in the reduction of its cost. Especially rapid is the increase of profits in the economy. In these conditions, the possibility cannot be excluded that by the end of the Seven Year Plan, money accumulation in the form of profits, on the basis of existing relations, will exceed accumulation in the form of turnover tax proceeds."

Although the sense of this remark is not self-evident—among others, the significance of the phrase "on the basis of existing relations" (*iskhodia iz tepereshnikh sootnoshenii*) is not clear—Zverev is assumed to be implying here approximate equality of the 1965S levels of profits and turnover taxes. Presumably, Zverev was referring to net profits, since profits data for other years he cites, as will be shown below, are so identified. My estimate of 1965S turnover tax proceeds is 50 billion rubles, suggesting a total net profits target of, say, 45–50 billions. Earlier I estimated total net profits in 1965S as 49–63 billion rubles on the basis of a blowup of the profits of four state sector branches, and as 44–56 billions on the basis of a residual calculation of deductions from state profits; I cited Garbuzov's 1962 statement that profits in 1965S would exceed 50 billion rubles and noted that the figure might represent a revised target (above, pp. 444–445). Suppose, then, that total net profits in 1965S were to be 47.5 billion rubles. Of this total I have already accounted for 12.3 billion rubles of retained profits (items 1.B and 1.C) and 1.0 billion rubles of tax on incomes of cooperatives and other organizations (Table G-3, sources for item 2.D). The residual, 34.2 billion rubles, consists of deductions from state sector profits. If the control for total charges against current product net of depreciation, but gross of the miscellaneous subsidies, is 120 billion rubles, we are left with 22.5 billion rubles apart from turnover taxes and all net profits. In turn, the 22.5 billion figure is composed of 5.4 billion rubles of collective farm retained income (above, p. 441), 1.6 billions of taxes on farm income (Table G-3, item 2.B), 5.7 billion rubles of enterprise charges for special funds (above, p. 445), and a remainder of 9.8 billion rubles of miscellaneous state sector revenues.

Thus, an estimate of the 1965S entry for item 3 may be constructed consisting of the following elements (billion rubles):

Tax on income of collective farms	1.6
Tax on income of cooperatives and other organizations	1.0
Deductions from state sector profits	34.2
Turnover tax	50.0
Miscellaneous revenues	9.8
	96.6

It must be noted that examination of the available data on "money accumulation" casts some doubt on the stability of the definition of the term. The problem may be outlined by considering information of two kinds—first, total "money accumulation" and major components up to 1960 plan, and second, major elements of "money accumulation" in 1965S.

Values of money accumulation and major components thereof for scattered years are presented in Table G-4. All entries are drawn from Zverev's books and articles and are listed according to the date of the source. Certain characteristics of the data may be summarized as follows:

(1) The profits figures clearly refer to net balance profits (see below, p. 469). Thus, Zverev declares, "For 1940 and 1950 profits are given net, that is, excluding losses. For 1956 losses in communal-housing economy, the coal and timber industries are subtracted from total profits." (*Finstroi*, 1957.) The second sentence appears to suggest a netting basis different from that used with respect to 1940 and 1950. However,

the figures for all three years correspond to those published in the statistical yearbooks (*NKh 1959* and later), with the minor exception of the figure for 1956. For that year, the yearbooks give a figure .07 rubles higher. The difference is negligible and may be attributable to revision on the basis of more complete data. The 1955 profits figures from Zverev 1958 and Zverev 1959 are identical with the yearbook figure.

(2) The turnover tax figures are the same as those encountered in budget documents and statistical yearbooks.

(3) Values of "other revenues" exhibit divergent values for 1940 and apparently inconsistent changes between years of the different series: compare the 1956 value in Zverev 1957a with the 1955 value in Zverev 1958 and 1959; 1957 plan in the former source with 1958 plan in the latter. Whatever accounts for these differences may also account for the 4 billion ruble reduction in 1958 plan total money accumulation between Zverev's second 1957 paper and his 1958 book.

Indeed, there does appear to have been a redefinition of the scope and content of "other revenues." As indicated, the category appears to include productive sector social insurance payments, customs revenues, incomes of credit institutions, local taxes on enterprises and organizations, and collective farm allocations to indivisible funds. In a still earlier 1957 article (*PKh,* 1957, No. 3, p. 17) Zverev declared that since profits of credit institutions form part of the separately indicated profits figures, "other revenues" include outlays of credit institutions. No reference to this peculiar departure from accounting netness is made in the later Zverev sources. Possibly it was eliminated by the 1958 volume. In that source a footnote (p. 112) indicates redefinition of money accumulation: "The figures have been made more precise (*utochneny*) compared with those published earlier by excluding MTS production outlays, losses of several production enterprises and of municipal-housing economy, payments through the MVT, and others." The 1957 and 1958 sources have component data for only one common year, 1940. Comparison of the entries in Zverev's tables for this year suggest that the revisions indicated in the 1958 source footnote applied to "other revenues."

It is assumed that MVT stands for *Ministerstvo vneshnei torgovli,* the Ministry of Foreign Trade, and that the payments in question are subsidies for the accounting losses incurred in exporting. Since the redefinition seems largely aimed at consistency in netting, it is possible that the difference between foreign trade accounting losses and profits is included with state-cooperative net profits, and the elimination of foreign trade subsidies from "other revenues" is designed to eliminate the type of awkward situation represented by the earlier treatment of credit institution outlays. Zverev omitted the quoted footnote in his 1959 book but reintroduced it, word for word, in his 1961 book.

A comparison of figures for "other revenues" in 1940, 1950, 1955, and 1956 with corresponding elements of SNIP calculations for those years (these are the years covered in common by SNIP calculations and Zverev's data) is also not encouraging (billion rubles):

	"Other Revenues"		*Corresponding*
	Zverev 1957a	*Zverev 1958 and Later*	*SNIP Income Items*
1940	1.86	1.45	2.40
1950	5.45		5.94/7.24
1955		4.37	9.64
1956	10.56		11.18

The SNIP data are taken from *SNIP 1940–1948,* pp. 22–23; *SNIP 1928–1948,* pp. 8–9; *SNIP 1949–1955,* p. 6; *SNIP 1956–1958,* p. 4. SNIP income categories covered are retained collective farm cash incomes; charges to enterprises for special funds, tax on collective farm incomes; miscellaneous budget incomes and customs revenues. For 1950 the figure after the slash includes income from sales of reparations.

The comparison suggests that SNIP estimates correspond more closely to the Zverev data of the 1957 articles than to those of his later work. However, the sample is too small for generalization. It should also be noted that the income components concerned include some for which SNIP estimates are especially difficult: for example, miscellaneous budget incomes, an estimate of which requires a more or less arbitrary distinction between current and noncurrent charges. Moreover, Zverev's data should exclude some nonproductive sector incomes included in the SNIP accounts.

(4) On the other hand, there appear to be certain inconsistencies between the scope of Zverev's profits figures and the requirements of national income accounting, especially Soviet accounting. If the profits figures are indeed of the balance type, they embrace not only sales of output but a variety of other types of income and losses: for example, housing, tax refunds or additional tax charges, fines and forfeits, capital gains and losses on inventories due to price changes (*SNIP 1956–1958,* pp. 74–75). In addition, the yearbook data are identified as the net profits of productive and nonproductive enterprises and organizations alike. If "money accumulation" is a form of the "net income of society,

representing part of the national income," presumably incomes of non-productive organizations should be excluded from the profits component.

(5) One datum may be adduced in support of Zverev's "money accumulation" target. In the spring of 1960, Garbuzov wrote: "The volume of the state budget is already now 773 billion [old] rubles, and at the end of the Seven Year Plan is to be 1.2 trillion [old] rubles" (*FinSSSR,* 1960, No. 5, p. 9). Garbuzov was apparently referring to revenues, since his base of comparison, 773 billion (old) rubles, was the 1960 plan volume of budget revenues (*Izvestiia,* October 31, 1959, p. 1). Note that the 1960 plan figure for revenues is within 5 percent of the 1960 plan figure for money accumulation. While the relation between budget revenues and money accumulation can vary—by virtue of changes in such items as retained enterprise and collective farm incomes or transfer payments by households, the close relation between Garbuzov's 1965S figure for budget revenues and Zverev's for money accumulation is reassuring. Indeed, given the expectation of a relatively slow growth of household transfer payments and a relatively rapid growth of enterprise retained profits, it is doubly reassuring that the figures imply a greater increase of "money accumulation" than of budget revenues.

In short there is evidence to disquiet us about Zverev's data on money accumulation in 1940–1960, but also some to reassure us about the 1965S total. Since the latter also makes reasonable sense relative to other information and estimates, as indicated earlier, the qualifications discussed should be borne in mind but need not undermine our estimate for the budget incomes in question.

4. *Net accounting profits of foreign trade organizations.*

Accounting profits on imports are assumed offset by accounting losses on exports.

5. *Allowance for subsidized losses, n.e.c.*

The 1958 estimate consists largely of subsidies to agricultural procurement. For 1965S a notional allowance of 1 billion rubles is set.

6. *Consolidated total charges against current product, net of depreciation.*

The sum of items 1–5.

7. *Depreciation.*

This figure is the sum of 1.8 billion rubles of depreciation allowances by collective farms (above, p. 441) and 12.7 billion rubles of allowances in the rest of the public sector.

The latter figure was obtained as follows: According to Budavei *et al.*

(*PKh,* 1959, No. 6, p. 20), allowances earmarked for capital repairs in this period were to be "more than 400 billion [old] rubles, of which more than 250 billion [old] rubles for productive capital of industry and construction. The fund of full replacement of fixed capital [from amortization allowances—A.S.B.] will be approximately the same sum." Unfortunately, it is not at all clear whether "approximately the same sum" refers to 25 or to 40 billion rubles.

It would seem likely that the referent is closer to 25 than to 40 billion rubles, on the following evidence: (1) amortization allowances were planned on the basis of an overall average norm of 5.5 percent of the value of capital, of which 2.3 percent was for investment and 3.2 percent for capital repairs (Filippov, *PKh,* 1960, No. 11, p. 39); (2) the actual distribution in 1958 and 1959 directed about 60 percent of allowances to capital repair (*NKh 1962,* p. 634).

The seven-year cumulated total of allowances is estimated on the assumption that the "more than" 40 billion rubles of allowances for repairs accounted for 60 percent of total allowances. The resulting figure, 70 billion rubles, in conjunction with the 1958 value, 7.06 billions, implies the 1965S entry in the table, on the assumption of a constant annual rate of growth.

8. *Consolidated total charges against current product.*

The sum of items 6 and 7.

9. *Transfer receipts.*

Identified with budget revenues from the population, shown in Table G-3, item 1. Insurance premiums are ignored; their value in 1958 was .05 billion rubles (above, p. 381).

10. *Consolidated net income.*

The sum of items 8 and 9.

TABLE G-1

ESTIMATION OF COLLECTIVE FARM MONEY INCOME IN 1965S FROM SALES TO STATE OF ELEVEN MAJOR FARM PRODUCTS AT 1958 PRICES

Product	State Procurement in 1965S (million tons) From All Sources	State Farm Deliveries	Purchases from Collective Farms	Collective Farm Purchase Prices (rubles per ton)	Value of Collective Farm Sales (billion rubles)
	(1)	(2)	(3)	(4)	(5)
Grain	52	21	31	64	1.98
Oil seed	3.92		3.45	148	.51
Potatoes	11.72		8.18	42	.34
Vegetables	8.4		5.20	78	.41
Sugar beets	81.00	5.00	76.00	23	1.75
Unginned cotton	5.70–6.10		4.96–5.31	337	1.67–1.79
Flax fiber	.53		.53	1664	.88
Meat, live weight	11.05	3.54	6.42	617	3.96
Milk	40.61	10.56	27.51	113	3.11
Wool	.54	0.18	.32	3761	1.20
Eggs [a]	10.00		5.71	62	.35
Eleven products					16.16–16.28

Note:

[a] Quantities in billion units, prices in rubles per thousand.

Sources:

Column 1: Given directly in the approved Control Figures, except for grain and vegetables. The target for grain is stated as somewhat higher than planned 1958 procurement. The latter is estimated as a little over 49 million tons based on planned deliveries from the RSFSR, Kazakhstan and the Ukraine—48.6 million tons (*Izvestiia*, November 6, 1958, p. 1)—and actual deliveries of the other republics of 1.0 million tons (*SKh*, p. 95). The target for vegetables is assumed to be twice the 1958 level (*SKh*, p. 90): Johnson and Kahan estimate the aggregate output target was twice the 1958 level and that most of the increase in output was to come from the public sector (Johnson and Kahan, *The Soviet Agricultural Program*, 1962, pp. 47–48).

Column 2: Except for sugar beets, entries in column 2 are obtained as the product of column 1 figures and shares of state farms in total procurements in 1965S cited by Khrushchev in *Plenum Tsk KPSS 15–19 dekabria 1958 goda*, p. 52. He also stated that state farm deliveries of sugar beets were to be more than four times greater in 1965S than in 1957. State farm deliveries of sugar beets came to 1.2 million tons in 1957 (total procurements less those from collective farms, as shown in *SKh*, pp. 61, 90; sugar beets are not produced in the private sector—*ibid.*, pp. 202–207).

Column 3: Grain and sugar beets: figures are the difference between columns 1 and 2. Oil seed: collective farm share in 1965S assumed the same as collective farm share of total sunflower seed procurements in 1958, 88 percent. Potatoes and vegetables: private sector sales assumed to increase by 10 percent, state farm deliveries by 150 percent, and collective farm sales obtained as residual. Cotton and flax: collective farm shares in 1965S assumed the same as in 1958, 87 and 99.5 percent, respectively. Meat, milk, and wool: private sector sales assumed to increase by 10 percent and collective farm sales obtained as a residual. Eggs: private sector sales assumed to increase by 10 percent, state farm deliveries by 100 percent and collective farm sales obtained as residual. Procurements of all products in 1958 taken from *SKh*, pp. 61, 90, 91, 102, 104, 106, 108, 110, 112.

Column 4: All prices are taken from Zverev, *Natsional'nyi dokhod i finansy SSSR*, 1961, p. 306, or from Table A-2.

Column 5: Column 3 times column 4.

TABLE G-2

COSTS AND PROFITS OF FOUR STATE SECTOR BRANCHES, 1958 AND 1965S (billion rubles)

	1958			1965S		
	Output	Costs	Profits	Output	Costs	Profits
Industry	127.2	116.4	10.8	229.0	185.4–199.0	30.0–43.6
Contract construction	13.2	12.4	.8	21.1	18.6	2.5
Railroad freight transportation	5.9	4.3	1.6	8.2	4.7	3.5
Retail trade	5.8	4.1	1.7	8.9	6.0	2.9
Total profits, four sectors			14.9			38.9–52.5

Sources:

Industry. 1958: Output is value of gross output at 1955 enterprise prices (net of turnover taxes), from *NKh 1964*, p. 123. Profits are from *Prom II*, p. 101, and represent net profits from sales; profits from all enterprise operations are .1 billion rubles lower (probably largely on account of housing losses).

1965S: The SYP called for an 80 percent increase in gross output and a decline of 11.5 percent in costs per ruble of marketed output. My calculation assumes that the cost target for all gross output was a reduction of 5–11.5 percent.

Construction. 1958: Output and profits from *NKh 1964*, pp. 524 and 747. Output is the value at estimate prices of construction-installation and other investment activities by contract organizations. For present purposes it is assumed that the estimate prices are equivalent to 1958 actual prices.

1965S: The volume of construction was to increase 60 percent by 1965S (*Pravda*, June 27, 1959, p. 3) and the Control Figures called for a 6 percent reduction in average cost in the seven-year period.

Railroad freight transportation. 1958: Output represents freight turnover (1302 billion ton-km, *NKh 1964*, p. 431) multiplied by an average freight rate of .45 kopecks per ton-km. The average freight rate was computed on the basis of statements by (1) Kreinin, *VE*, 1959, No. 8, p. 130, that cost represented on the average 73 percent of the price of railroad freight transport and (2), Perov, *PKh*, 1959, No. 3, p. 19, showing average cost of a freight ton-km in 1958 as .33 kopecks.

1965S: According to Perov (*ibid.*), cost per freight ton-km was to be reduced to .26 kopecks in 1965S. The 1965S goal for total freight turnover, the average of the range given in the Control Figures, is 1825 billion ton-km. Approximate confirmation of the implied increase in profits appears in a Soviet source claiming savings by 1965S from decreases in the cost of railroad shipments of more than 1.5 billion rubles (Rudoi and Lazarenko, *Razvitie transporta i sviazi v SSSR 1959–1965*, 1960, p. 73).

Retail trade. 1958: Selling costs, profits, and trade markup (selling costs plus profit) are taken from *Sovtorg II*, p. 154.

1965S: Retail trade was to increase 54 percent at current prices and 62 percent at 1958 prices (*NKh 1958*, p. 103). A 10 percent planned decline in costs is assumed.

TABLE G-3

STATE BUDGET REVENUES, 1958 AND 1965S
(billion rubles)

	1958		1965S	
Total revenues		67.24		115.0
1. From the population		6.83		6.0
A. State taxes	5.19		3.0	
B. State loans	1.06		2.2	
C. Lotteries	.31		.8 (C and D)	
D. Other	.28			
2. From the socialized sector		60.40		109.0
A. Turnover tax	30.45		50.0	
B. Collective farm income tax	1.03		1.6	
C. Social insurance revenues	3.26		5.0	
D. Income of MTS-RTS; income tax on cooperatives and other organizations, forest incomes; local taxes and fees; rental income from local soviet property; price differentials on agricultural machinery and parts; accounting profits on imports; payments by collective farms for MTS machinery	5.18		6.8–9.6	
E. Unidentified revenues	6.94		8.7–13.9	
F. Profits deductions, state enterprises	13.54		28.9–36.9	

Sources:

1958: Table C-1.

1965S: For total revenues, see above, pp. 41–42. Derivation of components is shown below.

1. *From the population.* The sum of components.

A. *State taxes.* The sum of .49 billion rubles of proceeds from the agricultural tax and 2.50 billions from the income tax, including the tax on bachelors, spinsters, and citizens with small families.

In his speech proclaiming the gradual abrogation of direct taxes (*Pravda*, May 6, 1960), Khrushchev indicated that the agricultural tax, essentially a tax on collective farmers, would remain in effect indefinitely. The yield in 1958 was 422 million rubles (*Gosbiudzhet I*, p. 9). The 1965S figure is estimated as increasing in proportion to the 14 percent increase in incomes of households from the private agricultural economy (above p. 425).

The estimate for income taxes was derived from data on the projected reductions as given in Khrushchev's tax speech and the text of the follow-up Supreme Soviet decree (*Pravda*, May 8, 1960). Abrogation of the income tax was to proceed in stages and be completed in 1965S. On October 1, 1965S taxes on monthly gross earnings of 100–200 rubles were to be eliminated but with partial reduction in net income as follows:

	Income increase after 10/1/65S	
Monthly base pay, rubles	*Increment in net pay, as percent of former tax*	*Increase in aggregate annual net pay, billion rubles*
100.1–120.0	79	.65
120.1–140.0	46	.26
140.1–160.0	29	.09
160.1–180.0	15	.02
180.1–200.0	max 10	.02

TABLE G-3 (continued)

In order to compute the tax paid by personnel in these categories, it is necessary first to determine the approximate employment levels in 1965S, N_i. N_i may be calculated from the equation

$$W_iN_i + A_i = W_i^*N_i$$

$$N_i = \frac{A_i}{W_i^* - W_i}$$

where for the ith pay category W_i and W_i^* are the old and new monthly net pay levels and A_i is the aggregate increase in net pay on a monthly basis. Two additional sets of information are necessary for this calculation—the average base pay in each of the listed categories and the magnitude of the tax. As to the first, I simply assume an average at the midpoint of each pay class. The second may be obtained from Soviet sources (e.g., *Ekonomicheskaia entsiklopediia–Promyshlennost' i stroitel'stvo*, 1964, II, Col. 510): for monthly wages and salaries of 100 rubles and over, the tax was 8.20 rubles plus 13 percent of the excess over 100 rubles. N_i may then be computed as follows:

			Increase in net pay			
			Per employee		*Aggregate*	
Monthly base pay, rubles	*Former monthly tax, rubles*	*Former net pay (W_i), rubles*	*As percent of old tax*	*($W_i - W_i^*$) rubles*	*million rubles*	*Employment (N_i), millions*
110	9.50	100.50	79	7.51	54.167	7.213
130	12.10	117.90	46	5.57	21.667	3.890
150	14.70	135.30	29	4.26	7.500	1.761
170	17.30	152.70	15	2.60	1.667	.641
190	19.90	170.10	8	1.59	1.667	1.048

The aggregate tax that would have been paid by personnel in these pay categories in 1965*S* is the product of the annual tax in each pay category and the computed employment levels. The sum of the annual tax proceeds so calculated is 2.08 billion rubles, of which 75 percent or 1.56 billion rubles is assumed to have been scheduled for the first nine months of 1965S.

Thus, workers and employees earning between 100.0 and 200.0 rubles would pay an estimated 1.55 billion rubles of income taxes in 1965S. In addition, workers and employees earning between 70.0 and 100.0 rubles, whose income tax rates were to be cut before that year, would still be paying some taxes in that year, as would those earning more than 200.0 rubles. To account for taxes from these categories of workers and employees, the total is raised to 2.5 billion rubles.

B. *State loans.* Identified with net savings, derived above, pp. 433–437. Until 1964 the annual increment in savings bank deposits was transferred to the budget in the form of purchases of state bonds. Here I ignore the role of voluntary insurance; premiums totaled only .05 billion rubles in 1958 (above, p. 381).

C. *Lotteries* and D. *Other.* Arbitrary estimate.

2. *From the socialized sector.* The difference between total revenues and revenues from the population.

A. *Turnover tax.* In the 1950s, turnover tax revenues increased much less rapidly than the value of retail trade (in current prices), as shown in these data (*NKh 1958*, pp. 699, 708, 899):

	Percent Increase in	
	Retail Trade [a]	*Turnover Tax Revenues*
1950–1953	19.8	3.2
1953–1955	15.4	(−)0.5
1955–1958	34.5	25.6

[a] Excluding commission trade.

TABLE G-3 (continued)

In large measure, especially with reference to the early 1950s, this pattern reflects the substantial retail price reductions effected primarily through decreases in the turnover tax. A projected SYP decrease in public catering prices amounted to 5.3 billion rubles (*NKh 1958*, p. 103), but in view of the large planned increase in retail profits (net of the price cut), it is not clear that turnover taxes should have suffered. Other factors affecting the likely proceeds target are: (1) anticipated changes in the structure of retail sales and consequent changes in the shares of commodity groups with different tax rates, and (2) planned changes in agricultural procurement prices. We know nothing about (2) and little about (1). Given the uncertainty, my estimate assumes an increase from the 1958 level roughly as large as the planned 62 percent increase in retail trade at constant prices.

B. *Collective farm income tax.* It is assumed that the effective income tax rate on collective farm money income was to decline from the 1956–1958 level of roughly 8 percent (*SNIP 1956–1958*, p. 98) to about 7 percent in 1965S. On December 18, 1958, the tax rate was reduced to a flat 12.5 percent on gross income net of essentially non-labor payments (*Vedomosti verkhovnogo soveta SSSR*, January 1, 1959, pp. 5–6). Zverev, then Minister of Finance, characterized this change as a reduction of the "existing [1958] tax rate . . . from 14 percent to 12.5 percent" (*Pravda*, December 23, 1958, p. 2). My estimate of collective farm money income in 1965S is 22.5 billion rubles (roughly the midpoint of a range derived above, p. 442).

C. *Social insurance revenues.* Estimated as increasing in proportion to the increase in the wage and salary bill, 53 percent (above, p. 415).

D. *Income of MTS-RTS*, etc. Obtained as follows (billion rubles; 1958 data from Table C-1):

	1958	*1965S*
Income of MTS-RTS	.97	.3–.5
Tax on cooperatives and other organizations	.63	1.0
Forest income	.23	.3
Local taxes and fees	.73	{1.1–1.7
Rental income from local soviet property	.13	
Price differentials on agricultural machinery and spare parts	.04	1.5–3.0
Accounting profits on imports	1.62	2.5–3.0
Payments by collective farms for MTS machinery	.83	.1
	5.18	6.8–9.6

MTS-RTS income. This income totaled almost 1 billion rubles in 1958 but declined to .18 billions in 1959. Although begun in 1958, the dissolution of the MTS was not completed in that year. Hence, it is necessary to use the 1959 figure, rather than those for previous years, as a rough guide to RTS incomes in 1965S. It is assumed that the RTS were expected to continue in operation through 1965S.

Tax on cooperatives and other organizations. Assumes an annual rate of growth of net income, and hence of tax, of 7 percent. Tax proceeds grew 18.7 percent per year in 1950–1955 and 5.5 percent in 1955–1958 (*Gosbiudzhet I*, p. 8).

Forest income. Revenue from this source varied little since 1950 (*Gosbiudzhet I*, p. 8).

Local taxes and fees; rental income. Assumes an increase of 25–100 percent.

Price differentials. Since the differentials were instituted at the end of 1958, a more appropriate base figure is that for 1959, 1.56 billion rubles. My estimate assumes the intention to continue the differentials indefinitely and takes into account the projected more than doubling of collective farm investment (below, p. 466).

Accounting profits on imports. The SYP called for a more than 50 percent increase in

TABLE G-3 (continued)

Soviet trade with the Socialist countries, while in his speech on the Plan to the 21st Party Congress, Khrushchev declared, "We can at least double the volume of our foreign trade." However, Soviet planners would not have counted on a proportional increase in import profits if they expected, as they seemed to, relative stability in the Soviet price level and price inflation abroad.

Payments for MTS machinery. It is a reasonable guess that the debt to the state for MTS machinery transferred to farms in 1958–1959 was expected to be liquidated by 1965S. The entry in the table is a token allowance for the possibility that my guess is wrong.

E. *Unidentified revenues.* Allows for an increase over the 1958 level of 25–100 percent.

F. *Profits deductions.* Residual, item 2 total less the sum of items 2.A through 2.E.

TABLE G-4

"MONEY ACCUMULATION," SELECTED YEARS, 1950–1960 PLAN

(billion rubles)

	State-Cooperative Profits	Turnover Taxes	Other Revenues	Total "Money Accumulation"
Zverev, 1957a				
1940	3.27	10.59	1.86	15.72
1950	5.22	23.61	5.45	34.28
1956	13.63	25.86	10.56	50.05
1957 approved plan	17.16	27.73	11.70	56.59
Zverev, 1957b				
1957 plan	..	..	..	56.59
1958 plan	..	..	..	62.55
Zverev, 1958				
1940	3.27	10.59	1.45	15.31
1955	12.58	24.24	4.37	41.19
1958 plan	19.20	30.15	9.26	58.61
Zverev, 1959				
1955	12.58	24.24	4.37	41.19
1958 approved plan	19.20	30.15	9.26	58.61
1959 plan	23.39	33.30	10.53	66.22
Zverev, 1961				
1940	3.3	10.6	1.4	15.3
1955	12.6	24.2	4.4	41.2
1960 plan	30.0	31.8	12.0	73.8

Sources:

1957a: Finstroi., p. 54.

1957b: PKh, 1957, No. 12, p. 14.

1958: Voprosy natsional'nogo dokhoda i finansov SSSR, 1958, p. 112.

1959: Khoziaistvennoe razvitie i finansy v semiletke, 1959, p. 48.

1961: Natsional'nyi dokhod i finansy SSSR, 1961, p. 131.

H

Sources to Table 4: 1965S

1. *Communal services.*

A. *Education, excluding R&D.* Obtained by subtracting 1 billion rubles of stipends from total current outlays of 12 billion rubles. The latter figure was obtained as follows:

The Control Figures and Khrushchev's speech to the 21st Party Congress provide the following information on SYP goals in the field of education: (1) the number of students in elementary and secondary schools was to increase by at most one-third, from 30 millions to 38–40 millions; (2) the number of pupils attending boarding schools was to jump from 180,000 to 2,500,000; (3) kindergarten enrollment was to grow by 84 percent, from 2,280,000 to 4,200,000; (4) higher educational institutions were to graduate 35 percent more specialists during the SYP period than in 1952–1958, 2,300,000 as compared with 1,700,000, whereas the number of specialists with higher education in 1965S was to total more than 4.5 million, or better than 50 percent more than in 1958; (5) during the seven years more than 4 million students were to be admitted to specialized secondary institutions. Since the corresponding level of admissions averaged 566,000 in 1956–1958 (*NKh 1959,* p. 745), the implied SYP period average of perhaps 600,000 represents a very small increase indeed.

The next step is to translate these goals into outlay values. In 1958 the state budget appropriation to "enlightenment" financed 86 percent of total expenditures on education excluding science, 6.90 of 8.02 billion rubles; an insignificant amount originated in social insurance funds and the rest from funds of enterprises, collective farms and other organizations (Tables D-1 and D-2; *NKh 1958,* p. 905). A breakdown of expenditure on education excluding science is available only for state budget outlays, but since they accounted for the overwhelming share of outlays from all sources, no great violence to the truth should be done if we assume that expenditures from other sources followed the same pattern. The distribution of budget outlays on enlightenment excluding science in 1958, by chapter and type (capital and current) may be shown as follows (billion rubles):

	All Outlays	*Capital Outlays Including Capital Repairs*	*Current Outlays*
1. General education			
A. Kindergarten	.52	.03	.49
B. Elementary and secondary schools	2.66	.29	2.37
C. Boarding schools	.11	.01	.10
D. Other	.69	.07	.62
E. Total	3.98		
2. Preparation of cadres			
A. Higher educational institutions	1.14	.12	1.02
B. Specialized secondary educational institutions	.54	.04	.50
C. Other	.67	.07	.60
D. Total	2.35		
3. Cultural-enlightment, press, art and broadcasting, miscellaneous	.57	.06	.51
Total	6.90	.69	5.21

The distribution of all outlays is taken from *Gosbiudzhet I,* pp. 21–23; capital outlays are estimated on the basis of 1957 proportions, calculated from *Raskhody,* pp. 49, 50, 53, 55, 57; capital outlays on items 1.D, 2.C, and 3 are assumed to account for the same proportion of all outlays as the average of other items, 10 percent.

The SYP goals reproduced earlier can be associated with outlay categories which account for about 72 percent of current budget expenditures on education excluding science in 1958. The relevant 1958 current outlays may now be multiplied by the growth factors of the Plan goals (enrollment in higher educational institutions is assumed to increase by 50 percent and in technicums, etc., by 10 percent):

	Billion Rubles	
	1958	*1965S*
Kindergarten	.49	.90
Elementary and secondary schools	2.37	3.16
Boarding schools	.10	1.40
Higher educational institutions	1.02	1.53
Specialized secondary institutions	.50	.55
	4.48	7.54

If the remaining budget and nonbudget current outlays on education excluding science were to increase in proportion—that is, from 2.13 (6.61–4.48) billion rubles in 1958 to 3.58 billions in 1965S—then aggregate current outlays from all sources on education excluding science would increase from 6.61 to 11.12 billion rubles. (In the period 1950–1958, budget outlays, current and capital, on all enlightenment excluding science rose faster than on general education and cadre training alone, thus implying relatively faster growth in the remaining components; see *Gosbiudzhet I,* pp. 21–22.) As an allowance for possibly higher expenditures per pupil or student, a round estimate of 12 billion rubles is adopted. All these figures include stipends.

Stipends alone are estimated as follows: The distribution of budget outlays on stipends in 1958 has been estimated (p. 401) as indicated below:

	Billion Rubles
Specialized secondary institutions	.192
Higher educational institutions	.365
Other	.093
Total budget	.650

Comparison of the value of stipends in the categories indicated with enrollment in specialized secondary and in higher educational institutions (above, p. 400) has shown some tendency to decline in the value of the stipend granted per enrollee in the period 1955–1958. However, this apparent decline was at least partly due to a decrease in proportion of students enrolled who received stipends. (Komarov, *Ekonomicheskie osnovy podgotovki spetsialistov dlia narodnogo khoziaistva,* 1959, p. 135; *Dostizheniia,* 1957, pp. 275, 278; *Tsifry 1958,* pp. 353, 356). For the purpose of estimating stipends in 1965S, I assume that total stipends distributed in specialized secondary and in higher educational institutions were planned to increase in proportion to enrollment, by 10 and 50 percent respectively. It is therefore assumed that any further decline in the proportion of students granted stipends was to be offset by an increase in the value of the average stipend.

The final estimate of the distribution of stipends is shown below. The indicated increases for other budget stipends, nonbudget stipends, and stipends to science are arbitrary estimates.

	Billion Rubles 1958	1965S
Budget stipends		
Specialized secondary institutions	.192	.21
Higher educational institutions	.365	.55
Science and other	.093	.18
Nonbudget stipends	.070	.10
Total stipends	.720	1.04
Less: stipends to science	.02	.04
Equals: stipends to education, excluding science	.70	1.00

B. *Health care and physical culture.* Obtained as follows (billion rubles; 1958 data from Table D-3):

	1958	1965S
Budget outlays on health and physical culture	4.11	6.4
Outlays from social insurance funds	.32	.5
Outlays by enterprises, collective farms, other organizations	.60	1.2
Total outlays	5.03	8.1
Less: capital outlays	.62	1.1
Equals: current outlays	4.41	7.0

Budget outlays. In his address to the 21st Party Congress, presenting the draft SYP, Khrushchev stated that "total state outlays on the further improvement of health care of our country's population" would reach almost 36 billion rubles during the SYP period. Khrushchev's remark is difficult to interpret. Presumably the outlays referred to did not include those by enterprises, collective farms, and other organizations and excluded, as well, capital repairs. But whether outlays from social insurance funds were included, or whether the planned expenditures were net or gross of new investment, is not clear. Assuming a constant annual rate of increase of expenditure, the alternative estimates for 1965S which can be inferred from Khrushchev's statement are shown below. (Capital outlays are crudely estimated on the assumption that half of new investment in 1958 originated in the budget with the other half distributed proportionally between social insurance funds and other sources; for investment see Table D-3.) The illustrative calculation yields impossible relations between net and gross investment in 1965S but suggests a rough order of magnitude level of 6 billion rubles.

	Billion Rubles	
	1958	*1965S*
Budget outlays only		
Gross of investment	4.11	6.0
Net of investment	3.91	6.2
Budget and social insurance fund outlays		
Gross of investment	4.43	5.7
Net of investment	4.15	6.0

What are the 1965S outlay implications of other Plan goals for health care? The Control Figures provided for a seven-year (centralized?) investment outlay of 7.7 billion rubles in education, culture and health, or 79 percent more than in 1952–1958. More than 25 billion rubles were to be invested in public health, social security, physical culture and sports, and the medical industry, or 80 percent more than was invested in these projects in 1952–1958. This investment was to result in increases in the number of hospital beds and nursery accommodations which were 100 percent and 150 percent, respectively, greater than the *increases* obtained in 1952–1958. The latter goal can be roughly translated into actual numbers of beds and accommodations as follows (*TsSU, Zdravookhranenie SSSR,* 1960, pp. 50 and 185; nursery places in 1954 from *NKh 1955,* p. 248):

	Thousands of Units	
	Hospital Beds	*Nursery Accommodations*
1950	1011	777
1954	..	862
1955	1289	907
1958	1533	1135

By interpolation (assuming constant annual rates of increase), we may estimate the number of beds in 1951 as 1,061,000 and the number of nursery places in that year as 798,000. Hence, the increase between 1951 and 1958 came to 472,000 beds and 337,000 nursery places. The corresponding SYP period increases are 100 and 150 percent, respectively, or 944,000 beds and 843,000 nursery places. Therefore, the number of beds in 1965S was to have been 62 percent and the number of nursery places 74 percent greater than in 1958.

The next step is to assess the relative importance of expenditures on these categories of health care. A breakdown of expenditures is available only for state budget outlays (*Gosbiudzhet I,* p. 23), but they account for roughly four-fifths or more of the total. (Physical culture expenditures are omitted here but they are negligible.) It is assumed that total operating outlays were to increase in proportion to the increase in the number of hospital beds and nursery places. The planned investment increase is estimated as 80 percent, the announced target increase in cumulated SYP state investment in public health, social security, physical culture and the medical industry, compared with the total for 1952–1958. The distribution of capital outlays in 1958 is estimated from information for 1956–1957 in *Raskhody,* pp. 73, 76. Budget outlays on health care in 1958 and 1965S may be distributed as follows (billion rubles):

	1958	*1965S*
Outlays on hospitals and dispensaries		
Capital outlays	.21	.38
Operating outlays	2.39	3.87
Total	2.60	4.25
Outlays on nursery schools		
Capital outlays	.02	.04
Operating outlays	.34	.59
Total	.36	.63
All outlays on hospitals, dispensaries and nursery schools		
Capital outlays	.23	.42
Operating outlays	2.73	4.46
Total	2.96	4.88
Other budget outlays on health care	1.11	?
Total budget outlays on health care	4.07	?

Thus budget outlays on the subcategories identified would increase to 4.88 billion rubles from the 1958 level of 2.96 billions. If other budget outlays on health care were to increase by no more than 2 percent a year, total budget outlays on health care in 1965S would amount to 6.2 billion rubles. This is roughly the outlay level inferred from Khrushchev's statement cited earlier. Note that other budget outlays on health care grew much more rapidly than the 2 percent postulated here for the SYP—12.9 percent between 1950 and 1955 and 4.2 percent between 1955 and 1958 (*Gosbiudzhet I,* p. 23). Continuation of the 4 percent rate of growth would mean a 6.34 billion ruble total for 1965S. Addition of expenditures on physical culture would raise the total to 6.4 billions.

Outlays from social insurance funds and *Outlays by enterprises, collective farms and other organizations.* Extrapolated from data for 1950–1958 in *NKh 1958,* p. 905, and *NKh 1959,* pp. 804–806.

Capital outlays. Assumed to increase by 80 percent, as indicated above (p. 463).

C. *Other.* Arbitrary estimate.

2. *Government administration.*

I assume no change in employment, a 25 percent increase in wages, and a small increase in material outlays between 1958 and 1965S. The SYP provided for a 15.5 percent increase in the number employed in the national economy as a whole and a decrease in the relative number employed in administration ("Sotsial'no-ekonomicheskie problemy . . . ," *VE,* 1960, No. 1, p. 105).

3. *Gross investment.*

A. *Fixed capital.* The 1958 and 1965S figures are the respective sums of the following components (billion rubles):

	1958	*1965S*
Public sector, excluding collective farms		
Centralized investment	19.92	35.2
Noncentralized investment	4.04	8.5
Project-design outlays	.56	.8
Capital repairs	5.83	9.7
Collective farms	3.04	6.2
	33.39	60.4

Centralized and noncentralized investment; project-design outlays. The 1958 values are from *NKh 1959,* pp. 542–543, adjusted to conform with the total for these three items found in later yearbooks (a difference of .01 billion rubles is involved). My 1965S estimate of centralized investment is derived from the SYP seven-year target of 194.0–197.0 billion rubles—I use the midpoint of that range—on the assumption of a constant annual rate of growth. The same assumption is used to compute the 1965S levels of noncentralized investment and project-design outlays. According to Broner (*Sovremennye problemy zhilishchnogo khoziaistva,* 1961, p. 126), the expected seven-year sum of centralized and noncentralized investment was 241.3 billion rubles. The centralized investment value in this total is probably the maximum of the announced range. By implication, the expected volume of noncentralized investment is 44.3 billion rubles.

According to Milykh and Nazarov (*Planirovanie proektno-izyskatel'skikh rabot v stroitel'stve,* 1961, p. 4), the seven-year total of project-design outlays connected with specific construction projects of state centralized investment was to be 4.8 billion rubles. It is believed that this figure is the appropriate SYP counterpart for the 1958 value cited above. That is, not all project-design outlays are considered an investment expenditure in Soviet accounting. Moreover, the official data (available only through 1960—*NKh 1959*, pp. 542–543 and *Kapstroi*, p. 48) identify project-design investment expenditures exclusively with investment from centralized funds, although according to Milykh and Nazarov (p. 16), some of these expenditures after 1959 are financed from noncentralized and capital repair funds. Outlays financed from centralized funds accounted for up to three-quarters of total project-design outlays (*ibid.*). Since the former made up only 2 or 3 percent of centralized fund investment in the 1950s, the value of project-design outlays financed from noncentralized funds was probably small. Moreover, it is possible that the failure to identify noncentralized fund outlays on project-design in the statistical handbooks is explained by their inclusion in identified noncentralized fund investment. This may also be true of project-design outlays connected with capital repairs. It would, then, be necessary to estimate only the 1965S value of project-design outlays directly connected with state investment.

Milykh and Nazarov provided no indication of the prices underlying the stated SYP target. The estimate price of project-design outlays is determined on the basis of a price handbook first introduced as of January 1, 1956 and subsequently substantially revised on January 1, 1958 (*ibid.*, p. 31). Presumably, both the 1958 and SYP target values of project-design outlays are expressed in the revised 1958 handbook prices. The official definition of the constant prices at which investment is valued reads as follows (for example, *NKh 1959*, p. 842): ". . . estimate prices of 1 July 1955 adjusted for new unit rates (*edinichnye rastsenki*) introduced in 1956 and also for the 1958 decrease of the norm of overhead expenditures and the 1959 decrease of prices for equipment installation." No specific mention is made of project-design price changes, but the use of a 1958 price list for these outlays is consistent with the post-1955 changes in other elements of estimate prices specified in the definition.

I make no allowance for warehouse stocks of equipment requiring installation. My 1958 estimate for this item is zero and no information is available on which to base a 1965S estimate.

Capital repairs. The seven-year total of capital repairs financed from amortization allowances was to be in excess of 40 billion rubles, as indicated earlier (above, p. 451). These repair funds accounted for 72 percent of all capital repairs in 1958, 79 percent in 1959, and 78 percent in 1960 (*NKh 1962,* p. 634 and above, p. 387). If the corresponding SYP relation was 75–80 percent, and assuming that "more than" 40 billion rubles means 42 billions, the total capital repair target would have been 52.5–56 billion rubles. I assume a target of 55 billions. The 1965S figure is again derived on the assumption of a constant annual rate of growth.

Collective farm investment represents in principle the allocation to the investment fund (see above, p. 392). The SYP called for 34.5 billion rubles, at estimate prices, of collective farm investment in the seven-year period. At estimate prices 1958 collective farm investment is officially reported (*NKh 1958,* p. 619; *Kapstroi,* p. 152) as 2.82 billion rubles. However, the 1958 figure is said to exclude capital repairs (e.g., *Kapstroi,* p. 7) whereas Koriunov (*Nedelimye fondy i kapital'nye vlozheniia kolkhozov,* 1960, p. 48) asserts that the SYP target includes capital repairs at least to buildings and structures. Collective farm outlays on capital repairs (including repairs to machinery) in 1958 came to .38 billion rubles (*ibid.,* p. 43). Thus the appropriate 1958 figure for comparison with the SYP target is about 3.2 billion rubles. Assuming a constant annual rate of growth, the 1965S value would be 6.6 billion rubles, a little more than double the 1958 level. I assume that allocations to the investment fund were to increase proportionally, from 3.04 billion rubles to 6.2 billions.

B. *Inventories.* The sum of .8 billion rubles of additions by collective farms to the working capital fund (three-quarters of the joint cultural and working capital fund figure shown on p. 441, the same proportion as in 1958) and 6.5 billion rubles of inventory investment in the rest of the public sector.

The Control Figures do not indicate a target for inventory investment in the SYP. Gorokhov (*Kommunist,* No. 15, October 1960, p. 51) made this cryptic statement immediately following a reference to the Plan goal for fixed capital investment: "Working capital (*oborotnye sredstva*) will conform (*sootvetsvovat'*) to the almost twofold increase in the volume of output." The reference to a doubling of output is mystifying, since the planned increase in national income was only 62–65 percent.

The Deputy Chairman of Gosbank's Administration, V. Ushakov, was somewhat more helpful: "According to preliminary calculations, based on the Control Figures for Development of the National Economy and on planned balances of raw materials, materials and finished output, short-term loans outstanding at the end of the Seven Year Plan period are to exceed [50] billion rubles, or increase by 50–60 percent." (*DiK*, 1960, No. 7, p. 71.) The meaning of the percentage increase range is not entirely clear: since in the previous paragraph Ushakov stated that loans outstanding at the end of 1958 totaled 32.01 billion rubles, to exceed 50 billion rubles at the end of 1965S, they would have to increase by more than 56 percent compared with the 1958 level. Ushakov's 1958 loan figure refers to Gosbank loans only; including loans by the construction bank as reported in the yearbooks (*NKh 1959*, p. 807; *NKh 1960*, p. 849) the 1958 total is 33.15 billion rubles. A 50 percent increase of that figure yields 49.7 billion rubles and a 60 percent increase 53.0 billions.

Since the relation between inventories and two sources of finance—bank loans and owned working capital—was close to unity in the 1950s (Moorsteen and Powell, *The Soviet Capital Stock, 1928–1962*, 1966, p. 129), it would be extremely helpful to know the intended role of owned working capital in the SYP period. Unfortunately such information has not been provided us. Mittel'man opined that owned working capital would increase less rapidly in the SYP period than would bank financing (*DiK*, 1958, No. 12, p. 43). However, he may have merely projected trends of the immediate past: in the middle 1950s the share of short-term loans in total sources of finance had been inching up (*VS*, 1957, No. 2, p. 94; *DiK*, 1958, No. 11, p. 31). Given the sharp planned increase in enterprise profits (above, pp. 444–445), an increase in the share of enterprise retained funds as source of finance would seem the more likely prospect.

A conservative estimate of the seven year growth of inventories would appear to be 50–60 percent, or 6–7 percent per year. At growth rates of 6.0 and 7.0 percent, the value of stock at the beginning of 1965S, given an end-1958 stock of 63.72 billion rubles (Table L-1) would be 90.39–95.62 billion rubles and at the end of 1965S, 95.81–102.32 billion rubles, implying inventory investment in 1965S of 5.42–6.70 billion rubles. The final estimate of 6.5 billions locates toward the upper end of the computed range.

4, 5, 6, 7. *R&D, internal security, defense, and outlays n.e.c., including statistical discrepancy.*

Residual, item 10 less the sum of items 1–3 and 9.

8. *Consolidated total value of goods and services, exclusive of sales to households.*

The sum of items 1 through 7.

9. *Transfer outlays.*

This is the sum of 1.0 billion rubles of stipends (above, p. 461), .5 billions of interest payments to households (an increase over the 1958 level of .25 billions in proportion to the estimated doubling of household savings—p. 437) and 15 billion rubles of pensions and allowances. The latter figure was estimated on the basis of the Plan goal for an increase of 67.4 percent in expenditures on certain social services and transfer payments, the so-called *vyplaty i l'goty* received by households. These expenditures cover pensions, stipends, insurance payments, grants-in-aid, free education and medical care, paid or reduced-price vacations in sanatoria and rest homes, etc. (*NKh 1960,* p. 874). In the absence of other information, pensions and allowances alone are assumed to increase from the 1958 level of 8.90 billion rubles by the indicated figure, rounded up to 15 billion rubles. No estimate is made of net new borrowings by households in 1965S for lack of information; the 1958 level was .08 billion rubles.

10. *Consolidated total outlays.*

Equals consolidated net income, Table 3, item 10.

I

Profits, Losses, and Subsidies in the State Sector

The Appendix consists of two sections. The first considers the available data on state sector profits and thereby attempts to estimate the total value of losses covered by conventional subsidies. In the second section, total conventional subsidies are distributed by branch of origin. These estimates, in turn, serve as a point of departure for the calculation in Appendix J of the incidence of subsidies by final use category of GNP.

The Profits Data

TYPES OF PROFITS

Soviet accounting distinguishes between two concepts of profit: "profit from sale of output" and "balance [sheet] profit" (or "profit from all enterprise activity"). The latter includes the former plus profit from sales of services and purchased materials as well as a variety of incomes and losses unrelated to sales. Examples of such incomes and losses are: from operation of enterprise housing; from operations of previous years (refunds or additional charges); write-offs of debts or receipts of previously written-off debts; fines and forfeits paid or received; rental of fixed assets; maintenance of unused production facilities; cancellation of orders; capital gains or losses on inventories of purchased materials; accidental loss or damage (*SNIP 1956–1958*, p. 75; *Finansovo-kreditnyi slovar'*, I, p. 238 and II, pp. 237–238).

For national income accounting, balance profits encompass too many extraneous elements, such as operations from previous years, write-offs, fines and forfeits. However, the best available series, in terms of clarity of identification and number of years covered, is one of balance profits, as will be shown below. Data on the other type of profits are scanty, ill-defined, and possibly of changing scope.

With regard to industrial net profits, there are only slight differences in actual values between balance profits and profits from sales: in the period 1958–1962, the only years for which we have data for both types of profit, net balance profits fell short of net profits from sales of output in all but the last year and by margins less than 150 million rubles (the totals were 10–15 billions); in 1962 balance profits were larger by 47 million rubles (*Prom II*, pp. 100–101). We know that the operation of enterprise housing typically is unprofitable: for example, (gross? net?) housing losses of industrial enterprises under the *sovnarkhozy* of 203 million and 235 million rubles were reported for 1960 and 1961 respectively (Zhevtiak, *Finansy promyshlennogo predpriiatiia*, 1963, p. 229; see also Birman, ed., *Finansy predpriiatii i otraslei narodnogo khoziaistva*, 1960, p. 528). Therefore, in aggregate other elements of industrial balance profits—that is, other than profits from sales—must have been positive and slightly smaller than housing losses (slightly larger in 1962). It is then likely that industrial balance profits only slightly overstate the magnitude of net profits appropriately entered in a national income account. Possibly this is also true of profits in other branches of the economy.

GROSS AND NET PROFITS

Beginning with *NKh 1959*, the statistical yearbooks have reported a profit series in absolute values for the state-cooperative sector by branch of the economy. The series is described as "net profits (after deducting all planned and unplanned losses)" (*NKh 1959*, p. 799; *NKh 1960*, p. 896; *NKh 1964*, p. 831) and plainly relates to balance profits. [This was first inferred by Nimitz (*SNIP 1956–1958*, pp. 76–77) from a variety of evidence. The inference was confirmed with the publication of *Prom II*. The latter source (pp. 100–101) gives both balance profits and profits from sales for all industry by branch. The balance profits figures are identical with the industry entries in the *NKh* series.] In the annual budget speeches by the Minister of Finance and in the follow-up articles generally written by or attributed to him, there appears a second series of planned and realized profits in the state sector, hereinafter termed "budget profits." For years prior to the 1957 industrial reorganization SNIP studies treated budget profits as intermediate between net and gross profits—net of losses within ministries or their chief administrations and gross of losses of chief administrations or ministries which were unprofitable as a whole. The effect of the 1957 reorganization could have been to make the *sovnarkhozy* (regional councils) the entity below which losses were netted out. However, a careful examination of the conflicting data seemed to indicate that after 1956 budget profits of industry were net of all losses (*SNIP 1956–1958,* pp. 74–81).

Finally there is a third series of gross profits obtained as follows: Beginning with the volume for 1961, the statistical annuals have published percentage distributions by use of state sector profits. The totals are indicated to "relate only to enterprises and economic organizations earning profits" (*NKh 1964,* p. 750), hence, presumably, to true gross profits. One of the listed channels of use is deductions to the budget. When the cited shares of gross profits deducted to the budget are divided by the known absolute values of the deductions, the result is the value of total gross profits. (The reported distributions of total gross profits contain two entries for a budget allocation: "deposited in the budget" and a component of this item, labeled "deductions from profits." It is assumed that the latter is the relevant category for our purposes. The difference between the two entries is 1.7 percent of total gross profits in 1958, rises to a high of 2.3 percent in 1960 and drops to 0.7 percent in 1962–1963.) The three series are shown in Table I-1.

[Not shown in Table I-1 is a possible alternative gross profits series, from Zverev, *Problemy tsenoobrazovaniia i finansy,* 1966, p. 78. The Zverev data are in absolute values and consist of total profits and their distribution among the following uses: deductions to the budget, increasing current assets, (fixed) capital investment, planned losses, enterprise fund, and other uses. There are a number of peculiarities in these data:

(1) The use categories differ somewhat from those given in the yearbooks, which are: deposited in the budget (of which, deductions from profits), capital investment and forming basic livestock herds, incentive funds of enterprises and economic organizations, increasing own current assets and financing planned losses of other enterprises, and other uses.

(2) For all years except 1960, Zverev's figures for deductions to the budget are smaller than the officially reported ones (see Table C-1) by margins of .2–1.6 billion rubles. Zverev's 1960 figure is 1.4 billion rubles larger than the officially reported figure. Possibly the Zverev figures omit deductions from previous years profits (or absorption of surplus working capital?).

(3) The relative distribution of profits in the Zverev data is different from that shown in the yearbooks, especially with respect to 1958–1961. Even thereafter, the relative distributions are not easily reconciled. Thus in the Zverev data, the sum of shares for increasing current assets and covering

planned losses is close to the share for the corresponding category in the yearbook distribution in 1962, 1963, and 1964, but this is not true of deductions to the budget in 1963, or of allocations to the enterprise fund (matched to the official distribution's incentive funds), or of the miscellaneous uses.

(4) Zverev's figures for total profits, which presumably are gross, are smaller than officially reported net profits in 1958–1959 and larger thereafter—by 4.1 billion rubles in 1960 and 1961, 4.2 billion in 1962, 6.0 billion in 1963 and 5.1 billion in 1964. Zverev's totals are considerably smaller than my computed gross figures (row 1 in Table I-1).

(5) Referring to these data in his text, Zverev calls them "balance of incomes and outlays of enterprises and ministries." Possibly this suggests something other than simple gross profits and their allocation.

Because of the uncertain interpretation of Zverev's figures, they are not further considered in my discussion.]

The difference between gross and net profits is entered in row 4 of Table I-1, that between gross and budget profits in row 5, and that between budget and net profits in row 6. If the three profits series can be meaningfully compared, one possible interpretation of rows 4 to 6 is that row 4 shows total losses in the state sector, row 5 represents conventional agency subsidies—that is, losses financed by intra-*sovnarkhoz* (or intra-ministerial) redistributions—and row 6 shows the volume of conventional budget subsidies. Under this interpretation budget profits are viewed as they were before the 1957 reorganization. There is some evidence in support of such an interpretation for the earlier years shown in Table I-1:

(1) Planned losses in 1960 incurred up to October 1 totaled 1.6 billion rubles (*Ekon.gazeta,* April 5, 1961, p. 2). It is not clear whether this refers to industry alone or to all state enterprises. For the year as a whole, planned losses should have been in the neighborhood of 2 billion rubles. My estimate of losses financed by redistribution in that year is 2.4 billion rubles.

(2) In 1962 budget outlays to cover above-plan losses exceeded 2 billion rubles (Pereslegin, *FinSSSR,* 1964, No. 10, p. 31). The 1962 entry in row 6 of Table I-1, identified with budget subsidies, is 2.3 billion rubles.

But how shall we interpret the negative entry for 1964 in row 6—that is, the fact that in that year budget profits are "netter" than net profits? Was there a change in definition of budget profits after 1962? If there was such a change, it may have been reversed in 1965: in that year realized budget profits at 37.2 billion (Garbuzov, *Izvestiia,* December 8,

1965, p. 4) are 1.1 billion rubles larger than net profits (*NKh 1965,* p. 757).

The problem with the 1963–1964 data evidently centers on industry. A comparison of the branch distributions of net and budget profits for 1964 (*NKh 1964,* p. 747 and *FinSSSR,* 1965, No. 1, p. 8) shows that only in industry and construction, lumped together in the budget profits table, do net exceed budget profits. The same comparison using 1963 data (*FinSSSR,* 1964, No. 1, p. 15), where industry and construction are separated, shows the anomaly only for industry.

The data for the period 1958–1962 also arouse misgivings. Thus the Soviet writer who provided the information just cited on 1962 budget subsidies, the financial official V. Pereslegin, is also responsible for some indirect evidence raising such doubts. In Table I-2, the reported percentage distribution of gross profits by type of use has been translated into absolute values, based on the computed total gross profits figures shown in Table I-1. These figures contradict data cited by Pereslegin in an earlier article—namely, that (1) only 8 billion rubles in 1958 and 9 billion in 1960 were expended by enterprises and organizations rather than over 9 and 10, respectively, as calculated in the table, and (2) allocations to incentive funds came to 1346 million rubles in 1958 and 1386 millions in 1960, compared with my 1.57 and 1.63 billion rubles (Pereslegin, *FinSSSR,* 1963, No. 5, p. 11).

However disturbing this inconsistency, it is not sufficient to discredit Table I-2 because Pereslegin's data are themselves difficult to interpret. If his percentage distribution for 1960, which is virtually identical to that used as the basis for my tables, is converted to absolute values with the aid of his ruble figure of allocations to incentive funds, the implied value of total gross profits is 25.2 billion rubles and that of profits deposited in the budget is 16.2 billion rubles. Both figures seem far too low—the first because it is distinctly smaller than budget profits in that year, 27.8 billions (whatever the correct interpretation of budget profits, they cannot be more "gross" than gross profits), and the second because it is smaller than deductions from profits (adjusted for deductions from the previous year's profits), 18.7 billion rubles. Pereslegin's implied gross profits figure may also be ruled out on the grounds that, compared with reported net profits, it implies total losses of only .8 billion rubles, no more than the *net* losses of the coal industry alone (*Prom II,* pp. 100–101). For these reasons, Pereslegin's data are not considered evidence of error in Tables I-1 and I-2.

Additional comparisons of entries in Table I-2 with other known values are possible. Since deductions from profits are the basis of the table and total deposits in the budget are not separately available, we may begin with row 2.A. At first glance, the computed allocations to fixed investment (including livestock) in Table I-2 seem too low. Planned use of enterprise profits for financing a part of *centralized* state investment accounts for upward of 90 percent of row 2.A in Table I-2, whereas realized *decentralized* investment alone was between 4 and 5 billion rubles in these years (CIA, *The Soviet Budget for 1962,* November 1962, p. 6). The comparison is somewhat misleading because decentralized investment is financed not only from profits directly but also from the incentive funds—that is, at one remove from profits, as well as from bank loans and even budget funds (Vasil'ev, *Kapital'nye vlozheniia za schet netsentralizovannykh istochnikov,* 1963, pp. 6 ff.; *Finansovo-kreditnyi slovar',* II, p. 365; Podshivalenko and Sher, eds., *Finansirovanie i kreditovanie kapital'nykh vlozhenii,* 1960, pp. 282–287). On the other hand, that part of row 2.A in Table I-2 representing outlays on forming basic livestock herds has no counterpart in the investment data, which exclude these outlays entirely (*NKh 1963,* p. 451, note).

The calculated values of profits allocated to incentive funds, row 2.B in Table I-2, appear reasonable. Official data on expenditures and end-year balances of incentive funds imply annual gross additions to state sector incentive funds of 2.05 billion rubles in 1959, 1.92 billions in 1960, 2.10 billions in 1961, and 1.95 billions in 1962; the 1958 figure cannot be computed for lack of data (*NKh 1962,* p. 629 and *NKh 1963,* p. 648). The direction of inequality between these values and row 2.B in Table I-2 is the expected one, since there are additional sources of incentive funds, apart from retained profits (*NKh 1963,* p. 714). We would also expect that profits are the predominant source; the above data show allocations from profits accounting for at least three-quarters of all gross additions.

Row 2.C in Table I-2 may be compared with row 5 of Table I-1. Until 1962, the direction of the inequality between the two series seems correct, since the latter was identified with losses financed by profit redistribution whereas the former includes additions to working capital as well. It is difficult to judge whether the 1958–1961 absolute differences are plausible. The problem is that we have no independent information from Soviet sources on allocations of retained profits to either of the uses indicated for row 2.C of Table I-2. We do know the volume of *planned* enterprise allocations from profits to increasing owned working capital norms (the designated minimum working capital needs of an enterprise; the other chief sources of finance are bank loans and *kreditory,* consisting of various debts), but from 1958 to 1960, the realized increases, financed from both retained profits and budget grants, were substantially larger than planned by .69, 1.08, and 2.2 billion rubles, respectively. Increases in 1961 and 1962 were only slightly higher than planned (CIA, *The Soviet Budget for 1961,* June 1961, p. 8, and *The Soviet Budget for 1962,* November 1962, p. 8; Garbuzov, *FinSSSR,* 1963, No. 1, p. 14). State outlays to cover own working capital shortages are given as 1126 million rubles in 1958, 1320 millions in 1959 and over 1500 millions in 1960 (Pereslegin, *Rezhim ekonomii v period stroitel'stva kommunizma,* 1962, p. 61). However, these figures presumably include unplanned subsidies. If we take planned enterprise allocations from retained profits as minimum estimates of realized allocations and subtract these from row 2.C of Table I-2, we should get maximum estimates of profits redistributed to cover losses of other enterprises. As the following tabulation shows, these ostensibly maximum estimates are lower than the presumed values of losses covered by redistribution, row 5 of Table I-1:

	Billion Rubles				
	1958	*1959*	*1960*	*1961*	*1962*
(1) Use of retained profits for increase of own working capital and financing planned losses of other enterprises (Row 2.C of Table I-2)	4.1	4.4	3.8	3.7	3.9
(2) Less: minimum estimates of retained profits allocated to increasing working capital [a]	1.8	1.7	2.1	2.2	2.0
(3) Equals: maximum estimates of losses covered by profit redistribution	2.3	2.7	1.7	1.5	1.9
(4) Row 5 of Table I-1	3.1	3.1	2.4	3.2	4.3

[a] The 1958 figure is from CIA, *The 1960 Soviet Budget,* November 1960, p. 26; figures for 1959–1962 are from CIA, *The Soviet Budget for 1961,* p. 8 and *The Soviet Budget for 1962,* p. 8.

Thus, suspicion attaches to either the gross profits series or the budget profits series or both. The conclusion is underscored when we consider that redistribution of profits serves profitable as well as unprofitable enterprises (Millionshchikov *et al., Otchisleniia ot pribyli,* 1964, p. 32; this applies to budget subsidies as well). Hence retained profits allocated for redistribution might well be larger than the actual losses covered by redistributions.

The data of Table I-1 can be faulted on other grounds. As indicated, the gross profits figures are obtained indirectly by means of a percentage distribution. All entries in the series for budget profits are preliminary data. The net profits data clearly refer to balance profits. This may be true of gross profits as well, since balance profits appear to be the basis for determining deductions from profits (*Finansovo-kreditnyi slovar'*, II, p. 237). If so, where in Table I-2 are to be found the profits used to finance losses of enterprise housing? Are these included in row 2.C of that table? Or possibly row 2.D?

I conclude that the suggested interpretation of rows 4–6 of Table I-1 as, respectively, total losses, losses subsidized by redistribution, and budget subsidies, cannot yet dispose of the questions raised. The major doubts appear to center on the scope and definition of the budget profit series, although the gross profit series must also be viewed with reserve, if only because of the absence of any discussion of it in the sources. Nevertheless, in the absence of other clarifying evidence, it will be assumed that entries in row 1 of Table I-1 are true gross profit totals.

Incidence of Conventional Subsidies by Branch of Origin

Total conventional subsidies are assumed to be given by entries in row 4 of Table I-1. It is necessary to estimate first, their origin by branch and second, their incidence by final use. The first task is performed here, the second in Appendix J.

Because of the availability of loss rates in various branches of industry in 1959, as well as of cost data emerging from Treml's reconstruction of the input-output table for that year (Treml, *The 1959 Soviet Intersectoral Flow Table,* 1964, I, p. 97), it is convenient to estimate industrial losses first in 1959. According to Kondrashev (*DiK,* 1962, No. 6, p. 29), the ratio of losses to cost in 1959 was 17.9 percent in coal production and 14.5 percent in iron ore mining. Soviet sources allude to losses in nonferrous ore mining but do not indicate the loss rate. The industrial price revision originally scheduled for 1963 called for a 15 percent increase in the average price of nonferrous ores (Bornstein, *Soviet Studies,* July 1963, p. 48). If the new prices were to provide, say, a 5 percent level of profit over costs, the loss rate before the price change was 9 percent. For 1959, a 10 percent loss rate is assumed.

It is also clear that there were substantial losses in other branches of heavy industry. In 1960, 39.1 percent of all gas producing enterprises in industry under *sovnarkhoz* jurisdiction, 18.5 percent of all chemicals enterprises, 15.7 percent of timber, wood, and paper, and 47.7 percent of all construction materials enterprises sustained losses (Bachurin and Kondrashev, *Tovarno-denezhnye otnosheniia v period perekhoda k kommunizmu,* 1963, p. 351). According to the same source, the corresponding percentages in the three branches for which we have 1959 loss rates were 32.4 percent of all ferrous ores enterprises, 50.7 percent of all nonferrous ore and 80.4 percent of all coal enterprises. It is assumed that the loss rate in gas production, chemicals (including rubber), timber, wood, paper, and construction materials (including glass), as a whole, was 5 percent.

Treml's reconstruction provides total gross outlays of the branches of industry under consideration, but at purchasers' prices. For a crude conversion to values at producers' prices, purchases by these branches from transportation-communication and trade-distribution are subtracted from branch outlays. (Only freight transportation and communication are deducted since only these outlays are considered productive in Soviet accounting.) It is necessary now to subtract profits and other noncost elements from branch outlays. Unfortunately, absence of data prevented Treml from breaking down national income originated in each branch. It is possible to deduct net profits (from *Prom II,* pp. 100–101) in all the branches except ferrous and nonferrous ores. Turnover taxes are levied in the gas industry and possibly with respect to chemicals too but probably not in the other branches. For my purposes, failure to make the required deductions should be of minor consequence.

The calculation of losses in these branches of industry may now be shown as follows (million rubles, except loss rate in percent):

	Ferrous Ores	*Nonferrous Ores*	*Coal*	*Gas, Chemicals, Timber, Paper, Wood, Construction Materials*
Gross outlays at purchasers' prices	562	828	6,381	28,817
Less: purchases from transport-communication and trade-distribution	99	63	1,674	5,140
Equals: gross outlay at producers' prices (approximate)	463	765	4,707	23,677
Less: net profits	. .	. .	(−)905	1,736
Equals: cost (approx.)	463	765	5,612	21,941
Loss rate, percent	14.5	10	17.9	5
Calculated losses	67	77	1,005	1,097

The sum of losses in the listed branches is 2.2 billion rubles. Subsidies to state agriculture in 1959 are estimated as .5 billion rubles.

[State farm losses in 1960 are said to have reached 600 million rubles (Kondrashev, *Tsena i stoimost' v sotsialisticheskom khoziaistve,* 1963, p. 307). Subsidies to state agriculture as a whole in 1961 must have exceeded .7 billions, since net profits of state agriculture and procurement together came to .34 billion rubles while budget profits of agriculture alone were 1.0 billions (*NKh 1962,* p. 627, and Lavrov, *PKh,* 1962, No. 2, p. 42). Net losses of state farms in 1963 rose to 1761 million rubles, of which 150 million rubles represented losses on housing (Emel'ianov and Marinko, *VE,* 1965, No. 9, p. 25). Subsidies of 1.7 billion rubles are also reported by Semenov (*VE,* 1965, No. 4, p. 20). Finally, according to Efimov and Karpov (*Kommunist,* 1966, No. 15, p. 76), state subsidies totaled in excess of 6 billion rubles "during the past six years." It is assumed that the reference is to 1960–1965.]

This leaves 2.2 billion rubles of other subsidies. On this basis and the indications that (1) the planned loss enterprises were concentrated in raw material branches of heavy industry (Bornstein, *Soviet Studies,* July 1963, p. 46), and (2) output of a number of products in consumers' goods industry was unprofitable (Malafeev, *Istoriia tsenoobrazovaniia v SSSR 1917–1963 gg.,* p. 334) conventional subsidies in 1959 are distributed as follows (billion rubles):

Heavy industry	3.4
Light industry	.5
Agriculture	.5
Other branches of economy	.5
	4.9

Subsidies to agriculture in other years are estimated as .2 billion rubles in 1958, .6 billion in 1960, .8 billion in 1961, 1.0 billion in 1962, 1.6 billion in 1963, and 1.0 billion in 1964. After deduction of these amounts from the estimates of total subsidies in Table I-1, subsidies to heavy industry, light industry and other branches of the economy are assumed proportional to the estimated 1959 distribution. The distribution of conventional subsidies for all years is then as follows (billion rubles):

	1958	*1959*	*1960*	*1961*	*1962*	*1963*	*1964*
Agriculture	.2	.5	.6	.8	1.0	1.6	1.0
Heavy industry	3.0	3.4	4.0	4.2	4.3	4.7	4.9
Light industry	.45	.5	.6	.65	.65	.7	.75
Other branches of the economy	.45	.5	.6	.65	.65	.7	.75
Total	4.1	4.9	5.8	6.3	6.6	7.7	7.4

TABLE I-1

STATE SECTOR PROFITS AND LOSSES, 1958–1964
(billion rubles)

	1958	1959	1960	1961	1962	1963	1964
1. Gross profits	23.36	27.02	30.16	32.45	36.43	37.52	41.40
2. Budget profits	19.64	23.24	27.8	29.3	32.1	30.4	33.2
3. Net profits	19.30	22.09	24.37	26.13	29.82	29.84	34.01
4. Gross minus net profits	4.06	4.93	5.79	6.32	6.61	7.68	7.39
5. Gross minus budget profits	3.12 [a]	3.14 [a]	2.4	3.2	4.3	7.1	8.2
6. Budget minus net profits	.94 [a]	1.79 [a]	3.4	3.2	2.3	.6	(−).8

Note:

[a] Adjusted for the inclusion in gross and net and exclusion from "budget" profits of profits earned by producer cooperatives, amalgamated with state industry in 1960.

Sources:

1. *Gross profits.* Computed as the quotient of the absolute value of deductions from profits divided by the share of such deductions in all profits earned by profitable enterprises and organizations. The shares are given in *NKh 1963*, p. 639; *NKh 1964*, p. 750; and *NKh 1965*, p. 758. The absolute values are official figures adjusted for deductions from the previous year's profits (p. 363).

2. *Budget profits.* 1958: Zverev, *PKh*, 1959, No. 1, p. 12 (1959 plan of 21.95 billion rubles exceeded 1958 actual by 2.31 billions). 1959: Garbuzov, *PKh*, 1959, No. 12, p. 6. 1960: Garbuzov, *FinSSSR*, 1961, No. 1, p. 8 (1961 plan of 30.2 billion rubles exceeded 1960 level by 8.6 percent; it is assumed that the implied 1960 figure refers to realized profits, since the 1960 target was 28.5 billions—Garbuzov, *PKh*, 1959, No. 12, p. 6). 1961: Garbuzov, *Izvestiia*, December 7, 1961, p. 4 (1962 plan of 32.9 billion rubles exceeded 1961 level by 12.2 percent; the 1961 target was 30.2 billions, as indicated above). 1962: Garbuzov in *Izvestiia*, December 11, 1962, p. 4 (1963 plan of 35.7 billions exceeded 1962 level by 11.3 percent; as indicated, the 1962 target was 32.9 billions). 1963: Garbuzov, *FinSSSR*, 1964, No. 1, p. 15. 1964: Garbuzov, *FinSSSR*, 1965, No. 1, p. 8.

3. *Net profits. NKh 1962*, p. 627 and *NKh 1964*, p. 747.

5. *Gross minus budget profits* and 6. *Budget minus net profits.* Net profits earned by producer cooperatives were .60 billion rubles in 1958 and .64 billions in 1959 (*NKh 1959*, p. 799). Entries in row 1 and 3 in these years are adjusted by these amounts. It seems doubtful that there was a significant distinction between net and gross profits for producer cooperatives.

TABLE I-2

DISTRIBUTION BY USE OF STATE SECTOR GROSS PROFITS, 1958–1964
(billion rubles)

	1958	1959	1960	1961	1962	1963	1964
1. Deposited in the budget	14.02	16.51	19.42	21.48	24.12	25.96	29.19
Of which: deductions from profits	13.62	15.94	18.73	20.80	23.86	25.70	28.73
2. Expended by enterprises and organizations							
A. Capital investment and formation of basic livestock herds	2.76	3.13	3.59	4.09	4.77	4.28	4.64
B. Allocated to incentive funds	1.57	1.73	1.63	1.65	1.89	1.69	2.24
C. Increase of own working capital and financing planned losses of other enterprises	4.13	4.40	3.80	3.73	3.93	3.98	3.35
D. Other uses	.89	1.24	1.72	1.49	1.71	1.61	1.99
E. Total	9.34	10.51	10.74	10.97	12.31	11.56	12.21
3. Total gross profits	23.36	27.02	30.16	32.45	36.43	37.52	41.40

Sources:
The data are computed from the sources described in Table I-1, sources for row1.

J

Factor Cost Adjustments: Basic Series

Table J-1 presents a calculation of GNP by use at adjusted factor cost. The calculation involves three groups of adjustments to the established-price values to obtain values at AFC: deduction of turnover taxes, addition of subsidies, and an adjustment for divergence of farm price levels. These are explained in turn below.

Turnover Taxes

The incidence of the turnover tax is estimated in Table J-2 in several steps:

(1) The following categories of final product are considered free of tax: extravillage farm market sales; imputed rent on privately owned housing; dues; services furnished by the private sector to households; other outlays for consumption; the wage component of government administration, R&D, internal security, communal services and household outlays on education, health care, physical culture, entertainment, and culture; consumption of farm income in kind; military pay and subsistence; livestock investment by households and collective farms; and the wage component of private housing construction.

(2) A nominal tax rate of 5 percent is applied to certain product categories as allowance for taxes on petroleum products, gas and electric power. Apparently, except for exports and additions to state reserves, all uses of fuel and power are subject to the tax.

According to Turetskii (*Ocherki planovogo tsenoobrazovaniia v SSSR,* 1959, pp. 134–135) the share of turnover tax in electricity rates charged in 1956 varied from 45–50 percent and averaged 15.8 percent. Proceeds from the turnover tax on petroleum products in 1959 have been estimated as 2.34 billion rubles (Belkin, *Tseny edinogo urovnia i ekonomicheskie izmereniia na ikh osnove,* 1963, p. 197, citing Broide, *Finansirovanie neftianoi i gazovoi promyshlennosti,* 1960, p. 101).

(3) Assumed tax rates of 20 and 40 percent, respectively, are applied to the materials component of (a) administration, R&D, internal security, and household outlays on entertainment and culture, and (b) communal services and household outlays on health and education. The 40 percent rate is a crude estimate based on (a) the share of food, office supplies (*kantseliarskie i khoziaistvennye raskhody*), other supplies and uniforms (*miakhkii inventar' i obmundirovanie*), in current material outlays (excluding investment) on education (about 90 percent) and health care (about 70 percent) in 1959 (Eidel'man, *Mezhotraslevoi balans obshchestvennogo produkta,* 1966, p. 166), and (b) an estimated average tax on taxable outlays of at least 50 percent. The latter is inferred from a variety of rates for individual products or product categories given in Smirnov, *Ekonomicheskoe soderzhanie naloga s oborota,* 1963, pp. 109 ff. A reduced rate of 20 percent is applied to material outlays in administration, R&D, internal security, and household outlays on entertainment and culture, on the assumption that taxable outlays on food are much less important in these categories than in health and education services.

(4) Sixty percent of household outlays on utilities is assumed to represent tax, based on a Soviet statement that "turnover tax is more than 50 percent of the price of matches, kerosene, electricity and gas for household needs. . . ." (*Ibid.,* p. 109.)

(5) Collective farm investment, exclusive of investment in livestock, is assumed to have been taxed at 15 percent for fixed and 20 percent for inventory investment, from 1958 through 1960. Thereafter the tax rate is assumed to have been cut 5 percentage points in each case. The basis for these assumptions is information on changes in prices paid by collective farms (*ibid.,* pp. 80–81), bearing in mind that much of the tax element in prices paid by farmers for investment goods was absorbed by the state budget not in the form of turnover taxes but as a price differential (Table C-1, sources for item 1.G(3)).

(6) The remainder of the tax is assigned to four categories of use in proportion to their values at established prices. The categories are:

state-cooperative sector retail sales, nonfarm wages in kind, the materials component of private housing construction, and a part of inventories in trade and procurement. The inventories in trade and procurement considered here are goods shipped (*tovary otgruzhennye*) and finished goods, the latter a component of the so-called "commodity-material values" (*tovarno-material'nye tsennosti*). It is believed that these are the stocks of consumers' goods on which the bulk of taxes applicable to inventory investment are likely to fall. Details of the calculation will be found in Table L-3.

The procedure just described embodies several departures from previous SNIP practice (cf. *SNIP 1956–1958,* pp. 131–133). The more notable changes introduced here are:

(1) Previous SNIP adjustments have included military subsistence in taxable product; in this study subsistence is assumed free of tax. This is also the conclusion of *The Soviet Financial System,* 1968, pp. 101–102. I assume that subsistence outlays under internal security are also free of tax.

(2) Because household outlays on "other services" are estimated in Appendix B by type of service, I am able to break out those outlays considered free of tax (private sector services) and the labor component of outlays on services akin to communal services, which are also broken down by labor and nonlabor components. In addition, taxes on utilities supplied to households are estimated independently.

(3) The procedure in previous SNIP studies relied on the estimation of an average tax rate (total turnover taxes divided by total taxable product) which was applied to taxable income in kind (military subsistence and nonfarm wages in kind), the nonwage component of government services, building materials sold to households, and state sector inventories excluding those in trade. In this study, use of the average rate is restricted to the four categories specified under point 6, above.

(4) Previous SNIP practice has been to distinguish between trade inventories and those in other state enterprises and organizations and to allow the former to bear a heavier implied tax rate. In this study the distinction is between trade and procurement on one hand, and other state enterprises on the other; and within trade and procurement, between goods shipped and finished goods on one hand, and remaining inventories on the other. It is believed that this procedure isolates the consumers' goods inventory investment subject to the heaviest tax burden.

Soviet data on the structure of turnover tax proceeds are generally scarce and what data there are cannot be directly used for my purposes. No information is available in Soviet sources on the incidence of the tax by use category. The closest approximation to such a breakdown is contained in Table J-3, showing the structure of tax proceeds by branch of industry origin.

The tax originating in "heavy" industry probably represents tax on petroleum products, gas, electric power, chemicals, construction materials, and other producers' goods sold to households and collective farms. (Fuel and power are taxed in almost all uses.) There appear to be two distinct classifications in the table, as may be seen by a comparison of the heavy industry shares for 1957 plan and 1960–1962 on one hand, and those for 1958, 1960, 1961, and 1962 on the other. The Bureau of the Census has conjectured that the difference may represent consumer durables. Possibly the difference in shares between the two groups includes other producers' goods sold to households or at retail. Since the preponderance of the available information relates to the apparently broader concept of "heavy" industry, that aggregate is used in what follows.

In Table J-2 the tax originating in heavy industry may be estimated as follows: (a) The tax originating in other than heavy industry is assumed to apply to items 1.A (retail sales), 3.B (nonfarm wages in kind), and 11.B(2)(a) (goods shipped and finished goods in trade and procurement); (b) For items 2.C(1)(b) (nonwage component of household outlays on health and education) and 6.B (nonwage component of communal services), the difference between a 20 percent and a 40 percent tax rate is a measure of tax which in Table J-3 would be found under consumers' goods industry; (c) Subtract the values obtained under (a) and (b) from the total tax. The total tax assumed to originate in heavy industry comes to 4.33 billion rubles in 1958 and 5.60 billions in 1962. The first figure is 3 percent larger and the second only 2 percent smaller than the indicated values in Table J-3. On the assumption that heavy industry tax includes tax levied on consumer durables and petroleum products as well as on producers' goods sold through the retail trade network, the comparison suggests that I have overstated heavy industry tax. On the other hand, the end product items listed under (a) and (b) do not exhaust the tax originating other than in heavy industry. The overstatement thus must be at least partly offset by understatement.

Subsidies

The final use incidence of subsidies, shown in Table J-4, is estimated as follows. In all cases, unless otherwise indicated, assignment is in proportion to values at established prices (net of turnover tax) of the indicated end uses, shown in Table J-2.

(1) As a preliminary step certain end-product categories are distributed into two major groups, according as they are assumed to be affected by conventional subsidies to heavy industry or light industry. Group I is further subdivided into three subclasses of descending relative significance of heavy industry product.

Group I. *End product related to heavy industry subsidies.*

IA

Defense except pay and subsistence
Materials component of private housing construction
Collective farm fixed capital investment, except livestock
State-cooperative fixed capital investment
State-cooperative other inventory investment (see Table J-2)

IB

Materials components of R&D and internal security
Collective farm inventory investment
Outlays n.e.c.; public sector statistical discrepancy

IC

State-cooperative retail sales
Paid rent
Materials component of household outlays on other services (excluding private sector services)
Nonfarm wages in kind
Military subsistence
Materials component of communal services and government administration
Increments of goods shipped and finished goods in trade and procurement

Group II. *End product related to light industry subsidies.*

State-cooperative retail sales
Materials component of household outlays on health and education

Nonfarm wages in kind
Military subsistence
Materials component of communal services and internal security
Increments of goods shipped and finished goods in trade and procurement

For group IC, the materials component is assumed as 50 percent of household outlays on transportation-communication and utilities and ⅔ of their outlays on other public sector services for consumption, in all cases net of turnover taxes. These rates are estimated on the basis of reported cost breakdowns for railroads (Ivliev, *Planirovanie na zheleznodorozhnom transporte,* 1961, pp. 98–101), communications (Vishnevskaia *et al., Ekonomika i planirovanie sviazi,* 1963, p. 206) and municipal services (Birman *et al., Finansy predpriiatii i otraslei narodnogo khoziaistva,* 1960, p. 547).

(2) The distribution by branch of origin of *conventional subsidies* is estimated in Appendix I. Heavy industry subsidies are apportioned among the elements of Group I (using arbitrary weights of 70:20:10), light industry and agriculture among Group II, and other branches among groups IA, IB, and IC.

(3) *MTS-RTS and procurement subsidies* (estimated above, pp. 371, 373 ff.) are distributed among Group II uses. I follow Nimitz (*SNIP 1956–1958,* p. 134) in regarding subsidies to procurement as in effect subsidies to the food and light industries, rather than to agriculture. Average realized farm prices are considered unaffected for the same reason. Hence, there is no need to revalue farm income in kind. With the abolition of payments in kind to the MTS the subsidy to these organizations (and their successors, the RTS) also no longer affect the value basis of income in kind.

(4) No information is available on the branch distribution of *wage reform subsidies* (estimated above, pp. 372–373), let alone on the incidence by final use. The incidence is inferred by a roundabout route:

(a) Subsidies could have been necessitated by one or more of three reasons: shortening of the work week with no reduction in pay, raising minimum wage scales, and changeover to new output norms and pay rates that raised the level of average wages and salaries. For the bulk of all workers and employees the changeover to a shorter work-week was completed in 1959–1960. The wage reform *per se,* including raising of minimum scales, was to be affected gradually, beginning with industry in 1959–1960 and continuing with construction in 1960, transport, communications, state agriculture, and research and design organizations in

1960–1961, and other branches of the economy in 1962. Minimum wages in the last named group were in fact not raised in 1962 but postponed to 1965 (CIA, *An Evaluation of the Soviet Wage Reforms 1956–1962,* August 1963, pp. 17–20; Khrushchev speech to the Supreme Soviet, *Pravda,* July 14, 1964, pp. 3–5). For my purposes, the impact of the wage and hour reform is assumed to have been restricted to heavy industry in 1958 and 1959, industry and construction in 1960, and transportation, communications, state agriculture, and R&D in 1961–1962. All of the small 1963 subsidy and half of the slightly larger 1964 subsidy are assumed to have affected all the aforementioned branches; the other half of the 1964 subsidy is regarded as affecting only health and education.

(b) The total of 1958 and 1959 subsidies and one-quarter of 1960 subsidies are allocated among Groups IA and IB with weights of 75:25. Remaining 1960 subsidies are apportioned among Group IC uses.

(c) Subsidies in 1961–1962 are distributed 10 percent to R&D and the remainder equally among transportation-communication and state agriculture—i.e., more or less in proportion to employment (*NKh 1962,* pp. 453–454). R&D subsidies affect R&D wages directly. Agriculture subsidies are assigned to Group II uses. Of the estimated transportation-communication subsidies 15 percent are assigned directly to the wage component of household outlays on this item and 85 percent are apportioned among all Group I uses (without weighting of subclasses). The 15 percent allocation is based on an estimate that gross revenues of transportation-communication in 1960 totaled about 22 billion rubles, in relation to which household outlays in that year (3.18 billions) come to 15 percent. In turn the gross revenue figure is obtained by blowing up a wage bill figure of 7 billion rubles, calculated from employment and wage data (*NKh 1964,* pp. 546, 555), by the share of wages in cost (about 40 percent, based on railroad data in Ivliev, *Planirovanie na zheleznodorozhnom transporte,* 1961, p. 98) and reported net profits of 4.4 billion rubles (*NKh 1962,* p. 627).

(d) The 1963 subsidy and half the 1964 subsidy are apportioned among Group I uses (without weighting of subclasses). The other half of the 1964 subsidy is assigned directly to the wage components of (i) household outlays on education, health and physical culture, and (ii) communal services excluding R&D.

(5) The *subsidy to housing* reflects the difference between rent paid (1.5 rubles per square meter of living space—see p. 335) and operating costs (net of amortization allowances) plus nominal profits. (The ad-

justment for underdepreciation is treated in Chapter 6). The size of the gap is estimated as 75 kopecks per square meter of living space per year, based on data supplied by Golt'sman, *Ekonomika kommunal'nogo khoziaistva uslugy, tarify,* 1966, p. 75. The equivalent rate per unit of floor space (see p. 339) is 53 kopecks. Absolute amounts are computed using the state-cooperative sector stock estimates developed earlier (p. 339) and are assigned directly to paid housing.

Additional support for the estimate of the housing subsidy is provided by Alekseev (*Ekonomika zhilishchnogo khoziaistva,* 1966, p. 25), who declares that the average operating cost (excluding capital repairs) per square meter of living space in the RSFSR in 1961 was 2.07 rubles. Other sources provide even higher estimates of the state subsidy to housing: for example, Rimashevskaia (*Ekonomicheskii analiz dokhodov rabochikh i sluzhashchikh,* 1965, p. 18), who cites a figure of 1.55 billion rubles per year, more than 3 times my estimate for 1964 (Table J-4). Rimashevskaia's figure seems much too high. Possibly it includes some investment outlays or imputed depreciation.

Strictly speaking, the reimbursement of operating losses on housing should be part of the conventional subsidy totals estimated in Appendix I. Hence, separate account here presumably involves double counting. However, the amounts estimated for "other branches of the economy" on p. 478 seem too small to encompass subsidies to housing as well as to all other branches except industry and agriculture.

(6) In Table J-4, all subsidies applicable to military subsistence are counted twice, once with reference to income in kind and again with reference to defense services. The same duplication appears in Table J-5 with respect to the farm price adjustment, discussed below.

In his calculation of AFC, Bergson reduced the value of military pay by the amount of subsidies and farm price adjustment incident on military subsistence as an element of defense services. (Bergson also allowed for turnover taxes on subsistence, as I do not, and therefore had to *increase* military pay by the amount of tax incident on subsistence.) He reasoned that whether or not the value of military services at current prices was appropriately reckoned from the viewpoint of the AFCS was a matter for separate consideration, hence that in the basic factor cost adjustments that value should be taken as unchanging (*SNIP 1937,* pp. 138–140; *SNIP 1940–1948,* pp. 220, 225). In his separate consideration of the appropriateness of the valuation of military services, Bergson took the 1937 relation of military services to civilian wages as a norm in comparison with which he found undervaluation of military services in 1944, limited overvaluation in 1940 and sizable overvaluation in 1948 (*SNIP 1940–1948,* pp. 60–61). Pay and subsistence per man in my accounts are reckoned at a constant 1090 rubles per year, whereas average wages and salaries in this period rose from 934–1081 rubles (pp. 295, 307). It seems difficult to decide whether military services are overvalued or undervalued at any point in this period and consequently what the direction of change is. Since the adjustments incident on military services are in any case small, I choose not to offset the adjustments by reducing military pay.

Farm Price Divergences

The reduction in state-cooperative sector retail sales resulting from the subtraction of turnover taxes and the addition of subsidies violates the canons of AFCS valuation because of the divergence created between state-cooperative and collective farm market price levels. Therefore, collective farm market sales must be reduced proportionally. Since this, in turn, implies a reduction in collective farm incomes, procurement prices must be adjusted correspondingly. The calculation is as follows:

(1) The net reduction in state-cooperative retail sales, in proportion to which collective farm market sales are to be reduced, is not just the difference between turnover taxes, T, and subsidies, S, incident on state-cooperative retail sales; it must also take into account the impact on state-cooperative sales of the increase in procurement prices by which it is necessary to compensate for the reduction in farm incomes through a reduction in collective farm sales.

(2) The total compensatory increase in procurement prices, P, is assumed to devolve, in proportion to values at established prices net of turnover taxes, on the Group II uses described in the section on adjustment for subsidies. Therefore, in any year the share of state-cooperative sales in the total value of output in that group is the proportion α of P falling on state-cooperative retail sales.

(3) Thus, the net reduction in state-cooperative sales may be defined as

$$kV = T - S - \alpha P$$

where V is the value of state-cooperative retail sales at established prices and k is the relative net reduction in V after all adjustments.

(4) As indicated, P is also equal to the net decline in collective farm market sales after the adjustment, the product of collective farm market sales at established prices, M, and the relative decline in these sales after adjustment, m. If there were no pre-existing disparities between the price levels of market sales and state-cooperative sales, m would equal k, the relative decline in state-cooperative sales. However, such disparities did exist and must be taken into account. Therefore, m is defined as

$$m = \frac{R - 1 + k}{R}$$

where R is the ratio of collective farm market to state-cooperative retail price levels. P may now be defined as

$$P = \frac{(R - 1 + k)M}{R}$$

(5) I can now compute k and P on the basis of the following values for the other variables (billion rubles except α and R which are ratios):

	V	T	S	α	R	M
1958	60.33	24.12	3.93	.864	1.06	4.43
1959	64.47	23.74	3.52	.854	1.04	4.23
1960	71.13	25.07	4.15	.910	1.06	4.00
1961	73.41	24.23	3.51	.901	1.12	4.31
1962	79.64	25.91	4.27	.907	1.15	4.36
1963	84.29	26.83	4.88	.907	1.20	4.29
1964	88.18	27.06	4.10	.865	1.25	4.42

Values of V, T and M are taken from Table J-2, those of S from Table J-4. Values of R are computed as follows:

a) Chapman (*Real Wages in Soviet Russia Since 1928,* 1963, p. 104) estimated that collective farm market prices were 60 percent higher than state-cooperative retail prices of food in 1940, citing a Soviet source supporting her 1940 estimate.

(b) The ratio of market to state retail food prices in the form of indexes on an average 1940 base may be computed from official sources as follows (*NKh 1961,* pp. 653, 665; *Sovtorg II,* pp. 165, 266; *NKh 1962,* pp. 533, 541; *NKh 1963,* p. 539; *NKh 1964,* p. 657; *NKh 1965,* pp. 652, 665; the 1962 figures in columns (1) and (2) are obtained by applying the percent increase of a 1952-based index to the 1940-based 1961 figures):

	1940 = 100		
	Index of Market Prices	*Index of State Retail Prices*	*Ratio of (1) ÷ (2)*
	(1)	*(2)*	*(3)*
1958	98	149	.66
1959	96	148	.65
1960	97	147	.66
1961	102	146	.70
1962	108	150	.72
1963	115	153	.75
1964	118	152	.78

(c) Multiplication of column (3) entries by the 1940 ratio described in (a) yields the value of *R*.

Therefore, computed values of *k* (ratio) and *P* (billion rubles) are:

	1958	*1959*	*1960*	*1961*	*1962*	*1963*	*1964*
k	.28	.28	.25	.22	.20	.18	.17
P	1.42	1.30	1.17	1.31	1.33	1.36	1.49

Values of P are allocated in Table J-5 in the proportions and to the uses designated Group II in the discussion of subsidies. *P* values are also the required net reductions in collective farm market sales and are so entered in Table J-5. Hence, except for the double counting of the adjustment falling on military subsistence, the sum of the adjustments in each year is zero.

(The foregoing description differs only in minor details from that provided by Bergson in *SNIP 1937,* pp. 140–142; *SNIP 1928–1948,* pp. 119–125; and *Real SNIP,* p. 132.)

TABLE J-1

CALCULATION OF GNP BY USE AT ADJUSTED FACTOR COST, 1958–1964
(billion rubles)

	1958				
	Value at Established Prices	Adjustment for Turnover Taxes	Adjustment for Subsidies	Adjustment for Farm Prices	Value at AFC
	(1)	(2)	(3)	(4)	(5)
1. Retail sales to households					
A. State-cooperative trade	60.33	24.12	3.93	1.23	41.37
B. Extravillage farm markets	4.43	—	—	−1.42	3.01
C. Total	64.76				44.38
2. Consumer services					
A. Housing	1.71	.03	.31	—	1.99
B. Dues	.91	—	—	—	.91
C. Other services	6.58	.69	.03	—	5.92
D. Total	9.20				8.82
3. Consumption of income in kind					
A. Farm income in kind	9.92	—	—	—	9.92
B. Nonfarm wages in kind	.50	.20	.03	.01	.34
C. Military subsistence	1.51	—	.16	.05	1.72
D. Total	11.93				11.98
4. Other outlays for consumption	3.00	—	—	—	3.00
5. Total outlays for consumption	88.89				68.18
6. Communal services	10.53	1.14	.19	.06	9.64
7. Government administration	1.20	.05	—	—	1.15
8. Gross investment					
A. Fixed capital	36.69	2.26	1.91	—	36.34
B. Inventories	7.90	1.51	.62	.06	7.07
C. Total	44.59				43.41
9. Research and development	2.06	.12	.25	—	2.19
10. Internal security	1.50	.07	.18	.01	1.62
11. Defense					
A. Pay and subsistence	4.11	—	.16	.05	4.32
B. Other	4.95	.25	.29	—	4.99
C. Total	9.06				9.31
12. Outlays n.e.c.; public sector statistical discrepancy	.23	.01	.11	—	.33
13. Gross national product	158.06	30.45	8.17	.05	135.83

TABLE J-1 (continued)

	1959				
	Value at Established Prices	Adjustment for Turnover Taxes	Adjustment for Subsidies	Adjustment for Farm Prices	Value at AFC
	(6)	(7)	(8)	(9)	(10)
1. Retail sales to households					
A. State-cooperative trade	64.47	23.74	3.52	1.11	45.36
B. Extravillage farm markets	4.23	—	—	−1.30	2.93
C. Total	68.70				48.29
2. Consumer services					
A. Housing	1.80	.03	.34	—	2.11
B. Dues	.94	—	—	—	.94
C. Other services	7.09	.78	.03	—	6.34
D. Total	9.83				9.39
3. Consumption of income in kind					
A. Farm income in kind	9.52	—	—	—	9.52
B. Nonfarm wages in kind	.55	.20	.03	.01	.39
C. Military subsistence	1.45	—	.13	.04	1.62
D. Total	11.52				11.53
4. Other outlays for consumption	3.19	—	—	—	3.19
5. Total outlays for consumption	93.24				72.40
6. Communal services	11.37	1.23	.16	.05	10.35
7. Government administration	1.12	.04	—	—	1.08
8. Gross investment					
A. Fixed capital	40.56	2.47	2.52	—	40.61
B. Inventories	9.41	2.00	.62	.08	8.11
C. Total	49.97				48.72
9. Research and development	2.31	.14	.15	—	2.32
10. Internal security	1.50	.07	.11	.01	1.55
11. Defense					
A. Pay and subsistence	3.95	—	.13	.04	4.12
B. Other	5.12	.26	.35	—	5.21
C. Total	9.07				9.33
12. Outlays n.e.c.; public sector statistical discrepancy	2.17	.11	.58	—	2.64
13. Gross national product	170.75	31.07	8.66	.04	148.38

TABLE J-1 (continued)

	1960				
	Value at Established Prices	Adjustment for Turnover Taxes	Adjustment for Subsidies	Adjustment for Farm Prices	Value at AFC
	(11)	(12)	(13)	(14)	(15)
1. Retail sales to households					
A. State-cooperative trade	71.13	25.07	4.15	1.06	51.27
B. Extravillage farm markets	4.00	—	—	−1.17	2.83
C. Total	75.13				54.10
2. Consumer services					
A. Housing	1.89	.04	.38	—	2.23
B. Dues	1.02	—	—	—	1.02
C. Other services	7.65	.85	.06	—	6.86
D. Total	10.56				10.11
3. Consumption of income in kind					
A. Farm income in kind	9.12	—	—	—	9.12
B. Nonfarm wages in kind	.60	.21	.04	.01	.44
C. Military subsistence	1.38	—	.12	.03	1.53
D. Total	11.10				11.09
4. Other outlays for consumption	2.66	—	—	—	2.66
5. Total outlays for consumption	99.45				77.96
6. Communal services	12.24	1.32	.18	.05	11.15
7. Government administration	1.09	.04	—	—	1.05
8. Gross investment					
A. Fixed capital	44.55	2.58	2.64	—	44.61
B. Inventories	4.80	.47	.32	.01	4.66
C. Total	49.35				49.27
9. Research and development	2.52	.15	.08	—	2.45
10. Internal security	1.50	.07	.06	.01	1.50
11. Defense					
A. Pay and subsistence	3.77	—	.12	.03	3.92
B. Other	5.23	.26	.34	—	5.31
C. Total	9.00				9.23
12. Outlays n.e.c.; public sector statistical discrepancy	5.62	.28	.74	—	6.08
13. Gross national product	180.77	31.34	9.23	.03	158.69

TABLE J-1 (continued)

	1961				
	Value at Established Prices	Adjustment for Turnover Taxes	Adjustment for Subsidies	Adjustment for Farm Prices	Value at AFC
	(16)	(17)	(18)	(19)	(20)
1. Retail sales to households					
A. State-cooperative trade	73.41	24.23	3.51	1.18	53.87
B. Extravillage farm markets	4.31	—	—	−1.31	3.00
C. Total	77.72				56.87
2. Consumer services					
A. Housing	1.97	.04	.40	—	2.33
B. Dues	1.12	—	—	—	1.12
C. Other services	8.48	.97	.13	—	7.64
D. Total	11.57				11.09
3. Consumption of income in kind					
A. Farm income in kind	9.36	—	—	—	9.36
B. Nonfarm wages in kind	.65	.21	.03	.01	.48
C. Military subsistence	1.31	—	.09	.03	1.43
D. Total	11.32				11.27
4. Other outlays for consumption	2.21	—	—	—	2.21
5. Total outlays for consumption	102.82				81.44
6. Communal services	13.23	1.43	.15	.05	12.00
7. Government administration	1.08	.04	—	—	1.04
8. Gross investment					
A. Fixed capital	47.07	2.54	2.72	—	47.25
B. Inventories	6.06	.81	.50	.03	5.78
C. Total	53.13				53.03
9. Research and development	2.90	.17	.49	—	3.22
10. Internal security	1.50	.07	.18	.01	1.62
11. Defense					
A. Pay and subsistence	3.57	—	.09	.03	3.69
B. Other	7.72	.39	.48	—	7.81
C. Total	11.29				11.50
12. Outlays n.e.c.; public sector statistical discrepancy	.30	.02	.15	—	.43
13. Gross national product	186.25	30.92	8.92	.03	164.28

TABLE J-1 (continued)

	1962				
	Value at Established Prices	Adjustment for Turnover Taxes	Adjustment for Subsidies	Adjustment for Farm Prices	Value at AFC
	(21)	(22)	(23)	(24)	(25)
1. Retail sales to households					
A. State-cooperative trade	79.64	25.91	4.27	1.21	59.21
B. Extravillage farm markets	4.36	—	—	−1.33	3.03
C. Total	84.00				62.24
2. Consumer services					
A. Housing	2.06	.04	.42	—	2.44
B. Dues	1.19	—	—	—	1.19
C. Other services	9.36	1.07	.12	—	8.41
D. Total	12.61				12.04
3. Consumption of income in kind					
A. Farm income in kind	9.55	—	—	—	9.55
B. Nonfarm wages in kind	.70	.23	.04	.01	.52
C. Military subsistence	1.47	—	.12	.03	1.62
D. Total	11.72				11.69
4. Other outlays for consumption	3.34	—	—	—	3.34
5. Total outlays for consumption	111.67	—	—	—	89.31
6. Communal services	13.83	1.49	.18	.05	12.57
7. Government administration	1.09	.04	—	—	1.05
8. Gross investment					
A. Fixed capital	49.43	2.67	2.75	—	49.51
B. Inventories	5.74	.69	.40	.02	5.47
C. Total	55.17				54.98
9. Research and development	3.30	.20	.28	—	3.38
10. Internal security	1.50	.07	.09	.01	1.53
11. Defense					
A. Pay and subsistence	4.00	—	.12	.03	4.15
B. Other	8.34	.42	.49	—	8.41
C. Total	12.34				12.56
12. Outlays n.e.c.; public sector statistical discrepancy	2.45	.12	.55	—	2.88
13. Gross national product	201.35	32.95	9.83	.03	178.26

TABLE J-1 (continued)

	1963				
	Value at Established Prices	Adjustment for Turnover Taxes	Adjustment for Subsidies	Adjustment for Farm Prices	Value at AFC
	(26)	(27)	(28)	(29)	(30)
1. Retail sales to households					
A. State-cooperative trade	84.29	26.83	4.88	1.24	63.58
B. Extravillage farm markets	4.29	—	—	−1.36	2.93
C. Total	88.58				66.51
2. Consumer services					
A. Housing	2.14	.04	.45	—	2.55
B. Dues	1.26	—	—	—	1.26
C. Other services	10.06	1.17	.05	—	8.94
D. Total	13.46				12.75
3. Consumption of income in kind					
A. Farm income in kind	9.39	—	—	—	9.39
B. Nonfarm wages in kind	.75	.24	.05	.01	.57
C. Military subsistence	1.36	—	.12	.03	1.51
D. Total	11.50				11.47
4. Other outlays for consumption	3.81	—	—	—	3.81
5. Total outlays for consumption	117.35	—	—	—	94.54
6. Communal services	15.33	1.66	.21	.05	13.93
7. Government administration	1.09	.04	—	—	1.05
8. Gross investment					
A. Fixed capital	51.64	2.81	2.78	—	51.61
B. Inventories	7.97	.87	.55	.02	7.67
C. Total	59.61				59.28
9. Research and development	3.80	.23	.29	—	3.86
10. Internal security	1.50	.07	.12	.01	1.56
11. Defense					
A. Pay and subsistence	3.70	—	.12	.03	3.85
B. Other	9.87	.49	.55	—	9.93
C. Total	13.57				13.78
12. Outlays n.e.c.; public sector statistical discrepancy	1.44	.07	.44	—	1.81
13. Gross national product	213.69	34.52	10.61	.03	189.81

TABLE J-1 (continued)

	1964				
	Value at Established Prices	Adjustment for Turnover Taxes	Adjustment for Subsidies	Adjustment for Farm Prices	Value at AFC
	(31)	(32)	(33)	(34)	(35)
1. Retail sales to households					
A. State-cooperative trade	88.18	27.06	4.10	1.29	66.51
B. Extravillage farm markets	4.42	—	—	−1.49	2.93
C. Total	92.60				69.44
2. Consumer services					
A. Housing	2.22	.05	.48	—	2.65
B. Dues	1.35	—	—	—	1.35
C. Other services	10.88	1.28	.10	—	9.70
D. Total	14.45				13.70
3. Consumption of income in kind					
A. Farm income in kind	9.67	—	—	—	9.67
B. Nonfarm wages in kind	.80	.24	.04	.01	.61
C. Military subsistence	1.24	—	.08	.02	1.34
D. Total	11.71				11.62
4. Other outlays for consumption	4.00	—	—	—	4.00
5. Total outlays for consumption	122.76	—	—	—	98.76
6. Communal services	16.83	1.82	.23	.06	15.30
7. Government administration	1.11	.04	—	—	1.07
8. Gross investment					
A. Fixed capital	57.11	3.01	3.03	—	57.13
B. Inventories	11.63	2.33	.73	.10	10.13
C. Total	68.74				67.26
9. Research and development	4.20	.25	.36	—	4.31
10. Internal security	1.50	.07	.12	.01	1.56
11. Defense					
A. Pay and subsistence	3.38	—	.08	.02	3.48
B. Other	9.60	.48	.54	—	9.66
C. Total	12.98				13.14
12. Outlays n.e.c.; public sector statistical discrepancy	1.11	.06	.37	—	1.42
13. Gross national product	229.23	36.69	10.26	.02	202.82

Sources:
Established price values from Table 6, adjustments from Tables J-2, J-4, and J-5.

TABLE J-2

INCIDENCE OF THE TURNOVER TAX BY FINAL USE CATEGORY, 1958–1964

	Tax Rate	1958 Outlays	1958 Tax	1959 Outlays	1959 Tax	1960 Outlays	1960 Tax	1961 Outlays	1961 Tax	1962 Outlays	1962 Tax	1963 Outlays	1963 Tax	1964 Outlays	1964 Tax
	(1)	(2)	(3)	(4)	(5)	(6)	(7)	(8)	(9)	(10)	(11)	(12)	(13)	(14)	(15)
1. Retail sales to households															
A. State-cooperative trade	[a]	60.33	24.12	64.47	23.74	71.13	25.07	73.41	24.23	79.64	25.91	84.29	26.83	88.18	27.06
B. Extravillage farm markets	—	4.43	—	4.23	—	4.00	—	4.31	—	4.36	—	4.29	—	4.42	—
C. Total		64.76		68.70		75.13		77.72		84.00		88.58		92.60	
2. Consumer services															
A. Housing															
(1) Imputed rent	—	1.10	—	1.14	—	1.18	—	1.21	—	1.24	—	1.26	—	1.29	—
(2) Paid rent	5	.61	.03	.66	.03	.71	.04	.76	.04	.82	.04	.88	.04	.93	.05
(3) Total		1.71		1.80		1.89		1.97		2.06		2.14		2.22	
B. Dues	—	.91	—	.94	—	1.02	—	1.12	—	1.19	—	1.26	—	1.35	—
C. Other services															
(1) Education, health, physical culture															
(a) Wages and equivalents	—	.50	—	.52	—	.55	—	.57	—	.60	—	.64	—	.69	—
(b) Nonwage costs	40	.16	.06	.17	.07	.18	.07	.19	.08	.20	.08	.21	.08	.23	.09
(2) Entertainment and culture															
(a) Wages and equivalents	—	.76	—	.77	—	.79	—	.84	—	.90	—	.94	—	.98	—
(b) Nonwage costs	20	.25	.05	.26	.05	.26	.05	.28	.06	.30	.06	.31	.06	.32	.06
(3) Transportation and communication	5	2.63	.13	2.90	.15	3.18	.16	3.66	.18	4.16	.21	4.49	.22	4.85	.24
(4) Utilities	60	.69	.41	.77	.46	.87	.52	.98	.59	1.09	.65	1.23	.74	1.35	.81
(5) Other public sector services for consumption	5	.84	.04	.93	.05	1.04	.05	1.16	.06	1.30	.07	1.41	.07	1.62	.08
(6) Private sector services	—	.75	—	.77	—	.78	—	.80	—	.81	—	.83	—	.84	—
(7) Total		6.58		7.09		7.65		8.48		9.36		10.06		10.88	
D. Total		9.20		9.83		10.56		11.57		12.61		13.46		14.45	

TABLE J-2 (continued)

	Tax Rate	1958 Outlays	1958 Tax	1959 Outlays	1959 Tax	1960 Outlays	1960 Tax	1961 Outlays	1961 Tax	1962 Outlays	1962 Tax	1963 Outlays	1963 Tax	1964 Outlays	1964 Tax
	(1)	(2)	(3)	(4)	(5)	(6)	(7)	(8)	(9)	(10)	(11)	(12)	(13)	(14)	(15)
3. Consumption of income in kind															
A. Farm income in kind	—	9.92	—	9.52	—	9.12	—	9.36	—	9.55	—	9.39	—	9.67	—
B. Nonfarm wages in kind	*	.50	.20	.55	.20	.60	.21	.65	.21	.70	.23	.75	.24	.80	.24
C. Military subsistence	—	1.51	—	1.45	—	1.38	—	1.31	—	1.47	—	1.36	—	1.24	—
D. Total		11.93		11.52		11.10		11.32		11.72		11.50		11.71	
4. Other outlays for consumption	—	3.00	—	3.19	—	2.66	—	2.21	—	3.34	—	3.81	—	4.00	—
5. Total outlays for consumption		87.89		91.54		97.66		100.85		109.49		115.05		120.76	
6. Communal services, excluding science															
A. Wages and equivalents	—	7.69	—	8.30	—	8.94	—	9.66	—	10.10	—	11.19	—	12.29	—
B. Nonwage costs	40	2.84	1.14	3.07	1.23	3.30	1.32	3.57	1.43	3.73	1.49	4.14	1.66	4.54	1.82
C. Total		10.53		11.37		12.24		13.23		13.83		15.33		16.83	
7. Government administration															
A. Wages and equivalents	—	.96	—	.90	—	.87	—	.86	—	.87	—	.87	—	.89	—
B. Nonwage costs	20	.24	.05	.22	.04	.22	.04	.22	.04	.22	.04	.22	.04	.22	.04
C. Total		1.20		1.12		1.09		1.08		1.09		1.09		1.11	
8. Research and development															
A. Wages and equivalents	—	1.44	—	1.62	—	1.76	—	2.03	—	2.31	—	2.66	—	2.94	—
B. Nonwage costs	20	.62	.12	.69	.14	.76	.15	.87	.17	.99	.20	1.14	.23	1.26	.25
C. Total		2.06		2.31		2.52		2.90		3.30		3.80		4.20	
9. Internal security															
A. Wages and equivalents	—	1.13	—	1.13	—	1.13	—	1.13	—	1.13	—	1.13	—	1.13	—
B. Nonwage costs	20	.37	.07	.37	.07	.37	.07	.37	.07	.37	.07	.37	.07	.37	.07
C. Total		1.50		1.50		1.50		1.50		1.50		1.50		1.50	

TABLE J-2 (continued)

10. Defense (explicit)															
A. Pay and subsistence	—	4.11	—	3.95	—	3.77	—	3.57	—	4.00	—	3.70	—	3.38	—
B. Other	5	4.95	.25	5.12	.26	5.23	.26	7.72	.39	8.34	.42	9.87	.49	9.60	.48
C. Total		9.06		9.07		9.00		11.29		12.34		13.57		12.98	
11. Gross investment															
A. Fixed capital															
(1) Households: livestock	—	.65	—	.47	—	.68	—	.72	—	.43	—	−.84	—	.45	—
(2) Households: private housing															
(a) Labor	—	1.77	—	2.04	—	1.83	—	1.58	—	1.38	—	1.19	—	1.10	—
(b) Materials	[a]	.88	.35	1.02	.38	.91	.32	.79	.26	.69	.23	.60	.19	.55	.17
(3) Collective farms: livestock	—	.46	—	.67	—	.80	—	.80	—	.86	—	.85	—	.90	—
(4) Collective farms: other	15/10	2.58	.39	2.66	.40	2.40	.36	2.40	.24	2.57	.26	2.54	.25	2.70	.27
(5) State-cooperative investment	5	30.35	1.52	33.71	1.69	37.93	1.90	40.78	2.04	43.50	2.18	47.30	2.37	51.40	2.57
(6) Total		36.69		40.56		44.55		47.07		49.43		51.64		57.11	
B. Inventories															
(1) Collective farms	20/15	.40	.08	.33	.07	.29	.06	.37	.06	.45	.07	.49	.07	.55	.08
(2) State-cooperative sector															
(a) Goods shipped and finished goods in trade and procurement	[a]	3.00	1.20	4.64	1.71	.62	.22	1.65	.55	1.30	.42	1.59	.51	6.61	2.03
(b) Other inventories	5	4.50	.23	4.44	.22	3.89	.19	4.04	.20	3.99	.20	5.89	.29	4.47	.22
(c) Total		7.50		9.08		4.51		5.69		5.29		7.48		11.08	
(3) Total inventory investment		7.90		9.41		4.80		6.06		5.74		7.97		11.63	
C. Total gross investment		44.59		49.97		49.35		53.13		55.17		59.61		68.74	
12. Outlays n.e.c.; public sector statistical discrepancy	5	.23	.01	2.17	.11	5.62	.28	.30	.02	2.45	.12	1.44	.07	1.11	.06
GNP		158.06	30.45	170.75	31.07	180.77	31.34	186.25	30.92	201.35	32.95	213.69	34.52	229.23	36.69

Notes:
Tax rate in percent; outlays and tax in billion rubles.
[a] Tax rate not explicitly calculated; tax computed as a share of residual obtained after deducting other components. See description in text of this appendix.

TABLE J-2 (continued)

Sources:

Tax rate. See text of this appendix.

Outlays. Table 6, except as noted below.

2.A. *Housing.* Above, p. 334.

2.C. *Other services.* Above, p. 354. The shares of wage and nonwage costs in health care, education and entertainment services are estimated as follows: According to Eidel'man, *Mezhotraslevoi balans obshchestvennogo produkta*, 1966, p. 166, current material outlays in 1959 (net of depreciation) were 1.57 billion rubles in education excluding science, press, and art and 1.47 billions in health care. It is not clear whether these figures encompass outlays from all sources or just budget expenditures. If the former is true, the figures may be compared with my estimates of current outlays, wage and material, of 6.30 and 4.85 billion rubles in respectively, education excluding science and health care plus physical culture (Tables D-1, D-2, and D-3); the error stemming from inclusion of press and art outlays should be insignificant for present purposes. Eidel'man's figures are 25 and 30 percent of the totals. Therefore, I estimate the share of material outlays as 25 percent in household outlays on education, health, and entertainment.

6–9. *Communal services, administration, R&D, internal security.* The share of nonwage costs in communal services is estimated as 27 percent, based on estimates of 25 percent for education and 30 percent for health care. See sources above for 2.C, "other services."

An alternative procedure of estimating the division between wage and nonwage costs is to extend the estimate for 1958 (assuming a 27 percent nonwage share) by indexes of employment and average earnings derived from official sources (*NKh 1962*, p. 454 and *NKh 1964*, pp. 547, 555; health and education earnings reported separately are averaged using employment as weights). The figure for 1964 so obtained is within 3 percent of the figure derived on the assumption of a constant percentage division of wage and nonwage costs.

The share of nonwage costs is estimated as 20 percent in administration, 25 percent in internal security, and 30 percent in R&D, based on the estimates for health and education as well as judgments on the relative importance of food and, for R&D, of test materials. The same close relation between 1964 wage costs derived on the assumption of constant wage cost shares and 1964 wage costs computed by extending the 1958 estimate with the aid of employment and wage indexes is obtained for R&D as it was for communal services. However, this is not true for administration, where the latter procedure yields a 1964 wage cost figure larger than total current outlays in that year. Evidently, the average earnings and employment series underlying the reputed budget outlays on administration differ from the series cited in the statistical yearbooks.

11. *Gross investment.*

A.(1) *Households: livestock.* Table 2, item 6.B.

A.(2) *Households: private housing.* Above, p. 361.

A.(3) *Collective farms: livestock.* Livestock investment is assumed to have accounted for 15 percent in 1958, 20 percent in 1959, and 25 percent in 1960–1964 of gross investment by farms (excluding acquisition of former MTS machinery), based on: Koriunov, *Nedelimye fondy i kapital'nye vlozheniia kolkhozov*, 1960, pp. 42–43; VNIIESKh, *Povyshenie urovnia razvitiia kolkhoznogo proizvodstva*, 1961, p. 91; *Gosudarstvennyi bank k XXII s"ezdu KPSS*, 1961, p. 61; Alekseeva and Voronin, *Nakoplenie i razvitie kolkhoznoi sobstvennosti*, 1963, p. 105; Nedelin, *Organizatsiia finansov kolkhoza*, 1964, p. 57.

A.(4) *Collective farms: other.* Total collective farms gross fixed investment (p. 387) less investment in livestock.

A.(5) *State-cooperative investment.* Above, p. 387.

B.(1) *Collective farms.* Above, p. 392.

B.(2) *State-cooperative sector.* Except for 1958, taken from Table L-3. The division of the total for 1958 between the indicated components is based on estimates by Moorsteen and Powell (*The Soviet Capital Stock*, 1928–1962, 1966, p. 457) that of total state-cooperative inventory investment in current prices of 9.21 billion rubles in 1958, 3.97 billions represented increments of inventories in trade and procurement. Data in Table

TABLE J-2 (continued)

L-1 below suggest that perhaps 90 percent of this must have been in finished goods and goods shipped, amounting to about 3.6 billion rubles in 1958. This figure is 39 percent of the Moorsteen–Powell total estimate. I assume 40 percent and therefore obtain a figure of 3.00 billion rubles for finished goods and goods shipped in procurement, given my total estimate of 7.50 billion rubles (p. 394).

Tax. The product of outlays and tax rate. The total tax is from Table C-1.

TABLE J-3

TURNOVER TAXES BY BRANCH OF ORIGIN, 1957–1962

<table>
<tr><th></th><th>Heavy Industry</th><th>Light Industry</th><th>Food Industry</th><th>Agricultural Procurement</th><th>Other</th><th>Total</th></tr>
<tr><td>1957 plan</td><td></td><td></td><td></td><td></td><td></td><td></td></tr>
<tr><td>Percent</td><td>7.0</td><td>30.0</td><td>38.3</td><td>13.0</td><td>11.7 [a]</td><td>100.0</td></tr>
<tr><td>Billion rubles</td><td>1.93</td><td>8.27</td><td>10.56</td><td>3.58</td><td>3.22 [a]</td><td>27.56</td></tr>
<tr><td>1958</td><td></td><td></td><td></td><td></td><td></td><td></td></tr>
<tr><td>Percent</td><td>13.8</td><td colspan="3">86.2</td><td></td><td>100.0</td></tr>
<tr><td>Billion rubles</td><td>4.20</td><td colspan="3">26.25</td><td></td><td>30.45</td></tr>
<tr><td>1960</td><td></td><td></td><td></td><td></td><td></td><td></td></tr>
<tr><td>Billion rubles</td><td>~5</td><td></td><td></td><td></td><td></td><td></td></tr>
<tr><td>1961</td><td></td><td></td><td></td><td></td><td></td><td></td></tr>
<tr><td>Percent</td><td>18</td><td colspan="4">82</td><td>100</td></tr>
<tr><td>Billion rubles</td><td>5.5</td><td colspan="4">25.4</td><td>30.92</td></tr>
<tr><td>~1960–1962</td><td></td><td></td><td></td><td></td><td></td><td></td></tr>
<tr><td>Percent</td><td>10</td><td colspan="2">70–75</td><td>10–12</td><td>3–10 [b]</td><td>100</td></tr>
<tr><td>Billion rubles</td><td>3</td><td colspan="2">22–24</td><td>3–4</td><td>1–4 [b]</td><td>31.74 [c]</td></tr>
<tr><td>1962</td><td></td><td></td><td></td><td></td><td></td><td></td></tr>
<tr><td>Percent</td><td>17.3</td><td>30.4</td><td>52.1</td><td></td><td>0.2 [a]</td><td>100.0</td></tr>
<tr><td>Billion rubles</td><td>5.70</td><td>10.08</td><td>17.16</td><td></td><td>.01 [a]</td><td>32.95</td></tr>
</table>

Notes:

[a] Residual.

[b] State trade organizations and consumer cooperatives.

[c] Average 1960–1962.

Sources:

Unless otherwise specified, values of the total tax are from Table C-1, with component values computed from the total tax and the percent distribution.

1957 plan. *SNIP 1956–1958*, p. 132.

1958, percent. Sitarian, *Natsional'nyi dokhod soiuznykh respublik*, 1961, p. 37.

1960. According to Turetskii (*FinSSSR*, 1963, No. 11, p. 42) about 14 billion rubles of profits and turnover tax in 1960 originated in heavy industry. Profits in heavy industry (reckoning as "heavy" all branches of industry other than "light" and "food") came to 8.7 or 8.9 billion rubles, depending on the concept of profit employed (*Prom II*, pp. 100–101).

1961, percent. Sitarian, *FinSSSR*, 1963, No. 10, p. 15.

1960–1962, percent. Allakhverdian, ed., *Finansy SSSR*, 1962, p. 202 and *Finansy v period stroitel'stva kommunizma*, 1963, p. 20.

1962, percent and values. Evdokimov, in MINKh, *Nauchnye zapiski aspirantov*, 1964, p. 165.

TABLE J-4
INCIDENCE OF SUBSIDIES BY TYPE AND FINAL USE CATEGORY, 1958–1964
(billion rubles)

End-use and Type of Subsidy	1958	1959	1960	1961	1962	1963	1964
1. State-cooperative retail sales							
Conventional	1.00	1.34	1.70	1.95	2.15	2.80	2.24
MTS-procurement	2.94	2.18	1.87	.90	1.54	2.04	1.82
Wage reform	—	—	.58	.66	.58	.04	.04
Total	3.93	3.52	4.15	3.51	4.27	4.88	4.10
2. Housing							
Conventional	.01	.01	.01	.01	.01	.01	.01
Wage reform	—	—	.01	—	—	—	—
Housing	.31	.33	.36	.38	.41	.44	.47
Total	.31	.34	.38	.40	.42	.45	.48
3. Household outlays on other services							
Conventional	.02	.03	.03	.04	.04	.04	.04
MTS-procurement	.01	.01	—	—	—	.01	—
Wage reform	—	—	.03	.09	.08	—	.05
Total	.03	.03	.06	.13	.12	.05	.10
4. Nonfarm wages in kind							
Conventional	.01	.01	.02	.02	.02	.03	.02
MTS-procurement	.02	.02	.02	.01	.01	.02	.02
Wage reform	—	—	.01	.01	.01	—	—
Total	.03	.03	.04	.03	.04	.05	.04
5. Military subsistence [a]							
Conventional	.04	.05	.05	.05	.06	.07	.05
MTS-procurement	.12	.08	.06	.02	.04	.05	.04
Wage reform	—	—	.02	.02	.02	—	—
Total	.16	.13	.12	.09	.12	.12	.08
6. Communal services							
Conventional	.05	.06	.07	.08	.09	.12	.10
MTS-procurement	.14	.10	.08	.04	.06	.09	.08
Wage reform	—	—	.03	.03	.02	—	.05
Total	.19	.16	.18	.15	.18	.21	.23
7. Government administration	—	—	—	—	—	—	—
8. Research and Development							
Conventional	.23	.12	.08	.37	.18	.29	.36
Wage reform	.02	.03	.01	.12	.10	—	—
Total	.25	.15	.08	.49	.28	.29	.36
9. Internal security							
Conventional	.14	.07	.05	.17	.08	.11	.11
MTS-procurement	.02	.02	.01	.01	.01	.01	.01
Wage reform	.01	.02	—	—	—	—	—
Total	.18	.11	.06	.18	.09	.12	.12
10. Defense							
A. Subsistence [a]							
Conventional	.04	.05	.05	.05	.06	.07	.05
MTS-procurement	.12	.08	.06	.02	.04	.05	.04
Wage reform	—	—	.02	.02	.02	—	—
Total	.16	.13	.12	.09	.12	.12	.08

TABLE J-4 (continued)

End-use and Type of Subsidy	1958	1959	1960	1961	1962	1963	1964
B. Other than pay and subsistence							
Conventional	.27	.29	.32	.45	.47	.54	.53
Wage reform	.02	.06	.02	.03	.03	.01	.01
Total	.29	.35	.34	.48	.49	.55	.54
11. Gross investment							
A. Materials component of private housing construction							
Conventional	.03	.04	.04	.03	.03	.02	.02
Wage reform	—	.01	—	—	—	—	—
Total	.03	.05	.04	.04	.03	.02	.02
B. Collective farm: excluding livestock							
Conventional	.13	.13	.13	.13	.14	.13	.14
Wage reform	.01	.03	.01	.01	.01	—	—
Total	.13	.16	.14	.14	.14	.13	.14
C. State-cooperative							
Conventional	1.65	1.90	2.33	2.39	2.45	2.60	2.83
Wage reform	.11	.41	.13	.15	.13	.03	.03
Total	1.75	2.31	2.46	2.54	2.58	2.63	2.87
12. Inventory investment							
A. Collective farms							
Conventional	.15	.06	.03	.17	.09	.13	.17
Wage reform	.01	.02	—	—	—	—	—
Total	.16	.07	.03	.17	.09	.13	.17
B. State-cooperative: goods shipped and finished goods in trade and procurement							
Conventional	.05	.10	.02	.04	.04	.05	.17
MTS-procurement	.15	.16	.02	.02	.03	.04	.14
Wage reform	—	—	.01	.01	.01	—	—
Total	.20	.25	.04	.08	.07	.09	.31
C. State-cooperative: other							
Conventional	.24	.25	.24	.24	.22	.32	.25
Wage reform	.02	.05	.01	.02	.01	—	—
Total	.26	.30	.25	.25	.24	.33	.25
13. Outlays n.e.c.; statistical discrepancy							
Conventional	.10	.45	.69	.15	.54	.44	.37
Wage reform	.01	.12	.05	—	.01	—	—
Total	.11	.58	.74	.15	.55	.44	.37
14. Total							
Conventional	4.14	4.95	5.85	6.35	6.66	7.77	7.45
MTS-procurement	3.52	2.63	2.11	1.02	1.74	2.30	2.14
Wage reform	.20	.75	.92	1.17	1.02	.10	.20
Housing	.31	.33	.36	.38	.41	.44	.47
All subsidies	8.17	8.66	9.23	8.92	9.83	10.61	10.26

Note:

[a] Subsidies applicable to military subsistence are counted twice, once with reference to income in kind and again with reference to defense services.

Sources:

Total subsidies of each type—estimated above, pp. 371, 478, and 487—are distributed as described in the text of this appendix.

TABLE J-5

ADJUSTMENT FOR FARM PRICES BY FINAL USE CATEGORY, 1958–1964
(billion rubles)

	1958	1959	1960	1961	1962	1963	1964
1. State-cooperative retail sales	1.23	1.11	1.06	1.18	1.21	1.24	1.29
2. Extravillage farm market sales	−1.42	−1.30	−1.17	−1.31	−1.33	−1.36	−1.49
3. Household outlays on health and education: materials	—	—	—	—	—	—	—
4. Nonfarm wages in kind	.01	.01	.01	.01	.01	.01	.01
5. Military subsistence [a]	.05	.04	.03	.03	.03	.03	.02
6. Communal services: materials	.06	.05	.05	.05	.05	.05	.06
7. Internal security: materials	.01	.01	.01	.01	.01	.01	.01
8. Increment of goods shipped and finished goods in trade and procurement	.06	.08	.01	.03	.02	.02	.10
9. Defense: subsistence [a]	.05	.04	.03	.03	.03	.03	.02
Total [a]	.05	.04	.03	.03	.03	.03	.02

Note:
[a] Adjustments cancel, except that adjustment incident on military subsistence is counted twice.

Sources:
See text of this appendix.

K

The Deflation of GNP by Use at Established Prices and Factor Costs

The first and largest part of this appendix discusses the deflators for individual end uses. The second part presents the calculation of GNP by use at two sets of prices, 1958 and 1964, in two variants, established prices and adjusted factor cost, and for AFC, at two alternative formulations.

The Deflators

Revaluation of the current-price data is generally by deflation. The major exception is farm income in kind, where physical quantities are reaggregated with 1958 and 1964 price weights.

HOUSEHOLD OUTLAYS

Retail sales in state-cooperative trade. These values are deflated by official retail price indexes (*NKh 1962*, p. 532; *NKh 1963*, p. 539; *NKh 1964*, p. 646). The index of state retail prices, which applies to all state and cooperative links in the retail trade network, excluding only collective farm market transactions, is said to be a given-year weighted harmonic mean of individual or group price index numbers of the form

$$R = \frac{\sum P_i Q_i}{\sum \frac{1}{k_i} P_i Q_i}$$

where k represents individual or group price index numbers of the form P_i/P_o. It appears that the published index numbers for the SYP period are linked, with values of the later year used as weights in each link (*Sovtorg II,* p. 487; Riauzov and Titel'baum, *Statistika torgovli,* 1961, pp. 204–205). Therefore, deflation of retail sales after 1959 by these index numbers will *not* yield a series at 1958 prices; a series at 1964 prices is similarly unobtainable for all years before 1964. In effect the price weights change continually and represent those of the year $i-1$:

$$\sum P_iQ_i \Bigg/ \frac{\sum P_iQ_i}{\sum\left(\frac{P_{i-1}}{P_i}\right)P_iQ_i} = \sum P_{i-1}Q_i$$

However, the official index shows small changes in these years and the computed hybrid series may be viewed as a sufficiently close approximation to the desired series.

Is the official index reliable? For years covering the early and middle 1950s and with 1940 as base year, the official index corresponds closely to measures computed by Chapman (*Real Wages in Soviet Russia Since 1928,* 1963, pp. 157–159). For later years no independent calculation is available. There is some question whether the official index takes adequate account of quality changes. For example, a number of visitors to the Soviet Union during the height of the food shortages in 1963–1964 reported quality deterioration that was not reflected in food prices. However, there is insufficient evidence to pursue the matter further.

Extravillage market sales. Soviet predilection for given-year weighted price indexes extends to all branches of retail trade; the official indexes of collective farm market prices also use given year weights, though made up of quantities rather than values (Beliaevskii, *Statistika kolkhoznoi torgovli,* 1962, pp. 72–73). Unlike the state retail price indexes, those for collective farm market prices do not appear to be constructed from annual links. It is true that annual changes in the 1940-based series are the same, allowing for rounding, as those for corresponding years in the 1952-based series (*NKh 1961,* p. 665; *NKh 1962,* p. 541; *Sovtorg II,* p. 266). However, this may mean no more than that the second series has been obtained directly from the first. On the other hand, a more relevant test is the following:

(1) Average prices and quantities in the major component groups of the official aggregate price and quantity indexes have been computed by Karcz. On the basis of these data, and using a Paasche index formula,

Karcz was able to reproduce the official aggregate price indexes with great fidelity (*American Economic Review,* June 1964, pp. 323–326).

(2) Using the same data (as shown in Table A-2) and the Paasche formula, I have computed the 1959 aggregate price index number on a 1958 base. The computed index number is 85, and that obtained from either the 1940-based or the 1952-based official series is 98.

(3) The one commodity group among those reported for which Karcz attempts no estimates is fruit. If fruit is included, based on my estimates in Table A-2, the computed index number rises to 88, still far below that implied by the official series.

(4) The difference cannot be attributed to the effect of omitting commodity groups for which component indexes have not been published (live animals, vegetable oil, mushrooms, honey, sugar, and so on). In Karcz's computed 1940-based index (in the mimeographed appendix to his article), the 1959 entry is 96.3 percent of the 1958 number—that is, comfortably close to the official 98 percent.

(5) That a 1940-based index and a 1958-based index imply different annual changes must, therefore, be due to differential weighting. That is, the 1958–1959 change in the 1940-based index is

$$\frac{\sum P_{59}Q_{59}}{\sum P_{40}Q_{59}} \bigg/ \frac{\sum P_{58}Q_{58}}{\sum P_{40}Q_{58}}$$

whereas the same change in the 1958-based index is

$$\frac{\sum P_{59}Q_{59}}{\sum P_{58}Q_{59}}$$

As deflators for collective market sales I use 1958-based and 1964-based price indexes with given year quantity weights, developed from the price and quantity data cited in Table A-2. The computed index numbers are as follows:

	1958 = 100	*1964 = 100*
1958	100.0	82.8
1959	88.4	73.7
1960	92.0	76.2
1961	94.9	79.1
1962	105.0	87.9
1963	109.1	92.6
1964	118.4	100.0

Housing. Since the value of housing services was computed as the product of the housing stock and a constant unit rental rate, there is no need for deflation here.

Dues. The deflator is average annual wages and salaries of workers and employees (above, p. 295).

Other services. Prices of these services appear to have changed little over this period. This is true of municipal services, including utilities, urban transportation, and the nonindustrial component of "everyday" services (Gol'tsman, *Ekonomika kommunal'nogo khoziaistva uslugi, tarify,* 1966, pp. 80–82). Comparison of two series relating to the industrial component of everyday services (largely repair and custom production of clothing and household goods)—output values at 1955 wholesale prices and receipts at current prices—imply price declines of 5 percent in 1960, 4 percent in 1961, and 8 percent in 1962 (*Prom II,* p. 414; *Sovtorg II,* p. 54). These changes are not inconceivable, but the two series are not entirely comparable. For example, the wholesale-price series omits the value of cloth sold by tailors, whereas the retail price series includes the value of all materials supplied by the artisans. (See the sources cited; also *Sovtorg II,* p. 486.) Travelers' reports indicate no change in prices of movie, theater, or concert tickets. I have seen no evidence of changes in tariffs for intercity passenger transportation, except with respect to airlines, where fares were reduced by an average 30 percent during the SYP period (Loginov, in *Zasedaniia Verkhovnogo soveta SSSR . . . 15–19 dekabria 1966 g.,* 1967, p. 334).

Farm income in kind. As previously indicated, farm income in kind is not deflated but revalued by reaggregating physical quantities at 1958 and 1964 prices. It is again assumed that the sum of values of the seven products is equivalent to the value of consumption of all products including those omitted—that is, that overstatement of consumption of the seven products offsets understatement of the global total through omissions of other products (see pp. 301–304). With regard to production expenses, only material purchases from collective farms are deflated, by the index applied below to other outlays for consumption.

Nonfarm wages in kind. No deflation is undertaken. The wages in question consist largely of free work clothing supplied in factories. The retail price index for "clothing and underwear" shows a 4 percent decline between 1958 and 1964, most of which occurred in 1961–1962. The decline is partially offset by the 3 percent increase in food prices between 1958 and 1963, most of which took place in 1962–1963, and to the extent that food is included in wages in kind (*NKh 1962*, p. 532; *NKh 1963*, p. 540; *NKh 1964*, p. 647).

Military subsistence. Deflation is unnecessary as the estimates assume a constant level of subsistence per man.

Other outlays for consumption. The outlays in question are believed to represent chiefly purchases in the intravillage farm market and from individual artisans. For the years 1959–1963 the figures at current prices also include errors and omissions in the values of other consumption components.

An index of intracollective farm market prices for the RSFSR has been presented in a Soviet source (Kuznetsov, *VS*, 1963, No. 12, p. 35) for the years 1960–1962, with 1959 = 100: 1960, 107; 1961, 124; 1962, 129. Zaslavskaia (*Raspredelenie po trudu v kolkhozakh*, 1966, p. 169) also indicates a continuing increase in the level of these prices from 1959 to 1964, but her data refer only to farms with cash wage accounting. On the other hand, for the entire USSR, an index based on six major products (grain, potatoes, vegetables, meat, milk, and eggs) shows the following pattern, with 1960 = 100: 1961, 95; 1962, 99; 1963, 107/108.

[This index is computed from data provided by Morozov in *Trudoden', dengi i torgovlia na sele*, 1965, pp. 265, 270, 288. Morozov cites sales in physical units, the percentage distribution of value of sales by product and prices for the single year 1963. (The prices are said to refer to 1961 but the discussion on p. 289 makes clear that this is an error and 1963 was intended.) On the basis of estimates of the total value of sales derived by Nimitz (*Incomes of Collective Farmers*), values for the six products are computed for each of the years in question and are then divided by the physical quantities to obtain average prices. The price index computed from these average prices utilizes 1960 quantities as weights. For 1963 two index numbers are computed—the first derived from the prices cited by Morozov, the second computed as indicated for the other years in the series.]

I have seen no data on the behavior of prices in other parts of the intravillage market nor in regard to purchases from individual artisans. On balance one suspects a rising trend. Arbitrarily, I assume an annual rate of price increase of 3 percent.

Private housing construction. Deflation is not attempted. The data used are official figures presumably valued at estimate prices. As such they should be roughly equivalent to a constant-price series. The index of estimate prices of state-cooperative construction-installation work

(1955 = 100) stood at 107 in 1956–1958, dropped to 106 in 1959, and remained at that level thereafter. (*Kapstroi*, p. 258; *NKh 1962*, p. 429, note; *NKh 1964*, p. 507, note.) A generally constant unit price is implied by comparison of private housing construction in terms of square meters of floor space put in place with the official ruble series. (See above, pp. 336, 338, 360.)

Farm investment in kind. Physical quantities (p. 304) are revalued at 1958 and 1964 prices (Table A-2, part D).

PUBLIC SECTOR OUTLAYS

Communal services, administration, and R&D. The wage component of these outlays (as estimated in Table J-2) is deflated by reported average annual wages and salaries in health and education (combined in proportion to employment), administration, and science (*NKh 1962*, p. 454 and *NKh 1964*, pp. 547, 555–556; gaps for 1959 and 1961–1962 are estimated by interpolation). The average earnings indexes are as follows: (1958 = 100):

	1959	*1960*	*1961*	*1962*	*1963*	*1964*
Communal services	100.1	100.3	102.6	105.0	107.5	112.6
Administration	100.8	101.7	104.7	107.9	111.2	113.8
Research and development	98.4	98.4	100.1	101.8	103.6	105.8

With regard to R&D pay, the yearbooks indicate a decline in average compensation between 1958 and 1960. I assume the decline took place in 1959 (based on Nimitz, *Soviet Expenditures on Scientific Research*, January 1963, p. 17, note 1) and that there was no change between 1959 and 1960.

There seems little point in attempting to deflate the materials component of current outlays in these categories. The official indexes of wholesale prices gross of turnover taxes show little change in the period under review (1949 = 100):

	1958	*1959*	*1960*	*1961*	*1962*	*1963*	*1964*
Heavy industry	59	61	61	59	59	59	58
Light and food industry	61	60	60	60	61	61	62
All industry	60	61	61	60	61	61	61

(Sources are *NKh 1962*, p. 145; *NKh 1963*, p. 137; *NKh 1964*, p. 155; Stoliarov, *O tsenakh i tsenoobrazovanii v SSSR*, 1963, pp. 111–112).

State-cooperative capital repairs (original data from p. 387). Information is lacking both on the structure of outlays at current prices and on the trend in costs and prices. It would seem clear from the extensive critical commentary of Soviet writers that capital repair is extremely labor intensive and inefficient relative to machinery production (for example, Bunich, *Osnovnye fondy sotsialisticheskoi promyshlennosti,* 1960, Chapter IV, esp. pp. 221–223; Khrushchev, *Pravda,* April 26, 1963, p. 3; Bunich, *Ekon.gazeta,* July 20, 1963, p. 18). Partial data for 1957 indicate that direct labor costs absorb one-quarter to one-third of capital repair funds while additional labor expenditures form part of shop, overhead, and "services" costs (Bunich, in NIFI, *Planirovanie i finansirovanie kapital'nogo remonta osnovnykh fondov,* 1958, p. 32). On this basis, it is assumed that wage costs account for half of capital repair outlays at current prices. The wage component is deflated by the official index of wages of industrial production workers (*NKh 1964,* p. 555; a separate series for repair personnel is not available):

1958—100.0	1961—107.8	1964—115.7
1959—102.6	1962—110.4	
1960—105.3	1963—113.1	

No attempt is made to deflate material costs. The official wholesale price index for all machine building and metal working (MBMW), excluding turnover tax, shows a 7 percent decline between 1958 and 1964 (*NKh 1963,* p. 136; *NKh 1965,* p. 166). On the reliability of this index see below, pp. 516–521.

Change in warehouse stocks of equipment requiring installation (p. 387). Again, deflation is not attempted: see the remarks immediately above with respect to material costs in capital repair.

State-cooperative new fixed investment. My "current-price" entries are in fact reported values at 1955 estimate prices (above, p. 392). There is no *ex post* current-price aggregate investment series in the available Soviet sources. Plan goals for so-called "financing" of the volume of state centralized investment, which includes small allocations for working capital increases in construction, are published in the annual budget speeches by the Minister of Finance to the Supreme Soviet (and in journal articles commenting on the budget, usually under the byline of the same Minister). The gap between planned "financing" and planned volumes, the latter valued at estimate prices, is always small, as the following tabulation shows (billion rubles):

	1958	1959	1960	1961	1962	1963	1964
Centralized investment, planned							
Volume	20.2	22.6	25.55	29.40	30.7	33.5	36.0
Financing	20.38	23.31	26.24	29.5	31.0	33.8	36.5

(Sources: *PKh*, 1959, No. 1, p. 6; *Pravda*, December 20, 1957; *Izvestiia*, October 28, 1959, p. 3; *PKh*, 1959, No. 12, p. 8; *Izvestiia*, December 21, 1960, p. 4; *FinSSSR*, 1961, No. 1, p. 17; *FinSSSR*, 1962, No. 1, p. 13; *FinSSSR*, 1963, No. 1, p. 12; *Pravda*, December 17, 1963, p. 3; *FinSSSR*, 1964, No. 1, p. 8. The last cites a "financing" figure for 1963 plan of 33.9 billion rubles.)

The sources of planned financing are budget allocations, retained profits, depreciation allowances, bank loans, "mobilization of internal resources" (which usually means net decrements in the value of uninstalled machinery), and cost decreases. For any given level of the planned volume of investment at estimate prices, failure to achieve the targets for "mobilization of internal resources" and construction cost decreases would require increased financing from other sources. Unfortunately, an *ex ante–ex post* comparison for these series or their components is not possible.

It is possible that for the period under review the difference between values at 1955 estimate prices and values at current prices may not be significant with respect to realized state-cooperative investment in "construction-installation," which accounts for around 60 percent of the sectors' new investment totals. For example, in 1958 the estimate-price value of construction-installation was 14.99 billion rubles; actual costs (*sebestoimost'*) of construction were 93.6 percent as large, or 14.03 billion rubles (*Kapstroi*, pp. 44, 263). Addition of profits earned in contract construction, which performs 85 percent of all state-cooperative construction-installation (*NKh 1962*, pp. 439, 627) raises the value in current prices to 14.85 billion rubles or 99 percent of the estimate-price value. (The profits figure used in this illustrative calculation represents balance profits, a concept explained in Appendix I. The appropriate value would be profits from sales, which are conceivably larger than balance profits.) The relation between actual costs of construction and the value of construction-installation at estimate prices varied little in subsequent years: the ratio was reported as .939 in 1959, .933 in 1960 (*Kapstroi*, p. 263); and may be estimated as .940 in 1961, .938 in 1962 and 1963, and .934 in 1964 (on the basis of a reported increase in costs of 0.8 percent in 1961 and decreases of 0.2 percent in 1962, 0.02 in

1963, and 0.4 percent in 1964—*NKh 1964,* p. 540. Estimate prices did not change after 1960).

[The preceding calculation is predicated on a particular interpretation of a footnote in *Kapstroi,* p. 263. Referring to the ratios of actual construction costs to values at estimate prices cited above, the footnote indicates the estimate price denominators are valued "at prices of the respective years." I take this to mean that the 1955 estimate prices were not retrospectively adjusted for the changes introduced in 1956, 1958, and 1959 (*Kapstroi,* p. 258). An alternative interpretation of the footnote is also possible: that the estimate prices incorporate input price changes but retain constant input norms. Official data claim no change in the index of wholesale prices of construction materials (*NKh 1962,* pp. 144–145; *NKh 1964,* pp. 154–155) but industrial wage rates did rise (*NKh 1964,* p. 555). If the input norms reflected in the estimate price denominators also changed there might be little justification for using these ratios to gauge the relation of "constant" estimate to current prices.

A simple test of these ratios in the years 1957–1960 does not contradict my assumption. That test consists in comparing the change in the ratios on one hand, with the change in (separately available) claimed decreases in actual construction-installation costs and indexes of estimate prices, on the other (*Kapstroi,* pp. 258–259):

	1956	*1957*	*1958*	*1959*	*1960*
Actual cost as percent of previous year's level	100	99	98	99	99
Index of estimate prices (July 1, 1955 = 100)	107	107	107	106	106
Estimate-price index as percent of previous year's level		100	100	99	100

The quotient of the figures in the last two rows in any year should yield the same annual change as is reflected in the series of ratios of actual to estimate cost. The results are as follows:

	Official Ratio of Actual to Estimate Cost in Given Year as Percent of that in Previous Year	*Same Ratio Computed from Separate Indicators*
1957	99.1	99
1958	99.0	98
1959	100.3	100
1960	99.4	99

Only the 1958 figures in the two columns diverge at all and the divergence is small.

My interpretation of the *Kapstroi* footnote may be wrong, but the data behave as if the assumption were in fact correct.]

As indicated, official statistics imply a slowly declining trend in actual construction costs. The statistical yearbooks report reductions in the cost of state-cooperative construction-installation in every year of the period 1957–1964 except 1961; in the latter year costs increased by a reportedly minute 0.8 percent (*NKh 1964,* p. 540). With regard to machinery acquisitions, the estimate price index shows no change from July 1, 1955 until 1959 when a percentage point decline appears; thereafter, presumably, no further change took place. The official index of wholesale prices refers to machine building and metal working (MBMW) as a whole. The index is roughly stable from 1958 on: Gross of turnover tax and with 1949 = 100, the index rises from 45 in 1958 to 48 in 1959, dropping back to 47 in 1960 and 45 in 1961–1964. Net of the tax—a more relevant indicator for most state-cooperative investment—the index declines from 45 in 1958–1959 to 44 in 1960–1962, 43 in 1963, and 42 in 1964 (*NKh 1963,* pp. 136–137; *NKh 1964,* pp. 154–155; *NKh 1965,* pp. 166–167; Stoliarov, *O tsenakh i tsenoobrazovanii v SSSR,* 1963, p. 112).

However, there is reason to question the reliability of the MBMW price index. For years through 1960 the MBMW index was calculated from values of gross output in current and constant prices. From 1961 on the index has been computed on the basis of a sample of products. The size of the sample is not indicated; we are told only that prior to 1961, when indexes for all other sub-branches of industry were computed by sampling, the sample encompassed 278 commodities. From 1961 on the sample was enlarged to cover 961 entities. It is not clear whether the increment represents only MBMW products or whether the structure of the total sample was altered (*NKh 1963,* p. 689; *NKh 1964,* pp. 804–805). Stoliarov, the head of CSA's division on price statistics, revealed that the industrial price index uses marketed output in 1956 as weights (*VS,* 1965, No. 3, p. 82). Presumably, this is true of the index for MBMW after 1960. Stoliarov did not indicate whether 1956 marketed outputs were used only for between-group or also for within-group weights. (In this connection, there are frequent complaints in the Soviet literature that prices of improved models are raised by a factor larger than the attained relative increase in productivity.) We have not been told whether the composition of the sample has remained constant or how CSA statisticians have treated qualitative change. Considering the degree of structural change that characterizes machine building, the use of constant weights in the construction of the MBMW price index is likely to hasten the index's obsolescence.

The proliferation of new products is indeed the crux of much of Soviet complaint on the *rising* cost of investment. Gatovskii pointed to "the inconsistency of the planned estimate value of construction with its actual value. The latter frequently exceeds the former by 1.5–2 times, and many large projects have cost the state 2–3 times more than planned" (*Ekon.gazeta,* 1965, No. 48, p. 6). Kvasha and Krasovkii, well known writers on problems of investment, bluntly charged a "concealed price inflation (*udorozhanie*) of equipment. The preponderance of new machines and instruments are not included in existing pricebooks, and temporary prices, embodying large expenditures on designing and mastering new models, lead to rising capital outlays per unit of equipment" (*VE,* 1964, No. 11, p. 12).

The extent of the alleged inflation of investment costs brought about by the high temporary prices on new equipment is suggested in the following rough calculation by the two authors (*ibid.,* pp. 12–13):

The share of nonseries equipment in the output of machine-building is about 50 percent. This equipment is valued entirely at temporary prices—as a rule, 30–40 percent higher than those adopted in the estimates. Thus, for the entire volume of equipment, series and nonseries, the inflation comes to about 15–20 percent. In addition, about 30 percent of equipment in the form of iron structures, steam conduits, etc., is produced directly on-site and is considered part of construction-installation. The equipment of this group also is valued at temporary prices. Outlays on equipment, including nonstandard, are 50–55 percent; thus, as a whole, the inflation of capital construction in the period after 1959 compared with the prices adopted in the estimates of 1955–1960 comes to about 10–12 percent.

A Gosplan official declared that machinery enterprise managers had an incentive to maximize the prices of new machines under conditions where premia were dependent on lowering production expenditures per ruble of "marketed" (*tovarnaia*) output. "As a result, the average price level of machinery . . . is constantly rising." (Matlin, *Tekhnicheskii progress i tseny mashin,* 1966, pp. 17–18.)

Nevertheless, the actual dimensions of the new product problem seem in dispute. A CSA survey of 86 *sovnarkhozy* showed that in 1961 "output valued at permanent handbook prices predominates in the structure of gross and marketed output of machinebuilding" (Stoliarov, *O tsenakh i tsenoobrazovanii v SSSR,* 1963, p. 169). Output at "permanent" prices accounted for 82.5 percent of marketed and 83.8 percent of gross production in the surveyed group. The proportion must vary sharply among machinery categories: According to Gabrieli (*VE,*

1963, No. 7, p. 61), roughly half of all agricultural machinery items (excluding tractors and automotive vehicles) were sold to collective and state farms at temporary prices.

Kvasha and Krasovskii, perhaps for cause, also ignored the role of the "mastering fund." The mastering fund was established in 1960, to be financed by deductions from production costs, in order to siphon off the pressure of higher costs in designing and producing new machinery. Prices of new machinery were to be set at levels corresponding to analogous existing models with some allowance for increased utility. Developmental and "mastering" costs were to be reimbursed from the mastering fund. From the beginning, however, significant classes of machinery were exempted: the fund was applicable only to "civilian production;" and within that category, tractors, agricultural machinery, large transport equipment (aircraft, ships, locomotives, mainline freight cars "and the like"), as well as experimental models produced to single order, were also excluded from consideration. (Basistov, *VE,* 1964, No. 5, p. 23; Riumin, in MFI, *Problemy finansovogo planirovaniia,* 1963, pp. 40–41.) For the classes of equipment covered, the mastering fund may not have been sufficient to the task (Vilkov, in AN SSSR, *Obshchestvenno neobkhodimye zatraty truda . . . ,* 1963, pp. 197–213, esp. pp. 210–211). Nevertheless, the official survey referred to earlier also found that "the procedure of reimbursing outlays on preparing and mastering production of new machinery out of a special fund insured a significant lowering of the price (*udeshevlenie*) of new products already in 1961 (on the average, according to the survey, by 14 percent)" (Stoliarov, *O tsenakh i tsenoobrazovanii v SSSR,* 1963, p. 170).

In a 1965 article, one of the two writers on investment quoted earlier, Kvasha, returned to the problem of the "unapparent (*neiavnyi*) rise in the investment price index" (in Venzher *et al., Proizvodstvo, nakoplenie, potreblenie,* 1965, pp. 121–123; the phrase quoted is from p. 121). He put the blame on two factors—multiple recosting (*pereosmechivanie*) of investment projects and increases in machinery prices. As to the first, there were evidently numerous cases of upward revision of estimate-price valuations on construction projects. Paradoxically, Kvasha also cites the findings of a survey relating to power projects that "on many sites an unfounded reduction in the estimate value of electric power stations is tolerated at the stage of working out and approving design targets." Presumably, although this is not made explicit, in the course of construction, estimate valuations have to be raised. (Some light is thrown on this phenomenon by Bukshtein in *Ekonomika stroitel'stva,* 1966, No. 8, pp. 53–54. According to him, design organizations are rewarded for lowering estimate costs and are not responsible for subsequent increases in estimate costs of the project due to faulty estimate costing in the design stage.) Kvasha provides no new information on the alleged inflation of machinery prices but refers again to the issue of new products and cites his and Krasovskii's 1964 estimate on the extent of the problem.

The other member of the team, Krasovskii, tackled the same problem, among others, in a book completed in early 1967 (*Problemy ekonomiki kapital'nykh vlozhenii,* 1967). Krasovskii also uses blunt terminology —for example, "mass phenomena of departure from constant 1955 prices" (p. 20), but gives the impression that the inflation affects construction as much if not more than equipment, and that in the former case the problem originates in the multiplicity of prices on local building materials (pp. 165–166). However, he also points to the longevity of "temporary" prices on new models and declares: "Facts show that in a number of branches of industry in recent years there is apparent an increase in the price (*udorozhanie*) of new machinery" (pp. 166–167).

If Kvasha and Krasovskii tend to stress price inflation, another recent reference takes a more evenhanded approach. Reporting to the Presidium of the Academy of Sciences (*Vestnik Akademii nauk SSSR,* 1967, No. 9, p. 13), Gatovskii declared that in many cases "prices of new equipment, owing to the imperfection of the price-setting system, are too low and do not insure normal profits to their producers." (We know, in fact, that operation below cost affected construction too, that some construction organizations were subsidized to cover costs over the level of estimate prices. See Efremov and Reinin, *Ekonomika stroitel'stva,* 1967, No. 12, p. 16.) Gatovskii also noted the contrary situation: "in other instances, prices reflecting high production cost of new products in the first years of their introduction [*osvoenie*—literally, "mastering"] sharply reduce the real effect of adopting new equipment."

Indeed, these two tendencies manifested themselves in the 1967 price reform. On one hand, a number of branches of machine building were considered to have swollen profit rates and therefore had their prices reduced, despite simultaneous increases in prices of a number of material inputs. Examples cited in this category are instruments, communications equipment, electrical machinery, and electronics; and these are obviously branches of the industry where qualitative change must be especially rapid. On the other hand, prices in a number of "metal-intensive" branches, especially tractors and agricultural machinery, were to be raised (*PKh,* 1967, No. 7, p. 17). The latter two branches, of course, are conspicuous for the slow pace of real product change.

From this and other evidence two conclusions may be drawn. (1) Temporary prices of new machinery models frequently were considerably higher than handbook prices of comparable older models which were used to draw up planned investment costs. (In addition to the sources cited, see also Allakhverdian, *VE,* 1965, No. 8, p. 83; Beliaev *et al., VE,* 1965, No. 11, p. 61; Shcherbitskii, in *Zasedaniia Verkhovnogo soveta SSSR . . . (7–9 dekabria 1965g),* 1966, p. 73.) By the nature of its construction, the MBMW wholesale price index is unlikely to reflect this development. (2) The increase in construction costs discussed by Soviet writers refers largely to the gap between plan and fulfillment—that is, to the continual underfulfillment of investment goals and cost reduction targets. For example, the claimed annual decreases in construction cost since 1958 have been 1 percent or less, whereas planned decreases are always considerably higher (*NKh 1964,* p. 540; see also Khachaturov, *VE,* 1963, No. 11, p. 31).

These inferences provide only a partial answer to the question of direct interest here: Does reported investment at estimate prices—which, as we have seen, are alleged to have changed only slightly after 1956, that change being a decrease in 1958–1959—reflect current price changes or do estimate prices approximate constant prices? If I read Kvasha and Krasovskii correctly, their answer appears to be, "neither." In addition to the excerpts from their work already cited, the following statements also seem relevant: "We are aware of price increases for many producers' goods but do not use indexes to convert to constant prices" (Krasovskii, *Problemy ekonomiki kapital'nykh vlozhenii,* 1967, p. 16; "we" is a general rather than a personal reference). On the other hand, Krasovskii estimates a considerable gap between a true current-price series and that in estimate prices: "It appears that until the introduction of new unitary valuations (*edinichnye rastsenki*) on the basis of 1967–1968 prices and for the period during which existing estimates will be recalculated, a temporary index of construction value in current prices of 1960–1965 (relative to 1955 constant prices) should be computed. One may presume that the magnitude of this index might be in the range 120–130. . . ." He acknowledges the crudity of the estimate but insists on the greater error involved in "naively relying on the stability and accuracy of 1955 estimate prices in force" (*ibid.*, p. 167). Such strictures to the contrary, both Kvasha and Krasovskii use the official data in contexts requiring constant-price series.

The evidence on this question is, in short, anything but conclusive. I am inclined to believe that for construction-installation and possibly "other investment" as well it may be safe to view estimate, current, and constant prices as virtually interchangeable in this period, at least for present purposes. We cannot be sure that the estimate-price values of equipment do not in fact constitute a current price series. There appears to be no reasonable basis for deflating the official data on investment in equipment, but in evaluating the calculated results (Chapter 6) I present some illustrative calculations to take account of possible investment price inflation in this period.

Collective farm investment. Little is known about price trends in collective farm construction. It is clear that a significant increase in the cost to farms of machinery and parts was instituted at the end of 1958: prices of machinery parts were raised 50–100 percent and prices of farm machines were also raised (above, p. 385). The increase was only partly reversed at the beginning of 1961 (Panin, *PKh,* 1964, No. 9, p. 76). One year later the government reduced prices to farms of construction materials, metals, and metal products, a reduction that allegedly saved the farms about 250 million rubles a year (MFI, *Problemy finansovogo planirovaniia,* 1963, p. 17). At the same time, however, some inflation also took place in the investment prices of new agricultural machinery (Gabrieli, *VE,* 1963, No. 7, pp. 59–61), and there was considerable grumbling in the Soviet press over the rising cost of capital repairs to farm machinery (for example, Pakhomov, *FinSSSR,* 1964, No. 10, p. 21; also Garbuzov, *FinSSSR,* 1965, No. 1, p. 13). On the basis of this information, the price index of collective farm investment in machinery, including capital repair of equipment, is assumed to have had the following pattern (1958 = 100):

1959	125	1962	110
1960	130	1963	113
1961	110	1964	116

The share of machinery investment (including equipment capital repair) in total gross investment excluding purchases of MTS machinery is estimated to have been 35 percent in 1958 and 1959 and 30 percent thereafter, based on published distributions of collective farm investment at current prices. (For 1958 and 1959, the sources are Koriunov, *Nedelimye fondy i kapital'nye vlozheniia kolkhozov,* 1960, p. 43, and VNIIESKH, *Povyshenie urovnia . . . ,* p. 91. Estimates for 1960 and 1961 derive from Alekseeva and Voronin, *Nakoplenie i razvitie kolkhoznoi sobstvennosti,* 1963, p. 105, while those for 1962–1964 are based on unpublished estimates by Sally Anderson. It is assumed that repairs to equipment in all years accounted for 70 percent of total capital repairs; this is the share reported for 1959.)

Earlier I suggested that outlays on livestock accounted for 15 percent of collective farm investment in 1958, 20 percent in 1959, and 25 percent thereafter (p. 502). These expenditures are deflated by a crude index of farm costs of producing a unit of livestock live weight (1958 = 100):

1959	100	1962	109
1960	108	1963	116
1961	100	1964	123

Livestock investment also takes place through purchases from the state, other collective farms, and households, but this aspect must be ignored because of the complete absence of information on the behavior of prices in these transactions.

[An index of collective farm livestock production costs is difficult to estimate because the available information refers to two different concepts and for generally different periods. One concept values collective farm labor at state farm wage rates and this type of cost data is virtually the only one available for years up to 1962. (Zverev, *Natsional'nyi dokhod i finansy SSSR,* 1961, p. 306; *NKh 1961,* p. 426; *NKh 1962,* pp. 333, 338–339). The second type values collective farm labor at actual distributions—cash and income in kind at retail prices—and relates mostly to 1962 and later (*NKh 1962,* pp. 338–339; *NKh 1964,* pp. 394–397). A link between the two types of data can be constructed from cost data of the second type supplied for 1958 and 1961 in *Ekon.gazeta,* February 9, 1963, p. 23, and for 1959–1962 by Studenkova, *Metodika ischisleniia sebestoimosti . . . ,* 1965, pp. 103–104. The Studenkova and *Ekon.gazeta* data enable us to compute a cost index for cattle for 1958–1962 (the latter providing 1958 and 1962 benchmarks, with intervening years filled in from the former source) and index numbers for hogs and sheep in 1961 on a 1958 base. Index numbers for hogs and sheep in 1960 are obtained by applying percentage changes in 1961, as given in *NKh 1961,* p. 426, to the 1961 index number. The actual costs for 1962, reported in *NKh 1962*, pp. 338–339 are then linked to the *Ekon.gazeta* data for 1961. Finally, 1964 entries are computed from the percentage change between 1962 and 1964, based on *NKh 1964,* pp. 396–397, applied to the 1958 index numbers. The results are as follows (1958 = 100):

	Index of Costs per kg of		
	Cattle	*Hogs*	*Sheep*
1959	92.8	..	..
1960	100.2	100.5	132.0
1961	92.7	94.2	120.7
1962	103.3	99.9	132.6
1963	..	..	..
1964	114.9	109.0	157.7

To average indexes for individual products I assume weights of 3:1 for cattle and hogs relative to sheep. In the absence of data for hogs and sheep in 1959, the index of farm costs is assumed unchanged in 1959 from the 1958 level. The index number for 1963 is interpolated between those for 1962 and 1964.]

Other components of collective farm investment are not deflated for lack of information on price trends.

State-cooperative sector inventory investment. See Appendix L.

Collective farm inventory investment. The appropriate deflator would combine an index of prices paid by farms for materials and parts with an index of costs of products produced on the farm. Prices of parts rose sharply in 1959 and were reduced in 1961, when prices of machinery and fuel were also reduced (above, p. 385, and Koroviakovskii, *Sovershenstvovanie sistemy gosudarstvennykh zagotovok . . . ,* 1963, p. 124). Additional price reductions took place in 1962 (above, p. 521). Collective farms are also supplied by the state retail market, where the overall level of prices declined slightly until 1961 and then rose by 2 percent in 1962 and 1 percent in 1963. Whether this trend also characterized farm purchases is not clear. Producers' goods are absent from the list of commodities for which individual price indexes have been published; the sole possible exception is kerosene, which is largely purchased for consumption. In any case, the average price of kerosene was the same in 1959 as in 1958, declined 4 percent in 1960, and remained at that level in 1961–1964 (*NKh 1962,* p. 532; *NKh 1963,* p. 540; *NKh 1964,* p. 647). Costs of production for livestock, as indicated, rose in 1960, dropped in 1961 and rose steadily thereafter. Farm reports suggest that immature livestock are a relatively significant part of collective farm inventories (*SNIP 1958–1962,* Part II, p. 190).

On balance, these fragmentary indications suggest some rise in prices and costs in 1959–1960, a decline in 1961 and increases thereafter. I hazard the following pattern (1958 = 100):

1959	103	1962	105
1960	105	1963	107
1961	100	1964	110

Internal security and defense. Military pay and subsistence values need not be deflated because they represent the product of estimated force levels and a constant level of pay and subsistence per man. The absence of information on price trends in the military sector and the crudity of my estimates of internal security preclude deflation of outlays on other than military personnel.

Outlays n.e.c.; statistical discrepancy. The deflator used is that implied by comparison of all other state-cooperative final outlays at both current and 1958 or 1964 prices. Among these outlays are communal services which include expenditures by collective farms, but no attempt is made to separate out the collective farm portion.

GNP at Constant Prices

Tables K-1 and K-2 present the values of GNP by use at 1958 and 1964 prices, obtained on the basis of procedures described in the previous section. Values at 1958 and 1964 factor cost, $\sum_u V_{58}Q_i$ and $\sum_u V_{64}Q_i$, are computed as, respectively

$$\sum_u V_{58}Q_{58}\frac{\sum_u P_{58}Q_i}{\sum_u P_{58}Q_{58}}$$

$$\sum_u V_{64}Q_{64}\frac{\sum_u P_{64}Q_i}{\sum_u P_{64}Q_{64}}\ .$$

That is, for any use category, *u*, of national output in year *i*, 1958–1964, an AFC value at 1958 (1964) prices is obtained as the product of the AFC value in 1958 (1964) multiplied by the quantity index of *u* at 1958 (1964) established prices. The indexes are computed from columns 1–7 of Tables K-1 and K-2; 1958 and 1964 factor cost values are taken or computed from Tables J-1, J-2, J-4, and J-5.

Table K-3, showing end-use indexes at 1964 prices, is computed from Table K-2 and represents the 1964 price counterpart of Table 18.

Constant AFC values are computed in Table K-4 by the alternative Method II:

$$\sum_u V_i Q_i \frac{\sum_u P_{58} Q_i}{\sum_u P_i Q_i}$$

$$\sum_u V_i Q_i \frac{\sum P_{64} Q_i}{\sum_u P_i Q_i}.$$

The rationale of these alternative calculations is developed on pp. 136–138.

TABLE K-1

GNP BY USE AT 1958 ESTABLISHED PRICES AND ADJUSTED FACTOR COST, 1958–1964
(billion rubles)

	Values at 1958 EP							Values at 1958 AFC						
	1958	1959	1960	1961	1962	1963	1964	1958	1959	1960	1961	1962	1963	1964
	(1)	(2)	(3)	(4)	(5)	(6)	(7)	(8)	(9)	(10)	(11)	(12)	(13)	(14)
1. Retail sales														
A. State-cooperative trade	60.33	64.92	72.13	75.03	80.20	84.29	88.18	41.37	44.52	49.46	51.45	55.00	57.80	60.47
B. Extravillage farm markets	4.43	4.79	4.35	4.54	4.15	3.93	3.73	3.01	3.25	2.96	3.08	2.82	2.67	2.53
C. Total	64.76	69.71	76.48	79.57	84.35	88.22	91.91	44.38	47.77	52.42	54.53	57.82	60.47	63.00
2. Consumer services														
A. Housing	1.71	1.80	1.89	1.97	2.06	2.14	2.22	1.99	2.09	2.20	2.29	2.40	2.49	2.58
B. Dues	.91	.93	.99	1.04	1.07	1.12	1.17	.91	.93	.99	1.04	1.07	1.12	1.17
C. Other services	6.58	7.09	7.65	8.48	9.36	10.06	10.88	5.92	6.38	6.88	7.63	8.42	9.05	9.79
D. Total	9.20	9.82	10.53	11.49	12.49	13.32	14.27	8.82	9.40	10.07	10.96	11.89	12.66	13.54
3. Consumption in kind														
A. Farm income in kind	9.92	9.76	9.38	9.39	8.60	8.32	8.58	9.92	9.76	9.38	9.39	8.60	8.32	8.58
B. Nonfarm wages in kind	.50	.55	.60	.65	.70	.75	.80	.34	.37	.41	.44	.48	.51	.54
C. Military subsistence	1.51	1.45	1.38	1.31	1.47	1.36	1.24	1.72	1.65	1.57	1.49	1.67	1.56	1.41
D. Total	11.93	11.76	11.36	11.35	10.77	10.43	10.62	11.98	11.78	11.36	11.32	10.75	10.39	10.53
4. Other outlays for consumption	3.00	3.10	2.51	2.02	2.97	3.29	3.35	3.00	3.10	2.51	2.02	2.97	3.29	3.35
5. Total outlays for consumption	88.89	94.39	100.88	104.43	110.58	115.26	120.15	68.18	72.05	76.36	78.83	83.43	86.81	90.42
6. Communal services	10.53	11.36	12.21	12.99	13.35	14.55	15.45	9.64	10.40	11.18	11.89	12.22	13.32	14.14
7. Administration	1.20	1.11	1.08	1.04	1.03	1.00	1.00	1.15	1.06	1.04	1.00	.99	.96	.96

TABLE K-1 (continued)

	Values at 1958 EP							Values at 1958 AFC						
	1958	1959	1960	1961	1962	1963	1964	1958	1959	1960	1961	1962	1963	1964
	(1)	(2)	(3)	(4)	(5)	(6)	(7)	(8)	(9)	(10)	(11)	(12)	(13)	(14)
8. Gross investment														
A. Fixed capital														
(1) Households														
(a) Farm investment in kind	.65	.50	.72	.72	.36	−.72	.36	.65	.50	.72	.72	.36	−.72	.36
(b) Private housing	2.65	3.05	2.74	2.37	2.07	1.79	1.66	2.33	2.68	2.41	2.08	1.82	1.57	1.46
(c) Total	3.30	3.55	3.46	3.09	2.43	1.07	2.02	2.98	3.18	3.13	2.80	2.18	.85	1.82
(2) State-cooperative	30.35	33.63	37.75	40.51	43.11	46.72	50.66	30.58	33.88	38.04	40.82	43.44	47.07	51.04
(3) Collective farm														
(a) Livestock	.46	.67	.74	.80	.79	.73	.73	.46	.67	.74	.80	.79	.73	.73
(b) Other	2.58	2.43	2.18	2.31	2.48	2.42	2.55	2.32	2.19	1.96	2.08	2.23	2.18	2.29
(c) Total	3.04	3.10	2.92	3.11	3.27	3.15	3.28	2.78	2.86	2.70	2.88	3.02	2.91	3.02
(4) Total	36.69	40.28	44.13	46.71	48.81	50.94	55.96	36.34	39.92	43.87	46.50	48.64	50.83	55.88
B. Inventories														
(1) State-cooperative	7.50	9.05	4.38	5.50	5.03	7.29	10.19	6.59	7.95	3.85	4.83	4.42	6.41	8.95
(2) Collective farms	.40	.32	.28	.37	.43	.46	.50	.48	.38	.34	.44	.52	.55	.60
(3) Total	7.90	9.37	4.66	5.87	5.46	7.75	10.69	7.07	8.33	4.19	5.27	4.94	6.96	9.55
C. Total	44.59	49.65	48.79	52.58	54.27	58.69	66.65	43.41	48.25	48.06	51.77	53.58	57.79	65.43
9. Research and development	2.06	2.34	2.55	2.90	3.26	3.71	4.04	2.19	2.49	2.71	3.08	3.47	3.94	4.29
10. Internal security	1.50	1.50	1.50	1.50	1.50	1.50	1.50	1.62	1.62	1.62	1.62	1.62	1.62	1.62
11. Defense														
A. Pay and subsistence	4.11	3.95	3.77	3.57	4.00	3.70	3.38	4.32	4.15	3.96	3.75	4.20	3.89	3.55
B. Other	4.95	5.12	5.23	7.72	8.34	9.87	9.60	4.99	5.16	5.27	7.78	8.41	9.95	9.68
C. Total	9.06	9.07	9.00	11.29	12.34	13.57	12.98	9.31	9.31	9.23	11.53	12.61	13.84	13.23
12. Outlays n.e.c.; public sector statistical discrepancy	.23	2.17	5.59	.30	2.41	1.41	1.07	.33	3.11	8.02	.43	3.46	2.02	1.54
GNP	158.06	171.59	181.60	187.03	198.74	209.69	222.84	135.83	148.29	158.22	160.15	171.38	180.30	191.63

Sources:
See the text of this appendix.

TABLE K-2

GNP BY USE AT 1964 ESTABLISHED PRICES AND ADJUSTED FACTOR COST, 1958–1964
(billion rubles)

	Values at 1964 EP							Values at 1964 AFC						
	1958	1959	1960	1961	1962	1963	1964	1958	1959	1960	1961	1962	1963	1964
	(1)	(2)	(3)	(4)	(5)	(6)	(7)	(8)	(9)	(10)	(11)	(12)	(13)	(14)
1. Retail sales														
A. State-cooperative trade	60.33	64.92	72.13	75.03	80.20	84.29	88.18	45.50	48.97	54.40	56.59	60.49	63.58	66.51
B. Extravillage farm markets	5.35	5.74	5.25	5.45	4.96	4.63	4.42	3.55	3.81	3.48	3.61	3.29	3.07	2.93
C. Total	65.68	70.66	77.38	80.48	85.16	88.92	92.60	49.05	52.78	57.88	60.20	63.78	66.65	69.44
2. Consumer services														
A. Housing	1.71	1.80	1.89	1.97	2.06	2.14	2.22	2.04	2.15	2.26	2.35	2.46	2.55	2.65
B. Dues	1.05	1.07	1.15	1.21	1.24	1.30	1.35	1.05	1.07	1.15	1.21	1.24	1.30	1.35
C. Other services	6.58	7.09	7.65	8.48	9.36	10.06	10.88	5.87	6.32	6.82	7.56	8.34	8.97	9.70
D. Total	9.34	9.96	10.69	11.66	12.66	13.50	14.45	8.96	9.54	10.23	11.12	12.04	12.82	13.70
3. Consumption in kind														
A. Farm income in kind	11.34	11.17	10.64	10.71	9.76	9.46	9.67	11.34	11.17	10.64	10.71	9.76	9.46	9.67
B. Nonfarm wages in kind	.50	.55	.60	.65	.70	.75	.80	.38	.42	.46	.50	.53	.57	.61
C. Military subsistence	1.51	1.45	1.38	1.31	1.47	1.36	1.24	1.63	1.57	1.49	1.42	1.59	1.47	1.34
D. Total	13.35	13.17	12.62	12.67	11.93	11.57	11.71	13.35	13.16	12.59	12.63	11.88	11.50	11.62
4. Other outlays for consumption	3.58	3.70	2.99	2.42	3.55	3.92	4.00	3.58	3.70	2.99	2.42	3.55	3.92	4.00
5. Total outlays for consumption	91.95	97.49	103.68	107.23	113.30	117.91	122.76	74.94	79.18	83.69	86.37	91.25	94.89	98.76
6. Communal services	11.50	12.40	13.33	14.17	14.56	15.86	16.83	10.45	11.27	12.12	12.88	13.24	14.42	15.30
7. Administration	1.33	1.24	1.19	1.15	1.14	1.11	1.11	1.28	1.20	1.15	1.11	1.10	1.07	1.07

TABLE K-2 (continued)

	Values at 1964 EP							Values at 1964 AFC						
	1958	1959	1960	1961	1962	1963	1964	1958	1959	1960	1961	1962	1963	1964
	(1)	(2)	(3)	(4)	(5)	(6)	(7)	(8)	(9)	(10)	(11)	(12)	(13)	(14)
8. Gross investment														
A. Fixed capital														
(1) Households														
(a) Farm investment in kind	.80	.62	.89	.89	.45	−.89	.45	.80	.62	.89	.89	.45	−.89	.45
(b) Private housing	2.65	3.05	2.74	2.37	2.07	1.79	1.66	2.41	2.77	2.49	2.16	1.88	1.63	1.51
(c) Total	3.45	3.67	3.63	3.26	2.52	.90	2.11	3.21	3.39	3.38	3.05	2.33	.74	1.96
(2) State-cooperative	30.81	34.10	38.27	41.05	43.70	47.41	51.40	30.99	34.30	38.49	41.29	43.95	47.69	51.70
(3) Collective farm														
(a) Livestock	.57	.82	.91	.98	.97	.90	.90	.57	.82	.91	.98	.97	.90	.90
(b) Other	2.75	2.58	2.30	2.45	2.63	2.57	2.70	2.62	2.46	2.19	2.33	2.50	2.45	2.57
(c) Total	3.32	3.40	3.21	3.43	3.60	3.47	3.60	3.19	3.28	3.10	3.31	3.47	3.35	3.47
(4) Total	37.58	41.17	45.11	47.74	49.82	51.78	57.11	37.39	40.97	44.97	47.65	49.75	51.78	57.13
B. Inventories														
(1) State-cooperative	8.00	9.66	4.71	5.98	5.33	7.44	11.08	6.85	8.27	4.03	5.12	4.57	6.37	9.49
(2) Collective farms	.44	.35	.30	.41	.47	.50	.55	.51	.41	.35	.48	.55	.58	.64
(3) Total	8.44	10.01	5.01	6.39	5.80	7.94	11.63	7.36	8.68	4.38	5.60	5.12	6.95	10.13
C. Total	46.02	51.18	50.12	54.13	55.62	59.72	68.74	44.75	49.65	49.35	53.25	54.87	58.73	67.26
9. Research and development	2.14	2.43	2.65	3.02	3.39	3.86	4.20	2.20	2.49	2.72	3.10	3.48	3.96	4.31
10. Internal security	1.50	1.50	1.50	1.50	1.50	1.50	1.50	1.56	1.56	1.56	1.56	1.56	1.56	1.56
11. Defense														
A. Pay and subsistence	4.11	3.95	3.77	3.57	4.00	3.70	3.38	4.23	4.07	3.88	3.68	4.12	3.81	3.48
B. Other	4.95	5.12	5.23	7.72	8.34	9.87	9.60	4.98	5.15	5.26	7.77	8.39	9.93	9.66
C. Total	9.06	9.07	9.00	11.29	12.34	13.57	12.98	9.21	9.22	9.14	11.45	12.51	13.74	13.14
12. Outlays n.e.c.; public sector statistical discrepancy	.24	2.24	5.77	.31	2.48	1.45	1.11	.31	2.87	7.38	.40	3.17	1.85	1.42
GNP	163.74	177.55	187.24	192.80	204.33	214.98	229.23	144.70	157.44	167.11	170.12	181.18	190.22	202.82

Sources:
See the text of this appendix.

TABLE K-3

INDEXES OF FINAL USE OF GNP AT 1964 PRICES—ESTABLISHED PRICES AND BASIC ADJUSTED FACTOR COST, 1959–1964

(1958 = 100)

	1964 EP						1964 AFC					
	1959	1960	1961	1962	1963	1964	1959	1960	1961	1962	1963	1964
1. Retail sales												
A. State-cooperative trade	108	120	124	133	140	146						
B. Extravillage farm markets	107	98	102	93	87	83						
C. Total	108	118	123	130	135	141	108	118	123	130	136	142
2. Consumer services												
A. Housing	105	111	115	120	125	130						
B. Dues	102	110	115	118	124	129						
C. Other services	108	116	129	142	153	165						
D. Total	107	114	125	136	145	155	106	114	124	134	143	153
3. Consumption in kind												
A. Farm income in kind	99	94	94	86	83	85						
B. Nonfarm wages in kind	110	120	130	140	150	160						
C. Military subsistence	96	91	87	97	90	82						
D. Total	99	95	95	89	87	88	99	94	95	89	86	87
4. Other outlays for consumption	103	84	68	99	110	112						
5. Total consumption	106	113	117	123	128	134	106	112	115	122	127	132
6. Communal services	108	116	123	127	138	146						
7. Administration	93	89	86	86	83	83						

TABLE K-3 (continued)

	1964 EP						1964 AFC					
	1959	1960	1961	1962	1963	1964	1959	1960	1961	1962	1963	1964
8. Gross fixed investment												
A. Households	106	105	94	73	26	61	106	105	95	73	23	61
B. State-cooperative	111	124	133	142	154	167						
C. Collective farms	102	97	103	108	105	108	103	97	104	109	105	109
D. Total	110	120	127	133	138	152	110	120	127	133	138	153
9. Inventory investment												
A. State-cooperative	121	59	75	67	93	139						
B. Collective farms	80	68	93	107	114	125						
C. Total	119	59	76	69	94	138	118	60	76	70	94	138
10. Total gross investment	111	109	118	121	130	149	111	110	119	123	131	150
11. R&D	114	124	141	158	180	196						
12. Internal security	100	100	100	100	100	100						
13. Defense	100	99	125	136	150	143	100	99	124	136	149	143
14. Outlays n.e.c.; public sector statistical discrepancy	933	2404	129	1033	604	463						
GNP	108	114	118	125	131	140	109	115	118	125	131	140

Source:
Table K-2. Omitted index numbers at 1964 AFC are by definition identical to corresponding index numbers at 1964 EP.

TABLE K-4

GNP BY USE AT 1958 AND 1964 AFC, 1958–1964, COMPUTED BY METHOD II
(billion rubles)

	1958 AFC							1964 AFC						
	1958	1959	1960	1961	1962	1963	1964	1958	1959	1960	1961	1962	1963	1964
1. Retail sales														
A. State-cooperative trade	41.37	45.68	51.99	55.06	59.62	63.58	66.51	41.37	45.68	51.99	55.06	59.62	63.58	66.51
B. Extravillage farm markets	3.01	3.31	3.08	3.16	2.89	2.69	2.48	3.64	3.98	3.71	3.79	3.45	3.16	2.93
C. Total	44.38	48.99	55.07	58.22	62.51	66.27	68.99	45.01	49.66	55.70	58.85	63.07	66.74	69.44
2. Consumer services	8.82	9.38	10.08	11.01	11.92	12.61	13.52	8.96	9.52	10.24	11.18	12.14	12.81	13.70
3. Consumption in kind	11.98	11.77	11.35	11.30	10.74	10.40	10.53	13.40	13.18	12.61	12.62	11.90	11.54	11.62
4. Other outlays for consumption	3.00	3.10	2.51	2.02	2.97	3.29	3.35	3.58	3.70	2.99	2.42	3.55	3.92	4.00
5. Total outlays for consumption	68.18	73.24	79.01	82.55	88.14	92.57	96.39	70.92	76.06	81.54	85.07	90.66	95.01	98.76
6. Communal services	9.64	10.34	11.12	11.76	12.09	13.15	13.92	10.61	11.38	12.24	12.94	13.30	14.46	15.30
7. Administration	1.15	1.07	1.04	1.00	.99	.96	.96	1.28	1.20	1.15	1.11	1.10	1.07	1.07
8. Gross investment														
A. Fixed capital														
(1) Households	2.98	3.23	3.18	2.87	2.23	.90	1.87	3.13	3.35	3.35	3.04	2.32	.73	1.96
(2) State-cooperative	30.58	34.25	38.31	41.01	43.52	46.98	50.96	31.04	34.72	38.83	41.55	44.11	47.67	51.70
(3) Collective farm	2.78	2.88	2.72	3.02	3.15	3.04	3.19	3.04	3.16	3.00	3.33	3.47	3.35	3.47
(4) Total	36.34	40.36	44.21	46.90	48.90	50.92	56.02	37.21	41.23	45.18	47.92	49.90	51.75	57.13

TABLE K-4 (continued)

	1958 AFC							1964 AFC						
	1958	1959	1960	1961	1962	1963	1964	1958	1959	1960	1961	1962	1963	1964
B. Inventories														
(1) State-cooperative	6.59	7.74	4.26	5.09	4.74	6.91	8.67	6.92	8.24	4.61	5.63	5.04	7.07	9.49
(2) Collective farm	.48	.32	.25	.48	.45	.51	.58	.53	.35	.27	.53	.49	.57	.64
(3) Total	7.07	8.06	4.51	5.57	5.19	7.42	9.25	7.45	8.59	4.88	6.16	5.53	7.64	10.13
C. Total	43.41	48.42	48.72	52.47	54.09	58.34	65.27	44.66	49.82	50.06	54.08	55.43	59.39	67.26
9. Research and development	2.19	2.33	2.48	3.22	3.34	3.77	4.15	2.27	2.44	2.58	3.34	3.37	3.92	4.31
10. Internal security	1.62	1.55	1.50	1.62	1.53	1.56	1.56	1.62	1.55	1.50	1.62	1.53	1.56	1.56
11. Defense	9.31	9.33	9.23	11.50	12.56	13.78	13.14	9.31	9.33	9.23	11.50	12.56	13.78	13.17
12. Outlays n.e.c.; public sector statistical discrepancy	.33	2.64	6.05	.43	2.84	1.78	1.37	.33	2.72	6.24	.44	2.92	1.82	1.42
GNP	135.83	148.92	159.15	164.55	175.58	185.91	196.76	141.00	154.50	164.54	170.10	180.87	191.01	202.82

Sources:

In general, the values in this table were obtained by deflating current AFC values (from Table J-1 directly, or from Tables J-2, J-4, and J-5) by the deflators discussed in the text of this appendix. Certain special situations are described more fully below.

3. *Consumption in kind.* Since there are no factor cost adjustments to EP values of farm income in kind, values of the latter are taken directly from Tables K-1 and K-2.

8.A. *Gross investment in fixed capital.*

(1) *Households.* Livestock investment also is not subject to factor cost adjustment, hence values are computed from p. 304. AFC values of private housing construction are derived by tracing through Tables J-2, J-4, J-5.

(2) *State-cooperative.* The deflation proceeds as follows:

(a) At current prices capital repairs account for 19.21, 18.39, 18.32, 18.42, 19.06, 21.06 and 21.21 percent, respectively, in the years 1958–1964 of all state-cooperative fixed investment (p. 387). It is assumed that these are also the shares of subsidies incident on state-cooperative fixed investment which can be assigned to capital repairs. The wage component of capital repairs is deflated as described on p. 513. Materials costs at current prices are augmented by subsidies in the manner described and diminished by turnover taxes, computed as 5 percent of all capital repairs at current EP (that is, at the same rate as for all state-cooperative investment—Table J-2).

(b) AFC values of state-cooperative fixed investment other than capital repairs are obtained by deducting turnover tax at the rate of 5 percent and adding the remainder of subsidies incident on this category.

(c) Thus, the values of the various components may be shown as follows (billion rubles):

TABLE K-4 (continued)

	Capital Repairs							
	Wages		Materials	Total		Other	Total	
	1958 AFC	*1964 AFC*	*1958 and 1964 AFC*	*1958 AFC*	*1964 AFC*	*1958 and 1964 AFC*	*1958 AFC*	*1964 AFC*
1958	2.92	3.38	2.96	5.88	6.34	24.70	30.58	31.04
1959	3.02	3.49	3.21	6.23	6.70	28.02	34.25	34.72
1960	3.30	3.82	3.57	6.87	7.39	31.44	38.31	38.83
1961	3.49	4.03	3.84	7.33	7.87	33.68	41.01	41.55
1962	3.76	4.35	4.22	7.98	8.57	35.54	43.52	44.11
1963	4.40	5.09	5.03	9.43	10.12	37.55	46.98	47.67
1964	4.71	5.45	5.51	10.22	10.96	40.74	50.96	51.70

(3) *Collective farms.* Current values of livestock investment, which is not subject to factor cost adjustment, are taken from Tables K-1 and K-2. "Other investment" is allocated between machinery and a residual in the proportions implied on p. 521, and current AFC values of "other investment" are distributed among the two components in the indicated proportions. The machinery investment deflator is that shown on p. 521; the residual component is not deflated. The values of the various components are as follows (billion rubles):

	Livestock		Machinery		Residual		Total	
	1958 AFC	*1964 AFC*	*1958 AFC*	*1964 AFC*	*1958 AFC*	*1964 AFC*	*1958 AFC*	*1964 AFC*
1958	.46	.57	.96	1.11	1.36	1.36	2.78	3.04
1959	.67	.82	.85	.98	1.36	1.36	2.88	3.16
1960	.74	.91	.67	.78	1.31	1.31	2.72	3.00
1961	.80	.98	.84	.97	1.38	1.38	3.02	3.33
1962	.79	.97	.89	1.03	1.47	1.47	3.15	3.47
1963	.73	.90	.86	1.00	1.45	1.45	3.04	3.35
1964	.73	.90	.66	.77	1.80	1.80	3.19	3.47

B. *Inventories.*

(1) *State-cooperative.* The deflation proceeds separately for goods shipped and finished goods in trade and procurement on one hand, and the remainder on the other. Current AFC values for the two categories are obtained by tracing through Tables J-2, J-4, J-5 and are then deflated by the EP ratios of values at constant prices to those at current prices, computed from Tables L-3 and L-4. The results are as follows (billion rubles):

	Goods shipped, etc.		Other inventories		Total	
	1958 AFC	*1964 AFC*	*1958 AFC*	*1964 AFC*	*1958 AFC*	*1964 AFC*
1958	2.06	(2.16)	4.53	(4.76)	6.59	6.92
1959	3.28	3.54	4.46	4.70	7.74	8.24
1960	.46	.44	3.80	4.17	4.26	4.61
1961	1.23	1.29	3.86	4.34	5.09	5.63
1962	.97	.97	3.77	4.07	4.74	5.04
1963	1.23	1.18	5.68	5.89	6.91	7.07
1964	4.74	4.99	3.93	4.50	8.67	9.49

Values for 1958 at 1964 prices enclosed within parentheses were computed by inflating current price AFC values by 5 percent. Such a procedure is necessary because 1958 state-cooperative inventory investment at 1964 prices had to be estimated independently (see p. 540). The 5 percent inflator was assumed after comparing constant current price ratios for the two categories in 1959 and 1961. The computed ratios are as follows:

	1959	*1961*
Goods shipped, etc.	1.086	1.065
Other	1.039	1.062

12. *Outlays n.e.c.; etc.* The deflation procedure is the same as that stated on p. 524.

L

The Deflation of State-Cooperative Inventory Investment

The first step in the procedure is to distribute end-year inventories at current prices by branch and, to some extent, by type (Table L-1). The next task is to compute annual increments at average prices of the given year. The price indexes required for this purpose and for revaluation of the resulting increments at constant prices are shown in the "A" entries in Table L-2. They are derived as follows:

(1) Where broken out, stocks of fuel are deflated by an index representing a simple average of official wholesale price indexes inclusive of turnover tax for coal and petroleum refining. (The official wholesale price indexes to which reference is made in this appendix are found in *NKh 1963*, pp. 136–137, Stoliarov, *O tsenakh i tsenoobrazovanii v SSSR,* 1963, pp. 111–112, and *NKh 1965,* pp. 166–167. Index numbers for coal in 1959 and 1961 have not been reported but are assumed unchanged from the 1958 and 1960 levels.) On a 1958 base, the reported and synthetic indexes are as follows:

	1958	*1959*	*1960*	*1961*	*1962*	*1963*	*1964*	*1965*
Coal	100	100	100	100	100	100	100	100
Petroleum refining	100	110	110	92	92	92	92	92
Fuels	100	105	105	96	96	96	96	96

(2) Goods shipped and other inventories in industry are deflated by the official wholesale price index for all industry. In this case, the appropriate indexes seem to be those excluding the turnover tax.

(3) Inventories in construction, other inventories in transport-com-

munication, all inventories in supply and sales, and other inventories in trade and procurement, are deflated by the official wholesale price index for heavy industry, again net of the tax.

(4) Goods shipped in state agriculture are deflated by a crudely estimated index of state farm delivery prices (1958 = 100): 1959, 100; 1960, 100; 1961, 110; 1962, 113; 1963, 118; 1964, 120; 1965, 144.

It is clear that prices paid state farms were raised in 1961–1962 (pp. 328–330) but no price indexes have been published and the movement of prices before that date is uncertain. Data supplied in a Soviet secondary source on state farm gross output per hectare at current and at 1958 prices imply a 20 percent decline in the prices underlying gross output in 1959 and increases of one percent in 1960, 12 percent in 1961, and 9 percent in 1962 (Studenkova, *Metodika ischisleniia . . .* , 1965, pp. 118–119). It is difficult to believe that so sharp a decline occurred in 1959, and in the absence of further information, the price level is assumed constant from 1958 through 1960. The estimated 10 percent increase in 1961 was instituted at the beginning of the year, while a further 5 percentage point rise is assumed to have occurred in June 1962.

In 1963 purchase and delivery prices of cotton, sugar beets, and potatoes were raised; increases set for purchase prices of beans may apply to delivery prices as well. The increase in cotton delivery prices was 12 percent and the increase in both purchase and delivery prices of sugar beets was 18 percent (*Zakupki sel'skokhoziaistvennykh produktov,* 1963, No. 4, p. 3; 1963, No. 5, p. 10; 1963, No. 10, p. 26; 1963, No. 11, p. 24). There were no changes in purchase prices of sugar beets, potatoes, cotton, and tobacco after 1963 (Belousov and Petrakov, *VE,* 1965, No. 11, p. 146); presumably, this is also true of delivery prices of these products. With 1952 = 100, the index of purchase prices in 1964 stood at over 350, according to Gumerov (*FinSSSR,* 1965, No. 8, p. 7). Given the 1962 index number of 332 cited by Stoliarov (*O tsenakh i tsenoobrazovanii v SSSR,* 1963, p. 106), Gumerov's figure implies an increase of about 6 percent in 1963–1964, most of which must have occurred in 1963. I assume that this description of purchase price changes is applicable to delivery prices as well.

A variety of changes in both purchase and delivery prices occurred in 1965. Unfortunately, these changes are too complex to be easily summarized and the reader must be referred to the sources cited for a more comprehensive review. In December 1964, prices of milk and cream were raised effective 1 January 1965 and further changes in these prices were introduced in the first quarter of 1965 (Karcz, *Soviet Studies,* October 1965, pp. 135–137). The March 1965 reform raised other prices as follows (Bush, in *New Directions in the Soviet Economy,* 1966, pp. 456–461):

Purchase prices of wheat and rye by 12 and 23 percent, respectively;

Delivery prices of wheat and rye by 25 and 32 percent, respectively;

Purchase and delivery prices of buckwheat by 50 percent, millet by 38 percent, rice by 36 percent, barley and oats by from 20 to 100 percent;

Purchase and delivery prices of cattle by 36 percent, hogs 32 percent, sheep and goats 33 percent;

Delivery prices of sunflower seed by from 129 to 221 percent.

The higher milk prices required budgetary subsidies in 1965 of 720 million rubles (*ibid.* p. 460). Given my estimate of the value of 1964 procurements of milk from all sources, about 4 billion rubles (Table A-1, part E), the overall price increase implied is 18 percent. The average increase for state farms has been reported as 19 percent, so we may assume a 17 percent increase in milk purchase prices. The various grain price increases are estimated to have averaged 25 percent for purchase prices and 35 percent for delivery prices. The average increase of purchase and delivery prices of livestock is estimated as 34 percent.

Using the value of 1964 sales to the state by collective farms and households (*NKh 1964,* p. 257) as weights, I estimate the average increase in all purchase prices as 15 percent. Similar value data for state farm deliveries are lacking: I assume an average increase of 20 percent, on the grounds that the price increases are generally higher for state farms and the products whose prices were raised are relatively more important in deliveries than in purchases.

(5) For the deflation of inventories of agricultural goods an index of state farm costs has been estimated. The index numbers for 1959–1962 are derived from data on state farm production outlays at current prices per ruble of gross output at constant prices (Studenkova, *Metodika ischisleniia sebestoimosti . . . ,* 1965, p. 118). These data show cost increases of 6.6 percent in 1960, 8.6 percent in 1961, and 9.1 percent in 1962, and seem consistent with other information on state farm productivity and costs (*Ekon.gazeta,* February 9, 1963, p. 23; Maniakin, *ESKh,* 1965, No. 2, p. 10). It is assumed that costs rose 5 percent in 1959, although in view of the sharp increase in prices of parts and

machinery at the end of 1958 (p. 385) the rise may have been steeper.

For 1963 and 1964 a 15 percent increase followed by a 6 percent decline in costs is assumed on the following evidence:

(a) For the two years together a net increase in costs of 6 percent is implied by a calculation of the average change in costs of producing 5 crop products (grain, cotton, sugar beets, potatoes, vegetables) and 5 livestock products (cattle, hogs, milk, eggs, wool).

[The 1962 data are taken from Studenkova, *Metodika ischisleniia sebestoimosti . . . ,* 1965, p. 103, and Maniakin, *ESKh,* 1965, No. 2, p. 10; the 1964 data are from *NKh 1964,* pp. 412–413. As weights in the calculation I employ state farm output in 1964 (*NKh 1965*, pp. 262, 264–265). Since state farm output of meat is not broken down by type, I compute outlays on meat output by assuming a 1964 unit cost of producing all meat of 800 rubles per ton of live weight, compared with the average delivery price of 750 rubles (Table A-2, part D). The average cost of producing a weight unit of large cattle increased 16 percent and that of hogs declined by 1 percent. I assume an average increase for all meat of 10 percent and thereby derive an average 1962 cost of 725 rubles per ton. Reported meat output in terms of slaughter weight is converted to a live weight measure using a coefficient of 1.6, derived from comparison of data in both units shown in *NKh 1960,* p. 378.]

(b) The two year cost change can be distributed between 1963 and 1964 for three livestock products as follows (Maniakin, *ESKh,* 1965, No. 2, p. 10):

	Cattle	*Hogs*	*Milk*
1963	+14	+19	+7
1964	+2	−16	+6

On the basis of the outlay structure implied in the calculation described under (a), the average increase in cost of livestock products is roughly estimated as 12 percent in 1963 and no change in 1964.

(c) Labor productivity on state farms increased 9 percent in the two years as a whole, declining 10 percent in 1963 and increasing 22 percent in 1964 (*NKh 1964,* p. 73).

State farm average costs in 1965 are estimated to have increased by 10 percent. A calculation of outlays parallel to that described under (a) above (using cost data from *NKh 1965,* pp. 428–429) implies an average increase of 11 percent. Labor productivity on state farms declined 8 percent in 1965 (*NKh 1965,* p. 71).

(6) Prices of parts held in state agricultural inventories are assumed

to have risen 50 percent at the beginning of 1959, remaining at that level until the beginning of 1961 when they were cut to 10 percent above the 1958 base (above, p. 521).

(7) Other nonagricultural inventories in agriculture are not deflated. A conceivable deflator is the wholesale price index of heavy industry, inclusive of tax, but this index is heavily influenced by changes in the subindex for petroleum refining. Other subindexes show little or no change.

(8) Goods shipped and finished goods in trade are deflated by the official wholesale price index, inclusive of turnover tax, for light and food industry.

(9) Goods shipped in procurement should be deflated by an index of prices paid procurement organizations. It is assumed that this index may be represented by the official index of light and food industry wholesale prices, net of turnover taxes.

(10) Finished goods in procurement are deflated by an index of prices paid by procurement organizations that for 1959–1962 averages the estimated index of state delivery prices, cited in numbered paragraph 4 above, with the official index of purchase prices paid households and collective farms (*SKh,* p. 117, and Stoliarov, *O tsenakh i tsenoobrazovanii v SSSR,* 1963, p. 106), extended as indicated in numbered paragraph 4. The three indexes are (1958 = 100):

	Delivery Prices	*Purchase Prices*	*Purchase and Delivery Prices*
1959	100	101	101
1960	100	101	101
1961	110	103	105
1962	113	112	113
1963	118	118	118
1964	120	120	120
1965	144	138	140

According to V. Boev, *PKh,* 1966, No. 11, p. 13, purchase and delivery prices together averaged 38 percent above the 1958 level in 1965, providing some support for my independent estimate of 40 percent.

On the basis of these deflators, I proceed to the computation of inventory increments at average prices of the given year (Table L-3). End-year stocks at currently prevailing prices are multiplied by the ratio of prices at the end of the previous year to prices at the end of the given year, yielding end-year stocks valued at prices of the end of the previous year. From these values I then subtract stocks at the end of the previous year at current prices and obtain inventory increments valued at prices at the end of the previous year. Finally, these increments are multiplied by the ratio of average prices for the year to prices at the end of the previous year, yielding increments at average prices for the year. (This procedure is essentially that of Bergson: see *Real SNIP,* Appendix G.) Since deflators have not been compiled for "other branches," the required values in Table L-3 have been computed on the assumption of proportionality to corresponding changes in the sums of other components (row 11).

Applied to the values of increments at average prices of the year, the deflators of Table L-2 ("A" entries) yield the values of inventory investment at 1958 and 1964 prices shown in Table L-4.

No values for 1958 are shown in Table L-4, nor is the 1958 increment calculated in Table L-3. Since the original estimate of inventory investment at current prices in 1958 was obtained independently, rather than as the difference between end-year stocks (above, pp. 393–394), it is not necessary to compute the value of the increment at average current prices, as is done for other years in Table L-3. By the same token, however, it is not possible to compute the value of the 1958 increment at 1964 prices by the procedure of Table L-4. The required value is set at 8.00 billion rubles, 7 percent higher than at current prices. In other years, the ratio of the value of the total increment at 1964 prices to the corresponding value at average prices of the year is 106.3 in 1959, 104.5 in 1960, 105.1 in 1961, 100.8 in 1962, and 99.4 in 1963.

TABLE L-1

STATE-COOPERATIVE INVENTORIES AT CURRENT PRICES AT THE END OF THE YEAR, BY BRANCH AND TYPE, 1958–1964
(million rubles)

	1958	1959	1960	1961	1962	1963	1964
1. Industry							
Goods shipped	3,740	3,924	4,042	4,244	4,172	4,746	5,125
Fuel	522	549	522	477	449	486	532
Other inventories	24,852	26,093	27,477	30,201	32,901	35,551	38,681
Total	29,114	30,566	32,041	34,922	37,522	40,783	44,338
2. Construction	2,263	2,631	2,916	3,276	3,529	3,835	4,211
3. Agriculture							
Goods shipped	24	29	26	58	69	97	85
Inventories of agricultural goods	2,630	3,288	4,466	5,971	7,213	7,776	8,916
Fuel	88	98	113	123	121	131	150
Parts	115	197	260	246	293	336	396
Other nonagricultural inventories	512	667	792	860	965	1,054	1,209
Total	3,369	4,279	5,657	7,258	8,661	9,394	10,756
4. Transportation-communication							
Fuel	131	151	171	147	123	126	..
Other inventories	789	916	1,059	1,069	1,174	1,242	..
Total	920	1,067	1,230	1,216	1,297	1,368	1,476
5. Supply and sales							
Goods shipped	2,121	2,341	2,299	2,230	2,160	2,410	2,657
Other inventories	4,232	5,116	6,214	6,426	6,994	8,305	8,993
Total	6,353	7,457	8,513	8,656	9,154	10,715	11,650
6. Trade							
Goods shipped	821	839	878	819	792	884	974
Finished goods	14,966	17,565	18,301	20,320	21,834	23,679	
Fuel	17	19	20	22	24	—[a]	27,958
Other inventories	1,521	1,637	1,728	1,870	1,904	1,897	
Total	17,325	20,060	20,927	23,031	24,554	26,460	28,932
7. Procurement							
Goods shipped	327	552	541	531	515	575	633
Finished goods	1,507	3,165	3,099	3,434	3,707	3,417	
Fuel	15	15	15	16	13	12	5,748
Other inventories	310	571	549	654	673	719	
Total	2,159	4,303	4,204	4,635	4,908	4,723	6,381
8. Subtotal, 7 branches	61,503	70,363	75,488	82,994	89,625	97,278	107,744
9. Other branches	2,216	2,996	2,479	2,308	2,504	2,756	2,846
10. All branches	63,719	73,359	77,967	85,302	92,129	100,034	110,590

Note:

[a] According to source, less than 0.1 (presumably, less than 0.05) percen t of stocks o "commodity-material values" in trade.

TABLE L-1 (continued)

Sources:

In Soviet statistics current assets are subdivided into five groups: "commodity-material values," goods shipped and services performed, money and bank accounts, claims (*debitory*), and miscellaneous assets. I define inventories as consisting of commodity-material values and goods shipped, with the following exclusions: goods shipped and services performed in construction and transportation-communication (the only two branches, it is believed, where the services indicated in the title of the asset subcategory are in fact to be found) and expenditures of future periods in all branches except construction. See the earlier discussion of this definition, p. 393.

"Inventories of agricultural goods" are the following components of commodity-material values in agriculture: seed, feed, livestock, unfinished agricultural production and supplies, and finished goods. "Other nonagricultural inventories" are the following components of commodity-material values in agriculture: raw and basic materials, purchased semifabricates, auxiliary materials, packing materials, small-valued and short lived instruments and tools, other production supplies, unfinished industrial and nonindustrial production. No attempt is made to separate out inventories of agricultural goods held in branches other than agriculture and procurement; the amounts are small and we have no information on the behavior of prices relating to these subsidiary agricultural inventories.

The data available in the Soviet sources cited below consist of ruble values for all years in the table of all current assets and of one of the major asset categories, commodity-material values—in both cases, by branch of the economy. With less complete branch and time coverage the sources also provide percentage distributions of current assets among the five categories as well as of just commodity material values. The latter distributions are set out in great detail. My procedure, in summary, is to estimate inventories for the seven branches identified in the sources by the application of the relevant percentage figures to the ruble values and to obtain inventories in the other unidentified branches residually, as the difference between inventories in all branches and those in the seven identified branches.

The details of the procedure may be set out as follows:

(1) The ruble values are taken from *NKh 1962*, p. 56 and *NKh 1964*, p. 751.

(2) The shares of goods shipped and services performed in all branches and in industry, construction, and agriculture, are given in *NKh 1962*, pp. 57–58 and *NKh 1964*, pp. 752–753. Shares of goods shipped and services performed in the other branches were taken from *NKh 1960*, pp. 94–95, for 1958–1959, and from *VS*, 1962, No. 11, p. 85, for 1960–1961. For 1962–1964, the missing shares were estimated on the assumption that the distribution of goods shipped among the four identified and the residual "other" branches was the same as in 1961, the last year for which complete information on this asset category is available. Note that the shares of industry, construction, and agriculture (for which 1962–1964 data are available) in the sum of the stock of goods shipped in these three branches remained relatively unchanged (industry, 92.4, 92.1, 92.1 percent in 1962, 1963, 1964, respectively; construction, 6.0, 6.0, 6.3 percent; agriculture, 1.6, 1.9, 1.6 percent).

(3) Expenditures of future periods and all items in the table other than goods shipped are components of the asset category commodity material values. Distributions for all branches, industry, construction and agriculture, in all years are found in *NKh 1962*, pp. 59–63 and *NKh 1964*, pp. 754–755, 762–763. Distributions for the other four identified branches are given in *NKh 1960*, pp. 99–101, for 1958–1959, in *VS*, 1962, No. 11, pp. 86–87, for 1960–1961, and in *VS*, 1964, No. 11, pp. 86–89, for 1962–1963. The latter source provides distributions for transportation and communication separately; my estimates are obtained on the assumption of a ratio of 7:3 for commodity material values in the two branches, respectively. Expenditures of future periods in 1964 in transportation-communication, supply and sales, trade, and procurement are assumed to account for the same proportion of the respective branch's stock of commodity-material values as in 1963; the sources show that 1963 proportions were almost always the same as in 1962, and for some branches, the same as in 1961.

TABLE L-2

DEFLATORS OF INVENTORY INVESTMENT, 1958–1965
(index numbers)

	1958	1959	1960	1961	1962	1963	1964	1965
1. Fuel								
A	100	105	105	96	96	96	96	96
B	103	105	100	96	96	96	96	
C		98	105	104	100	100	100	
D		102	100	96	100	100	100	
2. Goods shipped and other inventories in industry								
A	100	101	103	103	106	106	106	104
B	101	103	103	105	106	106	105	
C		98	100	98	99	100	101	
D		100	100	100	101	100	100	
3. Inventories in construction, etc.								
A	100	100	98	97	98	98	97	95
B	100	99	98	98	98	98	96	
C		101	101	100	100	100	102	
D		100	99	99	100	100	99	
4. Goods shipped in agriculture								
A	100	100	100	110	113	118	120	144
B	100	100	105	112	116	119	132	
C		100	95	94	97	97	90	
D		100	100	105	101	101	102	
5. Inventories of agricultural goods								
A	100	105	112	122	133	153	144	158
B	103	109	117	128	143	149	151	
C		94	93	91	90	96	99	
D		102	103	104	104	107	97	
6. Parts in agriculture								
A	100	150	150	110	110	110	110	110
B	150	150	110	110	110	110	110	
C		100	136	100	100	100	100	
D		100	100	100	100	100	100	
7. Other nonagricultural inventories in agriculture *								
8. Goods shipped and finished goods in trade								
A	100	98	98	98	100	100	100	98
B	99	98	98	99	100	100	99	
C		101	100	99	99	100	101	
D		99	100	100	101	100	100	
9. Goods shipped in procurement								
A	100	105	108	112	118	120	120	119
B	103	107	110	115	119	120	120	
C		96	97	96	97	99	100	
D		102	101	102	103	101	100	

TABLE L-2 (continued)

	1958	1959	1960	1961	1962	1963	1964	1965
10. Finished goods in procurement								
A	100	101	101	105	113	118	120	140
B	101	101	103	109	116	119	130	
C		100	98	94	94	97	92	
D		100	100	102	104	102	101	

Note:

A = Index numbers, average for the year, 1958 = 100.

B = Index number at the end of the year, average 1958 = 100.

C = Index number at the end of the previous year divided by the index number at the end of the given year.

D = Index number, average for the year, divided by the index number at the end of the previous year.

* = Values in this category are not deflated. See text of appendix.

Sources:

For the derivation of all A entries and of B entries for parts held in agriculture, see the text of this appendix. With the exception noted, B entries are obtained by averaging A entries.

TABLE L-3

CALCULATION OF STATE-COOPERATIVE INVENTORY INVESTMENT AT AVERAGE PRICES OF RESPECTIVE YEARS, 1959–1964
(million rubles)

	1958	1959				1960				1961			
	End-Year Stocks, Current Prices	End-Year Stocks, Current Prices	End-Year Stocks, Prices at End of Previous Year	Increment of Stocks, Prices at End of Previous Year	Increment of Stocks, Average Prices for the Year	End-Year Stocks, Current Prices	End-Year Stocks, Prices at End of Previous Year	Increment of Stocks, Prices at End of Previous Year	Increment of Stocks, Average Prices for the Year	End-Year Stocks, Current Prices	End-Year Stocks, Prices at End of Previous Year	Increment of Stocks, Prices at End of Previous Year	Increment of Stocks, Average Prices for the Year
	(1)	(2)	(3)	(4)	(5)	(6)	(7)	(8)	(9)	(10)	(11)	(12)	(13)
1. Fuel	773	832	815	42	43	841	883	51	51	785	816	−25	−24
2. Goods shipped and other inventories in industry	28,592	30,017	29,417	825	825	31,519	31,519	1,502	1,502	34,445	33,756	2,237	2,237
3. Inventories in construction; other inventories in transportation-communication, trade, and procurement; all supply-sales	11,236	13,212	13,344	2,108	2,108	14,765	14,913	1,701	1,684	15,525	15,525	760	752
4. Goods shipped in agriculture	24	29	29	5	5	26	25	−4	−4	58	55	29	30
5. Inventories of agricultural goods	2,630	3,288	3,091	461	470	4,466	4,153	865	891	5,971	5,434	968	1,007
6. Parts in agriculture	115	197	197	82	82	260	354	157	157	246	246	−14	−14
7. Other nonagricultural inventories in agriculture	512	667	667	155	155	792	792	125	125	860	860	68	68
8. Goods shipped and finished goods in trade	15,787	18,404	18,588	2,801	2,773	19,179	19,179	775	775	21,139	20,928	1,749	1,749
9. Goods shipped in procurement	327	552	530	203	207	541	525	−27	−27	531	510	−31	−32
10. Finished goods in procurement	1,507	3,165	3,165	1,658	1,658	3,099	3,037	−128	−128	3,434	3,228	129	132
11. Subtotal 1–10	61,503	70,363	69,843	8,340	8,336	75,488	75,380	5,017	5,026	82,994	81,358	5,870	5,905
12. Other branches	2,216	2,996	2,975	759	757	2,479	2,477	−519	−520	2,308	2,262	−217	−218
13. Total	63,719	73,359	72,818	9,099	9,083	77,967	77,857	4,498	4,506	85,302	83,620	5,653	5,687

TABLE L-3 (continued)

	1962				1963				1964			
	End-Year Stocks, Current Prices	End-Year Stocks, Prices at End of Previous Year	Increment of Stocks, Prices at End of Previous Year	Increment of Stocks, Average Prices for the Year	End-Year Stocks, Current Prices	End-Year Stocks, Prices at End of Previous Year	Increment of Stocks, Prices at End of Previous Year	Increment of Stocks, Average Prices for the Year	End-Year Stocks, Current Prices	End-Year Stocks, Prices at End of Previous Year	Increment of Stocks, Prices at End of Previous Year	Increment of Stocks, Average Prices for the Year
	(14)	(15)	(16)	(17)	(18)	(19)	(20)	(21)	(22)	(23)	(24)	(25)
1. Fuel	730	730	−55	−55	755	755	25	25	682 [a]	682 [a]	−73 [a]	−73 [a]
2. Goods shipped and other inventories in industry	37,073	36,702	2,257	2,280	40,297	40,297	3,224	3,224	43,806	44,244	3,947	3,947
3. Inventories in construction; other inventories in transportation-communication; all supply-sales	16,434	16,434	909	909	18,408	18,408	1,974	1,974	17,337 [b]	17,684 [b]	−724 [b]	−717 [b]
4. Goods shipped in agriculture	69	67	9	9	97	94	25	26	85	77	−20	−20
5. Inventories of agricultural goods	7,213	6,492	521	542	7,776	7,465	252	270	8,916	8,827	1,051	1,019
6. Parts in agriculture	293	293	47	47	336	336	43	43	396	396	60	60
7. Other nonagricultural inventories in agriculture	965	965	105	105	1,054	1,054	89	89	1,209	1,209	155	155
8. Goods shipped and finished goods in trade	22,626	22,400	1,261	1,274	24,563	24,563	1,937	1,937	28,932 [c]	29,221 [c]	4,658 [c]	4,658 [c]
9. Goods shipped in procurement	515	500	−31	−32	575	569	54	55	633	633	58	58
10. Finished goods in procurement	3,707	3,485	51	53	3,417	3,314	−393	−401	5,748 [d]	5,288 [d]	1,871 [d]	1,890 [d]
11. Subtotal 1–10	89,625	88,068	5,074	5,132	97,278	96,855	7,230	7,242	107,744	108,261	10,983	10,977
12. Other branches	2,504	2,461	153	155	2,756	2,745	241	241	2,846	2,860	104	104
13. Total	92,129	90,529	5,227	5,287	100,034	99,600	7,471	7,483	110,590	111,121	11,087	11,081

Notes:

[a] Excluding fuel in transportation-communication, trade, and procurement.

[b] Including fuel in transportation-communication and procurement; excluding "other inventories" in trade and procurement.

[c] All trade inventories, including fuel and "other inventories."

[d] Including fuel and "other inventories" in procurement.

Sources:

Columns 1, 2, 6, 10, 14, 18, 22. Table L-1.

Columns 3, 7, 11, 15, 19, 23, except other branches. Columns 2, 6, 10, 14, 18, 22, multiplied by C entries in Table L-2.

Columns 4, 8, 12, 16, 20, 24. The difference between columns 3, 7, 11, 15, 19, 23, and columns 1, 2, 6, 10, 14, 18.

Columns 5, 9, 13, 17, 21, 25, except other branches. Columns 4, 8, 12, 16, 20, 24, multiplied by D entries in Table L-2.

Values for other branches in columns 3, 7, 11, 15, 19, 23 are obtained by multiplying corresponding values in columns 2, 6, 10, 14, 18, 22, by the ratio of row 11 values in the first group of columns to their counterparts in the second group. The analogous procedure is used to obtain values for other branches in columns 5, 9, 13, 17, 21, 25.

TABLE L-4

STATE-COOPERATIVE INVENTORY INVESTMENT AT 1958 AND 1964 PRICES, 1959–1964
(million rubles)

	1959		1960		1961		1962		1963		1964	
	1958 Prices	1964 Prices	1958 Prices	1964 Prices	1958 Prices	1964 Prices	1958 Prices	1964 Prices	1958 Prices	1964 Prices	1958 Prices	1964 Prices
1. Fuel, seven branches	41	39	49	47	−25	−24	−57	−55	26	25	−76 [a]	−73 [a]
2. Goods shipped and other inventories in industry	817	866	1,458	1,546	2,172	2,302	2,151	2,280	3,042	3,224	3,724	3,947
3. Inventories in construction, other inventories in transport-communication, etc.	2,108	2,045	1,718	1,667	775	752	928	900	2,014	1,954	−739 [b]	−717 [b]
4. Goods shipped in agriculture	5	6	−4	−5	27	33	8	10	22	26	−17	−20
5. Inventories of agricultural goods	448	644	796	1,146	825	1,189	408	587	176	254	708	1,019
6. Parts in agriculture	55	60	105	115	−13	−14	43	47	39	43	55	60
7. Other nonagricultural inventories in agriculture	155	155	125	125	68	68	105	105	89	89	155	155
8. Goods shipped and finished goods in trade	2,830	2,830	791	791	1,785	1,785	1,274	1,274	1,937	1,937	4,658 [c]	4,658 [c]
9. Goods shipped in procurement	197	237	−25	−30	−29	−34	−27	−33	46	55	48	58
10. Finished goods in procurement	1,642	1,970	−127	−152	126	151	47	57	−340	−408	1,575 [d]	1,890 [d]
11. Subtotal 1–10	8,298	8,852	4,886	5,250	5,711	6,208	4,880	5,172	7,051	7,199	10,091	10,977
12. Other branches	755	805	−505	−543	−211	−229	147	156	235	240	96	104
13. Total	9,053	9,657	4,381	4,707	5,500	5,979	5,027	5,328	7,286	7,439	10,187	11,081

Notes:

[a] Excluding fuel in transportation-communication, trade, and procurement.

[b] Including fuel in transportation-communication and procurement; excluding "other inventories" in trade and procurement.

[c] All trade inventories, including fuel and "other inventories."

[d] Including fuel and "other inventories" in procurement.

Sources:

Except for "other branches," values are obtained by applying deflators in Table L-2 ("A" entries) to increments at average prices of the year in Table L-3 (columns 5, 9, 13, 17, 21, and 25). It is assumed that the relation between values at constant prices and at average prices for the year is the same for "other branches" as it is for the "subtotal, 1–10."

M

The Sensitivity of Various Series to the Magnitude of Public Sector Revenues

The determination of public sector incomes, and hence also of public sector outlays and GNP, is influenced to a varying degree by two essentially arbitrary decisions: (1) The amount of total state budget revenues in 1965S (p. 454) and (2) the share of residual public sector revenues in 1958–1964 (pp. 367 ff.) included in current income of the public sector (Table 3). In both (1) and (2) the alternatives imply corresponding changes in public sector outlays (Table 4) and therefore in the GNP accounts (Tables 5–6).

(1) The estimate of public sector incomes in 1965S is closely tied to an interpretation of statements by official Soviet sources with regard to total budget revenues in 1965S. It has been argued (above, pp. 41–42) that although that figure might possibly be as little as 110 or as much as 124 billion rubles, the more likely total is 115 billions. If the argument is wrong, how significant are the ensuing errors?

(2) Item 3.E in Table 3, "miscellaneous charges," is the sum of several small items of state budgetary revenue and of a very large item called "other revenues." In turn, figures for "other revenues" are obtained by taking 75 percent of residual budget revenues "from the socialist sector" (above, pp. 367 ff.). There is good reason to believe that much or most of these residual revenues are in fact current incomes and should be entered in the accounts. It is evident that neither 100 percent nor 0 percent of these revenues are on current account. Suppose,

however, that the appropriate share is not 75 percent but, say, 50 percent or, alternatively, 90 percent?

Calculations for 1965S, 1958, 1961, and 1964 are repeated, using the following alternative values: (1) total budget revenues in 1965S of either 110 or 120 billion rubles, compared with the existing estimate of 115 billions; (2) either 50 or 90 percent as the share of residual revenues included in current public sector income, compared with the existing estimate of 75 percent. Table M-1 shows the recalculated value of relevant entries in Tables 3–6 and 9–12. The remaining tables in this appendix are recalculations of other text and appendix tables affected by the hypothetical changes set out in Table M-1.

The recalculations are performed according to the procedure of the existing estimates as indicated in the sources to the relevant tables. The sole exception is for 1965S and with respect to Table 9. In the existing estimate, item 3.F accounts for 88.5 percent of the sum of items 1.B, 1.C, 1.D, and 3.F in Table 3. The added or subtracted 5 billion rubles of budget revenue are distributed between items 1.E and 3.F in the proportions .115:.885, or .6 and 4.4 billion rubles. Table M-3 confines itself to calculations for the 90 percent assumption because calculations for the 50 percent assumption yield nonsensical results (see p. 101).

The findings are as follows:

(1) *The 1965S accounts.* In absolute terms, total public sector incomes and outlays, residual public sector outlays, and GNP are altered by the same absolute amounts, 5 billion rubles. The relative impact is largest on the residual public sector expenditure item. For 1965S this residual encompasses other categories besides outlays n.e.c. because of information gaps, hence the visible impact is somewhat reduced. But 5 billion rubles is still 15 percent of the existing entry for rows 4–7 in Table 4. With regard to the revenue item immediately affected, row 3.F in Table 3, the alternatives imply changes of only ±5 percent, and on GNP the impact is reduced to only ±2 percent.

The effect of introducing one or the other of the alternative revenue estimates on the structural relations of Tables 30, 31, and 32 again can be generally foreseen. In regard to Table 30, the lower alternative means a reduction in the relative importance of taxes and other payments to the budget and corresponding increases in the other categories. To avoid the necessity of arbitrarily allocating the 5 billion ruble increment or decrement between income taxes and profits deduction on one hand, and other payments to the budget on the other, I restrict my consideration of items 1, 2, and 4 in Table 30 to the B variants. Changes here are of comparatively insignificant magnitude: the largest is a reduction of 1.2 percentage points in the share of payments to the budget. Much the same can be said of Table 32 where either alternative involves a single percentage point reduction (lower alternative) or increase (higher alternative) in the public sector's share of GNP originated and expended.

What significant sensitivity the results do display is restricted to Table 31. The alternatives involve a change of 3 percentage points in the share of other outlays in the total. The major compensation is in the relative weight of gross fixed investment where the lower alternative means an increase of more than 2 points and the higher alternative a decrease of 1½ points.

(2) *The accounts for 1958, 1961, and 1964.* In absolute terms, the use of the lower share, 50 percent, means a reduction in public sector "miscellaneous charges" of 1.74 billion rubles in 1958, 2.91 billion in 1961, and 3.23 billion in 1964. The higher alternative brings on a corresponding increase of respectively, 1.04, 1.75, and 1.95 billion rubles. These amounts are, of course, also the margin of difference for the relevant subtotals of Tables 3, 4, 5, and 6. Clearly, the relative impact is largest on the smallest affected entries, which turn out to be the volatile outlays n.e.c. of Table 4. Here the increments or decrements are multiples of the existing entries. Equally obviously, the relative impact is the smaller, the larger the absolute value of the affected entry. Thus, for the public sector "miscellaneous charges," the lower alternative means a decrease of 27 percent and the higher an increase of 16 percent, relative to the existing entries in Table 3. The relative impact is smallest on GNP where the changes are contained within the range −2 to +1 percent.

What would be the effects on the distributional patterns of Tables 11 and 13 of changes in the assumption under discussion? With respect to the structure of public sector revenues, Table 11, the lower alternative implies a reduction in the weight of taxes and other payments to the budget but an increase in the weight of all other elements. The converse is true of the higher alternative. Similarly, in Table 13, the 50 percent alternative involves a reduction in the share of outlays n.e.c. in the total but an increase in the relative weight of all other elements. Again, the converse is true of the 90 percent alternative. So much is clear intuitively. The magnitude of the changes resulting from substituting one of the alternative assumptions is also not unexpected. That is, changes are slight with respect to Table 11 (maximum: a percentage point reduction in the share of taxes and other payments to the budget with the 50 percent assumption) and to Table 13 (again the maximum change is a percentage point).

TABLE M-1

Sensitivity Recalculations of Affected Entries in Tables 3–6 for 1965S, 1958, 1961, and 1964 (billion rubles)

	1965S		1958		1961		1964	
	110 BR	120 BR	50%	90%	50%	90%	50%	90%
Table 3								
1.E. Total net retained income	17.1	18.3	←		n.a.			→
3.E. Miscellaneous charges	n.a.	n.a.	4.60	7.38	7.73	12.39	8.60	13.78
3.F. Total taxes and other payments . . . to the budget	90.6	99.4	50.28	53.06	60.58	65.24	75.19	80.37
6. Consolidated total charges against current product, net of depreciation	112.4	122.4	59.23	62.01	71.26	75.92	86.96	92.14
8. Consolidated total charges against current product	126.9	136.9	67.19	69.97	82.56	87.22	105.67	110.85
10. Consolidated net income	132.9	142.9	74.08	76.86	89.39	94.05	114.95	120.13
Table 4								
7. Outlays n.e.c.; statistical discrepancy	n.a.	n.a.	−1.51	1.27	−2.61	2.05	−2.12	3.06
4.–7. R&D, internal security, defense, outlays n.e.c.	28.9	38.9	←		n.a.			→
8. Consolidated total value of goods and services, exclusive of sales to households	116.4	126.4	64.13	66.91	77.43	82.09	101.13	106.31
10. Consolidated total outlays	132.9	142.9	74.08	76.86	89.39	94.05	114.95	120.13
Table 5								
Incomes								
2. Consolidated charges . . . against current product, net of depreciation	112.4	122.4	59.23	62.01	71.26	75.92	86.96	92.14
3. Net national product	236.9	246.9	148.36	151.14	172.04	176.70	207.29	212.47
4. Gross national product	251.4	261.4	156.32	159.10	183.34	188.00	226.00	231.18
Outlays								
7. Consolidated total value of goods and services . . . , exclusive of sales to households	116.4	126.4	64.13	66.91	77.43	82.09	101.13	106.31
8. Gross national product	251.4	261.4	156.32	159.10	183.34	188.00	226.00	231.18
Table 6								
12. Outlays n.e.c.; statistical discrepancy	n.a.	n.a.	−1.51	1.27	−2.61	2.05	−2.12	3.06
9.–12. R&D, internal security, defense, outlays n.e.c.	28.9	38.9	←		n.a.			→
13. Gross national product	251.4	261.4	156.32	159.10	183.34	188.00	226.00	231.18

TABLE M-2

RECALCULATION OF TABLES 11, 13, 30–32 FOR 1958, 1965S, 1961, AND 1964

(percent)

	1958		1965S		1961		1964	
	50%	90%	110 BR	120 BR	50%	90%	50%	90%
Tables 11 and 30								
1.B. Income of collective farms . . . , net of income tax	3.4	3.3	4.0	3.8	2.9	2.8	2.3	2.2
2.B. Net profits . . . , after income tax and profits deductions	7.7	7.4	9.2	8.5	5.7	5.4	4.6	4.4
3. Charges to enterprises	4.9	4.7	4.3	4.0	5.4	5.1	5.1	4.9
4.B. Taxes and other payments to budget including taxes and deductions	64.9	66.1	67.2	69.4	66.2	67.8	64.1	65.6
5. Depreciation	10.2	9.9	10.8	10.1	12.3	11.7	16.0	15.3
6.C. Total transfer receipts	8.9	8.6	4.5	4.2	7.4	7.1	7.9	7.6
7. Consolidated net income gross of subsidized losses, n.e.c.	←			100.0				→
Tables 13 and 31								
1. Communal services, excluding R&D	14.2	13.7	13.8	12.8	14.8	14.1	14.6	14.0
2. Administration	1.6	1.6	1.1	1.1	1.2	1.1	1.0	.9
3. Gross investment								
A. Fixed capital	45.1	43.4	45.4	42.3	49.2	46.8	47.8	45.8
B. Inventories	10.7	10.3	5.5	5.1	6.8	6.4	10.1	9.7
C. Total	55.7	53.7	50.9	47.4	56.0	53.2	58.0	55.5
4. Other outlays								
A. Military pay and subsistence	5.5	5.3	3.1	2.9	4.0	3.8	2.9	2.8
B. Other defense	6.7	6.4			8.6	8.2	8.4	8.0
C. Internal security	2.0	2.0	18.6	24.3	1.7	1.6	1.3	1.2
D. R&D	2.8	2.7			3.2	3.1	3.7	3.5
E. Outlays n.e.c., etc.	−2.0	1.7			−2.9	2.2	−1.8	2.5
F. Total	15.0	18.1	21.7	27.2	14.6	18.9	14.4	18.1
5. Transfer payments	13.4	12.9	12.4	11.5	13.4	12.7	12.0	11.5
6. Total outlays	←			100.0				→
Table 32								
Incomes								
Households	57.0	56.0	49.5	47.6			53.2	52.1
Public sector	43.0	44.0	50.5	52.4			46.8	47.9
GNP	100.0	100.0	100.0	100.0			100.0	100.0
Outlays					n.a.			
Households	59.0	57.9	53.7	51.6			55.3	54.0
Public sector	41.0	42.1	46.3	48.4			44.7	46.0
GNP	100.0	100.0	100.0	100.0			100.0	100.0

On the other hand, larger alterations would be required in Table 15, particularly in the share of outlays n.e.c.—declines of 2.3 to 3.2 percent and increases of 1.4 to 1.9 percentage points. The only other category for which tangible changes would be noted is gross fixed investment, with a maximum increase of 1.6 percentage points in 1961 (substituting the 50 percent assumption).

The time-pattern of the distribution of incomes and outlays appears not to be sensitive to the choice of the particular assumption. Even if it were believed that the share of residual budget revenues appropriately entered in the SNIP accounts is not uniform in all years, the conclusion would still hold generally true. The main exception, of course, is the relative importance of outlays n.e.c., on the accuracy of which it is necessary to retain a measure of detached skepticism. Nevertheless, the reader should also bear in mind that there are good reasons for believing that a consistently negative absolute level of outlays n.e.c. is highly unlikely (pp. 395 ff.); that a significant positive level is quite likely; hence, that if the 75 percent assumption is in error it is less likely to be an overestimate than an underestimate.

TABLE M-3

RECALCULATION OF TABLE 15 FOR 1958, 1961, AND 1964: 90 PERCENT ASSUMPTION
(percent)

	1958		1961		1964	
	EP	AFC	EP	AFC	EP	AFC
1. Consumption						
A. Retail sales	40.7	32.5	41.3	34.3	40.1	33.9
B. Consumer services	5.8	6.4	6.2	6.7	6.3	6.7
C. Income in kind	7.5	8.8	6.0	6.8	5.1	5.7
D. Other	1.9	2.2	1.2	1.3	1.7	2.0
E. Total	55.9	49.9	54.7	49.1	53.1	48.3
2. Communal services, excluding R&D	6.6	7.0	7.0	7.2	7.3	7.5
3. Administration	.8	.8	.6	.6	.5	.5
4. Gross investment						
A. Fixed capital	23.1	26.6	25.0	28.5	24.7	27.9
B. Inventories	5.0	5.1	3.2	3.4	5.0	4.9
C. Total	28.0	31.7	28.3	31.9	29.7	32.8
5. R&D	1.3	1.5	1.5	1.8	1.8	2.0
6. Internal security	.9	1.1	.8	.9	.6	.7
7. Defense	5.7	6.8	6.0	6.9	5.6	6.4
8. Outlays n.e.c., etc.	.8	1.1	1.1	1.5	1.3	1.7
GNP	← 100.0 →					

TABLE M-4

GNP IN 1958, 1961, AND 1964 AT CONSTANT PRICES UNDER VARYING ASSUMPTIONS ON SHARE OF INCLUDED RESIDUAL BUDGET REVENUES
(billion rubles)

		1958 prices		1964 prices	
Year	Assumed Share (%)	EP	AFC	EP	AFC
1958	50	156.32	. .	161.94	. .
	90	159.10	136.85	164.81	145.99
1961	50	184.15	. .	189.82	. .
	90	188.76	162.17	194.59	172.24
1964	50	219.72	. .	226.00	. .
	90	224.73	193.51	231.18	204.77

Sources:
1958 values at 1958 EP and 1964 values at 1964 EP are taken from Table M-1. The 1958 value at 1958 AFC and the 1964 value at 1964 AFC are taken from Table M-6. No entries are computed for the 50 percent assumption at constant AFC because, as indicated earlier, the results are absurd. Other entries are computed by deducting existing values of outlays n.e.c. from GNP, as shown in Tables K-1 and K-2 and substituting the deflated alternative values of outlays n.e.c. The deflation is accomplished as described in p. 524 on current EP values taken from Table M-1 and current AFC values taken from Table M-6.

TABLE M-5

RECALCULATION OF TABLE 33 FOR 1958, 1965S, AND 1964
(percent)

	1958		1965S		1964	
	50%	90%	110 BR	120 BR	50%	90%
1. State-cooperative retail sales	38.6	37.9	37.1	35.7	39.0	38.1
2. Consumer services	5.9	5.8	6.7	6.5	6.4	6.3
3. Consumption of income in kind; extravillage market sales; other outlays for consumption	12.4	12.2	8.5	8.2	8.9	8.7
4. Total consumption	56.9	55.9	52.3	50.3	54.3	53.1
5. Communal services, excluding R&D	6.7	6.6	7.3	7.0	7.4	7.3
6. Government administration	.8	.8	.6	.6	.5	.5
7. Gross investment						
A. Fixed capital	23.5	23.1	25.4	24.4	25.3	24.7
B. Inventories	5.1	5.0	2.9	2.8	5.1	5.0
C. Total	28.5	28.0	28.3	27.2	30.4	29.7
8. Other outlays						
A. Military pay and subsistence	2.6	2.6	1.6	1.6	1.5	1.5
B. Other defense	3.2	3.1	. .	. .	4.2	4.2
C. Internal security	1.0	.9	. .	. .	.7	.6
D. R&D	1.3	1.3	. .	. .	1.9	1.8
E. Outlays n.e.c.	−1.0	.8	. .	. .	−.9	1.3
F. Total	7.1	8.7	11.5	14.9	7.3	9.4
GNP	←	←	100.0	→	→	→

TABLE M-6

RECALCULATION OF AFFECTED ENTRIES IN TABLE J-1 FOR 1958, 1961, AND 1964: 90 PERCENT ASSUMPTION
(billion rubles)

	1958					1961					1964				
		Adjustment for					Adjustment for					Adjustment for			
	Value at EP	Turn-over tax	Subsi-dies	Farm prices	Value at AFC	Value at EP	Turn-over tax	Subsi-dies	Farm prices	Value at AFC	Value at EP	Turn-over tax	Subsi-dies	Farm prices	Value at AFC
1. Retail sales to households															
A. State-cooperative trade	60.33	24.07	3.93	1.23	41.42	73.41	24.15	3.51	1.14	53.91	88.18	26.98	4.09	1.29	66.58
B. Extravillage farm markets			← n.c. →			4.31	—	—	−1.27	3.04			← n.c. →		
C. Total	64.76				44.43	77.72				56.95	92.60				69.51
3. Consumption of income in kind															
B. Nonfarm wages in kind						.65	.22	.03	.01	.47			← n.c. →		
C. Military subsistence			← n.c. →					← n.c. →			1.24	—	.08	.03	1.35
D. Total										11.26	11.71				11.63
5. Total outlays for consumption	88.89				68.23	102.82				81.51	122.76				98.84
8. Gross investment															
A. Fixed capital			← n.c. →					← n.c. →			57.11	3.01	3.02	—	57.12
B. Inventories	7.90	1.51	.55	.06	7.00	6.06	.80	.41	.03	5.70	11.63	2.32	.66	.09	10.06
C. Total	44.59				43.34	53.13				52.95	68.74				67.18
9. R&D	2.06	.12	.14	—	2.08	2.90	.17	.30	—	3.03	4.20	.25	.22	—	4.17
10. Internal security	1.50	.07	.11	.01	1.55	1.50	.07	.10	.01	1.54	1.50	.07	.08	.01	1.52
11. Defense															
A. Pay and subsistence			← n.c. →					← n.c. →			3.38	—	.08	.03	3.49
C. Total											12.98				13.15
12. Outlays n.e.c.; statistical discrepancy	1.27	.06	.34	—	1.55	2.05	.10	.52	—	2.47	3.06	.15	.63	—	3.54
13. GNP	159.10	30.45	8.15[a]	.05	136.85	188.00	30.92	8.93[a]	.03	166.04	231.18	36.69	10.25	.03	204.77

Notes:

n.c. means no change.

[a] Difference from total shown in Table J-1 is due to rounding.

N

On the Reliability of Aggregate Household Incomes and Outlays

To test the reliability of the overall estimates in Tables 1 and 2 I make use of a number of statements that have appeared in Soviet sources with respect to changes in aggregate household money income in recent years.

The statements relevant here are:

(1) Money income of the population increased 42 percent from 1955 through 1960, not counting increases in income from curtailment of subscription loans, tax reduction, and increases of pensions (*Gosudarstvennyi bank SSSR k XXII s"ezdu KPSS,* 1961, p. 27).

(2) Taking into account the decrease in taxes and curtailment of bond subscriptions, money income of the population rose 16.8 billion rubles in the three years 1959–1961 and by almost 42 billion rubles or 87 percent since 1953 (Khrushchev, *Pravda,* March 6, 1962; Tsikoto, *Kommunizm i sel'skoe khoziaistvo,* 1963, pp. 13–14).

(3) Money income of the population rose more than 21 percent from 1958 through 1961 (Garbuzov, *Ekon.gazeta,* April 23, 1962, p. 9).

(4) Money income of the population rose 33 percent from 1957 to 1961 (Khrushchev, *Pravda,* March 17, 1962).

(5) Taking into account decreases in taxes and the curtailment of bond subscriptions, money income of the population in 1962 was 49 billion rubles greater than in 1953 (Lagutin, *ESKh,* 1963, No. 11, p. 56).

In none of the statements cited is "money income" defined. If the term is meant to cover the same aggregate as used in Soviet planning with reference to the "balance of money income and outlays" of the population, it could conceivably exclude current income from goods and services provided by households to households and include receipts from sales to secondhand shops and pawnshops (Sobol', *Ocherki po voprosam balansa narodnogo khoziaistva,* 1960: "Balance of Money Income and Outlays of the Population, Appendix to Table 5," insert before p. 227). However, the balance of money income and outlays is also drawn gross of transactions within the household sector; therefore, it is necessary to compute changes in income alternatively net and gross of intra-household-sector income. Receipts from sales to secondhand shops and pawnshops are probably negligible for present purposes.

In yet another statement on the change in money income, comparing 1955 and 1960, Khrushchev himself strongly implied concern with only the wage and salary bill, pensions, gains from tax cuts and from curtailment of bond subscriptions (*Plenum Tsentral'nogo komiteta Kommunisticheskoi partii Sovetskogo Soiuza, 10–18 ianvaria 1961 goda,* 1961, p. 523). In this sense, money income would exclude items 1.C, 2–6 of Table 1, part of item 8 (stipends and interest receipts), and perhaps item 2.B as well. It is possible that statement 1 refers only to wages and salaries, for in conjunction with a figure given by Khrushchev as the increase in the wage bill (17.1 billion rubles), it implies 1955 and 1960 levels of wages and salaries—40.7 and 57.8 billion rubles, respectively—that seem reasonable.

[The 1955 wage and salary bill was 43.1 billion rubles, the product of reported average employment of 50.2 millions (including 1.8 million members of producer cooperatives) and average earnings of 858 rubles per year (*NKh 1964,* pp. 545, 555). The 1960 wage and salary bill was 59.6 billions (Table 1). Exclusion of the earnings of producer cooperative members would reduce the computed values closer to those implied by Khrushchev.]

However, such a restricted scope cannot be true of statement 2, which implies levels of money income far too high for the narrow coverage. By extension, the limitation would seem inapplicable to statement 5 as well.

As an aid in handling the various statements, I define an aggregate called "gross basic money income"—the sum of items 1.A, 1.B, 2.A, 2.B, 3.A, and 4 in Table 1—and an aggregate called "net basic money income"—that is, basic income net of sales of goods and services to households by households.

[Intra-private-sector sales are defined as the sum of the value of services provided by the sector plus sales of farm products to households. For years covered in this study, estimates of private sector services for consumption will be found below, p. 354; construction services are computed as 60 percent of estimated hired labor services for private housing construction (see p. 361). The 1957 value of services is taken from *SNIP 1956–1958,* p. 58; the corresponding value for 1955 is estimated as .75 billion rubles, on the basis of 1956–1957 estimates in *SNIP 1956–1958*. Sales of farm products represent sales by households on extravillage farm markets less sales to institutions. The share of sales to institutions originating in household sales is assumed to be the same as in total market sales. Values are computed from *SNIP 1949–1955*, pp. 47 and 96; *SNIP 1956–1958*, pp. 37 and 53; and this study, Table A-1 and p. 334.]

In statements 2 and 5 above, "money income" is assumed to refer to the sum of basic income and transfer receipts (item 8.E of Table 1), less net bond purchases (part of item 8.A of Table 2) and direct taxes (item 8.B of Table 2). Statement 1 is taken to mean substantial exclusion of transfer receipts—that is, everything except stipends and interest on bank savings—as well as of the decrement in direct taxes. (I ignore new credits from banks, but these are too small to affect the results.) Statements 3 and 4 will be interpreted in both senses, that attached to statements 2 and 5 and that attached to 1.

The results are as follows:

Statement 1

	Calculated Percent Growth in Money Income Between 1955 and 1960
Gross basic	44.8
Net basic	50.6

If the 1955 values are correct, the 1960 estimates imply a relative increase that is 3–9 percentage points above the proclaimed growth. The aggregates for 1955 are calculated from *SNIP 1949–1955*, which was compiled from information available in late 1958 and early 1959. Probably the 1955 estimates could be revised with information now available, but whether up or down cannot be predicted *a priori*. As indicated, however, statement 1 may refer to little more than the wage and salary bill.

Statement 2 implies levels of money income of about 73 and 90 billion rubles in 1958 and 1961, respectively. Computed as indicated, the estimates provide corresponding figures as follows:

	1958		*1961*	
	Computed Money Income, Billion Rubles	*Percent Difference from Announced*	*Computed Money Income, Billion Rubles*	*Percent Difference from Announced*
Gross	78.6	+8	92.9	+3
Net	73.8	+1	88.4	−2

Unless statement 2 combines net income in 1958 with gross in 1961, the computed values understate the relative increase between the two years.

Statement 3, interpreted as defined in the pattern of statement 2, is slightly at variance with it. Statement 3 speaks of a growth of "more than 21" percent between 1958 and 1961; statement 2 implies an increase of 23 percent. If we apply the growth rate in statement 3 to the 16.8 billion ruble increase cited in statement 2, the theoretical 1958 aggregates would be (allowing for rounding) 78.5–79.6 billion rubles and those for 1961, 95.3–96.4 billion rubles. Acceptance of these figures would suggest that statements 2 and 3 should be interpreted in terms of gross rather than net basic income and my computed figures would then be roughly correct in 1958 and underestimated by 3–4 percent in 1961.

Statement 3 may also be interpreted as the sum of basic income plus stipends and bank interest only. The computed increases are then 16 percent using gross basic income and 18 percent with net basic income.

Under the varied interpretations, the computed percent changes in money income fall short of those indicated in statements 2 and 3. There is some reason to believe that such an understatement is to be expected and is not evidence of error in the estimates. In Table 1 the 1961 entry for item 4, other income currently earned, including the statistical discrepancy for the household account, shows a marked drop in 1961 relative to values in earlier years. It is possible that this drop reflects an increase in a negative income entry, increments to cash balances, for there is independent evidence (discussed in Chapter 4) of considerable increases in cash hoarding at this time.

Statement 4 implies an increase in 1958 over 1957 of either (roughly) 8 or 10 percent, depending on whether we use statement 2 or statement 3 as the match. If we compare the 1958 estimates of this study with those for 1957 by Nimitz in *SNIP 1956–1958* (the 1957 totals exclude net new bank loans, but these were of minor consequence in that year) using alternative interpretations of total money income, and either gross or net concepts, there are four possible values in each year, implying increases of 8 percent for either gross or net income defined as for statement 1 (basic income plus stipends and interest) and 11 percent for gross or net income as in statement 2 (basic income plus transfers, less net bond purchases and direct taxes).

Statement 5 is obviously a lineal descendant of statement 2, and both together imply an increase of money income of about 7 billion rubles in 1962. Computed as indicated appropriate to these statements, the estimates of Table 1 imply increases of 8.1 or 8.5 billion rubles of net income and 8.5 or 8.6 billion rubles of gross income. If 1961 income is understated, owing to deduction of additions to cash hoards, the true 1962 increment in money income may approach the theoretical 7 billion ruble figure more closely. On the other hand, it is possible that cash hoarding took place in 1962 as well as in 1961, as the discussion in Chapter 4 suggests.

O

Calculation of the Relative Undervaluation of Collective Farmer Incomes

Earnings of collective farmers in 1958 may be compared with wages of industrial workers in the same year as follows:

Labor input by able-bodied collective farmers in 1958 is estimated as 62.4 billion man hours. In that year there were approximately 26.8 million able-bodied collective farmers—members of collective farm households in the ages 16–59 for males and 16–54 for females, and whose main employment was on the collective farm; they spent an estimated 2328 hours each during the year on income-connected activities, excluding off-farm employment.

[The source is Nimitz, *Farm Employment in the Soviet Union, 1928–1963,* November 1965. The number of collective farmers is drawn directly from p. 112. The number of hours per man is estimated as follows: In budget sample households (the sample is stratified by type of farm and in this period covered 26,000 households in about 3 percent of the total number of collective farms—pp. 42–43) able-bodied collective farmers devoted an estimated 1634 hours during 1958 to work on the collective farm and 631 hours to work on their private plots (p. 83). However, the category of work on the plot excludes a number of productive activities, such as construction and repair of buildings and equipment, processing of output, and marketing (p. 44). To account for these excluded activities, time spent on the plot is raised by 10 percent or to 694 hours.

The same total input figure may be obtained from another table in the Nimitz study (p. 74) where man days worked by the able-bodied are given as 5146 million on the collective farm and 1991 million on the private plot. If the latter figure is blown up by 10 percent to account for the excluded activities discussed above, the joint total on farm and plot is raised to 7336 million man days. For the able-bodied the average number of hours worked on the collective farm per actual working day in 1958 came to 8.6 hours for men and 8.3 for women (p. 123). Assuming 8.5 hours per man day, the computed total number of man days implies 62.4 million man hours.

The two approaches are at least partly independent of each other. The figures on annual hours per man and aggregate man days originate in information from the budget sample, but the employment estimate is drawn from collective farm accounts.]

Collective farmer earnings consist of money payments from the farm, 5.00 billion rubles, net money income from sales of output by households, 6.22 billions, and income in kind at average realized farm prices, 10.57 billions (see Table 1 and p. 296). The last two items cover income of non-collective farmers as well. It is assumed on the basis of official data on the structure of sown area and of livestock products output and marketings that 90 percent of marketings by the private sector and 60 percent of its nonmarketed output originated in collective farmer households.

[Collective farmers accounted for 75 percent of the sown area in the private sector; 84 percent of the meat, 91 percent of the milk, 92 percent of the eggs, and 97 percent of the wool marketed by the sector; and 66 percent of the meat, 64 percent of the milk, 56 percent of the eggs, and 59 percent of the wool produced and not marketed by the sector. *SKh,* pp. 128, 334–337.]

On this basis, collective farmer income from sales comes to 5.60 billion rubles and income in kind 6.34 billions.

[Both sales and income in kind include output received by collective farmers from the farm as labor payment. Hence, the procedure used to estimate the collective farmer component of private sector income has a downward bias. An offsetting factor is the failure to deduct payments in kind to collective farm hired labor from sales and in kind income. As cash earnings of hired labor were only .25 billion rubles (p. 296), in kind allowances must have been small.]

All collective farmer incomes total 16.94 billions.

This volume of income was earned not just by the able-bodied but also by the overaged, disabled, and underaged members of collective farm households. In 1960, the overaged, disabled, and juveniles accounted for 8.0 percent of all man days worked on the farm, excluding labor on the plot (AN SSSR, *Puti povysheniia proizvoditel'nosti truda v sel'skom khoziaistve SSSR,* 1964, p. 60). Sample time budget data for 1959 indicate that the share of the overaged, disabled, and juveniles in all time spent by sample households on both the collective farm and the private plot came to 17 percent. (Nimitz, *Farm Employment in the Soviet Union, 1928–1963,* November 1965, p. 86). Allowing for lower unit earnings of the non-able-bodied, 10 percent of the aggregate 1958 income estimated in the previous paragraph may be attributed to the labor of the non-able-bodied. Total income of the able-bodied may be put at 15.25 billion rubles.

The in kind component of these income figures is valued at average realized farm prices. For a comparison of real income differentials, income in kind should be valued at retail prices less home processing costs. As an approximation to retail prices we may use collective farm market prices, bearing in mind that in 1958 market prices were slightly higher than retail prices (see above, pp. 490–491). Revalued at collective farm market prices, with an arbitrary allowance for home processing costs of 10 percent of the sales price, income in kind for all households would reach 18.40 billion rubles. The 60 percent share assumed to originate in collective farmer households comes to 11.04 billion rubles. Allowing for the income of the non-able-bodied, total able-bodied collective farmer income rises to, say, 19.5 billion rubles. Given total labor input of 62.4 billion man hours, earnings per hour averaged 31.3 kopecks. This figure is 63 percent of the hourly wage of industrial workers in 1958, which may be estimated as 49.6 kopecks (the average industrial wage in 1958 was 85.3 rubles per month, according to *NKh 1964,* p. 555, and it has been estimated that an annual average of 16,279 thousand wage earners worked 33.6 billion man hours in industry in 1958 [*New Directions in the Soviet Economy,* 1966, p. 783]); it is inferred to be slightly less than the average wage and salary in the food industry but farther short of the average wage and salary earned in light industry (average annual earnings [wages and salaries] in light industry in 1955 have been estimated as 82 percent of the industrial average; the corresponding ratio for the food industry was 69 percent in 1955 and 68 percent in 1959. Schroeder, *Soviet Studies,* January 1966, p. 316).

How did this relation change after 1958? Unfortunately, there is little information on the post-1958 distribution of private sector output and marketings. Between 1958 and 1962 there was a continuous drop in the collective farmer share within private sector totals with respect to sown area and livestock holdings. The drop was particularly marked in 1960, the year of a wave of conversions of collective to state farms, when the collective farmer's share of private sector sown area declined 17 percent. From January 1, 1959, to January 1, 1963, the collective farmer's share of private sector major livestock holdings declined between 11 and 16 percent (*NKh 1962,* pp. 252, 303–304). Therefore, for the period 1959–1962 I adopt the expedient of moving the 1958 share of private sector income—that is, from sales and in kind—originating in collective farmer households in proportion to the change in the collective farmer share of private sector sown area, as follows:

	1958	*1959*	*1960*	*1961*	*1962*
Percent	74.8	73.5	66.3	63.4	62.4
Index	100.0	98.3	88.6	84.8	83.4

No data have been published in the yearbooks on the post-1962 structure of private sector sown area or livestock holdings. I assume arbitrary small decreases in the share of collective farmers, reflecting continuing conversions of collective to state farms.

Thus, total earnings of collective farmers are estimated as follows (billion rubles, except where otherwise stated):

	1958	*1959*	*1960*	*1961*	*1962*	*1963*	*1964*
Incomes of the private sector from sales and in kind (Table 1)	16.79	16.32	15.78	16.12	17.33	16.47	17.12
Of which: by collective farmers in 1958	11.94						
Share of collective farmers, percent	71.1	69.9	63.0	60.3	59.3	58.0	57.0
Income of collective farmers from sales and in kind	11.94	11.41	9.94	9.72	10.28	9.55	9.76
Add: Money payments by collective farms (p. 296)	5.00	4.76	4.94	5.51	6.20	6.73	7.87
Equals: total incomes of collective farmers from work on the farm and their plots	16.94	16.17	14.88	15.23	16.48	16.29	17.63

Because of conversions and migration from the countryside, the able-bodied collective farmer labor force declined sharply after 1958, the overall reduction between 1958 and 1963 being almost one-quarter (Nimitz, *Farm Employment in the Soviet Union, 1928–1963,* November 1965, p. 112, Column 4). However, owing to an increase in labor input on the private plot, the decline in man hours was probably far smaller. Thus, total man days worked on farm and plot by all ages, including the non-able-bodied, declined only 9 percent between 1958 and 1962 (*ibid.,* p. 74). Assuming no change in the average length of the man day I then estimate the overall reduction in labor input by 1962 as 10 percent, of which I arbitrarily assign half to 1960 and the rest more or less equally to 1959, 1961, and 1962. The picture is less clear after 1962: man days of the private sector as a whole declined by 3.4 percent in 1963 and in 1964 increased by a bare 0.7 percent. Man days on collective farms dropped 3 percent in each of these two years (*ibid.,* p. 7, and unpublished estimates by Nimitz). In the absence of information on the ownership structure of private sector inputs or outputs, it is necessary to guess at the change in collective farmer labor input on both farm and plot. I assume a reduction in 1963 of 3 percent and no change in 1964.

In computing collective farmer earnings per man hour in relation to those of industrial wage earners after 1958, shown on p. 65, the data underlying the indexes are from the same sources as the computations for 1958 already described (with income in kind valued at average realized prices). The index numbers of the industrial wage in 1959 and 1961–1962 are obtained by interpolation between reported figures for 1958, 1960, and 1963.

P

Sources to Table 26

1. *SNIP gross fixed investment.* Table 2; pp. 387 and 464.

2. *Gross new investment, except livestock.*

A. *State-cooperative* and B. *Collective farms.* 1965S: p. 464. 1958–1964: *NKh 1962,* p. 435; *NKh 1964,* pp. 515, 517.

C. *Private housing.* Table 2.

3. *Gross new increments, except livestock.* The state-cooperative and collective farm figures for 1958–1964 are from *NKh 1963,* p. 448 and *NKh 1964,* p. 508. Values for 1965S in rows 3.A and 3.B are computed by applying the implied 1958–1965S increases in gross new investment to the 1958 gross increments.

The statistical yearbooks have not reported gross increments in private housing. For the first time, *NKh 1965* (p. 521) provided data from which gross increments of collective farm capital *plus* private housing could be computed; collective farm increments alone are not indicated. On the assumption that collective farm gross increments were not affected by the changes in valuation and coverage incorporated in *NKh 1965* data—this may be inferred from the identity of collective farm new investment data (*ibid.,* p. 536) with those in *NKh 1964* (p. 517)—we may subtract collective farm increments for 1958–1964 given in *NKh 1964* from the *NKh 1965* collective farm-private housing increments. The results, private housing increments, are almost always identical with the corresponding new investment figures to one decimal place. On this basis, the 1965S entry is set equal to that in row 1.C.

4. *Capital repairs.*

A. *State-cooperative.* Below, pp. 387 and 464.

B. *Collective farms.* 1958–1959: *Effektivnost kapital'nykh vlozheniia,* p. 47. 1960–1961: Alexseeva and Voronin, *Nakoplenie i razvitie kolkhoznoi sobstvennosti,* 1963, p. 105. 1962–1963: NIFI, *Organi-*

zatsiia finansov kolkhoza, 1964, p. 57, and AN SSSR, *Metody i praktika opredeleniia effektivnosti kapital'nykh vlozhenii i novoi tekhniki,* 1966, p. 34, cited by Anderson in an unpublished paper on collective farm accounts. 1964: Arbitrary estimate. 1965S: The 1958–1965S expected growth of capital repairs is assumed to be about the same as the expected growth of gross new investment, taking into account the repair requirements generated by the transfer of MTS machinery in 1958–1959.

C. *Private housing.* Estimated as .75 billion rubles in 1960 and projected back and forward in proportion to the change in the floor space of the private housing stock (p. 339). The 1960 estimate was obtained as follows: According to *NKh 1964,* p. 584, "amortization" of nonproductive capital as a charge to personal consumption was 2.9654 billion rubles in 1960. This represents real and imputed depreciation on all housing. (That the figure refers to housing is made clear on p. 579. Neither here nor in Eidel'man (*Mezhotraslevoi balans obshchestvennogo produkta,* 1966), who also cites these data (pp. 362–367), is it made explicit that all housing is involved, but the logic of the entry seems self-evident.) The Central Statistical Administration estimated that the value of all housing on 1 January 1960 was 94 billion rubles (*NKh 1959,* p. 67) and Norman Kaplan has inferred from Soviet sources an estimate for the private housing stock at the same date of 48 billion rubles (see above, sources for Table 8). Thus, private housing accounted for a little over half the total stock value. Applied to the reported depreciation figure, the ratio yields about 1.5 billion rubles as depreciation on private housing. Divided into an average 1960 value of the private housing stock of, say, 50 billion rubles, the 1.5 billion ruble figure implies a 3 percent depreciation coefficient. This seems reasonable, assuming a service life for private housing of 60 years (Moorsteen and Powell, *The Soviet Capital Stock 1928–1962,* 1966, p. 63) and allowing for capital repairs in the depreciation formula.

The 1965S figure is calculated from the 1958 figure, blown up by the 1958–1965S increase in imputed rent (pp. 335 and 430).

6. *Depreciation.*

A. *State-cooperative.* The sum of actual amortization allowances (pp. 379 and 450 above) plus imputed depreciation on some nonproductive capital. Not all state-cooperative capital is subject to amortization accounting or subject to the same extent. The major omission is of budget organization capital, overwhelmingly "nonproductive." The missing component is estimated as follows:

Eidel'man (*Mezhotraslevoi balans obshchestvennogo produkta,* 1966, p. 298) provides data for 1959–1963 showing the difference between the value of final (material) product and produced NMP. These differences represent the sum of depreciation (productive and nonproductive) and the book value of retirements (see item 8 below). If we subtract from these differences the value of depreciation on nonproductive capital (*NKh 1964,* pp. 584–585) and the residual value of retirements, the results should be depreciation on productive capital (billion rubles):

	1959	*1960*	*1961*	*1962*	*1963*
Difference between final material product and produced NMP	14.6	15.7	17.4	19.7	24.0
Subtract: nonproductive depreciation	4.9	5.5	6.1	6.8	7.5
Subtract: book value of retirements	1.7	1.1	1.2	1.8	1.2
Equals: productive depreciation	8.0	9.1	10.1	11.1	15.3

Figures for the book value of retirements are based on information provided by Eidel'man. The 1959 figure refers to the state sector alone (the problem of incompletely amortized withdrawals is probably almost entirely confined to the state sector) and is cited directly by him (p. 172). Entries for 1960–1962 are estimated from the 1959 value and another series cited by Eidel'man (p. 208), showing state-cooperative sector retirements, 1951–1962, at undepreciated original cost. The figure for 1963 is an estimate derived as an inference from a somewhat cryptic statement by Eidel'man. Noting that ratio of final material product to NMP was 1.106 in 1959, 1.108 in 1960, 1.114 in 1961, 1.120 in 1962, and 1.142 in 1963, he declares (p. 298): "The increase of the ratio of final product to NMP in recent years (*za poslednie gody*) was occasioned by the increase of amortization norms in 1963 and some increase in the writing off of old fixed capital in the preceding year, thereby increasing the sum of underamortized value." I take this to mean that the book value of retirements was higher in 1962 than previously and lower in 1963 than in 1962. Arbitrarily, the 1963 figure is assumed equal to the 1962 level.

The computed productive depreciation residuals account for 88–90 percent of all amortization allowances in the public sector (p. 379). This seems like a reasonable result except perhaps that the ratio might be higher in 1963 after the introduction of the new, higher depreciation rates (rates on nonproductive capital, largely buildings and structures, tend to be lower than those on productive capital). Possibly, the 1963 value is slightly understated relative to the others in the series. For the missing years, 1958 and 1964, I assume a ratio of productive depreciation to all amortization allowances of .9. For collective farms alone, the ratio probably should be a little higher, judging from the fact that the value of productive capital at the time of the census and revaluation (January 1, 1962) came to 92 percent of the total (*NKh 1961*, p. 421). I assume that the productive component of amortization allowances was 95 percent.

Thus, the nonproductive components of state-cooperative and collective farm amortization allowances were as follows (billion rubles):

	1958	*1959*	*1960*	*1961*	*1962*	*1963*	*1964*
Total	.8	1.0	1.1	1.2	1.5	1.8	1.9
Of which: collective farms	—	.1	.1	.1	.1	.1	.1
state-cooperative	.8	.9	1.0	1.1	1.4	1.7	1.8

The next step is to subtract these components from reported nonproductive depreciation (*NKh 1964*, pp. 584–585) to obtain the imputed values. For this purpose the reported series is extended to 1964 on the basis of capital stock indexes in *NKh 1964*, p. 68; the 1958 figure is an arbitrary estimate. Imputed nonproductive depreciation is assumed to apply only to state-cooperative capital. Subtraction of depreciation on private housing (item 6.C below) then yields the imputed values of state-cooperative depreciation on nonproductive capital. Finally, total state-cooperative depreciation is obtained by adding actual state-cooperative amortization allowances. The calculation is as follows (billion rubles):

	1958	*1959*	*1960*	*1961*	*1962*	*1963*	*1964*
Nonproductive depreciation, actual and imputed	4.3	4.9	5.5	6.1	6.8	7.5	8.0
Less: nonproductive component of all amortization allowances	.8	1.0	1.1	1.2	1.5	1.8	1.9
Equals: imputed nonproductive depreciation	3.5	3.9	4.4	4.9	5.3	5.7	6.1
Less: depreciation on private housing	1.4	1.5	1.5	1.5	1.6	1.6	1.6
Equals: imputed state-cooperative nonproductive depreciation	2.1	2.6	2.9	3.4	3.7	4.1	4.5
Add: state-cooperative amortization allowances	7.1	7.9	9.1	10.2	11.3	15.6	17.1
Equals: all state-cooperative depreciation	9.2	10.5	12.0	13.6	15.0	19.7	21.6

For 1965S the 1958 figure, 9.2 billion rubles, is inflated by the ratio of 1965S to 1958 amortization allowances, 180 percent.

B. *Collective farms.* Above, pp. 379 and 450.

C. *Private housing.* The 1960 value is explained above, in the sources to item 4.C. Other *ex post* entries are obtained by extending the 1960 value back and forward in time in proportion to the increase in the physical housing stock (p. 339). The 1965S figure is calculated from the 1958 figure, inflated by the 1958–1965S increase in imputed rent (pp. 335 and 430).

8. *Book value of retirements.* 1958–1963: See above, sources for item 6.A. The 1958 figure is obtained in the same way as the 1960–1962 figures. 1964: In the absence of other information, assumed unchanged from the 1963 level.

9. *Accidental losses.* A notional annual allowance of 1.0 billion rubles is assumed. Obviously, the actual amounts could vary widely around this figure. No information on these losses is available. The yearbooks lump them with the foreign trade balance in reporting the annual margin between produced and utilized NMP (see above, Chap. 7, note 41).

10. *Net investment.*

B. *Official data. VS,* 1966, No. 4, p. 96.

D. *Estimate for 1965S.* Takes into account the 1958–1964 margins between rows 7.D and 10.B.

Q

Public Sector Residual Outlays in 1965S and NMP by Final Use

Chapter 9 draws attention to the startling finding that "other outlays" of the public sector ("defense," internal security, R&D, outlays n.e.c. plus the public sector statistical discrepancy) in 1965S as estimated were to be more than 2½ times their 1958 level. The size of that increase meant a better than 60 percent increase in the relative weight of "other outlays" in GNP (Table 6). Values of the components of this amalgam were separately estimated for 1958 but, owing to absence of data, could not be separately estimated for 1965S. This appendix attempts to determine whether a clue to the distribution of "other outlays" in 1965S and to the credibility of the large 1958–1965S increase can be found in the reconstruction of the final use structure of NMP. The reconstruction, which also supplies comparative data for 1958 and 1964, is set out in Table Q-1.

The answer depends in part on the confidence that can be placed on the accuracy of the 1965S data. The reconstruction in Table Q-1 implies a 50 percent increase in personal consumption, compared with the 52 percent indicated in Table 35. Of course, there are some differences in the makeup of personal consumption in these two tables: as an element of GNP, household outlays include purchases of services as well as of goods. As an element of NMP, personal consumption excludes most services but includes depreciation on all housing, state-owned or private, actually costed or imputed, and an adjustment for the difference in method of valuing income in kind in the SNIP and official Soviet accounts. Nevertheless, these differences are outweighed by the elements common to personal consumption expenditures in Tables 35 and Q-1.

The similarity of the implied increases is, therefore, neither accidental nor proof of reliability of either table's values.

The 1965S entry for total institutional consumption—that is, total current material expenditures of the public sector, item 1.B(5)—is obtained as a residual, the difference between item 1.C, derived from official data, and item 1.A(9). If the values of the latter item may be assumed reasonably accurate, then the 1965S figures for total institutional consumption are indeed intriguing, for they imply an increase of about 150–200 percent in the SYP interval. After allowing for outlays on communal services (excluding R&D), housing, transportation-communication (not for production), other public sector services for consumption, and depreciation on nonproductive capital apart from housing, we find an institutional consumption residual, item 1.B(4)(c), whose 1965S level is 9 to 12 *times* as high as that of 1958!

I hasten to add that this residual in 1965S is extremely sensitive to error in the major components of consumption: a 5 percent understatement of total personal consumption in 1965S, all other things unchanged, means a reduction in the 1965S institutional consumption residual of one-half to two-thirds. A much larger error in the estimates of consumption apart from the residual is not likely, judging from the following evidence. The seven-year increase in the sum of items 1.A(9), 1.B(1)–(3) is 52 percent. Except that this group of expenditures excludes depreciation on the nonproductive capital of "institutions servicing households" and net investment of the household sector, it is identical to real incomes of the population, as Soviet statistics define that category. [Net, rather than gross, household investment is identified here to avoid double counting of depreciation on private housing. Depreciation on privately owned production capital is of course excluded from consumption, but whether it is also deducted to obtain real income is not clear.] In Appendix F it is estimated that the real income of collective farmers, workers, and employees was intended to increase by 54 percent. If, as is believed, incomes of the armed forces and of members of producer cooperatives are not included with those of workers and employees, addition of the omitted incomes to correspond with the scope of Table Q-1 would reduce the figure of 54 percent slightly. Addition of depreciation on nonproductive capital and household net investment would probably raise the 1958–1965S percentage increase in the sum of items 1.A(9) and 1.B(1)–(3). In short, a substantially larger 1965S than 1958 value for item 1.B(4)(c) is likely, but whether the true gap is as wide as indicated in Table Q-1 is highly conjectural.

A critical datum in the reconstruction of 1965S accumulation is net fixed investment, derived in a step by step buildup set out in Table 26. Inventory investment is estimated in Appendix H from fragmentary indications on expected changes in working capital liabilities. Table Q-1 also makes no allowance for increments in the stock of unfinished construction. Granted these figures, private sector inventories and state reserves were to have more than doubled over the Plan period, according to Table Q-1. As gross private agricultural output was not scheduled to increase by more than about one-seventh (Appendix E), it is a safe guess that state stockpiling was to increase considerably more rapidly than the sum of stockpiling and private inventory accumulation together. Again, however, the 1965S residual—in this case, item 2.B(2)—is sensitive to small errors in the other components of the total. A 10 percent error in the sum of items 2.A and 2.B(1) implies a 45 percent error in item 2.B(4). The conclusion is therefore similar to that drawn with respect to consumption: a substantially higher level of additions to state reserves in 1965S than in 1958 is possible and perhaps even probable, but far from certain.

Apart from estimating errors on other accounts, the 1965S figures may be off because of errors in the major subtotals for 1958 to which the announced percentage increase targets were applied to obtain absolute 1965S entries. The 1958 subtotals are taken from official sources but published in 1966. Up to that time no figures for 1958 were available. The 1959 figures were revised between first publication in the 1960 yearbook and republication in the 1961 yearbook (cf. *NKh 1960,* p. 154, and *NKh 1961,* p. 599). If this was true of the 1958 figures as well, the set available to planners in 1958–1959 and on which SYP targets were drawn may be quite different from that displayed in Table Q-1. The sensitivity of the residuals may be even greater than already indicated.

TABLE Q-1

NET MATERIAL PRODUCT BY USE, 1958, 1965S, AND 1964
(billion rubles)

	1958	1965S[a]	1964
1. Consumption fund			
A. Personal consumption of households			
(1) State-cooperative retail trade	60.33	98.2	88.18
(2) Utilities	.69	1.2	1.35
(3) "Industrial" services	.50	1.0	1.10
(4) Extravillage farm markets	4.43		4.42
(5) Income in kind	11.93	21.4	11.71
(6) "Other outlays for consumption"	3.00		4.00
(7) Farm income in kind valuation adjustment	.40	.5	.63
(8) Depreciation on housing	2.7	3.8	4.1
(9) Total	84.0	126.1	115.5
B. Material outlays in organizations servicing households, in science and administration			
(1) Education (excluding science), health care and other communal services	3.25	5.7	5.09
(2) Housing, transportation and communication, other public sector services for consumption	2.15	4.2	3.96
(3) Depreciation on nonproductive capital excluding housing	1.70	2.5	4.25
(4) Other			
(a) Science and administration	.86	..	1.48
(b) Residual	.1	..	.1
(c) Total	1.0	9–12	1.6
(5) Total	8.1	21–24	14.9
C. Total consumption fund	92.1	147–150	130.4
2. Accumulation fund			
A. Net increase of fixed capital	21.8	40	28.9
B. Net increase of inventories and reserves			
(1) Public sector inventory investment	7.90	7.3	11.63
(2) State-cooperative increment of unfinished construction	−.12	..	.85
(3) Increment of warehouse stocks of equipment requiring installation	—	—	.13
(4) Other: increment of collective farm unfinished construction, private agricultural stocks and state reserves	5.0	11	7.8
(5) Total	12.8	18	20.4
C. Total accumulation fund	34.6	58	49.3
3. Net material product utilized	126.7	205–208	179.7

Note:
[a] At 1958 prices.

Sources:
1958, 1964: Table 25.
1965S.
1. *Consumption fund.*
A. *Personal consumption.* Entries for items (1), (4), (5), (6) are taken from Table 6 and the sources to Table 20. Sources of other figures are as follows:
(2) *Utilities.* A ⅔ increase assumed, taking into account the 60 percent planned increase in the urban housing stock (p. 430) and the reported planned increase in the share

TABLE Q-1 (continued)

of new housing equipped with "conveniences" (*blagoustroistva*), from 75 percent in 1959 to 85 percent in 1965S (Broner, *Sovremennye problemy zhilishchnogo khoziaistva*, 1961, p. 116). Presumably, urban state housing is meant. Information on planned extension of utility service to rural households is lacking, but the Control Figures called for completion "in the main" of the electrification of collective farms by the end of the Plan period and for supply of electricity from the state power network to collective and state farms.

(3) *"Industrial" services.* The assumed doubling of the 1958 level is in line with the estimate of the increase in outlays on all "other services" (p. 433 ff.)

(7) *Income in kind adjustment.* Estimated as increasing roughly in proportion to private sector output (p. 425).

(8) *Depreciation on housing.*: A 40 percent increase is assumed, roughly in proportion to the estimated expected increase in the total housing stock (pp. 430–432).

(9) *Total:* Sum of components.

1.B. *Material outlays in organizations, etc.*

(1) *Education (excluding science), health, etc.* A 75 percent increase is estimated, roughly in proportion to the increase in public sector current outlays on communal services (Table 5).

(2) *Housing, etc.* Material outlays in socialized housing are increased by 75 percent over the 1958 level in proportion to the estimated increase in paid rent (p. 430). For other components, a doubling of the 1958 level is assumed, proportional to the change in household outlays on all "other services" (Table 4).

(3) *Depreciation on nonproductive capital excluding housing.* Estimate based on SYP targets in the field of health care and education (see pp. 458–463).

(4) *Other.*

(c) *Total.* Item 1.B(5) less the sum of items 1.B(1) through 1.B(3).

(5) *Total.* The difference between items 1.C and 1.A.

1.C. *Total consumption fund.* See sources for total NMP below.

2. *Accumulation fund.*

The figure for item 2.A is taken from Table 26, that for item 2.B(1) from pp. 466–467, and that for item 2.B(5) is the difference between items 2.C and 2.A. For the derivation of 2.C see sources for total NMP below. Item 2.B(4) is calculated as a residual, the difference between item 2.B(5) and the sum of items 2.B(1)–2.B(3).

3. *Net material product utilized.* The Control Figures directed a 62–65 percent increase in NMP and a 60–63 percent increase in the consumption fund. Although the accumulation fund target was not specified in the Control Figures, numerous contemporaneous Soviet sources (e.g., Sitarian, *FinSSSR*, 1959, No. 8, p. 12) indicate that the planned increase was 68 percent. The Control Figures did not define the concept of NMP to which the targets referred—that is, produced NMP or utilized NMP, the latter net of accidental loss or damage not charged to cost and of expenditures not distributed among consumption or investment. The former concept is suggested by the linking of the 62–65 percent target to the official series on growth of NMP at constant prices (*NKh 1959*, p. 77; *NKh 1960*, pp. 152, 873). However, the difference between produced and utilized NMP in 1958 amounts to 1.1 billion rubles (compare item 3 with *NKh 1964*, p. 575) and may have been expected to be similarly small in 1965S. In any case, allowing for rounding, application of the indicated percentage increases to the 1958 figures yields the following 1965S values (billion rubles):

Total consumption fund	146.9–150.5
Total accumulation fund	58.0– 58.3
NMP as sum of the above	204.9–208.8
NMP as 162–165 percent of 1958	204.6–209.6

The difference between the two sets of 1965S NMP figures is clearly insignificant. I therefore conclude that the Control Figures target for NMP applies to utilized as well as to produced NMP. The total accumulation fund in 1965S is taken to be 58 billion rubles and NMP is obtained as the sum of the accumulation and consumption fund entries.

Bibliography

Sources Cited by Short Title

SHORT TITLE	COMPLETE REFERENCE
1. *Books* (except where otherwise indicated, place of publication is Moscow)	
Dostizheniia	Tsentral'noe statisticheskoe upravlenie pri Sovete ministrov SSSR (TsSU SSSR), *Dostizheniia sovetskoi vlasti za 40 let v tisfrakh,* Gosstatizdat, 1957.
Finstroi	*Finansy i sotsialisticheskoe stroitel'stvo,* Gosfinizdat, 1957.
Gosbiudzhet I and *II*	Ministerstvo finansov SSSR, Biudzhetnoe upravlenie, *Gosudarstvennyi biudzhet SSSR i biudzhety soiuznykh respublik,* Gosfinizdat, 1962 (I) and Finansy, 1966 (II).
Kapstroi	TsSU SSSR, *Kapital'noe stroitel'stvo v SSSR,* Gosstatizdat, 1961.
NKh 1956 (1958, 1959, . . . 1965)	———, *Narodnoe khoziaistvo SSSR v 1956* (1958, 1959, . . . 1965) *godu,* Gosstatizdat, 1957 (1959, . . . 1962); Statistika, 1963–1966.
NKh RSFSR 1959 (1960, 1961, . . . 1963)	Tsentral'noe statisticheskoe upravlenie pri Sovete ministrov RSFSR, *Narodnoe khoziaistvo RSFSR v 1959* (1960, 1961, . . . 1963) *godu,* Gosstatizdat, 1960 (1961, 1962, 1963); Statistika, 1964.
Prom I and *II*	TsSU SSSR, *Promyshlennost' SSSR,* Gosstatizdat, 1957 (*I*) and Statistika, 1964 (*II*).
Raskhody	Ministerstvo finansov SSSR, Biudzhetnoe upravlenie, *Raskhody na sotsial'no-kul'turnye meropriiatiia po gosudarstvennomu biudzhetu SSSR,* Gosfinizdat, 1958.
Skh	TsSU SSSR, *Sel'skoe khoziaistvo SSSR,* Gosstatizdat, 1960.

SNIP . . .	
1928	Hoeffding, Oleg, *Soviet National Income and Product in 1928,* New York, Columbia University Press, 1954.
1937	Bergson, Abram, *Soviet National Income and Product in 1937,* New York, Columbia University Press, 1953.
1940–1948	——— and Hans Heymann, Jr., *Soviet National Income and Product, 1940–1948,* New York, Columbia University Press, 1954.
1940–1955	Hoeffding, Oleg and Nancy Nimitz, *Soviet National Income and Product 1949–1955,* Santa Monica, California, The RAND Corporation, RM-2101, April 1959.
1928–1948	Bergson, Abram, Hans Heymann, Jr., and Oleg Hoeffding, *Soviet National Income and Product, 1928–48: Revised Data,* Santa Monica, California, The RAND Corporation, RM-2544, November 1960.
Real SNIP	Bergson, Abram, *The Real National Income of Soviet Russia Since 1928,* Cambridge, Mass., Harvard University Press, 1961.
1956–1958	Nimitz, Nancy, *Soviet National Income and Product, 1956–1958,* Santa Monica, California, The RAND Corporation, RM-3112-PR, June 1962.
1965	Becker, Abraham S., *Soviet National Income and Product in 1965: The Goals of the Seven Year Plan,* Santa Monica, California, The RAND Corporation, RM-3520-PR, March 1963.
1958–1962, Part I	———, *Soviet National Income and Product, 1958–1962: Part I—National Income at Established Prices,* Santa Monica, California, The RAND Corporation, RM-4394-PR, June 1965.
1958–1962, Part II	———, *Soviet National Income and Product, 1958–1962: Part II—National Income at Factor Cost and Constant Prices,* Santa Monica, California, The RAND Corporation, RM-4881-PR, May 1966.
Sovtorg I and *II*	TsSU SSSR, *Sovetskaia torgovlia,* Gosstatizdat 1956 (I) and Statistika, 1964 (II).
Tsifry 1958	———, *SSSR v tsifrakh,* Gosstatizdat, 1959.
Tsifry 1959 (1960, 1961, . . . 1964)	———, *SSSR v tsifrakh v 1959* (1960, 1961, . . . 1964) *godu,* Gosstatizdat, 1960

	(1961, 1962, 1963); Statistika, 1964, 1965.
Vneshtorg . . .	Ministerstvo vneshnei torgovli SSSR, planovo-ekonomicheskoe upravlenie, *Vneshniaia torgovlia Soiuza SSR za . . .*
1959–1963	*1959–1963 gody,* Vneshtorgizdat, 1965.
1965	*1965 god,* Izdatel'stvo Mezhdunarodnye otnosheniia, 1966.

2. *Soviet journals and newspapers* (published in Moscow)

DiK	*Den'gi i kredit*
Ekon.gazeta	*Ekonomicheskaia gazeta*
ESKh	*Ekonomika sel'skogo khoziaistva*
FinSSSR	*Finansy SSSR*
PKh	*Planovoe khoziaistvo*
VE	*Voprosy ekonomiki*
VS	*Vestnik statistiki*

Other Works Cited

Note: Place of publication of all Soviet books is Moscow, unless otherwise stated. Complete references for abbreviated names of journals and books will be found in the *List of Short Titles.*

Agabab'ian, E. M., "O sinteticheskom pokazatele potrebleniia uslug," in V. F. Maier and P. N. Krylov, eds., *Planirovanie narodnogo potrebleniia v SSSR; sovremennye problemy,* Ekonomika, 1964, pp. 101–111.

Aganbegian, A. G., "Rost' proizvoditel'nosti truda v sel'skom khoziaistve—vazhneishee uslovie povysheniia material'nogo blagosostoianiia trudiashchikhsia," in Moskovskii gosudarstvennyi universitet, *Povyshenie proizvoditel'nosti truda—glavnoe uslovie rosta sel'skokhoziaistvennogo proizvodstva v semiletke,* Moskovskogo universiteta, 1960, pp. 109–134.

AN (Akademia nauk) SSSR, Institut ekonomiki, *Material'noe stimulirovanie razvitiia kolkhoznogo proizvodstva,* AN SSSR, 1963.

———, *Metody i praktika opredeleniia effektivnosti kapital'nykh vlozhenii i novoi tekhniki,* sbornik nauchnoi informatsii, vypusk 10, Nauka, 1966.

Akademiia obshchestvennykh nauk pri Tsk KPSS, *Puti povysheniia proizvoditel'nosti truda v sel'skom khoziaistve SSSR,* Nauka, 1964.

Aleksandrov, A. M., ed., *Gosudarstvennyi biudzhet SSSR,* Gosfinizdat, 1961.

Alekseev, Sergei A., *Ekonomika zhilishchnogo khoziaistva,* Stroiizdat, 1966.

Alekseeva, R. V. and A. P. Voronin, *Nakoplenie i razvitie kolkhoznoi sobstvennosti,* Ekonomizdat, 1963.

Alisov, M., "Vazhnye voprosy proizvodstva i realizatsii produktov sel'skogo khoziaistva," *Kommunist,* No. 15, October 1963, pp. 88–95.

Allakhverdian, Derenik A., *Finansy SSSR,* Gosfinizdat, 1958.

———, ed., *Finansy SSSR,* Gosfinizdat, 1962.

———, *Finansy v period stroitel'stva kommunizma,* Gosfinizdat, 1963.

———, "Nekotorye voprosy finansovogo planirovaniia," *VE,* 1965, No. 8, pp. 80–91.

Anchishkin, A. I., *Nalog s oborota—Konkretnaia forma pribavochnogo produkta sotsialisticheskogo proizvodstva,* Vysshaia shkola, 1962.

Annual Economic Indicators for the USSR. See U.S. Congress.

Arms Control and Disarmament Agency (ACDA), "Worldwide Defense Expenditures and Selected Economic Data, 1964," *Bulletin of the Atomic Scientists,* September 1966, pp. 44–48.

Bachurin, A. V., ed., *Finansy i kredit SSSR,* 2nd ed., Gosfinizdat, 1958.

——— and D. P. Kondrashev, eds., *Tovarno-denezhnye otnosheniia v period perekhoda k kommunizmu,* Ekonomizdat, 1963.

Badir'ian, G. G., ed., *Ekonomika, organizatsiia i planirovanie sel'skokhoziaistvennogo proizvodstva,* Ekonomizdat, 1963.

Balashov, A., "Razvitie deiatel'nosti potrebitel'skoi kooperatsii za semiletie, 1959–1965 gg," *Sovetskaia potrebitel'skaia kooperatsiia,* 1966, No. 3, pp. 28–33.

Baranov, V., "Razvivat' i sovershenstvovat' gosudarstvennoe strakhovanie," in *Voprosy gosudarstvennogo strakhovaniia,* Finansy, 1964.

Bashin, Maks L., *Planirovanie nauchno-issledovatel'skikh i opytnokonstruktorskikh rabot,* Ekonomika, 1966.

Basistov, A., "Ekonomicheskoe stimulirovanie vnedreniia novoi tekhniki," *VE,* 1964, No. 5, pp. 23–34.

Bauman, L. and V. Tolkushkin, "Ob uchete territorial'nykh razlichii gosudarstvennykh roznichnykh tsen," *VS,* 1965, No. 4, pp. 31–39.

Becker, Abraham S., *Soviet Military Outlays Since 1955,* The RAND Corporation, RM-3886-PR, July 1964.

Beermann, R., "The Parasites Law," *Soviet Studies,* Vol. 13, No. 2, October 1961, pp. 191–205.

Beliaev, V., Z. Okuneva, and N. Pen'kova, "Rezervy povysheniia fondootdachi v khimicheskoi promyshlennosti," *VE,* 1965, No. 11, pp. 57–63.

Beliaevskii, Igor' K., *Statistika kolkhoznoi torgovli,* Gosstatizdat, 1962.

Belik, Iu. A., *Natsional'nyi dokhod SSSR v semiletke,* Znanie, 1959.

———, "Velichestvennaia programma povysheniia zhiznennogo urovnia sovetskogo naroda," *PKh,* 1962, No. 1, pp. 3–13.

Belkin, Viktor D., *Tseny edinogo urovnia i ekonomicheskie izmereniia na ikh osnove,* Ekonomizdat, 1963.

Belousov, R. and N. Petrakov, "Ekonomicheskoe stimulirovanie proizvodstva i ispol'zovaniia mineral'nykh udobrenii," *VE,* 1965, No. 11, pp. 144–151.

Bergson, Abram and Simon Kuznets, eds., *Economic Trends in the Soviet Union,* Cambridge, Mass., Harvard University Press, 1963.

Birman, A. M., ed., *Finansy predpriiatii i otraslei narodnogo khoziaistva,* Gosfinizdat, 1960.

Boev, V., "Zakupochnye tseny i rentabel'nost' kolkhoznogo proizvodstva," *PKh,* 1966, No. 11, pp. 13–19.

Boiarskii, Aron Ia. *et al.*, eds., *Statisticheskii slovar',* Statistika, 1965.

Bolgov, A. V. *et al.*, eds., *Ekonomika sotsialisticheskogo sel'skogo khoziaistva*, Ekonomika, 1965.
Bol'shaia sovetskaia entsiklopediia, 2nd edition, Bol'shaia sovetskaia entsiklopediia, 1955.
Bor, Mikhail Z., "K voprosu o skheme planovogo balansa narodnogo khoziaistva," in AN SSSR, *Uchenye zapiski po statistike, tom 4. Voprosy balansa narodnogo khoziaistva i korreliatsii*, AN SSSR, 1959, pp. 50–62.
———, *Voprosy metodologii planovogo balansa narodnogo khoziaistva SSSR*, AN SSSR, 1960.
——— and A. Notkin, "Metodologicheskie problemy balansa narodnogo khoziaistvo," *VE*, 1961, No. 5, pp. 36–47.
Borisov, V., *Balans denezhnykh dokhodov i raskhodov naseleniia*, Finansy, 1965.
Bornstein, Morris, "The 1963 Soviet Industrial Price Revision," *Soviet Studies*, July 1963, Vol. 15, No. 1, pp. 43–52.
———, "The Reform and Revaluation of the Ruble," *American Economic Review*, March 1961, Vol. 51, No. 1, pp. 117–123.
——— "The Soviet Price System," *American Economic Review*, March 1962, Vol. 52, No. 1, pp. 64–103.
——— and others, *Soviet National Accounts for 1955*, Center for Russian Studies, The University of Michigan, 1961.
Bowles, W. Donald, "Pricing in Soviet Timber Sales," *Soviet Studies*, July 1961, Vol. 8, pp. 23–34.
Broner, David L., *Sovremennye problemy zhilishchnogo khoziaistva*, Vysshaia shkola, 1961.
Budavei, V., E. Ivanov, and K. Said-Galiev, "Rasshirennoe vosproizvodstvo osnovnykh fondov promyshlennosti SSSR v 1959–1965 godakh," *PKh*, 1959, No. 6, pp. 11–23.
Bukshtein, D., "Prichiny i sledstviia oshibok v smetnom dele," *Ekonomika stroitel'stva*, 1966, No. 8, pp. 53–54.
Bunich, Pavel G., "Amortizatsiia i voprosy finansirovaniia remonta i modernizatsii osnovnykh fondov," *VE*, 1959, No. 4, pp. 106–115.
———, "Amortizatsionnyi fond i obshchestvennye izderzhki proizvodstva," *VE*, 1960, No. 10, pp. 44–53.
———, ed., *Ekonomicheskaia rabota v finansovo-kreditnoi sisteme*, Finansy, 1965.
———, "Ispol'zovanie osnovnykh proizvodstvennykh fondov promyshlennosti," in P. Bunich, ed., *Ekonomicheskaia rabota v finansovo-kreditnoi sisteme*, Finansy, 1965, pp. 87–93.
———, *Osnovnye fondy sotsialisticheskoi promyshlennosti*, Gosplanizdat, 1960.
———, "Problemy kapital'nogo remonta osnovnykh fondov v promyshlennosti," in NIFI, *Planirovanie i finansirovanie kapital'nogo remonta osnovnykh fondov*, Gosfinizdat, 1958, pp. 5–35.
Burshtein, F. I. and V. T. Gusev, *Chto takoe mezhotraslevoi balans*, Ekonomizdat, 1963.
Bush, Keith, "Agricultural Reforms Since Khrushchev," in U.S. Congress,

Joint Economic Committee, *New Directions in the Soviet Economy,* 1966, pp. 451–472.

———, "Soviet Gold Production and Reserves Reconsidered," *Soviet Studies,* April 1966, Vol. 17, No. 4, pp. 490–493.

Campbell, Robert W., *Accounting in Soviet Planning and Management,* Cambridge, Mass., Harvard University Press, 1963.

Central Intelligence Agency, *A Comparison of Consumption in the USSR and the US,* Washington, D.C., January 1964.

———, *An Evaluation of the Soviet Wage Reform 1956–1962,* Washington, D.C., August 1963.

———, *Index of Civilian Industrial Production in the USSR, 1950–1961,* September 1963; *Supplement,* October 1963.

———, *Labor Supply and Employment in the USSR 1950–1965,* Washington, D.C., October 1960.

———, *The 1960 Soviet Budget,* Washington, D.C., November 1960.

———, *The Soviet Budget for 1961,* Washington, D.C., June 1961.

———, *The Soviet Budget for 1962,* Washington, D.C., November 1962.

Chandra, N. K., "Long-Term Economic Plans and Their Methodology," *Soviet Studies,* January 1967, Vol. 18, No. 3, pp. 296–313.

Chao, Kang, "Industrialization and Urban Housing in Communist China," *The Journal of Asian Studies,* May 1966, Vol. 25, No. 3, pp. 381–396.

Chapman, Janet, "The Minimum Wage in the USSR," *Problems of Communism,* September–October 1964, pp. 76–79.

———, *Real Wages in Soviet Russia Since 1928,* Cambridge, Mass., Harvard University Press, 1963.

Cohn, Stanley H., "Comment on 2½ Per Cent and All That," *Soviet Studies,* January 1965, Vol. 16, No. 3, pp. 302–316.

———, *Derivation of 1959 Value-Added Weights for Originating Sectors of Soviet Gross National Product,* Technical Paper RAC-TP-210, Research Analysis Corporation, McLean, Virginia, April 1966.

———, "The Gross National Product in the Soviet Union: Comparative Growth Rates," in U.S. Congress, Joint Economic Committee, *Dimensions of Soviet Economic Power,* 1962, pp. 69–89.

Comparisons of the United States and Soviet Economies. See U.S. Congress.

Current Economic Indicators for the USSR. See U.S. Congress.

Davies, R. W., G. R. Barker, and R. Fakiolas, in C. Freeman and A. Young, *The Research and Development Effort in Western Europe, North America, and the Soviet Union,* Paris, OECD, 1965.

Denezhnoe obrashchenie i kredit SSSR, Vysshaia shkola, 1965.

D'iachenko, V. P., ed., *Finansovo-kreditnyi slovar',* Vol. 1, Gosfinizdat, 1961; Vol. 2, Finansy, 1964.

D'iachkov, Mikhail F., *Statistika kapital'nogo stroitel'stva,* Gosstatizdat, 1962.

Dobb, Maurice, *Soviet Economic Development Since 1917,* 5th ed., London, Routledge and Kegan Paul, 1960.

Domar, Evsey D., *Essays in the Theory of Economic Growth,* New York, Oxford University Press, 1957.

———, "An Index-Number Tournament," *The Quarterly Journal of Economics,* May 1967, Vol. 81, No. 2, pp. 169–188.

Dimensions of Soviet Economic Power. See U.S. Congress.

Effektivnost' kapital'nykh vlozhenii v sel'skoe khoziaistvo, Sel'khozizdat, 1963.

Efimov, A., "Novye normy amortizatsii osnovnykh fondov," *VE,* 1959, No. 9, pp. 3–13.

——— and L. Ia. Berri, eds., *Metody planirovaniia mezhotraslevykh proportsii,* Ekonomika, 1965.

Efimov, V. and K. Karpov, "Sovkhozam—polnyi khoziaistvennyi raschet," *Kommunist,* No. 15, 1966, pp. 75–85.

Efremov, S. and S. Reinin, "Tseny—glavnyi ekonomicheskii rychag," *Ekonomika stroitel'stva,* 1967, No. 12, pp. 40–42.

Egereva, Lidiia I., *Balans proizvodstva i raspredeleniia produktsii sel'skogo khoziaistva,* Ekonomizdat, 1963.

———, "Ob"em i struktura valovoi produktsii sel'skogo khoziaistva," in M. Lemeshev, ed., *Ekonomicheskoe obosnovanie struktury sel'skokhoziaistvennogo proizvodstva,* Ekonomika, 1965, pp. 153–174.

Eidel'man, Moisei R., "Konechnyi produkt v mezhotraslevom balanse," *Ekonomika i matematicheskie metody,* 1967, Vol. 3, No. 4, pp. 533–538.

———, *Mezhotraslevoi balans obshchestvennogo produkta,* Statistika, 1966.

Ekonomicheskii ezhegodnik, god 1966. See S. P. Pervyshin, ed.

Emel'ianov, A. and I. Marinko, "Metodologicheskie voprosy perevoda sovkhozov na polnyi khozraschet," *VE,* 1965, No. 9, pp. 23–34.

Eremina, N. M. and V. P. Marshalova, *Statistika truda,* Statistika, 1965.

Erlich, Alexander, "Stalin's Views on Soviet Economic Development," in Ernest J. Simmons, ed., *Continuity and Change in Russian and Soviet Thought,* Cambridge, Mass., Harvard University Press, 1955, pp. 81–99.

Evdokimov, V., "K voprosu ob ekonomicheskom soderzhanii naloga s oborota v SSSR," in Moskovskii institut narodnogo khoziaistva (MINKh), im. G. V. Plekhanova, *Nauchnye zapiski aspirantov,* Finansy, 1964, pp. 165–178.

Fefilov, A. I., *Roznichnaia torgovlia v SSSR,* Gostorgizdat, 1957.

Figurnov, Sergei P., *Real'naia zarabotnaia plata i pod"em material'nogo blagosostoianiia trudiashchikhsia v SSSR,* Sotsekgiz, 1960.

———, *Stroitel'stvo kommunizma i rost blagosostoianiia naroda,* Sotsekgiz, 1962.

Filippov, Pavel R., *Novye normy amortizatsii,* Ekonomizdat, 1963.

———, "Sovershenstvovat' planirovanie amortizatsionnykh otchislenii," *PKh,* 1960, No. 11, pp. 39–43.

Finansovo-kreditnyi slovar'. See V. P. D'iachenko, ed.

Fonarev, E., *Raspredelenie i ispol'zovanie pribyli potrebitel'skoi kooperatsii,* Finansy, 1966.

Gabrieli, M., "Tsena i voprosy effektivnosti novoi sel'skokhoziaistvennoi tekhniki," *VE,* 1963, No. 7, pp. 59–69.

Galkin, I. G., *Voprosy ritmichnosti i zadela v stroitel'stve,* Gosstroiizdat, 1962.

Garbuzov, V., "Biudzhet novogo pod"ema ekonomiki i kul'tury strany," *PKh*, 1959, No. 12, pp. 3–15.

———, "Finansovaia sistema pered novymi zadachami," *FinSSSR*, 1961, No. 1, pp. 3–21.

———, "Gosudarstvennyi biudzhet SSSR i zadachi finansovykh organov na 1965 god," *FinSSSR*, 1965, No. 1, pp. 3–21.

———, "Novyi zakon o sel'skokhoziaistvennom naloge," *Finansy i kredit SSSR*, 1953, No. 9, pp. 9–15.

———, "Resheniia noiabr'skogo Plenuma TsK KPSS i zadachi finansovykh organov," *FinSSSR*, 1963, No. 1, pp. 3–19.

———, "Resheniia piatoi sessii Verkhovnogo soveta SSSR i zadachi finansovykh organov," *FinSSSR*, 1960, No. 5, pp. 1–15.

———, "Samaia prochnaia valiuta v mire," *Kommunist*, No. 1, January 1961, pp. 57–65.

———, "Uspeshnoe vypolnenie biudzheta—vazhnyi vklad v osushchestvlenie reshenii dekabr'skogo Plenuma TsK KPSS," *FinSSSR*, 1964, No. 1, pp. 3–19.

———, "Voprosy finansirovaniia i kreditovaniia sel'skogo khoziaistva v novykh usloviiakh," *FinSSSR*, 1959, No. 2, pp. 10–21.

Gass, Oscar, "Russia: Khrushchev and After," *Commentary*, November 1963, Vol. 36, No. 5, pp. 353–363.

Gatovskii, L., *Vestnik Akademii nauk SSSR*. See "Khoziaistvennaia reforma . . . "

Gel'rud, S. M., and A. F. Iakovleva, compilers, *Albom nagliadnykh posobii po kursu "Gosudarstvennyi biudzhet,"* Gosfinizdat, 1963.

Gladkov, N., "Kak opredeliat' razmer strakhovykh summ dlia dobrovol'nogo strakhovaniia stroenii grazhdan," *FinSSSR*, 1960, No. 1, pp. 74–77.

Glezerman, G., "V. I. Lenin o vzaimootnoshenii ekonomiki i politiki v stroitel'stve novogo obshchestva," *Kommunist*, No. 7, May 1963, pp. 30–40.

Gol'tsman, L. N., *Ekonomika kommunal'nogo khoziaistva, uslugi, tarify*, Ekonomika, 1966.

Gol'tsov, A. N., "Raspredelenie i ispol'zovanie trudovykh resursov kolkhozov," *Sotsialisticheskii trud*, 1960, No. 5, pp. 32–41.

———, "Raspredelenie i ispol'zovanie trudovykh resursov v sel'skom khoziaistve," in N. I. Shishkin, ed., *Trudovye resursy SSSR*, Ekonomizdat, 1961, pp. 85–127.

Gorokhov, K., "Finansy—vazhnyi rychag mobilizatsii vnutrikhoziaistvennykh rezervov," *Kommunist*, No. 15, October 1960, pp. 49–59.

Gosplan pri sovete ministrov SSSR, *Raschetnye i spravochnye materialy k obosnovaniiu proekta perspektivnogo plana razvitiia narodnogo khoziaistva SSSR na 1959–1965 gody* and *Formy i pokazateli k sostavleniiu proekta perspektivnogo plana razvitiia narodnogo khoziaistva SSSR na 1959–1965 gody*, in French translation in *Cahiers de l'Institut de Science Economique Appliquée, Le Plan Septennal Soviétique*, No. 107, Series G, No. 10, November 1960.

Gosudarstvennyi bank SSSR k XXII s"ezdu KPSS, Kratkii ocherk deiatel'-

nosti Gosbanka za period mezhdu XX i XXII s"ezdami KPSS, Gosfinizdat, 1961.

Greenslade, Rush V. and Phyllis Wallace, "Industrial Production in the USSR," in U.S. Congress, *Dimensions of Soviet Economic Power,* 1962, pp. 119–136.

Gritskov, M., "Zhiznenno neobkhodimaia mera," *Kommunist,* No. 9, 1962, pp. 40–45.

Grossman, Gregory, "The 'Time Factor': Two Aspects," *Problems of Communism,* May–June 1959, Vol. 8, No. 3, pp. 3–7.

Grushetskii, L., "Sovershenstvovat' metody ischisleniia sopostavimykh dannykh," *ESKh,* 1965, No. 3, pp. 90–93.

Gumerov, R., "Sovershenstvovanie tsen na kolkhoznuiu produktsiiu i ukreplenie khozrascheta v kolkhozakh," *FinSSSR,* 1965, No. 8, pp. 7–16.

Hoeffding, Oleg, "The Soviet Industrial Reorganization of 1957," *American Economic Review, Papers and Proceedings,* May 1959, Vol. 49, No. 2, pp. 65–77.

———, "Substance and Shadow in the Soviet Seven Year Plan," *Foreign Affairs,* April 1959, pp. 394–406.

Holzman, Franklyn D., *Soviet Taxation, The Fiscal and Monetary Problems of a Planned Economy,* Cambridge, Mass., Harvard University Press, 1955.

Horelick, Arnold L. and Myron Rush, *Strategic Power and Soviet Foreign Policy,* Chicago, University of Chicago Press, 1966.

Hunter, Holland, "Optimum Tautness in Developmental Planning," *Economic Development and Cultural Change,* July 1961, Vol. 9, No. 4, Pt. 1, pp. 561–572.

Iakovets, Iurii V., *Metodologiia tsenoobrazovaniia v gornodobyvaiushchei promyshlennosti,* Ekonomika, 1964.

Ignatov, I. D., *Puti razvitiia kolkhoznoi torgovli,* Gosplanizdat, 1959.

Ikonnikov, V. V., ed., *Denezhnoe obrashchenie i kredit SSSR,* 2nd ed., Gosfinizdat, 1954.

Institute for Strategie Studies, *The Military Balance 1962–1963,* November 1962.

———, *The Military Balance 1963–1964,* November 1963.

———, *The Military Balance 1964–1965,* November 1964.

———, *The Military Balance 1965–1966,* November 1965.

Iurkin, T., "Razvitie sovkhoznogo proizvodstva v RSFSR," *ESKh,* 1959, No. 3, pp. 38–47.

Ivliev, I. V., ed., *Planirovanie na zheleznodorozhnom transporte,* Transzheldorizdat, 1961.

Jasny, Naum, *Essays on the Soviet Economy,* New York, Frederick A. Praeger, 1962.

———, *Soviet Industrialization, 1928–1952,* Chicago, University of Chicago Press, 1961.

Johnson, D. Gale and Arcadius Kahan, *The Soviet Agricultural Program: An Evaluation of the 1965 Goals,* The RAND Corporation, RM-2848-PR, May 1962.

Kahan, Arcadius, "Soviet Statistics of Agricultural Output," in Roy D. Laird, ed., *Soviet Agricultural and Peasant Affairs,* Lawrence, Kansas, University of Kansas Press, 1963, pp. 134–160.

Kamenitzer, S., "Ekonomicheskie voprosy ispol'zovaniia proizvodstvennykh moshchnostei," *VE,* 1965, No. 8, pp. 3–12.

Kaplan, Norman M., "Capital Stock," in Abram Bergson and Simon Kuznets, eds., *Economic Trends in the Soviet Union,* Cambridge, Mass., Harvard University Press, 1963, pp. 96–149.

———, *Soviet Transport and Communications: Output Indexes, 1928–1962,* The RAND Corporation, RM-4264-PR, November 1964; *Supplement,* November 1965.

——— and Richard Moorsteen, "An Index of Soviet Industrial Output," *American Economic Review,* June 1960, Vol. 50, No. 3, pp. 295–318.

Kapustin, E. I., ed., *Obshchestvennye fondy i rost blagosostoianiia naroda v SSSR,* Sotsekgiz, 1962.

Karcz, Jerzy F., *A Compendium of Soviet Farm Prices in 1961* (mimeo.) Berkeley, University of California, Institute of International Studies, 1964.

———, "The New Soviet Agricultural Programme," *Soviet Studies,* October 1965, Vol. 17, No. 2, pp. 129–161.

———, "Quantitative Analysis of the Collective Farm Market," *American Economic Review,* June 1964, Vol. 54, No. 4, Part I, pp. 315–334.

———, "Seven Years on the Farm: Retrospect and Prospects," in U.S. Congress, Joint Economic Committee, *New Directions in the Soviet Economy,* 1966, pp. 383–450.

Kaser, Michael C., "Changes in Planning Methods During the Preparation of the Soviet Seven-Year Plan," *Soviet Studies,* April 1959, Vol. 10, No. 4, pp. 321–338.

———, The Nature of Soviet Planning; A Critique of Jasny's Appraisal," *Soviet Studies,* October 1962, Vol. 14, No. 2, pp. 109–131.

———, "The Reorganization of Soviet Industry and Its Effects on Decision Making," in G. Grossman, ed., *Value and Plan,* Berkeley, University of California Press, 1960, pp. 213–234.

Kassirov, Leonid N., *Planovye pokazateli i khozraschetnye stimuly proizvodstva v kolkhozakh i sovkhozakh,* Ekonomika, 1965.

Kats, Adol'f I., *Proizvoditel'nost' truda v SSSR i glavnykh kapitalisticheskikh stranakh,* Ekonomika, 1964.

Kats, Iakov D., *Ocherki statistiki truda,* Gosstatizdat, 1960.

Kerblay, Basile, "Entretiens sur la planification avec des économistes soviétiques," *Cahiers du Monde Russe et Soviétique,* May 1959, Vol. 1, No. 1, pp. 174–179.

Khachaturov, T., "Puti povysheniia ekonomicheskoi effektivnosti kapital'nykh vlozhenii," *VE,* 1963, No. 11, pp. 27–38.

Khlebnikov, V., "O dal'neishem ukreplenii ekonomiki kolkhozov," *VE,* 1962, No. 7, pp. 49–57.

———, "Rentabel'nost'—osnova ob"ektivnoi otsenki khoziaistvennoi deiatel'nosti kolkhozov i sovkhozov," *ESKh,* 1965, No. 11, pp. 37–47.

———, "Voprosy analiza rentabel'nosti sel'skokhoziaistvennogo proizvodstva," *VS,* 1965, No. 5, pp. 19–38.

"Khoziaistvennaia reforma i nauchno-tekhnicheskii progress," *Vestnik Akademiia nauk SSSR,* 1967, No. 9, pp. 12–17.

Khrushchev, Nikita S., *Stroitel'stvo kommunizma v SSSR i razvitie sel'skogo khoziaistva,* March 1962–March 1963, Vol. 7, Gospolitizdat, 1963.

Kirichenko, V. N., "Ukreplenie ekonomicheskoi sviazi promyshlennosti s sel'skom khoziaistvom," in N. A. Tsagolov, ed., *Razvitie kolkhoznoi sobstvennosti v period razvernutogo stroitel'stva kommunizma,* Ekonomizdat, 1961, pp. 118–129.

Komarov, V. E., *Ekonomicheskie osnovy podgotovki spetsialistov dlia narodnogo khoziaistvo,* AN SSSR, 1959.

Kondrashev, Denis D., "Razvitie systemy optovykh tsen v promyshlennosti," *DiK,* 1962, No. 6, pp. 23–33.

———, *Tsena i khoziaistvennyi raschet,* Sotsekgiz, 1961.

———, *Tsena i stoimost' v sotsialisticheskom khoziaistve,* Sotsekgiz, 1963.

Koriunov, Sergei N., *Nedelimye fondy i kapital'nye vlozheniia kolkhozov,* Gosfinizdat, 1960.

Koroviakovskii, Dmitrii Z., *Sovershenstvovanie sistemy gosudarstvennykh zagotovok sel'skokhoziaistvennykh produktov v SSSR,* Ekonomizdat, 1963.

Koshelev, F. P., "Sotsial'no-ekonomicheskaia priroda sel'skokhoziaistvennoi arteli i perspektivy ee dal'neishego razvitiia," *Vestnik Moskovskogo universiteta,* Seriia ekonomiki, filosofii, prava, 1958, No. 3, pp. 3–28.

Kotov, Fedor I., *Voprosy truda v semiletnem plane,* Gosplanizdat, 1960.

——— and P. Krylov, "Ob osnovnykh metodicheskikh polozheniiakh k sostavleniiu narodnokhoziaistvennykh planov," *PKh,* 1958, No. 9, pp. 11–24.

Kramish, Arnold, *Atomic Energy in the Soviet Union.* Stanford, California, Stanford University Press, 1959.

Krasovskii, V. P., *Problemy ekonomiki kapital'nykh vlozhenii,* Ekonomika, 1967.

Kreinin, A., "Problemy tsenoobrazovaniia na transporte," *VE,* 1959, No. 8, pp. 130–136.

"Kto ne rabotaet, tot ne est," *Kommunist,* No. 14, September 1960, pp. 13–21.

Kuleshov, V. U., *Sotsialisticheskoe vosproizvodstvo,* Vysshaia shkola, 1961.

Kuperman, Ia. M., *Oborotnye sredstva i proizvodstvennye zapasy stroitel'nykh organizatsii,* Ekonomika, 1964.

Kvasha, Ia. B., "Kapitaloemkost," in Vladimir G. Venzher *et al., Proizvodstvo, nakoplenie, potreblenie,* Ekonomika, 1965, pp. 112–174.

——— and V. Krasovskii, "Kapital'noe stroitel'stvo i problema vozmeshcheniia," *VE,* 1964, No. 11, pp. 8–16.

Lagutin, N., "O sootnoshenii pokazateli razvitiia promyshlennosti i sel'skogo khoziaistva SSSR," *VE,* 1960, No. 11, pp. 55–63.

——— and M. Lemeshev, "O likvidatsii sotsial'no-ekonomicheskikh i kul'-

turno-bytovykh razlichii mezhdu gorodom i derevnei," *ESKh,* 1962, No. 5, pp. 32–38.

Lavrov, Vasilii, "Gosudarstvennyi biudzhet—vazhnoe orudie planovogo rukovodstva," *PKh,* 1962, No. 2, pp. 38–50.

——— *et al., Finansy i kredit SSSR,* Finansy, 1964.

Lemeshev, M. Ia., ed., *Ekonomicheskoe obosnovanie struktury sel'skokhoziaistvennogo proizvodstva,* Ekonomika, 1965.

Levine, Herbert S., "The Centralized Planning of Supply in Soviet Industry," in U.S. Congress, *Comparisons of the United States and Soviet Economies,* pp. 151–176.

Levitskii, Iu. I., "Nepreryvnost' v planirovanii i vlianie priamykh sviazei na formirovanie godovykh planov predpriiatii," in Nauchno-issledovatel'skii ekonomicheskii institut, B. L. Goncharenko *et al.*, eds., *Nepreryvnost' v planirovanii i pokazateli gosudarstvennogo plana,* Ekonomizdat, 1962, pp. 54–62.

Liberman, Evsei, Comments on E. Gromov *et al., Vosproizvodstvo konechnogo obshchestvennogo produkta SShA,* in *Mirovaia ekonomika i mezhdunarodnye otnosheniia,* 1967, No. 12, pp. 141–142.

Linden, Carl A., *Khrushchev and the Soviet Leadership, 1957–1964,* Baltimore, Maryland, Johns Hopkins Press, 1966.

Loginov, E. F. See *Zasedaniia Verkhovnogo soveta . . . 15–19 dekabria 1966 g.*

Loza, P., "Sozdanie fonda amortizatsii v kolkhozakh," *VE,* 1960, No. 3, pp. 140–144.

Lukanina, E., *Rol' kredita v formirovanii osnovykh sredstv kolkhozov,* Finansy, 1965.

Maier, Vladimir F., *Zarabotnaia plata v period perekhoda k kommunizmu,* Ekonomizdat, 1963.

——— and P. N. Krylov, eds., *Planirovanie narodnogo potrebleniia v SSSR,* Ekonomika, 1964.

Maizel's, D. L., *Statistika kapital'nogo stroitel'stva,* Gosstatizdat, 1962.

Malafeev, A. N., *Istoriia tsenoobrazovaniia v SSSR (1917–1963 gg.),* Mysl', 1964.

Maniakin, V., "Preodolet' otstavanie v razvitii sel'skogo khoziaistva," *ESKh,* 1965, No. 2, pp. 1–12.

Mar'iakhin, G., "Pereraspredelenie sredstv naseleniia cherez finansovuiu sistemu," *FinSSSR,* 1960, No. 2, pp. 33–41.

Marinko, I. and N. Sabadakha, "Stimulirovanie intensifikatsii sel'skokhoziaistvennogo proizvodstva," *Ekonomicheskie nauki,* 1966, No. 5, pp. 57–67.

Markov, V., "Aktual'nye problemy ispol'zovaniia trudovykh resursov," *PKh,* October 1965, No. 10, pp. 1–8.

Maslakov, V., N. Filatov, and V. Barmin, *Finansy zhilishchnogo i kommunal'nogo khoziaistva,* Gosfinizdat, 1960.

Matlin, A., *Tekhnicheskii progress i tseny mashin,* Ekonomika, 1966.

MFI (Moskovskii finansovyi institut), *Problemy finansovogo planirovaniia,* sbornik statei, Gosfinizdat, 1963.

Millionshchikov, A. *et al., Otchisleniia ot pribyli,* Finansy, 1964.

Milykh, A. F. and F. N. Nazarov, *Planirovanie proektno-izyskatel'skikh rabot v stroitel'stve,* Gosplanizdat, 1961.
MINKh. See Evdokimov.
Miroshchenko, S. M., ed., *Gosudarstvennye dokhody,* Finansy, 1964.
Mitel'man, E., "Effektivno ispol'zovat' oborotnye sredstva," *DiK,* 1958, No. 12, pp. 37–46.
Moorsteen, Richard H., "On Measuring Productive Potential and Relative Efficiency," *Quarterly Journal of Economics,* August 1961, Vol. 75, No. 3, pp. 451–467.
——— and Raymond P. Powell, *The Soviet Capital Stock 1928–1962,* Homewood, Illinois, Richard D. Irwin, 1966.
Morozov, V., "O kolkhoznom rynke," *VE,* 1962, No. 2, pp. 58–67.
———, "O tsenakh vnutrikolkhoznogo rynka," *VE,* 1963, No. 8, pp. 144–150.
———, *Trudoden', den'gi i torgovlia na sele,* Ekonomika, 1965.
Morozova, I. A., *Balans narodnogo khoziaistva i metody ego postroeniia,* Gosstatizdat, 1961.
Nazarkin, K. I., ed., *Uchet i operatsionnaia tekhnika v Gosbanke,* Gosfinizdat, 1959.
Nazarov, F., "Sovershenstvovat' proektno-smetnoe delo," *PKh,* 1966, No. 7, pp. 69–76.
Nazarov, Ravino S., *Kolkhoznaia torgovlia,* Ekonomika, 1964.
Nedelin, S., "Nekotorye voprosy finansirovaniia i kreditovaniia sel'skogo khoziaistva v novykh usloviiakh," *FinSSSR,* 1965, No. 5, pp. 12–22.
Nemchinov, V. S., ed., *Primenenie matematiki v ekonomicheskikh issledovaniiakh,* Vol. 3, Mysl', 1965.
New Directions in the Soviet Economy. See U.S. Congress.
NIFI (Nauchno-issledovatel'skii finansovyi institut), *Organizatsiia finansov kolkhoza,* Finansy, 1964.
———, *Planirovanie i finansirovanie kapital'nogo remonta osnovnykh fondov,* Gosfinizdat, 1958.
Nikitin, V., "Prodavat' tovary melkim optom bez limita," *Sovetskaia torgovlia,* 1966, No. 6, pp. 35–37.
Nimitz, Nancy, *Farm Employment in the Soviet Union, 1928–1963,* The RAND Corporation, RM-4623-PR, November 1965.
———, *Soviet Expenditures on Scientific Research,* The RAND Corporation, RM-3384-PR, January 1963.
———, "Soviet Prices and Costs," in U.S. Congress, *Comparisons of the United States and Soviet Economies,* pp. 239–284.
———, "The Lean Years," *Problems of Communism,* May–June 1965, pp. 10–22.
Nove, Alec, "Some Thoughts While Reading the Soviet Press," *Soviet Studies,* July 1965, Vol. 17, No. 1, pp. 97–102.
———, "Statistical Puzzles Continue," *Soviet Studies,* July 1966, Vol. 18, No. 1, pp. 83–85.
———, "2½ Per Cent and All That," *Soviet Studies,* July 1964, Vol. 16, No. 1, pp. 17–21.

"Novym khoziaistvennym planam—vsestoronnee obosnovanie," *PKh,* 1963, No. 5, pp. 1–10.
Oldak, P. G., *Ekonomicheskie problemy povysheniia urovnia zhizni,* Ekonomizdat, 1963.
OECD (Organization for Economic Co-operation and Development), *National Accounts Statistics, 1955–1964,* Paris, 1966.
———, *Statistics of National Accounts 1950–1961,* Paris, 1964.
Pakhomov, A., "Puti snizheniia zatrat na ekspluatatsiiu tekhniki v kolkhozakh," *FinSSSR,* 1964, No. 10, pp. 19–23.
Pakhomov, Iu. N., "Novye tseny na sovkhoznuiu produktsiiu," *Sovkhoznoe proizvodstvo,* 1961, No. 4, pp. 5–7.
Palladina, M. and L. Grebennikova, "Garantirovannaia oplata truda v kolkhozakh," *VE,* 1966, No. 11, pp. 25–33.
Panin, N., "O sviazi natural'nykh i stoimostnykh pokazatelei pri planirovanii v kolkhozakh," *PKh,* 1964, No. 9, pp. 72–77.
Pankova, K., "K voprosy o perevode sovkhozov na polnyi khoziaistvennyi raschet," *VE,* 1966, No. 11, pp. 34–44.
Pereslegin, V., "Ekonomicheskie voprosy oborotnykh sredstv," *FinSSSR,* 1964, No. 10, pp. 30–39.
———, "Pribyl' i rentabel'nost' predpriiatii," *FinSSSR,* 1963, No. 5, pp. 8–17.
———, *Rezhim ekonomii v period stroitel'stva kommunizma,* Gosfinizdat, 1962.
Perov, G., "Sotsialisticheskoe vosproizvodstvo v period osushchestvleniia semiletnego plana," *PKh,* 1959, No. 3, pp. 3–26.
Pervushin, V. A., *Problema differentsiatsii proizvoditel'nosti obshchestvennogo truda,* Novosibirsk, Sibirskogo otdeleniia AN SSSR, 1963.
Pervyshin, S. P., ed., *Ekonomicheskaia nauka i khoziaistvennaia praktika. Ekonomicheskii ezhegodnik, god 1966,* Ekonomika, 1967.
Pesek, Boris P., "Economic Growth and Its Measurement," *Economic Development and Cultural Change,* April 1961, Vol. 9, No. 3, pp. 295–315.
Petrov, A. I., ed., *Kurs ekonomicheskoi statistiki,* 3rd edition, Gosstatizdat, 1961.
Le Plan Septennal Soviëtique. See Gosplan pri sovete ministrov SSSR.
Plenum Tsentral'nogo komiteta Kommunisticheskoi partii Sovetskogo soiuza, 15–19 dekabria 1958 goda; stenograficheskii otchet, Gospolitizdat, 1958.
Plenum Tsentral'nogo komiteta Kommunisticheskoi partii Sovetskogo soiuza, 10–18 ianvaria 1961 goda; stenograficheskii otchet, Gospolitizdat, 1961.
Pleshkov, A., "Nekotorye voprosy imushchestvennogo i lichnogo strakhovaniia," *FinSSSR,* 1966, No. 8, pp. 23–31.
Plyshevskii, Boris P., *Natsional'nyi dokhod SSSR za 20 let,* Mysl', 1964.
Podshivalenko, P., "Uporiadochit' tseny i raschety za oborudovanie," *Ekonomika stroitel'stva,* 1966, No. 1, pp. 32–39.
——— and I. D. Sher, eds., *Finansirovanie i kreditovanie kapital'nykh vlozhenii,* Gosfinizdat, 1960.
Povyshenie urovnia. See VNIIESKh.

Problemy ekonomiki truda, Ekonomika, 1965.
Riabushkin, Timon V., *Ekonomicheskaia statistika,* Statistika, 1966.
———, "Metodologicheskie voprosy balansa narodnogo khoziaistva," in AN SSSR, Moskovskii ekonomiko-statisticheskii institut, *Voprosy ekonomicheskoi statistiki,* Gosstatizdat, 1958, pp. 19–66.
———, "Voprosy istorii razvitiia balansovogo metoda v sovetskom soiuze," in Akademiia nauk SSSR, otdelenie ekonomicheskikh nauk, *Uchenye zapiski po statistike, tom 4. Voprosy balansa narodnogo khoziaistva i korreliatsii,* AN SSSR, 1959, pp. 21–49.
Riauzov, N. N. and N. P. Titel'baum, *Statistika torgovli,* 4th ed., Gosstatizdat, 1961.
Richter, Luba O., "Commentary," in Roy D. Laird, ed., *Soviet Agricultural and Peasant Affairs,* Lawrence, Kansas, University of Kansas Press, 1963, pp. 161–168.
Rimashevskaia, N. M., *Ekonomicheskii analiz dokhodov rabochikh i sluzhashchikh,* Ekonomika, 1965.
Riumin, S., "Sovershenstvovat' finansovoe planirovanie v promyshlennosti," in MFI, *Problemy finansovogo planirovaniia,* Gosfinizdat, 1963, pp. 31–49.
Riznik, A., "Svodnyi otchetnyi balans oborudovaniia i mashin," *VS,* 1965, No. 6, pp. 3–15.
Rogovtsev, Sergei E., *Planirovanie i finansirovanie novoi tekhniki na predpriiatii,* Ekonomika, 1965.
Roze, M., "Rasshirenie bytovykh uslug naseleniiu i kontrol' rublem," in P. Bunich, ed., *Ekonomicheskaia rabota v finansovo-kreditnoi sisteme,* Finansy, 1965, pp. 304–313.
Rudoi, E. F. and T. I. Lazarenko, *Razvitie transporta i sviazi v SSSR, 1959–1965,* Gosplanizdat, 1960.
Rumiantseva, A. V., *Obshchestvennye fondy kolkhozov,* Znanie, 1960.
Sarkisian, G., "Sblizhenie urovnei zhizni rabochikh i kolkhoznikov," *VE,* 1966, No. 6, pp. 73–81.
Schroeder, Gertrude, "Industrial Wage Differentials in the USSR," *Soviet Studies,* January 1966, Vol. 17, No. 3, pp. 303–317.
Semenov, V. N., *Khoziaistvennyi raschet i finansy sovkhozov,* Finansy, 1964.
———, "O finansirovanii zatrat na formirovanie osnovnogo stada v sovkhozakh," *DiK,* 1965, No. 4, pp. 39–42.
———, "Rentabel'nost' i finansy sovkhozov," *FinSSSR,* 1965, No. 4, pp. 27–33.
———, "Ukreplenie khoziaistvennogo rascheta—vazhnoe uslovie povysheniia effektivnosti sovkhoznogo proizvodstva," *VE,* 1965, No. 4, pp. 16–26.
Shchenkov, Serafim A., *Bukhgalterskii uchet v promyshlennosti,* 2d ed., Gosfinizdat, 1961.
Shcherbitskii, V. V. See *Zasedaniia Verkhovnogo soveta SSSR . . . 7–9 dekabria 1965g.*
Sidirova, M., "Formirovanie i planirovanie fondov obshchestvennogo potrebleniia v kolkhozakh," *VE,* 1961, No. 10, pp. 91–96.

Sigov, Ivglaf I., *Razdelenie truda v sel'skom khoziaistve pri perekhode k kommunizmu,* Ekonomizdat, 1963.

Singer, Hans, Review of Albert Waterson, *Development Planning—Lessons of Experience,* 1965, in *Economic Development and Cultural Change,* April 1967, Vol. 15, No. 3, pp. 369–371.

Sitarian, Stepan A., "Dvizhenie pribyli i naloga s oborota i biudzhet," *FinSSSR,* 1963, No. 10, pp. 12–21.

———, "Natsional'nyi dokhod i biudzhet v gody semiletki," *FinSSSR,* 1959, No. 9, pp. 9–18.

———, *Natsional'nyi dokhod soiuznykh respublik,* Moskovskogo universiteta, 1961.

——— and V. Afremov, "Ekonomicheskie osnovy i printsipy opredeleniia fiksirovannykh platezhei," *FinSSSR,* 1967, No. 4, pp. 8–15.

Sitnin, V., "Khoziaistvennaia reforma i peresmotr optovykh tsen na promyshlennuiu produktsiiu," *Kommunist,* No. 14, September 1966, pp. 37–46.

Smirnov, Aleksandr P., *Ekonomicheskoe soderzhanie naloga s oborota,* Sotsekgiz, 1963.

Smirnov, N., "Vliianie ekonomicheskikh form potrebleniia na velichinu neobkhodimogo produkta," in Ia. S. Kumachenko, *et al.,* eds., *Nekotorye ekonomicheskie problemy povysheniia effektivnosti proizvodstva,* Moskovskogo universiteta, 1966.

Sobol', Valerian A., *Ocherki po voprosam balansa narodnogo khoziaistva,* Gosstatizdat, 1960.

Sominskii, V., "Predpriiatie vstupaet v stroi—bystree ego osvaivat'," *Kommunist,* No. 10, July 1964, pp. 74–84.

Sonin, Mikhail Ia., *Vosproizvodstvo rabochei sily v SSSR i balans truda,* Gosplanizdat, 1959.

"Sotsial'no-ekonomicheskie problemy tekhnicheskogo progressa," *VE,* 1960, No. 1, pp. 92–106.

The Soviet Financial System. See U.S. Bureau of the Census.

Spravochnik partiinogo rabotnika, vypusk vtoroi, Gospolitizdat, 1959.

Statistical Abstract of the United States. See U.S. Bureau of the Census.

Statisticheskii slovar'. See Boiarskii.

Stigler, George J., *Capital and Rates of Return in Manufacturing Industries,* Princeton, N.J., Princeton University Press, 1963.

Stoliarov, Sergei G., *O tsenakh i tsenoobrazovanii v SSSR; statistiko-ekonomicheskie ocherki,* 2nd ed., Gosstatizdat, 1963.

———, in F.D., "V statisticheskoi sektsii Moskovskogo doma uchenykh," *VS,* 1965, No. 3, pp. 81–85.

Strana sovetov za 50 let. See TsSU.

Strumilin, S., "O differentsial'noi zemel'noi rente v usloviiakh sotsializma," *VE,* 1960, No. 7, pp. 81–97.

Studenkova, Natal'ia M., *Metodika ischisleniia sebestoimosti produktsii v kolkhozakh i sovkhozakh,* Ekonomika, 1965.

Suchkov, Aleksandr K., Ia. Sviderskii, and V. Paievskii, *Gosudarstvennye dokhody SSSR,* Gosfinizdat, 1960.

Sukharevskii, B., "Razvitie sfery obsluzhivaniia i stroitel'stvo kommunizma," *VE*, 1964, No. 10, pp. 3–14.

Tikidzhiev, R. and T. Rubinshtein, "Normy zadelov v proektirovanii i stroitel'stve," *PKh*, 1965, No. 7, pp. 39–44.

Titel'baum, N., "Pokupka tovarov organizatsiiami, uchrezhdeniiami i predpriiatiiami v roznichnoi torgovle," *VS*, 1961, No. 10, pp. 55–65.

Tiukov, Vasilii S. and Rafail A. Lokshin, *Sovetskaia torgovlia v period perekhoda k kommunizmu*, Ekonomika, 1964.

Treml, Vladimir G., "The 1959 Soviet Input-Output Table (As Reconstructed)," in U.S. Congress, Joint Economic Committee, *New Directions in the Soviet Economy*, pp. 257–270.

———, *The 1959 Soviet Intersectoral Flow Table*, Technical Paper RAC-TP-137, Research Analysis Corporation, McLean, Virginia, November 1964.

Tsagolov, N. A., ed., *Razvitie kolkhoznoi sobstvennosti v period razvernutogo stroitel'stva kommunizma*, Ekonomizdat, 1961.

Tsikoto, I. A., *Kommunizm i sel'skoe khoziaistvo*, Ekonomizdat, 1963.

TsSU (Tsentral'noe statisticheskoe upravlenie) pri Sovéte ministrov SSSR, *Itogi vsesoiuznoi perepisi naseleniia 1959 goda: SSSR*, Gosstatizdat, 1962.

———, *Srednee spetsial'noe obrazovanie v SSSR; staticheskii sbornik*, Gosstatizdat, 1962.

———, *Strana sovetov za 50 let; sbornik statisticheskikh materialov*, Statistika, 1967.

———, *Vysshee obrazovanie v SSSR; statisticheskii sbornik*, Gosstatizdat, 1961.

———, *Zdravookhranenie v SSSR; statisticheskii sbornik*, Gosstatizdat, 1960.

Turetskii, Shamai Ia., "Obshchestvenno neobkhodimye zatraty, pribavochnyi produkt i tseny," *FinSSSR*, 1963, No. 11, pp. 34–46.

———, *Ocherki planovogo tsenoobrazovaniia v SSSR*, Gospolitizdat, 1959.

———, *Razvitie uslug i printsipy tsenoobrazovaniia na bytovye uslugi*, Moskovskogo universiteta, 1966.

United Nations, Economic Commission for Europe, *Economic Survey of Europe in 1961, Part 2, Some Factors in Economic Growth in Europe During the 1950's*, Geneva, 1964.

———, Statistical Office, *Statistical Yearbook*, 1965, New York, 1966.

U.S. Bureau of the Census, *Long Term Economic Growth 1860–1965, A Statistical Compendium*, Washington, D.C., October 1966.

———, *The Soviet Financial System: Structure, Operation and Statistics*, by Daniel Gallik, Cestmir Jesina, and Stephan Rapawy, International Population Statistics Reports, Series P-90, No. 23, Washington, D.C., 1968.

———, *Statistical Abstract of the United States: 1964* (86th edition), Washington, D.C., 1964.

U.S. Bureau of Mines, *Minerals Yearbook, 1964, Vol. 1: Metals and Minerals (Except Fuels)*, Washington, D.C., 1965.

U.S. Congress, Joint Economic Committee, *Annual Economic Indicators for the U.S.S.R.*, Washington, D.C., February 1964.

———, *Comparisons of the United States and Soviet Economies*, Washington, D.C., 1959.

———, *Current Economic Indicators for the U.S.S.R.*, Washington, D.C., June 1965.

———, *Dimensions of Soviet Economic Power*, Washington, D.C., 1962.

———, *New Directions in the Soviet Economy*, Washington, D.C., 1966.

U.S. Department of Agriculture, *The USSR and Eastern Europe Agricultural Situation*, A Review of 1965 and Outlook for 1966, Washington, D.C., March 1966.

U.S. Department of Commerce, Office of Business Economics, *U.S. Income and Output*, A supplement to the *Survey of Current Business*, Washington, D.C., 1958.

Uriupin, F., "Vazhnyi etap v razvitii gosudarstvennogo strakhovaniia imushchestva kolkhozov i naseleniia," *FinSSSR*, 1960, No. 1, pp. 9–15.

The USSR and Eastern Europe Agricultural Situation. See U.S. Department of Agriculture.

Ushakov, V. I., in I. Levchuk, "Mezhvuzovskaia nauchnaia konferentsiia po voprosam kreditovaniia narodnogo khoziaistva, kreditnogo planirovaniia i kontrol'ia rublem," *DiK*, 1960, No. 7, pp. 71–75.

Vasil'ev, E. N., *Kapital'nye vlozheniia za schet netsentralizovannykh istochnikov*, Gosiurizdat, 1963.

Vasil'ev, S. S. *et al.*, *Ekonomika torgovli*, Gostorgizdat, 1962.

Venzher, V. G., "Osobennosti kolkhoznoi ekonomiki i problemy ee razvitiia," in Venzher *et al.*, *Proizvodstvo, nakoplenie, potreblenie*, Ekonomika, 1965, pp. 255–303.

Vernon, R., "Comprehensive Model-Building in the Planning Process: The Case of The Less-Developed Economics," *Economic Journal*, March 1966, Vol. 76, No. 301, pp. 57–69.

Vilkov, A. A., "Fond osoveniia novoi tekhniki i tseny na machiny," in AN SSSR, *Obshchestvenno neobkhodimye zatraty truda, sebestoimost' i rentabel'nost'*, AN SSSR, 1963, pp. 197–213.

Vintaikin, Z., "Ekonomika proizvodstva kartofelia," *ESKh*, 1963, No. 8, pp. 13–26.

Vishnevskaia, Valentina V. *et al.*, *Ekonomika i planirovanie sviazi*, Sviaz'-izdat, 1963.

VNIIESKh (Vsesoiuznyi nauchno-issledovatel'skii institut ekonomiki sel'skogo khoziaistva), *Povyshenie urovnia razvitiia kolkhoznogo proizvodstva*, Ekonomizdat, 1961.

Volin, Lazar, "Reforms in Agriculture," *Problems of Communism*, January–February 1959, Vol. 8, No. 1, pp. 35–43.

Volodarskii, L. M., *Statistika promyshlennosti i voprosy planirovaniia*, Gosstatizdat, 1958.

Voziakov, A. *et al.*, "Bank i povyshenie effektivnosti kapital'nykh vlozhenii," *FinSSSR*, 1966, No. 6, pp. 21–28.

Voznesenskii, Nikolai A., *Voennaia ekonomika SSSR v period otechestvennoi voiny*, OGIZ, 1948.

Vsesoiuznoe soveshchanie statistikov, 4–8 iunia 1957 g., Gosstatizdat, 1958.

Vorkunov, S., "O sblizhenii uslovii zhizni naseleniia derevni i goroda," *ESKh*, 1966, No. 5, pp. 93–99.

Wiles, Peter, "Are Adjusted Rubles Rational?," *Soviet Studies*, October 1955, Vol. 7, No. 2, pp. 143–160.

———, *The Political Economy of Communism*, Oxford, Basil Blackwell, 1962.

———, "A Rejoinder to All and Sundry," *Soviet Studies*, October 1956, Vol. 8, No. 2, pp. 134–143.

Willett, Joseph W., "The Recent Record in Agricultural Production," in U.S. Congress, *Dimensions of Soviet Economic Power*, pp. 91–114.

World Almanac and Book of Facts, New York, Newspaper Enterprise Association, Inc., 1967.

Wolfe, Thomas W., *Soviet Strategy at the Crossroads*, Cambridge, Mass., Harvard University Press, 1964.

Yanowitch, Murray, "The Soviet Income Revolution," *Slavic Review*, December 1963, Vol. 22, No. 4, pp. 683–697.

Zakonodatel'nye akty po voprosam narodnogo khoziaistva SSSR, Vols. I and II, Gosiurizdat, 1961.

Zaks, G. and M. Guterman, "Bankovskii kontrol' v individual'nom zhilishchnom stroitel'stve," *FinSSSR*, 1960, No. 5, pp. 70–74.

Zaleski, Eugène, *Planification de la croissance et fluctuations économiques en U.R.S.S., Tome 1, 1918–1932*, Vol. 1, Paris, SEDES, 1962.

Zasedaniia Verkhovnogo soveta SSSR, piatogo sozyva, vtoraia sessiia, 22–25 dekabria 1958 g.; stenograficheskii otchet, Verkhovnogo soveta SSSR, 1959.

Zasedaniia Verkhovnogo soveta SSSR, sed'mogo sozyva, vtoraia sessiia, 15–19 dekabria 1966 g.; stenograficheskii otchet, Verkhovnogo soveta SSSR, 1967; E. F. Loginov speech, pp. 333–339.

Zasedaniia Verkhovnogo soveta SSSR, shestogo sozyva, sed'maia sessiia, 7–9 dekabria 1965 g.; stenograficheskii otchet, Verkhovnogo soveta SSSR, 1966; V. V. Shcherbitskii speech, pp. 70–75.

Zaslavskaia, Tat'iana I., *Raspredelenie po trudu v kolkhozakh*, Ekonomika, 1966.

Zel'tser, P., "Rezervy uvelicheniia parka deistvuiushchego oborudovaniia," *VS*, 1963, No. 12, pp. 11–20.

———, "Uskorit' vvod v deistvie oborudovaniia," *PKh*, August 1964, No. 8, pp. 51–55.

Zhevtiak, Petr N., *Finansy promyshlennogo predpriiatiia*, Gosfinizdat, 1963.

Zverev, A. G., "Finansy SSSR za 40 let sovetskoe vlasti," *Finstroi*, pp. 5–84.

———, "Gosudarstvennyi biudzhet pervogo goda semiletki," *PKh*, 1959, No. 1, pp. 3–15.

———, "Gosudarstvennyi biudzhet SSSR na 1958 god," *PKh*, 1957, No. 12, pp. 13–25.

———, Gosudarstvennyi biudzet vtorogo goda shestoi piatiletki," *PKh*, 1957, No. 3, pp. 15–30.
———, *Khoziaistvennoe razvitie i finansy v semiletke (1959–1965 gg.)*, Gosfinizdat, 1959.
———, *Natsional'nyi dokhod i finansy SSSR*, Gosfinizdat, 1961.
———, *Problemy tsenoobrazovaniia i finansy*, Nauka, 1966.
———, *Voprosy natsional'nogo dokhoda i finansov SSSR*, Gosfinizdat, 1958.

Index

Selected RAND Books

BERGSON, ABRAM, *The Real National Income of Soviet Russia Since 1928,* Cambridge, Mass.: Harvard University Press, 1961.

BERGSON, ABRAM and HANS HEYMANN, JR., *Soviet National Income and Product 1940–48,* New York: Columbia University Press, 1954.

CHAPMAN, JANET G., *Real Wages in Soviet Russia Since 1928,* Cambridge, Mass.: Harvard University Press, 1963.

DINERSTEIN, H. S., *War and the Soviet Union: Nuclear Weapons and the Revolution in Soviet Military and Political Thinking,* New York: Frederick A. Praeger, Inc., 1959.

DORFMAN, ROBERT, PAUL A. SAMUELSON, and ROBERT M. SOLOW, *Linear Programming and Economic Analysis,* New York: McGraw-Hill Book Company, Inc., 1958.

DOWNS, ANTHONY, *Inside Bureaucracy,* Boston, Mass.: Little Brown and Company, 1967.

FAINSOD, MERLE, *Smolensk Under Soviet Rule,* Cambridge, Mass.: Harvard University Press, 1958.

GOLDHAMER, HERBERT and ANDREW W. MARSHALL, *Psychosis and Civilization,* Glencoe, Illinois: The Free Press, 1953.

HIRSHLEIFER, JACK, JAMES C. DEHAVEN, and JEROME W. MILLIMAN, *Water Supply: Economics, Technology, and Policy,* Chicago, Illinois: The University of Chicago Press, 1960.

HITCH, CHARLES J. and ROLAND N. MCKEAN, *The Economics of Defense in the Nuclear Age,* Cambridge, Mass.: Harvard University Press, 1960.

HORELICK, ARNOLD L. and MYRON RUSH, *Strategic Power and Soviet Foreign Policy,* Chicago, Illinois: University of Chicago Press, 1966.

JOHNSON, WILLIAM A., *The Steel Industry of India,* Cambridge, Mass.: Harvard University Press, 1966.

KERSHAW, JOSEPH A. and ROLAND N. MCKEAN, *Teacher Shortages and Salary Schedules,* New York: McGraw-Hill Book Company, Inc., 1962.

KOLKOWICZ, ROMAN, *The Soviet Military and the Communist Party,* Princeton, N.J.: Princeton University Press, 1967.

KRAMISH, ARNOLD, *Atomic Energy in the Soviet Union*, Stanford, Calif.: Stanford University Press, 1959.

LIU, TA-CHUNG and KUNG-CHIA YEH, *The Economy of the Chinese Mainland: National Income and Economic Development, 1933–1959*, Princeton, N.J.: Princeton University Press, 1965.

LUBELL, HAROLD, *Middle East Oil Crises and Western Europe's Energy Supplies*, Baltimore, Md.: The Johns Hopkins Press, 1963.

MARSCHAK, THOMAS A., THOMAS K. GLENNAN, JR., and ROBERT SUMMERS, *Strategy for R&D*, New York: Springer-Verlag New York Inc., 1967.

MCKEAN, ROLAND N., *Efficiency in Government Through Systems Analysis: With Emphasis on Water Resource Development*, New York: John Wiley & Sons, Inc., 1958.

MEAD, MARGARET, *Soviet Attitudes Toward Authority: An Interdisciplinary Approach to Problems of Soviet Character*, New York: McGraw-Hill Book Company, Inc., 1951.

MOORSTEEN, RICHARD, *Prices and Production of Machinery in the Soviet Union, 1928–1958*, Cambridge, Mass.: Harvard University Press, 1962.

NELSON, RICHARD R., MERTON J. PECK, and EDWARD D. KALACHEK, *Technology, Economic Growth and Public Policy*, Washington, D.C.: The Brookings Institution, 1967.

NOVICK, DAVID (ed.), *Program Budgeting: Program Analysis and the Federal Budget*, Cambridge, Mass.: Harvard University Press, 1965.

ROSEN, GEORGE, *Democracy and Economic Change in India*, Berkeley and Los Angeles, Calif.: University of California Press, 1966.

RUSH, MYRON, *Political Succession in the USSR*, New York: Columbia University Press, 1965.

SPEIER, HANS, *Divided Berlin: The Anatomy of Soviet Political Blackmail*, New York: Frederick A. Praeger, Inc., 1961.

WOLF, CHARLES, JR., *Foreign Aid: Theory and Practice in Southern Asia*, Princeton, N.J.: Princeton University Press, 1960.

WOLFE, THOMAS W., *Soviet Strategy at the Crossroads*, Cambridge, Mass.: Harvard University Press, 1964.

www.ingramcontent.com/pod-product-compliance
Ingram Content Group UK Ltd.
Pitfield, Milton Keynes, MK11 3LW, UK
UKHW040234290926
15471UKWH00002B/179

9 780520 321533